Phraseology and Discourse:
Cross Linguistic and
Corpus-based Approaches

Edited by

Antonio Pamies, José Manuel Pazos Bretaña,
Lucía Luque Nadal

Schneider Verlag Hohengehren GmbH

Scientific Board:

Antonio Pamies Bertrán, *University of Granada*, Spain
Dmitrij Dobrovol'skij, *Academy of Sciences*, Russia
Juan de Dios Luque Durán, *University of Granada*, Spain
Harald Burger, *University of Zürich*, Switzerland
Annelies Häcki Buhofer, *University of Basel*, Switzerland
Wolfgang Mieder, *University of Burlington*, Vermont, United States
Julia Sevilla Munõz, *University Complutense*, Madrid, Spain
František Čermák, Charles *University of Prague*, Czech Republic
Mirella Conenna, *University of Bari*, Italy
Rosemeire Monteiro, *Federal University of Ceará*, Fortaleza, Brazil
Carmen Mellado Blanco, *University of Santiago de Compostela*, Spain
Gloria Corpas Pastor, *University of Málaga*, Spain
Annette Sabban, *University of Hildesheim*, Germany
Carlos Crida, *National Kapodistrian University of Athens*, Greece

Cover art: Pilar Ortiz „Manhattan"
(oil painting, 50 cm × 20 cm)

Gedruckt auf umweltfreundlichem Papier (chlor- und säurefrei hergestellt).

Bibliografische Information der Deutschen Nationalbibliothek

Die Deutsche Nationalbibliothek verzeichnet diese Publikation in der Deutschen Nationalbibliografie; detaillierte bibliografische Daten sind im Internet über ›http://dnb.d-nb.de‹ abrufbar.

Phraseologie und Parömiologie ; Bd. 29

ISBN: 978-3-8340-1069-8

Schneider Verlag Hohengehren, D-73666 Baltmannsweiler 2012.

Homepage: www.paedagogik.de

Alle Rechte, insbesondere das Recht der Vervielfältigung sowie der Übersetzung, vorbehalten. Kein Teil des Werkes darf in irgendeiner Form (durch Fotokopie, Mikrofilm oder ein anderes Verfahren) ohne schriftliche Genehmigung des Verlages reproduziert werden.

© Schneider Verlag Hohengehren, Baltmannsweiler 2012.
Printed in Germany. Druck: Esser, Bretten

Index

Jean-Pierre COLSON	Phraséologie contrastive et linguistique de corpus: outils récents et perspectives	1
Salah MEJRI	Les pragmatèmes, entre théorie et description: le cas du du?a	11
Jorge BAPTISTA & Dolors CATALÀ	What glues idioms together may not be just statistics after all? The case for compound adverbs in Portuguese and Spanish	19
Maria CONCA & Josep GUIA	Propuestas teóricas y metodológicas para el estudio de las unidades frásicas en contexto	31
Mirella CONENNA	Expressions de médiation	43
František ČERMÁK	Animal phraseology: the case of dog and cat (a corpus-based study)	55
Moufida GHARIANI BACCOUCHE	La phraséologie, un mode de dénominations multiples	67
Kazumi KOIKE	Colocaciones complejas metafóricas	73
Márton NÁRAY-SZABÓ	Verbes supports et prédicats illocutoires	81
Andre VALLI; Alberto BRAMATI & Françoise NIN	Comprendre les métaphores ontologiques dans l'espace roman. le cas du français vers l'espagnol et l'italien	91
Zvonimir NOVOSELEC & Jelena PARIZOSKA	A Corpus-based study of similes and cognate adjectival forms in English, Swedish and Croatian	101
Berit BALZER	"Wenn du mich fragst…": hypotaktische Phraseoteexteme deutsch und spanisch	111
Mª Josefa MARCOS GARCÍA	Los complementos del verbo en las locuciones verbales fijas. estudio contrastivo en francés y en español	123
Ramón MARTÍ SOLANO	The current world economic crisis: phraseological equivalents and variants in English, Spanish and French	133
Attila CSERÉP	Idiom analyzability: an intuition-based study	143
Ai INOUE	Functional differentiation between hesitation fillers: the case of *you know what* and *let's say*	165
Krisztina GERÖLY	Satzwertige und satzübergreifende (textwertige) Phraseologismen in Texten der deutschen Gegenwartsliteratur	173
Günter SCHMALE	The conversational treatment of idiomatic expressions in German talk shows – A corpus-based study	181
Xabier ALTZIBAR ARETXABALETA	Locuciones adverbiales idiomáticas en euskera	193
Graciela GARCÍA DE RUCKSCHLOSS,	Variación fraseológica del español de Cuyo, Argentina	203
Makoto SUMIYOSHI	Non-compositionality and the emergence of a new phraseological unit: an analysis of have until X to V	211
Laura Mª ALIAGA AGUZA	Locuciones enunciados de valor específico en contextos reales del español	219

Łucja BIEL	Areas of similarity and difference in legal phraseology: collocations of key terms in UK and Polish company law	225
Rosa CETRO	Tourisme, sante et bien-être: analyse en phraséologie contrastive de quelques expressions du français et de l'italien.	235
Sylvia JAKI	Bier, Schweiß und Tränen - The activation of associative networks by lexical substitutions in phraseological units	247
Britta JUSKA-BACHER & Stefan MEIER	Die areale Verbreitung Sog. phraseologischer „Helvetismen"	257
Liliana MITRACHE	„Der Apfel fällt nicht leicht vom Stamm". Aspekte der Sprachstörungen bei Altersdemenz	267
G. Angela MURA	Las unidades fraseológicas irónicas: un esquema fraseológico en español	275
Ulrike PREUSSER	Stilistischer Fehlgriff oder funktionale Modifikation? – der Phraseologismen-Gebrauch in Sarah Kuttners *Mängelexemplar* (2009)	285
Justyna PIETRZAK	Motivación fónica en los fraseologismos italianos	295
Mario Garcia-Page	El nombre propio proervbial en la comparación estereotipada	303
Louisa BUCKINGHAM	"Poniendo en evidencia": an analysis of selected light verb constructions in Spanish in a Latin American newspaper corpus	309
Yara EL GHAYALINI, & Mahdi FENDRI	Léxico y frasemas figurados del aceite y la aceituna en árabe moderno	329
Esteban T. MONTORO	La fraseología especializada del área científica y socioeconómica del olivar y el aceite de oliva: entre la tradición y la modernidad	337
Mariam MROUE	La phraséologie du positionnement dans les écrits scientifiques	347
Alejandro PASTOR & Encarnación TABARES	Estudio de la variación topolectal de las UFE en el ámbito del derecho penal español e hispanoamericano	355
Christine SCHOWALTER	Die Paar Kröten, das sind doch alles nur Peanuts! Eine Analyse zur intra- und interlingualen Äquivalenz phraseologischer Einheiten in Pressetexten	367
Jean-Pierre COLSON	A new statistical classification of set phrases	377
Mª Luisa ORTIZ ALVAREZ, & Ana Paula RIBEIRO CÂMARA	La jerga de estudiantes brasileños universitarios: la tribu y la aldea	387
Sixta QUASSDORF	Quotations or anonymous phrasemes - that is the question!	399
Nils BERNSTEIN	Wo flinten im Korn und Hunde begraben liegen. zur epochenspezifischen Verwendung von Phraseologismen in moderner Lyrik	411

Mª Luisa SCHILLING	Nur über meine Leiche! - ¡Por encima de mi cadáver! enunciados fraseológicos alemanes y españoles que expresan recusación	421
Mª Carmen UGARTE GARCÍA	Pintadas y fraseología	431
Monia BOUALI	Les adjectivaux actualisateurs: étude contrastive français/ arabe	441

Foreword

Fixed multi-word units can be focused from different perspectives, which can be roughly classified into quantitative or qualitative approaches, though the reality of text corpora shows that things are far from being so clear-cut. Specialists from different countries and languages explain and debate their views and research on phraseology, according to the results of modern empirical studies on real spoken and written language. All these contributions help us to build a more updated panorama of current research on phraseology, a field which, far from being a closed list of non productive items, is becoming more and more complex because of its dynamic nature: moving from syntax to lexicon and from speech to language, over almost all kinds of metalinguistic borderlines.

In Jean-Pierre Colson's *Phraséologie contrastive et linguistique de corpus: outils récents et perspectives,* many examples of a given set phrase, especially a phraseme, can be retrieved only from very large corpora. While corpora of medium size can provide a general picture of some grammatical or cultural aspects of contrastive phraseology, it is necessary to use Web-driven corpora in order to access the full palette of set phrases in context. Recent developments, especially the WaCky project, open up new possibilities of checking the traditional hypotheses of contrastive phraseology against hard evidence. At the same time, huge linguistic corpora may shed a new light on the pivotal role of contrastive phraseology in language learning and translation studies.

Salah Mejri's *Les pragmatèmes, entre théorie et description: le cas du duʕa,* on the basis of Mel'cuk's typology of phrasemes, tries to validate the extreme diversity of the phraseological facts covered by the concept of *pragmateme*: utterances of any kind such as certain greetings or indications specific to certain writings, sequences like *no smoking* that whilst being transparent do not have identical sequences in the other languages, etc. After having specified the characteristics of pragmatemes, the author provides a first typology that takes into account the shared universal dimension of this phenomenon in the characterization and in the conditions of usage, and the idiomatic dimension of their linguistic realization in each language. In order to illustrate this last dimension, a particular type of pragmateme called "*duʕa*" has been chosen. The author describes its formal and semantic characteristics while providing a typology to be used as a reference in a systematic description of this phenomenon, and also considers the problems that these phrasemes pose in translation. Their strong idiomatic anchoring blocks their transfer from one language to another.

According to Jorge Baptista & Dolors Català -*What glues idioms together may not be just statistics after all? The case for compound adverbs in Portuguese and Spanish-* the construction of lexicon resources seems to be still an unavoidable bottleneck for the integration of multiword expressions in natural language processing systems, because of the costly and time-consuming task of identifying and formalizing them into computational lexicons. The problem becomes more difficult to tackle if one intends to build (semi-automatically) a lexicon directly from large-sized corpora. This contribution aims at investigating the distributional constraints between verbs and idiomatic, compound adverbs. Instead of looking for multiword idioms in texts, the opposite approach is taken, based on extensive lists of Portuguese and Spanish adverbs, the efficiency of several statistical measures is determined and applied on large-sized corpora.

The contribution of Maria Conca and Josep Guia, *Propuestas teóricas y metodológicas para el estudio de las unidades frásicas en contexto,* introduces and redefines some phraseological concepts, and describes the method of *phrasic concordance.* It proposes a system to develop rigorously phrasic corpus drawn from literary works and conduct proper phraseological analysis.

Mirella Conenna's *Expressions de médiation* shows the first results of an ongoing research project aimed at identifying the discourse(s) of mediation, the description of language used by mediators, and the creation of a French-Italian specialised dictionary. The study involves the analysis and comparison of two specialised corpora in the corresponding languages. The French corpus is composed of the *Rapports du Médiateur de la République française,* while the Italian corpus is composed of the *Relazioni del Difensore civico.* As a sample of the methodology, a detailed analysis of the expression "le médiateur de la république" is presented, taking into account its pattern of occurrence, and its behaviour as viewed through relevant sets of concordances. Some aspects of the analysis of the Italian corpus are also presented. The findings thus obtained may be exploited for translation purposes as well as for teaching purposes, and in particular for training mediators.

František Čermak's chapter, *Animal phraseology: the case of dog and cat (a corpus-based study),* investigates the fact that most languages use animal names to build their idioms on, especially those of dog and cat. An attempt will be made to inspect and compare their existence in the similes of four languages, namely Czech, English, French and German. Since a rather exhaustive coverage and description of these items is available in a dictionary form in Czech, this was made a starting point for the comparison. The main goal has been to inspect meaning of these similes, using a semantic framework used in the dictionary for all four languages. Hence, 63 broad semantic categories have been established and the four languages compared on this basis. It is interesting to note that despite the same extralinguistic basis quite a few differences are to be observed, due to different linguistic and cultural backgrounds.

The chapter by Moufida Ghariani Baccouche, *La phraséologie, un mode de dénominations multiples,* starts from some examples of unilexical and multiword denominations which either coexist or alternate in a perfect complementarity in natural languages (ex. Arabic/ French/English) and which are motivated by their morphology or their semantics. This contribution intends to show that multiword denominations are productive in the creation of new denominations but are in some cases replaced by alphanumeric ones which are rather scientific and neutral. The aim is to establish a certain typology of contexts motivating this or that choice.

The purpose of Kazumi Koike's work, *Colocaciones complejas metafóricas,* is to point out the existence of a special type of Spanish *complex collocations* which, used with metaphorical meaning, establish other links with their respective complements (*metaphorical complex collocations*). The base of a metaphorical complex collocation is not a noun, but a metaphorized compound (*cortina de humo* in *lanzar una cortina de humo sobre el escándalo*, or *balón de oxígeno* in *dar un balón de oxígeno al régimen de La Habana*). The existence of metaphorical complex collocations causes a borderline problem between collocations and verbal idioms, precisely because of their idiomatic meaning.

According to Márton Náray-Szabó (*Verbes supports et prédicats illocutoires*), light verb constructions have been a field of interest in many linguistic frameworks for the last three decades. Their structure and behaviour depends mainly on the semantic type of the predicative noun they contain. The author provides a description of a group of important nouns: the illocutionary predicates. After having delimited this class of phraseological units, their distributional properties are compared in two languages, French and Hungarian. The latter has traditionally been considered by linguists as one resisting to that kind of structure in general, but a thorough analysis can reveal a more complex image.

André Valli; Alberto Bramati & Françoise Nin (*Comprendre les métaphores ontologiques dans l'espace roman*) are interested in idioms including a verb and a noun referring to body parts, for instance, *avoir du nez* [*to have nose], which are organised in a network of ontological metaphors (Lakoff and Johnson, 1980). In the first part, they deal with the problems raised by these idioms, as far as linguistics theories are concerned. In the second, they analyze the relationships between these idioms and their equivalents in Spanish and Italian.

Zvonimir Novoselec's & Jelena Parizoska's chapter, *A corpus-based study of similes and cognate adjectival forms in English, Swedish and Croatian,* deals with the relationship between conventionalized similes with the structure [(*as*) + Adj. + *as* + NP] in English, Swedish and Croatian [e.g. eng. (as) *clear as crystal*, sw. *tung som bly* (*heavy as lead), cr. *hladan kao led* (*cold as ice)] and cognate adjectival forms, more specifically Noun-Adjective compounds such as eng. *crystal-clear* and sw. *blytung* (*lead heavy) and Adverb + Adjective collocations such as cr. *ledeno hladan* (lit. *icily cold*). Using corpus data, the authors examine the frequencies, collocational range and meaning of similes and adjectival forms in order to determine the degree of conventionality of each type of item and to identify the mechanisms underlying the process of creation of adjectival forms in the three languages. The aim is to show that similes and adjectival forms should be viewed on a scale of conventionality and grammaticalization. The frequencies of the two types of items as well as their semantic and syntactic differences raise the theoretical issue of the status of adjectival forms as idiomatic expressions, and the practical problem of items which are listed in dictionaries as canonical forms

Berit Balzer's work, *"Wenn du mich fragst...": hypotaktische Phraseotexteme deutsch und spanisch,* deals with subordinate clauses in German and Spanish which form a distinct group within the routine formulae, as they belong to pre-patterned speech and are invariable in their sequence. Sometimes they depend on a special verb in the main clause, but most often they can be uttered as separate adverbials. After presenting a variety of hypotactic clauses introduced by *wenn, wo*, and *wie*, as well as their possible Spanish counterparts, the point will is made that these clauses deserve to be treated as a subgroup within the syntactically heterogeneous type of formulaic discourse.

Mª Josefa Marcos García's contribution, *Los complementos del verbo en las locuciones verbales fijas,* is centered on the verbal fixed phrases in French and Spanish. A verbal fixed construction is constituted by several elements, of which the most important is a verb. The above mentioned verb, with his complements, forms a working unit that has its own meaning. In this study the author tries to establish a classification of the type of complements for every verb in the bilingual corpus.

Ramón Martí Solano's chapter, *The current world economic crisis: phraseological equivalents and variants in English, Spanish and French,* analyzes how the 2007 world economic crisis has given rise to a specific phraseology which is common to several European languages and which functions at different syntactic and pragmatic levels, depending on the language. Solely specifically designed corpora for each multi-word unit can yield empirical results for contrastive phraseology. This paper explores total and partial phraseological equivalents in English, Spanish and French and mainly focuses on the string the *bubble bursts*, its variants and its loan translations. The main hypothesis is that it is a high degree of lexicalisation of the nominal constituent of some predicate phraseological units that allows the wide-ranging scope of lexical-syntactical variation of the canonical forms.

In Attila Cserép's work, *Idiom analyzability: an intuition-based study,* native speakers' assumptions about the meaningfulness of idiom components have been examined in two online surveys. Participants tended to assign meaning to words, mostly relying on metaphorical conceptualizations, sometimes using substitute words based on common collocations or simply dividing the paraphrase and assigning meaning to the appropriate part of speech. When respondents were asked to formulate the paraphrases in their own words, they often provided holistic explanations. The results partially support conceptual metaphor theory.

Ai Inoue's contribution, *Functional differentiation between hesitation fillers: the case of "you know what" and "let's say",* presents the multifunction and polysemy of some frequently used phraseological units in line with different contexts. The items *you know what* and *let's say* serve the same function of hesitation fillers, although the actual words that constitute these phraseological units are completely different. Through the syntactic and lexical characteristics of *you know what* and *let's say* functioning as hesitation fillers, the lexical meanings of each component of these phraseological units seem to have been retained, which means that the core function of *you know what* and *let's say* survive. In addition, *you know what* and *let's say* do not function as synonymous hesitation fillers.

The main purpose of Krisztina Geröly's chapter, *Satzwertige und satzübergreifende (textwertige) Phraseologismen in Texten der deutschen Gegenwartsliteratur,* is to analyse sentence-worthed and sentence-overlapping (text-worthed) phraseologisms in the prose of German minority authors in the 80's and 90's of the 20th century from an intercultural perspective. There were 374 sentence-worthed and sentence-overlappinng phraseological items in the analyzed texts. These phraseological items can be divided in two categories: *phraseological transference* and *interference*. These phraseologisms have a culture-specified component, which does not have any equivalent in other languages. The analyzed items mainly have a pragmatical function: they express the attitude of characters in the novels to the contents of the texts.

For Günter Schmale (*The conversational treatment of idiomatic expressions in German talk shows: a corpus-based study*), corpus-based analyses of authentic conversational interaction, so far not the core interest of mainstream phraseological research, are essential in order to determine communicative functions of prefabricated expressions, but they are also indispensable so as to deliver a comprehensive description of multimodal aspects of phraseme usage. Based on a 32-hour-corpus of German television talk shows, this chapter studies the conversational treatment of formulaic expressions, i.e. reformulations (rephrasals and paraphrases), metadiscursive comments, play on words, and concomitant nonverbal activities, which very regularly "treat" idiomatic metaphorical and/or figurative expressions in the context of "public speaking" within German talk shows.

Xabier Altzibar Aretxabaleta's paper, *Locuciones adverbiales idiomáticas en euskera*, introduces and describes a list of Basque adverbial idioms of time, quantity and opinion. A distinction is made between idioms of a higher and lower degree of idiomaticity, and focus is set on the former for their high expressive value. There exist a considerable number of Basque idiomatic fixed expressions, and many of them are equivalent or similar to Spanish idioms. This fact is considered as evidence of linguistic and cultural connection between both languages.

The chapter by Graciela García de Ruckschloss, *Variación fraseológica del español de Cuyo*, introduces a comparative empirical investigation between phraseologisms found in a region of Argentina, and those found in the rest of the country and neighbour states, including Spain, with the final objective being lexicographical cataloging. By doing this, contrastive phraseological documentation is performed to incorporate the elements to the *Diccionario de regionalismos cuyanos*, a regional semasiological monolingual dictionary that contains the local variants of the peninsular Spanish registered in Cuyo.

Makoto Sumiyoshi's paper, *Non-compositionality and the emergence of a new phraseological unit...*, discusses the phraseological pattern *have until* X *to* V, which can be exemplified by *The banks have until the end of February to make a decision*. The discussion in this paper is organized around the following three interesting points displayed by the phraseological pattern. First, the unit expresses the time-limit meaning that is usually expressed by the preposition *by*, although what is denoted by *until* is the duration meaning. Second, as far as syntax is concerned, it is difficult to resort to traditional linguistic apparatuses such as intraposition to explain the emergence of the unit. It can be argued that *have until* is chosen as a unit without regard to its internal syntactic structure. Third, corpora research reveals that the preposition *till* is infrequently employed in the unit even though traditional grammar argues that *till* and *until* are exchangeable in most cases. This can be attributed to a stress clash caused by the sequence of *have till*.

The aim of Laura Mª Aliaga Aguza's *Locuciones enunciados de valor específico en contextos reales del español* is to make a pragmatic approach to the *specific value statements* in Spanish. For this purpose, the author establishes boundaries with adjacent structures, as *idiomatic phrases* and *sayings*. Secondly, focus is set on the practical analysis of such structures.

Łucja Biel: *Areas of similarity and difference in legal phraseology...*, discusses areas of similarity and difference in the phraseology of key terms in UK and Polish company law. The analysis is based on two comparable corpora of company law legislation. Similarities are motivated by the shared COMPANY-IS-A-PERSON metaphor and related conceptual scenarios, while differences arise from their system-specific instantiations, conditions-effects scripts and linguistic restrictions.

Rosa Cetro's work, *Tourisme, santé et bien-être...*, makes a contrastive phraseological analysis of some compound nouns or expressions containing the French word *tourisme,* or its Italian equivalent *turismo,* dealing with health and wellness. The aim of this research is to find which of these compound nouns is the most suitable to describe the tourism sector including thermalism, thalassotherapy and climatotherapy in both languages. After searching for these compound nouns in dictionaries, encyclopaedias, press and on Web pages, candidates are compared syntactically and semantically to establish their degree of equivalence.

Sylvia Jaki's chapter is called *Bier, Schweiß und Tränen - The activation of associative networks by lexical substitutions in phraseological units.* Newspapers and advertisements are replete with modified phraseological units involving mechanisms with one specific type of modification, lexical substitution. Using lexical substitution, writers can exploit various strategies on different meaning and form levels, in order to play with a large number of associations that are connected with both the canonical and the modified form. For the researcher, this implies looking at the formal, semantic and contextual relations between *substituens* and *substituendum*. Furthermore, exploring which relations hold between the meanings of the entire canonical and modified forms will prove to be as essential as reflecting upon the factors that influence modifiability, in particular figurativity.

Britta Juska-Bacher and Stefan Meier, in the chapter *Die areale Verbreitung Sog. phraseologischer Helvetismen,* observe that the geolinguistic distribution of phraseological helvetisms is not clearly defined. On the basis of empirical data gathered from about 1000 questionnaires (from Switzerland, Germany and Austria), they show that, in lexicographical practice, the term *helvetism* is used for different types of phrasemes: a first group which is exclusively known in (all areas of) Switzerland, a second group which is also known in Austria and/or parts of Germany, and a third group which is only known in some parts of Switzerland. We suggest that these different areal distributions should be considered by adding an element to the term *helvetism*, e.g. *austro-helvetism, regional helvetism*. For these classifications empirical data play an essential role.

Liliana Mitrache's paper „*Der Apfel fällt nicht leicht vom Stamm*". *Aspekte der Sprachstörungen bei Altersdemenz* contains a research on the connection between dementia and language disturbances. A typical language disturbance of senile dementia, which belongs to the early disease stage, is the *concretism*. This term describes the inability of the patient to understand abstract expressions, the words are understood only in their literal or strict sense. In this investigation this aspect of language disturbance in senile dementia is highlighted. The analysis uses proverbs and idioms, which are based upon neuropsychological tests, accomplished in the medical-geriatric competence centre Felix Platter-Hospital in Basel, Switzerland.

Giovanna Angela Mura, in her work *Las unidades fraseológicas irónicas: un esquema fraseológico en español,* aims to demonstrate the different discursive functions carried out by the Spanish phraseological pattern (*esquema fraseológico*) *¿será por + X?*. Drawing on theories developed by GRIALE (Grupo de Investigación para la Pragmática y la Ironía del Español, University of Alicante), the different uses of this phraseological *scheme*, which include future values, negative values and references to probability, can be observed.

Ulrike Preusser's text, *Stilistischer Fehlgriff oder funktionale Modifikation? – der Phraseologismen-Gebrauch in Sarah Kuttners Mängelexemplar,* examines the idea that literary texts continually represent revealing corpora for investigating the functions of idioms, which, however, is quite doubtable in some cases. This article attempts to reveal the implemented modifications of Sarah Kuttner's *Mängelexemplar* in such a way as to differentiate if these can be classified either functional or unmotivated.

Justyna Pietrzak, in *Motivación fónica en los fraseologismos italianos,* analyses phonic and rhythmic devices within phraseological units. A classification of phraseologisms is proposed according to their phonetic/prosodic motivation, including some phraseological units whose only motivation is phonic.

The main aim Mario García-Page's paper, *El nombre propio proverbial en la comparación estereotipada,* is to study some stereotyped comparatives containing a proverbial proper name that points out their typically Spanish origin. These expressions are *más feo que Picio, más listo que Cardona, más tonto que Abundio, escribir más que el Tostado, tener más cuento que Calleja,* and *saber más que Lepe*.

Louisa Buckingham's chapter, *"Poniendo en evidencia": an analysis of selected light verb constructions in Spanish in a Latin American newspaper corpus,* examines the relative idiomaticity of the noun component in light verb constructions (LVC), and discusses the relationship between idiomaticity and the degree of morpho-syntactic fixedness of the whole construction. The material was extracted from a seven-million-word corpus of contemporary newspaper texts from seven Latin American countries, and the study concentrates on LVC whose verbs are the most frequent *dar, poner, tener* and *tomar*. Results demonstrate that idiomaticity is not always a prerequisite for morpho-syntactic fixedness and that even fully idiomatic LVCs may display degrees of structural variation.

The paper by Yara El Ghayalini and Mahdi Fendri, *Léxico y frasemas figurados del aceite y la aceituna en árabe moderno,* studies the notional domain of olive tree in

Arabic idioms and lexicon (Tunisian dialect). The cultural impact of this tree is of high importance for research in ethnolinguistic phraseo-paremiology and metaphor studies.

Esteban T. Montoro's *La fraseología especializada del área científica y socioeconómica del olivar y el aceite de oliva: entre la tradición y la modernidad*, is also dedicated to olive trees and oil production terminology, including figurative expressions and jargon, across history up to the present times.

For Mariam Mroue (*La phraséologie du positionnement dans les écrits scientifiques*), the transdisciplinary scientific lexicon is a common lexicon for the entire scientific community, and it is related specifically to the writing and communication of scientific knowledge. This study examines the transdisciplinary collocations expressing the position of the author in his writing through a corpus of about two million words, made up of scientific articles and thesis of three scientific fields: linguistics, economics and medicine. The practical application of this study is to help foreign students in French universities to write their technical literature.

In the paper by Alejandro Pastor & Encarnación Tabares, *Estudio de la variación topolectal de las UFE en el ámbito del derecho penal español e hispanoamericano*, the authors present a systematic analysis of the main differences in the lexical selection of Spanish legal collocations, in relation to their counterparts in the different legal systems of the rest of the spanish-speaking countries. A corpus has been built consisting of specialized texts from criminal codes of all Spanish-speaking countries from Latin America and Spain. For the practice of translation diatopic variations in the field of specialized collocations are very important because usually the terms do not always select the same basis in the different legal systems that share Spanish as official language (e.g. the same collocation is not always used in the same communicative situations and with the same meaning).

Christine Schowalter's contribution, *Die Paar Kröten, das sind doch alles nur Peanuts!* is dedicated to the *toad* (ger. *Kröte*). In the German language a very small amount of money can be metaphorically designed as *Kröten* but, nowadays, as *Peanuts* as well. A first analysis concentrates therefore on the question if the two metaphors are similar and in which manner they could whether or not be replaced by each other. A second enquiry focuses then on the idiom *to swallow a toad* (ger. *eine Kröte schlucken*) and its cross-linguistic equivalence between several languages as English, German, French, Italian, Spanish and Portuguese. This part is based on articles from newspapers published in various countries in 2009.

In Jean-Pierre Colson's second contribution, *A new statistical classification of set phrases*, traditional classifications based on semantic criteria are confronted with the problem of borderline cases. They cannot be easily verified on large corpora nor used for automatic extraction. In this paper, a purely statistical classification is proposed, based on the association between the element parts of n-grams and on the frequency of the combination.

Mª Luisa Ortiz Alvarez and Ana Paula Ribeiro Câmara, in their work *La jerga de estudiantes brasileños universitarios: la tribu y la aldea,* examine slang as a group's linguistic resource ("tribe belonging"), more specifically, Brazilian youngsters' slang in a university context, its dynamism and its immense potential for reflecting socio-cultural practices and values. Expressions within this micro-system (*Brazilian university slang*), collected from *Orkut* web chats and recorded interviews with students, are analyzed in relation to their origin and meaning, as well as to their role in this emerging specific context.

Sixta Quassdorf's paper, *Quotations or anonymous phrasemes - that is the question!*, addresses the relationship between quotations and phrasemes. Simple answers cannot be given to this question, as quotations are a pragmatic rather than a structural phenomenon, i.e. their proper "existence" is context-sensitive. However, diachronic studies of usage reveal how word strings that are marked as quotations (or strongly resemble word strings in a literary work) are used outside their original context; they show if and how these word strings change over time and what these changes tell us about their phraseological status. A sample study of the verse line *I must be cruel, only to be kind,* from Shakespeare's *Hamlet,* demonstrates that, besides the emergence of deviating but recurrent formal and semantic properties, increased usage in new discourse contexts is especially indicative of a this development from a poet's word to a phraseological unit.

In Nils Bernstein's *Wo flinten im Korn und Hunde begraben liegen...* the author focuses the polemics in recent specialized literature about Lutz Röhrich's hypothesis of proverbs as the "rhetoric of the simple man". However, the use of many phraseological units, especially of conversational routines, is not adequate in the rather elaborated language of poetry. The counting of phraseological units in an anthology of ten volumes of German Poetry (ed. by Walther Killy et.al.) documents that they are very frequent in Modern Poetry of the 20th century. The increased frequency of occurrence can be used as a criterion for discriminating the language of poetry from everyday speech. Furthermore it proves the tendency of using colloquial language in Postmodern Poetry in terms of a deviation of concepts of conventional poetics. The article finally shows that phraseological units can be found in certain epochs of literary history.

Mª Luisa Schilling's contribution, *Nur über meine Leiche! - ¡Por encima de mi cadáver! enunciados fraseológicos alemanes y españoles que expresan recusación,* offers a contrasted analysis of German and Spanish psycho-social recusation routine formulas used to verbalize the linguistic expressions of denying and refusing. Furthermore, it analyses the linguistic structure of these routine formulae as well as their ilocutive value. Finally, it includes a contrasted analysis of the final results and a wide range of total and partial equivalences between both languages.

The chapter by Mª Carmen Ugarte García, *Pintadas y fraseología,* deals with Graffiti as a vehicle for the dissemination of new and old proverbs, along with other new manifestations of culture. In Spain, the study of the graffiti has been an exception, although some researches have seen the need to pay some attention to them. In this contribution external and internal form of graffiti are reviewed. Their external form uses mnemonic mechanisms, similar to proverbs, to attract the attention.

Last but not least, Monia Bouali's paper, *Les adjectivaux actualisateurs: étude contrastive français/ arabe*, describes these multi-word collocations or idioms performing the same function than adjectives (G. Gross: 1991). According to their use, they can be predicative (<*être*> *en colère* : *to be in anger: "angry") or non-predicative (<*être*> *de fer*: *to be [made] of iron). Previous linguistic studies generally focus on the first category. This work, deals specifically with adjectival collocations that realize the actualization of predicates, or arguments, in the elementary sentence. Whatever they be predicative or argumental, the *adjectivals* assume identification criteria specific to each use. The functioning of these items is described from a contrastive French / Arabic point of view.

These papers, selected from the materials and lectures from Europhras2010 (Granada, Spain), are complementary to two previously published books in the series *Phraseologie und Parömiologie*: *Linguo-cultural competence and phraseological motivation* (vol. 27, ed. by Antonio Pamies & Dmitrij Dobrovol'skij) & *Multi-lingual phraseography: second language learning and translation applications* (vol. 28, ed. by Antonio Pamies; Lucía Luque-Nadal & José Manuel Pazos).

PHRASÉOLOGIE CONTRASTIVE ET LINGUISTIQUE DE CORPUS : OUTILS RÉCENTS ET PERSPECTIVES

Jean-Pierre Colson
Institut libre Marie Haps (Bruxelles)
Université catholique de Louvain (Louvain-la-Neuve)

Abstract: There is nowadays a broad consensus on the recourse to corpora in linguistic research. This is, however, not a matter of evidence in contrastive phraseology, because many examples of a given set phrase, especially a phraseme (idiom) can only be retrieved from very large corpora. While corpora of medium size can provide a general picture of some grammatical or cultural aspects of contrastive phraseology, it is necessary to use Web-driven corpora in order to access the full palette of set phrases in context. Recent developments, especially the WaCky project, open up new possibilities of checking the traditional hypotheses of contrastive phraseology against hard evidence. At the same time, huge linguistic corpora may shed a new light on the pivotal role of contrastive phraseology in language learning and translation studies.

Key words: Contrastive phraseology, corpus linguistics, translation, stylistics

1. Introduction

La phraséologie contrastive embrasse un vaste domaine d'étude, qui touche notamment aux relations entre langue et cultures du monde, ainsi qu'à la traduction et à ses divers aspects théoriques et pratiques (Colson, 2008). Parmi les nombreuses applications possibles de la phraséologie contrastive figurent ainsi l'interaction entre langue et vision du monde, les relations entre l'histoire culturelle et la langue ; dans le domaine de la traduction, parmi d'autres : les techniques de repérage des phraséologismes en langue source, la phraséologie en langue cible, l'interférence entre phraséologie en langue source et en langue cible, les procédés de traduction des structures phraséologiques.

Si la linguistique a vocation de science, elle se doit aujourd'hui d'étayer ses diverses hypothèses par le biais des technologies toujours plus pointues accessibles aux chercheurs. Il existe à cet égard un large consensus à propos de l'importance des corpus linguistiques. Ces derniers ne sont plus l'apanage de la linguistique de corpus au sens strict (Sinclair, 1991) et sont largement utilisés dans d'autres domaines, qu'il s'agisse de linguistique appliquée (Wray, 2008) ou même de sémantique computationnelle (Baroni et al., 2010). Et pourtant, vouloir recourir aux corpus en phraséologie contrastive peut paraître une mission impossible. En effet, il est établi que des corpus gigantesques sont nécessaires afin de couvrir l'ensemble du spectre de la phraséologie, depuis les structures les moins figées et les moins idiomatiques (routines, collocations) jusqu'aux idiomes ou phrasèmes (Moon, 1998 ; Colson, 2003, 2007). Dans une perspective contrastive, cette exigence se retrouve multipliée par deux : le défi sera de constituer au moins deux corpus comparables et de taille très importante.

2. Corpus et études de cas en phraséologie contrastive

Des corpus de petite taille (de 1 à 5 millions de mots) ou de taille moyenne (de 5 à 50 millions de mots) ne peuvent dès lors ambitionner de résoudre les grandes questions théoriques qui sous-tendent la phraséologie contrastive, ni de fournir une multitude d'exemples pour étoffer les hypothèses. Qu'il s'agisse de langue de spécialité ou de langue générale, de tels corpus peuvent toutefois se révéler très utiles pour des études de cas à partir de structures phraséologiques fréquentes.

S'il est vrai que les structures les plus figées, figurées, idiomatiques ou opaques, souvent désignées sous l'appellation d'idiomes ou phrasèmes (Burger, 1998) sont à bien des égards des miroirs de la culture d'une langue, d'autres phraséologismes moins figés, et beaucoup plus fréquents, permettent également d'inférer nombre d'informations utiles à la phraséologie contrastive et à la traduction. Nous prendrons ici l'exemple de la structure française saisir + Substantif et de son pendant en langue néerlandaise *grijpen* + *Substantif*, à partir d'un corpus journalistique de taille moyenne dans chacune des deux langues[1]. Le tableau 1 ci-dessous reprend les occurrences les plus fréquentes pour l'équation de recherche.

11	occasion	11	hart
8	balle	11	leven
7	comité	11	lucht
6	justice	9	macht
5	juge	8	kans
5	opportunité	3	pen
5	tribunal	2	afgevaardigden
4	commission	2	hand
4	marché	2	telefoon
3	chambre	1	algemeen
3	chance	1	andere
3	conseil	1	basgitaar
3	perche	1	beest
3	réalité	1	bende
2	cour	1	bezoeker
2	film	1	bijna
2	gouvernement	1	broekspijpen
2	poids	1	bureaucraten
2	taureau	1	clubs
1	ampleur	1	divisie
1	ancienne	1	drugs
1	assemblée	1	drugsmaffia
1	attitude	1	erotiek
1	aubaine	1	fractie
1	ballet	1	gelegenheid
1	beauté	1	gesprek
1	bien	1	hongerstaking
1	bonheur	1	hoteliers
1	bruit	1	kano
1	bureau	1	keel
1	cargaison	1	kind
1	cause	1	kladden
1	complexité	1	kraag

Tableau 1. '*Saisir*' + Substantif et son équivalent néerlandais dans des corpus journalistiques

---

[1] Il ne s'agit dans cette expérience que d'un échantillon limité, à partir du terme de recherche (converti en expression régulière de Perl) : infinitif + article défini (français : LE, LA, L' ; néerlandais : DE, HET) + MOT. Le néerlandais étant à la fois SVO (sujet, verbe, objet) et SOV, l'ordre inverse a également été retenu pour cette langue (article défini + MOT + infinitif). Le corpus, d'environ 40 millions de mots dans chacune des deux langues, repose pour le français sur le journal *Le Soir* et pour le néerlandais sur le *NRC-Handelsblad*.

Avec toutes les réserves d'usage en raison de la taille limitée du corpus et de l'échantillon, nous pouvons observer les faits suivants. En combinaison avec *saisir / grijpen*, nous trouvons dans les deux langues, parmi les occurrences les plus élevées, plusieurs combinaisons nettement figées : *saisir l'occasion, saisir la balle (au bond), saisir l'opportunité*. Ceci est toutefois nettement plus marqué en néerlandais, où les 6 combinaisons les plus fréquentes sont figées ou font partie de structures figées : *naar het hart grijpen* (littéralement : 'saisir vers le cœur') : émouvoir ; *in het leven brengen* ('apporter en vie') : créer, mettre sur pied ; *uit de lucht grijpen*, ('saisir à partir de l'air') : inventer de toute pièce ; *de macht grijpen* : prendre le pouvoir ; *de kans grijpen* : saisir l'occasion ; *de pen grijpen* : saisir sa plume, se mettre à écrire.

Cet exemple illustre une différence importante entre la phraséologie du français et du néerlandais : la tendance, dans cette dernière, à construire davantage de locutions verbales (ou phrasèmes verbaux) à partir de verbes support et de substantifs concrets et hyperfréquents. Les corpus de taille moyenne suffisent largement à étayer de telles hypothèses.

Ceci vaut également pour les recherches visant à mettre en lumière les grandes caractéristiques culturelles qui sous-tendent la phraséologie d'une langue. Restons à l'exemple du néerlandais. Cette langue, à l'instar de son cousin germanique, l'anglais, avec lequel elle partage une tradition maritime bien connue, recourt volontiers au vaste domaine de la mer et de la navigation pour créer des structures phraséologiques. Si nous prenons pour point de départ un terme de base tel que *schip* (navire) ou *boot* (bateau), un corpus de taille moyenne nous fournira déjà une légion d'exemples significatifs.

1	attaque du bateau City of	5	buiten de boot te vallen
1	avec un bateau et qui	3	op een boot in de
1	charge du bateau et de	3	uit de boot te vallen
1	chargement de bateau faisait encore	3	uit de boot valt bij
1	charger le bateau qui sombre	3	uit de boot zouden vallen
1	chasse un bateau de pêche	2	binnen de boot worden gehouden
1	dans un bateau de pêche	2	buiten de boot dreigen te
1	dans un bateau plus petit	2	buiten de boot vallen en
1	dans un bateau qui coule	2	met de boot leverde gisteren
1	de ce bateau errant sur	2	om de boot te halen
1	de ce bateau et de	2	om de boot te missen
1	déserté un bateau qui tangue	2	om een boot permament te
1	devenu un bateau de sauvetage	2	om een boot te kopen
1	envoie un bateau prospecter du	2	op de boot naar Dover
1	envoya le bateau scientifique Sismik	2	op een boot te gaan
1	envoyait le bateau scientifique Sismik	2	uit de boot vallen omdat
1	et le bateau a tangué	2	zelf de boot te roeien
1	images du bateau de Greenpeace	1	120 per boot vanuit Lemmer
1	jours de bateau en partant	1	aan de boot en bepaalt
1	Le dernier bateau de la	1	aan de boot verbonden is
1	le grand bateau des sociétés	1	aan de boot waarmee hij
1	le prochain bateau en partance	1	aan een boot die vluchtelingen
1	lesquels un bateau plus ou	1	aan een boot met een
1	liaison par bateau à vapeur	1	al per boot zijn gevlucht
1	manquer le bateau de la	1	alleen de boot rechtop komen
1	mener le bateau à bon	1	alleen per boot naartoe kunt
1	Moscou par bateau au cours	1	als de boot die niet
1	ou par bateau ne bénéficient	1	als de boot op een
1	par ton bateau minable et	1	als de boot vastliep en
1	pas le bateau de la	1	als een boot zonder zee
1	prendre le bateau pour l	1	Amerika de boot te missen
1	que le bateau de son	1	anders je boot mist en
1	que le bateau retrouve son	1	avond een boot naar de
1	quitté son bateau pour se	1	bang de boot te missen
1	saborder le bateau dans lequel	1	basisschool de boot dreigen te
1	sur ce bateau ivre règnent	1	besloot de boot om te
1	sur le bateau français qui	1	besloten de boot niet in
1	sur le bateau le ramenant	1	bij de boot komt aanzwemmen
1	sur le bateau plus ou	1	bij de boot om de
1	sur le bateau qui les	1	bijvoorbeeld een boot voor de
1	tragédie du bateau City of	1	binnen de boot te houden
1	un unique bateau qui assure	1	blijft de boot van Bollius
		1	boot tegen boot waaruit dit

Tableau 2. '*Bateau / boot*' en contexte dans des corpus journalistiques

A titre d'illustration, le tableau présente, pour les mêmes corpus qu'au tableau 1, les structures les plus fréquentes en français et en néerlandais, répondant à l'équation de recherche : MOT MOT *bateau / boot* MOT MOT (*bateau / boot* précédés et suivis de deux mots).

Notons cette fois encore une différence assez marquée entre le français et le néerlandais pour l'échantillon étudié : le contexte de deux mots à gauche et à droite livre des fréquences plus élevées pour boot que pour bateau, et il s'agit pour plusieurs d'entre elles de phrasèmes (*buiten de boot vallen, uit de boot vallen* : rater une occasion, se retrouver sur le carreau ; *de boot halen / de boot missen*: ne pas rater / rater un rendez-vous).

Même si des constatations similaires peuvent être glanées aisément dans des corpus de taille moyenne, force est de constater que la récolte est plutôt maigre : les fréquences les plus élevées n'atteignent même pas la barre des 20 occurrences, considérée par John Sinclair (1991) comme le seuil minimal permettant à des lexicographes de travailler à partir d'un corpus. Comme nous l'avons souligné plus haut, des études plus poussées de phraséologie contrastive nécessitent des corpus de taille gigantesque et de nature comparable, dépassant les 500 millions de mots. Avec les progrès informatiques et le développement de la Toile, ceci ne relève plus de l'utopie.

3. La Toile comme Corpus : le projet WaCky

La Toile est utilisée depuis plusieurs années en tant que corpus linguistique au sens large, avec tous les problèmes que ceci comporte. Rappelons que selon Kilgariff & Grefenstette (2003), les avantages des corpus Web l'emportent largement sur leurs inconvénients.

Parmi les principaux défauts de la Toile utilisée comme corpus linguistique figurent le manque de contrôle du chercheur sur les données qu'il utilise (représentativité, équilibre des registres), ainsi que le caractère souvent stéréotypé et répétitif des pages web, où de nombreux éléments langagiers sont en réalité des formules dénuées d'intérêt linguistique : boutons de confirmation, encarts publicitaires, menus de page, messages d'erreur, codes informatiques etc.

Le projet WaCky (Baroni et al., 2009) offre l'originalité de créer des corpus de taille très importante (autour des 2 milliards de mots) dans plusieurs langues (actuellement anglais, allemand, français, italien, voir : http://wacky.sslmit.unibo.it/doku.php?do=show&id=start).

Contrairement à une utilisation directe de la Toile, il s'agit ici bel bel et bien d'un corpus assemblé par des linguistes selon des critères de sélection précis, et de nombreux filtres ont permis d'éliminer les pages qui ne comportent que des mentions répétitives ou des données chiffrées. Au bout du compte, le projet WaCky, appelé à s'étendre à d'autres langues, offre déjà à la phraséologie contrastive un outil de tout premier plan.

De tels corpus de grande taille livrent en effet de nombreux exemples pour la plupart des constructions figées, y compris les plus rares, c'est-à-dire les locutions verbales ou phrasèmes, à caractère idiomatique, non-compositionnel. Pour illustrer ce point, le tableau 3 présente les fréquences d'une vingtaine de phrasèmes verbaux français dans trois corpus : Le Monde Diplomatique (huit années, 19 millions de mots), Le Soir (2 années, 40 millions de mots) et le corpus WaCky français FRWAC (corpus Web ; 1,6 milliard de mots).

Phrasèmes verbaux et terme de recherche (S)	Monde	Soir	FRWAC
acheter chat en poche (S: chat en poche)	0	0	9
avoir d'autres chats à fouetter (S: d'autres chats à fouetter)	0	25	210
avoir /mettre la puce à l'oreille (S: la puce à l'oreille)	0	20	338
chat échaudé craint l'eau froide (S: chat échaudé craint l'eau froide)	0	5	28
chercher midi à quatorze heures (S: midi à quatorze heures)	0	6	66
couper les cheveux en quatre (S: les cheveux en quatre)	0	4	81
coûter les yeux de la tête (S: les yeux de la tête)	0	3	113
entre chien et loup (S: entre chien et loup)	3	3	92
faire la grasse matinée (S: la grasse matinée)	0	5	173
faire d'une pierre deux coups (S: d'une pierre deux coups)	5	23	380
faire peau neuve (S: peau neuve)	16	56	1927
garder une poire pour la soif (S: poire pour la soif)	0	7	40
jeter / mettre de l'huile sur le feu (S: huile sur le feu)	13	34	479
jeter de la poudre aux yeux (S: de la poudre aux yeux)	1	14	452
lâcher la proie pour l'ombre (S: proie pour l'ombre)	3	6	114
pousser le bouchon trop loin (S: le bouchon trop loin)	1	2	126
prendre la poudre d'escampette (S: la poudre d'escampette)	1	20	194
remettre / reporter aux calendes grecques (S: aux calendes grecques)	20	21	292
revenons à nos moutons (S: revenons à nos moutons)	0	0	251

Tableau 3 . Fréquence de 20 phrasèmes verbaux sur 2 corpus de journaux et sur le *FRWAC*

Notons que ces fréquences sont partielles, car seule la partie invariable du phrasème (indiquée par S dans le tableau) a été retenue comme terme de recherche, sans mot intermédiaire (ainsi, une éventuelle occurrence de « pousser le bouchon VRAIMENT trop loin » n'est pas reconnue par le test). Ces résultats sont néanmoins très probants : le gigantesque corpus FRWAC offre à chaque fois une fréquence nettement plus élevée que les corpus de journaux traditionnels. Même si la progression des fréquences ne répond pas à un strict principe mathématique, l'accroissement de la taille du corpus entraîne bel et bien une augmentation plus ou moins proportionnelle de la fréquence brute des phrasèmes.

En phraséologie contrastive, de tels corpus offrent des perspectives passionnantes : vérification des hypothèses théoriques de la phraséologie, recherches sémantiques multilingues, aide à la traduction, comparaison de structures figées. Nous nous limiterons ici à un exemple pratique. Comparons la structure *pour* + MOT (+1 ou 2 MOTS facultatifs) + *une solution* avec son équivalent anglais[2] *to* + MOT (+1 ou 2 MOTS facultatifs) + *a solution*. Les corpus WaCky nous offrent cette fois des fréquences impressionnantes.

733	pour trouver une solution		1089	to find a solution
159	pour obtenir une solution		289	to provide a solution
88	pour apporter une solution		117	to come up with a solution
84	pour proposer une solution		93	to offer a solution
62	pour tenter de trouver une solution		77	to develop a solution
48	pour parvenir à une solution		65	to reach a solution
46	pour bâtir une solution		64	to be a solution
37	pour aboutir à une solution		57	to deliver a solution
35	pour offrir une solution		55	to help you find a solution
31	pour fournir une solution		53	to seek a solution
26	pour vous proposer une solution		50	to produce a solution
24	pour arriver à une solution		48	to achieve a solution
21	pour essayer de trouver une solution		46	to create a solution
21	pour rechercher une solution		45	to finding a solution
18	pour développer une solution		41	to have a solution
18	pour donner une solution		37	to try and find a solution
14	pour choisir une solution		28	to negotiate a solution
14	pour vous apporter une solution		28	to work out a solution
13	pour créer une solution		26	to design a solution
13	pour imposer une solution		25	to arrive at a solution
11	pour autant une solution		24	to implement a solution
11	pour élaborer une solution		22	to help find a solution
10	pour cela une solution		22	to impose a solution
10	pour construire une solution		20	to propose a solution
10	pour vous une solution		19	to get a solution
9	pour avoir une solution		19	to identify a solution
9	pour chercher une solution		19	to see a solution
9	pour former une solution		19	to try to find a solution
9	pour mettre en oeuvre une solution		18	to agree a solution
9	pour mettre en place une solution		17	to look for a solution
9	pour moi une solution		17	to think of a solution
8	pour eux une solution		16	to obtain a solution
7	pour y apporter une solution		16	to tailor a solution
6	pour arriver à trouver une solution		15	to devise a solution
6	pour concevoir une solution		15	to suggest a solution
6	pour dégager une solution		12	to give a solution
6	pour déployer une solution		12	to make a solution
6	pour envisager une solution		12	to recommend a solution
6	pour évaluer une solution		11	to come to a solution
6	pour produire une solution		11	to discuss a solution
5	pour constituer une solution		11	to form a solution
5	pour délivrer une solution		9	to present a solution
5	pour déterminer une solution		9	to which a solution
5	pour devenir une solution		8	to achieve as comprehensive a solution
5	pour étudier une solution		8	to bring about a solution
5	pour la première fois une solution		8	to promise a solution
5	pour laquelle une solution		8	to work on a solution
5	pour lesquels une solution		7	to adopt a solution
5	pour mettre au point une solution		7	to build a solution
5	pour préparer une solution		7	to expect a solution

Tableau 4. Fréquence de la structure '*pour…une solution*'/ '*to…a solution*' sur les corpus WaCky

De tels échantillons permettent aux chercheurs en phraséologie contrastive et en stylistique comparée de vérifier les hypothèses théoriques. En l'occurrence, le tableau 4 illustre plusieurs différences marquées entre le français et l'anglais. Tout d'abord, le français recourt davantage à des verbes moins fréquents et plus abstraits dans ce type de structure (*parvenir à, bâtir, aboutir à, développer, créer, imposer, élaborer, concevoir, dégager, déployer, envisager, produire, constituer, délivrer, déterminer*) ; certes, l'anglais utilise aussi des verbes du même type (parfois équivalents), mais en nombre plus restreint (*develop, create, negotiate, design, implement, impose, propose, identify, devise*). Le nombre de verbes hyperfréquents est plus marqué en anglais (*reach, be, have, get, see, give, make, build*), de même bien sûr que les

---

[2] Il ne s'agit pas d'un équivalent complet, car la structure anglaise «to+verbe» ne correspondra pas toujours à un but ; d'autre part, celui-ci pourra aussi s'exprimer par «for+gérondif».

verbes support à préposition u phrasal verbs (*come up with, work out, arrive at, look for, think of, come to, bring about, work on*).

4. Extraction automatique et phraséologie contrastive

Parmi les récents développements du TAL (traitement automatique du langage, en anglais NLP), l'extraction automatique des structures figées et des termes composés constitue l'une des pistes les plus prometteuses. Les phraséologismes et termes composés binaires (souvent désignés par le terme générique de *collocations* en linguistique computationnelle), peuvent être extraits par des scores statistiques tels que le *log-likelihood*, le t-score, le PMI (*pointwise mutual information*) et une bonne vingtaine d'autres (pour un aperçu, voir Evert, 2004).

Les travaux en cours portent sur l'extension de tels score statistiques aux n-grammes plus élevés (séquences de 3, 4, 5 mots ou même davantage). La méthode proposée dans Colson (2010) est basée non sur la probabilité statistique, mais sur la proximité moyenne entre les éléments du n-gramme, et offre des scores de rappel et de précision tout à fait satisfaisants (supérieurs à 90 %). Un aperçu détaillé de cette problématique sortirait du cadre de cette contribution. Nous nous contenterons ici d'illustrer par un exemple tout l'intérêt que présente l'extraction automatique des phraséologismes pour les recherches contrastives.

L'extraction automatique permet notamment d'évaluer de manière objective le caractère naturel d'une production linguistique quelconque en examinant la proportion de phraséologismes qu'elle contient. Ceci s'avère particulièrement utile dans l'enseignement des langues, mais également dans le domaine de la traduction. A titre de simple expérience, le tableau 5 ci-dessous présente les résultats de l'extraction automatique à partir d'un texte de l'Union Européenne décrivant le rôle du Médiateur européen (http://www.ombudsman.europa.eu/atyourservice/couldhehelpyou.faces), dans ses versions anglaise, française, allemande et néerlandaise.

Langue	Mots	3+	3-	4+	4-	Total
FR	177	50	19	15	14	98
EN	172	40	14	13	5	72
DE	158	27	14	10	2	53
NL	184	38	14	7	4	63

Tableau 4. Extraction automatique des phraséologismes dans un texte relatif au Médiateur européen

Ce tableau reprend l'ensemble des phraséologismes de 3 et 4 mots (trigrammes et 4-grammes) extraits dans chaque version du texte (français, anglais, allemand, néerlandais), et distingue les scores élevés (3+ et 4+) des scores faibles (3- et 4-). Au total, il apparaît clairement que les versions française et anglaise du texte contiennent nettement plus de phraséologismes que les versions allemande et néerlandaise.

5. Conclusion

Les développements récents de la linguistique de corpus, et en particulier la création de corpus de taille gigantesque, repoussent aujourd'hui les limites du champ d'investigation de la phraséologie contrastive. Celle-ci pourra y gagner ses lettres de noblesse, d'autant que se profilent dans son entourage des domaines aussi passionnants que l'apprentissage des langues et la traductologie.

6. Bibliographie

BARONI, M., BERNARDINI, S., FERRARESI, A. & E. ZANCHETTA. (2009). "The WaCky Wide Web: A collection of very large linguistically processed Web-crawled corpora". In: *Journal of Language Resources and Evaluation 43 (3)*, p. 209-226.

BARONI, M., MURPHY, B., BARBU, E. & M. POESIO. (2010). Strudel: "A corpus-based semantic model based on properties and types". In: *Cognitive Science 34 (2)*, p. 222-254.

Burger, H. (1998). *Phraseologie. Eine Einführung am Beispiel des Deutschen*. Berlin: Erich Schmidt Verlag.

COLSON, J.-P. (2003). "Corpus Linguistics and Phraseological Statistics: a Few Hypotheses and Examples". In: Burger, H., Häcki Buhofer, A. & G. Gréciano (eds.), *Flut von Texten – Vielfalt der Kulturen. Ascona 2001 zu Methodologie und Kulturspezifik der Phraseologie*. Baltmannsweiler, Schneider Verlag Hohengehren, p. 47-59.

COLSON, J.-P. (2007). "The World Wide Web as a corpus for set phrases". In: H. Burger, D. Dobrovol'skij, P. Kühn & N. R. Norrick (eds.), *Phraseologie / Phraseology. Ein internationales Handbuch der zeitgenössischen Forschung / An International Handbook of Contemporary Research. Volume 2*. Walter de Gruyter, Berlin / New York, p. 1071-1077.COLSON, J.-P. (2008). "Cross-linguistic phraseological studies: An overview". In: Granger, S. & F. Meunier (eds.), *Phraseology. An interdisciplinary perspective*. John Benjamins, Amsterdam / Philadelphia, p. 191-206.

COLSON, J.-P. (2010). "Automatic extraction of collocations: a new Web-based method". In: S. Bolasco, S., Chiari, I. & L. Giuliano, *Proceedings of JADT 2010,Statistical Analysis of Textual Data, Sapienza University , Rome, 9-11 June 2010*. Milan, LED Edizioni, p. 397-408.

EVERT, S. (2004). *The statistics of word cooccurrences -word pairs and collocations*. Ph.D. thesis, University of Stuttgart.

KILGARIFF, A. & G. GREFENSTETTE, eds. (2003). "Web as corpus. introduction to the special issue". In: *Computational Linguistics. Volume 29*, p. 1–15.

MOON, R. (1998). *Fixed Expressions and Idioms in English*. Oxford: Clarendon Press.

SINCLAIR, J. (1991). *Corpus, Concordance, Collocation*. Oxford: Oxford University Press.

WRAY, A. (2008). *Formulaic language: pushing the boundaries*. Oxford: Oxford University Press.

LES PRAGMATEMES, ENTRE THEORIE ET DESCRIPTION. LE CAS DU DUƩA:[1]

Salah Mejri
Université de Paris-13, LDI (UMR 7187) – CNRS
Université de Manouba, TIL (00/UR/0201)

Abstract: It is on the basis of Mel'cuk's typology of phrasemes that we will try to demonstrate the extreme diversity of the phraseological facts covered by the concept of pragmateme: utterances of any kind such as certain greetings or indications specific to certain writings, sequences like no smoking that whilst being transparent do not have identical sequences in the other languages, etc.

After having specified the characteristics of pragmatemes, we will provide a first typology that takes into account the shared universal dimension of this phenomenon in the characterisation and in the conditions of usage, and the idiomatic dimension of their linguistic realisation in each language. In order to illustrate this last dimension, we choose a particular type of pragmateme called "*doua*". We will describe its formal and semantic characteristics while providing a typology to be used as a reference in a systematic description of this phenomenon. More particularly, we are considering the problems that these phrasemes pose in translation. Their strong idiomatic anchoring blocks their transfer from one language to another. The study of pragmatemes opens new prospects for the phraseological studies.

Key words: Pragmatemes; [duƩa:]; translation; phraseology

La notion de pragmatème est relativement récente dans les travaux consacrés au figement (Mel'cuk, 2011, Polguère, 2008). Le terme, on le doit à Mel'cuk et Polguère qui en donnent une définition qui le distingue des autres types de séquences figées (phrasèmes) sans en fournir une analyse détaillée. Nous reprenons ici ce concept pour l'interroger en tant qu'outil théorique permettant d'établir les caractéristiques de ce genre de SF à partir desquelles il serait possible d'en proposer une première typologie et d'étudier un cas particulier de pragmatème en arabe, le *duƩa:*.

1. Le pragmatème dans la théorie

On peut distinguer deux moments dans l'émergence du concept de pragmatème : un moment pendant lequel la notion était trop floue pour permettre d'isoler des éléments phraséologiques pertinents et le moment où l'on en a fourni une définition précise.

La période qui a précédé l'émergence du concept de pragmatème a connu plusieurs notions telles que formule, énoncé formulaire, salutations, prière, formules routinières, etc. Les exemples fournis pour illustrer ces notions sont de type : *je t'en prie, il n'y a pas de quoi, avec mes meilleures salutations, avec mes salutations distinguées*, etc. Il s'agit en réalité de

---

[1] Ce travail a bénéficié de l'appui des projets suivants :
PICS : Les phrasèmes nominaux de la langue générale : description et classification;
CAPES-COFECUB n° sh 651/09.
LIA, Langues, Traductions, Apprentissage, LDI-CNRS-TIL-Université de Manouba.

notions génériques et préthéoriques qui s'appliquent soit à n'importe quelle séquence polylexicale (comme c'est le cas de formule), soit à une formule consacrée par l'usage dans une situation énonciative précise renvoyant le plus souvent à l'oral (énoncé formulaire), soit à des catégories d'expressions spécifiques à des fonctions précises dans l'échange verbal (salutations, prières, etc.). Même si ces notions présentaient l'avantage d'attirer l'attention sur un usage particulier des séquences figées, elles n'avaient pas pour autant la précision nécessaire à une distinction pertinente entre les différents types de formules. Ainsi, on considérait *Bonne journée* ! comme une formule, tout autant que la séquence *politiquement correcte*, souvent suivie de l'expression selon la formule consacrée.

C'est avec Mel'cuk qu'on assiste à la naissance de la notion de pragmatème (2011) qui le situe dans la typologie générale des phrasèmes (SF). Pour lui, un phrasème est un syntagme non libre. Les phrasèmes se répartissent en deux catégories, ceux qui sont conditionnés pragmatiquement et ceux qui ne le sont pas. Ceux qui ne sont pas conditionnés pragmatiquement sont des phrasèmes sémantiques, qui se répartissent en phrasèmes sémantiquement compositionnels (les collocations et les clichés) et phrasèmes non compositionnels (les locutions, faibles, fortes et semi-locutions). Les phrasèmes conditionnés pragmatiquement sont les pragmatèmes. *Défense de stationner* illustre bien ce concept : il s'agit d'une SF dont l'emploi est conditionné par une situation énonciative précise. L'apport théorique de cette notion peut être ramené aux points suivants :
- l'intégration de la dimension pragmatique dans le classement des SF : jusque-là, seul le contenu sémantique de la séquence comptait ; les conditions d'énonciation des SF n'étaient pas prises en compte ;
- l'emploi comme critère de classement : un tel critère permet d'opérer des distinctions entre les différentes significations de la même séquence ;
- un degré de généralisation qui permet d'englober l'oral et l'écrit : si l'oral ne pose pas de problèmes, les pragmatèmes écrits sont souvent omis, comme c'est le cas pour *N.B.* (*nota bene* « notez bien »), *P.S.* (*post scriptum* « écrit après »), *i.e.* (*id est* « c'est-à-dire »), etc.
- la transversalité du concept : il s'applique à toutes sortes de séquences, quelles qu'en soient la nature et la dimension : *Défense de stationner, je n'y manquerai pas, de quoi je me mêle*, etc.

2. Les caractéristiques générales des pragmatèmes

Nous fournissons dans ce qui suit les principales caractéristiques des pragmatèmes :
a. Les pragmatèmes sont des SF. A ce titre, ils partagent toutes les caractéristiques des autres séquences :
- le degré de figement :
Fin prêt (séquence totalement figée emploi de *fin* comme adverbe)
Amitiés, mes amitiés, toutes mes amitiés (substitution de déterminants)
- l'existence de variantes :
Ferme-la ! La ferme !
Défense de stationner / Stationnement interdit
- la polylexicalité : les contraintes pragmatiques ne sont pas spécifiques aux pragmatèmes : une unité monolexicale peut connaître de telles contraintes. Par contre, la

polylexicalité est une caractéristique formelle des pragmatèmes : *à bientôt, Messieurs dames, marché conclu !*

b. Les pragmatèmes peuvent faire l'objet de reformulations libres ayant le même sens mais sans la contrainte pragmatique. La différence entre les deux réside dans la marque pragmatique du pragmatème. Dans la même langue, on peut avoir des variantes diatopiques qui peuvent être considérées comme des paraphrases d'une région à l'autre (Lamiroy, 2010 :114) :

Il n'y a pas de mal (Belgique, France, Suisse)
Il n'y a pas de souci (Belgique, France, Suisse)
Il n'y a pas de faute (Québec)
Il n'y a pas d'offense (Québec)

On peut également se contenter de reformulations qui laissent intact le sens analytique :

Stationnement interdit / Défense de stationner ≈ *Ne stationnez pas. Vous n'avez pas le droit de vous garer / Impossible de stationner* (Polguère, 2008 : 220)

c. Le sens analytique des pragmatèmes est transparent : cette caractéristique est la preuve que ce qui fait le pragmatème, ce n'est pas seulement son sens analytique, mais les contraintes d'emploi :

A nous deux !; C'est (bien) le cas de le dire !; A qui le dites-vous !

d. Partant du constat que le sens analytique, qui est véhiculé par les mots, ne suffit pas à lui seul pour créer le pragmatème, on peut concevoir sa structure sémantique d'une manière binaire : un sens linguistique auquel on ajoute un sens pragmatique. Le premier, qui est le résultat de la combinatoire syntactico-sémantique, est compositionnel, transparent : *C'est moi qui vous le dis !* Le second, c'est-à-dire celui qui prend en charge l'emploi de la séquence dans une situation d'énonciation précise, est plutôt opaque : dans l'exemple de *A nous deux !*, il s'agit de préciser la condition d'emploi, c'est-à-dire ici une situation d'affrontement, avec jugement de supériorité de celui qui emploie la formule, et avec l'intention de menacer.

Chacun des deux sens a une contrepartie formelle : le sens linguistique a pour support les constituants de la séquence ; la contrepartie du sens pragmatique est la forme linguistique telle qu'elle s'exprime à travers le figement. Dans les exemples suivants : *A qui le dites-vous !* et *que voulez-vous que je vous dise !*, la syntaxe interrogative et l'expression de l'exclamation sont les deux traits saillants qui caractérisent le figement de ces séquences et les rattachent telles quelles aux deux sens respectifs suivants :

- « confirmation et renforcement de ce qui a été dit avec implication de bonne connaissance par le locuteur de ce qui a été avancé » (Rey et Chantreau) ;
- « évidence de ce qui précède, caractère superflu de toute autre preuve » (idem).

e. Le caractère isolable du sens pragmatique :

Le test le plus simple pour isoler le sens pragmatique consiste à employer les pragmatèmes dans des situations inadéquates. Si cela donne une incongruité sémantique qui découle de l'inadéquation entre le pragmatème utilisé et la situation d'énonciation, on doit en conclure que le sens pragmatique de la séquence n'a pas été respecté. Dans l'échange suivant :

- *Dégage ou je te casse la gueule,*
- *Je t'en prie,*

L'incongruité est le résultat de l'inadéquation entre la menace contenue dans la première réplique et la formule de la seconde réplique employée normalement pour exprimer un remerciement ; ce qui confirme une telle analyse, c'est le test de la substitution au moyen de pragmatèmes équivalents à *je t'en prie* : aussi bien *il n'y a pas de quoi* (hexagonal) que *bienvenu* (Québécois) ont, dans ce cas, le même effet.

Comme le sens pragmatique est étroitement lié à l'aspect formel du pragmatème, c'est-à-dire son caractère figé en tant que formule consacrée par l'usage dans une situation précise, toute transformation qui touche à cet aspect remet en question la bonne formation de la séquence en tant que contrepartie formelle du sens pragmatique. Dans le paradigme suivant : *mes félicitations ! mes condoléances !* qui représente les séquences employées dans une situation où le locuteur présente à l'interlocuteur ses félicitations ou ses condoléances, etc., il suffit qu'on touche à la forme pour que la séquence soit incongrue : **ma félicitation !* (le nombre) ; **tes/ses félicitations !* (la personne), **ta/sa félicitation !* (les deux : le nombre et la personne). On peut ajouter un autre exemple phrastique :

- *Rappelez-moi au bon souvenir de vos parents.*
- *Je n'y manquerai pas.*

Dans le pragmatème *je n'y manquerai pas*, on ne peut toucher ni au déictique ni à l'anaphore ni au temps du verbe ni au forclusif de la séquence.

C'est cette contrepartie formelle qui assure l'ancrage des pragmatèmes dans l'idiomaticité. Découle de cette caractéristique un comportement particulier lors de la traduction : ce qui prévaut dans la traduction des pragmatèmes, c'est le sens pragmatique ; un autre argument pour illustrer la hiérarchie entre les deux sens et la primauté du sens pragmatique. Les équivalents de bonjour en dialectal tunisien [nha:rik tajjib] [sbe:hilxi:r] [nha:rik dagla wa hli:b] [sbe:h il fill] [sba:hinnu:r] sont très nombreux : نهارك طيّب، صباح الخير، نهارك دقلة و حليب، صباح الفلّ، صباح النّور etc. [littéralement : *journée bonne / matinée de bien/ ta journée de dates et de lait / matinée de seringua / matinée de lumière*, etc.].

3. Typologie des pragmatèmes

Toute typologie doit tenir compte des deux contenus, sémantique et pragmatique, des pragmatèmes. Sur le plan sémantique, puisque le contenu est compositionnel, on peut appliquer aux pragmatèmes la même analyse que celle des phrases canoniques qui considère que les constituants d'une phrase sont réductibles aux trois fonctions primaires. Dans *Le garçon joue au ballon*, *joue* assure la fonction de prédicat, *garçon* et *ballon* celle des arguments et *le*, *au* et la marque temporelle celle d'actualisateurs. On peut se servir de la même paraphrase pour appliquer une telle analyse à des pragmatèmes. Dans *défense de fumer* et *sens interdit*, on peut avoir respectivement les paraphrases suivantes :

Défense de fumer ≈ *Il est défendu de fumer*

Sens interdit ≈ *Il est interdit de circuler dans ce sens*

L'analyse des deux paraphrases[2] permet de dégager, à l'instar des phrases canoniques, un prédicat, respectivement *défendre* et *interdire* et des arguments (argument 1 : élidé ; argument 2 : *fumer* et *circuler*, lesquels représentent à leur tour des prédicats).

---

[2] On entend par paraphrase l'équivalent de la définition naturelle (R. Martin, 1990) à laquelle on a recours spontanément dans le discours pour remplacer l'unité linguistique paraphrasée. Sa forme, pour les pragmatèmes, peut varier selon le degré de synthèse du pragmatème : elle est proche du pragmatème quand il est plutôt analytique (*défense de fumer* ≈ *il est défendu de fumer*) ; elle s'en éloigne quand il est synthétique (*bon vent* ≈ *je souhaite (au marin) du bon vent*).

Dans la définition que donne Polguère des lexies pragmatiquement définies (=pragmatèmes), il y a lieu de retenir les éléments suivants :
- « ces syntagmes sont pour la plupart sémantiquement compositionnels » (Polguère, 2008 : 221) ;
- ces lexies « sont faites pour être utilisées dans un contexte d'énonciation donné. La caractérisation d'un tel contexte d'énonciation fait partie intégrante du signifié de ces lexies » (ibidem, p. 220) ;
- elles « peuvent être considérées comme pragmatiquement non compositionnelles » (ibidem, p. 221).

Compte tenu de ces éléments définitoires de la hiérarchie qui existe entre les deux contenus, sémantique et pragmatique, le second conditionnant le premier, l'analyse du contenu sémantique des pragmatèmes (en termes de prédicats, d'arguments et d'actualisateurs) serait insuffisante. Cela signifie qu'à lui seul, il ne serait pas pertinent pour dégager le contenu pragmatique du pragmatème (cf. les exemples de Lamiroy et alii. pour les expressions québécoises comme *il n'y a pas de faute* et *il n'y a pas d'offense* et les équivalents de *bonjour* en dialectal tunisien). Vu l'insuffisance de l'analyse prédicative du contenu compositionnel à rendre compte du contenu pragmatique et l'opacité de ce dernier, il serait plus adéquat de voir dans les pragmatèmes des prédicats synthétiques analysables en :
- un contenu pragmatique, hiérarchiquement supérieur et opaque, dont le rôle est d'assigner à la séquence figée les conditions de son emploi ;
- un contenu sémantique, compositionnel, déductible de celui des constituants grâce à une paraphrase équivalente.

Des pragmatèmes comme *la belle affaire !* et *sens interdit* s'analyserait comme suit :

	Contenu pragmatique	Contenu sémantique
La belle affaire !	Exclamation ironique	On dénie de l'importance à ce qui vient d'être dit
Sens interdit	Indication du code de la route	Il est interdit de circuler dans ce sens[3]

Partant de ces considérations, on peut opérer un premier classement qui repose sur ce qu'on pourrait appeler une prédication pragmatique ou énonciative qui sert de cadre à la prédication du contenu sémantique. Ainsi on aura :
- des salutations : *à bientôt, au revoir*, etc.
- des insultes : *va te faire voir, espèce de X*, etc.
- des invocations : *au nom du ciel, pour l'amour de Dieu*, etc.

Peut s'inscrire dans ce premier classement un second qui tient compte des contenus sémantiques des séquences. Ainsi aurions-nous des sous-classes sémantiques à l'intérieur des classes pragmatiques. Pour les consignes du code de la route, on aura par exemple des interdictions (*sens interdit*), des autorisations (*stationnement autorisé les jours impairs*), des obligations (*cédez le passage*), etc.[4]

---

[3] Les deux paraphrases sont plus ou moins proches formellement du contenu compositionnel de la séquence figée selon que la forme est plutôt analytique (*sens interdit*) ou synthétique (*la belle affaire !*).

[4] L'analyse du discours des G.P.S. est à ce titre très éclairant.

4. Un type particulier de pragmatème, le duʕa:[5]

Le Larousse arabe-français (1983) donne du mot arabe *duʕa:* les équivalents français suivants : *appel, invocation, oraison, prière, requête, supplication, souhait* et *vœux*. Si on mettait en relation le *duʕa:* avec ses équivalents dans une perspective onomasiologique, on y verrait un hyperonyme qui trahit une grande richesse en sous-classes sémantiques. Cela est confirmé par sa grande richesse en arabe en tant que genre qui se décline sous plusieurs formes :
- un genre littéraire bien codé qu'on rencontre dans des ouvrages consacrés aux prières, aux imprécations, aux bénédictions, etc. ;
- un genre religieux lié à des rites religieux comme les différentes prières : celle des grandes fêtes religieuses, celle de la pluie, celle du vendredi, celle des cinq prières quotidiennes, etc.
- une profusion de formules et de séquences figées qui ponctuent l'échange verbal quotidien.

C'est ce dernier type qui nous intéresse ici. Il existe aussi bien en arabe littéral qu'en dialectal. Pour les analyser, nous partons de l'idée que le prédicat pragmatique (contenu ou sens pragmatique) est *duʕa:* qu'on peut paraphraser par : *j'invoque Dieu, je prie Dieu*, etc. Deux grandes catégories sont à distinguer *le duʕa: pour* (bénédiction) et *le duʕa: contre* (imprécation contre, malédiction). Le premier est dénommé en tunisien *daʕ:lxir* « doua du bien », le second *daʕ:ʃʃar* « doua du mal ». Dans chacune des deux catégories sont versés les contenus sémantiques des séquences (sens compositionnel) :

[(barra:/rabbi:) junsrik] « Va ! [que] Dieu te rend[e] victorieux » (برّا، ربّي ينصرك)

[(barra:/rabbi:) jʒi:bik fi swa:b] « Va ! [que] Dieu te met[te] sur le droit chemin » (برّا، ربّي يجيبك في الصواب)

[(barra:/rabbi:) jsiddha fi wiʒhik] « Va, [que] Dieu ferme les portes devant toi » (برّا، ربّي يسدّها في وجهك)

[(barra:/rabbi:) jihlkik] « Va, [que] Dieu te corromp[e] » (برّا، ربّي يهلك)

Comme on le constate, l'attaque sert de marqueur formel au type *duʕa:*. Même si on peut en faire l'économie partiellement (l'un des deux éléments) ou totalement (les deux éléments), la forme raccourcie demeure reconnaissable.

Ainsi, la superposition des deux contenus, sémantique et pragmatique, donnerait lieu à des séquences comportant une double prédication étroitement liées, hiérarchisées et ayant des emplois où il n'est pas possible de dissocier les deux. L'imbrication des deux prédicats, le *duʕa:*, qu'il soit de bénédiction ou de malédiction, donne à ce genre de séquence une structuration prédicative comportant :
- un premier prédicat à valeur pragmatique qui consiste à faire un *duʕa:* pour ou contre quelqu'un,
- un second prédicat chargé de l'expression du contenu du *duʕa:*.

---

[5] Il s'agit d'un projet mené dans le cadre de l'unité de recherche TIL (00/UR/0201) et du laboratoire international associé-CNRS (LIA) entre le TIL et LDI, qui consiste à collecter des corpus oraux et écrits en arabe littéral et dialectal pour en effectuer l'analyse. L'objectif de ce texte est d'exposer les éléments théoriques retenus pour analyser les corpus.

Le premier a une valeur performative puisque le fait de prononcer un *duʃa:* implique l'accomplissement d'un acte, le second assure deux fonctions : préciser le contenu de l'acte et par conséquent orienter le *duʃa:* positivement ou négativement.

Nous comptons appliquer cette méthode d'analyse à la totalité des corpus collectés en vue d'en faire un classement selon qu'il s'agit d'un *duʃa:* pour ou d'un *duʃa:* contre, avec l'établissement de sous-classes sémantiques selon le contenu sémantique des séquences.

5. Conclusion

Il apparaît à la suite de cette démonstration que les pragmatèmes ont une structure duale comportant un contenu pragmatique qui en précise les conditions d'emploi dans une situation énonciative bien déterminée et un contenu sémantique qui est le fruit du sens compositionnel de la séquence. Les deux contenus sont hiérarchisés, le premier conditionnant l'emploi du second. L'interdépendance structurelle des deux contenus en fait un prédicat double : la simple énonciation d'un pragmatème donne lieu à l'expression d'une double prédication. Dans le cas du *duʃa:*, cela se traduit par une valeur performative véhiculée par le prédicat pragmatique, l'acte du *duʃa:* pour ou contre, et le prédicat sémantique qui exprime le contenu de l'acte langagier accompli. Il reste entre autres à démontrer :

- en quoi consiste la notion de double prédicat : en quoi est-elle différente de la prédication élémentaire, la prédication seconde et la prédication du second degré ? ;
- si le double prédicat est spécifique aux pragmatèmes ou s'il couvre d'autres réalités linguistiques ;
- si la dimension performative est limitée au seul type de pragmatème, *duʃa:*, ou si l'analyse proposée pour le *duʃa:* peut être généralisée.

6. Bibliographie

AS-SABIL, *Dictionnaire Arabe-Français, Français-Arabe*. 1983 Paris: Larousse.
LAMIROY, B., KLEIN, J.; LABELLE, J.; LECLÈRE; C., MEUNIER, A. & ROSSARI, C. (coords.) 2010 *Les expressions verbales figées de la francophonie. Les variétés de Belgique, France, Québec, Suisse*. Paris: Ophrys.
MARTIN, R. (ed.) 1990 *La définition*. Coll. *Langue et Langage*. Paris: Larousse /Centre d'études du lexique.
MEJRI, S. 1997 *Le figement lexical. Descriptions linguistiques et structuration sémantique*. Tunis: Publications de la Faculté des Lettres de La Manouba.
MEJRI, S. 2003 *Syntaxe et sémantique*, n°5, *Polysémie et polylexicalité*. Caen: Presses Universitaires.
MEJRI, S. 2006 « Structure inférentielle des proverbes ». In: Annelies Häcki Buhofer et Harald Burger (eds.), *Phraseology in Motion 1, Phraseology und Parönialogy, Band 19, Methoden und kritik*, Baltmannsweiler: Schneider Verlag: 175-187.
MEJRI, S. 2001 « La structuration sémantique des énoncés proverbiaux », *L'information grammaticale*, 88 (Paris, CILF): 10-15.
MEJRI, S. 2008 «Inférence et structuration des énoncés proverbiaux». In: D. Leeman (ed.) *Des topoï à la théorie des stéréotypes en passant par la polyphonie et l'argumentation dans la langue. Hommage à J.C. Anscombre*, *Langages*, Université de Savoie: 169-180.
MEJRI, S. 2011 « Opacité et idiomaticité des expressions figées : deux repères en traduction ». In: P. Mogorron Huerta & S. Mejri (eds.), *Opacité, idiomaticité, traduction*, Alicante: Université.
MEJRI, S. & François, J. (eds.) 2006 *Composition syntaxique et figement lexical*. Caen: Presses Universitaires.
MEL'CUK, I. 1984 *Dictionnaire explicatif et combinatoire du français contemporain. Recherches lexico-sémantiques*, Vol 1. Montréal: Presses Universitaires.
MEL'CUK, I. 2011 « Phrasèmes dans le dictionnaire ». In: J.-C. Anscombre & S. Mejri (dirs.) *Le figement linguistique. La parole entravée*. Paris-Genève: Honoré Champion: 41-62.
POLGUERE, A. 2008 *Lexicologie et sémantique lexicale. Notions fondamentales*, Montréal: Presses Universitaires.
REY, A. & CHANTREAU, S. 1989 [2006], *Dictionnaire des expressions et locutions*, Paris: LeRobert.

WHAT GLUES IDIOMS TOGETHER MAY NOT BE JUST STATISTICS AFTER ALL? THE CASE FOR COMPOUND ADVERBS IN PORTUGUESE AND SPANISH

Jorge Baptista
Universidade do Algarve/FCHS, L2F/INESC ID Lisboa
Dolors Català
Universitat Autònoma de Barcelona/DFFR, fLexSem

Abstract: The construction of lexicon resources seems to continue to be an unavoidable bottleneck for the integration of multiword expressions in natural language processing systems, because of the costly and time-consuming task of identifying and formalizing them into computational lexicons. The problem becomes more difficult to tackle if one intends to build (semi-automatically) a lexicon directly from large-sized corpora. This paper aims at investigating the distributional constraints between verbs and idiomatic, compound adverbs. Instead of looking for multiword idioms in texts, we take the opposite approach. Based on extensive lists of Portuguese and Spanish adverbs, we determine the efficiency of several statistical measures and apply these methods on large-sized corpora.

Key words: idioms, adverbs, Portuguese, Spanish, Computational Linguistics, Natural Language Processing

1. Introduction

In many Spanish (Català 2003) and Portuguese (Palma 2009) verb-adverbial idioms, such as in (1)[1]:

(1) pt: *O João fala pelos cotovelos* / sp: *Juan habla por los codos*
John speaks by the elbows 'to speak excessively'

there seems to be a strong distributional constraint between the verb and the adverb: not only is the verb unique for this prepositional phrase

(2) pt: **O João (conversa + diz + responde + murmura) pelos cotovelos*
sp: **Juan (conversa + dice + responde + murmura) por los codos*
John chats/says/answers/murmurs by the elbows

but it also lacks its normal syntactic frame, namely its 'theme/object' and 'addressee' complements :

(3) pt: *O João falou com a Ana sobre este assunto* (E + **pelos cotovelos*)
sp: *Juan habló con Ana sobre este asunto* (E + **por los codos*)
John spoke with Ana on this subject (by the elbows)

---

[1] An English word-by-word translation is provided to illustrate syntactic phenomena. A gloss in inverted comas may also be provided. The acceptability of this English translation is irrelevant for this paper. Each language is signaled in the examples by 'pt' or 'sp', for Portuguese and Spanish, respectively. Notations are straightforward: words between brackets and separated by '+' can vary in that given syntactic slot; *Prep* stands for preposition, *Adj* for adjective and so on; *C* stands for lexical constant; 'E' stands for the null string. Other notations are explained *in situ*.

Therefore, the prepositional phrase pt: *pelos cotovelos*/ sp: *por los codos* of (1) cannot be zeroed or the particular idiomatic meaning of the sentence would be lost.

In other cases, even if the verb is unique, such as in (4):

(4) pt: *O João riu-se às gargalhadas* / sp: *Juan se rió a carcajadas*
John laugh at (the) laughs, 'to laugh heartily'

the adverbial idiom looks like a mere quantifier, hence it can be zeroed without affecting the sentences overall acceptability. The syntactic structure of the verb remains unaltered in the presence of this idiomatic phrase:

(5) pt: *O João riu-se (da Ana + disso + E) às gargalhadas*
sp: *Juan se rió (de Ana + de eso + E) a carcajadas*
John laugh about Ana/that at (the) laughs, 'to laugh heartily'

However, it must be noted that in both sentences (1) and (4), these idiomatic phrases can be replaced by (quantifier) adverbs like pt: *muito*/sp: *mucho* ('very much', 'a lot') or pt: *demais*/sp: *demasiado* ('too much'), without changing the overall meaning of the sentence.

In order to build a computational lexicon of idioms, one has to ascertain if a given pair of words (and their variants) is just a chance (even if creative) word cooccurrence or if it is a relevant collocation. In this case, the lexicographer must decide whether to include in the lexicon the entire idiom pt:*falar pelos cotovelo*/sp:*hablar por los codos* as a frozen sentence (M. Gross 1982, 1996), that is, a verb with a frozen (adverbial) complement, even if the overall meaning of the verb pt: *falar*/*hablar* does not seem to be different from other contexts. The nature of the semantic relation between idioms and base verbs becomes, thus an important issue for linguistic description. On the other hand, in the case of pt: *rir às gargalhadas*/sp: *reír a carcajadas*, it may seem more adequate to consider the phrase as compound adverb (M. Gross 1986), even if it only operates on a single verb. One may consider this to be a collocation, in the sense of Mel'čuk (1994), expressing the lexical function MAGNUS of 'high degree' quantification.

The problem becomes more difficult to tackle if one intends to build (semi-automatically) a lexicon directly from large-sized corpora. Manning and Schütze (1999), among others, present basic statistical tools to rank candidate collocations in order to speed up the work of lexicographers in the task of compiling lists of compound words and other word combinations. Those methods seem to work fine when enough data is available. However, as it will be seen in the paper, they are less than effective to describe verb-adverb distributional constraints, such as the restrictions presented in the examples above.

This paper aims at investigating the distributional constraints between verbs and idiomatic, compound adverbs. Instead of looking for multiword idioms in texts, we take the opposite approach. Based on extensive lists of Portuguese and Spanish adverbs, we determine the efficiency of several statistical measures and apply these methods on large-sized corpora.

2. Related work

There is an extensive literature on the automatic discovery of multiword expressions (MWE) and their retrieval from texts, such as Church and Hanks (1990), Manning and Schütze (1999), or McKeown and Radev (2000), for an overview[2]. As concrete examples of the

---

[2] State-of-the-art research on MWE has been under the scope of the special interest group on the lexicon (SIGLEX: http://www.siglex.org/) of the Association for Computational

application of these methods, for example, in European Portuguese MWE, one can cite Dias (2008) and for the Brazilian variety Oliveira 2004 and Caseli (2009). Comparative studies between the two varieties based on the use of statistical methods are rare, but one can cite Baptista *et al.* (2011). On available lexicons of compound adverbs, for other languages than those under the scope of this paper, see Laporte and Voyatzi (2008), for French, and De Gioia (2001), for Italian.

3. Methods

We consider that extensive lexical coverage of Spanish compound adverbs has already been achieved by Català (2003). The dictionary of Spanish compound adverbs contains about 4,500 entries. These lexical items were formally classified according to the internal sequence of grammatical categories, based on the classes first presented by M. Gross (1982, 1986). The same methodology for collecting and classifying Portuguese compound adverbs was used by Palma (2009). The Portuguese dictionary of compound adverbs is currently composed of about 2,000 entries. This study, however, only described those compounds whose internal structure corresponds to prepositional phrases. Other studies are also available for the comparative forms of Portuguese (Ranchhod 1991), e.g. pt: [*comer*] *como um abade* '[eat] like an abbot' (='too much').

In order to study the distribution of verb-adverb combinations, the class PCPC was selected, which includes expressions such as pt/sp: *de cabo a rabo* 'from top to bottom, completely' and whose items are formed by the sequence *Prep C Prep C*. This class is composed of about 150 items both in Spanish and in Portuguese. Some entries were discarded because they consist of semi-productive strings where C is not a noun, such as demonstrative determiners (e.g. pt: *um após outro*/sp: *uno tras otro* 'one after another'), or numerals (e.g. pt: *um a um*/sp: *uno a uno* 'one by one'). Several compound temporal adverbs, mainly built around close sets of time-related nouns (e.g. pt: *dia a dia*/sp: *día a día* 'day by day') were also ignored. Other Portuguese compound temporal adverbs were not considered, since they involve internal adverbs (e.g. pt: *daqui a nada*/sp: *muy pronto* 'very soon', pt: *de agora em diante*/sp: *en lo sucesivo* 'from now on').

After this initial selection, the concordances of the remaining items were retrieved from the Spanish 152 million words *Corpus de Referencia del Español Actual* (CREA) of the Real Academia Española[3] and the Portuguese 190 million words CETEMPúblico corpus, available at Linguateca[4]. To the best of our knowledge, these are the two largest corpora publicly available for each language, which was the main reason for choosing them for this study. It should be noticed that the two corpora are not directly comparable, since the CREA includes texts from all geographical varieties of Spanish and many textual genres, including speech, while the CETEMPúblico is only composed of written journalistic material, from the

---

Linguistics (ACL: http://www.aclweb.org/) and the several workshops it has organized since the mid-90's.

[3] http://corpus.rae.es/creanet. The current version of the corpus contains precisely 152,558,294 words.

[4] http://www.linguateca.pt/cetempublico/ (189,575,095 words).

European variety of Portuguese. Differences in results are, therefore, to be expected. Table 1 presents the frequency of these adverbs in the corpora.

Table 1. PCPC distribution on the Spanish CREA and Portuguese CETEMPúblico corpora

	Spanish			Portuguese		
Frequency	Number of Entries	Count	% Total Count	Number of Entries	Count	% Total Count
0	32	0	0.000	-	-	-
1	11	11	0.001	4	4	0.001
2 to 9	15	65	0.005	21	106	0.017
11 to 99	37	1,607	0.115	43	1,726	0.269
100 to 199	10	865	0.062	5	797	0.124
200 to 499	5	1,862	0.134	3	1,035	0.161
>500	6	9,013	0.647	4	2,746	0.428
Total	117	13,926		80	6,414	

In the large corpus of contemporary Spanish, 32 out of 117 entries do not appear at all and 11 only appear once. On the other hand, among the 6 most frequent expressions totaling 9,013 occurrences, 5,658 alone correspond to the adverb sp: *poco a poco* 'little by little'. Only 12 adverbs show a frequency higher that 1 occurrence per million words. For the Portuguese, we retained a smaller number of entries (80), but the frequency classes are approximately the same. Also, due to the better research tools, we were able to factorize the search and grouped together many variants; this is why we do not show results for entries with zero occurrences. In this corpus, only 8 adverbs occur more than 1 time per million words.

3.1. Internal combinatorial constraints

Because of their small frequency, even in such a large corpus, it may be particularly difficult to automatically spot these compound adverbs in texts and retrieve them. Using the frequency list of the tokens of the corpus, the *t*-test and χ^2 (Manning and Schütze 1999)[5] measures were calculated for the two C-word combinations of each adverb with a non-null frequency in the corpus, thus ignoring the other grammatical components of the frozen adverb. Results are shown in Table 2:

---

[5] *Mutual information* (MI) (Church and Hanks 1990) is another statistic measure sometimes used to measure the combinatorial constraint between to word occurrences. Manning and Schütze (1999: 180-181), however, discuss the shortcomings of this statistics, basically due to its sensitivity to data sparseness, and conclude that it is not a good measure to capture dependency among word occurrences (in this case, the fixedness of the compound). Furthermore, unlike t-test and $\chi 2$, MI cannot be used in hypothesis testing, therefore, it was not used here.

Table 2. Internal combinatorial constraints (using *t*-test and χ^2)

	Spanish				Portuguese			
	t	%	χ^2	%	t	%	χ^2	%
TRUE	45	0.53	67	0.79	60	0.75	79	0.99
FALSE	40	0.47	18	0.21	20	0.25	1	0.01

In the Spanish corpus, 45 out of 85 (i.e. 0.53 %) of the idioms attained the threshold of the t-test (for α=0.005, p=2.575) to discard the null hypothesis (i.e. it is possible to say that those combinations did not occur by mere chance). However, as it is well known, the t-test presupposes a uniform distribution of the sample, so we compared it with the χ^2. As expected, only 18 items (21%) did not yield a statistically significant χ^2 result. This statistical measure seems, then, to be more efficient than the t-test in the discovery of this type of combinatorial patterns. However, even for such frozen combinations as PCPC adverbs, data from large-sized corpus is insufficient to capture about $^1/_5$ of these adverbial lexical entries.

In the Portuguese corpus, even if the total of items here tested is smaller (only 73 entries), results are significantly better, for only 21% of the adverbs were not captured by the t-test, while all entries were captured by χ^2 statistics.

In view of these results, it seems that the χ^2 statistics is a better tool than t-test to spot strings with two C elements that could be candidates to the status of compound adverb. Even so, the corpus homogeneity (in terms of the genres and language variety) may influence the effectiveness of these tools. Considering the Spanish heterogeneous corpus as against the more homogeneous Portuguese journalistic corpus, it seems that homogeneity may be related to better the results obtained with the latter.

3.2. Verb-adverb combinatorial constraints

In order to study the distribution of verb-adverb combinations, only up to 200 randomly selected occurrences of each adverb appearing more than 10 times in the Spanish corpus (0,065 occurrences per million words) were analyzed. The concordances were processed with the lexical resources for Spanish distributed with Unitex 2.0 (Paumier 2008), in order to extract all verb-adverb combinations in a window of up to 5 words.

For the set of occurrences of each adverb (#Corpus), the number of different verbs (V) was calculated, then the number of verbs appearing only once (V#1), twice (V#2), etc. was counted, up to verbs appearing 5 times (V#5) or more than 5 times (V#>5). Finally, the total dispersion rate (Disp) of the verbs among the concordances retrieved from corpus was calculated. Certain concordances from the Spanish corpus had to be discarded, since they did not contain any verb adverb combination. The calculation of the dispersion rate is based only in the manually validated concordances. For the Portuguese data, the corpus interface was used to retrieve the equivalent concordances. However, with this tool it is possible to obtain directly the distribution of the verbs occurring within that window distance from the target expression. Therefore, there was no need to discard any concordances.

A sample of the results, by decreasing dispersion rate, of adverbs appearing more than 10 times in the two corpora, is shown in Table 3 and
Table 4:

Table 3. Distribution of verb-adverb combinations in Spanish

ID	Adverb	#Corpus	V	V#1	V#2	V#3	V#4	V#5	V#>5	Disp
[0066]	de mar a	10	8	8	0	0	0	0	0	1.000
[0132]	de trecho en	27	22	21	1	0	0	0	0	0.957
[0104]	del principio	19	12	11	1	0	0	0	0	0.923
[0105]	de puerta a	11	9	8	1	0	0	0	0	0.900
[0100]	pieza por	38	32	29	2	1	0	0	0	0.889
[0051]	letra por	30	23	20	1	2	0	0	0	0.821
[0016]	de la cabeza	85	55	48	2	0	1	1	3	0.733
[0085]	paso por	31	20	16	1	2	0	1	0	0.714
[0013]	de buenas a	101	66	57	8	0	0	1	0	0.710
[0034]	de extremo a	57	38	31	4	1	1	0	1	0.691
[0077]	de par en	434	7	3	3	0	0	0	1	0.035

Table 4. Distribution of verb-adverb combinations in Portuguese

ID	Adverb	#Corpus	V	V#1	V#2	V#3	V#4	V#5	V#>5	Disp
[0022]	a cem à hora	10	10	10	0	0	0	0	0	1.000
[0040]	boca a boca	16	15	14	1	0	0	0	0	0.938
[0031]	de A a Z	12	11	10	1	0	0	0	0	0.917
[0029]	por amor à	11	10	10	0	0	0	0	0	0.909
[0030]	mano a mano	11	10	9	1	0	0	0	0	0.909
[0052]	gota a gota	21	19	18	0	1	0	0	0	0.905
[0026]	de homem para	10	9	8	1	0	0	0	0	0.900
[0027]	com água na boca	10	9	8	1	0	0	0	0	0.900
[0028]	tintim=por=tintim	10	9	9	0	0	0	0	0	0.900
[0043]	de orelha a	19	17	16	0	1	0	0	0	0.895

Table 5. Average distribution of verb-adverb combinations in Spanish and in Portuguese

PCPC in the Spanish Corpus							
	#1	#2	#3	#4	#5	#>5	Disp
#/N	0.346	0.098	0.062	0.034	0.021	0.438	0.454
#/V	0.895	0.155	0.057	0.025	0.022	0.078	

PCPC in the Portuguese Corpus							
	#1	#2	#3	#4	#5	#>5	Disp
#/N	0.598	0.093	0.067	0.030	0.027	0.186	0.694
#/V	0.822	0.080	0.039	0.014	0.010	0.033	

For lack of space, we summarize these results by showing average results both for Spanish and Portuguese in
Table 5. The columns indicate the frequency class, i.e., verb-adverb combinations from #1 up to more than #5 occurrences. The average results are given for the number of verb-adverb combinations over the total number of occurrences (#/N) and over the total number of different verbs found in those concordances (#/V).

4. Discussion

Results show that, in average, most verbs occurring with the PCPC adverbs appear only once: 89.5% in the Spanish corpus and a little less (82.2%) in the Portuguese corpus. Next frequency classes are all below 10%, except in Spanish, where there is in average 15% of verb-adverb combinations appearing twice. On the other hand, verb-adverb combinations appearing only once in the corpora constitute a significant proportion of all occurrences, especially in Portuguese (almost 60%), while in Spanish these correspond to 1/3 (approximately 35%) of all occurrences. These results may indicate that there are very few adverbs that show a strong selection on the verb.

The dispersion rate (Disp) is also interesting. Notice that the higher the dispersion rate, the harder it would be to establish a distributional preference of an adverb over a set of verbs it combines with. In average, Spanish verb-adverb combinations have Disp=0.456 while in Portuguese this average in much higher, Disp=0.694. In Spanish, there are only 4 adverbs with Disp>0.9 (and only one with Disp=1), while in Portuguese, there are 22 cases of Disp>0.9 (and 14 with Disp=1).

In Spanish, the most disperse cases, with Disp>9 are: *de mar a mar* (1.0), *de trecho en trecho* (0.957), *del principio al fin* (0.923) and *de puerta a puerta* (0.9). Looking to the concordances of the adverb sp: *de mar a mar* 'from sea to sea', where for each occurrence there is a different verb (Fig. 1):

Fig. 1. Concordances of sp: *de mar a mar* 'from sea to sea'

1. *Como parece dormida la guerra*, **de mar a mar.**
2. *a través de los Estados Unidos, de punta a punta,* **de mar a mar** , *y lo metía en líos, un lío tras otro, c 2004*
3. *de todas las riquezas* **esparcidas** *de sur a norte,* **de mar a mar** , *bajo este nuevo cielo descubierto [...]*
4. **De mar a mar** , *efectivamente, un espaci 1983*
5. *fundadores del imperio mexica, que* **llegaba de mar a mar** .
6. *sin ideas, como en los tiempos de Ortega,* **tendida de mar a mar** , *entre la Maladeta y Calpe.*
7. *"Tan gran era, que el su señorío durava et* **tenie de mar a mar** , *bien desde [...] de Taniar, que es 1985*
8. *y miles de cruces que hoy* **surcan** *el continente* **de mar a mar** .
9. *o imaginé, en aquellos días: - Una revolución* **de mar a mar** .
10. *interior secreto de espadas y orgasmo* **contenido** **de mar a mar** .
11. *que* **cruzan** *los Estados Unidos* **de mar a mar** , *ocultos en un vagón de mercancías*

One can see that not all contexts above are relevant for describing the distribution because in same examples there is neither verb nor other predicative element, the window being too small. However, even in such a small sample, it is possible to find out distributional regularities, namely the cooccurrence with **place-changing** or **movement** verbs like *cruzar* 'cross', *llegar* 'span', *surcar* 'sulcar' and *tender* 'spread'. Naturally, none of these intuitions about the distribution of this particular adverb can be captured by statistical methods because of the diminutive size of the sample. A similar phenomenon can be found in Portuguese adverb pt: *pé ante pé* 'to tiptoe' (Dist=0.777):

Fig. 2. Concordances of pt: pé ante pé 'to tiptoe'

1. *Uma senhora idosa,* [...] ***pé ante pé*** [...] **ultrapassou** *meia fila* [...] .
2. [...] *parece parada enquanto realmente* **anda** *pé ante pé* [...]
3. *ao lado das quais se deve* **passar** *pé ante pé, não vão elas sequer acordar levemente do seu inquieto sono* .
4. [...] *ouviu os pais levantarem-se, e* **irem***, pé ante pé, para a lareira,* [...]
5. [...] *foi este filme que* **caminha** *pé ante pé com demasiadas cautelas,* [...]
6. [...] *é* **caminhar** *pé ante pé, então o ministro* [...]
7. *uma guinada, a que teria sucedido um* **regresso** *pé ante pé à primitiva* [*concepção de Salazar*],
8. *Temos que* **ir** *pé ante pé,* [...]
9. [...] **Fujo** *pé ante pé* .

In this case, all verbs in the concordances are **place-changing** or **movement** verbs: *andar* 'walk', *caminhar* 'walk', *ir* 'go', *passar* 'pass', and *ultrapassar* 'bypass/surpass'; there is also one case of a predicative deverbal noun *regresso* 'return'. By using the semantic category of verbs co-occurring with a given adverb, it might be possible to reuse the t-test and χ^2 statistic measures to discover significant verb-adverb collocational patterns, However, to our knowledge, there is no (reproducible) semantic classification of verbs for any of these two languages available yet – even for the most commonly used verbs – so that one could use it to help describe the distribution of the verb-adverb combinations.

5. Conclusions and future work

Due to the lack of semantic descriptions, it is thus necessary to build *distributional profiles* for each compound adverb. For compound adverb pt: *pé ante pé* 'to tiptoe', this would correspond to something like:
- ***pé ante pé****: caminhar , ir* (2) *andar, fugir, passar, regresso, ultrapassar* (1)

However, automatically building distributional profiles of a given word/string is a non trivial task and requires a sophisticated parser. For example, in the concordance above, one has to consider the scope of the adverb that may appear before or after it (e.g. *ultrapassar*) as well its scope on elements other than verbs (e.g. *regresso* 'return', noun). The raw, non-edited distributional profile produced by simple pattern matching techniques like the ones here used may be clearly misleading; for example, using only the previously occurring verb, it would look like:
- ***pé ante pé****: caminhar, complicar, dar, dever, fazer, ir, olhar, parar, ter* (1)

Nevertheless, even so basic tools can, in some cases, be quite useful, like in the raw profile of adverb pt: [*abrir*] *de par em par* '[open] wide', where the collocational pattern with verb *abrir* 'open' is clearly evident:
- ***de par em par*:**   *abrir* (38), *despertar, enrolar, entrar, escancarar, evoluir, fazer, ir, murar, ocorrer, proporcionar, saber, temer, voltar* (1)

On the other hand, adverbs, especially compound adverbs, usually less ambiguous than simple words, with a relatively broad selection, could be used as a linguistic tool to better describe the semantically homogenous classes of predicates.

Acknowledgments

Research for this paper was partially supported by Fundação para a Ciência e a Tecnologia (FCT-MCTES, Portugal) under project REAP-PT (proj. ref. CMU-PT/HuMach/0053/2008).

6. References

BAPTISTA, J., VALE, O.& MAMEDE, N. 2011 "Identificação de expressões fixas em corpora: até onde podem ir os métodos estatísticos?". In: Shepherd, T.; Berber Sardinha, T. & Veirano Pinto, M. (Org.). *Linguística de Corpus: Sínteses e Avanços. Proceedings of the 7th Corpus Linguistics Conference (UERJ, Rio de Janeiro, 2009)*, Rio: Mercado das Letras: 159-172.

CASELI, H., VILLAVICENCIO, A., MACHADO & A., FINATTO, M. J. 2009 "Statistically-driven Alignment-Based Multiword Expression Identifications for Technical Domains". In: Proceedings of the *Workshop on Multiword Expressions (ACL-IJCNLP 2009)*, Suntec, Singapore: 1-8.

CATALA, D. 2003 *Les Adverbes Composés. Approches contrastives en Linguistique Appliquée*. (PhD Thesis). Barcelona: UAB.

CATALÀ, D. & BAPTISTA, J. 2007 "Spanish Adverbial Frozen Expressions". In: Proceedings of the Workshop *A Broader Perspective on Multiword Expressions (MWE 2007, Prague, June 2007), International Conference of the European Chapter of the Association for Computational Linguistics*: 33-40.

CHURCH, K. & HANKS, P. 1990 "Word association norms, mutual information, and lexicography". *Computational Linguistics* 16 (1): 22-29.

DE GIOIA, M. : 2001 *Avverbi idiomatici dell'Italliano. Analisi lessico-grammaticale*. Torino: Harmattan.

DIAS, G. 2005 "Extração automática de unidades polilexicais para o português". In: Sardinha, Tony (Org.) *A Língua Portuguesa no Computador*. São Paulo: Mercado das Letras: 155-184.

GROSS, M. 1986 *Grammaire transformationnelle du français : III – Syntaxe de l'adverbe*. Paris: ASSTRIL.

GROSS, M. 1982 "Lexicon Grammar". In: Brown, K.; Miller, J. (eds.): *Concise Encyclopedia of Syntactic Theories*. Cambridge: Pergamon: 244-258.

GROSS, M. 1982 Une classification des phrases figées du français. *Revue Québéquoise de Linguistique* 11(2) (Montréal: UQAM): 151-185.

LAPORTE, E. & VOYATZI, S. 2008 "An Electronic Dictionary of French Multiword Adverbs". In: Proceedings of *LREC'2008, Language Resources and Evolution Conference*. Workshop *Towards a Shared Task for Multiword Expressions (MWE2008, Marrakech)*: 31-39.

MANNING, C. & SCHÜTZE, H. 1999 [5th ed. 2003] *Foundations of Statistical Natural Language Processing*. Cambridge (MA): MIT Press.

MCKEOWN, K. & RADEV, D. 2000 "Collocations". In: Dale, Robert ; Moisl, Hermann & Somers, Harold (eds.). *Handbook of Natural Language Processing*. New York/Basel: Marcel Dekker: 507-523.

MEL'ČUK, I. 1994 "Fonctions lexicales dans le traitement du langage naturel". In: André Clas et Piérette Bouillon (réd.), *TA-TAO: Recherches de pointe et applications immédiates*, 1994, Beyrouth : FMA, 193-219.

OLIVEIRA, C., FREITAS, M. C., GARRÃO, M., ARANHA, C., & NOGUEIRA, C. 2004 "A extracção de expressões multi-vocabulares: uma abordagem estatística". *PaLavra* 12: 172-192, Rio de Janeiro: PUCRJ.

PALMA, CRISTINA. 2009 *Estudo Contrastivo Português-Espanhol de Expressões Fixas Adverbiais* (MA Thesis), Faro: UALG.
PAUMIER, S. 2008 *Unitex 2.0 User Manual*. Marne-la-Vallée: Université de Marne-la-Vallée/Institut Gaspard Monge.
http://www.igm.univ mlv.fr/~unitex/ UnitexManual2.0.pdf
RANCHHOD, E. 1991 "Frozen adverbs. Comparative forms *Como C* in Portuguese". In *Lingvisticae Investigationes* 11(1) [Amsterdam/Philadelphia: John Benjamins]: 141-170.

PROPUESTAS TEÓRICAS Y METODOLÓGICAS PARA EL ESTUDIO DE LAS UNIDADES FRÁSICAS EN CONTEXTO

Maria Conca
Josep Guia
Universitat de València

Abstract: By building on theories we have contributed elsewhere, this paper introduces new phraseological concepts, redefines ones that are known already, and describes the method of phrasic concordance. It offers a way to develop rigorously phrasic corpus drawn from literary works and conduct proper phraseological analysis.

Keywords: phrasic units, stylistic units, phrasic concordance, insertion modalities

1. Introducción

El estudio de las unidades frásicas (UFs) en contexto es un foco de interés para fraseólogos y paremiólogos,[1] sobretodo por la necesidad de analizar el significado contextualizado de estas unidades para la elaboración de diccionarios, la enseñanza de lenguas, la traducción, etc. El desarrollo de disciplinas lingüísticas que toman como base el uso de la lengua en su contexto (semiótica, pragmática, análisis del discurso, lingüística cognitiva...) ha contribuido eficazmente al avance del estudio fraseológico que nos ocupa.

El propósito de este trabajo es presentar un método general para la elaboración y el análisis de un corpus frásico a partir de un corpus textual literario, donde las unidades frásicas se encuentran usadas en contexto, que es la mejor manera de abordarlas para interpretar sus concretas significaciones discursivas.

2. Sobre algunos conceptos fraseológicos

Para abordar el estudio del frásico de un texto determinado partimos del concepto ya bien establecido de UF,[2] como una unidad pluriverbal que presenta las características de

---

[1] Cabe citar M. González Rey (1999), que analiza la riqueza discursiva de las expresiones idiomáticas; A. Naciscione (2001), que profundiza en aspectos teóricos y prácticos de la inserción de UFs en el discurso; G. Corpas y F. Mena (2003), que estudian la variación fraseológica en su uso discursivo; A. Zholobova (2004), que se ocupa de las modificaciones creativas de las UFs y de sus efectos estilísticos; A. Todirascu y C. Gledhill (2008), que presentan un método para la extracción y el análisis de colocaciones en contexto.

[2] Aunque ya venimos utilizando los términos *unidad frásica* y *frásico* en nuestros trabajos desde hace algunos años, creemos oportuno justificar esta decisión. Se trata de que el término *fraseología* pase a denominar estrictamente la disciplina y no su objeto de estudio, de manera que *frásico* remita al conjunto de las *unidades frásicas*, objeto de estudio de la fraseología, siguiendo una analogía útil: *Lexicología* (disciplina lingüística que estudia el léxico), *léxico* (conjunto de las unidades léxicas) y *unidad léxica* (objeto de estudio de la lexicología). Observemos que sería poco económico y hasta ilógico decir *unidad lexicológica y corpus lexicológico*, tal como ocurre cundo se dice *unidad fraseológica y corpus fraseológico*. A la

repetición, fijación e institucionalización. Seguimos la clasificación establecida por Gloria Corpas (1997),[3] pero ampliándola al *frásico generalizado*, que incluye las *unidades estilísticas* (también llamadas *unidades frásicas generalizadas*). Esta noción se nos ha planteado a partir del trabajo de localización e identificación de UFs en textos literarios (Guia, 2000), ya que en ellos aparecen expresiones semejantes a UFs, que aportan información relevante como elementos caracterizadores de estilo.

Así pues, más allá de las unidades frásicas (estrictas), una *unidad estilística* es una combinación estable de dos o más palabras que, configurada formalmente como las UFs, participa de alguna de las características de éstas. Responde básicamente a una creación propia del estilo de un autor, escuela, género, época... Puede estar configurada como sintagma (formalmente semejante a una locución) o como enunciado (formalmente semejante a una paremia). Para la identificación de las primeras se ha de tener en cuenta la repetición, mientras que para la identificación de las segundas es fundamental fijar la atención en la estructura parémica y en el significado metafórico.[4]

Volviendo al frásico estricto, una *fórmula* es un enunciado sin autonomía textual, con función subalterna y cohesiva del discurso, que aparece en contextos generalmente ritualizados (una salutación, una expresión de acuerdo con el interlocutor, la manifestación de un sentimiento o estado de ánimo, un inicio, un cambio de tema, un final...). Al margen de la diversa tipología de las fórmulas rutinarias (discursivas, psico-sociales, etc.),[5] las expresiones metalingüísticas que introducen o acompañan UFs no han sido vistas como fórmulas. Nosotros las denominamos *fórmulas de inserción frásica*,[6] definiéndolas como enunciados subordinados que contienen generalmente un verbo de dicción (decir, afirmar...) o un verbo de conocimiento (saber, leer, recordar...) y que aparecen en forma de cuña sobrepuesta en el discurso, con la función de presentar y a menudo valorar la UF que introducen.[7]

---

unidad lingüística objeto de estudio no se le debería aplicar el sufijo *–logos* antes de estudiarla.
[3] De acuerdo con Zuluaga (1980: 135-139, que no incluye las colocaciones) y Corpas (1997: 53-213), las UFs pueden ser *no enunciados* (colocaciones y locuciones) y *enunciados* (fórmulas y paremias). Las colocaciones pertenecen al ámbito de la norma, las locuciones al del sistema y los enunciados frásicos al del habla.
[4] Por ejemplo, el sintagma *cráneo privilegiado* (Timofeeva 2009), que puede considerarse en su origen como una unidad estilística de Valle Inclán, posteriormente, a la vista de su uso repetido por publicistas de ideología derechista, en contextos irónicos y descalificadores, cabría tipificarlo como una unidad estilística de una cierta escuela, más que como locución de la lengua.
[5] B. Alvarado y L. Ruiz (2008) estudian la delimitación y funciones de las fórmulas rutinarias del español hablado, llegando a la conclusión que, en general, las psico-sociales no manifiestan independencia.
[6] Estos enunciados se han denominado *presentadores* por diversos autores (Corpas 1997, 137) y también, en un sentido más amplio, *introductores* (Cermak 2005), pero, desde nuestra perspectiva, estos términos obvian la naturaleza frásica del objeto designado. Conca (1997) hablaba de *marcadores de inserción*, dejando también de lado su carácter frásico.
[7] Los patrones más habituales de las fórmulas de inserción frásica suelen ser las construcciones formadas por [Adv + V + SN]: *Como dice la gente*, *Como dice el refrán*; [V + SN]: *Afirma el proverbio*; [V + Conj]: *Dicen que*, *Es sabido que*. En general, predomina en

3. Unidades frásicas aisladas y en contexto

Ha sido habitual, en la práctica fraseográfica e incluso lingüística, estudiar las UFs de forma aislada o descontextualizada. Es evidente que, desde este enfoque, el análisis es limitado,[8] ya que no se puede ir mas allá de intentar analizar sus rasgos formales (constitución morfosintáctica y semántica) y, con ello, establecer la forma canónica (frente a las posibles variantes), las palabras clave y los recursos retóricos de una UF. Pero para realizar un estudio riguroso y completo de las UFs es necesario localizarlas en contexto y, si es posible, en mas de una ocurrencia. Solamente así se puede garantizar la autenticidad de las UFs,[9] dar definiciones precisas de acuerdo con su uso, clasificarlas adecuadamente, analizar las modalidades de inserción, comprender las funciones o significados discursivos,[10] encontrar equivalencias fiables en UFs de otras lenguas, etc.

En este sentido, los diccionarios que incluyen UFs con definiciones pero sin aportar referencias pragmáticas ni ejemplos reales de uso contextualizado, incurren en una falta de rigor (porque no justifican la autenticidad de la anotación) y en un defecto didáctico (porque no proporcionan instrucciones de uso).

Se nos podría objetar que las UFs que son formalmente invariables y presentan un alto grado de fijación, como las locuciones preposicionales, conjuntivas y algunas adverbiales,[11] no es necesario encontrarlas en contexto para analizarlas.

Por eso, este tipo de locuciones, que son de naturaleza gramatical, que realizan funciones de conexión oracional o textual y que tienen forma invariable, han sido desde antaño incorporadas a gramáticas y diccionarios, con definiciones precisas. Sin embargo, puestas en contexto, incluso este tipo de UFs pueden llegar a adquirir matices, valores pragmáticos, connotaciones diatópicas, etc.[12]

---

ellas la función metadiscursiva, pero también pueden tener función modalizadora, si aparecen elementos valorativos que manifiesten la actitud del hablante respecto de la UF introducida: *Como dice el viejo y sabio adagio.*

[8] Tal como afirma Anita Naciscione (2001a), las UFs "as isolated sentences do not reveal the wealth and variety of instancial use". Esta autora distingue entre el uso esencial o canónico de una UF ("the *core use* is the use of the phraseological unit in its most common form and meaning") y el uso estilístico singular ("the *instancial stylistic use* is a particular instance of a unique stylistic application of a phraseological unit in discourse resulting in significant changes in its form and meaning determined by the context").

[9] Sobre la cuestión de las falsas paremias, véase la "Introducción" de Delfín Carbonell a su *Diccionario panhispánico de refranes* (2002).

[10] La capacidad significativa de les UFs en contexto ha permitido a Alberto Zuluaga (1997) atribuirles lo que él llama *función inherente fraseológica*, una propiedad que las hace muy productivas en la comunicación y que el autor concreta en cuatro aspectos: *comunicabilidad, connotación, iconicidad y poeticidad.*

[11] Para el estudio de este tipo de locuciones véase el libro de E. T. Montoro del Arco (2006) y el manual de M. Garcia-Page (2008).

[12] Por ejemplo, usar las locuciones *malgrat tot, comptat i debatut, aixi doncs,* etc., en un contexto oral valenciano, connota al emisor, ante determinados oyentes reacios al uso (culto) de la lengua, como "catalanista".

4. Método de concordancias frásicas

Se trata de un método útil para la elaboración y el estudio de corpus frásicos obtenidos a partir de textos orales o escritos de una cierta extensión.[13] Dado que el corpus frásico se puede estudiar desde diferentes perspectivas (lingüística, cultural, estilística, contrastiva, etc.), el método implica la confección de una base de datos completa y bien organizada para poder atender estas necesidades y estudiar las UFs tanto de forma intrínseca como contextualizada.

Si en todas las ramas del conocimiento es necesario proceder con método, en el campo de la fraseología esta exigencia deviene más imprescindible, por las razones siguientes:

1) Las UFs intertextualizadas resultan a menudo difíciles de localizar, ya que pueden pasar por sintagmas u oraciones libres;

2) Inversamente, pueden tomarse construcciones libres de la lengua por UFs, cuando estas construcciones aparecen formuladas según esquemas frásicos;

3) De las UFs localizadas, se ha de buscar su forma canónica, es decir, su codificación más general y habitual;

4) La definición o significado canónico no siempre resulta fácil de determinar, especialmente cuando una UF se localiza por primera vez, ya que se hace necesario encontrar otras documentaciones para poder afinar el significado;

5) En muchos casos, son reacias a dejarse clasificar con facilidad, por lo que se deben tener muy en cuenta los aspectos sintácticos, semánticos y pragmáticos que presentan;

6) Es necesario analizar la modalidad de inserción, en conexión con la función discursiva o significado contextual; para ello, se ha de partir de un cotexto mínimo, que no siempre puede ser reducido;

7) Se ha de buscar documentación anterior, coetánea y, en su caso, posterior, posibilitando el estudio diacrónico de los cambios sufridos y el análisis sincrónico de su vigencia;

8) Se debe aportar documentación de codificaciones correspondientes en otras lenguas, valorando el grado de equivalencia;

9) Se ha de analizar cómo han sido trasladadas en las traducciones del texto que las contiene, consiguiendo así información sobre la competencia frásica del traductor y sobre las estrategias seguidas en la traducción. En resumen, que se debe seguir un método riguroso, procediendo paso a paso y rechazando las impresiones subjetivas y los planteamientos intuitivos, generalistas o globalizadores.

El *método de concordancias frásicas* consiste en localizar UFs (estrictas y generalizadas) en un texto, identificarlas, hacer el inventario completo (*corpus frásico*), validarlas a través de otras recurrencias concordantes (en el mismo texto o en otros) y estudiarlas bajo distintos enfoques. Estos enfoques pueden ser intrínsecos (forma canónica, palabras clave, estructura, recursos estilísticos, definición, clasificación) y contextuales (modalidades de inserción, funciones discursivas), además de contrastivos (documentación en la lengua del corpus y en otras lenguas, traducciones), sin olvidar el valor de las UFs como elementos caracterizadores de estilo, tanto por su calidad o naturaleza como por su cantidad o frecuencia de uso.

---

[13] Este método lo hemos aplicado al análisis estilístico en textos del siglo XV (Guia 1999, 2008) y en obras de autores contemporáneos, como Enric Valor y Vicent Andrés Estellés (Conca 2009), así como en trabajos fraseológicos contrastivos (Conca/Guia 2006).

5. Modalidades presenciales en la inserción de UFs

Cuando una UF en un texto presenta modificaciones creativas respecto de su forma y significado canónicos (alteración del orden de los constituyentes; sustituciones, omisiones o permutaciones léxicas; interpolación de otros elementos; cambios gramaticales; mutaciones semánticas; etc.), hablaremos de *presencia desautomatizada*, con dos casos extremos:

> *Presencia emboscada*: cuando se conserva algún elemento léxico de la UF y un cierto eco de su significado.[14]
> *Presencia mutada*: cuando se conserva algún elemento léxico de la UF pero se modifica el significado.[15]

Con independencia del grado de desautomatización, que afecta a la *integridad* de la UF, veamos diversas modalidades de presencia, referidas al *entorno* de la UF.

> *Presencia conectada*: Cuando la UF va precedida por un conector discursivo.[16]
> *Presencia formulada*: Cuando la UF va acompañada de una fórmula de inserción frásica.[17]
> *Presencia directa*: Cuando la UF no va precedida por ningún conector ni acompañada de fórmula de inserción alguna.[18]

---

[14] En *Tirant lo Blanc* (València, 1490) se lee: "Estigueren molt admirats com tan prest havien trobat lo que cercaven" (cap. 71), en donde se da una presencia emboscada del refrán *Qui cerca, troba*, documentado en otras obras catalanas del siglo XV y recogido en *Le dieci tavole dei proverbi* (Torino, 1535): *Qui cercha, trova*.

[15] En unos versos del poeta contemporáneo Vicent Andrés Estellés: "Pense en el teu cos com el cànter novell / que fa l'aigua fresca el món bell / serien els dies de l'aigua en cistella, / ja no series febrilment donzella", consideramos que hay presencia mutada de dos paremias: *Canteret nou fa l'aigua fresca* y *Amor de doncella, aigua en cistella*. En el primer caso, se conservan tres elementos léxicos, pero se combinan en una sintaxis libre que aporta nuevos significados. En el segundo, la reelaboración sintáctica y semántica de la paremia da lugar a una interpretación opuesta a su significado canónico.

[16] En *The Knight's Tale* de Chaucer (c. 1340-1400), aparece la locución verbal *To make virtue of necessity*: "Thanne is it wysdom, as thynketh me, / *To maken vertu of necessite*" (vs. 2189-2190), introducida mediante el conector "then" (en inglés moderno), a modo de desligamiento respecto al discurso anterior, seguida de la apelación a la voz de la sabiduría "is it wisdom" y de una expresión de refuerzo asertivo "as it semms to me".

[17] Muchos de los refranes contenidos en *El libro del buen amor* (siglo XIV) van precedidos de fórmulas de inserción como el primer verso de la estrofa 64: "Por esto diz' la patraña de la vieja fardida: / Non hay mala palabra, si non es a mal tenida; / Verás que bien es dicha, si bien fues' entendida; / Entiende bien mi libro: avrás dueña garrida".

[18] En *El Quijote* (siglo XVII), las intervenciones de Sancho Panza suelen contener refranes sin marcas metalingüísticas de presentación alguna. Así, el refrán *En otras casas cuecen habas, y en la mía, a calderadas* aparece de forma directa, en medio de dos frases sentenciosas: "No hay camino tan llano –replicó Sancho—que no tenga algún tropezón o barranco; en otras casas cuecen habas, y en la mía a calderadas; más acompañados y paniaguados debe de tener la locura que la discreción" (2ª parte, cap. 13).

Presencia cíclica: Cuando las UFs aparecen en el texto –en obras en verso, sobretodo– según una cadencia determinada (cada cierto número de versos, al final de cada estrofa, al final de cada párrafo, etc.).[19]

Presencia seriada: Cuando la UF forma parte de una serie de expresiones configuradas como UFs, con una misma función discursiva y una cierta sinonimia.[20]

Presencia inicial: Cuando la UF abre una secuencia discursiva (argumentativa, descriptiva, explicativa...) con la función de anunciar lo que se dirá en ella.[21]

Presencia conclusiva: Cuando la UF cierra una secuencia (argumentativa, descriptiva, explicativa...) con la función de resumen y/o moraleja de lo que en ella se ha dicho.[22]

Presencia parcial/total: Cuando la UF que figura en el texto es una colocación o locución integrante de una paremia. En este caso, sólo el contexto nos permite determinar si la referencia remite a la paremia completa o únicamente a la colocación o locución.[23]

---

[19] En *A Balade of Old Proverbs* (impresa en 1707), formada por ocho estrofas de seis versos, Charles C. Doyle (1975) ha puesto de manifiesto que, en cada estrofa, se enuncia y glosa un refrán como mínimo.

[20] En *El Quijote*, en boca de Sancho Panza, también se da a menudo una presencia seriada de UFs de diversa tipología, como en el siguiente fragmento del capítulo 33 de la segunda parte: "Eso de gobernarles bien –respondió Sancho--, no hay para qué encargármelo, porque yo soy caritativo de mío, y tengo compasión de los pobres; y a quien cuece y amasa no le hurtes hogaza; y para mi santiguada, que no me han de echar dado falso: soy perro viejo y entiendo todos tus, tus, y sé despabilarme a sus tiempos, y no consiento que me anden musarañas ante los ojos, porque sé donde me aprieta el zapato". En efecto, ahí se encuentran, entre otras: *A quien cuece y amasa, no le hurtes hogaza, Echar dado falso, A perro viejo, no hay tus, tus, Mirar a las musarañas, Saber (alguien) donde le aprieta el zapato.*

[21] Una de las obras de Chrétien de Troyes (escritas entre 1170 y 1181), comienza con la mención de un proverbio a modo de marcador sentencioso inicial del contenido de la obra: "Li vilains dit an son respit / que *tel chose a l'an an despit / qui molt valt mialz que l'an ne cuide*" (*Erec et Enide*, vs. 1-3).

[22] En *La Celestina* (siglo XV), encontramos la sentencia clásica *En el término medio está la virtud* como conclusión de un fragmento en donde Celestina describe el comportamiento de las mujeres enamoradas: "...rompen paredes, abren ventanas, fingen enfermedades, a los chirriadores quicios de las puertas hacen con aceytes usar su oficio sin ruydo. No te sabré dezir lo mucho que obra en ellas aquel dulçor, que les queda de los primeros besos de quien aman. Son enemigas del medio; contino están posadas en los extremos" (tercer acto).

[23] Hemos incluido la *presencia parcial* en esta relación (de modalidades presenciales que afectan al entorno de la UF) precisamente por la expresada necesidad de recurrir al contexto para identificar correctamente cual es la UF evocada. Por ejemplo, en el fragmento "Lo gregario salta donde menos se piensa. Lo egregio también salta donde menos se piensa, cuando se piensa desde el fetichismo del individuo" (*El País*, 2-10-1985; CREA), hay un par de inserciones desautomatizadas (permuta de componentes y sustitución léxica) del refrán *Donde menos se piensa, salta la liebre*, mientras que en el fragmento "Como decía anteriormente, donde menos se piensa hay gente que se presta a todas las maniobras" (Rigoberta Menchú, 1983; CREA), únicamente se usa la locución adverbial *donde menos se piensa*, sin referencia al refrán.

6. Metodología para la formación y el estudio de corpus frásicos.

Entendiendo la metodología como conjunto de criterios y pasos a seguir en la aplicación del método, en este apartado describimos dichos pasos con definiciones precisas. En primer lugar, observamos que, en el proceso de extracción de las unidades frásicas de un texto, se deben distinguir dos momentos: el de la localización y el de la identificación propiamente dicha.[24] Porque no es lo mismo intuir que, en tal pasaje o fragmento, hay inserida una UF que saber de qué UF se trata, cual es su forma canónica y cual su significado. La localización es condición necesaria para la identificación, pero no es condición suficiente. El fraseólogo puede tener la certeza de que una expresión de un texto es una UF (incluso porque se lo dice el propio texto con alguna fórmula de inserción explícita), pero la UF le será desconocida si no la encuentra repetida en otro lugar. En este caso, se tendrá que limitar a proponer, a modo de conjetura y a partir de la única ocurrencia conocida, una forma canónica y una definición, es decir, realizará una identificación hipotética provisional. Así pues, las tres fases iniciales del proceso son:

Localización: Es el hecho de detectar la presencia de una UF en un fragmento, con independencia de saber o no de qué UF se trata.
Identificación: Es el hecho de asignar a la UF localizada una forma canónica y una definición. Será *hipotética* cuando no se conozca ninguna otra recurrencia de la UF.
Validación: Es la confirmación de la identificación hipotética mediante la documentación pertinente.

En este proceso, el fraseólogo se puede encontrar con *espejismos frásicos*, es decir, con construcciones lingüísticas que pueden ser tomadas como UFs (por su estructura, rima, valor idiomático, carácter sentencioso, etc.) sin serlo.[25] La dificultad en la localización de UFs en un texto depende de las características del texto al que nos enfrentamos y de la competencia fraseológica de quien realice el trabajo. Sea como fuere, siempre es conveniente ayudarse de ciertas técnicas (o criterios de localización),[26] que clasificaremos tomando como base algunas

---

[24] En general, no se ha observado esta distinción, exceptuando A. Naciscione (2001b: 34-35) que marca diversas etapas en este proceso: "It is essential to establish a procedure for discovering instantial use [of the PU] in the flow of discourse and set out a sequence of directions in order to avoid subjective judgement as far as possible (...) A number of discrete steps can be singled out to aid the process of identification which can be divided into several phases: *recognition > verification > comprehension > interpretation* to enable the reader or listener to cope with the complexities of discourse".
[25] El paremiólogo Sebastià Farnés, en su meritorio vaciado frásico de obras clásicas catalanas, anotó como paremias algunos pareados del *Espill* que lo parecían pero que no lo eran (Guia 2008).
[26] Elisabeth Schulze-Busacker (1985: 16-18), para el vaciado de los proverbios de las ciento doce obras narrativas, comprendidas entre 1150 y 1300, que ha estudiado, ha seguido tres criterios de identificación: 1) Los elementos intrínsecos del proverbio en la línea de Greimas (1960), para quien el proverbio es "un bref énoncé de caractère universel, qui frappe par une formulation visiblement distincte du discours courant"; 2) Las marcas contextuales del proverbio inserido, como las fórmulas introductorias o conclusivas, la conjunción "car", etc.; 3) La concordancia entre el enunciado a identificar y algún proverbio ya recogido en alguno de los compendios medievales franceses. Anteriormente, Jacqueline y Bernard Cerquiglini

de las características intrínsecas de las UFs y apoyándonos en aspectos cotextuales y contextuales de la porción de texto observado.

A) Intrínsecas
1) Presencia de arcaísmos, palabras diacríticas o anomalías gramaticales.
2) Existencia de un sistema anafórico cerrado (para posibles paremias).
3) Manifestación de patrones frásicos prototípicos.

B) Cotextuales
4) La interpretación literal no da sentido al fragmento.
5) La expresión observada forma parte de una serie en donde hay alguna UF.
6) Va precedida de algún conector discursivo.
7) Va acompañada de alguna fórmula de inserción frásica.
8) Se encuentra abriendo o cerrando una secuencia discursiva.

C) Contextuales
9) La expresión observada es reconocida por el investigador como UF.
10) La UF no es reconocida por el investigador, pero éste la relaciona con otra UF, por ser concordante con ella en algún aspecto formal o conceptual.

Entre todos los criterios anotados, cabe destacar que los conectores (causales, consecutivos, adversativos, conjuntivos...) y las fórmulas de inserción frásica son de gran ayuda para localizar UFs en textos digitalizados, colocando en el buscador conectores o formas verbales de verbos de dicción o de conocimiento. Finalmente, en estrecha continuidad con la creación estricta del corpus frásico, se han de abordar la clasificación de las UFs y su interpretación.

Clasificación. Es la determinación del tipo de UF, establecida a partir de la forma canónica pero teniendo en cuenta el contexto.[27]
Interpretación. Es la función discursiva de la UF en el texto, para cuyo análisis se ha de tener en cuenta si es enunciado o no y las características cotextuales y contextuales (emisor, receptor, intención comunicativa...), además del significado habitual y los valores fraseológicos intrínsecos.[28]

(1976: 360-361) han propuesto criterios intrínsecos bajo la rúbrica "Spécifités internes", considerando elementos como el "binarismo", o el hecho de formar un "système anaphorique clos", así como "l'archaisme", es decir, "le toujours-déjà dit".

[27] Resulta necesaria esta atención al contexto porque es frecuente el caso de UFs que, en su primigenia configuración como pertenecientes a un lenguaje de especialidad, tienen un significado literal y son clasificables como colocaciones –es el caso de *marcar un gol* en el ámbito del fútbol o de *tener luz verde*, en el de la circulación de vehículos--, mientras que, incorporadas al sistema de la lengua y usadas metafóricamente más allá de su ámbito específico, tendrán que ser consideradas como locuciones.

[28] Para el estudio del significado contextual de las UFs véase el trabajo de G. Wotjak (2005, 128-131).

En resumen, la metodología propuesta permite y exige elaborar una base de datos informatizada, con un registro para cada UF que contenga suficientes campos para poder disponer de una información completa y abordar muchos otros aspectos. Estas bases de datos pueden ser de mucha utilidad para la confección de diccionarios, la traducción, el análisis del discurso, la enseñanza de lenguas, la determinación de estilos y de autorías, etc.

7. Referencias bibliográficas

ALVARADO, M. B. & RUIZ, L.. 2008 "Unidades de conversación y fraseología: acerca de la autonomía de las fórmulas rutinarias". In: G. Conde (ed), *Aspectos formales y discursivos de las expresiones fijas*, Frankfurt am Main: Peter Lang, 25-40.

CARBONELL, D. 2002 *Diccionario panhispánico de refranes*, Barcelona: Herder.

CERMAK, F. 2005 "Introductores textuales en paremias y otras unidades fraseológicas". In: J. Luque & A. Pàmies (eds), *La creatividad en el lenguaje: colocaciones idiomáticas y fraseología*, Granada: Granada Lingvistica: 235-255.

CERQUIGLINI, J. & B. 1976 "L'écriture proverbiale", *Revue des sciences sociales*, 163: 359-375.

CONCA, M. 1997 "Os estudios de fraseoloxía catalana: realidades e proxectos", In: X. Ferro (ed), *Actas do I Coloquio Galego de Fraseoloxía*, Santiago de Compostela: Centro Ramón Piñeiro: 139-167.

CONCA, M. 2006 "Identificació i anàlisi textual d'unitats fràsiques en l'obra poètica de Vicent Andrés Estellés". In: K. Faluba & I. Sziji (eds), *Actes del XIVè Col·loqui Internacional de Llengua i Literatura Catalanes* (Budapest, 2006), PAM, II: 137-150.

CONCA, M. & GUIA, J. 2006 "Análisis contrastivo del frásico de *Tirant lo Blanc* [València, 1490; Barcelona, 1497] y sus traducciones castellana [Valladolid, 1511] e italiana [Venezia, 1538, 1566, 1611]. Entre el calco, la equivalencia y la creación", *Cahiers du Prohemio*, 7: 195-215.

CORPAS, G. 1997 *Manual de fraseología española*, Madrid: Gredos.

CORPAS, G., MENA, F. 2003 "Aproximación a la variabilidad fraseológica de las lenguas alemana, inglesa y española", *ELUA*, 17: 181-201.

DOYLE, Ch. C. (1975 "On Some Paremiological Verses", *Proverbium*, 25: 979-982.

GARCIA-PAGE, M. (2008 *Introduccion a la fraseologia española: estudio de las locuciones*, Barcelona: Anthropos.

GONZÁLEZ REY, M. (1999 "La mise en discours des expressions idiomatiques françaises", *Paremia*, 8: 249-254.

GREIMAS, A. J. 1960 "Idiotismes, proverbes, dictons", *Cahiers de Lexicologie*, 2: 41-61.

GUIA, J. 1999 *Fraseologia i estil. Enigmes literaris a la València del segle XV*, València: Tres i Quatre.

GUIA, J. 2000 "Hacia una caracterización fraseológica de los estilos literarios". In: G. CORPAS (ed), *Las lenguas de Europa: Estudios de fraseología, fraseografía y traducción*, Granada, Comares, 75-93.

GUIA, J. 2008 *Principis teòrics i metodològics per a l'estudi de les unitats fràsiques en textos versificats. Anàlisi fraseològica de l'*Espill, València:Tesis doctoral en CD, PUV.

GUIA, J. & CONCA, M. 2008 "Unitats fràsiques en textos versificats. Notícia de l'*Espill*, obra catalana del segle XV de gran interès fraseològic". In: G. Conde (ed), *Aspectos formales y discursivos de las expresiones fijas*, Frankfurt am Main: Peter Lang, 53-75.

MIEDER, W. BRYAN, G. B. 1996 *Proverbs in World Literature: A Bibliography*, New York: Peter Lang.

MONTORO DEL ARCO, E. (2006 *Teoría fraseológica de las "locuciones particulares"*, Frankfurt: Peter Lang.

NACISCIONE, A. 2001a "Phraseological Units in Literari Discourse: Implications for Teaching and Learning", *Cauce. Revista de Filología y su Didáctica*, 24: 53-67.

NACISCIONE, A. 2001b *Phraseological Units in Discourse: Towards Applied Stylistics*, Riga: Latvian Academy of Culture.

SCHULZE-BUSACKER, E. 1985 *Proverbes et expressions proverbiales dans la littérature narrative du Moyen Âge français*, Genève/Paris: Slatkine.

TIMOFEEVA, L. 2009 "Las unidades fraseológicas". In: L. Ruiz Gurillo & X. A. Padilla (eds), *Dime como ironizas y te diré quién eres. Una aproximación pragmática a la ironía*, Frankfurt: Peter Lang: 193-217.

TODIRASCU, A. & GLEDHILL, C. 2008 "Collocations en contexte: extraction et analyse contrastive", *Texte et Corpus*, 3: 137-148.

WOTJAK, G. 2005 "¿Qué significado podemos atribuir a las unidades fraseológicas? In: J. Luque & A. Pàmies (eds), *La creatividad en el lenguaje: colocaciones idiomáticas y fraseología*, Granada: Granada Lingvistica: 121-147.

ZHOLOBOVA, A. 2004 "El uso creativo de las unidades fraseológicas en contexto", *Interlingüística*, 15 (2): 1407-1411.

ZULUAGA, A. 1980 *Introducción al estudio de las expresiones fijas*, Frankfurt: Peter Lang.

ZULUAGA, A. 1997 "Sobre las funciones de los fraseologismos en textos literarios", *Paremia*, 6: 631-640.

EXPRESSIONS DE MÉDIATION

Mirella Conenna
Université de Bari « Aldo Moro »

Abstract: This study shows the first results of an ongoing research project aimed at identifying the discourse(s) of mediation, the description of the language used by mediators, and the creation of a French-Italian specialised dictionary. Our analysis focuses on the figure of the *Médiateur de la République française*. The study involves the analysis and comparison of two specialised corpora in the corresponding languages. The French corpus is composed of the *Rapports du Médiateur de la République française*, while the Italian corpus is composed of the *Relazioni del Difensore civico*. As a sample of our methodology, we present here a detailed analysis of the expression "le médiateur de la république", taking into account its pattern of occurrence, and its behaviour as viewed through relevant sets of concordances. Some aspects of the analysis of the Italian corpus are also presented. The findings thus obtained may be exploited for translation purposes as well as for teaching purposes, and in particular for training mediators.

Key words: French-Italian translation; mediator training courses; specialized phraseology; ombudsman terminology; corpus linguistics

1. Le(s) discours de la médiation : un aperçu de la situation en France et en Italie

Cette étude s'insère dans le cadre d'un projet de recherche en cours (Conenna & Vergne 2006 ; Vergne 2010)[1] visant à identifier le(s) discours de la médiation en français et en italien et à les analyser systématiquement. Le repérage et le classement des termes et des expressions de la médiation sont finalisés à la constitution d'un dictionnaire spécialisé bilingue.

Depuis quelques années, en France et en d'autres pays, la figure du médiateur est répandue dans une si grande variété de situations que l'on a même parlé d'un phénomène d'« ombudsmania », avec une référence au mot qui est utilisé en anglais ainsi qu'en d'autres langues pour indiquer cette fonction de « justice de proximité » (Labiano & Lernout 2004) qui s'inspire du modèle scandinave. Dans la vie de tous les jours, les gens savent, de plus en plus, qu'en cas de litiges, d'obstacles sociaux, de problèmes familiaux etc., ils peuvent recourir aux services d'un médiateur pour une solution à l'amiable des conflits. En Italie, les circonstances sont différentes. D'abord, il y a un certain retard de la mise en place, pourtant prévue, des médiateurs institutionnels. Puis, lorsque ces nouvelles figures devaient apparaître ou, dans certains cas, commençaient à s'installer et à fonctionner, des restrictions budgétaires ont, paradoxalement, déterminé la suppression d'un grand nombre de médiateurs locaux . Tout cela engendre, sur le plan linguistique, un véritable flou lexical qui demande une organisation cohérente.

---

[1] « Il discorso della mediazione fra terminologia e traduzione », projet CPDA101713/10 financé par l'Université de Padoue. Je codirige avec Michele De Gioia (Université de Padoue) une équipe de recherche dont font partie Mario Marcon (Université de Padoue), Sara Vecchiato (Université d'Udine), Michel Vergne (Université de Bari «Aldo Moro»).

Notre enquête s'articule en deux axes : le premier prévoit le catalogage préalable des textes provenant du domaine de la médiation afin d'établir une typologie discursive (De Gioia & Vecchiato à paraître) ; le deuxième envisage l'analyse des éléments linguistiques, notamment des termes et des expressions, qui permettront de définir la médiation comme un « discours spécialisé » (Humbley et al. 1993 ; Gotti 2003 ; De Gioia 2007 ; De Gioia à paraître). En revanche, nous cherchons ici à donner une réponse à la question essentielle de nos démarches, celle qui avait déclenché notre curiosité : « Un médiateur, comment parle-t-il ? ». Notre but est donc de localiser les expressions récurrentes, de montrer quelques traits distinctifs de cette langue, de constater si elle a toujours les qualités de clarté et de transparence qu'elle devrait avoir. C'est ce que suggère Six, auteur d'un livre qui est une référence dans le domaine de la médiation, lorsqu'il indique, même sur le plan langagier, le modèle nordique du médiateur ; il s'exprime ainsi à propos de l'ombudsman du Danemark :

> *On fait très attention, dans les bureaux du médiateur, à ne pas noyer le plaignant dans un jargon juridique, à parler une langue que tout le monde peut comprendre – et l'ombudsman, par ailleurs, ne se prive pas de critiquer les autorités qui s'expriment de manière insaisissable !* (Six 2001 : 66).

Notre projet s'est d'abord développé sur le français. Dans ces pages, nous nous focalisons sur la figure (et les textes) du Médiateur de la République française, dont la mission – depuis son institution en 1976 – est d'améliorer les relations entre l'administration et les citoyens.

Pour la partie italienne de notre enquête, nous avons choisi la figure (et les textes) du *Difensore civico* qui se rapproche davantage de celle du Médiateur de la République. En effet, selon la loi[2], le « *difensore civico [...] svolge un ruolo di garante dell'imparzialità e del buon andamento della pubblica amministrazione* »[3] ; l'on rapproche ouvertement cette figure de celle du médiateur : « *Sulla scia del modello nordico dell'ombudsman, commissario parlamentare di garanzia* »[4]. Le *difensore* est donc le résultat d'une « *duplice formula : protettore dei diritti dell'uomo, come di 'mediatore' fra cittadino e burocrazia* »[5].

Quant à leurs compétences, le Médiateur de la République et le *difensore civico* sont des auxiliaires qualifiés en droit administratif.

En Italie, on constate toutefois le manque d'une figure institutionnelle nationale ainsi qu'une diffusion non homogène des médiateurs, qu'ils soient institutionnels ou non institutionnels (postes requis auprès de centres culturels, établissements scolaires et universitaires, centres d'accueil d'immigrés, écoles, hôpitaux, etc.). Face à ce manque, on assiste à une demande croissante de formation de médiateurs à tous les niveaux institutionnels (collectivités territoriales, gouvernements régionaux, universités, etc.). De ces facteurs dépendent certes, sur le plan strictement linguistique, les incohérences que nous avons mises en relief : soit un vide lexical, soit un désordre terminologique dû à une multiplication des étiquettes donnant lieu à un « chaos » d'appellations. Nous avons illustré ailleurs (Conenna à paraître) le cas de l'expression *mediatore europeo*, calque reconnu de l'équivalent français

---

[2] Cf. la loi concernant l'institution du *difensore civico* (*legge* 142/1990).

[3] « Le *difensore civico* [...] joue un rôle de garant de l'impartialité et du bon fonctionnement de l'administration publique » (c'est nous qui traduisons).

[4] « Dans le sillage du modèle nordique de l'ombudsman, commissaire parlementaire de garantie » (c'est nous qui traduisons).

[5] Cf. le site web www.difesacivica.it. « double formule: protecteur des droits de l'homme, comme de 'médiateur' entre citoyen et bureaucratie » (c'est nous qui traduisons).

médiateur européen et de la confusion qui dérive de son emploi, du moment que la figure juridique correspondante en Italie serait le *difensore civico*. Et si nous prenons en considération le cas du *difensore civico*, nous retrouvons la même inadéquation, parce que l'expression est souvent considérée comme un synonyme du mot *ombudsman*. Par exemple, on parle de « *Ombudsman (o difensore civico)* »[6] pour expliquer la création de l'*ombudsman bancario*, équivalent italien du *médiateur de la banque* français.

2. Un corpus bilingue de textes de la médiation

Les sources des deux corpus de textes spécialisés que nous avons constitués sont les *Rapports du Médiateur de la République française* (dorénavant MEDIAREP) et les *Relazioni del Difensore civico* (dorénavant DICIV). Ces comptes-rendus annuels peuvent en effet être considérés comme des textes de référence : « Le Médiateur est surtout connu grâce à la diffusion et à la médiatisation de son rapport annuel »[7]. Nous allons présenter les critères de constitution des deux corpus et certaines données quantitatives, qui sont plus détaillées pour le français car l'analyse du lexique italien fera l'objet d'une autre étude.

2.1 Analyse du corpus français MEDIAREP

Le corpus français MEDIAREP (396.894 occurrences, 11.783 types) est constitué de 4 rapports annuels couvrant la période 2005-2008.

2.1.1 Fréquence des mots simples

Au départ, nous avons pris en compte les 30 premières formes nominales et adjectivales[8] les plus fréquentes. Pour ce faire, nous avons utilisé le logiciel Unitex[9].

Mot	Fréquence
Médiateur	1317
République	1173
droit	427
droits	411
cas	389
loi	387
Annuel	334
rapport	308

---

[6] Cf. le site web http://edu.pattichiari.it/Banca/ombudsma n.kl
[7] Cf. le site web www.vie-publique.fr. Une anecdote : le dimanche 21 février 2010 le rapport du Médiateur de la République fait la une du journal *Le Monde*.
[8] Nous avons filtré manuellement la liste afin de ne pas retenir d'autres parties du discours (verbes, adverbes, prépositions etc.). Nous avons également gardé les différences de casse, afin de mieux localiser les attestations dans les rapports (titres, indices, tables des matières, corps du texte etc.) dans nos études à venir.
[9] Cf. le site web http://igm.univ-mlv.fr/~unitex/

délégués	306
services	298
réforme	295
personnes	283
administration	260
Situation	218
sociale	211
dossiers	209
service	196
régime	187
public	187
médiateur	181
réclamations	180
effet	179
travail	178
retraite	174
France	169
demande	169
secteur	165
publics	159
Accès	157
Vie	156

Fig. 1. Les 30 premiers mots simples français.

À l'aide d'un simple script PERL, nous avons ensuite détecté les co-occurrents des formes *médiateur/Médiateur* (1.515 occurrences), veillant à retenir les co-occurrents en première position à droite et à gauche, ainsi que leurs fréquences respectives. Nous avons donc constaté une fréquence élevée des occurrences *le médiateur/le Médiateur*, ce qui nous a mené à lire les concordances calculées à l'aide d'Unitex. Nous avons ainsi trouvé 490 concordances[10], et nous les avons triées manuellement d'après la fonction de sujet ou de complément que l'occurrence *le médiateur* jouait à l'intérieur de ses contextes. Dans les cas où les concordances ont montré la fonction de sujet, nous avons effectué un deuxième tri des concordances sur le verbe (forme active ou passive, modes et temps) pour montrer les préférences discursives de réalisation caractérisant le genre textuel *rapport annuel*.

---

[10] Contexte de 60 caractères à gauche et 100 caractères à droite.

Expressions de médiation 47

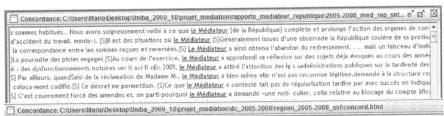

Fig. 2. Captures d'écran des concordances françaises et italiennes sous Unitex.

2.1.2. Les appellations du Médiateur de la République

Nous avons commencé par l'analyse des expressions qui correspondent à la dénomination même de l'objet de notre recherche, le médiateur (de la République). Parmi les appellations du médiateur, nous avons repéré, bien évidemment, *Médiateur de la République française* :
   En juin 2008, le Médiateur de la République française s'est rendu en Albanie et en
   Macédoine sur invitation...
avec ses formes abrégées, *Médiateur de la République* :
   Le Médiateur de la République a approuvé la décision du préfet...
ainsi que *Médiateur* tout court :
   ... à la réflexion menée par le Médiateur tout au long de l'année 2007, à la demande
   du gouvernement...
L'appellation la plus fréquente correspond à la forme *Médiateur de la République* qui est donc l'expression la plus significative. C'est ce que met en relief une citation montrant une sorte d'abréviation manquée, accentuée par les crochets :
   Nous avons soigneusement veillé à ce que le Médiateur [de la République] complète
   et prolonge l'action des organes de contrôles existants...
Nous avons aussi trouvé cette forme avec insertion du nom propre :
   Inspiré par les exemples de ses homologues européens, le Médiateur de la
   République, Jean-Paul Delevoye, avait d'ailleurs indiqué, lors de son audition...

2.1.2.1 Les structures d'occurrence des appellations du Médiateur de la République

Nous indiquons de manière schématique les résultats de notre analyse. L'appellation *Le Médiateur de la République* est généralement employée avec des verbes à la forme active :
   N_0 (=: Le Médiateur de la République) V (*Forme active ou passive*)

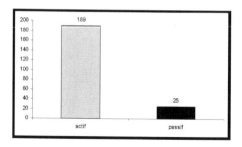

Fig. 3. Co-occurrences de l'expression *Le Médiateur de la République* et des verbes à la forme active et passive.

Nous avons trouvé plusieurs structures dont nous détaillons l'occurrence de deux appellations du médiateur – *Le Médiateur de la République* et *Le Médiateur* – ainsi que les modes et les temps verbaux impliqués. En ce qui concerne la première appellation, nous avons trouvé :
N_0 (=: Le Médiateur de la République) V (*indicatif*)

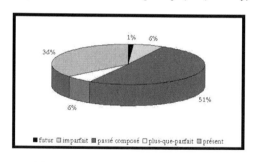

Fig. 4. Pourcentages des temps verbaux.

N_0 (=: Le Médiateur de la République) V (*indicatif, passé composé*)
  Le Médiateur de la République a approuvé la décision du préfet et saisi lui aussi le procureur de la...
N_0 (=: Le Médiateur de la République) V (*indicatif, présent*)
  ... le Médiateur de la République alerte les autorités sur les dérives provoquées bien souvent par un...
N_0 (=: Le Médiateur de la République) V (*indicatif, imparfait*)
  le Médiateur de la République alertait également les médias qui ont repris ce thème des...
N_0 (=: Le Médiateur de la République) V (*indicatif, futur*)
  ... c'est au niveau national que le Médiateur de la République, une fois informé par ses délégués, pourra intervenir auprès...
N_0 (=: Le Médiateur de la République) V (*indicatif, plus-que-parfait*)
  Auditionné en février 2008 par la commission Le Garrec, le Médiateur de la République avait de nouveau rappelé les carences et les effets injustes...

N_0 (=: Le Médiateur de la République) V (*subjonctif, présent*)
... *il est regrettable que le Médiateur de la République ne soit pas davantage en mesure de susciter un véritable débat...*
N_0 (=: Le Médiateur de la République) V (=: être) (E + Adv) W
Le Médiateur de la République est également doté d'un important pouvoir de proposition de réformes...
N_0 V N_1 (=: le Médiateur de la République)
La société de dépannage a alors saisi, courant octobre, le Médiateur de la République. Celui-ci est intervenu auprès du préfet aux fins de...
N_0 V (E + W) par N_x (=: le Médiateur de la République)
Ces exemples prouvent l'urgence de la réforme demandée par le Médiateur de la République pour l'harmonisation des régimes des trois fonctions publiques.

En ce qui concerne la deuxième appellation, nous avons trouvé :
N_0 (=: Le Médiateur) V (*forme active ou passive*)

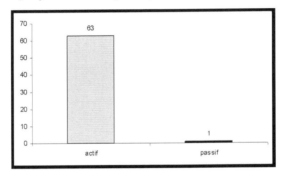

Fig. 5. Co-occurrences de l'expression *Le Médiateur* et des verbes à la forme active et passive.

N_0 (=: Le Médiateur) V (*indicatif*)

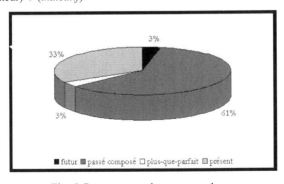

Fig. 6. Pourcentages des temps verbaux.

N_0 (=: Le Médiateur) V (*indicatif, passé composé*)
   En 2005, le Médiateur a attiré l'attention des administrations publiques sur la tardiveté des...
N_0 V N_1 (=: le Médiateur)
   Le litige dont est également souvent saisi le Médiateur concerne l'ouverture des droits à indemnisation chômage.
N_0 V (E + W) par N_x (=: le Médiateur)
   ... à la réflexion menée par le Médiateur tout au long de l'année 2007, à la demande du gouvernement...

2.2 Éléments d'analyse du corpus italien : l'appellation du *difensore civico*

Le corpus italien est constitué de 20 *relazioni* de 5 *Difensori civici* couvrant la période 2005-2008 ; autrement dit, 5 séries de *relazioni annuali* (1 série = 1 *difensore civico* + 4 *relazioni annuali*).

	Occurrences	Types
Abruzzes	324.303	10.916
Basilicate	99.227	6.227
Marches	141.571	9.426
Piémont	289.081	7.922
Toscane	461.897	12.678
DICIV	**1.316.081**	**23.769**

Fig. 7 Occurrences et types du corpus DICIV et de ses sous-corpus régionaux.

Comme pour le français, nous avons établi les listes de mots simples les plus fréquents, toujours à l'aide d'Unitex. Nous avons ensuite comparé les listes de mots simples de chaque sous-corpus régional (les *relazioni* des *difensori civici* pour les régions suivantes : *Abruzzes, Basilicate, Marches, Piémont, Toscane*), en nous concentrant encore une fois seulement sur les noms (communs et propres)[11] et sur les adjectifs.

Excepté quelques spécificités locales, concernant entre autres les noms des provinces d'intervention des *difensori civici*, les listes des 30 noms et adjectifs les plus fréquents ont montré un noyau lexical commun à chaque région, qui relève du domaine administratif (ex. *attività, parte, regionale*).

Dans une deuxième phase, nous avons regroupé les cinq sous-corpus pour former un corpus unique (DICIV), aboutissant à une seule liste de mots (fig. 8). Cette liste a été filtrée en respectant les critères qui ont été retenus pour la constitution des 5 listes précédentes.

---

[11] Concernant les noms propres, nous avons également retenu des sigles comme AN pour Ancona, ASUR pour *Azienda Sanitaria Unica Regionale*. Nous remarquons que ces sigles ne comparaissent pas dans la liste DICIV. Ils sont très souvent caractéristiques d'une région en particulier, et donc ils gardent une basse fréquence.

Mot	Fréquence
Difensore	2.573
civico	2.040
regionale	1.507
art	1.269
parte	1.250
legge	1.167
Ufficio	1.012
Regione	1.003
attività	991
Civico	943
Comune	889
cittadini	888
accesso	797
anno	795
stato	786
comma	779
intervento	712
casi	709
Comuni	698
diritto	692
caso	688
Consiglio	635
Richiesta	634
richiesta	630
locali	611
materia	603
atti	590
pratiche	562
ufficio	543
servizio	529

Fig. 8 Les 30 premiers mots simples italiens.

C'est l'appellation du *Difensore* (2.573 occurrences)[12] qui est en tête de liste. Dans cette dernière, *Difensore* est immédiatement suivi de l'adjectif *civico* (2.040 occurrences)[13], nous suggérant non seulement une récurrence significative de l'expression *Difensore civico* (2.639

---

[12] En rajoutant les occurrences de la forme *difensore*, le nombre total s'élève à 2.992 occurrences.
[13] En rajoutant les occurrences de la forme *Civico*, le nombre total s'élève à 2.983 occurrences.

occurrences)[14], mais surtout un usage très limité de la forme réduite *Difensore* (36 occurrences)[15] en tête nominale.

Dans une perspective contrastive, on constate donc un résultat similaire pour la langue française où nous avons une haute fréquence de l'expression *Médiateur de la République* (1.080 occurrences) et une fréquence plus basse de la forme réduite *Médiateur* (323 occurrences)[16]. Toutefois, si les appellations complètes en italien et en français sont les plus utilisées, le rapport d'usage entre les deux langues diffère. Pour l'italien, *Difensore* représente 0,9% des appellations totales identifiées, alors que pour la langue française ce rapport est plus élevé puisque *Médiateur* représente 29% des appellations totales[17] (Marcon & Vergne à paraître).

2.3. Quelques remarques

Premièrement, à partir de l'analyse des appellations du Médiateur de la République, nous avons remarqué :
a) la préférence pour l'appellation complète: *Médiateur de la République*, ainsi que – en ce qui concerne les verbes – pour la forme active et le mode indicatif (présent et passé composé) ;
b) l'emploi de plusieurs verbes à haute fréquence :
demander (346)
saisir (157)
recevoir (138)
informer (124)
émettre (100)
présenter (96)
proposer (93)
intervenir (87)
disposer (68)
transmettre (47)
poursuivre (45)
participer (44)
c) la présence de quelques expressions figées, surtout adverbiales (*en tout état de cause, le cas échéant* etc.) ;
d) la haute fréquence de compléments introduits, à gauche de l'expression considérée, par des participes passés, comme le verbe *saisir*. Par exemple :
Saisi du dossier, le Médiateur de la République est intervenu auprès de la direction des affaires criminelles et des grâces du ministère de la Justice.
Deuxièmement, la comparaison français-italien de nos données montre des équivalences terminologiques ponctuelles qu'il faudra observer systématiquement. Voici un exemple

---

[14] Ce résultat ne prend pas en considération les différences de casse.
[15] Résultat obtenu par la lecture des concordances.
[16] Résultat obtenu par la lecture des concordances.
[17] La somme *Difensore civico* e *Difensore* représente 100%. Il en va de même pour *Médiateur de la République* et *Médiateur*.

concernant les équivalents sémantiques *ces dysfonctionnements* et *situazioni di cattiva amministrazione* :

> Devant ces dysfonctionnements, le Médiateur de la République a remis en cause l'ensemble de la chaîne de traitement des amendes.

> *Il Difensore Civico, peraltro, nell'affrontare le situazioni di cattiva amministrazione, agisce con un contatto concreto teso alla risoluzione dei problemi e favorisce in questo modo la comprensione e la cooperazione fra cittadini e pubblica amministrazione.*

Troisièmement, sur le plan discursif, nous avons détecté également la trace des actions menées par le médiateur (ses dialogues, ses enquêtes etc.), ce qui nous amène à considérer le discours de la médiation comme une forme de discours rapporté.

3. Conclusion et perspectives

Nous avons présenté une analyse linguistique fondée sur un corpus spécialisé, afin d'étudier le(s) discours de la médiation. Nous avons mis en lumière des expressions fréquentes dans le lexique du Médiateur de la République française ainsi que de son homologue italien, le *Difensore civico*.

Nous envisageons d'améliorer l'extraction des lexiques sur base statistique (Marcon à paraître), afin de comparer les données résultant de notre analyse avec d'autres analyses menées sur des textes français provenant de médiateurs différents, comme le médiateur européen ou le défenseur des enfants (Marcon 2007). Aussi, faudra-t-il mener une analyse détaillée du corpus italien, afin de construire un dictionnaire bilingue français-italien de la médiation.

Dans l'optique contrastive, il serait souhaitable d'élargir l'enquête à d'autres langues et de constituer des lexiques plurilingues. L'intérêt d'une communication multilingue n'est pas moindre : désormais, même les sites institutionnels s'internationalisent. Par exemple : un site officiel[18] montre les codes en vigueur traduits en anglais et en espagnol. En outre, depuis 2004, on publie les traductions en anglais du *Rapport du Médiateur de la République*, où, par ailleurs, l'on traduit cette expression par *The Mediator of the French Republic* ; on aurait supposé plutôt le choix traductif de *ombudsman*, terme qui, comme nous l'avons vu, est le plus diffusé dans le monde anglophone, et qui est également utilisé pour dénommer le médiateur européen (*The European Ombudsman*).

Enfin, les différents apports de notre projet pourront être exploités en traduction et aussi en didactique, notamment pour la formation des médiateurs.

---

[18] Cf. le site web www.legifrance.gouv.fr.

4. Références

COLONNA, N. 2009 *Parcours dans l'univers linguistique de la médiation*. Tesi di Laurea specialistica. Università degli Studi di Bari « Aldo Moro ».

CONENNA, M. 2010 « Médiation/Traduction ». Communication présentée au colloque *Jean-René Ladmiral: une oeuvre en mouvement*, 3-4 juin 2010, Université de Paris-Sorbonne.

CONENNA, M. & VERGNE, M. 2006 « Traitement automatique multilingue du lexique de la médiation ». In S. Petrilli (ed.) *Comunicazione, Interpretazione, Traduzione*. Mimesis : 445-453.

De GIOIA M. 2007 « Figement et discours spécialisés ». In G. Bellati, G. Benelli, P. Paissa, C. Preite (eds) *« Un paysage choisi ». Mélanges de linguistique française offerts à Leo Schena/Studi di linguistica francese in onore di Leo Schena*. Torino/Paris: L'Harmattan: 141-151.

De GIOIA, M. [à paraître] Les termes sont-ils des expressions figées? *Cahiers de recherche de l'École Doctorale en Linguistique française*, Milano : Lampi di stampa.

De GIOIA M. & VECCHIATO S. [à paraitre] Pour une typologie des discours de la médiation.

GUILLAUME-HOFFNUNG, M. (2000) [1995] *La médiation*. Que sais-je? Paris : PUF.

HUMBLEY, J., MOIRAND, S., ALI BOUACHA, A., BEACCO, J.-C. & COLLINOT, A. (éds) 1993 *Parcours linguistiques de discours spécialisés : Colloque en Sorbonne les 23-24-25 septembre 1992*. Berne: Peter Lang.

LABIANO, P. & LERNOUT, M. 2004 *La justice de proximité pour résoudre les litiges du quotidien*. Paris: Vuilbert.

MARCON, M. 2007 *La médiation "enfant": du texte aux mots*. Tesi di Laurea triennale. Università degli Studi di Bari « Aldo Moro ».

MARCON, M. [à paraître] Mots-clés de médiation. Extractions statistiques du lexique de la médiation.

MARCON, M. & VERGNE, M. [à paraître] Estrazione e analisi del lessico del difensore civico italiano.

PAUMIER, S. 2006 *Unitex 2.0*. (http://www-igm.univ-mlv.fr/~unitex/) (30-05-2010).

SIX, J.-F. 2001 [1990] *Le temps des médiateurs*. Paris : Le Seuil.

VERGNE, M. 2010 « La situation de médiation dans l'apprentissage d'une langue ». *Lingua viva* X : 15-30.

ANIMAL PHRASEOLOGY: THE CASE OF DOG AND CAT
(A CORPUS-BASED STUDY)

František Čermák
Charles University, Prague

Abstract: Most languages use animal names to build their idioms on, including those of two common animals, dog and cat. In the following, an attempt will be made to inspect and compare their existence in four languages in similes only, namely Czech, English, French and German. Since a rather exhaustive coverage and description of these is available in a dictionary form in Czech, this was made a starting point for the comparison. The main goal has been to inspect meaning of these similes, using a semantic framework used in the dictionary for all four languages. Hence, 63 broad semantic categories have been established and the four languages compared on this basis. It is interesting to note that despite the same extralinguistic basis quite a few differences are to be observed, due to different linguistic and cultural backgrounds.

Key words: Paremiology, cat-proverbs, dog-proverbs, similes, corpus, metalanguage, anthropomorphism.

1. Introduction: Animals in Phraseology.

Due to general and long-term appearance of some animals in any culture or society it seems reasonable to suppose that their names are also used in the phraseological stock of various languages. Because of obvious differences of these cultures and roles these animals play there, one can easily compare roles of (almost) universal animals, such as *dog* and *cat*, in different languages and their phraseology.

Let us first have a look at these animals outside the phraseology, namely in a large corpus, such as The Czech National Corpus (SYN2005) and the British National Corpus, both having about 100 million words. To make this preliminary comparison short, only Word Sketches of these will be used, limited to **adjective collocations** of *dog* and *cat* in both languages.

Going by frequency only joint collocations of *dog* (pes) and *cat* (kočka) in Czech include *toulavý* (stray), *věrný* (faithful), *opuštěný* (abandoned/ditched), *hladový* (hungry), *velký* (great) (followed by colour names, such as *bílý* (white)). In the corresponding English collocations for *dog* and *cat*, one gets *black, big, strange, nice, great (dog/cat)*. However, apart from *great*, no adjective collocations in one language matches the other. Of course, the starting assumption was that adjectives may signal a rather straightforward association that the users might have to the two animals. As this has not turned true it may be taken as a warning about making too simple conclusions.

Differences, rather than correspondeces, in the collocations for each animal only, should then be of little surprise. Thus, the Czech *dog* is accompanied by the adjectives *hlídací, lovecký, spráskaný, zakopaný, štěkající* (guard(dog), hunting, whipped, buried, barking) etc., while the Czech *cat* by *angorská, perská, předoucí, siamská, šedivá* (Angora, Persian, purring, Siamese, grey). The English *dog* has the company of *sleeping, mad, dear, faithful, beloved*, while the English *cat* that of *Siamese, female, contented, purring, sleek*. While there are only two adjectives used with *cat*, namely *Siamese* and *purring*, that are used in both languages with high frequency, there is none for the *dog*, all adjectives being different. It does suggest a rather different view of the two animals in both languages, too.

Animal names are very common in **phraseology**, too. There are hundreds of Czech idioms employing for example *dog* or *cat* as a constituent, other languages being similar. Since it seems that these two animals are so common, they have become the goal of a comparative study in several languages included in a dictionary form, the focus having been here on similes only (*Slovník české frazeologie a idiomatiky. Přirovnání*, F. Čermák, J. Hronek, J. Machač, eds., 2009 Praha, 2nd ed.). The similes published here are provided by equivalents in English, French and German.

2. Structures: Similes, Their Form and Variants

There are 34 dictionary articles having the word *kočka/ kocour* (cat/he-cat) as a component and 42 articles using the component *pes* (dog), out of which 63 Czech similes have been chosen for a further examination. It was, then, the Czech language that was chosen as a point of departure, as no comparable collection and description of what is in current, contemporary use was found in other languages, offering also equivalents in other languages. This means

(1) that an equivalent in the three remaining languages may not always be found, and
(2) that those similes in the three languages having these components, that are not used in Czech, have not been considered (for examples see below).

Form of the similes is, basically, the same in all four languages, based, mostly, on the structure (**Cd**)-**R**-**Tc**-**c**-**Ct**, i.e.

Comparandum + Relator + Tertium comparations + Comparator + Comparatum,
such as in (*Sie =Cd*, supplied by the context) *ist* (a verb/adjective =*R*) *müde* (explicit feature used for comparison =*Tc*) *wie* (*like/comme/jako =c*) *ein Hund* (model/prototype referred to =*Ct*).

Despite the attempt to find **equivalents** in the three languages (all of the co-authors responsible being native speakers), the search has not been successful in all cases (see the Appendix). On the other hand, some equivalents may not have the form of a simile.

Some of the similes may have alternatives, such as *kocour* (*tom-cat*, next to *cat, kočka*) or *čokl* (*dog*, deprecating) in Czech, the English *cur* or the German *hundemüde, Katzenwäschen,* etc.

3. Meaning and Function.

The choice of the two animals (cat and dog) for the similes inspected here is due to their rather different distribution. While there are only two types of **meaning** (be tired, be finnicky, be sweet-toothed) where both animals take part, though the expressions are not synonymous, the rest is quite different. On the one hand it seems that only

- similes based on the *dog* component express fighting, suffering or loyalty,
- while the *cat* component is reserved for those expressing perfidiousness, scratching or walking quietly,

but the overall picture is much more rich (see the Appendix).

While no detailed examination of the type of meaning of the similes included have been undertaken, at least two general semantic groups can be singled out, namely

A physical movements, looking, seeing, appearance, tastes, washing, fighting etc.
B behaviour and psychological properties (insincerity, loyalty), acting as, feelings (depression), expressions, talking, understanding, anger, hatred, etc.

An attempt has been made to cover these meanings by a brief description in a metalanguage (based on but not quite equal to real meaning, its definition to be found in the source dictionary), e.g.

scratching   *mít drápy jako kocour*
E have claws like a *cat* **G** Krallen wie eine *Katze* haben **F** !avoir des griffes de *chat*

where the metalinguistic description is related to a Czech startup simile followed by equivalents in English, German and French. In those equivalents that are based on either *cat* or *dog*, these components are marked by italics, such as the English have claws like a ***cat***. On the other hand, should an equivalent exist that does not have the structure of a simile, it is preceded by an exclamation mark, such as **!avoir des griffes de *chat***.

Functionally, most similes of the type examined have an obvious anthropomorphic character expressing those types of meaning that are exclusively related to man, human being. In text, these similes are used for other persons (2nd person mostly), accordingly (with a possible exception of *být utahaný jako pes, be tired like a dog*, where the simile can be used by the speaker about himself/herself). For a more detailed description, a comparative study based on a corpus is necessary.

Pragmatically, it is obvious (again, without a detailed corpus-based study) that most of these cat and dog similes express mainly a negative evaluation of the person used as Comparandum in text, such as *rvát se jako psi, fight like dogs, sich wie die Kesselflicker raufen, se battre comme des chiens*.

Semantic range of the similes inspected covered 63 broad types of meaning whose survey is offered in the Appendix.

In at least a brief attempt to find out about the **use of these similes in corpus**, first data on *dog* in Czech may serve as a first illustration. Thus

- Out of all of 283 occurences (uses) of the phrase *like a dog* (jako pes) it seems that only under 10 % belong to phraseology and are part of idioms.
- The most common similes based on *dog* (*pes*) are those expressing loyalty (26%), tiredness (24%), though the combination *like a cat and dog* is also prominent.

Obviously, a detailed study of the use of similes is a different resarch foled, however, which deserves to be undertaken.

4. Summary: Four Languages Compared: Main Features

Comparing the data of the 63 Czech similes and their equivalents in English, German and French, the following aspects have been inspected:

(a) degree of correspondence in the use of cat/dog and their equivalents or its absence,
(b) existence or non-existence of (any) equivalent.

Thus, English equivalents show (a) correspondence to Czech in 37 cases against 26 cases of its absence, i.e. use of other, non-cat-or-dog equivalents, (b) there is only one case where an equivalent is missing, e.g. *(být) mlsný jako kocour/kočka* (literary: be finnicky as a cat).

In German, there are (a) 40 cases of a cat-and-dog equivalence with 23 non-equivalent cases, while (b) 10 equivalents are missing altogether.

French shows (a) 33 cases of equivalence and a rather high number of a different possibility, while (b) there are 10 cases where no equivalent is offered at all.

It is obvious that the highest correspondence, regardless of a cat-and-dog equivalence or other, is to be found between Czech and English, while Czech-French correspondence seems to be the lowest. However, if the type of equivalents is considered, the highest (cat-and-dog) correspondence is found between the Czech and German.

One more general observation based on the data presented may seem interesting: While similes based on the cat component tend to be expressions of, basically, more physical nature (seeing, scratching, walking), the dog component seems to appear more often in expressions having a more abstract character (be useless, behave rigorously, feel depressed), though not exclusively. What sort of motivation is to be found here in the behaviour of these familar animals is very much an open question.

On the other hand, looking for possible similes in the three target languages, one does find a few in dictionaries, that are not covered in the Czech startup data. Thus, for

English (NODE) has *like a cat on a hot tin roof, like the cat that's got (or who's stolen) the cream, look like something the cat brought in, dressed (up) like a dog's dinner, like a dog with two tails*

German (Duden) the following are registered: *bekannt sein wie ein bunter/scheckiger Hund, wie ein Hund leben, frieren wie ein junger Hund,* while the

Finally, **French** (Le Robert) offers these: *arriver comme un chien dans un jeu de quilles, recevoir qn comme un chien dans un jeu de quilles*

5. Literature

ČERMÁK, F. 2009 "Česká přirovnání". In: *Slovník české frazeologie a idiomatiky 1 Přirovnání*, 483-507

ČERMÁK, F.; HRONEK, J. &MACHAČ, J. (dir.) *Slovník české frazeologie a idiomatiky 1 Přirovnání* Leda Praha 2009 (2nd ed., = *A Dictionary of Czech Phraseology and Idiomatics*, Vol 1: Similes).

6. Appendix

1-scratching	mít drápy jako kocour E have claws like a *cat*	G Krallen wie eine *Katze* haben	F !avoir des griffes de *chat*
2-scratching	škrábat/drápat jako kocour E scratch like a *wildcat*	G kratzen wie eine *Wildkatze*	F -
3-squinting	mhouřit oči jako kocour E squint like a *cat*, !screw one's eyes up	G (blinzeln), die Augen zusammenkneifen wie eine *Katze*	F -
4-goggling, gawking	vyvalovat oči jako když kocour sere do řezanky E !his eyes are popping out of his head	G (die Augen herausdrehen)	F (rouler des yeux ronds)
5-looking expectantly	o(b)lizovat se jako kocour E !lick one's chops, (enjoy/relish one's food)	G -	F !se lècher les babines
6-defence by scratching	bránit se/škrábat jako (divoká) kočka E spit/scratch like a wild cat	G sich wehren/kratzen wie eine *Wildkatze*	F -
7-washing superficially	mýt se jako kočka E !have a *catlick*	G !*Katzenwäschen* machen	F !faire une toilette de *chat*
8-falling, landing	dopadnout jako kočka na všechny čtyři E land on all fours like a *cat*	G wie eine *Katze* auf die Füsse/alle Viere fallen	F !retomber sur ses pieds
9-walking quietly	chodit/našlapovat jako kočka E !go with *cat-like* tread	G wie eine *Katze* schleichen	F marcher comme un *chat*
10-curling	svinout se/stočit se/stulit se (do klubíčka) jako kočka E A curl up like a *cat*	G sich einkuscheln wie ein *Kätzchen*	F se pelotonner comme un *chat*
11-seeing well	mít oči jako kočka E have eyes like a *cat*, !have the eyes of a *cat*	G Augen wie eine *Katze* haben	F !avoir des yeux de *chat*
12-defending oneself, be viable	mít život (tuhý) jako kočka E have nine lives like a cat	G zäh wie eine *Katze* sein, !ein zähes Leben haben	F -
13-fight furiously	rvát se/servat se (o něco) jako psi E scrap/fight like *dogs*	G sich wie die Kesselflicker raufen	F se battre comme des *chiens*

14-beat so. cruelly	zbít/seřezat někoho jako psa n. zabít/zastřelit někoho jako psa E !knock the living daylights out of so. !beat. so. to a pulp/jelly	G j-n abknallen/ erschiessen wie einen (tollen) Hund	F abattre/ tirer qn comme un *chien*
15-be skinny/lean	(být) hubený/vyzáblý/vychrtlý jako pes E be as thin as a rake/lath	G dürr/ knochig sein wie eine Ziege	F être maigre comme un coup de trique
17-look ridiculous/funny	sluší mu to/tomu to sluší jako psovi uši E it suits him as a saddle suits a sow, !he looks a right sight	G das passt wie die Faust aufs Auge/der Arsch auf die Pfanne	F ça lui va comme un tablier à une vache
18-be sweet-toothed, finnicky	(být) mlsný jako kocour/kočka E -	G !eine *Naschkatze* sein	F être gourmand comme une *chatte*
19-be sweet-toothed, finnicky	olizovat se/chodit kolem něčeho jako mlsný pes E !lick one's chops, (enjoy/relish one's food)	G -	F !se lècher les babines
20-be insincere/ perfidous	(být) falešný jako kočka E be as deceitful as a snake in the grass	G falsch wie eine *Katze* sein, !katzenfreundlich sein	F être hypocrite comme un *chat*
21-be strict/ rigorous	být (na někoho) jako pes E !have it in for so.	G !zu j-n *hundsgemein* sein	F ! être toujours sur le dos de qn
22-be agile/lithe	(být) mrštný jako kočka E be as lithe as a *cat*	G flink/geschmeidig wie eine *Katze* sein	F être souple comme un *chat*
23-be forsaken/ abandoned	(být) opuštěný jako pes E be like an outcast	G !einsam und verlassen/allein sein	F être abandonné comme un *chien*
24-be tired	(být) utahaný jako pes/čokl E!be *dog*-tired, !be knackered/dead beat	G müde wie ein Hund sein, !*hundemüde* sein	F !être à bout de souffle, ! être vanné
25-be tired	(být) utahaný jako kočka E !be *dog*-tired	G müde wie ein Hund sein, !*hundemüde* sein	F !être à bout de forces
26-be loyal/faithful	(být) (někomu) věrný jako pes E be like a faithful *hound*	G treu wie Gold/ ein *Hund* sein	F être fidéle comme un *chien*
27-be furious	(být) vzteklý jako pes	G wie ein toller	F être comme un

62 František Čermák

	E be like a rabid *dog*, be as cross as two sticks	*Hund* sein	*chien* enragé
28-be unfree, restrained	*být (někde) (uvázaný) jako pes u boudy/na řetěze* n. *být někde jako uvázaný* E it's like being in prison, !be chained up	G angebunden sein wie ein *Kettenhund*	F être comme un *chien* à la chaine
29-be useless	*být někde platný jako pes v kostele* E be about as useful as a Toby jug without a handle, feel/be like a ham sandwich at a Jewish wedding	G wie das fünfte Rad am Wagen sein	F !être la cinquiéme roue de la charette
30-be drunk/en	*byl (tak) vožralej, že říkal psovi slečno* E !he was so drunk he opened his collar to piss	G -	F -
31-be hungry	*(být) hladový jako pes* n. *mít hlad jako pes* E (be starving), !I could eat a horse	G hungring wie ein Wolf sein	F !avoir une faim *canine*
32-suffer	*zkusit/zkoušet jako pes/víc než pes/zvíře* n. *mít se (někde) jako/hůř než pes* E !lead a *dog*'s life, (suffer agonies)	G leben wie ein *Hund*	F !mener une vie de *chien*
33-be depressed/ dejected	*být/chodit jako zpráskaný/zbitý pes* E slink off like a whipped *cur*, !have that *hangdog* look	G herumlaufen wie ein geprügelter *Hund*	F !avoir un air de *chien* battu
34-look triumphantly	*koukat (se)/dívat se na někoho jako kočka na myš* E watch so. like a *cat* watching a mouse	G jn anstarren wie die Klapperschlange ein Kaninchen/wie ein Raubtier sein Opfer	F !on dirait un *chat* qui guette une souris
35-feel contempt	*připadat si/být jako prašivý pes* E be (made to) feel like a leper	G -	F -
36-express contentment	*příst jako kočka* E purr like a *cat*	G schnurren wie eine *Katze*	ronronner comme un *chat*
37-act strictly	*být (na někoho) jako pes*	G !zu j-n	F ! être toujours

Animal Phraseology: The Case of Dog and Cat (a Corpus-based Study)

	E !have it in for so.	*hundsgemein* sein	sur le dos de qn
38-torment cruelly	hrát si/pohrávat si s někým jako kočka s myší E !play (a game of) *cat-and-mouse* with so.	G !mit jm *Katz* und Maus spielen	F jouer avec qn/sa victime comme un *chat* avec une souris
39-not dare to start, hesitate how to begin	chodit kolem/okolo něčeho jako (kočka) kolem/okolo horké kaše E !beat about the bush	G irgendwo wie die Katze um den heissen Brei herumstreichen	F !tourner autour du pot, !ne pas savoir par quel bout prendre qch
40-suck up to, nuzzle	někomu lísat se (k někomu) jako kočka E fawn like a *cat*	G !ein Schmeichel*kätzchen* sein	F -
41-speak sharply, snap	být/utrhnout se/utrhovat se na někoho jako na psa E treat so. like a mangy *cur*	G -	F injurier comme un *chien*
42-act contemptuously	jednat/zacházet s někým jako se psem n. jednat/zacházet s někým hůř než se psem E !treat so. no better than a *cur/dog*, treat so. like dirt	G j-n schlechter als einen *Hund* behandeln	F traiter qn comme un *chien*/du poisson pourri, traiter qn pire qu'un *chien*
43-give contemptuously	hodit/házet někomu něco jako psovi (kost) E toss so. sth like a *dog* a bone	G -	F jeter qch á qn comme à un *chien*
44-be irritated/angry	ježit/zježit/naježit vousy jako kocour E !bristle up, !get one's hackles up prskat jako kočka/kocour E spit like a *cat*	G die Barthaare aufstellen wie ein Kater G fauchen wie eine Katze	F (se hérisser) F -
45-splutter	prskat jako (divoká) kočka E spit like a wild *cat*	G fauchen wie eine Wildkatze	F -
46-splutter, be angry	prskat jako kocour see under kočka		
47-fume, rage	hnát se/rozehnat se za někým/vrhnout se na někoho jako vzteklý pes E go after so./let fly at so. like enraged bull	G hinter j-m hersein wie ein wildgewordener Rüde	F se jeter sur qn comme un *chien* enragé
48-recover, disregard	oklepat se/otřepat se/otřást se jako pes	G sich wie ein *Hund* schütteln	F se secouer comme un

49-scold, tongue-lash	E !shrug it off, !barely bat an eyelid, !make light of it vynadat/nadávat někomu jako psovi E !curse so. up hill (and) down dale	G -	barbet qui sort de l'eau F injurier qn comme un chien/du poisson pouri
50-expect eagerly	svítit očima jako kočka E !his eyes are shining like a cat's	G mit den Augen funkeln wie eine Katze	F !avoir des yeux de chat
51-lurk	číhat na něco/někoho jako kočka na myš E watch so. like a cat watching a mouse	G auf etw lauern wie die Katze vor dem Mäuseloch	F guetter qn comme un chat guette une souris
52-fight, brawl	tahat se/rvát se o něco jako psi o kost E scrap/fight like dogs	G sich wie die Kesselflicker raufen	F se battre comme des chiens
53-rush, order about	honit někoho jako psa E !slavedrive so., !keep so. at it	G -	F chasser qn comme un chien
54-run out	vyvádět/vyletět jako vzteklej pes E carry on/rant like nobody's business	G -	F -
55-rage, be seething	vyvádět/vyletět jako vzteklej pes E carry on/rant like nobody's business	G -	F -
56-pursue	hnát se/rozehnat se za někým/vrhnout se na někoho jako vzteklý pes E go after so./let fly at so. like enraged bull	G hinter j-m hersein wie ein wildgewordener Rüde	F se jeter sur qn comme un chien enragé
57-talk continuously	mlít hubou jako pes ocasem E !her tongue never stops wagging	G !sie macht viel Wind um das, was sie sagt	F parler comme un moulin
58-sing off-key	mít hlas/zpívat/hrát jako když tahá kočku za ocas/šlape kočce na ocas E have a voice like a piece of coke under the door, (vulg) have a voice like a cow giving birth to a roll of barbed wire	G das ist, als wenn man einer Katze auf den Schwanz tritt	F -

59-write illegibly	škrábat/drápat/psát/mazat jako kocour E scratch like a *wildcat*	G kratzen wie eine *Wildkatze*	F -
60-work incompetently	jde mu to jako psovi pastva n. dělá (to) jako když se pes pase E be about as good at/with sth as a duchess with a shovel	G -	F -
61-not comprehend, be useless	být někde platný jako pes v kostele E be about as useful as a Toby jug without a handle, feel/be like a ham sandwich at a Jewish wedding	G wie das fünfte Rad am Wagen sein	F !être la cinquiéme roue de la charette
62-hate each other	mají se rádi jako kočka s myší E !they lead a *cat*-and-dog life	G -	F -
63-die disgracefully	chcípnout/pojít (někde) jako pes za plotem/u cesty E die like a *dog*	G wie ein *Hund* verrecken	F mourir/crever comme un *chien*

LA PHRASÉOLOGIE, UN MODE DE DÉNOMINATIONS MULTIPLES

Moufida Ghariani Baccouche
Rencontres Linguistiques Méditerranéennes (Tunis)

Abstract: Starting from some examples of unilexical and multiword denominations which either coexist or alternate in a perfect complementarity in natural languages (ex. Arabic/ French/English) and which are motivated by their morphology or their semantics, this paper intends to show that multiword denominations are productive in the creation of new denominations but are in some cases replaced by alphanumeric ones which are rather scientific and neutral. The aim is to establish a certain typology of contexts motivating this or that choice.

Key words: Derivational morphology, phraseological fixedness, figurative terminology

0. Introduction

Les recherches menées surtout ces derniers temps sur la phraséologie ont montré clairement que le mode de dénomination des réalités qui nous entourent ne saurait se limiter à la monolexicalité. Les expressions polylexicales ont autant d'importance dans le fonctionnement du langage humain et son économie générale. Ces deux modes de dénomination ne sont nullement contradictoires ou exclusifs, ils coexistent ou alternent dans une parfaite complémentarité. En effet, plusieurs réalités sont exprimées en même temps par l'un ou l'autre des deux modes de dénomination comme nous le verrons plus loin à partir de quelques spécimens dénominatifs. Nous focaliserons par la suite sur l'analyse des exemples récents de dénominations multiples d'une maladie dans les médias à caractère pandémique; il s'agit de *la grippe porcine/ mexicaine/ AH1N1*.

1. Dénominations monolexicales

La langue dispose de plusieurs dénominations monolexicales pour les mêmes référents avec une motivation tant au niveau de la morphologie qu'au niveau du sémantisme des mots.

1.1 Dénominations motivées par la morphologie des mots

Prenons comme exemples des dénominations de maladie : *jaunisse / hépatite* qui désignent la même maladie. La désignation *jaunisse* relève du niveau de la langue courante et doit son origine à l'ictère, terme médical qui exprime la coloration jaune de la peau due à la présence dans le sang et dans les tissus, notamment dans la peau, de pigments biliaires (cf. *Petit Larousse* illustré, 1989). Quant à la dénomination *hépatite*, elle fait partie de la langue spécialisée, la langue médicale : *hêpar*; *hêpatos* (du grec) foie, *-ite*, étant le suffixe servant à former des noms indiquant un état maladif (exemple: *gastrite, méningite*).

Nous retrouvons en arabe le même mécanisme descriptif dans la dénomination. En effet, la *jaunisse* est désignée en arabe dans la langue courante par le terme *bu$\underline{s}$offi:r*, littéralement «le père du jaunissement». Quant aux locuteurs bilingues, ils recourent souvent à l'emprunt du terme français *hépatite*, courant dans la langue spécialisée.

1.2 Dénominations motivées par le sémantisme des mots

Nous pensons ici aux euphémismes. Rappelons qu'un euphémisme, (du grec : *euphêmismos,* emploi d'un mot favorable) est une manière adoucie ou atténuée d'énoncer un mot, une expression ou une idée trop crue ou choquante pour ménager la susceptibilité de l'interlocuteur. L'euphémisme peut aller, dans l'antiphrase, jusqu'à l'emploi d'un mot ou d'un énoncé qui exprime le contraire de ce qu'on veut dire (cf. *Dictionnaire de linguistique,* Larousse, 1989 et *Petit Larousse illustré,*1989). Nous citerons en arabe les exemples suivants :

bija:đ, littéralement : «blancheur» pour *fħamm* (charbon noir).
ribħ, littéralement : «gain», pour *milħ* (sel).
ʕIdit jiddik, littéralement : «le compte de ta main» pour *χamsa* (le chiffre 5)
ʕIdit jidi :k, littéralement : «le compte de tes mains» pour *ʕaʃra* (le chiffre 10)

Le verbe *mourir* en arabe : *ma :t,* semble être dur à énoncer; pour cela son équivalent : *twaffa,* provenant de la troncation de l'expression : *tawaffa:hu-lla:h,* littéralement : «Dieu a mis fin à ses jours», semble pouvoir atténuer le choc par la référence à la volonté divine.

2. Dénominations mono/polylexicales

Dans ce processus dénominatif caractérisé par l'alternance des deux types de dénomination, les dénominations polylexicales sont plus motivées de par leur polylexicalité. Le mot arabe *ʃukran,* «merci», alterne avec une expression polylexicale revêtant une certaine connotation religieuse, *ba:raka-lla:hu fi:k,* dont la transposition serait : «que Dieu te bénisse», ou bien, *allah- iχalli :k* «que Dieu te garde», ou encore *jaʕti:k issaħħa,* «qu'Il te donne la santé».

Le verbe *mourir* en arabe *ma:t,* cité plus haut, étant un terme qu'on préfère éviter, est souvent remplacé par des euphémismes dans des dénominations multiples ayant également une connotation religieuse, telles que *: iddwa :m lil-lah,* «l'éternité pour Dieu», *(fula:n) jʕi:ʃ ra:sik,* littéralement «(un tel) vive ta tête». *sa:ħib-l-ama:na hazz ama:ntu* littéralement «le propriétaire du dépôt a repris ce qu'il a confié».

D'autres expressions sont à caractère euphémistique, par exemple en arabe, pour dire de quelqu'un qu'il est malade : *mri:đ,* on utilise souvent l'expression *ma jiqdirʃ,* littéralement «il est dans l'incapacité». Pour un non-voyant : *aʕma,* on dirait : un tel est *bʕini:h* «avec ses yeux», ou *bṣir,* terme de l'arabe littéraire qui veut dire «un bon voyant»; de même pour un sourd : *atraʃ,* un tel est *b-wiðni:h* « avec ses oreilles» et pour un paralysé : *muqʕad,* un tel est *b-saqi:h* «avec ses jambes»

Ces dénominations plurielles que nous retrouvons dans la plupart des langues naturelles fonctionnent dans beaucoup de situations de la vie courante comme euphémismes tirant de l'embarras ou de la gêne ceux qui choisissent de les utiliser à bon escient. Un Français dirait par exemple de quelqu'un qui vient de décéder *: il nous a quittés* ou *il a rendu l'âme*; par contre il se retiendra de dire crûment *: il est mort.* Il en est de même pour l'anglais dans : *to breathe one's last, to lose one's life, to meet one's maker.*

D'autres dénominations polylexicales, toujours dans le même contexte, ont une connotation péjorative ou chargée d'ironie; c'est ce qui explique l'existence d'expressions comme *kuθr-ilhamm jđaħħak,* littéralement : «l'excès de malheur fait rire».

Pour revenir à l'arabe, on dirait pour *mourir,* non sans une note de dérision, une manière d'atténuer l'effet de la mort: *blaʕ zru:su* «il a avalé ses molaires», ou encore *twassad-l-*

mχadda, «il a posé la tête sur l'oreiller». De même le français dirait pour *mourir : passer l'arme à gauche, casser sa pipe, boire le bouillon de minuit, manger les pissenlits par les racines*». Quant à l'anglais, il utilise d'autres images ou tropes non moins expressives telles que : *to kick the bucket, to snuff it*.

3. Dénominations polylexicales

En fait, chaque dénomination polylexicale a sa motivation. Les expressions arabes suivantes : *sba-ħ-l-χi:r/-innu:r/-fill*, littéralement «une matinée de bien/de lumière/de jasmin»; *nha:rik tajjib*, «ta journée est bonne»; *nha :rik digla wa ħli:b*, «que ta journée soit de dattes et de lait», où nous remarquons le recours à des éléments odoriférants ou culinaires savoureux, ont le même contenu performatif, c'est-à- dire saluer le matin, mais leurs motivations comportent deux sens, le sens littéral, celui des mots qui les composent, et le sens idiomatique, c'est-à-dire le sens global : bonjour. Il est à noter ici que cette expression a une connotation religieuse du fait que c'était l'habitude du prophète Mohammed de commencer sa journée par un petit déjeuner comportant des dattes et du lait.

Ainsi la langue dispose-t-elle dans son fonctionnement économique de plusieurs modes de dénomination des réalités. En jouant sur la dualité monolexicalité/polylexicalité, la langue recourt à toutes les possibilités combinatoires dans la faculté de dénomination multiple comme nous venons de le voir. En effet, elle semble très productive dans différents domaines de la vie courante, des plus simples jusqu'aux activités spécialisées et scientifiques. C'est ce que nous proposons d'examiner dans ce qui suit en essayant de répondre à la question suivante :

4. Comment les dénominations plurielles sont-elles actives dans le processus néologique?

Certaines dénominations polylexicales ont vu le jour à la suite de certains évènements : épidémies, tragédies naturelles, maladies, telles que *la grippe aviaire, la vache folle, la grippe asiatique, la grippe espagnole*, etc. Nous allons considérer ici le cas de la dernière épidémie qui a suscité une grande campagne médiatique partout dans le monde : *la grippe porcine* appelée également *la grippe mexicaine* ou *du Mexique* et finalement *la grippe AH1N1*. Dans les medias arabes, c'est le terme *influenza-l-χana:zi:r*, «la grippe des cochons» qui a circulé les premiers temps avant d'être remplacé par la dénomination scientifique consacrée officiellement, *la grippe AH1N1*. On pourrait également remarquer que le terme *influenza*, pris de l'anglais et en particulier du vocabulaire de spécialité, a été choisi plutôt que le terme *flu*, terme médical, qu'on retrouve dans *bird flu, Asian flu, et swine flu*.

4.1 comment expliquer ces dénominations plurielles?

La polylexicalité aurait une motivation explicative, d'où la structure relationnelle : N+adjectif. Remarquons que ces qualificatifs sont des pseudo adjectifs puisqu'ils présentent des caractéristiques particulières : on ne peut pas les employer comme attributs, ni les antéposer, ni les intensifier.

Dans les dénominations *grippe mexicaine, grippe espagnole, grippe asiatique*, la motivation est à caractère géographique. Quant aux autres dénominations, *grippe aviaire* ou *bird flu, grippe porcine* ou *swine flu*, la motivation trouve son origine dans l'espèce animale. Donc, il n'y aurait pas eu de motivation sans la polylexicalité.

Pour résumer on peut dire que la structure N+adjectif est un moule indiquant la relation entre la grippe et l'endroit géographique, ou la grippe et l'espèce, c'est-à-dire l'animal concerné.

Nous retenons de tout cela deux points importants : la littéralité et la polylexicalité dans *grippe porcine, grippe aviaire, grippe espagnole*, sont des éléments dénominatifs définitoires. D'autre part, le sens du sémème définitoire est le genre prochain, c'est-à-dire l'hyperonyme, ou la classe, auquel on ajoute les sèmes spécifiques.

Ces dénominations polylexicales à connotation géographique ou renvoyant à l'espèce, ont vite été abandonnées, au profit de la dénomination *grippe AH1N1*, composée de lettres et de chiffres.

4.2 Pourquoi le recours à des dénominations alphanumériques?

En fait ces formules chimiques confèrent à la dénomination un statut savant, une autorité scientifique. Cette motivation qui s'éloigne de la littéralité est de nature opaque et donc savante et neutre. Ce qui explique d'autre part le choix et l'adoption officielle de la dénomination *AH1N1*, ce sont probablement les retombées négatives des connotations *mexicaine, porcine, espagnole*. A titre d'exemple, les autorités égyptiennes ont procédé à l'extermination de tous les porcs élevés par les coptes «chrétiens» créant ainsi un malaise entre musulmans et chrétiens. Dans ce cas les retombées négatives sont de nature économique, mais également religieuse. Quant aux Mexicains, ils ont protesté contre l'usage de l'expression *grippe mexicaine*, contestant cette origine qui ne manque pas de conséquences économiques négatives : tourisme, échanges commerciaux, etc.

5. Conclusion

Après cet examen de quelques spécimens de dénominations multiples dans les trois langues étudiées, peut-on dégager une certaine typologie de ces expressions polylexicales dans leur ancrage discursif?

L'examen de ces spécimens de dénomination nous autorise à établir une certaine typologie de contextes motivant l'emploi ou le choix de l'une ou l'autre des dénominations et leur ancrage discursif.

Un ensemble d'expressions plus ancrées dans le discours populaire est motivé par sa transparence sémantique grâce à la référence géographique, animale, etc.

Un ensemble d'expressions sémantiquement opaques, moins motivées, réservées au discours scientifique, permettent, entre autres, un positionnement neutre, revêtant ainsi plus d'autorité et contribuant par voie de conséquence à éviter les éventuelles retombées négatives.

6. Bibliographie

BACCOUCHE, T. 2006 «Le concept de figement en linguistique arabe», *Composition syntaxique et figement lexical*, Caen: Presses Universitaires: 219-226.

BACCOUCHE,T., MEJRI, S. & GHARIANI BACCOUCHE, M. 1998 «Du sacré au profane: le parcours d'une lexicalisation», *Le figement lexical*, Tunis: CERES: 121-131.

COWIE, A. P. MACKIN, R. & McCAIG, I. R. 1983 *Oxford Dictionary of Current Idiomatic English, vol. I. Phrasal Verbs, Vol. II. Phrases,Clauses and Sentence Idioms,* Oxford: Oxford University Presss.

DICTIONNAIRE DE LINGUISTIQUE, 1989 Paris: Larousse.

GHARIANI BACCOUCHE, M. 2001 *L'idiomaticité en anglais : considérations théoriques et pratiques,* Lille: Atelier National de reproduction des thèses.

GRÉCIANO, G. 1983 *Signification et dénomination en allemand. La sémantique des expressions idiomatiques,* Recherches Linguistiques, IX, Metz: Université.

GROSS, G. 1996 *Les expressions figées en Français,* Paris, Ophrys.

MEJRI, S. 1997 *Le figement lexical,* Tunis: Publications de la Faculté des Lettres de la Manouba.

MEJRI, S. 2003 «La stéréotipie du corps dans la phraséologie. Approche contrastive», in Harald Burger, Annelies Hâck Buhofer et Gertrud Gréciano, *Flut von Texten-Vielfalt der Kulturen,* (Phraseologie und Parömiologie, Band 14) Baltmannsweiler: Schneider Verlag Hohengehren: 203-217.

PETIT LAROUSSE ILLUSTRÉ, 1989 Paris: Larousse.

COLOCACIONES COMPLEJAS METAFÓRICAS

Kazumi Koike
Universidad Takushoku (Tokio, Japón)

Abstract: The purpose of this paper is to point out the existence of a special type of Spanish complex collocations which, used with metaphorical meaning, establish other links with their respective complements (*metaphorical complex collocations*). The base of a metaphorical complex collocation is not a noun, but a metaphorized compound (*cortina de humo* in *lanzar una cortina de humo sobre el escándalo*, or *balón de oxígeno* in *dar un balón de oxígeno al régimen de La Habana*). The existence of metaphorical complex collocations causes a borderline problem between collocations and verbal idioms, precisely because of their idiomatic meaning.

Key words: Complex collocations, verbal idioms, metaphorization

1. Objetivos

En nuestros trabajos anteriores (Koike 2006 y 2008a) hemos estudiado aquellas colocaciones léxicas que, empleadas con valor metafórico, establecen otros vínculos con sus respectivos complementos (p.ej., *subir por la escalera del éxito, escalar las cimas del poder*); a dichas construcciones las hemos denominado *colocaciones metafóricas*. En el presente artículo queremos llamar la atención sobre la existencia de otro tipo de colocaciones metafóricas que presentan un comportamiento semántico similar. Se trata de aquellas colocaciones verbonominales cuya base es una locución nominal formada a partir de un compuesto sintagmático.

En los ejemplos (1a), (2a) y (3a) aparecen los compuestos sintagmáticos *balón de oxígeno, cortina de humo* y *bola de nieve*, que se emplean con sus respectivos significados metafóricos:

(1a) La condena a la intensificación del embargo norteamericano a Cuba centra los debates de una cumbre iberoamericana que […] una vez más servirá para dar *un balón de oxígeno* al régimen de La Habana (CREA). [coloc. compleja metafórica]
(1b) Se gestionó a todos los niveles que subieran un *balón de oxígeno* porque Luis se estaba asfixiando con un fuerte ataque de asma (CREA). [compuesto sintagmático]
(2a) E invocar este argumento equivale a correr *una cortina de humo* sobre el verdadero problema, y a desviar el asunto de su fondo real (CREA). [coloc. compleja metafórica]
(2b) (*Una cortina de humo* ha ido creciendo hasta desdibujar las siluetas de los objetos y las personas. Detrás de esta *cortina de humo* que avanza hacia y por el patio de butacas se vienen gritos espeluznantes (CREA). [compuesto sintagmático]
(3a) De tanto hablar, habéis hecho *una bola de nieve* de un incidente sin importancia (DP, s.v. *bola*). [coloc. compleja metafórica]
(3b) Hay nieve "mojada" y nieve "seca". La "mojada" está hecha de copos grandes y más húmedos. Esta es la mejor nieve para hacer *bolas de nieve* (CREA). [compuesto sintagmático]

Como puede apreciarse, los compuestos sintagmáticos *balón de oxígeno*, *cortina de humo* y *bola de nieve* en (1a), (2a) y (3a) están metaforizados y no significan lo mismo que en (1b), (2b) y (3b). En los ejemplos de la serie (a) hay colocaciones complejas formadas por un verbo y un compuesto metaforizado, pero éstas no conservan sus significados literales, porque lo que se da en (1a) no es un balón de oxígeno "real", lo que se corre en (2a) tampoco es una cortina de humo "visible", y lo que se hace en (3a) tampoco es una bola de nieve "tangible". Teniendo en cuenta su estructura, denominamos a estas combinaciones *colocaciones complejas metafóricas*.

2. Dos tipos de colocaciones metafóricas

Las colocaciones complejas metafóricas presentan el mismo comportamiento semántico que las colocaciones simples metafóricas tratadas en Koike (2006 y 2008a). Así, el compuesto sintagmático metaforizado *cortina de humo* ('artificio de ocultación', DRAE) puede combinarse con verbos como *lanzar, extender, tender, correr*, etc., formando una colocación compleja, la cual, a su vez, sufre otra metaforización al introducir, por ejemplo, el complemento *sobre el escándalo*. El único elemento que se emplea con significado recto en *lanzar una cortina de humo sobre el escándalo* es el sustantivo *escándalo* que funciona como complemento, puesto que el significado de *lanzar una cortina de humo* en esta combinación tiene un valor metafórico ('ocultar').

Este proceso semántico es idéntico al que presenta la colocación metafórica *escalar las cimas* cuando ésta, usada con significado metafórico ('alcanzar'), incorpora el complemento preposicional *(del poder)*. Al igual que en el caso citado, el único elemento que interviene con significado recto en esta combinación léxica es el sustantivo *poder,* que funciona como modificador del SN. El siguiente esquema ilustra el paralelismo en la estructura semántica entre las dos colocaciones metafóricas:

[*escalar* [*las cimas*]$_{\text{metaforizado}}$]('alcanzar')$_{\text{coloc. simple metafórica}}$ *del poder*
[*lanzar* [*una cortina de humo*]$_{\text{metaforizado}}$]('ocultar')$_{\text{coloc. compleja metafórica}}$ *sobre el escándalo*

3. Tipo de locución nominal

Como es de suponer, no todas las colocaciones complejas con locución nominal conforman colocaciones con valor metafórico. Así, la locución *visto bueno* ('aprobación', DFDEA) no puede generar dichas colocaciones, aunque sí una colocación compleja con valor funcional (*dar el visto bueno a algo*, 'aprobar').

El tipo de locución nominal que puede aparecer junto con un verbo en las colocaciones complejas metafóricas es limitado. En términos generales, solo aquellos compuestos sintagmáticos metaforizables que suelen combinarse con determinados verbos pueden conformar colocaciones complejas metafóricas como las que se estudian aquí. Por ejemplo, el compuesto *oro negro* ('petróleo', DFDEA) no es capaz de producir una colocación metafórica, mientras que *piedra angular* ('piedra que forma la esquina en la unión de dos paredes', DS) sí constituye una colocación compleja cuando se emplea con significado metafórico y se coloca con el verbo *poner* (*poner la piedra angular de algo*).

El compuesto sintagmático utilizado con significado metafórico lo consideramos como un tipo de locución nominal (Koike 2009). La combinación de un verbo con un compuesto sintagmático es una colocación compleja léxica (p.ej., <u>cortar el cordón umbilical</u> *que une un bebé a su madre*), mientras que la de un verbo con el mismo compuesto metaforizado (convertido en una locución nominal) produce una colocación compleja metafórica (p. ej., *cortar el cordón umbilical con alguien*).

En Koike (2006: 53-54) hemos señalado que los sustantivos utilizados en las colocaciones simples metafóricas no son sustantivos abstractos, sino sustantivos que, en su mayoría, designan 'objetos físicos' (*bastón, timón, riendas, muro, bandera, estandarte, copa, máscara, careta, puerta*, etc.) o 'fenómenos físicos' (*fiebre, pulso, temporal*, etc.) y que son susceptibles de ser empleados con significado metafórico, lo cual explica que el compuesto sintagmático conforme una colocación compleja metafórica. Del mismo modo que un sustantivo concreto se metaforiza al combinarse con determinados verbos, un compuesto sintagmático que se comporta como un sustantivo concreto sufre una metaforización al colocarse con ciertos verbos, creando así una colocación compleja metafórica. Así, tanto el sustantivo *puerta* en (4) como el compuesto *piedra angular* en (5) no se emplean con su significado recto, sino metafórico:

(4) Este acuerdo *abre la puerta a nuevas negociaciones* (DS, s.v. *puerta*).
(5) Ellos *han puesto* no la primera piedra, sino *la piedra angular de la Feria para Niños* [...] (CREA).

La nómina de locuciones nominales que crean colocaciones complejas metafóricas no es muy extensa si se tienen en cuenta el reducido número de compuestos sintagmáticos metaforizables y la presencia obligada de un verbo colocativo para producir estas combinaciones. La lista siguiente recoge locuciones nominales formadas a partir de un compuesto sintagmático capaces de conformar colocaciones complejas metafóricas:

balón de oxígeno ('alivio que se recibe en una situación comprometida', DRAE), *bola de nieve* ('noticia que va adquiriendo más detalles y más importancia al pasar de boca en boca', DFDEA), *cheque en blanco* ('libertad de actuación'), *compás de espera* ('interrupción temporal de un proceso o actividad en espera de algo', DS), *cordón umbilical* ('elemento que sirve de unión entre una entidad y otra de la que esta depende', DFDEA), *cortina de humo* ('artificio de ocultación', DRAE), *cuenta atrás* ('la del tiempo cada vez menor que falta para un acontecimiento previsto', DRAE), *marcha atrás* ('acción de desistir de hacer algo', DS), *pistoletazo de salida* ('principio, más o menos solemne de una actividad', DS), *punto culminante* ('punto más importante, de mayor intensidad, esplendor, etc.', DP), *punto final* ('hecho o palabras con que se da por terminado un asunto, una discusión, etc.', DRAE), *punto muerto* ('momento de interrupción', DS), *puñalada trapera* ('traición o mala pasada', DFDEA), *recta final* ('última etapa o último período de alguna situación', DClave), *salto atrás* ('retroceso en sentido moral o físico', DRAE), *vía muerta* ('situación de paralización en un proceso', DRAE), etc.

4. Verbo colocativo

Un compuesto sintagmático metaforizado puede aparecer en diversos entornos sintácticos. Frente a los casos anteriores, donde funcionaba como complemento de un verbo predicativo, puede ser sujeto gramatical o parte del sujeto (6), el atributo en una oración copulativa (7) o un constituyente de un sintagma preposicional (8), etc.:

(6) La *columna vertebral* de la programación de Radio 5 "Todo Noticias" es la información a través de los boletines de noticias y los avances informativos en forma de titulares (CREA).
(7) Los senadores quieren que sea una *caja de resonancia* del malestar social y un cauce para mejorar la televisión (CREA).
(8) Inmersos en un tenso *compás de espera* [...] los inversores limitaron sus tomas de posición (CREA).

El compuesto sintagmático *vía muerta* puede aparecer en varios entornos sintácticos (*las vías muertas de la estación, Las estaciones tienen vías muertas*, etc.), pero la colocación compleja metafórica se produce solo al combinarse éste, con significado metafórico, con verbos como *entrar* (*en*) o *dejar* (*en*):

(9) "El pacto autonómico suscrito por el PSOE y el Partido Popular *entró en vía muerta* el mismo día de la firma (CREA).
(10) La pareja, sin embargo, *deja en vía muerta* la posibilidad de contar con el hipotético paquete que maneja Javier de la Rosa (CREA).

Por otro lado, hay compuestos sintagmáticos que eligen el mismo verbo tanto con significado recto como con significado metafórico, como es el caso de *cordón umbilical,* que puede colocarse, entre otros, con el verbo *cortar* con ambos sentidos ('conjunto de vasos que une la placenta de la madre con el vientre del feto para la nutrición de este hasta el momento del parto' y 'elemento que sirve de unión entre una entidad y otra de la que esta depende', DFDEA):

(11) La policía *cortó el cordón umbilical* y trasladaron a la madre y al niño al hospital Clínico (CREA). [verbo + compuesto sintagmático = coloc. compleja léxica]
(12) El propio Manuel Garnacho, secretario general de construcción, señaló a este diario que "ya advertí a Méndez que *cortara el cordón umbilical con Redondo,* que él era ahora el secretario general del sindicato" (CREA). [verbo + locución = coloc. compleja metafórica]

5. Estructuras formales

Los posibles esquemas que puede adoptar una colocación compleja metafórica son los siguientes:

I. [verbo transitivo + locución nominal]$_{\text{coloc. compleja metafórica}}$ + prep. + $SN_{\text{CI/C. de régimen/modificador}}$
[[*dar*] [*un balón de oxígeno*]$_{\text{metaforizado}}$]('ayudar') $_{\text{metaforizado}}$ *al presidente*
II. [verbo transitivo + prep. + locución nominal]$_{\text{coloc. compleja metafórica}}$ + SN_{CD}
[[*dejar*] [*en vía muerta*]$_{\text{metaforizado}}$]('paralizar')$_{\text{metaforizado}}$ *el pacto autonómico*$_{\text{CD}}$
III. [verbo intransitivo + prep. + locución nominal]$_{\text{coloc. compleja metafórica}}$ + SN_{sujeto}
[[*entrar*] [*en vía muerta*]$_{\text{metaforizado}}$]('paralizarse')$_{\text{metaforizado}}$ *el pacto autonómico*$_{\text{sujeto}}$

I. El esquema más frecuente es la combinación de un verbo transitivo con una locución nominal. En esta estructura la colocación metafórica introduce un complemento mediante una preposición, el cual puede ser un complemento indirecto (*dar un balón de oxígeno a alguien*), un complemento de régimen preposicional *(lanzar una cortina de humo sobre algo,* abrir un *compás de espera en algo*) o un modificador de la locución nominal (*hacer una bola de nieve de algo*).

II. El segundo esquema es la secuencia formada por un verbo transitivo y un sintagma preposicional del que forma parte la locución nominal, como es el caso de *dejar en vía muerta (algo)*. En esta colocación metafórica el elemento variable funciona como complemento directo del verbo.

III. El último esquema consiste en un verbo intransitivo y un sintagma preposicional del que forma parte la locución nominal. A veces entre el segundo y el tercer esquema existe la relación de transitivo e intransitivo que se observa en la pareja *dejar en vía muerta* (*algo*) y *entrar en vía muerta*. En este caso, el complemento directo del segundo esquema pasa a ocupar la posición de sujeto en el tercero.

6. Estructura semántica

Hemos analizado el compuesto sintagmático metaforizado como locución nominal precisamente por su significado metafórico. Estas locuciones nominales formadas a partir de un compuesto sintagmático sufren otra metaforización al emplearse en las colocaciones metafóricas. Por ejemplo, el compuesto *recta final* en (13) conserva su significado recto ('último tramo antes de la meta', DRAE), pero en (14) se emplea con significado metafórico:

(13) Los caballos *entran* ya *en la recta final* (DS, s. v. *recta*).
(14) Las dos compañías gallegas del sector pesquero y alimentario *entraron* ya *en la recta final de la negociación* (CREA).

En (14) el compuesto *recta final* está empleado en sentido metafórico y, además, la colocación compleja *entrar en la recta final* está metaforizada al combinarse con el modificador *de la negociación*; de este modo en esta secuencia se produce una doble metaforización: la de *recta final* y la de la colocación compleja *entrar en la recta final*. Este proceso semántico es el mismo que se advierte en la colocación simple metafórica *escalar las cimas del poder*.

Las colocaciones complejas metafóricas tienen en común este fenómeno de doble metaforización con las colocaciones simples metafóricas estudiadas en Koike (2006). El esquema siguiente ilustra la doble metaforización existente en las expresiones *entrar en la recta final de la negociación* y *escalar las cimas del poder*:

[[*las cimas*]$_{\text{metaforizado}}$ *del poder*]
> [*escalar las cimas*]('alcanzar')$_{\text{coloc. simple metafórica}}$ (*d*)*el poder*]
[[*la recta final*]$_{\text{metaforizado}}$ *de la negociación*]
> [*entrar en la recta final*]('ir a finalizar')$_{\text{coloc. compleja metafórica}}$ *de la negociación*

Desde el punto de vista semántico, las colocaciones complejas metafóricas presentan valores funcionales porque tienen un significado equivalente al de un verbo simple. Por ejemplo, *lanzar una cortina de humo* tiene el significado de 'ocultar' en *lanzar una cortina de humo sobre el escándalo*.

Hay locuciones nominales que pueden conformar colocaciones complejas con valor pasivo (p. ej., *recibir un balón de oxígeno, recibir la luz verde*).

Algunas de las colocaciones complejas metafóricas presentan valores aspectuales diversos, como el incoativo (p. ej., *entrar en vía muerta*), el durativo (p. ej., *seguir en un compás de espera*), etc.

7. Problema de límites

Dadas la complejidad semántica y formal de una colocación compleja, existen combinaciones difíciles de clasificar.

Hay colocaciones complejas que se metaforizan sin complemento; es el caso de *dar el do de pecho* o *lanzar un globo sonda*, cuyo tratamiento entraña cierta dificultad, ya que puede ser una colocación compleja ([*dar*]$_V$ + [*el do de pecho*]$_{compuesto}$, [*lanzar*]$_V$ + [*un globo sonda*]$_{compuesto}$,) o una colocación compleja metafórica ([*dar el do de pecho*]$_{coloc.\ compleja\ metafórica}$, [*lanzar un globo sonda*]$_{coloc.\ compleja\ metafórica}$) convertida en una locución verbal.

(15a) Lamentablemente, el tenor desafinó al *dar el do de pecho* (DP, s. v. *do*). [colocación compleja léxica]
(15b) Tienes que *dar el do de pecho* en tu examen (DS, s. v. *do*). [locución < coloc. compleja metafórica]
(16a) *Han lanzado un globo sonda* para investigar el ozono del Polo Sur (DS, s.v. *globo*). [colocación compleja léxica]
(16b) Inmediatamente, Pedro se retractó de lo que había dicho a su amigo y por eso tuve la sensación de que sólo había querido *lanzar un globo sonda* para ver si me estaba enterando de lo que hablaba (CREA). [locución < coloc. compleja metafórica]

En nuestra opinión, *dar el do de pecho* es una colocación compleja cuando significa 'dar una de las notas más agudas que alcanza la voz del tenor' y una locución verbal con base colocacional cuando significa 'hacer máximo esfuerzo por conseguir una cosa'. Lo mismo puede decirse de *lanzar un globo sonda*, que es una colocación compleja cuando tiene el significado de 'lanzar un globo no tripulado para estudiar fenómenos meteorológicos' y una locución formada a partir de una colocación metafórica cuando significa 'difundir una noticia con el objetivo de observar la reacción que produce y obrar en consecuencia'.

Por otra parte, hay locuciones catalogadas como verbales que podría analizarse como colocaciones complejas metafóricas. Es el caso de la expresión *poner punto final a algo*, que es una colocación compleja formada por el verbo *poner* y el compuesto sintagmático *punto final*, cuya estructura semántica es idéntica a la de otras colocaciones complejas metafóricas:

[[*poner*]$_V$ + [*punto final*]$_{metaforizado}$]('finalizar')$_{coloc.\ compleja\ metafórica}$ *a la discusión*

8. Conclusiones

Hemos apuntado la existencia de un tipo especial de colocaciones complejas que, empleadas con valor metafórico, establecen otros vínculos con sus respectivos complementos. A continuación se resumen las principales características formales y semánticas de las colocaciones complejas metafóricas:

a) Al igual que las colocaciones simples metafóricas, las colocaciones complejas metafóricas son un tipo de colocaciones polisémicas que presentan dualidad semántica cuando introducen un complemento con determinado rasgo semántico.

b) Estas colocaciones complejas se caracterizan formalmente por ser composicionales, dado que la locución nominal que funciona como núcleo sintáctico del SN puede aparecer con sentido metafórico en otros contextos sin formar colocaciones verbonominales.

c) Las locuciones nominales que se emplean preferentemente en esta clase de colocaciones son originariamente compuestos sintagmáticos que se comportan como sustantivos concretos; el paso del significado originario al metafórico se logra gracias a la presencia de un complemento.

d) Aunque la doble especialización semántica que se produce tanto en la base de la colocación como en el verbo colocativo es un proceso semántico que caracteriza a las colocaciones complejas metafóricas, éstas se dan como resultado de una metaforización que afecta al conjunto de la colocación compleja.

e) La presencia de colocaciones complejas metafóricas plantea un problema de límites entre las colocaciones y las locuciones, en virtud precisamente del significado idiomático que presentan.

9. Siglas utilizadas

CREA = Real Academia Española, *Corpus de Referencia del Español Actual* (CREA) [en línea] <http://corpus.rae.es/creanet.html> [2007-2009]
DClave = Maldonado González, Concepción (dir.) (1999): *Clave. Diccionario de uso del español actual*, Madrid: SM.
DFDEA = Seco, Manuel y otros (eds.) (2004): *Diccionario fraseológico documentado del español actual*, Madrid: Santillana.
DP = Marsá, Francisco (dir.) (1982): *Diccionario Planeta de la lengua española usual*, Barcelona: Planeta.
DRAE = Real Academia Española (2001): *Diccionario de la lengua española,* Madrid: Espasa-Calpe.
DS = Gutiérrez Cuadrado, Juan (dir.) (1996): *Diccionario Salamanca de la lengua española*, Madrid: Santillana.

10. Bibliografía

GARCÍA-PAGE SÁNCHEZ, MARIO 2005 «Colocaciones simples y complejas: diferencias estructurales», en R. Almela, E. Trives y G. Wotjak (eds.). *Fraseología contrastiva con ejemplos tomados del alemán, español, francés e italiano,* Murcia: Universidad: 145-167.

GARCÍA-PAGE SÁNCHEZ, MARIO 2008 *Introducción a la fraseología española. Estudio de las locuciones,* Barcelona: Anthropos.

KOIKE, KOIKE 2001 *Colocaciones léxicas en el español actual: estudio formal y léxico-semántico,* Alcalá de Henares /Tokio: Universidad de Alcalá & Takushoku University.

KOIKE, KOIKE 2005 «Colocaciones complejas en el español actual». In: R. Almela; E. Trives & G. Wotjak (eds.): *Fraseología contrastiva con ejemplos tomados del alemán, español, francés e italiano,* Murcia: Universidad: 169-184.

KOIKE, KOIKE 2006 «Colocaciones metafóricas». In: E. de Miguel; A. Palacios & A. Serradilla (eds.), *Estructuras léxicas y estructura del léxico,* Frankfurt: Peter Lang: 47-59.

KOIKE, KOIKE 2008a «Colocaciones atípicas», *LEA,* 30/1: 87-107.

KOIKE, KOIKE 2008b «Locuciones verbales con base colocacional», *Revista de Filología,* 26: 75-94.

KOIKE, KOIKE 2009 «Las locuciones nominales del español», *Language Studies,* 121: 1-45.

PENADÉS MARTÍNEZ, INMACULADA 2001 «¿Colocaciones o locuciones verbales?», *LEA,* 23/1: 57-88.

REAL ACADEMIA ESPAÑOLA Y ASOCIACIÓN DE ACADEMIAS DE LA LENGUA ESPAÑOLA 2009 *Nueva gramática de la lengua española,* Madrid: Espasa.

RUIZ GURILLO, LEONOR 2002 «Compuestos, colocaciones, locuciones: intento de delimitación». In: A. Veiga et al. (eds.), *Léxico y gramática,* Lugo: Tris Tam: 327-339.

VERBES SUPPORTS ET PRÉDICATS ILLOCUTOIRES

Márton Náray-Szabó
Université Péter Pázmány
Piliscsaba, Hongrie

Abstract: Support verb (or light verb) constructions have been a field of interest in many linguistic frameworks for the last three decades. Their structure and behaviour depends mainly on the semantic type of the predicative noun they contain. We will give an account here on a group of highly important nouns these days: the illocutionary predicates. After having delimited this class, we will compare their distributional properties in two languages, French and Hungarian. This latter language has traditionally been considered by linguists as one resisting to that kind of structure in general, but a thorough analysis can reveal a more complex image.

Key words: light verb constructions, support verbs, illocutionary predicates, distribution, French, Hungarian.

1. Présentation

Un des phénomènes de la phraséologie qui constitue un groupe particulier dans la «Mischklassifikation» (classification mixte) burgerienne (Burger et al. 1982: 30-31), les constructions à verbe support (CVS), présentent des particularités uniques non seulement du point de vue du figement sémantique, mais au niveau lexical et syntaxique aussi. Elles se composent essentiellement de deux parties: la première est verbale (verbe support) et sert à préciser les circonstances de la seconde, qui est un prédicat nominal, qui en serait incapable tout seul. Le fait que ces constructions existent dans bien des langues incite à voir les différences du fonctionnement entre langues, en particulier entre des langues appartenant à des familles différentes.

Au lieu d'entrer en discussion sur les avantages et les désavantages des différentes approches, nous nous contentons ici de renvoyer le lecteur à un certain nombre d'ouvrages représentant les plus importantes écoles ayant traité du sujet jusqu'à l'heure actuelle.

Les structuralistes allemands ont reconnu dans les années 80 qu'en allemand, et surtout dans le registre formel, il s'observe un type d'unité phraséologique non encore décrit suffisamment, qui contient des verbes qu'ils appellent verbes fonctionnels («Funktionsverben», von Polenz 1987: 70). Dans ces constructions, ils supposent l'existence d'un nom d'action ou d'état qui est actualisé dans la phrase grâce à un verbe sémantiquement affaibli, mais dans une bonne partie des cas, il est préférable en langue standard de remplacer ces expressions par un verbe simple synonyme. Cependant, ils reconnaissent certaines valeurs aspectuelles à ces verbes (Hentschel & Weydt 2003: 86).

En Hongrie, après quelques descriptions sommaires et simplistes (du genre «Ne dites pas ceci, mais dites cela», Bíró et al. 1978), les linguistes se sont penchés sur la question à la fin des années 90 pour la première fois (Keszler 1995, Dobos 2009). Sous l'influence des linguistes allemands, certains adoptent une attitude restrictive plutôt que descriptive (Gósy & Heltai 2005).

Les générativistes entament une analyse en profondeur sur les CVS presqu'en même temps que les structuralistes (Grimshaw & Mester 1988), mais s'y intéressent surtout du point de vue de l'attribution des cas et des théta-rôles (rôles sémantiques) par le verbe, et non à ses valeurs supplémentaires dans la construction. Dans un cadre complètement différent, mais suivant le même type de raisonnement, la grammaire lexico-fonctionnelle se tourne vers la problématique de l'aspect aussi (Butt & Geuder 2001).

Mel'čuk et ses disciples partent de relations lexicales concrètes, qu'ils appellent fonctions, dont deux sont à assimiler à la notion de verbe support (Polguère 2003: 139-141).

Nous avons choisi l'approche du lexique-grammaire (Daladier 1978, Giry-Schneider 1987, Gross, M. 1981, Gross, G. 1996a, Gross, G. 1996b), vu les fondements de sa définition, le nombre des critères, et son applicabilité pour rendre compte systématiquement des phénomènes sémantiques aussi bien que syntaxiques. Pour le raisonnement détaillé de notre choix, nous nous référons ici à une de nos études (Náray-Szabó, 2010).

2. Prédicats nominaux illocutoires

C'est une classe qui se définit au niveau de son contenu pragmatique, et certains reconnaissent son caractère prédicatif aussi (Leech 1983: 203). Si on reformule cette définition, on peut constater qu'il s'agit de prédicats dont le signifié consiste à réaliser un acte qui change le monde extérieur par sa prononciation même. Sémantiquement, elle constitue une sous-catégorie des verbes de parole, dont certaines définitions sont basées sur ses propriétés distributionnelles (Dubois & Dubois-Charlier 1997, Eshkol 2002, Vivès 2004, pour les verbes de parole en général), mais on peut trouver également quelques distributions qui sont spécifiques aux prédicats illocutoires. Après avoir examiné le problème de plus près, il nous semble pertinent de faire la délimitation des noms illocutoires par rapport à trois autres classes connexes: les prédicats constatifs, psychologiques et perlocutoires. Les premiers sont difficiles à utiliser avec certains verbes comme *revenir sur*:

(1) Luc est revenu sur *(sa promesse + son conseil + son affirmation + sa décision + son opinion)*

(2) Luc est revenu sur *(?sa constatation +?son rapport + *son histoire + *son renseignement)*

Les groupes de prédicats illocutoires ont chacun un groupe correspondant parmi les prédicats constatant un état psychologique (Leech 1983: 211-212), mais ces derniers ne sont pas naturels avec la construction *dire ce que* + futur proche:

(3) Luc a dit ce qu'il *(allait affirmer + allait conseiller + allait promettre) à Léa*

(4) ?*Luc a dit à Léa ce qu'il *(allait penser + allait souhaiter à Léa* (ici: 'désirer la réalisation de qc') + *allait décider de faire)*

On a enfin la classe des prédicats perlocutoires: ils expriment un acte qui a des conséquences résultant des paroles du locuteur. Nous proposons le test *ne pas entendre*:

(5) Luc a *(fait une affirmation + fait une promesse + donné un ordre) à Léa, mais Léa ne l'a pas entendu(e)*

(6) *Luc a *(persuadé + dissuadé + consolé) Léa, mais Léa ne l'a pas entendu*

D'ailleurs, ces prédicats peuvent être classifiés aussi selon des critères transformationnels (Levin 1993), pragmatiques (pour l'anglais: Leech 1983: 201-226, et pour le français: Martins-Baltar 1995) ou selon leurs composants sémiques par exemple (Wierzbicka 1989).

Verbes supports et prédicats illocutoires 83

Dans cette étude préliminaire, notre objectif est de décrire cette classe de noms prédicatifs et de mettre en relief le rôle des CVS dans sa délimitation à base distributionnelle. Nous avons effectué notre analyse en comparant deux langues, le français et le hongrois à cet égard, afin de constater les similitudes et de mettre en relief certaines différences typologiques entre les deux langues. Les tests délimitatifs proposés ci-dessus sont valables pour les deux langues.

3. Le cadre du lexique-grammaire

Comme nous l'avons déjà annoncé dans la présentation, notre analyse s'inscrit dans le cadre du lexique-grammaire fondé par M. Gross (Gross, M. 1975, 1998). A certains points, le traitement des CVS dans cette théorie a été complété par G. Gross (Gross, G. 1996a, Gross, G. 1996b), notamment au niveau de la délimitation et de l'aspectualité.

Ainsi, on définit les verbes supports comme des éléments servant à l'actualisation des prédicats nominaux dans la phrase, qui en portent les marques morphologiques comme celles du temps, du mode, de la personne, du nombre, de l'aspect et de l'intensité. Le verbe n'est plus sélecteur d'arguments, comme en grammaire générative, c'est seulement le nom qui l'opère, vu le caractère prédicatif qui appartient à lui seul. A côté des verbes supports basiques (neutres) comme *faire, donner, dire, adresser,* on distingue des variantes aspectuelles, converses (changement de position du sujet et du complément grâce à un verbe actif dénotant la même action, dirigée en sens inverse), stylistiques et d'intensité. Exemples: *répéter* (aspectuelle), *recevoir* (converse), *marmonner* (stylistique), *accabler de* (d'intensité). Dans les CVS construites avec une variante, la paraphrase avec le verbe support de base est toujours possible:

(7) *Luc a répété son remerciement à Léa. (=Il le lui a adressé encore une fois.)*
(8) *Léa a reçu un remerciement de Luc. (=Il lui en a adressé un.)*
(9) *Luc a marmonné quelques mots de remerciement à Léa. (=Il l'a exprimé de façon à peine audible.)*
(10) *Luc a accablé Léa de remerciements. (Il lui en a adressé même un peu trop.)*

Par contraste, les verbes pleins ayant pour complément direct un de ces noms prédicatifs ne forment pas de CVS, la paraphrase est donc impossible:

(11) *Luc a (écrit+envoyé) des remerciements à Léa. ≠ Il lui en a adressé.*
(12) *Léa a refusé le remerciement de Luc. ≠ Léa l'a reçu. = Il lui en a adressé.*

Pour les causatifs et les copules non plus:

(13) *Luc a arraché une promesse à Léa.≠ Elle en a fait une.*
(14) *Ces quelques mots hébétés (constituent un + équivalent à un + sont un + servent de) remerciement pour Léa. ≠ *Les mots hébétés adressent un remerciement à Léa.*

D'autre part, dans la majorité des cas, il existe un verbe simple étymologiquement apparenté au nom prédicatif qui équivaut, à certains réserves près, à la CVS:

(15) *Luc a remercié Léa. = Luc a adressé son remerciement à Léa.*

4. Les propriétés des CVS en LG

Pour rendre claire la définition, il convient d'apporter des précisions à deux endroits: nous devons bien tracer les frontières entre CVS et expressions figées verbales d'une part, et entre CVS et constructions transitives libres de l'autre. A deux exceptions près, tous les tests suivants sont cités de G. Gross (G. Gross 1996b: 72-78). Ainsi, par contraste avec les expressions figées, la détermination dans les CVS est (relativement) variable *(Luc a fait (une+ cette) promesse; Lux a fait (la+E) promesse de reconstruire la maison)*, l'adjonction d'un adjectif ou parfois d'un adverbe d'intensité sont possibles *(Luc a fait une promesse solennelle; Luc a très peur)*, ainsi que la formation d'une subordonnée comparative en *que*, celle d'une relative ou d'une phrase passive *(Luc a fait plus de promesses que Léa; la promesse que Luc a faite; Cette promesse a été faite par Luc)*. L'effacement du verbe support avec adjonction d'un déterminant possessif ou d'un complément de nom produit une phrase sémantiquement équivalente *(Luc a fait une promesse → la promesse de Luc; sa promesse)*. Contrairement aux constructions libres, on observe l'impossibilité de la nominalisation *(*l'adressement d'un remerciement;* ceci n'est pas valable pour le hongrois: *köszönet nyilvánítása, köszönetnyilvánítás)*, l'interdiction de l'extraction et de l'interrogation en *que (*c'est une promesse que Luc a faite; Qu'a fait Luc? – Une promesse)*. En outre, Langer (Langer 2004) indique que la coordination avec un nom n'est possible que s'il appartient au même type de prédicats *(Luc a fait une proposition et une offre (*et un gâteau))*. Dans des cas rares, comme le suggère Giry-Schneider (Giry-Schneider 1987: 31), la montée de l'adverbe est également permise *(Luc a fait une proposition sérieuse à Léa = Luc a fait sérieusement une proposition)*.

5. Enquête sur les CVS à noms illocutoires

Les recherches se sont déroulés sur deux corpus: *Frantext* pour le français et *MNSz* pour le hongrois (corpus national hongrois), en prenant seulement des textes de 1950 à nos jours. Une centaine de prédicats illocutoires fréquents et à structure sémantique simple ont été choisis en français, contrastés avec des équivalents hongrois. En voici leur distribution:

Type illocutoire	Prédicats français	Prédicats hongrois
Assertifs	46	45
Directifs	31	29
Commissifs	9	9
Expressifs	31	44
Total illocutoires	117	127

Dans un premier temps, il importe de mentionner qu'une bonne partie de ces noms sont polysémiques. Dans la majorité des cas, cette polysémie est régulière: ils sont susceptibles d'exprimer un acte de langage (l'action), sa version textuelle (l'objet) ou le contenu propositionnel (le résultat) de l'acte, ou au moins deux de ces trois (cf. Grimshaw 1990):

(16) *Luc a fait une déclaration.* = *Luc a commis un acte.*
(17) *Luc a signé sa déclaration* = *Luc a signé un document.*
(18) *Luc parlait de sa déclaration faite hier.* = *Luc parlait du contenu de sa déclaration faite hier.*

Types	Exemples de polysémie régulière (acte de langage, texte, contenu)
ASSERTIFS	*Déclaration /nyilatkozat, témoignage /tanúvallomás, attestation /igazolás, jugement/ítélet, dénonciation /feljelentés, critique /kritika*
DIRECTIFS/	*Proposition/javaslat, invitation /meghívás/meghívó, demande /kérés*

ROGATIFS	/kérvény, recours /fellebbezés, commande /megrendelés, ordre /parancs, approbation /jóváhagyás, autorisation /meghatalmazás, permission /permis /engedély, accord /megállapodás, interview /interjú
COMMISSIFS	Garantie/garancia, offre/ajánlat
EXPRESSIFS	Plainte /panasz, réclamation /reklamáció

A part cela, il existe des cas spécifiques de polysémie irrégulière aussi, que nous avons regroupés sous quatre types.

Sens secondaire	Exemples de polysémie (tous existent en hong. aussi)
Acte juridique	Déclaration, jugement, plaidoyer, dénonciation, accusation, opposition, recommandation, recours, accord, plainte, réclamation
Acte religieux	Confirmation (hong. bérmálás), prière (hong. ima), bénédiction, malédiction, révélation (divine) (hong. kinyilatkoztatás)
Groupe d'élus	Opposition, conseil
Prestation	Assurance, garantie, offre

Comme on peut le voir, dans presque tous les cas, l'équivalent hongrois présente la même type de polysémie. On a toutefois des exemples où le hongrois a plusieurs lexèmes pour exprimer tel ou tel emploi du mot français: *invitation* = *meghívás* ('acte verbal') / *meghívó* ('document'), *demande* = *kérés* ('acte verbal') /*kérvény* ('document'), *confirmation* = *megerősítés* ('acte verbal') /*bérmálás* ('acte religieux'), *prière* = *kérés* ('acte verbal') /*ima* ('acte religieux'), *révélation* = *nyilvánosságra hozatal* ('acte verbal ou écrit') / *kinyilatkoztatás* ('acte divin'), ou vice versa: *permission* /*permis* = *engedély*. Dans tous les cas, seuls les emplois 'acte verbal', 'acte juridique' et 'acte religieux' sont pris en considération, vu que les autres ne sont pas prédicatifs.

Deuxièmement, nous avons examiné dans les deux corpus le nombre d'occurrences de verbes supports rattachés aux noms illocutoires. Ensuite, notre objectif a été d'y observer la fréquence de ces verbes par rapport à celle des verbes en général. Ce rapport montre à quel degré les textes du corpus tendent à utiliser des CVS plutôt que d'autres verbes. Enfin, nous nous sommes intéressé à quel degré ces noms sont susceptibles d'être modifiés par des adjectifs. Toutes ces données contribuent à comprendre le poids des CVS parmi les distributions possibles.

Type de syntagme	Corpus français %	Corpus hongrois %
Vsup + Npréd	12,51	11,29
Vplein + Nréd	15,59	16,92
Npréd ADJ	17,91	25,24
Vsup/V	41,06	36,69

La fréquence des CVS par rapport à la totalité des résultats et par rapport à ceux construits avec un verbe (quelconque) est légèrement supérieure pour le français, par contre celle des verbes pleins et des adjectifs se prouve plus élevée dans le corpus hongrois. Evidemment, ces données doivent être vérifiées sur un échantillon de noms plus ample pour être plus représentatives. Parmi les verbes supports les plus souvent enregistrés dans *Frantext*, nous avons certains dont les équivalents hongrois ont une fréquence également exceptionnelle dans *MNSz (autocritique /önkritika, autorisation /felhatalmazás, serment /eskü)*. Il importe en outre de mentionner que selon le rapport entre verbes supports et verbes en général, on trouve des pairs de noms équivalents aussi qui ont des fréquences pareillement importantes: *assurance /megnyugtatás, condoléances /részvét, remerciement /köszönet*.

Troisièmement, nous avons passé en revue un à un les verbes supports basiques et leurs variantes, ainsi que les verbes pleins et les adjectifs. Nous avons distingué quatre types pragmatiques de noms illocutoires dans le corpus: les assertifs, les directifs ou rogatifs, les commissifs et les expressifs. Les premiers expriment une affirmation, les deuxièmes l'engagement de l'interlocuteur, les troisièmes celui du locuteur lui-même à faire quelque chose et les derniers un sentiment verbalement manifesté (Leech 1983: 205-206). Les plus importants verbes supports de base sont (dans les deux langues):

- *faire/tenni, donner /adni, dire /mondani* pour les assertifs
- *donner /adni, adresser /fordulni, faire /tenni, formuler /megfogalmazni, dire/mondani* pour les directifs et rogatifs
- *faire/tenni* et *donner /adni* pour les commissifs et
- *faire/tenni, dire /mondani, adresser /fordulni, donner /adni, présenter/mutatni, exprimer /kifejezni, marquer /jelezni* pour les expressifs

En plus, les deux langues possèdent une bonne vingtaine de verbes, plus spécifiques pour un certain sous-groupe de noms: *végezni* ('exécuter'), *hozni* ('apporter'), *emelni* ('soulever'), *részt venni* ('participer'), *viszonozni* ('retourner'), *osztani* ('partager'), *elkövetni* ('commettre').

Les variantes aspectuelles sont d'un nombre à peu près égal dans les deux langues *(commencer/kezdeni, entamer/belefogni, finir/befejezni, répéter/ismételni, maintenir/ fentartani)*, mais le hongrois en a certains que nous n'avons pas relevé dans le corpus français *(osztogatni, sorolni* ('distribuer', 'énumérer')). Une variante converse, comme nous l'avons vu, est une CVS où le sujet est coréférent au complément du verbe de base, et le complément au sujet de celui-ci. En voici les plus importants dans les corpus: *recevoir /kapni, avoir /bírni, bénéficier /részesülni, encaisser /nyerni*. Parmi les variantes stylistiques, ce sont avant tout les noms assertifs et les directifs pour lesquels on constate une richesse nettement plus grande dans les textes hongrois. On a en commun *risquer /megkockáztatni, avancer /előállni, émettre /hallatni, marmonner /mormolni, lâcher /megereszteni, déposer/ benyújtani, user /élni, infliger /sújtani*, mais le hongrois en possède en outre: *kerülni* ('procéder'), *adagolni* ('alimenter en portions'), *elkövetni* ('commettre'), *elragadtatni magát* ('s'emporter'), *hangot adni* ('extérioriser', 'exprimer de vive voix'), *keveredni* ('se mêler'), *bocsátkozni* ('se lancer'), *előterjeszteni* ('présenter'), *nyújtani* ('tendre/offrir'). Les verbes supports d'intensité ajoutent une valeur supplémentaire de force ou de vitesse au nom illocutoire: *accabler/elhalmozni, crier/kiáltani*. Les noms illocutoires expressifs hongrois en comptent un nombre particulièrement élevé, dont certains sont bien expressifs au sens stylistique aussi: *csapni* ('claquer'), *zengeni* ('résonner'), *kipréselni* ('extraire'), *kitörni* ('éclater en'), *kanyarítani* ('arrondir'), *lendülni* ('se lancer'), *elmerülni* ('plonger dans'), *ráönteni/rázúdítani* ('verser/répandre sur'), *szórni* ('semer'). Les causatifs, par contre, ne se comptent pas parmi les variantes sémantiques des verbes supports, comme nous l'avons montré dans la section 3 ci-dessus, mais en sont une transformation. Citons à titre d'exemple: *demander /kérni, provoquer /provokálni, arracher /(ki)kényszeríteni, appeler /felszólítani, entraîner /kiváltani*.

Nous avons exclu des verbes supports les verbes qui ne sont ni basiques ni des variantes, et qui prennent en général le nom prédicatif comme un vrai complément direct. Ce sont donc des verbes pleins: *répondre /válaszolni, justifier /igazolni, accepter/elfogadni, rejeter /elutasítani, refuser /visszautasítani, confirmer /megerősíteni, appuyer /támogatni, résister /ellenállni, obtenir /megszerezni, enfreindre /megszegni*. Une paraphrase par un verbe simple est souvent possible, ce qui montre le fait qu'il s'agit bien de deux prédicats et pas d'un seul:

(19) Luc a accepté le conseil de Léa. = Luc a accepté ce que Léa lui avait conseillé.

Les principaux adjectifs modifiant les noms illocutoires, qui sont bien plus fréquents dans les CVS hongroises que dans les françaises, sont les suivants: dans le corpus français, *simple, grand, faux, public, social, politique, total, absolu,* dans le hongrois, *hivatalos, jogos, írásbeli, szóbeli, politikai* ('officiel', 'justifiable', 'écrit', 'oral', 'politique').

6. Conclusion

Nous avons montré une batterie de 16 tests pour délimiter les CVS dans le cadre théorique du lexique-grammaire (2 dans la section 3, et 14 dans 4). L'exemple des noms prédicatifs illocutoires s'est avéré une parfaite illustration des particularités principales intralinguistiques et interlinguistiques, dont les polysémies régulière et irrégulière ou la présence des variantes aspectuelles, converses, stylistiques et intensives. Au niveau quantitatif, au vu de ce tout petit échantillon, dont certes la taille devrait être multiplié par des dizaines, voire des centaines, le français tendrait légèrement plus à recourir à l'emploi de CVS en rapport avec les prédicats illocutoires, mais cette tendance serait largement contrebalancée par la richesse exceptionnelle du hongrois quant aux types de verbes supports de base et des variantes aspectuelles, stylistiques et intensives, surtout au niveau des constructions sur des noms assertifs et expressifs. Tout cela n'est pas une caractéristique de la seule langue soutenue ou officielle, mais selon le témoignage des corpus, de presque tous types de textes. Il serait donc une erreur, à notre avis, de sous-estimer l'importance, voire de bannir systématiquement les CVS illocutoires hongrois des structures possibles, quoi qu'il en soit le registre ou le domaine. La présente étude a tenté de faire un premier pas vers les preuves.

6. Bibliographie

BURGER, H., HÄCKI BUHOFER, A., SIALM, A., ERIKSSON, B. 1982 *Handbuch der Phraseologie*, Berlin/New York: Walter de Gruyter.
BUTT, M., GEUDER, W. 2001 «On the (semi)lexical status of light verbs». In: Corver N., Riemsdijk H. (éds.), *Semi-lexical categories: the function of content words and the content of function words.* Berlin/New York: Mouton de Gruyter (coll. «Studies in generative grammar 59»).
DALADIER, A. 1978 *Problèmes d'analyses de nominalisations et de groupes nominaux complexes en français.* Thèse de 3e cycle, Université Paris 7.
DOBOS, CS. 2009 *Funkcióigés szerkezetek.* Miskolc: Passzer 2000 Kiadó.
DUBOIS, J., DUBOIS-CHARLIER, F. 1997. *Les Verbes français.* Paris: Larousse-Bordas.
ESHKOL, I. 2002 *Typologie sémantique des prédicats de parole.* Thèse de doctorat. Villetaneuse: Université Paris 13.
FRANTEXT. http://www.frantext.fr/
GIRY-SCHNEIDER, J. 1987 *Les prédicats nominaux en français: les phrases simples à verbes supports.* Genève: Droz.
GÓSY, M., HELTAI, P. 2005 «A terpeszkedő szerkezetek hatása a feldolgozásra». *Magyar Nyelvőr* 129: 473-487.
BÍRÓ, Á., GRÉTSY, L., KEMÉNY, G. 1978 *Hivatalos nyelvünk kézikönyve.* Budapest: s.n.
GRIMSHAW, J., MESTER, A. 1988 «Light Verbs and Theta - Marking». *Linguistic Inquiry* 19: 2..
GRIMSHAW, J., MESTER, A. 1988 «Light Verbs and Theta-Marking». *Linguistic Inquiry* 19: 2: 205-232.
GRIMSHAW, J. 1990 *Argument Structure.* Cambridge: MIT Press.
GROSS, G. 1996a «Prédicats nominaux et compatibilité aspectuelle *Langages* 121: 54-72.
GROSS, G. 1996b *Les expressions figées. Noms composés et autres locutions.* Paris: Ophrys.
GROSS, M. 1975 *Méthodes en syntaxe. Le régime des constructions complétives.* Paris: Hermann.
GROSS, M. 1981 «Les bases empiriques de la notion de prédicat sémantique». In: *Langages* 63. 7-52.
GROSS, M. 1998 «La fonction sémantique des verbes supports». In: *Travaux de linguistique* 37. 25-46.
HENTSCHEL, E., WEYDT, H. 2003 *Handbuch der deutschen Grammatik.* Berlin: Walter de Gruyter.
KESZLER, B. 1995 «A mai magyar nyelv szófaji rendszerezésének problémái». *Magyar Nyelvőr* 119: 293–308.
LEECH, G. 1983 *Principles of Pragmatics.* London: Longman.
LEVIN, B. 1993 *English Verb Classes and Alternations: A Preliminary Investigation.* Chicago: The University of Chicago Press.
MARTINS-BALTAR, M. 1995 «Enoncés de motif usuels: figures de phrase et procédés de déraison». In: Martins-Baltar, M. (éd.) *La locution en discours.* Paris: E.N.S. Fontenay/Saint-Cloud.
MNSz: Magyar Nemzeti Szövegtár. Váradi, T. 2002 «The Hungarian National Corpus». In: *Proceedings of the 3rd LREC Conference,* 385-389, Las Palmas, Espagne: s. n., http://corpus.nytud.hu/mnsz

NÁRAY-SZABÓ, M. 2010 «Verbes supports et contrastivité: théorie et usage». In: Mańkowska, A., Giermak-Zielinska, T. (éds.) *Des mots et du texte aux conceptions de la description linguistique.* Warszawa: Wydawnictwa Uniwersytetu Warszawskiego. 351-358.

POLGUERE. A. 2003 *Lexicologie et sémantique lexicale.* Montréal: Presses Universitaires de Montréal.

VIVES, R. 2004 «Les prédicats de dire en français: bref sondage sur les préférences des locuteurs». *Langages* 154: 74-86.

VON POLENZ, P. 1987 «Funktionsverben, Funktionsverbgefüge und Verwandtes: Vorschläge zur satzsemantischen Lexikographie». In: *Zeitschrift für germanistische Linguistik* 15: 2: 169-189.

WIERZBICKA, A. 1989 *English Speech Act Verbs: A Semantic Dictionary.* Sydney: Academic Press.

COMPRENDRE LES METAPHORES ONTOLOGIQUES DANS L'ESPACE ROMAN: LE CAS DU FRANÇAIS VERS L'ESPAGNOL ET L'ITALIEN

André Valli (*Université de Provence*)
Alberto Bramati (*Università degli Studi di Milano*)
Françoise Nin (*Université de Provence*)

Abstract: We are interested in idioms including a verb and a noun referring to body parts, for instance, *Avoir du nez*, which are organised in a network of ontological metaphors (Lakoff and Johnson, 1980). In the first part, we are dealing with the problems raised by these idioms, as far as linguistics theories are concerned. In the second part, we present a corpus of french idioms including the nouns *oeil* and *nez*, then we analyse the relationships between these idioms and their equivalents in Spanish and Italian.

Key words: Ontological metaphors, body-parts, somatic idioms, fixed verbal constructions, contrastive phraseology.

0. Introduction

On connaît l'intérêt suscité par la phraséologie et en particulier par l'étude des phénomènes locutionnels (Martins-Baltar 1977). Dans cette communication, nous nous intéressons aux constructions verbales figées en français, en italien et en espagnol contenant un nom «partie du corps»[1] comme *Mener quelqu'un par le bout du nez*. Les travaux de Lakoff et Johnson 1980 et plus récemment de Lakoff 1987 ont attiré l'attention des linguistes sur le rôle primordial de la métaphore dans la mise en place de nos conceptualisations. On rappelle que ces travaux sont ainsi à l'origine d'un regain d'intérêt pour l'étude des locutions figées, en particulier les expressions contenant un Npc, qui déclenchent, selon F. Bercker (1992 : 126), «des égalités qui permettent de structurer notre expérience d'une chose en termes d'autre chose, d'employer des concepts moins complexes relevant de notre perception/ interaction avec *moi + les autres + le monde*, pour exprimer des concepts plus complexes ou abstraits». Bercker fait en outre remarquer que l'ensemble des constructions figées concernant les parties du corps «semble s'organiser autour d'un réseau de métaphores qui dépendent toutes à divers degrés, de ce que Lakoff et Johnson appellent la *métaphore ontologique* qui consiste à concevoir une notion concrète ou abstraite comme une entité, objet ou substance» (1992 : 126).

Le problème crucial que posent ces expressions est que, par définition, elles sont figées – leur construction est fixe – et d'autre part, leur sens n'est pas compositionnel, ce qui devrait soulever, a priori, un problème spécifique d'intercompréhension et donc une difficulté de traduction, sauf à supposer que les locuteurs de langue romane aient tendance à développer des processus de conceptualisation de leur expérience du monde sensible relativement proches. Nous avions adopté cette hypothèse dans deux précédentes études – l'une (Valli et Villagenes-Serra 1998) portant sur les métaphores ontologiques de l'espagnol et du français et l'autre (Valli et Bramati 2009) sur les métaphores du français et de l'italien – qui avaient abouti à une confrontation intéressante entre les deux listes de constructions verbales figées

---

[1] Dorénavant : Npc.

dégageant des cas fréquents d'homologies totales ou partielles, i.e. les structures grammaticales sont identiques ou presque (différence de déterminant, de modificateur, de préposition ou de verbe). Nous poursuivons cette recherche ici en nous proposant de confronter trois listes de constructions verbales figées contenant un Npc en français, en italien et en espagnol.

1. Description linguistique des métaphores ontologiques françaises contenant un Npc

Le cadre théorique de cette étude qui s'intéresse au problème posé par la locution aux théories linguistiques – déviance de la locution/systématicité de la langue : non-substitualité, non-permutabilité, double lecture, non prédictibilité – est emprunté principalement aux travaux de M. Gross (1983, 1988, 1993), sans ignorer ceux plus récents d'I. Mel'čuk (2003).

1.1 Un point sur la définition et la description des constructions figées en français.

L. Danlos (1988) définissait le figement par l'opacité du sens et la fixité des éléments, en premier lieu les déterminants. M. Gross (1993) insiste pour sa part sur le caractère non compositionnel des phrases figées qui les définit comme dans cet exemple :
 [1] se boucher les yeux
On retiendra le bilan dressé par M. Gross à propos de la notion formelle de figement: étant donnée une expression, on la dira figée quand deux de ses termes (au moins) sont indissociables, autrement dit figés l'un par rapport à l'autre[2].

1.2 Les formes des phrases figées contenant un Npc

On observe une grande variété formelle de ces phrases figées, mais un point commun: cette notation se généralise, selon M. Gross, à des phrases dont le figement n'est pas complet. Dans les expressions retenues dans cette étude, le syntagme contenant un Npc au moins est figé, les autres syntagmes peuvent être figés également ou libres. Mais, d'autre part, il faut noter que le figement du lien entre le verbe et le groupe nominal est variable : ainsi, dans les phrases qui suivent, un des SN figés peut être le sujet ou un complément de rang 1, 2 ou 3, ou un complément de nom, un éventuel second complément pouvant être libre ou figé :
 [2] la moutarde lui monte au nez
 [3] se boucher le nez
 [4] avoir quelqu'un dans le nez
 [5] tirer les vers du nez

---

[2] Mel'čuk (2003) propose une caractérisation de la construction verbale figée fondée uniquement sur la non-compositionnalité du sens de l'expression. Par conséquent, une expression AB ayant le sens S est un « phrasème complet» (locution figée, angl. *Idiom*) si et seulement si une des deux conditions suivantes est remplie : 1. S n'inclut ni A ni B ; 2. S inclut A mais n'inclut pas B, et A « n'est pas dans la position communicativement dominante» (25). Autrement dit, pour Mel'čuk un *phrasème complet* est une expression AB dont le signifié soit n'inclut ni le signifié de A ni le signifié de B (ex., *traîner quelqu'un dans la boue*) soit inclut le signifié de A mais A n'est pas l'élément qui «résume» le sens du phrasème (ex. *mener quelqu'un par le bout du nez*).

[6] mener quelqu'un par le bout du nez

La détermination du figement peut faire difficulté : dans l'exemple

[7] mettre quelque chose sous les yeux de quelqu'un

les arguments que retient Gross pour analyser les exemples suivants comme des phrases figées sont de trois ordres: 1) la restriction du complément : elle n'est pas évidente puisqu'il existe

[8] mettre quelque chose sous le nez de quelqu'un

mais on ne peut faire varier la préposition :

[9] ? mettre quelque chose devant le nez / les yeux de quelqu'un

2) le blocage du verbe qui refuse toute substitution

[10] *poser quelque chose sous le nez / les yeux de quelqu'un

3) l'opacité du sens : un locuteur non francophone de naissance aura du mal à comprendre l'expression

[11] avoir quelqu'un dans le nez

1.3 Problèmes d'identification des formes figées : constructions verbales vs suites adverbiales

L'expression

[12] coûter les yeux de la tête

pose un problème, celui des constituants figés qui ne sont pas des arguments, sujet ou objet du verbe, mais des modificateurs, des «adverbes» au sens de M. Gross (1986),[3] qui marquent, par une structure figée, soit une qualité d'intensité, comme dans l'exemple ci-dessus,[4] soit une expression de manière, comme dans l'exemple suivant:

[13] faire quelque chose les yeux fermés

Dans ces deux expressions, à la différence de la construction verbale figée, le lien qui crée le figement est au sein du groupe nominal et non entre le groupe nominal et le verbe, qui est libre.[5]

2. Les constructions verbales figées françaises contenant les Npc *œil* et *nez*. Analyse d'un corpus

Pour établir le corpus français des constructions verbales figées contenant les deux Npc *œil* et *nez*, nous avons d'abord étudié le corpus mis au point à l'Université de Provence par André Valli et ses collaborateurs dans les années quatre-vingt-dix ; à partir de ce noyau, nous avons ensuite consulté les sources lexicographiques suivantes : 1) un dictionnaire des expressions et locutions (Rey et Chantreau 1997) ; 2) trois dictionnaires de la langue françaises (*Petit Robert* 1997, *Grand Robert* 2005, *TLF*) ; 3) enfin, pour les cas douteux, nous avons consulté le web,

---

[3] M. Gross, *Grammaire transformationnelle du français. 3 - Syntaxe de l'adverbe*, Asstril, Paris.
[4] Ce type d'adverbe figé correspond à la fonction lexicale Magn définie par I. Mel'čuk (*Dictionnaire explicatif et combinatoire du français contemporain*, vol. 1, Presses de l'Université de Montréal, Montréal, 1984).
[5] G. Gross introduit, pour ce type de figement, la notion de « suite métaphorique figée» (*Les expressions figées en français*, Ophrys, Paris, 1996, p. 15).

par le truchement de Google, et, si nécessaire, quelques locuteurs natifs. Nous avons ainsi construit un corpus français de 144 constructions verbales figées, dont 97 contenant le Npc *oeil* et 47 contenant le Npc *nez*.

Voici la liste des principales structures syntaxiques figées que nous avons repérées dans notre corpus : chaque structure est présentée d'abord sous forme de schéma formel[6] suivi du nombre d'occurrences entre parenthèses, et exemplifiée ensuite par une construction verbale figée contenant soit *oeil* soit *nez*.

ŒIL (97)
1. **N0 V C1 (Npc)** (27)
ouvrir les yeux
2. **N0 V Prép. C1 (Npc)** (5)
tourner de l'œil
3. **N0 V C1 (Npc) Prép. N2** (21)
faire les gros yeux à qqn
4. **N0 V N1 Prép. C2 (Npc)** (17)
manger qqn des yeux
5. **N0 V C1 (Npc) [Prép.] C2** (12)
ne plus avoir que ses yeux pour pleurer
6. **N0 V C1 Prép. C2 (Npc)** (12)
avoir le compas dans l'œil

NEZ (47)
1. **N0 V C1 (Npc)** (15)
avoir le nez fin
2. **N0 V Prép. C1 (Npc)** (4)
passer sous le nez de qqn
3. **N0 V C1 (Npc) Prép. N2** (8)
fourrer son nez dans qqch
4. **N0 V N1 Prép. C2 (Npc)** (4)
avoir qqn dans le nez
5. **N0 V C1 (Npc) [Prép.] C2** (5)
fourrer son nez partout
6. **N0 V C1 Prép. C2 (Npc)** (5)
fermer la porte au nez de qqn [7]

D'après les données collectées, les deux structures syntaxiques les plus fréquentes dans notre corpus sont donc les suivantes : 1) la structure à deux arguments «N0 V C1 (Npc)» dont nous avons repéré 27 occurrences pour *oeil* (28%) et 15 occurrences pour *nez* (32%) ; 2) la structure à trois arguments «N0 V N1 Prép N2» dans ses quatre variantes (3, 4, 5, 6) dont nous avons repéré 62 occurrences pour *œil* (64%) et 22 occurrence pour *nez* (47%). La somme des constructions verbales figées françaises ayant recours à ces deux structures syntaxiques atteint, dans le cas de *œil*, 89 occurrences, soit 92%, et, dans le cas de *nez*, 37 occurrences, soit 79, autrement dit l'immense majorité des constructions verbales figées dans les deux cas.

3. Les expressions espagnoles et italiennes correspondant aux constructions verbales figées françaises contenant les noms «parties du corps» *œil* et *nez*

Pour établir quelles expressions espagnoles et italiennes correspondent aux constructions verbales figées françaises de notre corpus, nous avons procédé de la façon suivante : 1) nous avons travaillé dans une seule direction, i.e. du français respectivement vers l'espagnol et vers l'italien ; 2) comme nous l'avions fait pour le français, nous avons utilisé plusieurs sources :

---

[6] Dans un schéma formel, le symbole C indique, comme chez M. Gross, un argument figé ; si cet argument figé est représenté par un nom «partie du corps», le symbole C est suivi par le symbole Npc entre parenthèses.

[7] Dans notre corpus, nous avons repéré aussi des structures syntaxiques plus complexes (ex., «C0 lui V Prép. C1 (Npc), à N» correspondant à *La moutarde me monte au nez*), dont les occurrences sont toutefois très rares. C'est pourquoi nous avons préféré remettre leur présentation à une phase ultérieure de notre recherche.

des dictionnaires bilingues français-espagnol et français-italien,[8] des dictionnaires monolingues espagnols et italiens,[9] des dictionnaires des locutions espagnoles et italiennes,[10] les corpus de l'espagnol et de l'italien disponibles sur le web[11] et, pour finir, la compétence linguistique de quelques locuteurs natifs espagnols et italiens ; 3) pour chaque construction verbale française, nous avons retenu la construction verbale figée espagnole ou italienne la plus proche tant du point de vue sémantique que du point de vue syntaxique.

3.1 Critères de correspondance syntaxique[12]

Les différents types de relations syntaxiques entre constructions verbales figées françaises et constructions correspondantes espagnoles et italiennes ont été repartis en cinq classes : (**a**) homologie totale ; (**b**) homologie partielle ; (**c**) expression figée espagnole ou italienne contenant un autre Npc ; (**d**) expression figée espagnole ou italienne ne contenant pas de Npc ; (**e**) absence d'expression figée en espagnol ou en italien.

a) L'«homologie totale» (HT) correspond à «une identité totale sur le plan syntaxique» entre la construction figée française et la construction figée espagnole ou italienne, «comprenant la même partie du corps et développant les mêmes significations, littérale et métaphorique» (Valli, Villagenes Serra 1998, p. 187). Voici quelques exemples d'abord pour l'espagnol et ensuite pour l'italien:

[14] être tout yeux   ser todo ojos
[15] mettre son nez dans qqch   meter la nariz / las narices en algo[13]
[16] parler aux yeux   parlare agli occhi
[17] faire les yeux doux à qqn   fare gli occhi dolci a qno

Dans certains cas, l'absence de correspondance entre la structure syntaxique de la construction française et celle de la construction espagnole ou italienne tient à une règle grammaticale : c'est le cas, par exemple, de la traduction en espagnol ou en italien des certains déterminants (partitifs ou possessifs) qui introduisent les Npc en français :

[18] avoir des yeux de lynx   tener ojos de lince
[19] avoir des yeux de lynx   avere occhi di lince
[20] mettre son nez dans qqch   meter la nariz en algo
[21] ne plus avoir que ses yeux pour pleurer   avere solo gli occhi per piangere

---

[8] Pour l'espagnol : : Larousse 1995; pour l'italien : Boch 2000 ; DIF 2002 ; Garzanti 2003.
[9] Pour l'espagnol : RAE 1992 ; M. Moliner 1997 ; pour l'italien : Treccani 1997 ; GRADIT 2000 ; DISC 2005.
[10] Pour l'espagnol : Bruitrago Jimenez A., *Dichos y frases hechas*, Madrid 1997 ; Pénet C. et Gómez C., *¡No me digas! Les six mille et une expressions de l'espagnol parlé*, Marne la Vallée, 1995 ; pour l'italien : Quartu B.M., *Dizionario dei modi di dire della lingua italiana*, Rizzoli, Milano 2000.
[11] Pour l'espagnol : RAE, Banco de datos, Corpus CREA, consultable en ligne sur le site de la RAE.
[12] Faute d'espace, nous ne présenterons pas les problèmes d'ordre sémantique tels que la polysémie des constructions verbales figées ou les différences de registre de langue.
[13] Nous avons classé les constructions dont la seule différence tient au nombre du nom « partie du corps» parmi les homologies totales.

Nous avons donc classé ce type de relation, où l'absence de correspondance au niveau du déterminant est imposée par la grammaire, parmi les homologies totales. De même pour certains compléments prépositionnel : bien que le système prépositionnel de l'espagnol et de l'italien soient semblables au système français, il existe tout de même des différences d'ordre grammatical. Ainsi, en espagnol, le complément d'objet direct désignant une personne doit être précédé de la préposition *a* :

[22] regarder qqn dans les yeux   mirar a alguien en los ojos

Un verbe de mouvement, comme *echar* dans l'exemple suivant, ne peut être suivi d'une préposition indiquant une position (*en*, *sobre*...), mais d'une préposition marquant le terme du mouvement :

[23] jeter les yeux sur qqn   echar el ojo a alguien

Même si une des valeurs dérivées de la préposition espagnole *de* est de marquer un complément de moyen, en général, l'équivalent du français «de N» est rendu par «con N», comme dans l'exemple suivant :

[24] dévorer qqn des yeux   devorar con los ojos

En italien aussi, la préposition française *de* qui introduit un complément «de N» à valeur de moyen/manière ne se traduit pas par l'une des prépositions correspondantes, *di* ou *da*, mais par la préposition *con* :

[25] manger qqn des yeux   mangiare qno con gli occhi

Une règle grammaticale est aussi à l'origine de la traduction de certaines prépositions françaises à valeur locative : p. ex., le complément locatif français «à N» est souvent traduit en italien par «in N» même si la préposition italienne *a* peut elle aussi avoir un sens locatif :

[26] jeter de la poudre aux yeux de qqn   gettare polvere negli occhi di qno

Nous avons classé ces relations imposées par la grammaire parmi les homologies totales.

b) L'«homologie partielle» (HP) correspond à une identité de structure syntaxique à un élément près. Cet élément qui diffère peut être soit le déterminant du Npc :

[27] jeter les yeux sur qqch   echar un ojo a algo
[28] fermer les yeux sur qqch   chiudere un occhio su qsa

soit le modificateur du Npc :

[29] avoir l'oeil aux aguets   tener el ojo tan largo
[30] avoir l'oeil aux aguets   avere l'occhio vigile

soit une préposition :

[31] faire qqch les yeux fermés   hacer algo a ojos cerrados
[32] ne pas en croire ses yeux   non credere ai propri occhi

soit un deuxième complément figé du verbe :

[33] ne pas avoir les yeux en face des trous   no tener ojos en la cara
[34] ne rien voir qu'avec les yeux de qqn   vedere tutto con gli occhi di qno

soit le verbe lui-même :

[35] boire qqn des yeux   comerse a alguien con los ojos
[36] boire qqn des yeux   mangiare qno con gli occhi

Nous avons aussi considéré comme des homologies partielles les cas où la construction figée espagnole ou italienne, tout en gardant le même Npc, présente plusieurs variantes au niveau des autres éléments de la structure, comme dans les deux exemples suivants où les éléments qui changent sont le verbe, la préposition et le déterminant du Npc:

[37] avoir qqn à l'oeil   no quitarle ojo a alguien
[38] avoir qqn à l'oeil   tenere qno d'occhio

c) Dans quelques cas, l'expression homologue en espagnol ou en italien d'une construction verbale figée française est une construction figée contenant un autre Npc, comme dans les exemples suivants :
    [39] baisser le nez   bajar los ojos / la cabeza
    [40] baisser le nez   abbassare gli occhi / la testa

d) Dans d'autres cas, l'expression homologue en espagnol ou en italien d'une construction verbale figée française est une construction figée ne contenant aucun Npc, comme dans l'exemple suivant :
    [41] avoir un (coup+verre) dans le nez   coger una mona
    [42] ne pas avoir les yeux en face des trous   non vederci dal sonno, dalla stanchezza

e) Le dernier type de relation que nous avons repéré dans notre corpus correspond au cas où il n'existe pas en espagnol ou en italien une construction verbale figée équivalente à une certaine construction figée française : dans ce cas-là, il faut avoir recours à la définition sémantique de la construction française.

3.2 Tableau des correspondances entre constructions verbales figées françaises, espagnoles et italiennes

Résultats	œil = 97 ESP	% ESP	œil = 97 ITA	% ITA	nez = 47 ESP	% ESP	nez = 47 ITA	% ITA
HT	29	30	47	48,5	7	15	17	36
HP déterminant	1		2		1		3	
HP modificateur	7		16		2		1	
HP préposition	4		3		2			
HP (C1 ou C2)	2		1		1			
HP verbe	7		7		8		1	
HP combinaisons	26		9		15		3	
total HP	47	48,5	38	39	29	61.5	8	17
total HT + HP	76	78,5	85	87,5	36	76.5	25	53
HP Npc	1	1	1	1	2	4.5	14	30
Autre constr. verb. figée	1		6		3		1	
Absence d'expr. figée	19		5		6		7	
total	20	20.5	11	11,5	9	19	8	17

Les données affichées dans le tableau montrent d'abord le nombre globalement élevé de métaphores ontologiques ayant une construction homologue ou quasi-homologue dans les trois langues romanes. En ce qui concerne plus particulièrement la relation entre le français et l'italien, les données du tableau montrent que pour un locuteur italien la compréhension des constructions verbales figées françaises contenant *œil* est beaucoup plus aisée que celle des constructions verbales figées françaises contenant *nez*. En particulier, 48,5% des constructions françaises contenant *œil* sont dans une relation d'homologie totale (HT) avec les constructions italiennes correspondantes, alors que seulement 36% des constructions françaises contenant *nez* sont dans cette relation avec les constructions italiennes correspondantes. Mais si l'on considère les données globales concernant les HT et les HP, la différence entre les deux Npc paraît évidente : en effet, 87,5% des constructions françaises contenant *œil* sont dans une relation d'HT ou d'HP avec les constructions italiennes correspondantes, ce qui montre que la métaphore ontologique de l'œil se retrouve de façon très stable dans les deux langues ; au contraire, seulement 53% des constructions françaises contenant *nez* sont dans une relation d'HT ou d'HP avec les constructions italiennes correspondantes. En fait, dans 30% des constructions figées françaises contenant ce Npc, *nez* est remplacé dans la construction correspondante italienne par un autre Npc (dans la plupart des cas, *faccia, muso, occhi*). Sur la base de ces résultats, notre hypothèse est que l'existence en italien de constructions figées contenant *occhio* équivalentes aux constructions figées françaises contenant *œil* tient au fait que cette partie du corps est considérée comme un organe des sens dans les deux langues, alors que dans les constructions figées françaises le nom *nez* est considéré non seulement comme un organe de sens mais aussi comme un élément du visage, ce qui permet de la remplacer en italien par un autre élément du visage ou par un nom désignant le visage lui-même (il apparaît alors une relation de métonymie «partie/tout»).

En revanche, les résultats du tableau montrent que la compréhension par un locuteur espagnol des constructions verbales figées françaises est sensiblement équivalente que le Npc soit *œil* (78,5 %) ou *nez* (76.5 %). Cependant, 30 % des constructions françaises contenant *œil* sont dans une relation d'homologie totale (HT) avec les constructions espagnoles correspondantes, alors que seulement 15 % des constructions françaises contenant *nez* sont dans cette relation avec les constructions espagnoles correspondantes. Mais il faut tenir compte du fait que le nombre d'expressions sur lesquelles nous avons travaillé est plus du double concernant *œil* par rapport à *nez*. Nous ne saurions affirmer, par conséquent, que les expressions portant sur *œil* sont plus prévisibles et plus faciles à interpréter, pour un locuteur de langue espagnole que celles portant sur *nez*. Si l'on compare les deux langes cibles (italien et espagnol), il semblerait que, pour les cas examinés, l'italien soit souvent plus proche du français que l'espagnol : respectivement 48.5% et 30 % d'HT pour *œil*, et 36% et 15% pour *nez*. Cela est confirmé par le fait que seulement 11.5 % en italien contre 20.5 % en espagnol pour *œil* et 17 % en italien contre 19 % en espagnol pour *nez* ne sont pas dans une relation d'HT ni d'HP avec les constructions françaises. Dans la plupart de ces cas, il n'existe pas de construction figée correspondante en espagnol.

L'étude menée sur les différents types de construction nous a aussi permis de constater que, lorsque les deux langues cibles n'ont pas d'équivalent (HT ou HP) avec le français, elles sont en revanche souvent proches l'une de l'autre (HT ou HP).

Une étude portant sur un plus grand nombre de cas et sur d'autres parties du corps semble maintenant indispensable pour corroborer ou infirmer ces tendances et peut-être découvrir des régularités, entre langues, même pour ces expressions figées et métaphoriques, permettant de faciliter plus régulièrement le passage d'une langue à l'autre.

4. Bibliographie

BERCKER, F. 1992 «Alouette, gentille alouette... Parties du corps et constructions figées». In: Perrin I. (dir.), *Approche énonciative de l'énoncé complexe*, Louvain, Peters-Bibliothèque de l'information grammaticale: 119-143.

DANLOS, L. 1988 «Les expressions figées construites avec le verbe être Prep». *Langages*, 90: 23-39.

GROSS, M. 1983 «Les déterminants dans les expressions figées». *Langages*, 79: 89-117.

GROSS, M. 1988 «Les limites de la phrase figée». *Langages*, 90: 7-23.

GROSS, M. 1993, «Les phrases figées en français». *L'information grammaticale*, 59: 36-42.

LAKOFF, G. & JOHNSON, M. 1980, *Metaphors we live by*, Chicago: The University of Chicago Press (trad. fr., *Les métaphores dans la vie quotidienne*, Paris, Editions de Minuit [1985]).

LAKOFF, G. 1987, *Women fire and dangerous things*, Chicago, The University of Chicago Press.

MARTINS-, M. 1977 «Repères dans les recherches actuelles sur la locution». In: Martins-Baltar M. (éd.), *La locution entre langue et usages*, Fontenay/Saint-Cloud, ENS Editions: 19-52.

MEL'CUK, I. 2003 «Les collocations : définitions, rôle et utilité», dans Grossmann F. et Tutin A. (eds), *Les collocations. Analyse et traitement*, Travaux et recherches en linguistique appliquée, Série E, n. 1, Amsterdam: De Werelt,: 23-31.

VALLI, A. ET BRAMATI, A. 2009 «Traduire les métaphores ontologiques dans l'espace roman. Le cas du français vers italien» . In: *Actes des 8es Journées scientifiques «Passeurs de mots, passeurs d'espoir : lexicologie, terminologie et traduction face au défi de la diversité», Lisbonne, 15-17 octobre 2009* (à paraître).

VALLI, A. ET VILLAGENES SERRA, E. 1998 «Locutions figées comprenant un nom "partie du corps" en espagnol et en français» . In: Mejri S. *et al.* (éds), *Le figement lexical, Rencontres linguistiques Méditerranéennes, Tunis, les 17-18 et 19 septembre 1998*, p. 177-206.

A CORPUS-BASED STUDY OF SIMILES AND COGNATE ADJECTIVAL FORMS IN ENGLISH, SWEDISH AND CROATIAN

Zvonimir Novoselec
Jelena Parizoska
University of Zagreb

Abstract: This paper deals with the relationship between conventionalized similes with the structure *(as)* + adjective + *as* + NP in English, Swedish and Croatian (e.g. (as) clear as crystal, tung som bly ('heavy as lead'), hladan kao led ('cold as ice')) and cognate adjectival forms, more specifically noun-adjective compounds such as crystal-clear and blytung ('lead heavy') and adverb + adjective collocations such as ledeno hladan (lit. icily cold). Using corpus data, we examine the frequencies, collocational range and meaning of similes and adjectival forms in order to determine the degree of conventionality of each type of item and to identify the mechanisms underlying the process of creation of adjectival forms in the three languages. The aim is to show that similes and adjectival forms should be viewed on a scale of conventionality and grammaticalization. The frequencies of the two types of items as well as their semantic and syntactic differences raise the issue of the status of adjectival forms as idiomatic expressions, and the issue of items which are listed in dictionaries as canonical forms.

Key words: Similes, adjectival forms, corpus, conventionality, dictionary

1. Introduction

The traditional definition of idioms as units whose components and syntactic structure are fixed has been challenged by corpus-based studies, which have shown that many idioms have one or more variant forms (Moon 1998; Cignoni, Coffey and Moon 2002; Langlotz 2006). Among the idiomatic expressions which show relative variability cross-linguistically are similes containing an adjective and a noun phrase, for example in English *(as) solid as a rock*, in Swedish *svart som natten* ('black as night'), in Croatian *čist kao kristal* ('clean as crystal'). In English and Swedish similes may have cognate noun-adjective compounds, e.g. *rock-solid* and *nattsvart* ('night-black'), a number of which are conventionalized lexical units. Noun-adjective compounds are typically listed as variants of similes, while some are lexical items in their own right. In the latter case, the cognate simile may be listed as an independent item or it may not be listed at all.

In Croatian similes rarely have parallel noun-adjective compounds such as *rock-solid*. However, corpus data show that there are adverb + adjective collocations associated with similes, as in the following example:[1]

(1) Radnja se fokusira na sudbinu kristalno čiste ljubavi dvoje mladih ljudi...

---

[1] All examples are drawn from three corpora: the British National Corpus, the Swedish corpus PAROLE (http://spraakbanken.gu.se/parole/) and the Croatian National Corpus (http://www.hnk.ffzg.hr).

'The plot revolves around the story of the pure love (lit. crystally clean love) of a young couple...'

Croatian is different from English and Swedish in that adjectival forms of the type illustrated in (1) are listed in neither general dictionaries nor dictionaries of idioms.[2] Thus, dictionary entries show that the relationship between similes and cognate adjectival forms in terms of conventionality is treated in different ways: they may be regarded as variants (and are therefore grouped together under the same headword) or as independent items.

Corpus data from all three languages show that in cases where similes and parallel adjectival forms co-exist, the latter may occur with a different set of nouns and have different meanings. For example, the English simile *light as a feather* and its Swedish counterpart *lätt som en fjäder* mean 'very light in weight' and typically refer to physical entities (objects or humans). On the other hand, the adjectival forms *feather-light* and *fjäderlätt* also collocate with abstract nouns, as shown by the following examples:

(2) Long's playing in the Concerto possesses *feather-light* dexterity with sly, wittily contrasted phrasing...
(3) Ett *fjäderlätt* handlag, tyngd i replikerna ...
'A feather-light skill in running the show, tough in replies...'

In examples (2) and (3) the compound relates to an activity which involves very little effort.

Dictionary entries and corpus evidence raise two important issues concerning the relationship between similes with the structure *(as)* + adjective + *as* + NP and cognate adjectival forms. First, in cases where a simile and an adjectival form co-exist in a given language, which of the two items should be considered the canonical form? Second, can there be a unified account of the mechanisms underlying the creation of adjectival forms associated with similes and the range of meaning which they have?

Using corpus data, we aim to show that similes and parallel adjectival forms exhibit different degrees of conventionality. We will also show that the syntactic and semantic differences between similes and adjectival forms are related to grammaticalization. All of this is significant for their lexicographic treatment.

The paper is organized as follows. Section 2 deals with some essential theoretical points concerning the mechanisms underlying the similarity of structural and semantic properties of similes in English, Swedish and Croatian. Section 3 presents the results of the corpus studies, followed by a discussion. The final section is the conclusion.

2. Theoretical background

In English, Swedish and Croatian there are a number of similes with the structure *(as)* + adjective + *as* + NP, which have similar components and similar meanings. For example, the expressions *cold as ice, kall som is* and *hladan kao led* all use the adjective 'cold' and the noun denoting frozen water to refer to a thing or substance of very low temperature, e.g. a drink, hands, feet, etc. These expressions can also be used to describe a person lacking feeling

---

[2] It should be noted that all Croatian dictionaries, including the recent ones, are based on hand-collected data.

and friendliness. The question arises: How can the similarity of the lexical make-up and meaning of idiomatic expressions in different, even unrelated languages, be accounted for? Cognitive linguistic research has shown that it can be attributed to the universality of some mechanisms motivating idiomatic expressions, which derives from universal aspects of human experience (Lakoff 1987; Kövecses 2000; Kövecses 2002). For example, English, Swedish and Croatian all use the cold domain in the conceptualization of emotions. This is reflected in the fact that conventionalized similes referring to lack of affection, *cold as ice, kall som is* and *hladan kao led*, have similar components.

It has also been show that, although they represent relatively stable constructions, similes exhibit considerable potential for variation across languages (cf. e.g. Clausén 1993; Moon 1998, 2008; Fink 2002; Omazić 2002). One group of variants are adjectival forms, for instance in English noun-adjective compounds such as *crystal-clear* and adverb + adjective collocations such as *ledeno hladan* (lit. icily cold) in Croatian. This group of lexical units have not been the focus of phraseological studies, but just a small section of larger studies. Thus, investigations into variation of similes have not dealt with the frequency of adjectival forms in comparison with similes, and their semantic and syntactic properties.

These issues are explored in the remainder of the paper. Given the universality of some mechanisms motivating similes in English, Swedish and Croatian, it can be assumed that common mechanisms underlie the process of creation of adjectival forms associated with similes.

3. Results

We used idioms dictionaries, general dictionaries and learner's dictionaries of English, Swedish and Croatian (see sources) to identify similes with the structure *(as)* + adjective + *as* + NP, which are considered to be conventionalized lexical items.[3] Altogether, we obtained 454 similes: 191 English, 74 Swedish and 207 Croatian items.

We conducted a study of the initial set in three corpora – the British National Corpus (BNC), PAROLE and the Croatian National Corpus (CNC). We looked for units which follow the pattern *(as)* + adjective + *as* + NP and cognate adjectival forms, i.e. noun-adjective compounds and/or adverb + adjective collocations. The entire sample contains 1761 English, 663 Swedish and 421 Croatian examples. We looked at the data concerning: 1) the frequencies of listed similes and parallel adjectival forms, and 2) their semantic and syntactic properties – the nouns that similes and adjectival forms occur with, the range of meaning of each type of item, and their attributive and predicative use.

The presented results should be taken as tendencies because of the considerable differences in the corpora. First, the British National Corpus and the Croatian National Corpus total about 100 million tokens each, while PAROLE is considerably smaller, with about 19 million tokens. Second, neither the Croatian National Corpus nor PAROLE are balanced: 70% of the texts in each corpus are journalistic and neither corpus contains spoken texts.

3.1. Frequencies of listed similes and cognate adjectival forms in corpora

---

[3] Of the twelve dictionaries used in this study, seven dictionaries use corpora and five dictionaries are citation-based.

The results show that the majority of listed similes which occur in the corpora do not have cognate adjectival forms (74.5% of the English sample, 84.4% of the Swedish sample and 72.4% of the Croatian sample). Table 1 gives numbers of similes and parallel adjectival forms occurring in each of the three corpora.

	BNC	PAROLE	CNC
	No. of items	No. of items	No. of items
(as) + adjective + *as* + NP	109	27	21
(as) + adjective + *as* + NP and parallel adjectival form	37	5	8
Total	146	32	29

Table 1. Similes and parallel adjectival forms in BNC, PAROLE and CNC

In English about 25% of the listed similes occurring in the British National Corpus co-exist with noun-adjective compounds. In the Swedish corpus PAROLE there are 5 such items altogether: *död som en sten* ('dead as a stone'), *frisk som en nötkärna* ('healthy as the kernel of a nut'), *smal som en sticka* ('thin as a splinter'), *svart som natten* ('black as night') and *tung som bly* ('heavy as lead'). Among the 8 similes which have parallel adjectival forms in the Croatian National Corpus are *bijel kao snijeg* ('white as snow') and *mek kao svila* ('soft as silk').

Although the number of similes which co-exist with cognate adjectival forms is relatively small, in such cases adjectival forms occur more frequently. This is shown in Table 2.

	BNC		PAROLE		CNC	
	No. of tokens	%	No. of tokens	%	No. of tokens	%
(as) + adjective + *as* + NP	229	21.9%	11	10.2%	43	43.4%
Adjectival form	818	78.1%	97	89.8%	56	56.6%
Total:	1047	100%	108	100%	99	100%

Table 2. Frequencies of parallel forms in BNC, PAROLE and CNC

In more than half the cases involving parallel forms in English, the noun-adjective compound is considerably more frequent than the simile. A case in point is *clear as crystal*, which occurs 6 times in the British National Corpus, while *crystal-clear* occurs 135 times. In Swedish, two compounds, *stendöd* ('stone-dead') and *nattsvart* ('night-black'), are more frequent than their counterparts: the adjectival forms have 22 and 57 tokens respectively, while *död som en sten* ('dead as a stone') and *svart som natten* ('black as night') each occur only once. An example from Croatian is the adjectival form *kristalno čist* ('crystally clean'), with 31 tokens. By comparison, its counterpart *čist kao kristal* ('clean as crystal') occurs in the corpus only once.

Finally, the results show that a number of Swedish similes which are listed as conventionalized items fail to occur, while parallel adjectival forms are found in the corpus. Thus, of 74 listed similes, 32 do not occur in PAROLE. Of these, roughly 43% have cognate compounds in the corpus. In addition, some of these items occur relatively frequently. For example, the listed simile *hård som en sten* ('hard as stone') fails to show up in PAROLE. By comparison, the corpus has 190 tokens of *stenhård* ('stone-hard'). In the English sample, there are a 4 adjectival forms associated with listed similes which fail to occur in the corpus: *paper-dry, pig greedy, death-pale, velvet-smooth*. Each of these items occurs only once in the British National Corpus. In Croatian there are 7 adjectival forms associated with similes which do not occur in the Croatian National Corpus, among which is *nebeskoplav* ('sky-blue', 74 tokens).

3.2. Semantic and syntactic properties of similes and adjectival forms

Corpus evidence shows that there are considerable differences between similes and cognate adjectival forms in terms of nouns they occur with, the range of meaning, and attributive and predicative use.

The results show that in cases involving parallel items, adjectival forms may be used with a wider set of nouns. For example, the English simile *solid as a rock* refers to physical entities, objects (example (4)) and humans (example (5)):

(4) Enormous family sofa, solid as a rock, potential heirloom. Bargain!
(5) As solid as a rock and a very tough competitor, Clohessy would have been a perfect choice, particularly after going through the pre-Tour fitness regime.

The compound *rock-solid* has can also be used with nouns referring to objects and humans. In addition, it is used with abstract nouns, as illustrated by the following example:

(6) ...it proclaimed itself with the modesty of an institution whose confidence in its purposes was rock-solid.

Similarly, the Swedish items *svart som natten* ('black as night') and *nattsvart* ('night-black') both refer to objects that are black in colour (e.g. car, hair) or places where one cannot see very well (e.g. road). Unlike the simile, the compound can be used of a human to refer to their unpleasant character. In Croatian, the items *čist kao kristal* ('clean as crystal') and *kristalno čist* ('crystally clean') are both used to refer to a substance which is completely transparent (e.g. water). The collocation *kristalno čist* is also used of a person's reputation. Thus, the results show that in all three languages similes typically occur with concrete nouns, whereas adjectival forms occur with both concrete and abstract nouns.

Corpus evidence shows that in all three languages similes typically refer to physical properties such as colour (*crven kao krv* ('red as blood')), weight (*smal som en sticka* ('thin as a splinter')), health (*pigg som en mört* ('brisk as a roach')) and posture (*straight as a ramrod*).

Some similes can also relate to emotions (*tough as leather*, 'insensitive') and character (*hard as iron*, 'unyielding').

On the other hand, most adjectival forms referring to physical properties can also relate to abstract domains, which is not the case with similes. For example, the Swedish compound *nattsvart* denotes dark colour and can also refer to a depressing situation, as shown by the following example:

(7) *Hedlund målar upp en nattsvart bild där egentligen ingen lösning gives för Ryssland.*
'Hedlund paints a grim (lit. night-black) picture in which no solution for Russia is actually given'

Similarly, the Croatian item *mrtvački blijed* (lit. corpse pale) relates to very light colour, and it can also be used of a person to indicate that they seem much less good in comparison with someone else. Thus, corpus evidence shows that adjectival forms have a wider range of meaning than similes.

Finally, the results show that in cases involving parallel forms, similes always function as complements of verbs, whereas adjectival forms are also used as modifiers. Table 3 gives numbers of attributive and predicative use of adjectival forms.

	Attributive	Predicative
BNC	65.6%	34.4%
PAROLE	63.9%	36.1%
CNC	70%	30%

Table 3. Attributive and predicative use of adjectival forms in BNC, PAROLE and CNC

In the majority of the examples in each of the three languages adjectival forms occupy the prenominal position, which is associated with permanent and characteristic properties (Radden and Dirven 2007: 149), e.g. *a rock-solid tent*. On the other hand, similes exclusively appear in predicative position and refer to temporary properties, as in *The door was solid as a rock*. Thus, while both similes and adjectival forms express qualification, the latter have an epistemically closer relationship with the nominal element.

4. Discussion

Corpus evidence shows that a relatively small number of listed similes occurring in each of three corpora have cognate adjectival forms, more specifically noun-adjective compounds such as *crystal-clear* and *nattsvart* and adverb + adjective collocations such as *ledeno hladan*. However, in cases where similes and adjectival forms co-exist, the latter are considerably more frequent. Furthermore, a number of similes appearing in dictionaries which have been used in this study fail to show up, whereas cognate adjectival forms are found in corpora, some of which occur relatively frequently. The results thus confirm that a number of adjectival forms in all three languages are conventionalized lexical items. Moreover, in light of the frequency counts of the two types of items, the traditional status of similes as canonical forms is called into question. This is especially true of cases where the adjectival form is considerably more frequent than the parallel simile (e.g. *crystal-clear*) and cases where a given simile fails to occur in the corpus (e.g. *hård som en sten* ('hard as stone')). Our findings show that similes and adjectival forms exhibit different degrees of conventionality. We therefore suggest that the relationship between these two types of items not be classified in terms of canonical form vs. variant, but that they be viewed on a scale conventionality with open ends. This can be tied in with the difference between frequency of occurrence and prototypicality (Geeraerts 1988: 122): certain usages of lexical items are more frequent because they prototypical; they are not prototypical because they are frequent.

The results also show that in all three languages a number of parallel adjectival forms are used with a wider set of nouns and have a wider range of meaning. We argue that similar underlying mechanisms are responsible for the meaning change that adjectival forms undergo and the type of nouns that they may occur with. We suggest that it is the result of grammaticalization (Hopper and Traugott 2003; Heine and Kuteva 2004). While similes exhibit the characteristics of source forms in terms of structure (long phrases), limited collocational range (concrete nouns) and syntactic function (only predicative), adjectival forms are grammaticalized: they are structurally simpler, they are used in new contexts (i.e. with abstract nouns), and their meanings are more schematic, perhaps even subjectified (Langacker 2006). This is additionally confirmed by the fact that adjectival forms mostly occur in prenominal position.

The results of this study raise two important issues: 1) the status of adjectival forms as conventionalized expressions and 2) the forms which are listed in dictionaries as canonical forms. In English and Swedish noun-adjective compounds are conventionalized lexical units, which is reflected in dictionary entries: a number of such forms are listed as independent items. Moreover, in a few minor cases the simile is listed as a variant of the adjectival compound (cf. the entries *bone-dry* in *Cambridge International Dictionary of Idioms* 1998 and *sockersöt* ('sugar-sweet') in *Svenska ordbok utgiven av Svenska Akademien* 2009).On the other hand, in Croatian dictionaries adjectival forms do not occur at all, which suggests that there is no relationship between similes and units such as *ledeno hladan* ('icily cold'). The frequencies of adjectival forms in the Croatian National Corpus indicate that a number of such items are conventionalized and should therefore be included in dictionaries. This is especially important in organizing entries in bilingual dictionaries. As regards the criteria for establishing the canonical form, our results suggest that we need to use corpus evidence, more specifically frequencies, to determine the level of conventionality of different types of idiomatic expressions.

5. Conclusion

Based on the data from the British National Corpus, the Swedish corpus PAROLE and the Croatian National Corpus, we have established that a substantial number of similes with the structure *(as)* + adjective + *as* + NP co-exist with parallel adjectival forms, which occur more frequently. Our findings also show that adjectival forms in English, Swedish and Croatian share similar semantic and syntactic properties: they are used with a wider set of nouns than similes, they have a wider range of meaning and they prototypically occupy the prenominal position. This indicates that similar mechanisms underlie the process of the creation of adjectival forms, i.e. that they are grammaticalized.

On a more general level, we have shown that similes and adjectival forms are lexical units which exhibit different levels of conventionality. We therefore believe that dictionary entries should provide a more schematic account of forms that idioms occur in to allow for variability.

6. References

CIGNONI, L., COFFEY, S. & MOON, R. 2002 "Idiom Variation in English and Italian: two corpus-based studies". *Languages in Contrast* 2/2: 279-300.
CLAUSÉN, U. 2005 "Jämförelsekonstruktioner i Svensk konstruktionsordbok – struktur, variation och funktion". *Nordsike Studier i Leksikografi 6*. Tórshavn: Nordisk Forening for Leksikografi: 75-85.
FINK-ARSOVSKI, Ž. 2002 *Poredbena frazeologija: pogled izvana i iznutra*. Zagreb: FF Press.
GEERAERTS, D.1988 Where does prototypicality come from? In: B. Rudzka-Ostyn (ed.), *Topics in Cognitive Linguistics*. Amsterdam/Philadelphia: John Benjamins: 207–229.
HOPPER, P. J. & CLOSS TRAUGOTT E. 2003 *Grammaticalization. 2nd Edition*. Cambridge: Cambridge University Press.
HEINE, B. & KUTEVA T. 2004 *World Lexicon of Grammaticalization*. Cambridge: Cambridge University Press.
KÖVECSES, Z. 2000 *Metaphor and Emotion. Language, Culture, and Body in Human Feeling*. Cambridge University Press.
KÖVECSES, Z. 2002 *Metaphor: A Practical Introduction*. New York: Oxford University Press.
LAKOFF, G. 1987 *Women, Fire and Dangerous Things*. Chicago-London: The University of Chicago Press.
LANGACKER, R. W. 2006 Subjectification, grammaticization, and conceptual archetypes. In: A. Athanasiadou, C.s Canakis & B. Cornillie (eds.) *Subjectification: Various Paths to Subjectivity*. Berlin/New York: Mouton de Gruyter: 17-40.
LANGLOTZ, A.s 2006 *Idiomatic Creativity*. Amsterdam-Philadelphia: John Benjamins.
MOON, R. 1998 *Fixed Expressions and Idioms in English. A Corpus-Based Approach*. Oxford: Clarendon Press.
MOON, R. 2008 Conventionalized *as*-similes in English: A problem case. *International Journal of Corpus Linguistics* 13/1: 3-37.
OMAZIĆ, M. 2002 O poredbenom frazemu u engleskom i hrvatskom jeziku. *Jezikoslovlje* 3/1-2: 99-129.
RADDEN, G. & DIRVEN, R. 2007 *Cognitive English Grammar*. Amsterdam-Philadelphia: John Benjamins.

7. Sources

ANIĆ, V. 2004 *Veliki rječnik hrvatskoga jezika*. Zagreb: Novi Liber.
Bonniers svenska ordbok (2006). Stockholm: Bonniers.
BNC The British National Corpus.
Cambridge Advanced Learner's Dictionary. Third Edition. 2008 Cambridge: Cambridge University Press.
Cambridge International Dictionary of Idioms 1998 Cambridge: Cambridge University Press.
COWIE, A.P.; MACKIN R. & McCAIG, I.R. (1985). *Oxford Dictionary of Current Idiomatic English. Volume 2*. Oxford: Oxford University Press.
The Croatian National Corpus http://www.hnk.ffzg.hr

FINK ARSOVSKI, Ž. et al. (2006). *Hrvatsko-slavenski rječnik poredbenih frazema*. Zagreb: Knjigra.
Longman Idioms Dictionary (2001). Harlow: Longman.
Macmillan English Dictionary for Advanced Learners: International Student Edition (2002). Oxford: Macmillan Education.
MENAC, A.; FINK-ARSOVSKI, Ž. & VENTURIN, R. 2003 *Hrvatski frazeološki rječnik*. Zagreb: Naklada Ljevak.
Norstedts svenska ordbok 2003 Stockholm: Norstedts.
Svensk ordbok utgiven av Svenska Akademien 2009 Stockholm: Norstedts.
Svenskt språkbruk 2003 Stockholm: Norstedts.
The Swedish PAROLE Lexicon. http://spraakbanken.gu.se/parole/

"WENN DU MICH FRAGST... " : HYPOTAKTISCHE PHRASEOTEXTEME DEUTSCH UND SPANISCH

Berit Balzer
Universidad Complutense (Madrid)

Abstract: This article deals with subordinate clauses in German and Spanish which form a distinct group within the routine formulae as they belong to pre-patterned speech and are invariable in their sequence. Sometimes they depend on a special verb in the main clause, but most often they can be uttered as separate adverbials. After presenting a variety of hypotactic clauses introduced by WENN, WO, and WIE, as well as their possible Spanish counterparts, the point will be made that these clauses deserve to be treated as a subgroup within the syntactically heterogeneous type of formulaic discourse.

Key words: hypotactic structure, formulaic language, German-Spanish phraselogy

1. Einleitung

Eine relativ große Anzahl an formelhaften Phraseologismen im Deutschen tut sich syntaktisch durch ihre Nebensatzstruktur hervor. Im Gegensatz zu Redewendungen sind diese phraseologischen Einheiten invariabel, also formelhaft und in ihrer Sequenz fixiert. Sie treten jedoch nicht, wie Routineformeln dies tun, in einer bestimmten Sprechsituation als Reaktion auf eine vorangegangene Äußerung des Gesprächspartners auf, sondern können nach Belieben in den mündlichen und schriftlichen Dikurs eingeflochten werden und sind relativ selbständig, d.h. im Gegensatz zu nicht phraseologischen Satzadverbialen ist ihr logischer Bezug zum Matrixsatz meist elidiert. Ein solches Phraseotextem beinhaltet entweder einen relativ hohen Grad an Idiomatizität und Bildhaftigkeit (z.B. „wenn alle Stricke reißen") oder lässt sich eher als ein strukturelles Teil-Idiom ohne Bildspender auffassen (z.B. „wenn dem so ist"). Bei diesem Gegenstand unserer Ausführungen wirft sich also zunächst das Problem seiner Klassifikation auf. Vorausschicken kann man, dass es sich bei den behandelten Textemen wohl tatsächlich um Routineformeln handelt, die aber auch außerhalb einer Dialogsituation geäußert werden können. Aufgrund ihrer Plastizität wären sie marginal dem beschreibenden, ausmalenden Charakter der Redewendungen zuzuordnen, doch können sie im Unterschied zu diesen nie im Infinitiv benannt werden[1]. Burger (1998:53) führt unter seiner Klassifikation der Routineformeln u.a. auch die Beispiele *soweit ich weiß* und *wie schon gesagt wurde* an, die eine hypotaktische Struktur besitzen und eine gesprächssteuernde Funktion haben, nämlich im ersten Fall als „Vagheitsindikator" und im zweiten als „äußerungskommentierende Metakommunikation". Burgers Feststellung, dass Routineformeln „syntaktisch gesehen [...]sehr heterogen" sind und neben anderen auch „situationsunabhängige kommunikative Funktionen in mündlichen und schriftlichen Texten

---

[1] Es sei darauf hingewiesen, dass auch unter den Redewendungen mit Verbkern eine umfangreiche Gruppe von nicht infinitivfähigen Phrasemen besteht wie z.B. diejenigen mit fester Subjektstelle und obligatorischem Dativobjekt wie: „jdm. geht ein Licht auf" (**jdm. ein Licht aufgehen), wobei das Verb im Tempus, nicht jedoch in der Personalform der 3. Person Singular abwandelbar ist.

haben" (Burger 1998:52), trifft für die von mir behandelte Gruppe ebenfalls zu. Allerdings ist die exakte Beschreibung dieser kommunikativen Funktion, wie wir sehen werden, nicht ganz problemlos[2].

2. Korpus und Vorgehensweise

Ich habe die von mir untersuchten hypotaktischen Phraseotexteme je nach Subjunktor in drei Typen von Wendungen gegliedert: 1) solche, die eine gegenwärtige oder zukünftige Bedingung ansprechen und mit WENN eingeleitet sind; 2) solche, die sich auf eine Örtlichkeit beziehen und mit WO eingeleitet werden; 3) solche, die über den Anschluss mit WIE einen Vergleichssatz einleiten. Dabei habe ich nur weiterführende Angabesätze, also keine Gliedsätze, behandelt. Durch WAS oder WARUM eingeleitete Texteme bilden in der Regel von einem Verb im Matrixsatz abhängige Gliedsätze und stellen einen eher verschwindend kleinen Anteil innerhalb des hypotaktischen Strukturtyps dar. Die Relevanz einer derartigen Abgrenzung von anderen Phraseologismen dürfte außer Frage stehen, denn ihre Geläufigkeit ist in beiden Sprachen durch Suchmaschinen leicht nachweisbar. Da die Hypotaxe durch ihre Verb-Endstellung im Deutschen vom didaktischen Gesichtspunkt her auffällig ist, sollte die Suche nach einem Äquivalent in der Übersetzung nicht nur über die Semantik, sondern auch über eine syntaktisch vergleichbare PE laufen[3]. Zunächst habe ich das Phänomen, ausgehend vom Deutschen, anhand von zwanzig Beispielen analysiert und dabei zwölf strukturelle Übereinstimmungen mit dem Spanischen gefunden. Aus dem umgekehrten Blickwinkel fällt die im Vergleich höhere Anzahl von spanischen Phraseotextemen (42) auf, von denen 30 im Deutschen kein Gegenstück haben. Dies überrascht keineswegs angesichts der höheren Anzahl an PE im Spanischen gegenüber dem Deutschen[4]. Unter Phraseotextem versteht man, nach Kurt Günther[5], ein satzartiges, phraseologisches Konstrukt, das als Ganzes fixiert ist. Diese Bedingung wird von hypotaktischen Routineformeln erfüllt[6]. Meine Belege entnehme ich hauptsächlich aus dem Corpus der geschriebenen Sprache des COSMAS II (einer Datenbank des IDS Mannheim), die spanischen Belege entstammen CREA, einer vergleichbaren Datenbank der Real Academia Española. Ich stelle sowohl Volläquivalenzen als auch Teil- und Nulläquivalenzen in unserem Sprachenpaar vor.

---

[2] Földes (2007:424) bezeichnet diesen Typus unverbindlich als „phraseologische / phraseologisierte Teilsätze" und führt als einziges Beispiel *wissen, wo Barthel den Most holt* an.

[3] Die Studie von Gaudino (2010) umfasst nur die spanische Hypotaxe in Bezug auf Kausalität und Finalität.

[4] Siehe die 16.000 intendierten Einträge des Projekts zu einem Spanisch-deutschen Wörterbuch der Redewendungen eines Forschungsteams der Uni Köln unter der Leitung von Prof. Aina Torrent-Lenzen gegenüber den ca. 4000 Einträgen in Balzer/Moreno/Piñel/Raders/Schilling, *Kein Blatt vor den Mund nehmen. No tener pelos en la lengua. Diccionario fraseológico alemán-español*, Madrid: Editorial Idiomas 2010.

[5] Günter, Kurt, *Die Phraseologie der russischen Sprache*, Leipzig: Enzyklopädie 1992.

[6] Sie sind nicht nur in ihrer syntaktischen Abfolge fixiert, sondern besitzen auch eine feste Satzbetonung, z.B.: **Wenn du 'mich fragst...** Diese besondere Prosodie ist ein unabdingbarer Teilaspekt der meisten Formeln.

3. WENN

Der Subjunktor WENN kann im Deutschen bekanntlich sowohl konditional als auch temporal verwendet werden. Je nach Kontext ist er daher oft schwer vom spanischen SI oder CUANDO zu unterscheiden[7]. In unserem ersten Beispiel stimmt das spanische Gegenstück *por si las moscas* syntaktisch nicht ganz mit der deutschen Satzadverbiale überein, denn es zeigt eine phraseologisch feste Sequenz in Form einer Satzellipse:

| **Wenn alle Stricke reißen**, gibt es da immer noch meine Freundin in Hamburg... (*Mannheimer Morgen*, 01.08.2007) | Pues me gasto ahora ocho perras que tengo **por si las moscas**... (Ramón Sender, *Imán*, 1930) |

Der deutsche Bildspender „Strick" ist wohl aus dem Dachdecker- oder Bergsteigerberuf entnommen und bezieht sich auf die letzte Absicherung, die einen, wenn alles andere fehlschlägt (*si todo falla*), vor dem Absturz bewahrt[8]. Die bedeutungsähnliche deutsche Formel *wenn es hart auf hart kommt / geht* weist wiederum eine Gemination innerhalb einer verbalen Wendung auf, bei welcher der Stellenwert von *hart* sich laut Lutz Röhrich auf die Fähigkeit, Schicksalsschläge auszuteilen und einzustecken, bezieht. Der Sinn ist sehr ähnlich wie der von *wenn alle Stricke reißen* und meint wohl „wenn man in Bedrängnis kommt":

| Eine Reihe von Senatoren könnte nämlich, **wenn es hart auf hart kommt**, für und nicht gegen Clinton stimmen. (Salzburger Nachrichten, 28.7.1995) | El albergue puede ser [...] refugio, [...] piedras salientes y, **en el peor de los casos**, incluso un simple trozo de plástico echado sobre los hombros... (Antonio Faus, *Diccionario de la montaña*, 1963) |

Hier wäre ein spanisches *poniéndose en lo peor* angebracht, wobei eine *gerundio*-Struktur durchaus auch als nebensatzartiges Gebilde angesehen werden kann. Die Idee, dass im äußersten Notfall noch irgendein Mittel zur Verfügung steht, wird gemeinsprachlich mit *en el peor de los casos* oder in Nebensatzstruktur mit *si todo falla* wiedergegeben oder auch durch

---

[7] Man denke an Sätze wie folgende, die eine Interpretation von seiten des Übersetzers erforderlich machen: **Wenn** es aufhört zu regnen, mache ich einen Spaziergang. →**Im Falle, dass** es aufhört... (**Si** para/ **en caso de que** pare de llover...) →**Sobald** es aufhört zu regnen, mache ich einen Spaziergang. (**En cuanto** / **tan pronto** pare de llover, daré un paseo. → **Cuando** pare de llover...) Auf spanisch variiert der Modus vom Indikativ zum *subjuntivo*, je nachdem, ob das WENN konditional oder futurisch interpretiert wird.

[8] Die spanische Anspielung auf *moscas* (Fliegen) lautet eigentlich als ganzer Satz "*por si las moscas pican*" (falls die Fliegen stechen) und bezieht sich auf eine Legende, nach der im Jahre 1285 vom Grab des heiligen Narciso von Gerona aus ein Schwarm Fliegen auf das französische Heer, das Gerona belagern wollte, losgegangen sein soll, was zu panischer Flucht aus Angst vor der Verbreitung der Pest führte.

eine wenig geläufige temporale Nebensatzstruktur: *cuando todo corra turbio*[9] [wörtlich etwa: „wenn alle Wasser trüb fließen"]. Losgelöst aus einem ehemaligen denotativen Wortlaut und als rein elliptisch, bzw. deiktisch sind auch folgende Phraseotexteme zu betrachten, bei denen die Zuordnung nur locker sein kann.

Und **wenn ich es dir sage**, Mädchen. Sie stand vor mir, leibhaftig. (*Braunschweiger Zeitung*, 20.04. 2007)	La vida no es tan fea, después de todo, y **si te lo digo yo**... MUCHACHO: La vida es una porquería... (Carlos Gorostiza, *El caso del hombre de la valija negra*, 1951)

Wenn ich es dir sage bekräftigt eine hier durch „es" anaphorisierte Aussage, betont deren Glaubwürdigkeit und heischt Zustimmung. Das spanische *como lo oyes*, kann eine Reaktion auf eine Geste der Verwunderung des Gesprächspartners sein (...me gustó Paco, **como lo oyes**, yo era una niña (Miguel Delibes, *Cinco horas con Mario*, 1966:102). Ein weiteres Beispiel:

Denn 'Casino' ist im Französischen männlich –es heißt 'le casino'.- Und **wenn dem so ist**, dann hat die weibliche ‚-e-Endung am Anhängsel nichts verloren. (*Mannheimer Morgen*, 12.12.2006)	La harina es la misma y, **si esto es así**, hay que atribuir la mala calidad a defectos de fabricación. (*ABC*, 12-1-1946)

Wenn dem so ist weist eine erstarrte deiktische Dativform auf. *Si esto es así* kann alternativ durch *de ser así* oder *en este caso* ausgedrückt werden. Beide haben ebenfalls deiktischen Charakter. Auf spanisch funktionieren *si te lo digo yo* und *como lo oyes* pragmatisch sehr ähnlich, nämlich um der eigenen Aussage Nachdruck zu verleihen, während durch *wenn du mich fragst* vom Sprecher vorausgeschickt wird, dass er bescheiden, aber auch ungefragt, seine abweichende Meinung zu einem Thema äußern möchte. Es ist also eine rein rhetorische Formel, die im Spanischen ein hypotaktisches Gegenstücke besitzt[10]:

Also, **wenn du mich fragst**, ich sehe keine Wellen. (H. Hartwig, *Suse an Bord*, 2002:100)	Y, en el fondo, **si quieres que te sea franco**, no lo deseo... (B. Ortiz de Montellano, *Epistolario* 1999:278)

Als konditional ist auch folgendes Phraseotextem zu verstehen, das im Deutschen so viel besagt wie das adverbiale *en el mejor de los casos* oder hypotaktisch *si me apuras*:

---

[9] Cervantes, *Don Quijote, Teil II*, Kap. XXIII: "...y **cuando todo corra turbio**, menos mal hace el hipócrita que se finge bueno que el público pecador..." (...und **schlimmstenfalls** stiftet doch der Heuchler, der sich fromm stellt, weniger Schaden, als wer öffentlich sündigt...)

[10] Pragmatisch gesehen wäre *fuimos muy amigos y*, **por lo que a mí respecta**, *seguimos siéndolo* (J. Ribera, *La sangre de mi hermano*, 1988:69) eine weitere Möglichkeit, die aber dem deutschen **was mich betrifft** näher steht.

Also geeignet für Kleinkinder und, **wenn es hochkommt**, Kinder vielleicht bis zehn... (*Frankfurter Rundschau*, 06.05.1998)	Hoy un Seiscientos lo tiene todo el mundo, hasta las porteras, **si me apuras**, que a la vista está. (Miguel Delibes, *Cinco horas con Mario*, 1966:40)

Wenn es hochkommt bedeutet laut Röhrich „alles eingerechnet, im äußersten Fall, darüber hinaus bestimmt nicht", stammt also aus dem Kalkulationsbereich. Die Anapher „es" verweist zurück auf eine nicht genannte Größe –wiederum ein typisches Merkmal für Idiomatizität[11]. *Si me apuras* („wenn du mich bedrängst") könnte als falscher Freund zu *wenn du mich fragst* interpretiert werden. Es bezieht sich in obigem Beispiel aber auf eine genaue Berechnung im Sinne von *genau genommen*. Eine exakte Deckungsgleichheit liegt vor in folgendem Beleg:

Morgen früh, **wenn Gott will**, wirst du wieder geweckt... (*Braunschweiger Zeitung*, 8.10.2008)	Mañana, **si Dios quiere**, comulgaré... (Angel Vázquez, *La vida perra de Juanita Narboni*, 1976:143)

Ein Beispiel für eine exakte Entsprechung in konditionaler Verwendung wäre folgendes:

Zwar wurden die Feuer, **wenn ich mich recht entsinne**, korporalschaftsweise angelegt... (W. Alexis, *Als Kriegsfreiwilliger nach Frankreich*, 1815)	Ella [...] ponía una ópera de Puccini, **si mal no recuerdo**... (Juan Goytisolo, *Estela del fuego que se aleja*, 1984:165)

Hier hat das spanische Adverb *mal* seinen festen Platz vor der Verneinung und nicht am Satzende, wie es in der Allgemeinsprache üblich wäre. Ebenso sind Adverb und Verb in der deutschen Sequenz fixiert (weder „richtig" noch „korrekt" und auch nicht „daran denke")[12].

Im temporalen Sinn eines mit WENN eingeleiteten Nebensatzes erscheint in allen Fällen im Spanischen der Modus *subjuntivo*. Ausgedrückt wird, dass etwas niemals (oder am Sankt Nimmerleinstag) passieren wird. Dafür gibt es im Spanischen das geläufige Konstrukt:

Wenn Ostern und Pfingsten auf einen Tag fallen... Soll heißen: Wer's glaubt, wird selig. Das wird nie und nimmer passieren! (Hanno Gerke, *Ev. Kirchengemeinde*, 11.05.05, Zugriff: 05.03. 09)	¡Como no me poseas para **cuando las ranas críen pelo**...! (Vicente Blasco Ibáñez, *Traducción de las Mil y una noches*, 1906)

[11] Lutz Röhrich verweist auf den biblischen Ursprung dieses Phraseotextems in Psalm 90,10: „Unser Leben währet siebzig Jahr, und wenn's hochkommt, so sind's achtzig Jahr".

[12] Für irrealisierbare Bedingungssätze gibt es im Deutschen ein ganzes Geschwader von scherzhaften Vorgaben, wobei der Hauptsatz häufig unausgesprochen bleibt: **Wenn meine Tante Räder hätte**, (dann wäre sie ein Omnibus); **Wenn der Onkel kein Schwänzel hätt**, (dann wär er die Tante); **Wenn der Hund nicht gemusst hätte**, (dann hätte er den Hasen gekriegt); **Wenn Dummheit weh täte**, (da/dann müsste er/sie ununterbrochen schreien).Das Spanische ist für solche Situationen vergleichsweise weniger einfallsreich. Der humoristische Hinweis *si sale con barbas, San Antón, y si no, la purísima Concepción* ist parömisch und bedeutet so viel wie „ganz egal, was dabei herauskommt".

Häufig wird für diese Idee im Spanischen statt einer Hypotaxe eine Nominalgruppe verwendet (*en la semana que no tenga viernes*). Beide Beispiele sprechen eine Situation an, die sich nach menschlichem Ermessen niemals ereignen kann, nämlich, dass Fröschen ein Fell wächst oder dass es eine Woche ohne Freitag gibt. Dazu existieren noch etliche Varianten - der Volksmund ist diesbezüglich sehr kreativ- wie die religiös konnotierten *cuando San Juan baje el dedo*[13] (wenn Johannes der Täufer den Finger senkt) und *cuando vengan los nazarenos* (wenn die Nazarener kommen) oder das saloppe *cuando meen las gallinas* (wenn die Hühner pinkeln). Will man sich auf den Zeitpunkt beziehen, zu dem ein Unglück bereits geschehen ist, also um Kritik an der zögerlichen Vorgehensweise von jemandem zu üben, dann wäre die Bedeutungsentsprechung zu *wenn das Kind in den Brunnen gefallen ist* ein Sprichwort:

Kein Thema, mit dem man sich im Vorfeld beschäftigt, sondern erst, **wenn das Kind in den Brunnen gefallen ist.** Erst Krisen schaffen hier offenbar das Problembewusstsein.(*VDI-Nachrichten*, 09.02.2007)	Al asno muerto, la cebada al rabo (Samaniego, *Fábula V*, 1784: 116)

Samaniego selbst erläutert in der Fabel die Bedeutung als "dar el consejo cuando llega tarde" (den Rat erteilen, wenn er zu spät kommt). Die Semantik stimmt also mit der deutschen überein, auch wenn die parömische Struktur auf spanisch nicht einmal ein Verb beinhaltet[14]. Das andere mögliche spanische Pendant, *a toro pasado*, ist nur oberflächlich vergleichbar, denn erstens bedeutet es nicht „wenn das Unglück schon geschehen ist", sondern „wenn die Gefahr vorüber ist", und zweitens ist seine Struktur nicht hypotaktisch, sondern adverbial. Aber in generelleren Zusammenhängen wäre es eine mögliche Wahl für den Sprecher: *¡Y me lo dices ahora, a toro pasado!* (Und das sagst du mir erst jetzt, wo schon alles überstanden ist).

Wenn derjenige, von dem gerade die Rede ist, im selben Moment erscheint, sagt man:

Lala, da bist du ja! Hab dich schon lang nicht mehr gesehen. **Wenn man vom Teufel spricht!** Hab erst vorhin nach dir gefragt! (*Neue Kneipen braucht das Land*, http://forum.kijiji.de/post-591374.html.Zugriff: 5.3.09)	Mira, en **hablando del rey de Roma**, por allí asoma... (Antonio Díaz-Cañabate, *Paseíllo por el planeta de los toros*, 1970:42)

Die spanische *gerundio*-Form lautet nach Iribarren eigentlich *en mentando al rey de Roma, luego asoma*. *Rey* ist dabei eine Verballhornung von *ruin* (=der Böse). Weder konditional noch temporal, sondern vielmehr konzessiv ist der Wert folgender Nebensatzstruktur: ‚Und

---

[13] D.h. „auf unbestimmte Zeit". Iribarren (2005:34) dokumentiert die Variante *hasta que San Juan baje el dedo*.

[14] Auch hier belegt Lutz Röhrich einen gemeinsamen Ursprung der generelleren Wendung „den Brunnen zudecken / zuschütten, wenn das Kind / das Kalb hineingefallen ist" aus der klassischen Literatur: *accepto damno ianum claudere* und verfolgt dessen Spur bei den Schildbürgern und in einer Abbildung von Pieter Breughel.

wenn du dich auf den Kopf stellst, diese Gelegenheit lasse ich mir nicht entgehen', zischelte Cora. (Selige Witwen, *Mannheimer Morgen*, 30.6.2001). Hierfür gibt es mehrere hypotaktische Entsprechungen: *te pongas como te pongas* (stell dich an, wie du willst), *por mucho que te empeñes* (so sehr du dich auch bemühst), *ni aunque me aspen* (auch wenn sie mich aufs Rad flechten). Außerdem kann letzteres nur über die eigene Person gesagt werden, ist also pragmatisch fixiert. So viel zum spanischen Konditionalsatz mit *subjuntivo* oder SI[15].

4. WO

Lokale Nebensätze werden mit diesem unterordnenden Adverb eingeleitet. Im Spanischen gibt es mehrere Vollentsprechungen für die Bedeutung „weit abgelegen und schwer zu erreichen":

| So sitzen die Spittaler nun ziemlich frustriert oben am Berg, **wo sich die Füchse gute Nacht sagen**...(*Neue Kronen-Zeitung*, 14.2.1995:17) | Vivía en la calle de Tabernillas, que para los madrileños del centro es **donde Cristo dio las tres voces**...(Benito Perez-Galdós, *Fortunata y Jacinta*, 1887) |

Hierzu existieren auch die Varianten *donde Dios perdió el gorro* und *donde el diablo perdió el poncho*. Das spanische Pendant zu den Tieren im tiefen Wald ist neutestamentarischen Ursprungs und bezieht sich auf die Wüste, wo Christus dreimal dem Teufel entsagte. Semantisch gleichwertig, aber in der Struktur nicht deckungsgleich sind:

| Werner [...] wurde von uns Kindern oft mit dummen Sprüchen geneckt: ‚In Buxtehude, **wo die Hunde mit dem Schwanz bellen**...' (Ulrich Rakoún, *Das Haus der toten Stimmen*, 2005:52) | Ellos ofrecieron dinero para instalarse en un piso nuevo **en el quinto pino**...(Angel Palomino, *Torremolinos*, 1971:30) |

Ursprünglich bezog sich dieses deutsche Phraseotextem nur auf die Stadt Buxtehude und ihre Kirchenglocken[16]. Inzwischen wird es aber allgemeinsprachlich im Sinne von „weit abgelegen und rückständig" gebraucht. Die Adverbiale *en el quinto pino* („beim fünften Pinienbaum") ist im Spanischen heute so geläufig wie im Deutschen *in der Pampa*. Das

---

[15] Für gleichartige Gebilde aus der entgegengesetzten Perspektive muss zumindest auf eine unterschiedliche Verwendung von *si* im Spanischen hingewiesen werden, da diese Konjunktion sowohl WENN als auch OB bedeuten kann: *si a mano viene* (wenn es gelegen kommt, [eigentl.: wenn es zur Hand ist]); *si bien se mira* (wenn man es recht betrachtet); *si tan largo me lo fías* (wenn du mich so lange warten lässt, [eigentl.: wenn du es mir so lang anschreibst]); *si son galgos o son podencos* (ob es Rosen oder Nelken sind, [eigentl.: ob es Windhunde oder Vorstehhunde sind]); *si es no es* (so unscheinbar, dass man es übersieht); *si los hay* (emphatisierend).

[16] Die „Hunte" ist im Niederdeutschen der Glockenklöppel, und der „Schwanz" eine Verlängerung des Zugseils. „Bellen" bedeutet soviel wie läuten, siehe das englische *the bell*-die Glocke.

nächste lokale Beispiel läuft in beiden Sprachen vom Sinn und der Struktur her parallel, wenn auch zwischen dem deutschen und dem spanischen Verb ein leichter Bedeutungsunterschied besteht (nicht „zusammenlaufen", sondern „sich kreuzen"). Beide Konstrukte beziehen sich auf ein organisatorisches Zentrum der Macht, der Planung, der Anordnung, usw.:

| Die Deutschen haben gelernt, ohne das eine Zentrum auszukommen, **wo alle Fäden zusammenlaufen**...(*Frankfurter Rundschau*, 30.7.1999:8) | El secuestro en un mundo **donde se entrecruzan todos los hilos** de la corrupción y el delito de una manera espeluznante... (www.latinoseguridad.com/LatinoSeguridad/Reps/Secuestro.shtml) |

Die letzten Belege aus dieser Gruppe weisen eine unterschiedliche Struktur auf: der Nebensatz im Deutschen erscheint auf spanisch als Redewendung: „Nein, das ist kein Ort, **wo der Kaiser zu Fuß hingeht**..." (*Mannheimer Morgen*, 24.11.2005, Ressort: Sport) ("ir al excusado, visitar al / ir a hablar con el señor Roca"). In beiden Sprachen wird verhüllend auf das „stille Örtchen" angespielt. Im deutsche Beleg ist die Wendung allerdings remotiviert, nämlich in Bezug auf „Kaiser" Franz Beckenbauer, der sich einem bestimmten Fußballstadion nur per Hubschrauber nähert. *El excusado* spricht ein Tabu an, das den Sprecher vom Nennen des Ortes entbunden, „excusado", hat. *El señor Roca* ist ein Euphemismus für die bekannteste aller spanischen Sanitärmarken Roca, eine Kloschüssel, die man einfach nur besucht oder mit der man sogar Zwiesprache hält. Ebenfalls euphemistisch und nur auf spanisch hypotaktisch formuliert wäre die Umschreibung für den „verlängerten Rücken": "...**donde la espalda pierde su (casto) nombre**..." (Moreno Torres, 1990:93), eigentl.: „wo der Rücken seinen keuschen Namen verliert".

Einige Phraseotexteme hängen von bestimmten Verben im Obersatz ab (*jdn. dahin wünschen* oder *jd. soll bleiben*) und entsprechen dem Sprechakt „Zurückweisung, Verwünschung". Im folgenden Kontext ist ihr Gebrauch allerdings eher diskursiver Natur:

| Was haben Sie sich eigentlich gedacht in Ihrem klugen geschulten Kopf, als Sie Ihren Professor dahin begleiteten, **wo der Pfeffer wächst**... (Uwe Johnson, *Mutmaßungen über Jakob*, 2000:115) | Don Fermín hubiera deseado a su madre **a cien leguas**. No podía ocultar la impaciencia (Leopoldo Alas "Clarín", *La Regenta*,1885:413) |

Ebenfalls von mehreren Verben wie *zeigen/klarmachen/wissen* abhängig, also relativ locker fixiert, ist das folgende Beispiel, das ebenso wie das spanische Gegenstück auf eine Zurechtweisung Bezug nimmt:

| Es war mal nötig, dass er klar gemacht hat, **wo der Hammer hängt**... (*Hamburger Morgenpost*, 5.9.2007:6) | No se meta conmigo [...] porque yo le diré **cuántas son cinco**... (Pío Baroja, *Susana y los cazadores de moscas*, 1938) |

Anstatt mit DONDE ist das spanische Pendant hier mit CUANTO eingeleitet. Eine Alternative wäre die Redewendung *cantarle a alg. las cuarenta*, die ebenfalls eine Zurechtweisung beinhaltet. Vom kreativen Umgang mit der Sprache zeugt unser letzter deutscher Beleg in dieser Gruppe, dessen Herkunft auf das Jahr 1958 durch Max Frischs *Homo Faber* festzumachen ist, der aber gute Chancen hat, in die allgemeine Umgangssprache aufgenommen zu werden, und zwar im Sinne von „überall, sich rasch vermehrend": **Wo man hinspuckt**, nix als Pisa-Deppen...www.muenzblog.de/2-euro-gedenkmuenze-10-jahre-euro-wwu-emu-2009/ (Zugriff:8.3.2009). Im Spanischen könnte hier ein transparentes *por donde mires* („wohin du auch siehst") stehen. In diese Gruppe mit DONDE gehören hingegen keine Parömien wie *donde las dan las toman* („wie du mir, so ich dir") oder *donde comen dos comen tres* („wo zwei essen, kann auch ein Dritter essen"), auch wenn sie häufig formelhaft als Kommentar gebraucht werden.

5. WIE

Dieses modale Adverb leitet typischerweise modale Nebensätze vergleichender Art ein. Der einzige phraseologische Beleg für das Deutsche ist folgender mit variierbarem Genus:

Ein Trucker Pin-up, **wie es im Buche steht**...(*Berliner Morgenpost*, 16.9.99)	Comíamos **como Dios manda** (A. Zamora Vicente, *A traque barraque*, 1972:184)
Er ist ein Realist **wie er im Buche steht**...(Hansi Hartwig,*Suse an Bord*, 2002:79)	...que eres un cabronazo **de tomo y lomo** (Juan Marsé, *Últimas tardes con Teresa*, 1966:163)
Eben eine Naturkonstante, **wie sie im Buche steht**...(*Spektrum direkt*, 1.12.02)	Esto es una verdad **como una casa** (Juan Marsé, *Últimas tardes con Teresa*, 1966:163)

Das Maskulinum steht hierbei doppelt so oft wie das Femininum, das Neutrum erscheint nur in seltenen Fällen, z.B. „ein Pin-up, wie es im Buche steht". Mit dem Buch wird auf das Gesetzbuch, das biblische Buch Mose, angespielt, in dem ein Kanon vorgeschrieben steht. Insofern entspricht das spanische *como Dios manda* in etwa dem biblischen Ursprung der deutschen Formel und ist darüber hinaus auch syntaktisch vergleichbar, während andere semantisch gleichwertige Strukturen keine finite Verbform enthalten. So sind die obigen spanischen Nominalformen (*de tomo y lomo* und *como una casa*) als „beachtlich" oder „bedeutend" und „groß und offensichtlich" zu interpretieren und würden auch in einen negativ konnotierten Kontext passen, was bei *como Dios manda* unmöglich ist (Du bist ein Egoist, **wie er im Buche steht**. - Eres un egoísta ***de tomo y lomo***; Das ist ein Fehler, **wie er im Buche steht**.- Es un error ***como una casa***.)

Die gesprächsüberleitende Floskel „wie dem auch sei" hat zwar einen hypotaktischen Satzbau, steht jedoch häufig losgelöst von einem Obersatz. Dasselbe ist der Fall bei ihrem spanischen Gegenstück *sea como fuere*. In beiden Fällen ist die erstarrte Kasus- und Modusform typisch für Phraseotexteme. Im folgenden Beispiel steht *el otro* (der andere) anonym für das unpersönliche „man" oder „irgendjemand":

La calle es de quien la trabaja, **como dijo el otro**. (Rosario Castellanos, *El eterno femenino*, 1975:148)	Der Markt ist, **wie man so schön sagt**, in Bewegung... (*Rhein-Zeitung*, 11.3.06)

Des weiteren leitet *como si* auch irreale Vergleichssätze ein und entspricht dem deutschen „als ob", nur ist in folgendem Beispiel der Bildspender ein ganz anderer:

| Hay un gato negro en su puerta, aseándose, **como si no hubiese roto un plato**... (Angel Vázquez, *La vida perra de Juanita Narboni*, 1976) | Der ausgebildete Schutz- und Sprengstoff-spürhund *sieht aus,* **als ob er kein Wässerchen trüben könnte**, aber Vorsicht ist geboten... (*Mannheimer Morgen*, 16.7.2005) |

Die sehr rentable Gruppe der phraseologischen Vergleiche, eine der produktivsten Typologien überhaupt, bringt eine Reihe von Phraseotextemen hervor. Diese scheinen im Spanischen jedenfalls häufiger als im Deutschen in der Nebensatzform vorzukommen[17].

6. Schluss

Da bei einer adäquaten Übersetzung nicht nur semantische und imagologische Kriterien, sondern auch formal syntaktische in Betracht gezogen werden sollten, halte ich eine Gegenüberstellung dieses vergleichbaren Phänomens in unserem Sprachenpaar für äußerst relevant, wobei neben der vergleichbaren Struktur und der Frequenz im Gebrauch auch noch der exakte Stellenwert eines jeden dieser Phraseoteхteme auf einer Skala verglichen werden sollte, die von maximaler Opazität bis zur maximalen Transparenz reichen kann[18].

---

[17] Folgende spanischen Belege können im Deutschen lediglich paraphrasiert werden: **como Dios / su madre le trajo al mundo** (nackt wie Gott ihn schuf); **como si dicen misa** (ohne zuzuhören); **como cuando enterraron a Zafra** (regnen wie bei Zafras Beerdigung); **como Dios da a entender a alg.** (nach bestem Wissen, ohne viel nachzudenken); **como Dios pintó a Perico** (mühelos); **como dos y dos son cuatro** (allem Anschein nach); **como quien entra en una cuadra** (ungehobelt, ohne Schliff, rüpelhaft); **como quien oye llover** (ohne jdm. / einer Sache Beachtung zu schenken); **como sardina que lleva el gato** (sehr schnell); **como quien tiene un tío en América** (verschwenderisch); **como quien no quiere la cosa**- (wie ungewollt, unwillkürlich).

[18] Ein weiterer Schritt, der unternommen werden sollte, besteht in der Untersuchung der von einem Hauptverb *wissen* (*saber*) im Obersatz abhängigen Nebensätze. Diese können durch verschiedene Subjunktoren eingeleitet sein: ...jeder in der Union ‚weiß jetzt, **was die Glocke geschlagen hat**'(*Frankfurter Rundschau*, 27.4.1998:3) - *¡Que ya tiene edad para saber* **cuántas son cinco!** (Jesús Alvarez Arroyo, *Un solo son en la danza*, 1982:18); wissen wollen, **was die Semmeln kosten** (querer saber la verdad); Wir wollen wissen, was den Bürger interessiert **und wo ihn der Schuh drückt**. (*Braunschweiger Zeitung*, 26.10.2005) - *Don Juan es hombre y sabe* **dónde le aprieta el zapato** (Arturo Uslar Pietri, *La visita en el tiempo*, 1990:271). Und auch die überaus plastischen und humoristischen Anspielungen auf jemandes Unwissenheit: nicht wissen, **warum die Frösche keine Schwänze haben**; jd. weiß nicht, **was der Elefant gefressen hat**, bis er so groß geworden ist. Vergleichbar wären hier eventuell die verbalen Redewendungen *"no saber de la misa la media"* oder *"no tener ni pajolera idea de algo"*.

7. Bibliographie

BURGER, H. 1998 *Phraseologie. Eine Einführung am Beispiel des Deutschen*. Berlin: Erich Schmidt.

COSMAS II, Version 1.6.2. (Corpus Management and Analysis System. https://cosmas2.ids-mannheim.de/cosmas2-web/

DOMÍNGUEZ, J. M. und VALLE, M. 2004 *Moderna fraseología en su contexto*, Stuttgart: Schmetterling Verlag.

DUDEN 11 1998 *Duden, Redewendungen und sprichwörtliche Redensarten: Wörterbuch der deutschen Idiomatik* / bearb. von Günther Drosdowski und Werner Scholze-Stubenrecht, Mannheim / Leipzig / Wien / Zürich: Dudenverlag.

FÖLDES, C. 2007 „Phraseme mit spezifischer Struktur", in: Burger / Dobrovol'ski / Kühn / Norrick, *Phraseologie. Ein Handbuch*, Berlin: De Gruyter, Ss. 424-435.

GAUDINO FALLEGGER, L. 2010 *Hypotaktische Konstrukte im gesprochenen Spanisch. Theorie und Empirie*, Wilhelmsfeld: Gottfried Egert Verlag.

GÜNTHER, K. 1998„Zur Begriffsfindung in der Phraseologie: Die Termini Lexem, Phrasem, Textem, Phraseotextem", in: *EUROPHRAS 95: Europäische Phraseologie im Vergleich: Gemeinsames Erbe und kulturelle Vielfalt*. Ed. Wolfgang Eismann. Bochum: Norbert Brockmeyer, Ss. 283-293.

IRIBARREN, J. M. 1990 *El porqué de los dichos*, Pamplona: Gobierno de Navarra 2005 (13ª).

MORENO TORRES, F. (Hg.) 1990 *Lexikon der spanischen Redewendungen spanisch/ deutsch. Expresiones idiomáticas*, Eltville am Rhein: Bechterminz Verlag.

REAL ACADEMIA ESPAÑOLA: Datenbank CREAonline: http://corpus.rae.es/creanet.html

RÖHRICH, L. 1994 *Lexikon der sprichwörtlichen Redensarten. 3 Bde.*, Freiburg [Breisgau] / Basel / Wien: Herder.

LOS COMPLEMENTOS DEL VERBO EN LAS LOCUCIONES VERBALES FIJAS. ESTUDIO CONTRASTIVO EN FRANCÉS Y EN ESPAÑOL

María Josefa Marcos García
Universidad de Salamanca

Abstract: Our paper contribution is centred on the verbal fixed phrases. It is a study of two languages: French and Spanish. A verbal fixed construction is constituted by several elements, of which the most important is a verb. The above mentioned verb, with his complements, they form a unit capable of working and meaning for her itself. In our study we try to establish a classification of the type of complements that presents every verb in our bilingual corpus. We will see that French and Spanish present many similarities in this type of phrases.

Key words: Verbal fixed phrases, verb complements, morphosyntactic semantic study, French, Spanish.

1. Introducción

Ante la gran variedad de unidades fraseológicas, los especialistas han intentado establecer una clasificación. En la bibliografía consultada, las clasificaciones que nos parecen más útiles para el objetivo de nuestro trabajo son las de González Rey (2002:71) y Corpas Pastor (1996:51). En ambas clasificaciones encontramos tres grupos de unidades. González Rey distingue colocaciones, expresiones idiomáticas y paremias. Corpas Pastor, por su parte, habla de colocaciones, locuciones y enunciados fraseológicos. Las locuciones verbales fijas pertenecen al segundo grupo y son definidas por González Rey como "Construction d'un ensemble polylexical formé autour d'un noyau verbal" (González Rey 2002:178)

Este tipo de construcciones se ilustra con ejemplos como:

(1) Buscar las pulgas / Chercher des puces
(2) Hablar para el cuello de la camisa / Parler dans sa moustache
(3) Perder la cabeza / Perdre la tête

2. Características de las locuciones verbales fijas

Las locuciones verbales fijas presentan una serie de características comunes. Una de las características más importantes es su alto grado de fijación. Dicha fijación se manifiesta por una serie de rasgos como la invariabilidad de los componentes (4a), los componentes léxicos no son conmutables (4b), ni permutables (4c) ni extraíbles (4d), además, no se puede realizar una transformación pasiva (4e), finalmente, no se puede realizar una nominalización (4f). (Ruiz Gurillo 1997:113)

(4) Dorar la píldora
(4a) *Dorar las píldoras
(4b) *Dorar la cápsula
(4c) *La píldora la están dorando
(4d) *La píldora que doraste no ha servido de nada
(4e) *La píldora fue dorada
(4f) *El dorar de la píldora

Desde el punto de vista morfosintáctico estas construcciones también comparten una serie de rasgos. Se trata de unidades autosuficientes para funcionar y para significar: posee predicado y argumentos que construyen su propio significado y el significado de la frase, además, pueden formar los predicados de las frases en las que se insertan.

En ocasiones, la propia estructura presenta *casillas vacías* que representan actantes que han de ser actualizados.

Gaston Gross señala que "aucune locution verbale n'a de structure interne spécifique". (G. Gross 1996:70). [1]

Esta característica acerca a las locuciones verbales fijas a los grupos verbales libres. Por esta razón, encontramos algunas características que las locuciones verbales comparten con los grupos verbales.

La primera de estas características es la posibilidad de tener un CD e incluso CC. Otra característica es que siempre se incluye una forma verbal que puede ser conjugada. Por último, Gastón Gros considera que existe un grado de fijación variable:

- El elemento fijo es un CD, no hay otro complemento: *Porter le chapeau*
- El CD es fijo y el CI es libre: *Graisser la patte à qqn.*
- El CD es libre y el CI es fijo: *Passer qqn. à tabac*
- Los dos complementos son fijos: *Prendre des vessies pour des lanternes*

La última cuestión que queremos mencionar relacionada con la estructura sintácticca de las locuciones verbales son los diferentes patrones sintácticos que, según Corpas (1997:103), son los más frecuentes:

- Verbo copulativo + atributo: *Ser el vivo retrato de alguien*
- Verbo + complemento circunstancial: *Dormir como un tronco*
- Verbo + suplemento: *Oler a cuerno quemado*
- Verbo + objeto directo con complementación opcional

3. Descripción del corpus

El punto de partida de nuestro corpus es el extenso corpus bilingüe presentado en su estudio por Pedro Mogorrón (2002). A partir de este material hemos llevado a cabo una selección de locuciones que hemos clasificado en función del número de actantes del verbo:

[1] Conclusión a la que ya había llegado Maurice Gross. (1993)

Intransitivos: (A1) Sujeto + verbo
Transitivos: (A1 + A2) Sujeto + verbo + CD
Transitivos: (A1 + A2 + A3) Sujeto + verbo + CD + CI

Las locuciones que forman nuestro corpus están construidas con los siguientes verbos:

Intransitivos: *Caer / tomber; Costar / coûter; Dormir / dormir; Hablar / parler; Ir / aller; Jugar / jouer; Pasar / passer; Vivir / vivre.*
Transitivos: *Beber / boire; Buscar / chercher; Comer / manger; Mirar / regarder; Perder / perdre; Saber / savoir; Ver / voir.*
Transitivos: *Decir / dire; Llevar / mener; Mandar / envoyer.*

4. Tipos de complementos

El objetivo de nuestro trabajo es llevar a cabo un estudio morfosintáctico en el que intentamos ver cuales son los tipos de complementos que acompañan a los verbos analizados en un tipo de construcciones caracterizadas, como hemos señalado antes, por un alto grado de fijación. Este estudio basado en el funcionamiento morfosintáctico se ve completado por un análisis semántico que permite establecer la significación que dichos complementos aportan al verbo de la locución.

4.1. Verbos Intransitivos: (A1) Sujeto + verbo

a) El primer recurso que hemos encontrado en este grupo de verbos es la comparación. La estructura de esta comparación es: *como + N, SN; comme + N, SN*. A través de ella, se completa el significado del verbo con complementos circunstanciales que aportan significados diferentes.

- Complemento circunstancial de cantidad

(5) Caer como chinches / moscas
    Tomber comme des mouches
    Caen muchos

Complemento circunstancial de modo

(6) Dormir como un angelito
    Dormir comme un ange
    Dormir plácidamente

(7) Dormir como un bendito[2]

---

[2] Existen otras variantes de esta locución que coinciden en ambas lenguas. El significado no varía y la construcción del verbo es la misma, sólo cambia el segundo término de la comparación.
Dormir como un leño / Dormir comme une bûche

Dormir comme un bienheureux
Dormir ininterrumpidamente, profundamente

(8) Ir como una seda / Ir sobre ruedas
Aller comme sur des roulettes
Ir las cosas (muy) bien

(9) Vivir como un rey / reina
Vivre comme un roi
Vivir (muy) bien

b) Otro tipo de complemento que acompaña a los verbos intransitivos es el sintagma preposicional: Prep. + *N, SN*. En este caso, hemos establecido una distinción entre las locuciones que presentan la misma estructura en las dos lenguas y las que se construyen de forma diferente.

Entre las locuciones que coinciden en ambas lenguas, el sintagma preposicional realiza la función de un complemento circunstancial, que tiene diferentes significados.

- Complemento circunstancial de causa

(10) Caerse de sueño
Tomber de sommeil
Estar agotado por causa del sueño

- Complemento circunstancial de modo

(11) Hablar entre dientes[3]
Parler entre ses dents
Hablar muy bajo

(12) Ir de mal en peor
Aller de mal en pis
Ir cada vez peor

- Complemento circunstancial de finalidad[4]

Dormir como un lirón / Dormir comme un loir
Dormir como una marmota / Dormir comme une marmotte
Dormir como un tronco / Dormir comme une souche

[3] En este caso observamos una pequeña diferencia en la presencia del posesivo en francés, término que no existe en español.

[4] Es la frase francesa la que nos lleva a pensar que se trata de un complemento de finalidad. Aunque en español la preposición utilizada en estos casos suele ser *para*, consideramos que, semánticamente, ambas lenguas pueden ser interpretadas del mismo modo.

(13) Hablar por hablar
Parler pour parler
Hablar por no callar
Parler pour ne rien dire
Hablar para no decir nada

En el caso de las locuciones que son diferentes también encontramos complementos circunstanciales de diversos tipos.

- Complemento circunstancial de modo

(14) Hablar con el corazón en la mano
Parler à cœur ouvert
Hablar sinceramente

Esta locución está basada en una metáfora semejante en ambas lenguas, a partir de la idea de *corazón*, sin embargo el tipo de sintagma es diferente. La preposición que introduce el sintagma es diferente y el español utiliza un determinante que está ausente en francés; además, el español añade un CC de lugar *en la mano*, mientras que el francés completa el significado del nombre con el adjetivo *ouvert*.

(15) Hablar sin ton ni son
Parler à tort et à travers
Hablar de forma desconsiderada

(16) Hablar para el cuello de la camisa
Parler dans sa moustache / Parler dans la barbe
Hablar muy bajo

También esta locución se basa en una metáfora en ambas lenguas, sin embargo, el término utilizado es diferente, así como la preposición que introduce el sintagma, Además, el francés introduce una variación en el determinante: dans *sa* moustache / dans *la* barbe.

- Complemento circunstancial de lugar

(17) (No) caer en saco roto
Ne pas tomber dans l'oreille d'un sourd
(No) Aprovechar los consejos

La locución en ambas lenguas es completamente diferente, tanto en los términos, *saco roto / oreille d'un sourd*, como en la estructura. Mientras en español aparece un SN[5] sin determinante, el francés utiliza un sustantivo precedido de un artículo y completado por un complemento del nombre.

---

[5] Formado por un nombre y un adjetivo.

c) Por último, encontramos verbos que van seguidos solamente de un SN (N; det + N; det + N + CN)

- Sujeto / CD

(18) Caer chuzos (de punta)
Tomber des cordes
Llover muy fuerte

Aunque el valor semántico de los complementos es de un CC de cantidad, sintácticamente la locución funciona de forma muy diferente. En la frase del español consideramos que se trata de un verbo acompañado de su sujeto: *Caen chuzos (de punta)*. En francés, pensamos que se trata más bien de un CD. Se trata de un uso impersonal del verbo *tomber* semejante al del verbo *pleuvoir*, donde el sujeto es un pronombre *il* con un valor puramente gramatical. Además, el significado es el mismo en ambos casos: *il pleut des cordes / il tombe des cordes*[6]

-CC de cantidad

(19) Costar una cosa un ojo de la cara
Coûter les yeux de la tête
Costar mucho

La única diferencia entre ambas lenguas es la alternancia entre el plural y el singular de *ojo / yeux*.

4.2. Verbos transitivos: (A1 + A2) Sujeto + verbo + CD

a) También en este tipo de verbos la comparación es un recurso frecuente. Como en el caso de los verbos intransitivos, se expresa con la estructura *como + N, SN; comme + N, SN*. En los ejemplos de nuestro corpus esta comparación expresa un complemento circunstancial de cantidad

(20) Beber como un cosaco [7]

---

[6] Esta locución ha sido motivo de reflexión entre los especialistas relacionándola con la variante *pleuvoir des cordes*. Gaston Gros considera que la expresión *pleuvoir des cordes* se ha creado a partir de *tomber des cordes*. Para el lingüista, la extensión del verbo es, en ambos casos, un CD que semánticamente conlleva un matiz de intensidad. Además, se trata de una locución fija, lexicalizada, puesto que, el verbo *pleuvoir* puede aparecer solo (*il pleut*), sin embargo, la extensión no puede utilizarse junto a otros verbos (*pleurer des cordes). En nuestra opinión, esta idea se ve más clara aún con el verbo *tomber*. Dicho verbo no puede utilizarse solo con esta misma estructura (*il tombe).

[7] Hemos encontrado algunas variantes de esta locución:
Beber como si no tuviera fondo / Boire comme un trou
Beber como un tonel / Boire comme un tonneau
Beber como una esponja / Boire comme une éponge

Boire comme un polonais
Beber mucho

(21) Comer como un pajarito
Manger comme un oiseau
Comer poco

b) Otra estructura presente en este grupo de verbos es un complemento directo seguido de un complemento circunstancial.

(22) Buscar una aguja en un pajar
Chercher une aiguille dans une botte / meule de foin
Pretender algo muy difícil

4.3. Verbos transitivos: (A1 + A2 + A3) Sujeto + CD + CI

a) El primer grupo de locuciones presentan solamente un complemento directo junto al verbo

(23) No decir ni palabra
Ne dire mot
Callar

(24) Llevar la batuta
Mener la danse
Dirigir

b) Frente al grupo anterior, otras locuciones utilizan un verbo de este grupo pero únicamente con un complemento indirecto.

(25) Decir a los cuatro vientos
Dire aux quatre vents
Divulgar sin reserva

c) Otro tipo de locuciones combinan el complemento directo con el complemento circunstancial.

(26) Mandar una cosa al diablo
Envoyer au diable
Desentenderse

d) Finalmente, hemos encontrado locuciones en las que se combinan los tres ripos de complementos: complemento directo, complemento indirecto y complemento circunstancial.

(27) Decirle una cosa a alguien en la cara
Dire à quelqu'un ses quatre vérités
Decir lo que se piensa

En este último ejemplo vemos que el francés, con una estructura más cerrada, no presenta el CC que contiene la locución española.

Tanto esta locución como la (26) son ejemplos de las *casillas vacías* a las que hacíamos referencia más arriba. *Una cosa, a alguien, à quelqu'un* son sintagmas a los que se da un contenido cuando las locuciones se utilizan en el discurso.

5. Conclusiones

A modo de conclusión, queremos señalar que, en nuestro corpus, existen muchas similitudes entre el francés y el español. Las mayores diferencias entre ambas lenguas aparecen en los verbos intransitivos que funcionan con un sintagma preposicional.

En cuanto a los tipos de complementos encontrados hemos observado una gran presencia de locuciones construidas con una comparación formada con *como / comme*. La comparación aparece con verbos intransitivos y con verbos transitivos de dos actantes. Semánticamente, esta comparación tiene un valor de CC.

El CC es el complemento que se repite en las locuciones construidas con verbos intransitivos.

En los verbos transitivos hemos encontrado una presencia frecuente del CD, a menudo seguido de otros complementos: complemento indirecto y complemento circunstancial.

6. Bibliografía

CORPAS PASTOR, G. 1996 *Manual de fraseología española*. Madrid: Gredos.
GONZÁLEZ REY, I. 2002 *La phraséologie du français*. Toulouse: Presses Universitaires du Mirail.
GROSS, G. (1996): *Les expressions figées en français (noms composés et autres locutions)*. Paris: Ophrys
GROSS, M. 1993 "Trois applications de la notion de verbe support", *L'information grammaticale* 59: 36-41.
MARCOS GARCÍA M.J. 2008 "Descripción formal de las unidades fraseológicas en francés y en español.". In: Conde Tarrío G. (ed.): *Aspectos formales y discursivos de las expresiones fijas*. Frankfurt: Peter Lang: 199-218.
MOGORRÓN HUERTA, P. 2002 *La expresividad en las locuciones verbales en francés y en español*. Alicante: Universidad.
RUIZ GURILLO, L. 1997 *Aspectos de fraseología teórica española*. Valencia. Universidad.

THE CURRENT WORLD ECONOMIC CRISIS: PHRASEOLOGICAL EQUIVALENTS AND VARIANTS IN ENGLISH, SPANISH AND FRENCH

Ramón Martí Solano
University of Limoges, France

Abstract: The 2007 world economic crisis has given rise to a specific phraseology which is common to several European languages and which functions at different syntactic and pragmatic levels depending on the language. We claim that solely specifically designed corpora for each multi-word unit can yield empirical results for contrastive phraseology. This paper explores total and partial phraseological equivalents in English, Spanish and French and mainly focuses on the string the bubble bursts, its variants and its loan translations. Our main hypothesis is that it is a high degree of lexicalisation of the nominal constituent of some predicate phraseological units that allows the wide-ranging scope of lexico-syntactic variation of the canonical forms.

Key words: Contrastive phraseology, phraseological equivalents, lexicalisation, idiom variants, collocations

1. Introduction

The current world economic crisis started in 2007 in the United States and was largely the result of financial and real estate speculation. The crisis rapidly spread to many other countries and just one year later it developed into a worldwide phenomenon. The enormous amount of texts produced principally in the media was unquestionably characterised by a common phraseology. Economic crises lend themselves to the use of metaphors, imagery and figurative language which are not only pervasive and recurring but which are also shared by a considerable amount of languages and are definitely motivated by "intertextual phenomena" (Dobrovol'skij & Piirainen, 2006: 34).

2. Contrastive phraseology

Having as a general background the research done by Dobrovol'skij and Piirainen on contrastive phraseology, we subscribe to the concept of cross-linguistic uniformity of idioms in European languages (Piirainen, 2005: 45). Three different types of sources of total or partial phraseological equivalents must be taken into consideration when describing and analysing such a phenomenon, namely loan translations, common metaphorical source domains and common cultural tradition. Table 1 presents a selection of idioms from the same thematic group shared by the three languages in question. Although they may look like full or absolute equivalents at a first glance, a detailed corpus analysis shows that their syntactic, pragmatic and collocational behaviour differs from one language to another. These partial equivalents are "idioms of L1 and L2 which have identical or near-identical meanings, but do not fully correspond in syntactic and lexical structure, or imagery basis." (Dobrovol'skij, 2000: 372). Many other idiomatic expressions related to this topic have obviously been encountered during the course of this study. Expressions such as *a sinking ship*, *go belly up* or *go to the wall* are simply very scarcely represented or not represented at all in the English corpus and for that reason they have not been considered for inclusion[1]. The same situation applies to the equivalent expressions in French and in Spanish.

Table 1. Common phraseological units from the same thematic group, i.e. economic crisis

English	Spanish	French
the bubble bursts	*estalla la burbuja*	*la bulle éclate*
tighten your belt	*apretarse el cinturón*	*se serrer la ceinture*
kill the goose that lays the golden eggs	*matar la gallina de los huevos de oro*	*tuer la poule aux œufs d'or*
green shoots	*brotes verdes*	*pousses vertes*

3. Corpora and research methodology

Given the prevalence of this type of phraseology in the written press, we decided to use corpora coming from newspaper articles from the British daily *The Guardian*, the Spanish newspaper *El País* and the Belgian daily *Le Soir*. For searching the corpora we have used *Concgram 1.0.*, a programme recently developed by Chris Greaves for the automatic identification of phraseological variation. This programme allows to "identify all the co-occurrences of two or more words irrespective of constituency and/or positional variation in order to more fully account for phraseologial variation and provide the raw data for identifying lexical items and other forms of phraseology." (Greaves, 2009: 2). This piece of research is therefore a corpus-based analysis of the main and relevant lexical and grammatical associations of a sub-group of multi-word units related to this topic and their co-occurrence patterns.

3.1. The English corpus

The research started with the creation of a corpus of English texts by using the filters provided by the electronic archives of *The Guardian*. The idea was to have a very specific corpus spanning a period of one year[2], limited to the business section of the newspaper and using the lemma BUBBLE as the target word. The result is a corpus of over 130,000 words specifically

---

[1] There are no occurrences of *a sinking ship* in our corpus. There is only one occurrence of *go belly up* and two occurrences of *go to the wall*.
[2] For practical reasons we chose what has been described as the highest peak of the crisis, a period somewhere between the summers of 2008 and 2009.

designed to analyse the string *the bubble bursts* (its canonical form, the potential variants and the main collocations of the nominal constituent) in business and financial contexts. By doing so it was easy to avoid possible occurrences of other related but semantically different bigrams such as *burst someone's bubble*, which is defined in the *Oxford Dictionary of Idioms* as follows: "shatter someone's illusions about something or destroy their sense of well-being". The latter is rather infrequent and tends to be used in fiction whereas the former is extremely frequent and appears mainly in newspapers, according to a search carried out in the *British National Corpus*[3].

Table 2. Results of the English corpus *the bubble bursts*

Categories	Examples	N° of tokens
lemma	*bubble*	221
bigram	*bubble burst*	49
collocations	*housing bubble*	34
	property bubble	17
	dotcom bubble	11

3.2. The Spanish corpus

The same criteria were used for the other two corpora. For the Spanish corpus, exactly the same filters were applied. The lemma BURBUJA was used to create a corpus of over 130,000 words, limited to the business section of the newspaper and for the same period of time. Here are the results which are, by the way, strikingly similar both quantitatively and qualitatively showing practically no frequency differences across both languages (Colson, 2008: 198):

Table 3. Results of the Spanish corpus *estalla la burbuja*

Categories	Examples	N° of tokens
lemma	*burbuja*	196
bigram	*estalla burbuja*	47

---

[3] There are only 4 occurrences of *shatter one's bubble* compared to 23 occurrences of *the bubble bursts*, 15 of which are to be found in the newspaper/magazine section of the corpus.

collocations	burbuja inmobiliaria	55
	burbuja de la vivienda	4
	burbuja de Internet	3
	burbuja de las puntocom	1

3.3. The French corpus

Unfortunately articles cannot be accessed in the electronic archives of the main French national newspapers *Le Monde* and *Le Figaro*, which would have provided a similar corpus to the English and Spanish ones. The national Belgian newspaper *Le Soir* has been used instead to create the French corpus. As the amount of articles was substantially and comparatively low, the time span was widened to the years 2008 and 2009 and a text database was created of about half the size of the other two databases totalling approximately 65,000 words. The lemma BULLE was used as the target word to search for strong patterns and the analysis of lexical collocations.

Table 4. Results of the French corpus *la bulle éclate*

Categories	Examples	N° of tokens
lemma	bulle	114
bigram	bulle éclate	53
collocations	bulle immobilière	28
	bulle internet	22
	bulle monétaire	5

The interlinguistical comparison of the results of the three corpora (Tables 2, 3 and 4) shows a striking homogenization of the use of the same multi-word unit. The number of lemmas is similar in both the English and the Spanish corpus (221 and 196 respectively), whereas it is much higher in the French corpus (a total of 144) if we consider the fact that the latter is half the size of the other two. The *property/housing bubble* and the *dotcom bubble* are the two main collocations to be found in the three corpora, which accounts for the standardisation of these co-occurrences across languages.

4. The lexicalisation of the nominal constituent *bubble/burbuja/bulle*

Some nominal constituents become lexicalised and are used independently from the string to which they formerly belonged. Our main hypothesis is that it is a high degree of lexicalisation of the nominal constituent of some predicate phraseological units that allows the wide-ranging scope of lexico-syntactic variation of the so-called canonical forms, at least in English.

According to the *Oxford English Dictionary* in its 1989 edition, *bubble* is defined as "Anything fragile, unsubstantial, empty, or worthless; a deceptive show. From the 17th c. onwards the term is often applied to delusive commercial or financial schemes, such as *the Mississippi bubble* or *the South Sea bubble*[4]." The word thus came to mean a kind of financial hoax at that early stage to gradually approach the sense, as is the case today, of the word *boom*, a period of sudden economic growth.

This is clearly not the case with the other two languages. As far as Spanish is concerned, the word *burbuja* is registered in the *Diccionario de la Real Academia Española* with only one figurative sense as illustrated by the only example supplied in the dictionary entry "Los poderosos viven en una burbuja de impunidad", which literally translates as "People in power live in a bubble of impunity". However, the comprehensive *Diccionario de uso del español* by María Moliner in its 2008 edition registers the loan translation with the same meaning as it has in English although this new sense was not still registered in, for instance, the 2000 edition of the same dictionary. So we are to infer that the word must have been used in Spanish with this new sense some time between these two dates. The only seven examples of *burbuja inmobiliaria* (property bubble) found in the CREA[5] are all from newspaper sources and are attested in the years 2002, 2003 and 2004, which definitely corroborates the lexicographic hypothesis.

As for French, the situation is similar to that in Spanish. The *Trésor de la Langue Française informatisé* does not register any figurative sense of the word except for its use as a constituent of the rather infrequent expression *coincer la bulle* meaning to rest or to be idle. It is not until 2001 that the first occurrence of *bulle immobilière* can be found in the archives of the French national newspaper *Le Monde* in an article published on 16 January of that year in the business section entitled "L'euro reprend des forces avant l'échéance historique du 1er janvier 2002" to be precise. The new sense can be found, however, in the French dictionary *Le Petit Robert* in its 2007 edition, which clearly shows a parallel lexicographic pattern similar to its Spanish counterpart.

5. Phraseological variants

The commonest and most obvious variant on the phrase *the bubble bursts* is, needless to say, the substitution of the verbal constituent. First of all, synonymous verbs show differences not only in focus or degree but also in register, which, by and large, accounts for a great deal of phraseological variation. The change of polarity is, in its turn, achieved by the use of alternating verbs such as *grow, develop, expand* or *inflate*. But what is most interesting is the

---

[4] **Mississippi Bubble:** a financial scheme in 18th-century France that triggered a speculative frenzy and ended in financial collapse. The scheme was engineered by John Law, a Scottish adventurer, economic theorist, and financial wizard who was a friend of the regent, the Duke d'Orléans. **South Sea Bubble:** the speculation mania that ruined many British investors in 1720. The bubble, or hoax, centred on the fortunes of the South Sea Company, founded in 1711 to trade (mainly in Slaves) with Spanish America, on the assumption that the War of the Spanish Succession, then drawing to a close, would end with a treaty permitting such trade.

[5] CREA stands for *Corpus de Referencia del Español Actual*, a synchronic corpus for Spanish of over 154,000,000 words.

use of *bubble* as the agent of a transitive verb as shown in (1) with the verb *to funnel*, which clearly shows an extremely high degree of syntactic complexity connected to the nominal constituent:

> *(1) There was nothing resembling an investment boom until the dot-com **bubble** at the end of the decade **funnelled** vast sums of capital into crazy internet schemes.* (The Guardian, 12/11/2008)

The range of verb variants is certainly narrower in the other two languages: *estallar, reventar, hincharse, romperse, formarse* and *desinflar* are the only six verbs used in Spanish with various degrees of frequency[6]. The same thing applies to related or unrelated nouns such as *estallido, pinchazo, reventón, explosión, formación* and *generación*. As regards French, the variation is even smaller: *éclater, exploser, péter* and *dégonfler* and their corresponding nouns *éclatement, explosion, pet* and *dégonflement* represent the limited number of variants on the canonical form of the string. The most recurrent collocations of *bubble/burbuja/bulle* both as the nominal constituents of the idiom and as independent lexicalised words coincide in the three languages. However, two special collocations seem to be specific to Spanish if compared to the other two: *burbuja educativa* (educational bubble) and *burbuja del ladrillo* (the brick bubble, a metonymic realisation of *burbuja inmobiliaria*, the housing bubble, a variant form which denotes a more informal language register). The overall results show across-the-board similarities between the three languages concerning this idiom although minor culture-specific and language-specific variants reveal interesting pragmatic or contextual adaptations.

6. *To tighten one's belt*

To tighten one's belt is another idiom that has been widely used, but definitely not as much as *the bubble bursts*, and which belongs to the common stock of European phraseology. Here are just a few examples of equivalents in other European languages: Spanish *apretarse el cinturón*, French *se serrer la ceinture*, German *den Gürtel enger schnallen*, Italian *tirare la cinghia*, Portuguese *apertar o cinto* or Greek σφίγγω το ζωνάρι. Nominalisation and adjectivisation of predicate phraseological units are extremely common in English unlike in Spanish or in French which show major grammatical constraints and, thus, normally tend to express the same sense by other linguistic means. *Trail-blazing* from *blaze a trail*, *whistle-blowing* from *blow the whistle* or *sabre-rattling* from *rattle your sabre* are but a few examples of this common practice. Examples (2) and (3) show the nominal forms of the idiom in the English corpus. No equivalent forms have been found either in the Spanish or in the French corpus.

> *(2) Britain's consumers lost the spending habit last month as a combination of indifferent spring weather and **belt-tightening** to combat the recession kept them out of the shops.* (The Guardian, 18/06/2009)

---

[6] The English corpus yields a total of 18 different verb variants, namely *burst, prick, puncture, pop, explode, implode, blow up, go pop, create, grow, develop, expand, deflate, inflate, fuel, funnel, collapse, pump up*.

*(3) The biggest US carmaker, General Motors, is implementing **belt-tightening** measures ranging from the factory floor to the boardroom as it scrambles to bolster its cash position by $15bn (£7.5bn) to cope with plummeting car sales.* (The Guardian, 16/07/2008)

7. To klll the goose that lays the golden eggs

This idiom, which originated in one of Aesop's Fables and was later readapted in France by La Fontaine, and which exemplifies the common cultural and literary tradition of European languages, is the least used of the four selected in English whereas it seems to be favoured in the other two languages as found in the archives of the three newspapers. The idiom, which can be paraphrased as "Greed destroys the source of good", is illustrated in (4) by the use of a variant form in the Spanish corpus:

*(4) Y justo ahora, cuando **la burbuja ha estallado**, cuando se han acabado las ganancias multimillonarias, **cuando la gallina de los huevos de oro está muerta y enterrada**, qué casualidad.* (El País, 31/05/2009)

The above variant could be translated as "when the golden-egg goose is dead and buried". It should be noticed that it is used co-textually with *la burbuja ha estallado* ("the bubble has burst") and is inserted in the same syntactic frame, namely a temporal subordinate clause introduced by *cuando* ("when") as a sort of stylistic reiteration. The fact that no occurrences have been found in the English corpus and just one occurrence in the Spanish corpus and one in the French corpus clearly calls for the creation of specific corpora in order to empirically give evidence of across-language phraseological comparisons.

8. *Green shoots*

A very recent idiom in English and an even more recent loan shift in the other two languages, *green shoots* can somehow epitomise what can be referred as 'mass media intertextuality'. The original metaphor is associated to the renewal of life in deciduous trees in the spring. The conceptual correspondence works well in the three languages but the novelty of the phrase in Spanish and in French often makes necessary the addition of metalinguistic extensions of the type 'as they say', 'what's been called', etc.

*(5) A pesar de los **brotes verdes** que dicen ver algunos, el Fondo Monetario Internacional (FMI) aseguró ayer que Europa no **doblará la esquina** de la crisis hasta la segunda mitad de 2010.*[7] (El País, 13/05/2009)

Example (5) from the Spanish corpus illustrates the inclusion in the same contextual environment of another loan shift from English *to turn the corner* ("doblará la esquina" in bold type in the text), which, not having the same metaphoric entailment in Spanish, loses part

---

[7] "Despite the **green shoots** that some people say they can see, the International Monetary Fund announced yesterday that Europe will not **turn the corner** until the second half of 2010." (our own translation).

of its idiomaticity for the sake of clarity by the addition of the phrase "de la crisis" (of the crisis).

9. Conclusion

Special corpora need to be designed in order to address specific research questions. When observed in the light of these corpora, across-language phraseological equivalents show relevant association patterns which can be extremely similar from a quantitative and a qualitative point of view. Concerning the multi-word unit *the bubble bursts* and its Spanish and French equivalents, English shows a higher degree of verb variation which evidences what Gläser defines as phraseo-stylistics (Gläser, 1986). The processes of nominalisation and adjectivisation of the "belt-tightening" type seem to be particular to English. Parallel corpora in other languages would shed some light on the extent of this phraseological specificity. Although phraseological equivalents tend to share a common syntactic, pragmatic and collocational behaviour, minor culture-specific variants appear. Finally, whether some of the loan shifts will eventually become institutionalised and widespread in French and Spanish only time and meticulous research work will tell.

10. References

COLSON J.-P., 2008 "Cross-linguistic phraseological studies" in S. Granger and F. Meunier (eds) *Phraseology: An Interdisciplinary Perspective*, Amsterdam/Philadelphia: John Benjamins: 191-206.
DOBROVOL'SKIJ D. & PIIRAINEN E. 2006 "Cultural knowledge and idioms" in F. Mena-Martínez (ed.) *International Journal of English Studies*, Vol. 6, n° 1: 28-42.
DOBROVOL'SKIJ D. 2000 "Idioms in contrast: a functional view" in G. Corpas Pastor (ed.) *Las lenguas de Europa: estudios de fraseología, fraseografía y traducción*, Granada: Comares: 367-388.
GLÄSER, R. 1986 "A plea for phraseo-stylistics" in D. Kastovsky & A. J. Szwedek (eds) *Linguistics across Historical and Geographical Boundaries 1: Linguistic Theory and Historical Linguistics.* Berlin/New York/Amsterdam: Mouton: 41-52.
GREAVES Ch. 2009 *Concram 1.0.: A Phraseological Search Engine.* Amsterdam/Philadelphia: John Benjamins.
PIIRAINEN E., 2005 "Europeanism, internationalism or something else? Proposal for a cross-linguistic and cross-cultural research project on widespread idioms in Europe and beyond" in *Hermes*, n° 35: 45-75.

10.1. Dictionaries

Diccionario de la Real Academia, http://www.rae.es/rae.html.
Diccionario del Uso del Español, 2000, Madrid: Gredos.
Diccionario del Uso del Español, 2008, Madrid: Gredos.
Le Petit Robert, 2007, Paris: Collins.
The Oxford Dictionary of Idioms, 2004, Oxford: Oxford University Press.
The Oxford English Dictionary, 1989, Oxford: Clarendon Press.
Trésor de la langue française informatisé, http://atilf.atilf.fr/tlf.htm.

IDIOM ANALYZABILITY: AN INTUITION-BASED STUDY[1]

Attila Cserép
University of Debrecen

Abstract: Native speakers' assumptions about the meaningfulness of idiom components were examined in two online surveys. Participants tended to assign meaning to words, mostly relying on metaphorical conceptualizations, sometimes using substitute words based on common collocations or simply dividing the paraphrase and assigning meaning to the appropriate part of speech. When respondents were asked to formulate the paraphrases in their own words, they often provided holistic explanations. The results partially support conceptual metaphor theory.

Key Words: Decomposability, analyzability, conceptual metaphor, English idioms

1. Introduction

Idioms were regarded as noncompositional, long words in the past, but there is growing evidence that idiomatic expressions comprise a heterogeneous class. One division commonly recognized is that of decomposable versus nondecomposable, also known as analyzable versus unanalyzable, or idiomatically combining expressions versus idiomatic combinations (Dobrovol'skij 2007: 807). The former permit decomposition of their idiomatic senses. In *back the wrong horse*, *back* means something like 'support' and *horse* means 'thing, person', while *wrong* has one of its usual senses. In contrast, *chew the fat* 'chat' is nondecomposable. It was Nunberg (1978: 125-127) who first introduced this distinction.

At first sight, analyzability depends on what meaning the speaker attaches to the whole expression. The ODI (Siefring 2005: 12) defines *back the wrong horse* as 'make a wrong or inappropriate choice', which helps associate *wrong* with 'wrong or inappropriate', but it is less obvious whether native speakers would want to treat *horse* 'choice' and *back* 'make' as semantically autonomous in the given senses. However, as Dobrovol'skij (2007: 813) argues, it is the underlying mental image that matters, not the meaning paraphrase. The scenario of betting on horses is mapped onto a more abstract scene of supporting a loser.

Decomposability has been examined in a number of psycholinguistic experiments that asked speakers to classify idioms in terms of the contribution of each idiom component to the overall figurative meaning (Gibbs and Nayak 1989, Gibbs et al. 1989a, 1989b, Titone and Connine 1994, Libben and Titone 2008, Tabossi et al. 2008). Rather than having to specify this semantic contribution, the participants were asked to judge whether idiom components contribute to the overall meaning or not, and whether the meaning that a given component conveys is closely or more metaphorically related to the literal referent of the same component. Typically, respondents were presented with the idiom and its meaning paraphrase, as well as – in many cases – the categories "normally decomposable", "abnormally decomposable", "nondecomposable" together with brief descriptions of these categories and illustrative examples. In *pop the question*, *question* is closely related to 'marriage proposal', while in *spill the beans*, *beans* is metaphorically related to 'secret' (Gibbs and Nayak 1989, Gibbs et al. 1989a.) In two judgment tasks, decomposability was assessed on 5-point or 7-point scales (Cutting and Bock's 1997, Tabossi, Fanari and Wolf 2008).

The purpose of this study is to see whether the distinctions between degrees of decomposability also manifest themselves when speakers are asked to explicitly provide a meaning paraphrase for a given idiom component, rather than simply mark a point on a scale or place an expression in a pre-determined category. I prepared two online surveys ("Idioms 1" and "Idioms 2") using the tools on the SurveyMonkey website (http://www.surveymonkey.com/). Idioms collected from previous studies were used to make online questionnaires and the links were sent to various contacts in the US.[2] Although the online method did not ensure a strict control over participants, the instructions explained that American English native speakers were needed to complete the surveys.

2. Idioms 1

2.1 Material and procedure

The first survey included the same V + NP expressions that are found in Gibbs and his co-researchers' experiments reported in Gibbs and Nayak (1989), Gibbs at al. (1989a), Gibbs et al. (1989b), as well as Hamblin and Gibbs (1999). A total of 53 idioms were put in sentential contexts and participants were asked to provide the meaning of idiom components. No restrictions were placed on how the paraphrase is formulated, participants were free to use single words or phrases, one or more than one. The sentences were taken from A. Makkai, M.T. Boatner, J.E. Gates (2004) *A Dictionary of American Idioms* (http://www.sky-net-eye.com/eng/english/idioms/american), a recent edition of the same dictionary that was the source of examples in Gibbs and his colleagues' experiments. Each screen presented an example sentence, with one idiom component and space for the paraphrase below the sentence. The verbs to be paraphrased were given in the same inflectional form as in the example. The first 53 screens presented the idioms with either the verbal or the nominal component as the test item, the next 53 screens showed the example sentences in the same order with the other component as the test item. It was thought that focusing on one idiom component at a time would reduce the complexity of the task. This approach caused some difficulty in data interpretation (see Section 2.2).

One of the disappointing findings about "Idioms 1" was that many speakers who started the survey skipped a number of questions. Out of 109 respondents only 14 completed the whole questionnaire (12.8%). This may have been due to lack of information about the number of questions and my optimistic estimation of the completion time. Therefore, the online material was divided into two equal sections after some time: "Idioms 1a" and "Idioms 1b". Dividing the survey reduced the time spent on it and improved the completion rates ("Idioms 1a": 37 (67.3%) out of 55, "Idioms 1b": 20 (83.3%) out of 24). The instructions were as follows:

> WARNING: If you are not a native speaker of American English, do not take this survey!
>
> This study explores people's understanding of idiomatic expressions such as "kick the bucket". Below you will find a number of sentences

including idiomatic expressions. One component of the expression is listed below the example sentence. You have two tasks: first, judge whether the given component contributes to the expression's figurative meaning. For example, we can say that in the phrase "pull strings" each component has a meaning that it contributes to the overall meaning of the idiom: "pull" means something like 'exert, use' and "strings" means something like 'influence'. Note that we are not talking about replacing the words of the expression: "pull" cannot be replaced with "exert" or "use", since "exert/use strings" sounds odd and is not normally used. Despite this, "pull" expresses part of the meaning of the whole idiom. If the component has no meaning in the given example, write "No meaning" in the space provided. If you think that the given component has a meaning in the sentence, your second task is to paraphrase/explain that meaning. You can use single words or phrases to paraphrase the meaning, but please note that you are asked to explain only the meaning of the component!

Some of the answers were ignored, especially when the participant admitted not being familiar with the expression or when the whole expression was included in the paraphrase such as ' "swallowed his pride" means to be humble' (see Section 2.2). Although all the examples were taken from an idiom dictionary of American English, some speakers were unfamiliar with some idioms, such as *pay the fiddler* (a variant of *pay the piper*), *hit the sauce*, *lay an egg* or *make the scene*, or otherwise commented that the sentence sounds strange. Unnatural sentences may slip through the net of lexicographers even in recently published dictionaries.

I made a deliberate effort to judge each response to a given constituent without considering responses to the other constituent of the same idiom. Thus, a given paraphrase of *gave* in *The ball team gave Joe the sack because he never came to practice* was classified as much as possible without considering either the response to *sack* coming from the same speaker or all the responses to *sack*. As a result, I did not place great weight on the consistency of answers from the same participant. That is why I did not exclude responses to a given word when the other word of the same idiom was not paraphrased or was claimed to have no meaning. Also, I did not exclude non-matching responses from a given speaker to the two constituents of an idiom (*cleared* 'removed', *air* 'minds'). However, this technique caused difficulty in data interpretation, especially where one of the components was left without paraphrase.

2.2 Responses and their interpretation

'No meaning' responses indicate that the given idiom constituent is meaningless, but the rest of the responses do not necessarily mean that the speaker assigns some sense to the word in the idiom. Two major types of responses were interpreted as 'No meaning': holistic and literal paraphrases.

Many of the answers were holistic paraphrases of the whole expression, rather than that of a single word. Some examples are shown below. Meaning explanations given by different speakers are labeled by different letters, while the item to be explained is in bold (it was printed in normal type in the online version). The paraphrases are shown in single quotation marks, with the original spelling retained.

(1)   *He packed his car and hit the road for California.*
        hit   (a) ' "Hit the road for" means headed to'
                         (b) 'traveled'

(2)   *Mother and Father went out and told the children to hold the fort.*
        hold   'protect/look after/don't make a mess..of the house'

These holistic paraphrases may be interpreted in different ways. First, the respondent believes that the given idiom component has the given sense. In terms of decomposability, this option could mean that the idiom component has its own meaning, which is the same as the meaning of the whole expression. This is very unlikely. Second, it could also mean that the idiom is non-decomposable, because the meaning paraphrase is viewed as evidence that the expression has a holistic sense that cannot be broken down and the respondent – more or less unwittingly – identified this holistic sense. Third, the participant misinterpreted the task or wasn't paying attention and provided the meaning of the whole expression. Evidence that this was the case comes from answers that specifically included the whole expression in the meaning explanation, as in (1a) above. Misinterpretation of the task resulted in the speaker deliberately explaining the whole idiom, these responses were therefore ignored. Not all answers that contained the complete idiomatic phrase were discarded. For example, 'to "play the market" has singular meaning' was one of the paraphrases provided for *market*. This was included in the analysis, since it explained that the components have no individual meanings. The treatment of the holistic responses depends on which of the above assumptions the researcher has. I generally worked under the second assumption.

Despite the holistic meaning explanation, an idiom could still be viewed as analyzable if the paraphrase implies decomposition. In (2) above, 'of the house' is added to complete the meaning explanation, but it is clear that this addition is not meant to be part of the sense of the verbal component *hold*. Elsewhere it was more difficult to decide whether a holistic paraphrase was divisible into meaning chunks. Whenever in doubt, I also checked the response given by the same participant (more precisely, IP address, since there was no way the paraphrase could be traced back to the actual person) to the other component of the same idiom. If this response was unsupportive, the paraphrase was considered unanalyzable into meaning elements.

(3)   *The gang raised the roof with their singing.*
        raised   'created a ruckus'

(4)   *Al had a steady girlfriend, but John was playing the field.*
        playing   'investigating several potential options'

The meanings in both (3) and (4) are decomposable in principle ('create' + 'ruckus', 'investigating' + 'several potential options'). While the response to *roof* coming from the same speaker who provided the explanation in (3) read 'the permanent covering of a house or building', the meaning assigned to *field* by the respondent in (4) was 'several potential options'. The former gives the literal sense of *roof*, not a synonym of *ruckus*, 'created a ruckus' was therefore treated as holistic. In contrast, the meaning explanation in (4) was considered to be analyzable (*playing* 'investigating' + *field* 'range of options').

The use of a pronoun implies the semantic autonomy of the noun, because pronouns stand for meaningful noun phrases. Thus, when *buried* is explained as 'pretended that it did not exist', not only the verb *bury* but also the noun *hatchet* ("it") emerge as meaningful. When one of the constituents was left undefined by the same participant, I was usually cautious and decomposed only when the paraphrase was clearly decomposable. Interpreting open-ended answers is inevitably subjective and there is no way of knowing what the speaker had in mind.

Since the idioms are all verbal expressions, there is less temptation to treat an answer as holistic if it is nominal.

(5)   The *ball team gave Joe the sack because he never came to practice.*
        sack   (a) 'firing, losing the job'
                (b) 'dismissal'
                (c) 'dismissed Joe'

The paraphrases in (5) denote what happens to Joe, and could arguably be viewed as holistic, but only (c) was treated as such, because (a) is a noun and (b) is a nominal expression and they could correspond to the noun *sack*. One of the reasons for assigning the holistic-like nominal sense to the noun alone may be the transparency of the noun and the presence of a general verb such as *give* or *get*, whereas I was more reluctant to assign holistic-like nominal senses to opaque nouns, especially if the verb was semantically more specific. 'Chat' or 'small talk' as the senses of *fat* and 'small talk' or 'conversation' as paraphrases of *breeze* were considered holistic unless the corresponding paraphrase of the verb suggested otherwise, as in the case of *chew* 'spend time on' paired with *fat* 'light conversation'.

Similarly to holistic paraphrases, the interpretation of an idiom constituent in the literal sense may also be viewed as evidence that the given constituent has no independent (figurative) sense.

(6)   *The two men had been enemies a long time, but after the flood they buried the hatchet.*
        hatchet   'small axe-like tool with which enemies can hurt each other'

The sense of *hatchet* in (6) cannot be integrated into the idiomatic meaning, and the noun is therefore not considered meaningful. However, there may be a number of reasons why a speaker thinks a word has a literal reading. First, some words preserve their literal sense in the expressions (*perish the **thought**, swallow one's **pride**, **promise** the moon*). Second, the literal sense of a component may be very closely (metonymically, less often metaphorically) related to the idiom's usual interpretation: *button one's **lip**, eat one's **words**, pop the **question**, hit the **road**, paint the **town** red*. It is not unlikely that some speakers view the nouns in these highly transparent idioms as basically literal.[3] Nine participants out of 51 (17.6%) defined *words* with the single item 'words' and five more used it in their paraphrase. 18 out of 72 (25%) interpreted *road* as 'road' or 'highway/freeway' and eight more used these words together with items such as 'trip', 'path' or 'journey' in their response. Third, the context may allow a literal reading.

(7) Bob had spent all his money and got into debt, so now he must pay the fiddler.
 pay 'give money to someone in exchange for something received'

(8) The policeman lined his pockets by taking bribes.
 pockets (a) 'pockets'
 (b) 'pockets- where keep money' [*sic*]

Pay is usually figurative in the expression *pay the fiddler*, but the literal meaning fits the context of spending money and getting into debt (7). *Fiddler* is then mapped onto someone who gives credit. *Line one's pockets* can be interpreted metonymically as denoting the process of getting rich, but an alternative reading is possible in (8) by taking the noun in its literal sense and regarding the verb as a metaphor for the act of filling the pockets with money. Fourth, Conceptual Metaphor Theory claims that metaphor is a cognitive mapping between a usually abstract entity and a concrete, physical object referred to by the noun.

If this is so, the abstract process denoted by the verb may be felt to be a physical act. Thus, the verb may have its literal sense, rather than any other abstract non-literal senses, as in (9) and (10).

(9) If you break a window, do not pass the buck; admit that you did it.
 pass 'give to others, not keep (buck being blame)'

(10) Mary gave John the bounce after she saw him dating another girl.
 gave 'handed to, presented with (this isn't the metaphorical part)'

Finally, a speaker may interpret the expression in a peculiar, noncanonical sense (*cool one's heels*-**cool** 'get cold from waiting').

Many paraphrases of idiom components were consonant with the underlying metaphors, as discussed in Conceptual Metaphor Theory. Thus, *torch* was variously defined as 'romantic emotions' or 'love' and the fort is appropriately mapped onto the home in a context such as (2) above. But some of the responses seemed to be lexical substitutes that did not befit the conceptual mechanism motivating the idiom.

(11) The ball team gave Joe the sack because he never came to practice.
 sack 'pink-slip'

(12) The gang raised the roof with their singing.
 roof 'normal sound level'

(13) For a moment I actually believed that his wife had royal blood. Then I realized he was pulling my leg
 pulling 'disguising'
 leg 'the truth'

Pink-slip is a term that collocates with *give*; nevertheless, it substitutes *sack* rather than paraphrases it in (11). Similarly, *roof* is part of a metaphorical phrase based on metonymy in which the result (roof coming off) stands for the cause (making a lot of noise) in (12). Since *roof* is a physical boundary, it may be re-conceptualized as a psychological noise-boundary, a kind of threshold or level, though it is not, strictly speaking, the noise level itself. The components of *pull sb's leg* are unmotivated, yet one of the speakers provided the paraphrases in (13).

2.3 Results and discussion

Below is a statistical summary of the results. Each table includes idioms of the same type as classified by Gibbs and his co-researchers and shows what percentage of the speakers in my survey assigned no meaning to the verbal (V) or nominal (N) component. "Holistic" excludes responses that can be broken down. "Literal" means that the given constituent is understood in its literal sense instead of the idiomatic sense (if any). Where the idiomatic sense allows a literal interpretation of a constituent either in typical uses of the idiom (*promise* in *promise the moon*), or in the given context (*pay* 'give money to someone in exchange for something received' in *Bob had spent all his money and got into debt, so now he must pay the fiddler*) this sense is not included in the tables.

Table 1a. Percentage of responses showing lack of semantic autonomy

Normally decomposable	No meaning (%)		Holistic (%)		Literal (%)		Total (%)	
	V	N	V	N	V	N	V	N
button one's lip	3.8	4.8	13.5	1.6	0	0	**17.3**	**6.3**
clear the air	3.9	21.7	3.9	0	0	3.3	**7.8**	**25**
close the books	16.7	7.7	15.4	5.8	1.3	0	**33.3**	**13.5**
eat one's words	8.9	7.8	5.4	9.8	0	0	**14.3**	**17.6**
hit the jackpot	10.4	5.2	11.9	12.1	4.5	6.9	**26.9**	**24.1**
lose one's grip	19.7	5.9	11.3	2	2.8	2	**33.8**	**9.8**
miss the boat	10.2	10.7	10.2	0	4.1	1.8	**24.5**	**12.5**
open the door	11	7.9	45.1	7.9	0	3.2	**56**	**19**
perish the thought	11.8	10.2	8.2	5.1	0	0	**20**	**15.3**
play the market	5.7	12.8	1.9	2.6	0	0	**7.5**	**15.4**
pop the question	8.5	7.1	2.4	5.4	1.2	0	**12.2**	**12.5**
rack one's brains	8.4	8.9	18.1	10.7	0	0	**26.5**	**19.6**
swallow one's pride	1.6	7.8	3.3	5.9	0	0	**4.9**	**13.7**

Normally decomposable idioms are those whose components refer to some parts of the idiomatic meaning, and this relation between (the literal meaning of) the component and the idiomatic sense is relatively straightforward (Gibbs, Nayak, Bolton and Keppel 1989: 59). Therefore, the idioms in Table 1a are expected to have low percentage figures, as their components are assumed to be meaningful. As can be seen, most totals for verbs and nouns are relatively low.

Three of the components stand out: the verbs *close* (*close the books*), *lose* (*lose one's grip*) have slightly higher figures, while *open* (*open the door*) is much higher than the rest. *Close* was defined as 'stop selling' by several speakers and this paraphrase was regarded as holistic and nondecomposable when *books* was paraphrased as 'register' or 'sales records' or when it was not defined. This may have been too cautious an approach, and if these answers were treated as nonholistic (*close* 'stop' + *books* 'selling (tickets)'), the total percentage for *close* would drop to 25.6. A similar treatment of holistic responses to *lose* is not feasible.

Responses to *open* were difficult to classify. A number of paraphrases were treated as holistic, whenever *door* was not paraphrased. These include answers built on the pattern of verb of giving/creating + noun meaning 'opportunity/access' ('creates possibilites' [*sic*], 'allows access to', 'creates opportunities', 'gives opportunity', etc.) and responses such as 'allows' or 'makes available/possible'. But note that the absence of a paraphrase is not the same as a response of 'No meaning'. If we assigned 'creates/gives' to *open* (and 'opportunity/access' to *door*), the percentage of holistic responses would drop to 28.6 and the total to 39.6, and if 'allows' or 'makes available/possible' were viewed as the sense of *open* alone, then the holistic percentage would further sink to 15.4 and the total to 26.4. Combinations of 'make possible/available' (*open*) and 'opportunity' (*door*) can be found among the answers, but there is no evidence for 'allow' + 'opportunity', though pairs such as 'allows' + 'beginning, start' or 'allows' + 'way' or 'allows for' + 'opportunities' do occur.

Finally, it is interesting to note that there are speakers who find these idiom components meaningless, especially items such as *question*, *words*, *pride* or *thought*, which preserve their literal meanings.

Table 1b. Percentage of responses showing lack of semantic autonomy of V and N

Abnormally decomposable	No meaning (%)		Holistic (%)		Literal (%)		Total (%)	
	V	N	V	N	V	N	V	N
bury the hatchet	8.8	7.1	2.5	5.4	1.3	5.4	12.5	17.9
carry a torch	16.4	11.5	14.8	7.7	3.3	3.8	34.4	23.1
crack the whip	35.8	19	18.9	11.4	11.3	8.9	66	39.2
grease the wheels	7.8	15.9	23.5	4.3	7.8	2.9	39.2	23.2
hit the sack	17.3	8.3	3.8	1.4	0	0	21.2	9.7
hold the fort	9.1	13.3	3.4	1.7	1.1	1.7	13.6	16.7
lay an egg	44.7	52.8	10.5	8.3	5.3	5.6	60.5	66.7
line one's pockets	11.1	17.5	12.1	4.8	1	0	24.2	22.2
paint the town	50	18.8	12	8.3	12	0	70	27.1
pay the fiddler	14.9	20.8	12.8	2.1	0	6.3	27.7	29.2
pass the buck	9.6	17.7	15.4	5.1	1.9	1.3	26.9	24.1
promise the moon	10.2	5.2	0	0	0	1.3	10.2	6.5
pull the plug	25.5	17.4	11.8	8.7	5.9	2.9	43.1	29
push the panic button	46.2	14.3	11.5	28.6	11.5	12.2	69.2	55.1
spill the beans	8.6	16.7	1.7	0	0	0	10.3	16.7
steal sb's thunder	6.6	5.8	11.5	5.8	0	5.8	18	17.3
wear the pants	21.3	12.5	21.3	3.6	4.3	7.1	46.8	23.2

Abnormally decomposable idioms also have meaningful components, but their literal senses are less directly, more metaphorically related to the idiomatic sense than those of normally decomposable idioms (Gibbs et al. 1989a: 59). Some of the idioms in the above table are very similar to normally decomposable ones, judging by the statistics. The figures of *bury the hatchet, hit the sack, hold the fort, promise the moon, spill the beans* and *steal sb's thunder* fall within the same range as those of many normally decomposable idioms. In fact, these expressions contain fairly transparent metaphors, or straightforward literal senses (*promise*).

Note that the distinction between normally and abnormally decomposable idioms is assumed to reside in motivation, the transparency of the word's contribution, not the word's contribution *per se*. Thus the figures of abnormally decomposable idioms should not exhibit a marked difference from the percentages in Table 1a, since they are not directly related to opacity. The mean percentage for normally decomposable verbs is 21.9, the mean for nouns is 15.7. The means for abnormally decomposable verbs (34.9) and nouns (26.3) are slightly higher. The data collected is unsuitable for an analysis of speakers' views on the metaphoricity and transparency of components. Furthermore, normally decomposable idioms are frequently assumed to have only literally related components or at least one literal constituent (see Titone and Connine 1994: 256, Libben and Titone 2008: 1106, Tabossi et al. 2008: 315), but *lose one's grip, miss the boat, hit the jackpot* and *play the market* seem to have figurative components.

Table 1c. Percentage of responses showing lack of semantic autonomy of V and N

Nondecomposable	No meaning (%)		Holistic (%)		Literal (%)		Total (%)	
	V	N	V	N	V	N	V	N
chew the fat	15	26	38.3	24	3.3	4	**56.7**	**54**
face the music	6.6	1.9	5.3	0	1.3	1.9	**13.2**	**3.8**
get the eye	9.4	1.2	9.4	10.6	0	0	**18.9**	**11.8**
give the ax	38.9	22.5	11.1	18.8	0	2.5	**50**	**43.8**
give the bounce	41.3	15.7	15.9	27.5	3.2	0	**60.3**	**43.1**
give the sack	42.3	28.4	19.2	24.3	4.6	4.1	**66.2**	**56.8**
hit the road	5.7	20.8	39.6	5.6	1.9	0	**47.2**	**26.4**
hold one's peace	5.3	8.2	14	6.1	0	0	**19.3**	**14.3**
kick the bucket	57.1	54.5	32.7	12.7	2	3.6	**91.8**	**70.9**
make the scene	25.4	9.1	7.9	6.8	4.8	0	**38.1**	**15.9**
pack a punch	5.4	2	5.4	7.8	0	0	**10.7**	**9.8**
play the field	14.5	8.4	5.5	2.4	3.6	2.4	**23.6**	**13.3**
pull sb's leg	43.9	55.1	42.1	16.3	7	6.1	**93**	**77.6**
raise the roof	33.8	36.4	20	8.1	9.2	6.1	**63.1**	**50.5**
rock the boat	0	9.4	22.7	5.7	3	3.8	**25.8**	**18.9**
shed some light	10	6.9	32	13.8	6	0	**48**	**20.7**
shoot the breeze	39.2	46.6	43.1	31	3.9	6.9	**86.3**	**84.5**
speak one's mind	6.1	3.6	4.1	0	0	0	**10.2**	**3.6**

I expected high percentages in Table 1c, indicating that these components have no meanings. Yet, only some of the components can be considered meaningless (*kick* and *bucket*, *pull* and *leg*, *shoot* and *breeze*). Most other items carry various meanings. The figures for *face the music*, *get the eye*, *hold one's peace*, *pack a punch*, *play the field*, *rock the boat*, *speak one's mind* are particularly low, and these expressions should be reclassified as (normally or abnormally) decomposable. Percentages in the range of 40 to 60 can be interpreted as indicating native speakers' disagreement in treating the given word as devoid of meaning. It is noteworthy that a classic example of nondecomposable idiom – *chew the fat* – is meaningful for some speakers, *chew* denoting talking and *fat* referring to the content (topics, ideas, gossip, news).

Table 1d. Percentage of responses showing lack of semantic autonomy of V and N

?	No meaning (%)		Holistic (%)		Literal (%)		Total (%)	
	V	N	V	N	V	N	V	N
break the ice	15	10.3	8.3	1.1	1.7	1.1	25	12.6
cook sb's goose	24.5	29.5	0	9.1	0	0	24.5	38.6
cool one's heels	27.1	47.7	41.7	0	12.5	11.4	81.3	59.1
get the picture	4.9	1.9	0	7.4	1.2	1.9	6.2	11.1
hit the sauce	16	13	6	1.4	2	0	24	14.5

The idioms listed in Table 1d were put into contradictory categories in previous classifications. *Break the ice* is normally decomposable in Gibbs and Nayak (1989: 133) and Gibbs et al. (1989a: 67), while Gibbs et al. (1989b: 591) regard it as abnormally decomposable, but Hamblin and Gibbs (1999: 36) view it as nondecomposable. The figures in Table 1d show it to be decomposable. *Cook one's goose* is either abnormally decomposable (Gibbs and Nayak 1989: 133) or nondecomposable (Gibbs et al. 1989a: 67, Gibbs et al. 1989b: 592, Hamblin and Gibbs 1999: 36), the figures favor the former. *Cool one's heels* is classified as normally decomposable (Gibbs et al. 1989a. 67) or nondecomposable (Gibbs and Nayak 1989: 133, Gibbs et al. 1989b: 592), and the survey figures suggest nondecomposability, though speakers disagreed about the noun. *Get the picture* was judged as normally decomposable (Gibbs et al. 1989a. 67, Gibbs et al. 1989b: 591) and nondecomposable (Hamblin and Gibbs 1999: 36). *Hit the sauce* was also treated as normally decomposable (Gibbs and Nayak 1989: 133, Gibbs et al. 1989b: 591) and nondecomposable (Gibbs et al. 1989a. 67). Both idioms seem to be decomposable. Participants had no problem identifying *sauce* with alcohol and *picture* with understanding or idea.

The above discussion treated the verbs and nouns separately, although the literature focuses on the whole idiom. Therefore, I went through the answers and calculated the mean percentage for the entire idiomatic expression.

Table 2. Mean percentage of responses showing lack of semantic autonomy (V + N)

Idiom	Mean	Idiom	Mean
speak one's mind	6.9	lose one's grip	21.8
face the music	8.5	grease the wheels	22.1
get the picture	8.7	rock the boat	22.4
swallow one's pride	9.3	rack one's brains	23.1
pack a punch	10.3	close the books	23.4
play the market	11.5	hit the jackpot	25.5
button one's lip	11.8	make the scene	27.0
pop the question	12.4	paint the town	30.0
bury the hatchet	13.2	cook sb's goose	31.6
spill the beans	13.5	line one's pockets	31.8
get the eye	15.4	shed some light	34.4
eat one's words	16.0	wear the pants	35.0
clear the air	16.4	crack the whip	35.1
hold one's peace	16.8	lay an egg	36.5
promise the moon	17.2	hit the road	36.8
pass the buck	17.6	open the door	37.5
perish the thought	17.7	give the ax	46.9
steal sb's thunder	17.7	give the bounce	51.7
pay the fiddler	18.3	chew the fat	55.4
miss the boat	18.5	raise the roof	56.8
play the field	18.5	give the sack	61.5
break the ice	18.8	push the panic button	62.2
hold the fort	19.1	cool one's heels	70.2
hit the sauce	19.3	kick the bucket	81.4
pull the plug	20.0	pull sb's leg	85.3
carry a torch	21.3	shoot the breeze	85.4
hit the sack	21.5		

3. Idioms 2

3.1 Material and procedure

The survey reported above relied on speakers' own paraphrases. The purpose of the second survey was to see whether speakers can decompose idioms, when they have to choose from pre-formulated paraphrases. As in the first experiment, a number of respondents skipped some questions. A total of 27 (46.6%) out of 58 participants completed the whole survey. Unfortunately, the low number of responses detracts from the reliability of the statistics.

Thirty-four idioms of various patterns were tested in an online multiple choice task. Most idioms were taken from Langlotz (2006), these varied not only in their grammatical structure but also in their opacity (degree of motivation) and decomposability.

Motivated idioms were of two types. One in which the constituents taken independently were motivated (constituental motivation) and one in which the whole phrase was motivated but the independent components were not (global motivation).

Langlotz's (2006) list was expanded with idioms that contained cranberry items, words occurring only in the given expression, and idioms with one component keeping its literal interpretation. The complete list is shown below (18 V + NP idioms, 9 V + PP idioms, 2 Adj/N + N idioms, 4 PP idioms and 1 V + N + P idiom).

Table 3. The idiom list

Decomposable, global and constituental motivation	Decomposable, global but not constituental motivation
swallow the bitter pill	gain ground
make headway	rock the boat
weather the storm	miss the boat
jump on the bandwagon	upset the applecart
catch the wave	skate on thin ice
a dead end	the home stretch
	step into sb's shoes

Nondecomposable, global motivation	Nondecomposable, opaque
drop the ball	chew the fat
grease the wheels	bite the bullet
drag one's feet	come a cropper
prime the pump	bite the dust
not get to first base	go for broke
put down roots	with flying colors
	give up the ghost

One constituent cranberry	One constituent literal
out of kilter	know the score
in cahoots	talk shop
put the kibosh on	pay through the nose

Miscellaneous
cut to the bone
in cold blood

Most idioms had each of their (lexical) constituents tested separately, and some V + PP idioms had two or three of their components presented together as test items. As a result, a total of 96 questions comprised the survey. Each screen showed one question consisting of an example sentence taken from the *Cambridge Dictionary of American Idioms* or the *Corpus of Contemporary American English*, the idiom constituent(s) to be tested and a choice of four meaning paraphrases as response options in a drop-down menu, as in (14). Of the four responses, one was "No meaning", another paraphrased the literal sense of the test item and two provided figurative senses. One of the figurative senses was supposed to be unrelated to the idiomatic meaning, while the other was assumed to be related. Randomization of the order of the meaning options and questions was done manually.

(14) *A number of smaller city museums have really jumped on the bandwagon.*
  on the bandwagon   carried by the wagon
  asking for donation
  involved in the trend
  No meaning

I attempted to provide consistent paraphrases. Once a certain meaning option was used to paraphrase a word (*bandwagon* 'trend'), longer idioms chunks containing the same word also included this meaning option in their paraphrase (*on the bandwagon* 'involved in the trend'). The instructions were as follows:

> This study explores people's understanding of idiomatic expressions such as *kick the bucket*. Below you will find a number of sentences including idiomatic expressions. You have several tasks. First, please read the sentence and determine if you are familiar with the expression. If so, you will be asked to complete several other questions. If the expression is not familiar to you, indicate this by writing "Not familiar" in the comment box and go on to the next example.
>
> After determining that an idiom is familiar, you must now consider the separate parts of the expression. One component of the expression is listed below the example sentence. You have two tasks: first, judge whether the given component contributes to the expression's figurative meaning. For example, we can say that in the phrase *spill the beans* each component has a meaning that it contributes to the overall meaning of the idiom: *spill* means something like 'reveal' and *beans* means something like 'secret'. Note that we are not talking about replacing the words of the expression: *spill* cannot be replaced with *reveal*, since "reveal the beans" sounds odd and is not normally used. Despite this, *spill* expresses part of the meaning of the whole idiom.
>
> In other cases it is difficult to attach a figurative meaning to the parts of an idiom: *kick the bucket* means 'die', but neither *kick* nor *bucket* seem to carry meanings that they contribute to the meaning 'die'. If you think that the component has no meaning in the given example, choose "No meaning" from the drop-down menu. If you think that the given component has a meaning in the sentence, your second task is to choose from among the options offered in the drop-down menu.
>
> When the word listed in the drop-down menu can function as verb or noun, assume that it has the same part-of-speech category as the selected idiom component. Choose a meaning if you feel the given component can be said to have that meaning or a very similar meaning.

3.2 Results and discussion

Below is a tabular presentation of the most frequent responses. The first column shows the idiom, while the row below the heading uses part of speech labels to indicate which word in the idiom is paraphrased. In addition to the response, the percentage figure is shown together with the number of speakers selecting the given option. Where two or more idiom components comprised the test item, this is separately listed in the first column.

Table 3a. Overview of the most common responses

Decomposable, global and constituental motivation				
Idiom	Verb	Preposition	Adjective/Noun	Noun
swallow the bitter pill	accept 93.5% (29)		unpleasant 98.0% (49)	fact 76.9% (20)
make headway	achieve 94.4% (34)			progress 100.0% (30)
weather the storm	survive 100.0% (35)			difficult situation 100.0% (30)
jump on the bandwagon	No meaning 41.2% (14)	involved in 42.3% (11)		trend 100.0% (33)
jump on	become involved in 100.0% (30)			
on the bandwagon		involved in the trend 93.5% (29)		
catch the wave	exploit 83.3% (30)			opportunity 69.6% (16)
a dead end			not developing 85.3% (29)	situation 50.0% (15)

The expressions in Table 3a are well-motivated and parts of the meaning are assumed to be easily assignable to the components. For example, consistent with Conceptual Metaphor Theory, *swallow* is interpreted as 'accept'.

Low percentage figures (40 to 60) are a sign of disagreement among the participants. Although the majority did not treat *jump* as meaningful, several speakers interpreted it as 'spring' (32.4% (11)) or 'become' (26.5% (9)). The notion of disagreement, however, is tricky. A speaker may choose an option because it is believed to be an appropriate expression of the semantic content carried by the test item, or because it is the best paraphrase of all the versions offered, or simply because one option is supposed to be chosen. To give participants some leeway, I instructed them to choose a meaning paraphrase if "the given component can be said to have that meaning *or a very similar meaning*" [emphasis mine]. I also included a space for comments, and though it was originally meant for comments of familiarity, some participants used it to express their views on the appropriacy of certain paraphrases. *Jump*, for example, could best be defined as 'join' according to nine respondents. Interestingly, the strategies adopted by those nine speakers were different. Some did not select any of the meaning options, others chose 'become', 'spring' and 'No meaning'. Those who did not choose any option still believe that this idiom component is meaningful, although this is not

Idiom analyzability: an intuition-based study 157

reflected in the statistics.[5] This example raises the important issue of what is tested: decomposability or the appropriacy of the paraphrase? I believe it would be self-deception to claim that only decomposability is tested.

Note also that despite the majority 'No meaning' response to the word *jump*, the idiom chunk *jump on* did not cause any disagreement, as it was unanimously "defined". This suggests that in V + PP constructions the verb alone could be felt to be insufficient to convey a particular meaning. "Involved in" was the most popular choice for *on*, but it was closely followed by 'No meaning' (38.5% (10)), suggesting the insufficiency of the preposition alone as well, though to a lesser extent.

Another item with a low figure is *end* in *a dead end*. Although 'situation' is the most frequent response (and it is the one that was expected), 'final part of an object' (26.7% (8)) and 'No meaning' (23.3% (7)) were also selected. This is surprising in light of the transparency of the phrase.

Table 3b. Overview of the most common responses

Decomposable, global but not constituental motivation				
Idiom	Verb	Preposition	Adjective/Noun	Noun
gain ground	achieve 100.0% (30)			progress 96.3% (26)
rock the boat	upset 96.7% (29)			situation 91.2% (31)
miss the boat	fail to take advantage of 96.6% (28)			chance 91.4% (32)
upset the applecart	spoil 59.4% (19)			situation 96.4% (27)
skate on thin ice	act 64.3% (18)	No meaning 51.9% (14)	risky 94.3% (33)	situation 57.7% (15)
skate on	act 63.6% (21)			
thin ice			risky situation 98.1% (51)	
on thin ice		in a risky situation 100.0% (31)		
the home stretch			final 93.5% (29)	phase 77.6% (38)
step into sb's shoes	get 81.5% (22)	into 82.8% (24)		position 100.0% (27)
step into	get into 82.4% (28)			
into sb's shoes		into our position 100.0% (30)		

As predicted by the literature, the idioms in Table 3b are decomposable. Most responses confirmed my expectations. I will focus here on the low percentages again.

It seems that the verb alone expresses the same meaning as the verb and preposition together in *skate on thin ice*, rendering the preposition meaningless. Note, however, that the second most common choice for *on* was 'involved in' (33.3% (9)). What is remarkable is that *ice* 'situation' was selected only by a little more than half of the participants, and it was judged meaningless by several speakers ('No meaning' 34.6% (9)). The figures for *thin ice* and *on thin ice* suggest that *thin ice* is more easily mapped onto the target domain than *ice* alone.

Table 3c. Overview of the most common responses

Nondecomposable, global motivation				
Idiom	Verb	Preposition/ Particle	Adjective/Noun	Noun
drop the ball	miss 65.5% (19)			opportunity 78.1% (25)
grease the wheels	support 83.9% (26)			development 76.9% (20)
drag one's feet	delay 88.6% (31)			action 63.3% (19)
prime the pump	support 78.9% (15)			development 83.3% (25)
not get to first base	reach 96.9% (31)	as far as 83.3% (25)	initial 93.5% (29)	phase 85.0% (34)
get to	reach as far as 100.0% (27)			
first base			initial phase 100.0% (27)	
to first base		as far as the initial phase 100.0% (33)		
put down roots	establish 71.4% (20)	No meaning 85.2% (23)		relationships 84.0% (21)
put down	establish 97.1% (34)			
down roots		No meaning/ relationships 50.0% (15)		

All the idiom components in Table 3c were considered meaningful by the respondents, which is an unexpected finding, if these expressions are classified as nondecomposable. The results suggest that either the phrases are decomposable or semantic analysis is conducted in ways that are not predicted by the literature. Langlotz (2006) treats *put down roots*, *grease the wheels* and *prime the pump* as exhibiting latent isomorphism, i.e. decomposability that is masked by metonymy but often emerges in context. As can be seen, the majority of respondents assigned meanings to the components of these idioms in contexts such as (15)-(17), except *down*, which was judged to be meaningful in combination with the verb *put*.

(15)   Easy credit does grease the wheels of the American economy.

(16)   Even though they're trying to prime the pump with lower interest rates, it's our viewpoint it isn't going to do much to stimulate growth in our area.

(17)   He hasn't put down roots anywhere because he has trouble making new friends.

Not get to first base and *drop the ball* are likewise decomposable, though some suggested 'responsibility' as the sense of *ball* or selected the option 'let fall' for *miss* (24.1% (7)). However, it is not clear why *drag one's feet* is analyzed, since it does not seem to be so easily decomposable as the others. The association between *drag* and 'delay' is much stronger than that between *feet* and 'action'. What is also surprising is that half of the respondents regarded *down roots* as meaningful, even though it is not a syntactic constituent.

Table 3d. Overview of the most common responses

Nondecomposable, opaque				
Idiom	Verb	Preposition/ Particle	Adjective/Noun	Noun
chew the fat	chat 76.7% (23)			topic (of conversation) 75.8% (25)
bite the bullet	accept 89.7% (26)			unpleasant situation 71.8% (28)
come a cropper	No meaning 72.7% (16)			failure 58.8% (10)
bite the dust	cease 50.0% (15)			existence/No meaning 44.4% (12)
go for broke	commit 43.8% (14)	No meaning 53.1% (17)	total commitment 60.0% (18)	
go for	commit/risk 44.4% (12)			
for broke			total commitment 52.0% (13)	
with flying colors			great 70.0% (28)	success 63.3% (19)
give up the ghost	No meaning 52.0% (13)	No meaning 81.5% (22)		functioning 77.4% (24)

give up	relinquish 57.7% (15)	
up the ghost		No meaning 56.5% (13)

The data in Table 3d is even more surprising, given that these idioms are unmotivated. Though the percentage figures are not high, indicating native speaker disagreement, it is still confusing to see that the majority choice is not 'No meaning' in most cases. Furthermore, 'No meaning' is only the third most common response behind 'metal projectile' 17.9% (7) for *bullet*, 'risk' 34.4% (11) for *go* and 'everything' 16.7% (5) for *broke*. Despite the opacity of the underlying metaphor, participants tend to view the above constituents as conveying some meaning, though their confidence level is lower. Speakers seem to attach a sense to a component even in defiance of the mappings in the metaphor. Bullets are not thought to correspond to the situation, nor dust to existence, nor colors to success, yet speakers seem to make those connections. Do they remotivate the idiom?

There is some evidence that language users can find motivation. *Fat* is taken to refer to conversational topic, perhaps because another word related to the category of food (*meat*) also refers to information content, as a respondent commented: "also 'meat' as in 'content'." Additionally, chewing metonymically relates to mouth movement, itself standing metonymically for speaking; moreover, ideas, as well as the carriers of those ideas (words), are often conceptualized as food items.

Table 3e. Overview of the most common responses

Miscellaneous				
Idiom	Verb	Preposition /Particle	Adjective/Noun	Noun
cut to the bone	reduce 87.1% (27)	to 59.4% (19)		minimum 96.4% (27)
in cold blood		with 46.4% (13)	lacking 48.4% (15)	emotion 76.7% (23)
out of kilter		not in (a state) 72.7% (24)		good condition 85.7% (24)
in cahoots		involved in 64.5% (20)		partnership 96.3% (26)
put the kibosh on	put 75.0% (18)			end, stop 96.6% (28)
know the score	be aware of 100.0% (36)			facts 93.1% (27)
talk shop	chat 93.3% (28)			trade, profession 91.7% (33)
pay through the nose	give money 98.3% (57)	too much 96.7% (29)		

What the expressions in Table 3e show is that participants can identify words that keep their literal senses and regard even cranberry words as meaningful. The words *kilter*, *cahoots* and *kibosh* occur only in the given expressions. Speakers were least confident when they had to decide on prepositions.

4. Conclusion

The statistics in these experiments are based on a subjective interpretation of the data and should be viewed as merely indicative. Nevertheless, a number of interesting points have emerged. The overall results confirm the view that speakers regard many idiom constituents as meaningful items, not as empty words. There is a stronger tendency to assign meaning to idiom components that are presumed to be meaningless than to assign no meaning to what are regarded as semantically autonomous constituents in the literature. Words – whether as components of idioms or not – are meaningful. Most paraphrases are consistent with underlying metaphorical conceptualizations, but speakers also assign meanings that seem to be substituting words and phrases independently of the metaphors. If this is proved to be true, decomposition may rely not only on the underlying image, but on the paraphrase as well. Meaning assignment can also take place in opaque idioms, though there is more disagreement among language users. Vega Moreno (2007: 148) notes that "[t]he set of beliefs that people take to license idiom meaning need not be that which motivated the meaning of the idiom back in history but just a set of assumptions which helps them to make (synchronic) sense of its current meaning". There is some evidence supporting this view. Although *kick the bucket* is unmotivated, one of the respondents said "*bucket* may be the container of life". The role of analyzability in the syntactic variability and psycholinguistic processing of idioms and the extent of native speaker agreement on the degree of analyzability are still under debate (Libben and Titone 2008: 1104, Tabossi et al 2008: 319). Native speaker agreement was not measured rigorously, but of the 96 idioms parts examined in the second experiment native speakers disagreed about 20.8% (20 of them), if disagreement is equated with 40-60 percent of speakers selecting the same meaning option.

5. Notes

1 This study was funded by a Fulbright Research Grant (Grant Number 1207202), which was administered by the Bureau of Educational and Cultural Affairs, U.S. Department of State (ECA) with the cooperation of the Hungarian-American Commission for Educational Exchange (Fulbright Commission) in Hungary and the Council for International Exchange of Scholars (CIES) in the United States.
2 One participant sent the answers in a Word document, and these responses were input into the online survey manually.
3 Since idioms are complex linguistic units, with the literal and figurative senses activated to various degrees, partially depending on context, the figurative and literal senses of words co-exist. Though the literal sense is usually backgrounded, it may be activated to such an extent that speakers assign the literal rather than the non-literal meaning to a given constituent, especially if the two are metonymically related.
4 Three respondents who commented that 'join' is a good paraphrase left the question unanswered. If we added them to the group of 'become', 'No meaning' would still be the most

popular. If we added them to the group of 'spring', 'No meaning' and 'spring' would have equal numbers (and percentages) of supporters.

6. Abbreviation

ODI Siefring, Judith. (ed.) 2005 (2nd edition). *The Oxford Dictionary of Idioms*. Oxford: Oxford University Press.

7. References

CUTTING, J.C; & BOCK, K. 1997 "That's the way the cookie bounces: Syntactic and semantic components of experimentally elicited idiom blends". *Memory and Cognition* 25/1: 57-71.

DAVIES, M. 2008– *The Corpus of Contemporary American English (COCA): 410+ million words, 1990-present*. http://www.americancorpus.org.

DOBROVOL'SKIJ, D. 2007 "Cognitive approaches to idiom analysis". In: Burger, H.; Dobrovol'skij, D.; Kühn P. & Norrick. N. R. (eds.) *Phraseologie/Phraseology. 2. Halbband/Volume 2*. Berlin / New York: Walter de Gruyter: 789-818.

FINLEY, R. 1999–2010 *SurveyMonkey.com*. Portland, Oregon USA. http://www.surveymonkey.com/.

GIBBS, R. W. Jr. & N.P. NAYAK. 1989. "Psycholinguistic studies on the syntactic behavior of idioms". *Cognitive Psychology* 21/1: 100-138.

GIBBS, R. W. Jr.; NAYAK N. P.; BOLTON J. L. & KEPPEL M. E. 1989 "Speakers' assumptions about the lexical flexibility of idioms". *Memory and Cognition* 17/1: 58-68.

GIBBS, R. W. Jr.; NAYAK,N. P. & CUTTING, C.. 1989 "How to kick the bucket and not decompose: analyzability and idiom processing". *Journal of Memory and Language* 28/5: 576-593.

HAMBLIN, J. L. & GIBBS, R. W. Jr. 1999 "Why you can't kick the bucket as you slowly die: verbs in idiom comprehension". *Journal of Psycholinguistic Research* 28/1: 25-39.

HEACOCK, P. (ed.) 2003 *Cambridge Dictionary of American Idioms*. Cambridge and New York: Cambridge University Press.

LANGLOTZ, A. 2006. *Idiomatic creativity: A cognitive-linguistic model of idiom-representation and idiom-variation in English. Appendix E: Analysis of lexicogrammatical variants of SPF-idioms*. http://www.idiomatic-creativity.ch/.

MAKKAI, A.; BOATNER M.T.; & GATES, J.E. 2004 *A Dictionary of American Idioms*. Hauppage: Barron's. http://www.sky-net-eye.com/eng/english/idioms/american.

NUNBERG, G D. 1978. *The Pragmatics of Reference*. Bloomington: Indiana University Linguistics Club.

TABOSSI, P.; FANARI, R. & WOLF K. 2008 "Processing idiomatic expressions: effects of semantic compositionality". *Journal of Experimental Psychology: Learning, Memory, and Cognition* 34/2: 313-327.

VEGA MORENO, R. E. 2007 *Creativity and Convention: The Pragmatics of Everyday Figurative Speech*. Amsterdam / Philadelphia: John Benjamins.

FUNCTIONAL DIFFERENTIATION BETWEEN HESITATION FILLERS: THE CASE OF *YOU KNOW WHAT* AND *LET'S SAY*

Ai Inoue
National Defense Academy (Yokosuka, Japan)

Abstract: This study focuses on the functional differentiation between hesitation fillers particularly the usages of *you know what* and *let's say* in present-day spoken English. Inoue (2007) presents the multifunction and polysemy of frequently used phraseological units (*you know what*, *here we go/here we go again*, and *let's say*) in line with different contexts. According to her work, *you know what* and *let's say* serve the same function of hesitation fillers although the actual words that constitute these phraseological units are completely different. Through the syntactic and lexical characteristics of *you know what* and *let's say* functioning as hesitation fillers, the lexical meanings of each component of these phraseological units seem to have been retained, which means that the core function of *you know what* and *let's say* survive. In addition, *you know what* and *let's say* do not function as synonymous hesitation fillers.

Key words: *hesitation fillers, lexical meaning, semantic weakened*

1. Introduction

It is widely known that hesitation fillers such as *er*, *see*, and *let me see* are one of the characteristics of spoken English (see Leech and Svartvik 2002:11). Research on hesitation fillers has been carried out mainly from the viewpoint of discourse markers; such research merely examines the types of hesitation fillers that are used. Unfortunately, very little research has been done on pursuing the essential quality of a hesitation filler.

I have been conducting research on the polysemous and multifunction of phraseological units frequently used in spoken English to help improve the English proficiency of non-native speakers of English, and the descriptions of phraseological units in dictionaries. As one of my works, I studied the multifunction and polysemy of *you know what* and *let's say* in 2007. On the basis of the observations obtained from Inoue (2007), *you know what* has seven distinctive functions(opener, topic changer, emphasizer, the mixture of topic changer and emphasize, information supplier, substitute, and hesitation filler) and *let's say* has four distinguishable functions(to give an example, to introduce metaphors, to offer a revision of a former utterance, and hesitation filler). Each function of *you know what* and *let's say* is closely related to each syntactic and phonetic characteristic (Please see Inoue 2007:148, 194). Also, the function of *you know what* and *let's say* overlap in a hesitation filler even though the component words of each phraseological unit are different (it is positioned in the middle of the sentences, its tone is level-pitch, and *well* is occasionally observed as a typically co-occurring word).

Inoue (2007) is also devoted to the expansion of their core functions to their extended functions. In the case of *you know what*, it comprises the result of the ellipsis of the proposition. Further, given the syntactic feature of *you know what*, we can say that the missing proposition is the message the speaker wants to convey. In other words, its core function is intensification; by omitting the proposition, *you know what* gives suspense to the listener and gives a strong, intensified sense of anticipation to the hearer. The expansion from the core function of *you know what* to its extended functions may be ordered as is shown in (1)

(1) emphasizer → mixture of the topic changer and emphasizer → opener, topic changer, → information supplier → hesitation filler [Inoue 2007:149]

(1) yields the following observations. The growth into the peripheral function of *you know what* is due to the degree of intensification. In addition, as the outlying function develops, the lexical or literal meaning of *you know what* suffers the semantic process of bleaching and the degree of intensification weakens (*ibid.*).

In the case of *let's say*, (2) shows the semantic development of *let's say* taking the syntactic feature of *let's say* into consideration (See Inoue 2007:208f for details).

(2) to introduce metaphor → to give an example → to offer a revision of the former utterance → hesitation filler [Inoue 2007:208]

Similar to the semantic expansion of *you know what* in (1), the expansion into the peripheral function of *let's say* is attributable to the degree of the introducing metaphor. Further, the lexical or literal meaning of *let's say* seems to have been weakened as its function is growing into the peripheral one.

This study clarifies the behaviour of *you know what* and *let's say* as hesitation fillers particularly focusing on the following research questions. (a) Do the function of *you know what* and *let's say* remain exactly the same when they are used as hesitation fillers?, (b) Does the lexical meaning of each component of *you know what* and *let's say* seem to have been lost or weakened as Inoue (2007:150, 208) mentions?

2. What is a hesitation filler?

Leech and Svartvik (2002:11) refer to hesitation fillers as voice-filled pauses and describe them as one of the features of genuine spoken English's features.

Quirk *et al.*(1985:1474) explain hesitation fillers as follows: 'Informal conversation is characterized by an overtly uncompleted pairing, especially through unfinished *but*-coordinations. These often occur where one speaker is effectively inviting another participant to speak. It can give a pleasantly apologetic and self-effacing tone'.

Inoue (2007:150, 208) mentions that 'a hesitation filler just works in order to fill the pause and does not convey any meaning'.

3. Data used in the research

The data used in this research is the "Larry King Live" Corpus (henceforth the "LKL" corpus)[1]. The number of words as of August 2009 that I used in this research is about 30,000,000 running words.

---

[1] "LKL" corpus consists of the downloaded transcripts of "Larry King Live" and "Larry King Weekend" on CNN since 1994.

4. Behaviour of *you know what* and *let's say* as hesitation fillers

4.1 (a) Do the functions of *you know what* and *let's say* remain exactly the same when they are used as hesitation fillers?

4.1.1 *you know what*

Please observe the following examples (underlined by the author).

(3) KING: You like working with her?
FORD: She's delightful.
KING: She's a princess.
FORD: She is **so** -- you know what, she is **so** sweet and **so** nice, I think viewers just love Connie... [Oct., 1999]

(4) KING: Have you ever been asked to do something that you had to say no because of your faith?
M.OSMOND: Sure. I've been offered a lot of money to do things.
KING: Like what?
D.OSMOND: Tell us. I'd like to know that.
M.OSMOND: It's **just** - you know what, what's the point? You know, I think a little mystery is a beautiful thing. [Aug., 1999]

(5) KING: Are you scared?
WILLIAMS: ... and I'm not a weak person. I'm just ill right now, and I'm going to get through it and I am going show some of those other victims and sufferers of this disease that - you know what? - I know your pain, I **really** do. God knows, I know your pain.... [Aug., 1998]

(6) KING: Are you saying you were not impressed?
GREENFIELD: Well, I - you know what? I...
KING: Was it a major apology to you?
GREENFIELD: What it was was the most unusual and difficult speech any public figure has ever had to give.... [Aug., 1998]

Admittedly, all the examples above contain the syntactic and phonetic characteristic of hesitation fillers as have been mentioned in Inoue (2007). Furthermore, (3), (4) and, (5) serve to illustrate that the words in bold type implying intensification, such as *so*, *just*, and *really*, are observed in the passages near *you know what* when *you know what* functions as a hesitation filler. It can be easily imagined from the above that the core function of *you know what*, i.e., emphasis, seems to have survived. In other words, in (3), (4), and (5), *you know what* functions as both a hesitation filler and an emphasizer. However, in (6), *you know what* is used differently. *You know what* mainly works as a hesitation filler since markers showing intensification are not observable in the passages around *you know what*. Hence, the lexical meaning of each component of *you know what* seems to have been weakened.

In summary, *you know what* has two functions: to fill a pause and to emphasize what a speaker is going to say next in case it is used as a hesitation filler. It is rare to find *you know what* merely just filling a pause in the "LKL" Corpus. This means that the two functions are not clearly separate but gradually evolve when *you know what* serves as a hesitation filler.

4.1.2 *let's say*

Let us observe the following examples:

(7) KING: And do you have any thoughts on the Democratic vice president?
G. BUSH: No.
KING: None at all. No person you're particularly worried about or...
G. BUSH: No, sir.
KING: And the announcement **will** be made - **probably, well,** let's say - we can expect to get - what will be the setting of the vice presidential announcement? Will it be in his or her place? [Jul.,2000]

(8) KUCINICH: ...And furthermore, as the debate continues, I think that more and more Americans are going to want to know who will deliver not-for-profit health care, who will deliver jobs for all because, let's face it - let's say, Larry - let's go right to the debates in 2004. **If** the Democratic nominee standing next to George Bush said there were weapons of mass destruction, voted for the war, supports a continuation of the occupation, doesn't have a plan to get out and is for sending another 40,000 troops... [Feb., 2004]

(9) KING: All right. Alan Dershowitz, what does his reputation mean to - let's say - just you as a citizen?
DERSHOWITZ: Well, it's - I think it again raises some doubts, but probably it won't be admissible as evidence. Profiling is not science.... [Aug., 1998]

(10) KING: Was it difficult to not be what you had become known as?
THE ARTIST: You mean...
KING: I think - **well,** let's say - the only other famous person I know who did this was Cassius Clay.... [Dec.,1999]

As a syntactic feature of *let's say* as hesitation fillers, we find that words implying metaphors, such as *will, probably, if, hypothetical,* and *hypothetically,* are found in the contexts around *let's say.* As with *you know what,* the core function of *let's say,* i.e., to introduce a metaphor, and its function of filling a pause seem to have been retained in (7) and (8). In (9) and (10), *let's say* has the same syntactic feature as mentioned in Inoue (2007); as such, the core function of *let's say* seems to have been weakened, and it merely fills a pause.

It is thus clear that like *you know what, let's say* has two functions: introduction a metaphor (core function) and acting as a hesitation filler. As stated earlier, the two functions gradually evolve and are not clearly separate.

It is probably safe to mention that *you know what* and *let's say* behave differently when they function as hesitation fillers; the evidence for this lies in the syntactic features of each phraseological unit mentioned above. I submitted the following questionnaire to native speakers of English (two Canadians, four Americans, and one English) to confirm that this proposal pertaining to *you know what* and *let's say* as hesitation fillers can be supported.

(11) Could you read the following contexts and fill either *you know what* or *let's say* in the following blanks?
    a. A: You like working with her?
       B: She's delightful.

A: She's a princess.
B: She is so - (   ), she is so sweet and so nice, I think viewers just love Connie.

b. A: Have you ever been asked to do something that you had to say no because of your faith?
B: Sure. I've been offered a lot of money to do things.
A: Like what?
B: Tell us. I'd like to know that.
A: It's just - (   ), what's the point? You know, I think a little mystery is a beautiful thing.

c. A: And do you have any thoughts on the Democratic vice president?
B: No.
A: None at all. No person you're particularly worried about or...
B: No, sir.
A: And the announcement will be made - probably, well, (   ) - we can expect to get - what will be the setting of the vice presidential announcement? Will it be in his or her place?

d. A: And furthermore, as the debate continues, I think that more and more Americans are going to want to know who will deliver not-for-profit health care, who will deliver jobs for all because, let's face it - (   ), Larry - let's go right to the debates in 2004. If the Democratic nominee standing next to George Bush said there were weapons of mass destruction, voted for the war, supports a continuation of the occupation,....

e. A: Are you saying you were not impressed?
B: Well, I - (   ) I...
A: Was it a major apology to you?
B: What it was was the most unusual and difficult speech any public figure has ever had to give, and I don't - and - by the way, I think to judge this on a scale of, you know, rhetoric 8, cosmetology 6,....

f. A: All right. Alan Dershowitz, what does his reputation mean to - (   ) - just you as a citizen?
B: Well, it's - I think it again raises some doubts, but probably it won't be admissible as evidence. Profiling is not science.

(12) Table 1; Result of the informant elicitations done in (11)

	you know what	*let's say*	others	sum
(11a)	3	4	you know(1)	7
(11b)	5	2	you know(1)	7
(11c)	2	5		7
(11d)	3	3	you know(1), neither (1)	7
(11e)	3	4		7
(11f)	2	5	you know(1)	7

The answers in the "LKL" transcripts are given by the coloured columns in Table 1. There are five things worth noting in this table. Firstly, except for (11a), the results obtained are considerably supported. Secondly, *let's say* is preferably used even though intensifiers such as *so* are observed in the case of (11a). The reason why the informants chose *let's say* instead of *you know what* is that the speakers merely wanted to fill the pause without emphasizing what they were going to say next as there was a pause after the utterance *she is so -*. Thirdly, (11d) is an example where words typically co-occurring with *you know what* and *let's say* are not observed. In this case, when no markers were found, the informants found it difficult to judge as to which of the phraseological units was appropriate. Fourthly, four informants chose *let's say* in the case of (11e) which was unlike in the transcript. This is because *well*, a word typically co-occurring with *let's say,* is observed here. Lastly, *let's say* was chosen more often than *you know what* in all examples. This leads to the assumption that *let's say* has a higher probability of serving as a hesitation filler than *you know what*.

4.2 (b) Does the lexical meaning of each component seems to have been lost or weakened?

As mentioned in the previous section, the lexical meaning of each component of *you know what* and *let's say* does not always seem to have been lost even when *you know what* and *let's say* function as hesitation fillers. Consequently, I shall be proposing a further modification to Inoue (2007:150, 208)'s remarks (a hesitation filler merely fills the pause and does not convey any meaning) as follows: a hesitation filler not only fills the pause but also conveys the meaning of the core function of each phraseological unit.

4.3 Other findings concerning *you know what* and *let's say* in the "LKL" Corpus

In addition to the features of *you know what* and *let's say* revealed from the data in the "LKL" Corpus, the following interesting findings were made.
When I counted how many times each phraseological unit is repeatedly used in the corpus, the number of functions of *you know what* is much larger than that of *let's say*. However, as for the percentage of each phraseological unit working as a hesitation filler, the figure for *let's say* (about 0.9%) almost doubles that of *you know what* (about 0.5%). Given this observation, I can raise the following two queries. (c) Why is *let's say* used as a hesitation filler more often than *you know what*? (d) Are there any features whose presence allows some phraseological units to be more easily used as hesitation fillers than others?

4.3.1 (c) Why is *let's say* used as a hesitation filler more often than *you know what*?

It seems very difficult to accept that *you know what* is less used as a hesitation filler even though the functions of *you know what* are more numerous. On the other hand, it is easier to assume that *let's say* is used as a hesitation filler since it has a function – to give an example – that is semantically close to a hesitation filler.
From this point, it follows that the distance between the core function of each phraseological unit and the most peripherally located hesitation filler significantly affects the ease of occurrence of hesitation fillers. In other words, the greater the distance between the core function of each phraseological unit and a hesitation filler, the lesser the probability of the occurrence of the hesitation filler. Please look at (13) and (14).

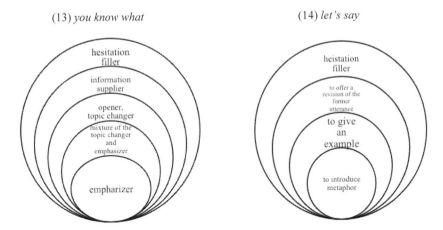

Comparing the distance between the core function and hesitation fillers in (13) and (14), I find that the distance is much less in (14). Consequently, it is safe to mention that *let's say* works as a hesitation filler much more often than *you know what*.

4.3.2 (d) Are there any features whose presence allows some phraseological units to be more easily used as hesitation fillers than others?

As mentioned above, the distance between the core function of a phraseological unit and a hesitation filler has heavy influence on the phraseological units' inclination to be hesitation fillers.

5. Concluding remarks

On the basis of the syntactic observations of *you know what* and *let's say*, I can conclude that hesitation fillers still have the core function of a phraseological unit and that *you know what* and *let's say* behave differently even though they have the same function as hesitation fillers. Hence, I need to correct the explanation for hesitation fillers given in Inoue (2007) and to make the suggestion that the lexical meaning of each component of the phraseological units does not seem to have been lost. This interpretation is also supported by the results of the informant elicitations. This research also mentioned that the probability of the occurrence of a hesitation filler mainly depends on the distance between the core function of each phraseological unit and a hesitation filler.

Acknowledgement

This research is supported by a Grant-in-Aid for Scientific Research(B) (20320089) (KAKENHI). I appreciate the support provided by the Japan Society for the Promotion of Science, the Ministry of Education, Culture, Sports, Science and Technology.

6. References

INOUE, A. 2007 *Present-day Spoken English: A Phraseological Approach*. Tokyo: Kaitakusha.
LEECH, G. & SVARTVIK, J. 2002 *A Communicative Grammar of English*, 3rd edition. London: Longman.
QUIRK, R., S. GREENBAUM, G. LEECH & SVARTVIK, J. 1985 *A Comprehensive Grammar of the English Language*. London: Longman.

SATZWERTIGE UND SATZÜBERGREIFENDE PHRASEOLOGISMEN IN TEXTEN DER UNGARNDEUTSCHEN GEGENWARTSLITERATUR

Krisztina Geröly
Pécs, Ungarn

Abstract: The main purpose of this paper is to analyse sentence-worthed and sentence-overlapping (text-worthed) phraseologisms in the prose of German minority authors in the 80's and 90's of the 20th century from an intercultural aspect: There were 374 sentence-worthed and sentence-overlappinng phraseological items in the analyzed texts. *These phraseological items can be divided in two categories: phraseological transference and interference.* These phraseologisms have a cultur-specified component, which does not have any equivalent in other languages. The analyzed items mainly have a pragmatical function: they express the attitude of characters in the novels to the contents of the texts.

Key words: Sentence-worthed phraseologisms, sentence-overlapping phraseologisms, culture-specified components, phraseological transferences and interferences.

1. Einleitung: Forschungsprämisse, –ziele und –methoden

Als Ausgangspunkt des vorliegenden Beitrags diente eine eigene Untersuchung, die an Phraseologismen von Texten der ungarndeutschen Gegenwartsliteratur unter kontaktlinguistischem Aspekt durchgeführt wurde (Geröly 2009: 89ff.). In diesem Projekt wurden sämtliche Typen von Phraseologismen in ungarndeutschen Texten einbezogen: sowohl satzgliedwertige als auch satzwertige. Bei der Forschung (Geröly 2009: 89ff.) kam ich zum Ergebnis, dass auch satzübergreifende sowie textwertige sprachliche Einheiten als Phraseologismen betrachtet werden können. Deshalb habe ich eine zweite Untersuchung durchgeführt, in die lediglich satzwertige und satzübergreifende phraseologische Einheiten einbezogen wurden. Diese Untersuchung hat sich zum Ziel gesetzt, die Erscheinungsformen und Rolle von den vorher erwähnten Phraseologismen in Texten der ungarndeutschen Gegenwartsliteratur, diese sprachlichen Konstruktionen nach ihrer Kulturspezifik sowie territorialen Verbreitung zu gruppieren.

Als Korpusgrundlage zur Untersuchung dienten Texte ungarndeutscher Autoren der 80-er und 90-er Jahre des 20. Jh.-s. Korpus: 281 satzwertige und satzübergreifende phraseologische Einheiten: davon insgesamt 8 satzübergreifende.

Die Forschung machte eine empirische Untersuchung erforderlich, in der die einzelnen Kontaktphänomene in EDV gespeichert wurden. In dieser Forschung wurde mit einer synchronisch–vergleichenden Methode gearbeitet. Um den Ursprung der Kontaktphänomene möglichst genau festzustellen, brauchte man inter– bzw. intralinguale Untersuchungen durchzuführen. Als Kontrolle wurden in die Untersuchung deutsche und österreichische Kontaktpersonen als Gewährspersonen von unterschiedlichem Alter, Geschlecht und Schulung einbezogen.

2. Phraseologismen-Bestimmungen

Die Meinungen gehen daran auseinander, welche sprachlichen Einheiten als Phraseologismen aufgefasst werden können, wo die Grenze eines Phraseologismus liegt. Es gibt Linguisten, nach denen Phraseologismen als feste Wortgruppen unterhalb der Satzebene definiert werden können (Földes 1996: 14).
Burger/ Buhofer/ Sialm (1982: 1)/ Dobrovol'skij/ Piirainen (1996, 2002) unterscheiden Phraseologismen im engeren und im weiteren Sinne. Unter Phraseolgismen im engeren Sinne werden nicht satzwertige Wortgruppen mit unterschiedlicher syntaktischer Struktur und mehr oder weniger ausgeprägter Umdeutung der Komponenten verstanden.
Phraseologismen im weiteren Sinne können durch folgende Eigenschaften charakterisiert werden: Festgeprägtheit (Stabilität), Satzwertigkeit, teilweise Idiomatizität. Zu dieser Gruppe gehören satzwertige Ausdrücke u.a. Sprichwörter und Antisprichwörter, Sagwörter, Lehnsprichwörter, geflügelte Worte.

Burger (2003: 37) klassifiziert Phraseologismen aufgrund ihrer Struktur folgendermaßen:

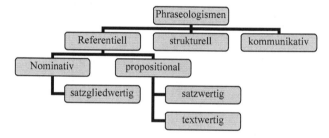

Nach seiner Aufteilung gehören auch propositionale Einheiten zu Phraseologismen: Darunter versteht er einerseits satzwertige andererseits textwertige phraseologische Einheiten.
  Phraseologische Einheiten, die das Kriterium der Idiomatizität erfüllen, sind feste Phrasen und topische Formeln (Sprichwörter und Gemeinplätze). Nach Kühn (2009: 78) können satzwertige und nichtsatzwertige Phraseologismen als vorgeprägte Ausdrücke in ihrer pragmatischen Perspektive definiert werden. Nach Pilz (2009: 117ff.) gehören Sprichwörter und Gemeinformeln zu satzwertigen Phraseologismen. Bukovĉan (2009: 71ff.) betont den semantischen Mehrwert von Phraseologismen. Wie Mieder (2006) feststellt, können satzwertige und satzübergreifende sprachliche Einheiten wie z.B. Aforismen, geflügelte Worte auch als Phraseologismen eingestuft werden: sie werden propositionale Phraseologismen genannt. Nach meiner Klassifizierung gehören propositionale (sowohl satzwertige als auch textwertige) Ausdrücke zu Phraseologismen, da diese Strukturen die Hauptmerkmale der Phraseologismen (Stabilität und Idiomatizität) erfüllen.

3. Phraseologismen in den ungarndeutschen Texten

Nach Földes (1997: 159) können Texte der ungarndeutschen Gegenwartsprosa durch „verschiedene Manifestationen von Mehrsprachigkeit und Sprachenkontakten" charakterisiert werden. Er kommt zum Ergebnis, dass diese Texte weniger Phraseologismen enthalten als binnendeutsche Texte von gleicher Art. Im vorliegenden Beitrag wird darauf eine Antwort gesucht, in wie weit die zitierte Feststellung von Földes für die im vorliegenden Beitrag analysierten Phraseologismen gilt.

4. Zur Terminologie: Phraseologische Transferenzen und Interferenzen

In der Sprachkontaktforschung bzw. der Zwei- und Mehrspachigkeit–Forschung unterscheidet man Interferenzen und Transferenzen in allen sprachlichen Ebenen. Manche Linguisten verwenden diese Termini als synonym. Im vorliegenden Aufsatz werden diese zwei Termini im unterschiedlichen Sinne gebraucht. Unter phraseologischer Transferenz wird verstanden, wenn ein Phraseologismus oder eine phraseologische Komponente aus dem Ungarischen oder aus einer ungarndeutschen Mundart in die analysierten Texte übernommen (transferiert) wird, während im Falle der phraseologischen Interferenz ein Phraseologismus nach dem Vorbild des Ungarischen oder einer ungarndeutschen Mundart gebildet wird.

5. Satzwertige Phraseologismen im Untersuchungskorpus: Sprichwörter und Gemeinplätze

Die in den analysierten Texten vorhandenen Sprichwörter und Gemeinplätze haben in allen ungarndeutschen sowie in standarddeutschen Sprachvarietäten eine Äquivalente.
Diese Gruppe von Phraseologismen drücken allgemeine Wahrheit aus und erreicht ihre Effektivität durch Wiederholung und Austausch der phraseologischen Komponenten.
Die in den analysierten Texten vorhandenen Sprichwörter und Gemeinplätze haben in allen ungarndeutschen sowie in standarddeutschen Sprachvarietäten eine Äquivalente.
Diese Gruppe von Phraseologismen drücken allgemeine Wahrheit aus und erreicht ihre Effektivität durch Wiederholung und Austausch der phraseologischen Komponenten.
(1) "Da heißt es irgendwo, daß *aus den Ersten die Letzten und aus den Letzen die Ersten werden.*" (Rittinger: Heut wär ich ein Herr von ..., In: Verschiedene Verhältnisse, S. 178).
Im angeführten Beleg geht es um eine phraseologische Interferenz aus dem Ungarischen in die ungarndeutschen Texte. Darunter verstehe ich, dass ein Phraseologismus in den Texten nach dem Beipiel eines ungarischen Phraseologismus mit derselben Bedeutung gebildet wird.
Bukovčan (2009: 78) betont die pragmatische Fuktion von satzwertigen und satzübergreifenden Phraseologismen: Diese sprachlichen Einheiten verfügen über eine semantische Mehrwert. Sie sind feste Satzkonstruktionen mit lehrhafter Tendenz und werden als eigene Mikrotexte zitiert (Fleischer 1982: 83). Diese Strukturen sind stark von volkskundlichen und kulturgeschichtlichen beherrscht. Man kennt ihre konkrete Herkunft.
Eine wichtige Rolle dieser phraseologischen Einheiten besteht darin, Gefühle, Einstellungen auszudrücken, sie haben eine pragmatische Rolle. In den analysierten Texten kommen in diesen Phraseologismen Gefühle der Figuren der ungarndeutschen Erzählungen zum Ausdruck, wie in folgenden Belegen:
a, Die Erleichterung der Figur der Novelle wird im folgenden Phraseologismus zum Ausdruck gebracht:
(2) "Der Liesl *war ein großer Stein vom Herzen gefallen.*" (Mikonya: Die Bäuerin und ihr Knecht, In: Krähen auf dem Essigbaum, S. 71).
b, Die Enttäuschung über die geschehenen Ereignisse

(3) "Stellte meinen Spaten unter den Birnbaum **und in mir wurde auf einmal alles zunichte.**" (Fischer: Asyl im Weinberg In: Tiefe Wurzeln S. 135).
c, Die Traurigkeit der Figur wegen dem Geschehenen
(4) "Der Lang Stefi —hieß die Antwort, und *im stillen Inneren weinte mein Herz*, trauerte, und es trauert noch immer demnach, der die Seele unserer Blasmusik war." (G. Wittmann: Musikanten, spielt auf! In: Tiefe Wurzeln S.81).

Eine wichtige Perspektive von satzwertigen und satzübergreifenden Phraseologismen ist ihre Historizität, die historische Umgebung in der sie entstanden sind. In unseren Belegen sind die wichtigsten Motive *der Krieg* und *die Aussiedlung* und damit im Zusammenhang die negativen Gefühle. Wiederholung und Rheime in den phraseologischen Komponenten drücken die Betonung der Gefühle Angst, Enttäuschung aus: wie im folgenden Beleg die verbale Komponente *flieg* und die substantivische *Krieg*.

(5) "Flogen die Maikäfer, so folgte der Spruch:
Flieg, Maikäfer, flieg,
Dein Vater ist im Krieg!" (Wittmann: "Du frugst mich danach ...", In: Tiefe Wurzeln, S. 73).

Im folgenden Beleg wird die phraseologische Komponente *Maikäfer* personifiziert: in diesem satzwertigen Phraseologismus handelt es sich um eine Person, deren Vater im Krieg ist und dieser Mensch muss wegen dem Krieg fliehen.

Die unter den Punkten a, b und c angeführten Phraseologismen sind von arealer Verbreitung: sie sind im ganzen ungarndeutschen Sprachraum verbreitet.

6. Distributionskategorisierung von Phraseologismen

Phraseologismen können nicht nur aufgrund ihres Aufbaus, sondern auch nach ihrer Distributionskategorisierung klassifiziert werden (Piirainen 2009: 362). Sie unterscheidet darin Phraseologismen die in einem Dorf, in einer regionalen Umgangssprache, in einer Standardvarietät, in einem Staatsgebiet, im gesamten Geltungsbereich einer Sprache, in mehreren Einzelsprachen oder in Sprachen mehrerer Kontinente gebraucht werden. In unserem Fall handelt es sich nach ihrer Aufteilung von satzwertigen und satzübergreifenden Phraseologismen einer ungarndeutschen Ortsmundart (Phraseologismen von kleinräumiger Verbreitung) oder einer regionalen Umgangssprache. Die unter dem Punkt 4 zitierten Phraseologismen sind von regionaler Verbreitung, während die folgenden phraseologischen Einheiten von kleinräumiger Verbreitung sind.

(6) "Verse sagtest Du auch, in unserem schwäbisch-bayerischen Dialekt, wie:
Zepplujka tanz i gean
mit a jungn feschn Hean
mit 'n oldn mog i net
liaba tanz i Zeppl net."
(Wittmann: "Du frugst mich danach ...", In: Tiefe Wurzeln, S. 74).

Über die satzwertigen Phraseologismen weiß man woher diese Konstruktionen stammen, man kennt ihre Herkunft. Diese phraseologischen Einheiten haben kulturspezifische phraseologische Komponenten (Zepplujka, Zeppl), die innerhalb einer Ortsmundart verbreitet sind. Dieser Phraseologismus ist für eine bairisch-österreichische ungarndeutsche Mundart charakteristisch. Der zitierte Phraseologismus drücken eine subjektive Stellungnahme zu einer spezifisch ungarndeutschen Tanz aus.

In den analysierten satz- und textwertigen Phraseologismen kann eine Komponente als kulturelle Transferenz (Ethnorealia) eingestuft werden, da für diese Komponente aus kulturellen Gründen keine Äquivalent im Binnendeutschen gibt, sogar ist es unmöglich eine Äquivalent für diesen Lexem in einer anderen Sprache zu finden, deshalb werden diese phraseologischen Komponenten aus dem Ungarischen oder aus einer ungarndeutschen Mundart in die anaiysierten Texte transferiert.

In diesem transferierten textwertigen Phraseologismus ist *Zepplujka* oder *Zeppl* eine Ethnorealia. Beide beziehen sich auf dieselbe phraseologische Komponente. Aus etymologischer Hinsicht kann das Lexem Zeppl entweder auf eine transferierte phraseologische Komponente aus dem österreichischen *Zeperl–Polka* oder dem *Zeppel Polka* aus Banat und Batschka zurückgeführt werden. Im Falle des *Zeperl–Polkas* handelt es sich um eine österrreichische Polka, während *Zeppel–Polka* ein Kreistanz aus der Banat und Batschka ist (Fillafer/ Hoi/ Riedl 1997: 28). Von diesen zwei Vermutungen halte ich es — wegen der ungarndeutschen Beziehungen — für wahrscheinlicher, dass es sich in diesem Beleg um einen Tanz aus dem Banat und der Batschka handelt. Die phraseologische Komponente *Zeppl* oder *Zepplujka* ist ein Symbol für die ungarndeutsche Nationalitätenidentität.

Zu satz- und textwertige phraseologischen Transferenzen gehören ebenfalls Phraseologismen mit Zitatencharakter (Lüger 1999: 325). In meinem Korpus geht es in diesem Fall um Zitattransferenzen, d.h. dass ein berühmtes Zitat von eines ungarischen Dichters oder Schriftstellers in die ungarndeutschen Texte transferiert wird:

(7) „Ti Vavusch hot uf ihrem Kepäck in oner Eck khockt un hot nar an tes ketenkt, was sie uf ten Wagon kschriewe hot:

'Szülőföldem szép határa,

meglátlak –e valahára?" (Márnai – Mann: Ti verlaareni Homet. Tr Apschied. In: Hometskschichte S. 83).

Dieser satzwertige Phraseologismus mit Zitatencharakter ist eine phraseologische Transferenz, die ursprünglich aus einem ungarischen Volkslied transferiert wurde, und dieses Lied wurde später von dem ungarischen Dichter, Károly Kisfaludy in einem Gedicht bearbeitet. Der Phraseologismus mit Zitatencharakter kann als Symbol für das Heimweh und die Heimatliebe von Vavusch (der Hauptfigur der Novelle) betrachtet werden.

Wie es auch aus den angeführten Belegen hervorgeht, können satzwertige Phraseologismen durch die Verwendung einer ungarndeutschen Mundart oder durch eine aus dem Ungarischen oder aus einer ungarndeutschen Mundart transferierte kulturspezifische phraseologische Komponenten dazu beitragen, den Nationalitätencharakter der Texte wiederzuspiegeln. Diese Feststellung ruft die weiterführende Frage hervor, welche Rolle wohl Phraseologismen aus textlinguistischer Sicht erfüllen.

Eine weitere Klasse der ungarndeutschen satzwertigen und satzübergreifenden Phraseologismen bilden Kinderreime und Spiele, die vor allem pragmatische Rolle in den analysierten Texten haben. Diese Phraseologismen dienen dazu Gefühle (wie z.B. Lustigkeit, Unsicherheit) der Sprecher (in unserem Fall der Figur der Erzählung) auszudrücken. Die Gefühle werden durch verschiedene Stilmittel — wie im folgenden Beispiel Aufzählung, Alliteration ausgedrückt.

(8) „Und die Kinderspiele? Beim Zupfen der Margaretenblume hieß es:

Was soll ich werden?

Kaiser, König, Edelmann,

Bürger, Bauer, Bettelmann,
Schuster, Schneider, Leinenweber,
Doktor, Kaufmann, Totengräber?" (G. Wittmann: "Du frugst mich danach ..., In: Tiefe Wurzeln, S. 73).

Im angeführten satzübergreifenden Phraseologismus wird die Ungewissheit der Figur durch die gleichzeitige Anwendung mehrerer Stilmittel dargestellt: Alliteration und Rheime in den phraseologischen Komponenten.

Die im Korpus angeführten satzübergreifenden Phraseologismen waren für die binnendeutschen und österreichischen Gewährspersonen unbekannt. Das kann darauf zurückgeführt werden, dass diese Phraseologismen sowohl unter lexikalisch–semantischem als auch unter morphosyntaktischem Aspekt kulturspezifisch sind: sie sind von binnendeutschen phraseologischen Konstruktionen unterschiedlich: Sie haben entweder eine kulturspezifische phraseologische Komponente wie im Beleg 7 oder der ganze Phraseologismus ist durch seinen Inhalt kulturspezifisch.

4. Zusammenfassung und Ausblick

Wie aus der durchgeführten Analyse hervorgeht, besteht die Bedeutung der satzwertigen und satzübergreifenden Phraseologismen vor allem in ihrer Kulturspezifik und Historizität. Die Kulturspezifik kommt entweder in einer phraseologischen Komponente (wie im Beleg 7 *Zepplujka* oder *Zeppl* oder im Beleg 8 die ungarische phraseologische Komponente *szülőföld* (auf Deutsch *Heimat*). Damit steht ihre Ditributionskategorisierung im engen Zusammenhang: die untersuchten Phraseologismen sind entweder im ganzen ungarndeutschen Sprachraum verbreitet oder ihre Verwendung beschränkt sich auf eine gewisse Region oder auf ein kleines Dorf. Diese satzwertigen und satzübergreifenden Konstruktionen spielen in den Texten eine pragmatische Rolle. Diese Konstruktionen haben die Fuktion, die Meinung oder die Einstellung des Sprechers (in unserem Fall der Figuren der Novellen) zum Gesagten auszudrücken.

Es wäre wohl interessant, Verwendung und Rolle von satzwertigen und satzübergreifenden Phraseologismen in weiteren Texten der geschriebenen und gesprochenen Sprache von ungarndeutschen Minderheiten zu untersuchen und die unterschiedlichen Forschungsergebnisse miteinander zu vergleichen. Es könnte weiterhin zu wertvollen Ergebnissen führen, den Phraseologismengebrauch von deutschen Minderheiten in den Nachbarländern von Ungarn durchzuführen.

5. Literatur

ÁTS, E. (Hrsg.) 1974 *Tiefe Wurzeln. Eine ungarndeutsche Anthologie.* Budapest: Literarische Sektion des Demokratischen Verbandes der Deutschen in Ungarn.
BUKOVĈAN, D. 2009 "Phraseologie im mehrsprachlichen Diskurs". In: Földes, Cs. (Hrsg.): *Phraselogie disziplinär und interisziplinär.* Tübingen: Narr: 71-86.
BURGER, H. 2003 *Phraseologie. Eine Einführung am Beispiel des Deutschen.* Berlin: Erich Schmidt.
BURGER, H.; HÄCKI-BUHOFER, A. & SIALM, A. 1982 *Handbuch der Phraseologie.* Berlin /New York: De Gruyter.
DOBROVOL'SKIJ, D., PIIRAINEN, E. 1996 *Symbole in Sprache und Kultur. Studien zur Phraseologie aus kultursemiotischer Perspektive.* Bochum: Universitätsverlag.
EISMANN, W. (2009). "Situationsspezifische Redensarten". In: Földes, Cs. (Hrsg.): *Phraselogie disziplinär und interisziplinär.* Tübingen: Narr: 117-129.
FILLAFER, K., HOI, R. & RIEDL, M. 1997 *Tänze aus Kärnten.* Kärnten/ Klagenfurt/ Villach: Landesarbeitsgemeinschaft Österreichischer Volkstanz
FLEISCHER, W. 1982 *Phraseologie der deutschen Gegenwartssprache.* Leipzig: VEB Bibliographisches Institut.
FÖLDES, C. 1996 *Deutsche Phraseologie kontrastiv. Intra– und interlinguale Zugänge.* Heidelberg: Julius Groos Verlag (Deutsch im Kontrast; 15).
FÖLDES, C. 1997 "Sprachkontakteinflüsse auf die ungarndeutsche Gegenwartsliteratur — dargestellt an phraseologischem Material". In: Moelleken; Wolfgang; Weber & Peter (Hrsg.): *Neue Forschungsarbeiten zur Kontaktlinguistik.* Bonn: Dümmler (Plurilingua; 19): 159-174.
FÖLDES, C. (Hrsg.) 2010 *Phraseologie disziplinär und interdisziplinär. Europhras 2006;* Tübingen: Narr.
GERÖLY, K. 2006 "Spachkontaktenflüsse auf die ungarndeutsche Gegenwartsliteratur. Skizze eines Forschungsvorhabens". In: *Deutschunterricht für Ungarn, 2006/1, 2.* Budapest: Ungarischer Deutschlehrerverband: 132-138.
GERÖLY, K. 2009 "Erscheinungsformen und Rolle von Phraseologismen in Texten der ungarndeutschen Gegenwartsliteratur". In: Földes, Csaba (ed.): *Disciplinary and Interdisciplinary Phraseology. Selected papers of the EUROPHRAS conference in Veszprém 2006;* Veszprém: University of Pannonia, University Press: 89-97.
LÜGER, H. 1999 *Satzwertige Phraseologismen. Eine pragmalinguistische Untersuchung.* Wien: Edition Praesens
MÁRNAI-MANN, N. 1979 *Hometskschichte.* Budapest: Verband der Ungarndeutschen.
MICHAELISZ, J. 1994 *Zauberhut.* Budapest: Verband der Ungarndeutschen.
MIEDER, W. 2006 *„Andere Zeiten, andere Lehren." Sprichwörter zwischen Tradition und Innovation.* Baltmannsweiler: Schneider Verlag.
MIKONYA, J. 1994 *Krähen auf dem Essigbaum. Erzählungen, Gedichte.* Budapest: VudAK.

THE CONVERSATIONAL TREATMENT OF IDIOMATIC EXPRESSIONS IN GERMAN TALK SHOWS – A CORPUS-BASED STUDY

Günter Schmale
Université de Lorraine-Metz

Abstract: Corpus-based analyses of authentic conversational interaction, so far not the core interest of mainstream phraseological research, are essential in order to determine communicative functions of prefabricated expressions by taking into account contextual, situational and sequential factors, but they are also indispensable so as to deliver a comprehensive description of multimodal aspects of phraseme usage by taking into account segmental, suprasegmental and nonverbal phenomena closely linked to the production of a phraseological expression. Based on a 32-hour-corpus of German television talk shows, the present article studies the conversational treatment of formulaic expressions, i.e. reformulations (rephrasals and paraphrases), metadiscursive comments, play on words, and concomitant nonverbal activities, which very regularly "treat" idiomatic metaphorical and/or figurative expressions in the context of "public speaking" within German talk shows.

Key words: Idiomatic expressions, corpus-based approach, conversational treatment (types and functions): reformulation, metadiscursive comments, word puns, concomitant nonverbal activities, German talk shows

1. Necessity of Corpus-Based Analyses

Hartmut Feilke who developped the somewhat visionary idea of "idiomatische Prägung" (~ "idiomatic moulding") of language, stipulating that basically any type of language production, not just phraseological expressions, is to some extent based on pre-fabricated language material (cf. Feilke 1998), believes that

It is far more important to use a phraseological expression in an adequate syntactic construction and in the right situation rather than reproduce it verbatim. (Feilke 2004: 59)[1]

And Elisabeth Gülich (2008), within her concept of "prefabricated turn-construction units as a resource for conversational interaction", points out that:

"… using prefabricated expressions is not just a question of reproducing ready-made linguistic constructions which the speaker might prefer (or not) to a freely created construction (following an "idiom principle" or an "open-choice principle"). It is in fact, like any other recourse to different means of discourse production, e.g. reformulations, part of the speaker's formulation/verbalization work and as such subject to conversational treatment." (Gülich 2008: 877)[2]

---

[1] My translation of the German passage: "*Pragmatisch weit wichtiger aber als die getreue Reproduktion ist es, den Phraseologismus überhaupt syntaktisch und situativ passend unterzubringen.*" (ibid.)

[2] My translation of: "[…] *le recours au préformé n'est pas simplement une activité de reproduction d'éléments 'préfabriqués' que le locuteur peut préférer ou non à une production libre ou créative (selon un 'idiom principle' ou un 'open choice principle'),*

Both Feilke's and Gülich's highly usage-oriented approaches necessarily imply that phraseological phenomena have systematically to be analyzed on the basis of representative corpora, preferably taken from the domain of conversational interaction. Such corpus-based studies on the conversational use of *formulaic expressions*, to use a now widespread term for prefabricated expressions[3] (cf. e.g. Kuiper 2009 or Wray & Perkins 2000) which shall be specified later on in this paper, are essential not only in order to determine communicative functions of prefabricated expressions by taking into account contextual, situational and sequential factors, they are also indispensable for a variety of other reasons, viz. so as to

- determine the current actual form a formulaic expression (= FE) majoritarily used within the speech community and which is often not the one lemmatized in dictionaries;
- deliver a comprehensive description of multimodal aspects of FE usage, i.e. taking into account not only segmental, but also suprasegmental and non verbal phenomena closely linked to the production of a FE;
- provide a thorough account of collocational, connotational and situational factors of FE use;
- give a detailed record of the sequential position of FEs, i.e. are they in initial, second or final position?, what is their relation to preceding, concomitant or following verbal and/or nonverbal activities? etc.

2. The Use of German Talk Shows as a Corpus

However, in spite of this obvious necessity of corpus-based studies of conversational material, comparatively extremely little research work has been carried out so far on the use of FEs in authentic conversational interaction (cf. e.g. Dausendschön-Gay, Ulrich; Gülich, Elisabeth & Krafft, Ulrich 2007; Drew & Holt 1998; Gülich 2008; Gülich & Krafft 1997; Kallmeyer & Keim 1986, 1994; and some others). This is why a study on the use of FEs was undertaken on the basis of thirteen different talk shows from German television as a form of – even though more or less institutionalized – conversational interaction, thus allowing to systematically account for the multimodal nature of FE use. Initially it was intended to study the frequency of use and functions of proverbs in conversational interaction, but – unfortunately or rather: fortunately for what was discovered subsequently – only a very small number of 8 genuine proverbs appeared in the 32-hour corpus, e.g. *Wer im Glashaus sitzt, soll nicht mit Steinen werfen (People in glass houses should not throw stones); Neue Besen kehren gut (New brooms sweep clean)* or *Wo Rauch ist, ist auch Feuer (There is no smoke without fire)*. However, what was discovered in the corpus was the fact that formulaic idiomatic expressions in general on a syntagmatic or phrasal level were quite systematically "referred to" by means of preceding, following or even concomitant verbal or non verbal activities. In other words, idiomatic expressions (= IE) are "conversationally treated" within specific conversational

---

mais il fait partie – tout comme le recours à d'autres procédés de production discursive (p.ex. la reformulation) – du travail de formulation et est soumis à un traitement interactif."

[3] Which is certainly more appropriate than "fixed expression", given the very flexible nature of phrasemes. In conversational terms one might rather prefer the term "prefabricated turn-construction units".

sequences, i.e. they are being reformulated, literally rephrased or non-literally paraphrased, or they reformulate themselves another idiomatic expression, they are commented on via metadiscursive activities, they are (word)played with, they are illustrated by non-verbal activities.These five types of "conversational treatment" shall be presented and studied via transcript excerpts of relevant conversational sequences, *viz.* two types of reformulations, rephrasals (pt. 3) and paraphrases (pt. 4), metadiscursive comments (pt. 5); play on words (pt. 6) and finally concomitant non-verbal activities (pt. 7).[4]

3. Rephrasals of Idiomatic Expressions

Reformulating rephrasals of the semantic type "x R x", i.e. an IE is, except for necessary deictic modifications, literally reused in the same or the following expression, have to be subdivided into auto-rephrasals by the producer of the initial IE, and hetero-rephrasals by another participant in the or a following utterance.[5] Example (1) provides an instance of auto-rephrasal, whereas (2) is a case of hetero-rephrasal of an idiomatic expression.

(1) A journalist's opinion on Nuremberg's football players self confidence. (Dopa/7-3/5)[6]

01	J	in dieser Saison hat Nürnberg zu Haus noch nie gewonnen
		this season Nuremburg has not won a single match at home

02	J	wie willst du denn da **mit=nem breiten Kreuz** äh nach Dortmund fahren [...]
		how to you expect them to play away in Dortmund bursting with confidence

03	J	wenn du zu Hause NIE gewinnst
		when you NEVer win a single match at home

04	J	ja wie sollst du dort auswärts (.) **mit breitem Kreuz** dastehn
		how do you want them to be bursting with confidence when you're playing away

(2) Talk show host Meiser (M) asking Elke (E) about her ex-boyfriend (HM/19-3/8)

01	M	sechs Jahre wars der Mann ihrer Träume obwohl der immer auf ihrer Tasche lag
		for six years he was the man of your dreams though you knew he was taking advantage of you

---
[4] Cf. Schmale (2001a) for an exhaustive treatment of the different types mentioned (and some others).
[5] Cf. Schmale (2001b) on the analyses of rephrasals.
[6] Sequences in bold letters are those being the centre of the analyses. Capital letters indicate strong accentuation. All other transcription signs have been eliminated in order to simplify transcriptions and to gain space.

| 02 | | und dann haben sie (den) **in die Wüste geschickt** |
| | | *but then you sent him packing* |

| 03 | E | dann hab ich ihn **in die Wüste geschickt** |
| | | *yeah then I sent him packing* |

Now what are the functions of this auto-rephrasal of *mit breitem Kreuz*[7] in (1) and of the hetero-rephrasal of *in die Wüste geschickt* in (2)? Obviously, they are not identical on an *illocutionary level*: whereas J supports his own argument in (1) by rephrasing the metaphorical expression initially produced, E's simply confirms M's statement by rephrasing his idiomatic expression in (2). However, by reusing the host's IE literally E implicitely produces a manifestation or reciprocity – *"I reuse the expression, even the whole turn you produced, which implies that I do not reject it, most likely even agree with it and ... with you."* This would be the function of the rephrasal on the level of the *social relationship* between interactants. The function both (1) and (2) share is situated on the *cognitive level* – what I propose to call the "cognitive relief" function. In fact, both IE-producer himself and IE-reproducer/rephraser choose to reuse a metaphorical, expressive[8] phrase which perfectly renders the intended meaning; the (re)user is thus relieved of the production of a – semantically and stylistically (*cf.* its expressiveness) – equivalent expression.

4. Paraphrases of idiomatic expressions or by idiomatic expressions

The corpus contains three different types of paraphrases of the "x R y" type, i.e. an idiomatic expression is being paraphrased by a semantically equivalent non-formulaic expression (pt. 4.1), a non-formulaic expression is being paraphrased by an idiomatic one (pt. 4.2), or an idiomatic and/or formulaic expression is being paraphrased by another idiomatic and/or formulaic expression (pt. 4.3.)[9].

   4.1 x_{IE} R y_{non-FE} – Non-formulaic paraphrases of idiomatic expressions
   (3) A guest denies living in an illusory world (BS/19-3/3)

| 01 | BS | ((asking guest)) behauptest du einige Frauen machen ihren Job äh schlecht |
| | | *((host asking ZU)) do you mean that some women don't do their jobs properly* |

| 02 | G | das kann ich nich beurteilen ich sag nur **jedem Tierchen sein Plaisierchen** |
| | | *I can't judge that*   *all I'm saying is each to his own* |

---

[7] Another case of deviation of the lemmatized dictionary form which would be *mit breiter Brust*, nevertheless not a subject of conversational negociation by participants.
[8] Via the image it contains. Cf. Schmale (2010, forthcoming) on the expressiveness of idiomatic expressions.
[9] Cf. Schmale (2007) on different types of paraphrases of IEs.

| 03 | G | jeder soll **so leben wie er es für richtig hält** |
| | | *everybody should live the way they think is right* |

(4) German girl Lil is madly in love with her American friend (Ara/30-6/3)

| 01 | L | es gibt niemanden der irgendwie:: (-) **ihm das Wasser reichen** kann sozusagen |
| | | *there's absolutely nobody   fit to hold a candle to him so to speak* |

| 02 | A | **was ist denn so toll an ihm,** |
| | | *what's so fantastic about him* |

| 03 | L | das kann man schwierig irgendwie erklären weil er is einfach MEIN **Traumtyp** |
| | | *it's difficult to explain   because he's just the man of my dreams* |

Again, an example each of an auto-paraphrase (3) and a hetero-paraphrase (4) as to their conversational and communicative functions shall be analyzed. In both cases the non-formulaic paraphrase seems to occupy an explanatory function: in (3), G explains himself his IE by producing a perfectly transparent non-formulaic paraphrase of it; in (4), via her question, A implicitely reformulates L's IE by means of a simple adjective, *viz. toll*. But why this semantic specification? As for (3), G probably considers that the meaning of the IE is not obvious to every spectator; on the other hand, he is definitely aware of the fact that he is publicly speaking on television and thus wishes to demonstrate communicative competence. He does so by showing that he is able to paraphrase his own expression adequately and by lenghtening his own statement, thus extending his appearance on television. Especially length of utterance seems to be an important factor in public media-based speaking – in general, one does not have to be too short to be taken seriously. As for the host's (A) implicit hetero-paraphrase in (4), her specifying reformulation of L's IE might imply that she considers L's use of *niemand kann ihm das Wasser reichen*[10] as imprecise considering that this IE normally depicts objective practical or intellectual competence, but not personal preference on a purely affective level which is meant by L when talking about her lover. It is A's role as a host to clarify such situations for her public.

4.2 x_{non-FE} R y_{IE} – Idiomatic paraphrases of non-formulaic expressions

Extracts (5) and (6) show that idiomatic expressions themselves can be used to paraphrase another preceding (part of a) turn.

(5) Jacky talking about her husband who is thinking of leaving her (Ara/4-2/2)

| 01 | A | ja liebst du ihn oder liebst du ihn nich |
| | | *do you love him or don't you love him* |

---

[10] Literally : nobody is fit to give him a glass of water.

	02	J	& <<laughing slightly> ich lieb ihn aber **ich kann ihn ja auch nich festhalten**
			of course I do love him but I can't hold him back either

	03	J	**ich kann ihn ja nich in Ketten legen>**
			I can't put him in chains;

(6) J tells M that her husband (=H) is still kind, polite, helpful; H comments on this (HM/3-6/13)

	01	H	**& man gibt zurück was man bekommt**
			you give in return what you are being given

	02	M	ey das war n schöner Spruch nich
			wow that's a nice saying isn't it

	03	M	**so wie man in=den Wald hinein (-) ruft so schallt es heraus**
			you reap what you sow don't you

J's idiomatic auto-paraphrase in (5) has first of all an argumentative function in that she strengthens her non-formulaic statement *ich kann ihn ja auch nich festhalten* by the highly metaphorical and expressive[11] idiomatic expression *ich kann ihn ja nich in Ketten legen*. On the other hand, as in (3), Jacky is definitely aware of the fact that she is speaking on television, thus making stylistic efforts and lengthening her turn. As to host M's turns in (6); both his metadiscursive evaluation of H's turn (cf. l. 02) and his subsequent hetero-paraphrase (l. 03), they are most certainly to be explained by the fact of public media-based speaking and M's role as talk-show host. In order to entertain his spectators, it is for him to make comments on his guests and to show his competence by paraphrasing their statements in terms of proverbial "folk wisdom".[12]

4.3 x_{IE1} R y_{IE2} – Idiomatic / formulaic paraphrases of an idiomatic / formulaic expression

Let us finally look at an example of an idiomatic auto-paraphrase of another (partially) idiomatic expression; there is no instance of hetero-paraphrase for this type of reformulation.

(7)   Bettina reports that, soon after her wedding, her husband moved in with another woman, but often came back to see his wife. Host B. Schäfer cannot believe it (BS/3-6/2)

---

[11] Rated as such by native German test persons (cf Schmale, in press) who are, however, far from rating any pictorial and/or metaphorical expression as more expressive than its non-formulaic equivalent. Quite often the contrary is the case, especially when subjects consider an expression as old-fashioned or not straightforward enough.

[12] Nobody seemed to notice that M inverted the logical relation expressed in H's utterance: you return what you are being given (H) – what you get in return depends on what you give (M).

01	BS	so einen würd ich doch **laufen lassen** warum hast du überhaupt geheiratet
		but a bloke like that I'd send him off why did you get married to him

02	BS	also was bedeutet dir die Ehe
		what does marriage mean to you

03	B	((explains her reasons for this marriage))

04	BS	ja aber dann würd ich so einen doch **in=nen Wind schießen**
		yes but a bloke like that I would send him packing

05	BS	und **laufen lassen** wenn der mir sowas antut
		and send him off if he did this to me

Host BS first produces *laufen lassen* (l. 01) which is only slightly metaphorical, as the image used does not necessarily depict a concrete state of affairs (according to Burger's 2010 definition of metaphore), being consequently not very expressive. This might be the reason why BS then, following her guest's explanation (cf. l. 03), uses an expression with a much stronger image ("bildstark"), i.e. *in den Wind schießen*, which, however, is not metaphorical[13]. To finish her turn BS then reuses the initial faintly metaphorical expression (cf. l. 05). As to the functions of the two paraphrases[14]: within a sequence of emphatic language use BS increases the expressivity of her statement on B's marriage; on the other hand, especially as she is the host, she demonstrates her communicative competence by producing alternative – idiomatic – formulations within a multi-unit turn.

5. Metadiscursive comments on idiomatic expressions

Schmale (2009) describes eight types of metadiscursive comments on IEs; due to space restrictions two types only shall be analyzed hereafter. Generally speaking metadiscursive comments are used by the producer of an idiomatic expression in order to clarify the intended meaning of his utterance and thus guide the hearer's interpretation of it.[15] At the same time, the producer of the comment displays his own competence as a speaker, i.e. as someone who knows that an expression is formulaic and generally used within the speech community. On the other hand, as a sort of precautionary measure, he points out that the IE, belonging to "folk wisdom", is not of his own invention and that he cannot be held responsible for it.

(8) Lesbian Andrea (= A) talking to "hetero" guests (IC/2-2/13)

---

[13] As it does not concretely represent the abstract state of affairs meant by the producer, in other words: the image used is in no way transparent like for instance *Strike while the iron is hot*.

[14] Or of the paraphrase and the rephrasal of *laufen lassen* ? Which, sequentially speaking, is nevertheless a paraphrase of *in den Wind schießen*.

[15] Which does in no way suggest that the speaker « commands » the hearer's interpretation, but he can try.

01	A	aber ich denke einfach mal **kennt ihr nich den Spruch**
		but I just think *don't you know the expression*

02	A	**leben und leben lassen** (-) lasst sie doch; lasst sie doch einfach
		live and let live *just let them* *just let them*

In this case, A employs what might be called a "metalinguistic term", viz. *Spruch (motto)*, other members of this type are *Phrase (hackneyed phrase)* or *Floskel (set phrase)*, hightlighting that the following expression is prefabricated and frequently used.

(9) Host Hans Meiser (M) talking to his guests living on social security (HM/2-2/1)

01	M	wir zahlen ja alle Steuern und von diesen Steuern leben sie
		we all have to pay taxes *and you live on these taxes*

02		und **sie leben damit wie die Made im Speck** sacht so mancher
		and you live like a bee in clover many people would say

Post-positioned *sacht so mancher* in (9) belongs to the second type of metadiscursive comments, indicating what might be called "common use" and, implicitely, the formulaic nature of the IE thus qualified.

6. Play on words with idiomatic expressions

Three types of wordplay involving formulaic expressions were discovered in the corpus: modification of a phraseme constituent; re-use of a constituent in a following utterance; use of an IE in a specific communicative situation.[16] The following sequence (10) contains an example of the most common type of puns involving IEs, i.e. the one alluding to a – apart from very specific contexts, normally *virtual* – literal meaning of an IE.

(10) Host Meiser introduces his guest Mrs. Ortwein (HM/19-3/13)

01	HM	es gibt tatsächlich so etwas wie::: medizinische Wunder
		they're in fact things like… medical miracles

02		**sie war 1984 total blind** (--) **vor Liebe**; inzwischen kann sie wieder sehn
		in 1984 she was totally blind … for love but now she can see again

03		((Lachen im Publikum)) aus Berlin Anneliese Ortwein herzlich willkommen

---

[16] Cf. Schmale (2005a) for a more detailed presentation of the different types of wordplay with IEs.

		((audience laughing)) from Berlin Anneliese Ortwein welcome to the
show		

Host Meiser does this by deliberately introducing a rather lengthy pause (for conversational standards) after *blind* which cannot but induce his spectators to literally interpret *she was totally blind*. The emerging play on words is due to his adjoining of the prepositional phrase *vor Liebe* which means that she was not physically *blind*, but metaphorically *blind for love;* the audience acknowledges the pun by laughing. Play on words with IEs, almost exclusively reserved to the talk show host, has its main function in the entertainment of the spectators, and, as a side effect, in the demonstration of the host's competence and dominant role.

7. Non-verbal activities concomitant to the production of an idiomatic expression

To finish our review of different types of conversational treatment of IEs in German televised talk shows a type of treatment will be presented which has so far been neglected by phraseological research, *viz.* concomitant non-verbal activities to the production of IEs (cf. Schmale 2005b). Again, several types can be distinguished: non-verbal *emblems* having a univocal signification like non-verbal quotation marks; very frequent *batons*, i.e. rythmic movements using hands, head or the whole body; and the type represented in example (11): the non-verbal *illustration* of (a constituent of) an idiomatic expression.

(11) Host Bio asks MR about her feelings when she found her father at last (Bio/2-2/5)

01	MR	also ich sag ihnen ehrlich mir i::s **<<macht eine grosse Kreisbewegung>**
		I can tell you quite frankly <<making a big circular movement with both hands>

02		**SO ein Stein> von meinem Herzen gefallen**
		it took such a load> off my mind

In fact, the "pseudo-identifier" *SO*, strongly accentuated by speaker MR, would be without a precise reference if it were not for MR's non-verbal gesture, i.e. the big circular movement with both hands, which illustrates the intensity of her feeling of relief. It is interesting to note that the gesture is perfectly synchronized with the noun-phrase *SO ein Stein* which it illustrates. As to the functions of non-verbal activities produced simultaneously to the utterance of an IE: via the illustration of verbal turn-constructional elements, they clarify or even intensify the speaker's intended meaning and thus try to guide the hearer's interpretation of the speaker's turn – like metadiscursive comments, but probably less consciously.

8. Conclusion – Public "media-based" speaking and "conversational treatment"

Apart from specific semantic, argumentative, conversational or social functions which have been analyzed for the different types of IE treatment, the basic common feature of the talk show sequences studied seems to reside in the fact that the conversational treatment of IEs takes place in a public and/or media-based context.[17] Speakers, in particular the talk show host, have to demonstrate their communicative competence and possibly their dominance by treating IEs by the means identified, i.e. reformulations, metadiscursive comments, wordplay, and the production of concomitant non-verbal activities.

The eleven conversational excerpts analyzed show that it is not formulaic expressions in general which are being conversationally treated by participants, but specifically idiomatic expressions with a non-compositional meaning, and even more specifically those idiomatic expressions which contain an image and/or a metaphor. Idioms like to *drop a brick* or *to put one's foot in it* are pictorial, but not metaphorical, as the image does not represent a concrete model of the abstract state of affairs designated (cf. Burger 2010). Others are figurative, i.e. contain an image corresponding to a concrete model and are thus metaphorical, like *The early bird catches the worm* or *All that glitters is not gold*.

Out of 190 formulaic expressions "treated" in the 32-hour corpus, 122, i.e. 2/3, contain an image and/or a metaphore. In order to verify the hypothesis that figurative and/or metaphorical idiomatic expressions are treated prioritarily, any formulaic referential expression in two talk shows of the corpus were systematically collected. It turned out that out of 199 untreated FEs in *"Ich weiß, dass du mich betrügst..."* only 17, i.e. less than 10%, were figurative/-metaphorical; and in "Ich liebe nur mich selbst" only 13 out of 109. Instances of non-treated idioms are *auf Abstand gehen (to keep one's distance), gespannt wie ein Flitzebogen (to be dying with suspense), im Spiel sein (to be involved), die Gerüchteküche brodelt (the rumour mill is buzzing), Blut lecken (to taste blood)*, etc. These might not be treated, even though they are figurative or even metaphorical, because speakers do not consider the image/metaphor as one needing conversational treatment, probably, the image is faded or worn out to a point that they are not even aware of its figurativeness any more.

Extensive corpus-based studies of conversational interaction will have to determine which IEs are concerned or not by conversational treatment. And – a possibly daring hypothesis to finish this contribution with – this might be one way to determine the IEs which can be taught without any danger to foreign language learners. In fact, those which are *not* treated by native speakers as inconspicuous formulaic expressions are those which may be used by non-natives as there is no or less risk to transgress the borderline to native territory.

---

[17] Cf. Köster (2008) who points out that the study of media-related aspects of phraseme use in talk shows has been neglected in my prior work.

9. References

BURGER, H. 2010⁴; 1998 *Phraseologie. Eine Einführung am Beispiel des Deutschen*. Berlin: Erich Schmidt.

DAUSENDSCHÖN-GAY, U.; GÜLICH, E. & KRAFFT, U. 2007 "Vorgeformtheit als Ressource im konversationellen Formulierungs- und Verständigungsprozess". In : Hausendorf, H. (Hrsg.) : *Gespräch als Prozess. Linguistische Aspekte der Zeitlichkeit verbaler Interaktion* (= Studien zur Deutschen Sprache 37). Tübingen : Narr, 181-219.

DREW, P. & HOLT, E. 1998 "Figures of speech: Figurative expressions and the management of topic transition in conversation". *Language in Society* 27: 495-522.

FEILKE, H. 1998 "Idiomatische Prägung". In: Barz, I. & Öhlschläger, G. (Hg.): *Zwischen Grammatik und Lexikon*. Tübingen: Niemeyer: 69-80.

FEILKE, H. 2004 "Kontext – Zeichen – Kompetenz". In: Steyer, K. (Hg.): *Wortverbindungen – mehr oder weniger fest*. Berlin: de Gruyter: 41-64.

GÜLICH, E. 2008 "Le recours au préformé: une ressource dans l'interaction conversationnelle". In: Durand, J.; Habert, B. & Laks, D. (dir.) *Congrès mondial de linguistique française. Paris, 9-12 juillet 2008*. Paris: ILF/EDP Sciences: 93. Disponible en ligne http://www.linguistiquefrancaise.org/index.php?option= article&access=doi&doi=10.1051/cmlf08315 (16/11/2009).

GÜLICH, E. & KRAFFT, U. 1997 "Le rôle du préfabriqué dans les processus de production discursive". In: M. Martins-Baltar (ed.). *La locution entre langue et usages*. Fontenay-aux-Roses: ENS: 241-276.

KÖSTER, Lutz 2008 "Phraseme in audiovisuellen Medien". In: Burger, H.; Dobrovol'skij, D.; Kühn, P. & Norrick, N.R. (eds.): *Phraseology. An International Handbook of Contemporary Research*. Berlin / New York: De Gruyter: 275-284.

KUIPER, K. 2009 *Formulaic Genres*. London: Palgrave MacMillan.

SCHENKEIN, J. N. 1978 "Sketch of an Analytic Mentality for the Study of Conversational Interaction". In: *Studies in the Organization of Conversation Interaction*. New York /San Francisco /London: Academic Press: 1-6.

SCHMALE, G. 2001a *Le traitement conversationnel de phrasèmes dans les talk-shows de la télévision allemande*. Université de Nantes: Unpublished Monography.

SCHMALE, G. 2001b "Rephrasages comme traitement conversationnel de phrasèmes dans les talk-shows de la télévision allemande". *Beiträge zur Fremdsprachenvermittlung*, 39: 47-71.

SCHMALE, G. 2005a"Wortspiele mit phraseologischen Ausdrücken in deutschen Talkshows". *Deutsch als Fremdsprache* 4: 215-219.

SCHMALE, G. 2005b "Nonverbale Aktivitäten bei der Äußerung von Phraseologismen". *Studia Germanica Universitatis Vesprimiensis* 9/2: 159-173.

SCHMALE, G. 2007 "Paraphrases phraséologiques dans la conversation". In: Kara M. (ed.): *Usages et analyses de la reformulation. Recherches Linguistiques* 29: 163-175.

SCHMALE, G. 2009 "Metalinguistic Comments and Evaluations of Phraseological Expressions in German Talk Shows". *Textes & Contextes*, 4, Varia 2009. URL: http://revuesshs.u-bourgogne.fr/textes& contextes/document.php?id=877 (16/05/2010).

SCHMALE, G. (in press). "Ist ein idiomatischer Ausdruck immer expressiv? Korpusbasierte und fragebogengestützte Beobachtungen zu einer verbreiteten Prämisse". To be published in October 2010 by Kuiper, Koenraad (ed.): *Yearbook of Phraseology*. Mouton de Gruyter.

WRAY, A. & PERKINS, M. R. 2000 "The functions of formulaic language. An integrated model". *Language & Communication* 20: 1-28.

LOCUCIONES ADVERBIALES IDIOMÁTICAS EN EUSKERA[1]

Xabier Altzibar Aretxabaleta
Universidad del País Vasco
Euskal Herriko Unibertsitatea

Abstract: In this paper we present a list of Basque adverbial idioms of time, quantity and opinion. We make a distinction between idioms of a higher and lower degree of idiomaticity, and we focus our attention on the former for their high expressive value. We find that there exists a considerable number of Basque idiomatic fixed expressions, and that many of them are equivalent or similar to Spanish idioms. We consider this fact as evidence of linguistic and cultural connection between both languages.

Key Words: Phraseology, Basque idioms

1. Introducción

El estudio de los fraseologismos puede ser fructífero para el uso de la lengua, para la enseñanza de la misma o la traducción, o también como elemento de información para analizar otros muchos aspectos de las relaciones lingüísticas o culturales. En el caso del euskera (lengua vasca o vascuence), el conocimiento y uso de los fraseologismos es necesario para la revitalización del idioma. Conviene tener en cuenta que este idioma está en contacto con el español (en el Estado español), y que, siendo éste mayoritario incluso en la Comunidad Autónoma Vasca y la Comunidad de Navarra, las interferencias sobre el euskera son continuas. Además, el euskera está actualmente en un proceso de unificación y normalización, que requiere un lenguaje más formal pero también más expresivo.

Los adverbios son importantes en el uso de la lengua. Por ej., en los medios de comunicación los adverbios sirven para especificar el tiempo en que ocurren los hechos, el lugar, modo, grado, cantidad, etc.; el periodista cuenta los hechos o las opiniones según tal o cual fuente de información o punto de vista, restringiendo o reforzando el valor de verdad de la aserción, etc. Pues bien, en todos estos aspectos los adverbios son auxiliados por las locuciones adverbiales. Villasante, presidente de Euskaltzaindia–Real Academia de la Lengua Vasca, decía lo siguiente (la traducción es mía):

"En el fondo, existen razones, razones profundas, que explican la génesis y el uso de las expresiones fijas. La primera: la lengua no tiene, generalmente, suficientes palabras para expresar todas las ideas, con sus pliegues y matices, y esa escasez la remedia por medio de las expresiones fijas. Por ej., la lengua es demasiado parca en adverbios, y ese vacío lo llena, en

---

[1] Este trabajo es fruto del proyecto de investigación "Inguruko erdaren interferentzia eta kalkoak hedabideetako hizkeran (Interferencias y calcos de las lenguas vecinas en el euskera de los medios de comunicación)", financiado por la Universidad del País Vasco / Euskal Herriko Unibertsitatea (UE08/05). Abreviaturas: A: Azkue; I: Izagirre; (lit.): literalmente; M: Mocoroa (véase Bibliografía); /: indica palabra alternativa.

cierta medida, con las expresiones fijas. Y, en segundo lugar, ahí está la ley de la expresividad. El ser humano no se contenta con expresar sus pensamientos con brevedad y sin energía; quiere expresarlos de un modo incisivo, con viveza, con sal y pimienta. El modo de hablar desprovisto de estas expresiones suele resultar claro, sí, pero insulso. No tiene la fuerza y viveza del otro." (Villasante: *Euskararen auziaz* [Sobre la cuestión del euskera] 1988, pág. 193).

Conviene aclarar qué entendemos por "locuciones adverbiales idiomáticas" en euskera. Según Corpas, las locuciones son unidades fraseológicas del sistema de la lengua con fijación en la forma y significado, que no constituyen enunciados completos, y, generalmente, funcionan como elementos oracionales (1997:88-89). Pero faltan estudios específicos que definan morfosintácticamente las locuciones del euskera. De todos modos, convengamos en que las locuciones adverbiales son, tanto en español como en euskera, aquellas unidades fraseológicas que, en general, funcionan como complementos circunstanciales (de tiempo, lugar, grado, cantidad, modo, opinión), o tienen algunas otras funciones (adverbios ordenadores, conjuntivos, de afirmación o negación, etc).

En cuanto al calificativo de "idiomáticas" aplicado a las locuciones, es, de hecho, una redundancia, porque las locuciones son idiomáticas en sí, en mayor o menor grado; en nuestras listas hemos incluido las locuciones en general, no sólo las "idiomáticas". Sin embargo, utilizamos este calificativo como un reclamo o gancho para llamar la atención y destacar el papel de las locuciones de sentido figurado o metafóricas (muchas veces contienen una imagen), que son menos denotativas o menos claras en una escala semántica, y cuyo significado es fruto de un proceso de abstractización o idiomatización mayor. Por ello, nos valdremos de las expresiones "menos idiomática" y "más idiomática" para diferenciar las locuciones, aunque somos conscientes de que esta división puede ser demasiado esquemática (algunas temporales pueden considerarse intermedias, "cuasi-idiomáticas"; véase 2.1 y 2.3). Por ej., entre las locuciones equivalentes al español *nunca*, consideramos que *behin ere ez* '(lit.) ni una vez') es "menos idiomática" que *oiloak arrautza beltza egin orduko* '(lit.) cuando la gallina ponga un huevo negro') y ésta "más idiomática" que aquella.

Como consecuencia de la falta de una definición morfosintáctica de las locuciones euskéricas topamos con un problema: cómo identificar las locuciones. Como es sabido, el euskera no es una lengua románica, y, por tanto, no tiene preposiciones; es, más bien, una lengua aglutinante que funciona con sufijos o casos. Por ej., para formar adverbios se utilizan generalmente sufijos (*-ki/gi, -to, -ro, -ka, -ik, -la,* etc.) o casos (*-z, -n, -ra, -tik,* etc.). Estos sufijos y/o casos –que equivalen a las preposiciones– se posponen al núcleo o palabra base, formando un todo inseparable. Por ej., de *behin* 'una vez' se forma la locución *behingo batean* 'de una vez', 'inmediatamente', pero también su sinónimo *behingoan*; el artículo *-a* de este último y el numeral *bat* de aquél cumplen funciones similares. Otras veces, al núcleo se posponen palabras enclíticas formando una única palabra, como consecuencia de la lexicalización (*nolerebait < nola + ere + bait* 'de algún modo'). De modo que las locuciones pueden estar formadas por varias palabras que se escriben separadas (*behingo batean, esku beteka* '(lit.) a manos llenas', 'en abundancia') o bien juntas (*behingoan, nolerebait*). ¿Quiere decir esto que en euskera una locución puede estar formada por una sola palabra?

En cualquier caso, sería interesante el estudio morfosintactico de las locuciones del euskera y de otros idiomas diferentes a los románicos e indoeuropeos. Como podremos ver en los ejemplos, muchas de las estructuras sintácticas de las locuciones adverbiales se basan en la reduplicación intensiva (*egunean-egunean* 'diariamente', '(lit.) en el día-en el día'), en construcciones comparativas de diverso tipo (sobre todo con los términos *baino, bezala/lez, adina, beste,* superlat. *-en*, u otras de patrón sust. + *bete* 'lleno' + sust. 'en abundancia', en construcciones negativas (*egundaino ez* 'nunca jamás', '(lit.) no hasta el día de hoy'), o bien distributivas, disyuntivas y correlativas (con las partículas *edo* 'o' y *eta* 'y') o pospositivas (*ikusita bat* 'nada más ver(lo)', '(lit.) visto y uno'). Muchas de estas estructuras pueden parecer complejas, pero también pueden ser flexibles y estilizables. Existe multiplicidad de variantes formales y dialectales, que no podemos especificar aquí por falta de espacio.

En este artículo pretendemos mostrar una serie de listas básicas de locuciones adverbiales y señalar la importancia de las "idiomáticas", relacionandolas con sus equivalentes o similares del español. Hemos escogido tan sólo algunos grupos de locuciones: las temporales correspondientes a *nunca, antiguamente, inmediatamente,* las de cantidad correspondientes a *abundantemente* y las de opinión correspondientes a *en opinión, probablemente, aparentemente, en verdad, evidentemente, sin duda.* La mayoría de las locuciones de nuestras listas están recogidas de diversos diccionarios y recopilaciones: Azkue (1969), Izagirre (1981), DGV-OEH (1987-2005), Mocoroa (1990), el diccionario de refranes de Garate (1990) y otras fuentes. Pero algunas otras no están señaladas o consideradas como locuciones en esas fuentes, por lo que hemos tenido que identificarlas entre la selva de ejemplos. Para ello, nos hemos valido de muchos ejemplos del repertorio de Mocoroa (el DGV-OEH no lo ha utilizado como fuente), y también algunos de Azkue e Izagirre, en casos que nos parecen válidos y claros, y los hemos marcado con las abreviaturas M, A, I. Las locuciones figuran generalmente en la forma unificada de la lengua (*euskera batua*). Como método, en cada una de los cinco series diferenciaremos, *grosso modo*, entre las locuciones "menos idiomáticas" y las "más idiomáticas".

2. Locuciones adverbiales temporales

2.1. En este primer apartado mencionaremos las locuciones correspondientes al español *nunca* 'en ningún tiempo'. Las "menos idiomáticas" están formadas por una serie de palabras denotativas que expresan conceptos abstractos relacionados con el tiempo o la vida: *behin* 'una vez', *inoiz* 'nunca', *egun* 'día', 'hoy', *sekula* 'siglo' (significado arcaico), 'jamás', *mende* 'siglo', 'época', 'tiempo', *denbora* 'tiempo', *bizi* 'vida', y combinaciones de varias de ellas. Son las siguientes: *behin ere + ez, behin ez behin* 'ni una vez', *inoiz (ere) + ez, sekula (ere) + ez* 'nunca', *egundaino + ez* o *egundo + ez* '(lit.) hasta hoy no', *inoizko mendetan + ez* 'en ninguna época', *egun eta mende + ez, menderen mendetan/mendez + ez, sekula sekulorutan + ez* '(no) en los siglos de los siglos', *egun eta (santa) sekulan + ez* o *ez egun eta ez sekulan* 'ni hoy ni nunca' (M 60280, 60282, 60283), *sekula santan* o *santa sekulan + ez, sekula guztian + ez, -en denboran/denbora guztian + ez* '(lit.) (no) en todo el tiempo de X' (persona) y *sekula bizian + ez* 'jamás en la vida', estas últimas muy similares o equivalente a la locución española *en la vida* o *en (toda) su/tu/...vida*. Excluimos de la lista las correspondientes a *nunca más, ya más nunca*, como por ej. *inoiz gehiago + ez, gehiagoren gehiago + ez* etc. Obsérvese que todas estas locuciones necesitan de la partícula de negación *ez* 'no' que precede al auxiliar verbal; sin *ez*, muchas de ellas significan 'siempre'. Estas locuciones "menos idiomáticas" son de registro más amplio y más reproducibles.

En cambio, hay otro grupo de locuciones plenamente idiomáticas, que contienen imágenes visuales y visualizables de la fauna y elementos atmosféricos del mundo rural vasco, son más coloquiales y se usan más bien en contextos restringidos: generalmente, cuando los mayores quieren hacer callar a los niños parlanchines o preguntones, o, simplemente, cuando no se quiere contestar directamente a la pregunta ¿cuándo? Estas locuciones son cuasi-enunciados y provienen de las paremias o están en relacion directa con ellas. Por ej., *oiloak arrautza beltza egin orduko* (A 330) '(lit.) antes que / en cuanto la gallina ponga un huevo negro' es muy similar a la española *Cuando los gallos pongan huevo* (Santiago de Cuba) y parecida a la francesa *Quand les poules auront des dents*. Una de sus variantes es el refrán infantil *Oilo beltzak arrautza beltza egin artean hago isilik* 'estáte callado hasta que la gallina negra ponga un huevo negro', o su gemela *Oilo txuriak arrautza beltza egin artean hago isil* 'estáte callado hasta que la gallina blanca ponga un huevo negro', ambas recogidas en la misma localidad (Errezil, Gipúzkoa), y que, según Azkue, su colector, se dice a los niños charlatanes (A 256 Callar, 301 Huevo).

Otra locución, que no hemos encontrado en diccionarios (salvo el de Izagirre) debe de ser *oiloak piz egiterako o oiloak txiz egin baino lehenago* o similar, ya que existe el refrán, algo más basto que el anterior, *Oiloak piz egiterako adiskidatuko haiz* 'te reconciliarás para cuando la gallina orine' de Errezil (A 294 Gallina) o su variante *Adiskidatuko dira oiloak txiz egin baino lehenago* de Legazpi (A 319 Orina). Según Elexpuru (2004), en Bergara a los niños, para que callen, se les dice *Umiak, ixilik oilluak txixa eiñ arte* 'Niños, callad (o 'los niños deben callar') hasta que las gallinas orinen'. Todas estas variantes equivalen a la locución española *Cuando las gallinas meen*.

Asimismo, están relacionadas con las paremias o se utilizan como tales las siguientes locuciones: *haizerik ez den urtean* '(lit.) el año que no haya viento' (cfr. la paremia *Hator haizerik ez den urtean!,* que, según Garate, quiere decir *Véte a freir espárragos*) y también *kea atzera datorrenean etxera* '(lit.) cuando el humo vuelva a casa' (M 60308), relacionada con la paremia *Kea badoa eta ez dator gehiago* 'el humo se va y no vuelve' (Según Garate el humo es símbolo de la vida). Otra similar es *asto arrak umea egin orduko* (I 644) o *katarrak umea egin orduko* 'cuando/antes que el burro (o el gato macho) críe'.

Algunas de las locuciones usuales equivalentes o semejantes a las euskéricas mencionadas son, en español, las siguientes: *cuando la(s) rana(s) críe(n) pelo(s), cuando las vacas vuelen, cuando Colón/San Juan baje el dedo* (Buitrago:2002), *cuando San Pedro baje el dedo* (Santiago de Cuba). En esta ciudad son también usuales las siguientes: *El día que tengas un choncholí blanco* (el choncholí o totí es un ave de color negro), *cuando el manco eche dedos, cuando el mar se seque, cuando el pescado camine*.

2.2. Entre las locuciones correspondientes a *antiguamente, hace mucho tiempo*, las "menos idiomáticas" estan formadas por palabras que denotan tiempo (*antzina* 'antiguamente', *aspaldi* 'hace mucho tiempo', *behinola* 'un día', 'hace mucho tiempo', *mende* 'tiempo', ' época', 'siglo'; *ordu* 'hora') y son las más usadas: *antzina-antzina, antzina-antzina baten* (M 60602), *antzin(a) hartan/haietan* (M 60.603, 60610), *antzina (e)ta behinola, aspaldi bate(a)n, aspaldi handian,* a*spaldi eta aspaldi, aspaldiko denboran/denboretan, orain (dela/duela) aspaldi* 'ahora hace mucho tiempo', *behinola bate(a)n, mendeen/mendetako gauean* (equivalente a la locución española *en la noche de los tiempos*), *mende zaharretan* 'en los viejos tiempos/siglos', *bertze orduz* '(lit.) en otra hora', equivalente a *otrora* (arcaico).

Las locuciones "más idiomáticas" se usan en registros muy restringidos, generalmente son fórmulas de comienzo de cuentos: *Gauza guziek/abereek hizketan zekiten denboran* '(lit.) 'cuando todas las cosas hablaban/sabían hablar', *Behiala, hegaztiak mintzo zirenean* 'Hace mucho tiempo, cuando las aves hablaban/sabían hablar', *Urlia denboran* 'en tal tiempo' (recogida por Barandiaran), *Peru ta Mariren aldian* 'en los tiempos de Peru y Mari' (personajes de cuentos) (M 60835-60837).

He aquí algunas locuciones españolas, semejantes a las vascas mencionadas: *en tiempos de Maricastaña* o *allá en/por los años de Maricastaña*, (con los verbos suceder, pasar) *en tiempos del rey que rabió* (Buitrago:2002), (ser de) *antes de la guerra* (Varela-Kubarth:1996), *cuando se hacía la mili con lanza, cuando Franco era corneta/cabo*.

2.3. Las locuciones correspondientes a *rápidamente, velozmente, inmediatamente, en seguida, de repente*, etc. son abundantes. Entre ellas hay un grupo de locuciones formadas por palabras que expresan rapidez (*arin, laster, azkar, fite, bizkor* 'rápidamente', 'velozmente', *berehala* 'inmediatamente') y son las "menos idiomáticas": *arin batean, laster asko, laster bai/baino laster, laster baino lasterrago, laster batean, laster ere laster, laster eta bertan* 'inmediatamente', *azkar batean, azkar asko, berehalako batean, bizkor-bizkor*.

Otro grupo de locuciones estan formadas por palabras denotativas que relacionan el tiempo y el espacio con la rapidez: *behin* 'una vez', *istant* 'instante', *gaur/egun* 'hoy', *bihar* 'mañana (día que sigue al de hoy)', *goiz* 'mañana (parte del día)', *gau* 'noche', *orain* 'ahora', *gero* 'después', *atze* 'atrás', 'pasado', *beta* 'tiempo', *han* 'allí', *bertan* 'allí mismo', 'inmediatamente', *bat* '(lit.) uno', que expresa la idea de 'inmediatamente'. De modo que podríamos denominar "cuasi-idiomáticas" a estas locuciones: *behingo batean, istant batean, gaurtik/egunetik biharrera* 'de hoy a mañana' (I 450), *goizetik gauera/gauerakoan/arrats(era)* 'de la noche a la mañana' (M 64022-64023), *egun batetik bestera/bertzean* 'de un día a otro' (M 64221), *gauetik goizera* (equivalente a la locución española *de la noche a la mañana*), *gauetik egunera* 'de la noche al día' (menos usada), *geroko utzi gabe* 'sin dejar para después' (M 63763), *geroko/gerora begira egon gabe* '(lit.) sin estar mirando a después' (M 63765-63766), *atzera begira egon gabe* 'sin estar mirando atrás' (M 63768), *bertatik bertara* 'inmediatamente' '(lit.) de ahí mismo a ahí mismo', *bertatiko bate(a)n* 'de repente', *han (orduko) hemen* '(lit.) [antes que] allí aquí', (M 63661-63665), *bat-batean, bat-batera, bet-betan, halako batean* 'de repente', y construcciones con participio + *(e)ta bat* 'inmediatamente después de' o infinitivo + *-tzeko beta gabe / -tzeko asti barik* 'sin tiempo para (+ verbo)' (M 63753-63756).

Las locuciones idiomáticas son tanto o más abundantes que las "menos idiomáticas" o "cuasi-idiomáticas" (aunque no tan usadas), al contrario de lo que ocurre con las correspondientes al español *nunca* y *antiguamente* (2.1, 2.2). Los somatismos forman un grupo numeroso; sobre todo, los formados con *begi* 'ojo': *begien/begiak itxi-ireki batean* o *begi(ak) iste-irekitze batean* y todas sus variantes (*begien iste batean, begi idek-heste batez, begi irekian/ireki batean, begi itxi bate(a)n, begia hets artean, begiak hesteko artean, begiak hets-idek artean), begiak itzul artean, begi itzuli batean, begi-kliska batean, begi-kolpe batez*. Algunas de estas locuciones son equivalentes y otras más o menos similares a las españolas *en un abrir y cerrar de ojos* y *en un pestañeo* o a la francesa *en un clin d'oeil*.

Tampoco faltan los somatismos formados con las palabras *aho* 'boca', *hitz* 'palabra', *buru* 'cabeza', *arnasa* o *hats* 'aliento', 'respiración' y otras relacionadas (*hots* 'ruido', 'sonido', 'golpe'): *hitzetik/ahotik hortzera* '(lit.) de la palabra/boca a los dientes' (M 64064-64067, 64068), que también significa 'frecuentemente', *ahotik eskura/sudurrera* 'de la boca a la mano/nariz' (M 64062, 63946), *hitz/berba batetik bestera* 'de una palabra a otra' (M 63736) o sus variantes (*hitz batetik bestean, hitz batetarik bertzean*), *burua/begia itzul(tzeko) artean* '(lit.) en el tiempo que se tarda en volver la cabeza' (M 63927, 63935), *arnasa hartzeko beta/asti gabe/barik* 'sin tiempo para respirar' (M 63754, 63773), *arnas(a) hots batean* '(lit.) en un golpe de respiración' (M 63961), *arnasa batean* (M 64121) o *hats batean*, estas últimas equivalentes al español *en un soplo/suspiro* y similares a *como una exhalación*. Otras locuciones relacionadas con las anteriores son *ito-itoka* 'a toda prisa', '(lit.) ahogando(se)' y *hots batean* 'de golpe' (M 63957-63960).

Son también abundantes las locuciones comparativas (comparaciones con animales, elementos atmosféricos, culturales y religiosos), formadas con palabras como *ziztu/histu/txistu* 'saliva', 'silbido', 'velocidad', *tximista* 'relámpago', 'rayo', *txori* 'pájaro', *aida* 'voz con que se llama a las vacas para que avancen', etc.: *ziztu bizian/biziz/handian* 'a gran velocidad', *txistua baino arinago* (M 63710, 64193-64195), *ehun deabruen histuan* lit. 'a la velocidad de cien diablos', *ehun puten histuan* 'a la velocidad de cien putas' (coloquial) (Duhau:2003:154) y *tximista batean* y sus variantes *(tximista(k) bezala/legez, tximistaren pare, tximistak hartuta/harturik, tximistak egiten, tximista baino lehen*), todas estas últimas equivalentes o similares a la española *como un rayo*.

Otras locuciones son: *txoria baino arinago* (M 64196) 'más ligero/veloz que el pájaro', *aida bate(a)n*. Nada escasas son las que mencionan inicio y final de oraciones religiosas: *aitaren egin orduko* 'antes de santiguarse', *aitaren batean*'(lit.) en un decir "En el nombre del Padre"', *Jesus batean* 'en un decir Jesús', *amen* (o *Jesus* o *Jesus amen*) *esan orduko* (o *esan arte*) 'antes de decir amén/Jesus', *inomine batean* y sus variantes *(inomine santan, inomine santi batean)*.

Algunas de ellas son equivalentes y otras similares a las españolas *en un decir Jesús, en un decir amén, en un santiamén, en menos que se santigua/persigna un cura loco, en menos que se reza un credo, en un credo, en una avemaria*.

No escasean las locuciones onomatopéyicas y las provenientes de onomatopeyas: *di-da (batean)* (similar a la española *en un pis-pas*), *ti-ta, tink-tank, zirt edo zart, zizt-zazt, takada batean* 'de un tirón', 'en una tacada' (la onomatopeya *tak* denota un golpe o una acción rápida). No faltan tampoco las construcciones con sintagmas negativos en correlación, de patrón "Ni X ni Y": *ez bat eta ez bi* '(lit.) ni uno ni dos' (M 64049-64052), *ez agur eta ez adio* 'a todo correr', '(lit.) ni saludo ni adiós' (M 64154, 64061); *ez non eta ez han* 'de pronto', 'inopinadamente', '(lit.) ni dónde ni allí' (M 64056-64058).

A pesar de esta abundancia relativa, habitualmente se emplean unos pocos; en los medios de comunicación los más oídos son *ziztu bizian, bertatik bertara, hitzetik hortzera* (que significa también 'frecuentemente') y *di-da batean*.

Hemos mencionado bastantes locuciones españolas equivalentes o similares a estas vascas. Otras son: *en un periquete, en un tris, en menos que canta un gallo, en un dos por tres*.

3. Locuciones adverbiales de cantidad

Las locuciones equivalentes al español *abundantemente* están formadas por palabras que denotan abundancia (*asko* 'mucho', *gehiegi/larregi/lar/sobera* 'demasiado', *aski* 'bastante', 'suficiente', *adina/beste* 'tanto como', *nasai* 'abundante', 'pródigo', *makina bat* 'muchas personas/cosas', *mundu* 'mundo', 'multitud de gente') por lo que las consideramos como "menos idiomáticas". Por ej.: *asko-asko, asko eta asko, asko eta gehiegi/larregi/la* '(lit.) mucho y demasiado', *lar ere/be lar* 'realmente demasiado', *aski eta sobera* 'suficiente y demasiado', *nahi/gura beste/adina, nahi(ko) guz(t)ia, nahiko beste* 'tanto como se quiera', 'en abundancia', *makina bat* (+ sust.(pers.), generalmente *jende*), *mundu bat, mundu bete* 'multitud de gente'.

Las locuciones que expresan 'lleno de', 'colmado de' (personas/cosas) están formadas por palabras como *bete* 'lleno', *mukuru* 'colmo', 'montón', 'colmado (de)', *leher* 'abundancia/exceso de', '(a) reventar', *blai* 'calado', 'colmado', *txil-txil* 'lleno', y palabras con sentido figurado como *lepo* 'cuello', 'lleno', 'en abundancia', *josita* 'cosido', 'clavado', 'lleno': *txil-txil, mukuru bete* 'lleno hasta el colmo' (equivalente a la locución española *a(l) colmo*), locuciones de patrón sintactico sust. + *bete* + sust. como *galtza(k) bete lan* 'con mucho trabajo', '(lit) con los pantalones llenos de trabajo' (?), *kolko(a) bete diru* '(lit.) con el seno lleno de dinero', construcciones pospositivas como *-z lepo(raino)* (con los verbos *egon/bete* 'estar'/'llenar', expresos o no; es equivalente a la locución española *hasta el cuello*), *-z leher(ra), -z josita* o *-en emana* 'afluencia', 'multitud', y reduplicaciones intensivas como *blai-blai* (con algunas restricciones de uso), *bete-betean* 'plenamente', 'a rebosar', *bete-beterik* o *mukuru-mukuru*.

Entre las "más idiomáticas" hay somatismos, comparaciones, reduplicaciones onomatopéyicas etc. Los somatismos están formados por las palabras *lepo* 'cuello' ya mencionado, *esku* 'mano', *ezker* 'izquierda', 'mano izquierda', *eskuin* 'derecha', 'mano derecha', *buruko ile* 'pelos de la cabeza': *ezker-eskuin* '(lit.) a izquierda y derecha' (equivalente a la española *a diestro y sinistro*), *esku beteka/betez* (equivalente a *a manos llenas*).

Algunos somatismos tienen construcción comparativa: *buruko ileak baino X* (sust.) *gehiago, buruan ileak adina* con sus variantes (*buruan/buruko ileak/uleak beste/lez* etc.) 'tantos como pelos de/en la cabeza', equivalente a la locución española *como (o más que) pelos hay (*o *tengo) en la cabeza*.

Comparaciones con insectos que viven en sociedades: *erlea legez/bezala* 'como las abejas', *txindurria bezala* o *inurria lez* 'como las hormigas' y *txindurria(k) baino ugariago* '(lit.) más abundantemente que las hormigas' (M 72317, 72318, 72319), *eltxoa bezala* 'como los mosquitos' (M 72310-72313), similar a la española *como moscas*. Otras locuciones comparativas: *arrautza bezala (betea)* '(lit.) lleno como el huevo' (M 72489, 72490), *zeruan izar (den) bezainbat* (M 72069) o *zeruan izar(rik) (den/dagoen) baino gehiago* 'tantos como/más que estrellas en el firmamento' (M 72068).

Otras locuciones similares que denotan 'abundancia': *dozenan hamabi* '(lit.) doce en la docena' (M 72049), *dozenan hamahiru* '(lit.) trece en la docena', *naizu-naizu* 'en extrema abundancia' '(lit.) quieres-quieres'.

Hay también un grupo que locuciones, que se combinan generalmente con el verbo *bizi* 'vivir' que relacionan la abundancia con vivir a placer: *esne-mamitan/esnetan* '(lit.) en nata de leche / en leche', *azal-apainetan* '(lit.) en afeites', *uren gaineko bitsean/bitsetan* '(lit.) en la espuma' o *urre bitsean* '(lit.) en baño de oro'. Finalmente, las reduplicaciones onomatopéyicas forman otro grupo: *barra-barra / bar-bar* 'abundantemente'.

Hemos citado varias locuciones equivalentes españolas. Algunas otras son: *a tutiplé, a troche y moche* 'sin medida' (*a trocha y mocha* en Cuba).

4. Locuciones adverbiales de opinión

Las locuciones de opinión equivalentes al español *en opinión (de X)* están formadas por palabras usuales y más bien denotativas (*uste* 'opinión', 'presunción', *iritzi* 'juicio, opinión', *arabera* 'según', 'conforme a', *irudi* 'aspecto, apariencia', 'parecer, opinión') y alguna otra más figurativa como *begi* 'ojo'. Se utilizan sobre todo en construcciones pospositivas, con el genitivo *-en* precedido: *-en ustez* (por ej. *nire ustez* 'en mi opinión', *zure ustez* 'en tu opinión' etc.), con sus variantes (*-en ustean/ustetan*), *-en iritziz/iritzian*, *-en arabera*, *-en irudiko/irudiz* 'al parecer (de)'; *-en begietan/begitako* 'en opinión (de)'. Fuera de estas construcciones pospositivas, hay otras locuciones como, por ej. *uste denez, uste den bezala/lez* 'como se cree', *oraingo ustez* 'según se cree ahora'. Existen también algunas locuciones, a caballo entre las de opinión u otras, que son cuasi-enunciados, como por ej. *nik erran behar banu (o guk esan behar bagenu)* 'en mi (o: en nuestra) modesta opinión', '(lit.) si yo tuviera (o nosotros tuvieramos) que decir' (M 21152, 85994), *nik dakidala* (o *guk dakigula*, etc.) o *nire jakinean* (o *gure jakinean*) 'que yo sepa' (o 'que nosotros sepamos').

A continuación mencionaremos algunas locuciones adverbiales de opinión restrictivas del valor de verdad de la aserción (tomamos esta terminología de Bosque–Demonte (eds.):1999); en concreto, las correspondientes al español *probablemente, al parecer, aparentemente, en verdad* y *sin duda*. No es siempre fácil distinguir claramente entre ellas. De hecho, en euskera algunas locuciones pueden tener un significado ambivalente, un tanto difícil de discernir en un texto escrito (véase los casos de *nonbait ere* y *nolabait ere* unas líneas más abajo) y, por otro lado, se advierte una cierta abundancia o exceso de variantes. Estas locuciones estan formadas generalmente por palabras denotativas; son, pues, "menos idiomáticas".

Locuciones equivalentes a *probablemente, al parecer, seguramente, por lo visto*: *seguru/ziur asko, segur aski* 'probablemente', '(lit.) con bastante seguridad', las locuciones vizcaínas *aren baten* 'seguramente' (M 85968) y *eritxi baten (iritzi batean* en euskera unificado) 'al parecer', '(lit.) en una (misma) opinión', *nolabait ere* 'de algun modo', 'seguramente' (M 86055-86061), *nonbait ere* 'seguramente', 'por lo visto', 'supuestamente', 'sin duda', *ikusten denez* 'por lo visto', '(lit.) como se ve'.

Locuciones equivalentes a *aparentemente*: *itxura denez* '(lit.) como es apariencia' y todas sus variantes (*itxura den lez, itxura batean/batera, itxura dagoenez/daukanez, (gauzak) itxura duenez, itxura guztien arabera, itxuraz behintzat* 'al menos en apariencia'), *antza denez, agi danez/ danean* 'según parece'.

Por último, entre las locuciones que refuerzan el valor de verdad de la aserción, las equivalentes a *en verdad*: *egia esan* y sus variantes *(egia esateko/esatera/esanda)* 'a decir verdad', *egiari zor* 'en deuda con la verdad' (en boga recientemente). Equivalentes a *evidentemente*, s*in duda*: *duda(rik) gabe/barik, zalantza(rik) gabe/barik, igarri-igarrian* 'muy conocidamente', 'sin la menor duda', *nabarmen-nabarmen* '(lit.) muy notoriamente', *bistan denez/dena* 'como/que está a la vista', *noski baino noskiago* 'evidentemente', '(lit.) más claro que claro'; de uso similar es *argi (e)ta garbi* 'muy claramente'.

5. Conclusiones

El euskera cuenta con un patrimonio locucional nada desdeñable, como podemos comprobar en estas listas de locuciones adverbiales. Hemos querido llamar la atención sobre las locuciones más plenamente idiomáticas, por su abundancia en algunas series adverbiales, por su interés lingüístico-cultural y para resaltar el valor expresivo de las mismas. Porque, aunque algunas locuciones corren peligro de desaparición, las locuciones son necesarias (como el resto de los fraseologismos) para dar fuerza expresiva al lenguaje, de ahí su valor práctico para la comunicación. Por eso, nos parece que el euskera necesita un buen diccionario de locuciones euskéricas (en formato electrónico, al menos), con sus correspondientes en español, francés e inglés.

Hemos comprobado también que muchas locuciones euskéricas son equivalentes o similares a las del español, lo que pone de manifiesto la estrecha relación linguística y cultural que ha existido y existe entre ambas lenguas. Asimismo, estamos seguros de que existen locuciones equivalentes y similares a las del euskera en otras lenguas, y para un mejor conocimiento de las locuciones en general y las del euskera en particular sería interesante la comparación morfosintáctica y semántica de locuciones de lenguas diferentes.

6. Bibliografía

AZKUE. R.M. 1969 "Esakerak/Modismos". *Euskalerriaren Yakintza*, III. Madrid: Espasa Calpe: 233-351.

BOSQUE, I. & DEMONTE, V. (eds.) 1999 *Gramática descriptiva de la lengua española*. Real Academia Española, colecc. Nebrija y Bello. Madrid: Espasa.

BUITRAGO, A. 2002 *Diccionario de dichos y frases hechas*. Madrid: Espasa Calpe.

CORPAS, G. 1997 *Manual de fraseología española*. Madrid: Gredos.

DGV-OEH. Véase Michelena, L.

DUHAU, H. 2003 *Hasian hasi. "Birdena" edo bigarren partea. Beskoitzeko euskara*. Donibane Lohizune: Akoka.

ELEXPURU, J.M. 2004 *Bergara aldeko hiztegia. Leintz-Aramaio, Oñati eta Eibar aldeko berbekin osotuta*. Bergarako Udala.

GARATE, G. 1998 *Atsotitzak. Refranes. Proverbes. Proverbia*. Fundación BBK.

IZAGIRRE, K. 1981 *Euskal lokuzioak espainolezko eta frantsesezko gida-zerrendarekin*. Hordago.

http://intza.armiarma.com; www.erabili.com/lantresnak/esamoldeak/esamoldeak;

MICHELENA, L. 1987-2005 *Diccionario General Vasco–Orotariko Euskal Hiztegia*. Bilbo, Euskaltzaindia. http://www.euskaltzaindia.net/oeh;

MOCOROA, J. M. 1990 *Ortik eta emendik. Repertorio de locuciones del habla popular vasca, oral y escrita, en sus diversas variedades. Analógicamente clasificado por categorías y conceptos a base de los cuadros e índices de A. Pinloche y F. Brunot*. Labayru—Eusko Jaurlaritza—Etor. www.erabili.com/lantresnak/esamoldeak/mokoroa;

VARELA, F. & KUBARTH, H. 1996 *Diccionario fraseológico del español moderno*. Madrid: Gredos.

VILLASANTE, L. 1988 *Euskararen auziaz*. Colección Eleizalde.

VARIACIÓN FRASEOLÓGICA DEL ESPAÑOL DE CUYO, ARGENTINA

Graciela García de Ruckschloss
Inst. de Inv. Lingüísticas y Filológicas Manuel Alvar
Universidad Nacional de San Juan, República Argentina

Abstract: In this work, we introduce a comparative investigation between phraseologisms found in the Cuyo region, Argentina, and those found in the rest of the country and neighbour states, including Spain, with the final objective being lexicographical cataloging. By doing this, we perform contrastive phraseological documentation to incorporate the elements to the *Diccionario de Regionalismos Cuyanos*, a regional semasiological monolinguistic dictionary that contains the local variants of the peninsular Spanish registered in Cuyo.

Keywords: Spanish phraseography; dialectal phraseology; phraseological variation

En la región de Cuyo, Argentina, cuando aludimos al hecho de faltar a clase sin autorización o al trabajo sin motivos importantes, empleamos la locución *hacerse la chupina*[1], que en el centro del país equivale a *hacerse la rata*, *la sin cola*, *la rabona* (esta última también en España, pero con la forma *hacer rabona*), en el norte, a *hacerse la yuta*[2], en Perú, a *hacerse la vaca*, en Chile, a *hacerse la chancha*, en el español peninsular general, a *hacer novillos* y en el español peninsular regional a *hacer pirola* (en Zaragoza). Los fraseologismos sirven para comprender el pensamiento y la realidad de un pueblo, su cultura y sus relaciones sociales, ya que constituyen la parte más característica de la lengua. En esta comunicación presentamos un estudio comparativo entre los fraseologismos registrados en la región de Cuyo, por un lado, y los registrados tanto en el resto del país y en los países vecinos como en España, por otro, con el objetivo final de catalogación lexicográfica. Así, damos cuenta de la exploración fraseológica contrastiva adoptada para incorporar estas unidades al *Diccionario de Regionalismos Cuyanos*, un diccionario semasiológico parcial, monolingüe, que recopila las variantes regionales del español peninsular que se registran en la región de Cuyo. Respecto de la zona objeto de estudio, planteamos este trabajo con una visión regional; consideramos un corpus de fraseologismos registrados en la región de Cuyo, conformada tradicionalmente por las provincias de San Juan, Mendoza y San Luis, a las cuales se agrega la provincia de La Rioja, debido a ciertos fenómenos lingüísticos comunes.

En relación con las fuentes, trabajamos con la "Segunda Encuesta sobre el Habla Regional, 1950", un corpus escrito constituido por encuestas léxico-etnográficas, cuyo objetivo específico fue el de conocer y afianzar las particularidades del español de Argentina.[3] Para establecer la contrastividad diatópica, hemos aplicado criterios lexicográficos similares a los establecidos por Haensch y Werner. Realizamos la selección contrastiva sobre la base del

---

[1] *chupino, na*. (Del quechua *chupa*, cola) adj. ∅ Ref. a un animal, que no tiene cola o que la tiene más corta de lo normal en su especie (DRSJ).
[2] *yuta*. f. rur. Especie de perdiz sin cola (DASyJ).
[3] Estos materiales forman parte del Fondo Berta Vidal de Battini (FONVIBA), un Corpus Documental y Bibliográfico inédito, declarado Patrimonio de la Universidad Nacional de San Juan, en resguardo del Instituto de Investigaciones Lingüísticas y Filológicas Manuel Alvar.

cotejo con diccionarios españoles generales que registran fraseologismos, con diccionarios de americanismos y de países vecinos, y con diccionarios de argentinismos y de regionalismos del resto del país. Asimismo, consideramos diccionarios fraseológicos españoles, americanos y argentinos. A continuación, presentamos, a través de tablas, una muestra representativa de la exploración fraseológica contrastiva.

1. Criterios de exploración fraseológica contrastiva

1.2 La UF no se registra en el español peninsular (ver tabla 1).

En este grupo incluimos los fraseologismos en cuya composición intervienen voces de creación prehispánica, provenientes de lenguas indígenas, o voces de creación local. Consideradas con un criterio diferencial, poseen el rado máximo de contrastividad frente al sistema lingüístico de referencia, esto es, el español de España, puesto que han tenido su origen histórico en América. Se trata de palabras indígenas procedentes, en un alto porcentaje, de las lenguas andinas quechua y aimara (debido a su condición de lengua general), y, en un ínfimo número, de la lengua mapuche. En cuanto a los campos semánticos donde se observa una mayor presencia de vocablos indígenas, podemos mencionar, en primer lugar, la fauna, luego, la flora, y después, los referidos a vestimenta, alimento y utensilios domésticos (los más apropiados para la productividad fraseológica).

1.2. La UF está constituida por algunas unidades léxicas que presentan acepciones que no se registran en el español peninsular (ver tabla 2).

Dentro de este criterio, incluimos las palabras que son usadas en el español peninsular, pero que acá adoptan, además, otro/s sema/s en función de las realidades que designan. Por otra parte, es importante destacar que ocupan el porcentaje más elevado en los diccionarios parciales.

1.3. La UF está formada por algunas unidades léxicas que presentan, en el español peninsular, un uso restringido a una determinada región o bien que no tienen un uso actual (ver tabla 3).

Este apartado contiene las voces que, en los diccionarios generales de la lengua, tienen marcas de restricción regional y/o cronológica. Sin bien, no representan un porcentaje elevado, se dan algunos casos de palabras de uso regional, en desuso o poco usadas en España pero que nosotros preservamos vivas en el uso cotidiano de la lengua.

1.4. La UF posee una misma o similar estructura sintáctica que la del español peninsular, pero presenta variantes léxicas pertenecientes a un mismo campo semántico o a campos semánticos distintos (ver tabla 4).

Dentro de este ítem, consideramos las UFs que coinciden en sus significados fraseológicos y, en buena parte, también en su estructura y componentes pero que difieren en alguna palabra. También incluimos aquí las UFs que vehiculizan ideas metafóricas diferentes.Si bien hemos presentado solo una muestra de la metodología que empleamos para seleccionar e incluir los fraseologismos al *Diccionario de Regionalismos Cuyanos*, estimamos que es suficiente para exponer la factibilidad de los criterios que proponemos. De la lectura de las tablas se desprende que este muestreo de fraseologismos es factible de ser incluido en nuestro vocabulario parcial puesto que, de las veinte unidades presentadas, trece no figuran en ninguno de los repertorios generales ni particulares consultados. De las siete restantes, hay tres que sí se registran pero con marcación geográfica para San Juan y San Luis. Lo cual nos lleva a confirmar el uso regional de esas unidades. Es nuestro propósito elaborar un vocabulario parcial cuyas UFs sean incluidas siguiendo determinados criterios de contrastividad, lo cual implica clarificar el panorama que presentan las obras lexicográficas regionales. Tarea que, creemos, no está emprendida (o al menos, publicada) para la región de Cuyo, tal como se desprende de la lectura crítica de los diversos diccionarios de cuyanismos y de argentinismos consultados. Con este estudio comparativo de los fraseologismos, pretendemos contribuir al tratamiento descriptivo de la fraseología en nuestra región, y al mismo tiempo, proponer un marco de encuentro que tienda a afianzar la unidad desde la diversidad. "No es nuestro interés el marcar fronteras lingüísticas, ni destacar originalidades nacionales, ni alzar banderolas regionales. Muy por el contrario. El conocimiento de los frutos de la creación lingüística entre nosotros nos llena de orgullo pues nos muestra como contribuyentes activos a la renovación y enriquecimiento de la lengua común" (Barcia & Pauer, 2010: 31).

2. Bibliografía

10700R= RODRÍGUEZ MARÍN, F. 1914 *Todavía 10.700 refranes más*. Madrid: Prensa Española".

AT= ROJAS, E. 1976 *Americanismos usados en Tucumán*. Tucumán: Universidad Nacional de Tucumán.

CEVS= Di LULLO, O. 1946 *Contribución al estudio de las voces santiagueñas*. Santiago del Estero: López.

DA= MALARET, A. 1942 *Diccionario de americanismos*. Buenos Aires: Academia Argentina de Letras.

DAAH= ABAD de SANTILLÁN, D. 1976 *Diccionario de argentinismos de ayer y de hoy*. Buenos Aires: TEA.

DANB= SEGOVIA, L. 1911 *Diccionario de argentinismos, neologismos y barbarismos*. Buenos Aires: Coni.

DASyJ= OSÁN, M.; PÉREZ SÁEZ, V. 2006 *Diccionario de americanismos en Salta y Jujuy*. Madrid: Arco-Libros.

DEA= SECO, M.; ANDRÉS, O., RAMOS, G. 1999. *Diccionario del español actual*. Madrid: Aguilar.

DEAr= HAENSCH, G. & WERNER, R.2000. *Diccionario del español de Argentina*. Madrid: Gredos.

DEChi= MORALES PETTORINO et al. 1984 *Diccionario ejemplificado de chilenismos*. Univ. de Playa Ancha.

DGA= SANTAMARÍA, F. 1942 *Diccionario General de Americanismos*. Méjico: P. Robredo.

DiFHA= BARCIA, P. & PAUER, G. 2010 *Diccionario fraseológico del habla argentina*. Bs.As: Emecé.

DiHA= ACADEMIA ARGENTINA de LETRAS. 2003 *Diccionario del habla de los argentinos*. Bs. As: Planeta.

DMLC= CABALLERO, R. 1947 *Diccionario de modismos de la lengua castellana*. Buenos Aires: El Ateneo.

DP= ARONA, J. de. 1938 *Diccionario de peruanismos*. París: Descleé de Brouwer.

DR= CAMPOS, J. & BARELLA, A. 1993 *Diccionario de refranes*. Madrid: Espasa Calpe.

DRSJ= QUIROGA, C.; GARCÍA de RUCKSCHLOSS, G. et al. 2006 *Diccionario de Regionalismos de San Juan*. AAL.

DRAE= REAL ACADEMIA ESPAÑOLA. 1992 *Diccionario de la Lengua Española*. Madrid: Espasa Calpe.

DRS= SOLÁ, J. V. 1950 *Diccionario de regionalismos de Salta*. Buenos Aires: Amorrortu.

DUE= MOLINER, M. 1966 *Diccionario de uso del español*. Madrid: Gredos.

DAVV= GONZÁLEZ, A. 2006 *Breve diccionario argentino de la vid y del vino*. Bs. As: AAL.

EDI= ALONSO, M. 1958*Enciclopedia del idioma*. Madrid: Aguilar.

ID= BARCIA, P. 2006*Un inédito Diccionario de Argentinismos del siglo XIX*. Bs. As: AAL.

MiDU= ANL. 2006 *Mil dichos, refranes, locuciones y frases del español del Uruguay*. Montevideo: ANL.

MiPEU= ACADEMIA NACIONAL de LETRAS. 2003 *Mil palabras del español del Uruguay*. Montevideo: ANL.

PChi= LAVAL, R. 1928 *Paremiología chilena*. Santiago de Chile: Universo.
R= MOYA, I. 1944 *Refranero*. Buenos Aires: Imprenta de la Universidad.
ReFCo= CARRIZO, J. M. 1941 *Los refranes y las frases en las coplas populares*. Bs. As: ICU.
ReGIE= MARTÍNEZ KLEISER, L. MCMLIII. *Refranero general ideológico español*. Madrid: Aguirre Torre.
VC= VILLAFUERTE, C. 1961 *Voces y costumbres de Catamarca*. Buenos Aires.
VRFP= CORREAS, G. 1924 *Vocabulario de refranes y frases proverbiales*. Madrid: Tipogragía de la "RABM"

Anexo:

tabla 1 *Chileno y bueno*[4]; *Como el mate de las Morales*[5]; *Como los perros de Pituil; Hacer cutamear / cutamiar; Lindo pial si no se chusque*[6]; *Muchas pitillas para un solo trompo; No tan grueso que no es para chuce; No se apure que no es minga*[7].
tabla 2 *Andar/estar chispeado/ curado/ farreado/ picado/ punteado; A vaquita echada; Domar el chivo ; Quedarse con el cominillo*[8]/ *pica*.[9]
tabla 3 *Ardiles*[10] *quiere la guerra; Es al ñudo tironear cuando la cobija es corta /No hay que estirarse más de lo que dan las cobijas; Buey solo bien se lambe*.
tabla 4 *Dios castiga y/pero no se le ve la guasca.*[11]; *Mal de muchos, consuelo de tunturuchos.; Más vale cata en mano que cien volando; Champa*[12] *de la misma vega; No hay que contar con la chuspa*[13] *sin pillar el avestruz.*[14]

---

[4] Con sus variantes: *chileno y bueno, no se ha visto*; *chileno y bueno, el que no se lleva la cincha se lleva el freno; chileno y bueno, si no se va con la mula se va con el freno*.
[5] La locución completa es *ser como el mate de las Morales, que nunca llegó a cebarse*.
[6] chusquear. tr. rur. p. us. ≠ Resbalar. (DRSJ). Con sus variantes: *lindo pial si no se sale; lindo pial si no se corta; lindo pial si no se zafa*.
[7] minga. (Del quech. minc'ay, alquilar gente) f. ∅ Reunión de amigos o vecinos para realizar el trabajo común de la siega del trigo, sin más remuneración que la comida y bebida a cargo del patrón (generalm. acompañadas con cantos y bailes) (DRSJ).
[8] cominillo. m. Cizaña. // 2. Arg., Chile. Escrúpulo, recelo (DRAE).
[9] pica. f. coloq. Arg. y Ur. Rivalidad (DRAE)
[10] ardil. m. p. us. ⊕ *Ardid*. (DRSJ)
[11] guasca. (Del quech. *huasca*, soga) f. ∅ Lonja o tira de cuero que se emplea en tareas rurales para diversos fines, como atar o azotar. (DRSJ)
[12] champa. (Del quech.) f. ∅ Pan formado por el pasto y por la tierra adherida a sus raíces. (DRSJ)
[13] chuspa. (Del quech. *ch'uspa*, bolsa) f. ∅ Pequeña bolsa fabricada con el buche del avestruz o la vejiga del guanaco, que se utiliza para guarda objetos, especial., dinero o tabaco. (DRSJ)
[14] Con sus variantes *no hay que contar con la chuspa sin antes bolear el avestruz; no hay que contar con la chuspa, antes de pillar el avestruz; no hay que contar con la chuspa, estando el avestruz en el campo; no hay que ofrecer la chuspa sin bolear el avestruz; no hay que vender la pluma antes de bolear el avestruz*.

Anexo tabla 1

	Dicc. esp. generales			Dicc. de americanismos y de países vecinos					Dicc. argentinismos				Dicc. regionalismos resto del país					Dicc. fraseols esp				Dic. fr. amer.		Diccionarios fr. argentinos			
DRAE	EDI	DEA	DUE	DGA	DA	DECh	MiPEU	DP	DiHA	DID	DAAHB	DANB	DEAr	DRS	AT	DASyJ	DVC	CEVS	VRFP	ReGlE	10 7 00 R	DR	PCfri	MiDU	DfFHA	DMLC	R	RefCo
Chileno y bueno fr. prov. Se usa para desconfiar de la veracidad o certeza de alguien o de algo	–	–	–	–	–	–	–	–	–	–	–	–	–	–	–	–	–	–	–	–	–	–	–	–	–	–	–
Como el mate de las Morales. loc. adv. rur. Señala una cosa prometida y nunca cumplida	+[5]	–	–	–	–	–	–	–	–	–	+	–	–	–	–	–	–	–	–	–	–	–	–	–	–	+[4]	–
Como los perros de Pitui. loc. adv. rur. Muy pobre	–	–	–	–	–	–	–	–	–	–	–	–	–	–	–	–	–	–	–	–	–	–	+	–	–	+	–
Hacer cutamear / cutamiar. loc. vb. rur. Aplicar un castigo	–	–	–	–	–	–	–	–	–	–	–	–	–	–	–	–	–	–	–	–	–	–	–	–	–	–	–
Lindo pial si no se chusque. fórm. Comenta lo bueno de algo, si durara.	–	–	–	–	–	–	–	–	–	–	+[6]	–	–	–	–	–	–	–	–	–	–	–	–	–	–	–	–
Muchas pitillas para un solo trompo. enunc. v. esp. Da a entender que lo que se ambiciona no puede alcanzar para todos.	–	–	–	–	–	–	–	–	–	–	–[9]	–	–	–	–	–	–	–	–	–	–	10	–	+[7]	–	+[8]	–
No tan grueso que no es para chuce. fórm. Censura palabras subidas de tono	–	–	–	–	–	–	–	–	–	–	–	–	–	–	–	–	–	–	–	–	–	–	–	–	–	–	–
No se apure no es minga. fórm. Sirve para detener al precipitado en cualquier acción o decisión	–	–	–	–	–	–	–	–	–	–	–	–	–	–	–	–	–	–	–	–	–	–	–	–	–	–	–

Variación fraseológica del español de Cuyo, Argentina... 209

tabla 2

Dicc. esp. generales				Dicc. americanismos y países vecinos					Dicc. argentinismos					Dicc. regionalismos resto del país							Dicc. fraseols esp					Dic. fr. amer.			Diccionarios fr. argentinos				
DRAE	EDI	DEA	DUE	DGA	DA	DECh	MPEU	DP	DHA	ID	DAAHB	DEAr	DRS	ART	DASvJ	VC	CEVS	VRFP	ReGlE	1078OR	DR	PChi	MDU	DFHA	DMLC	R	ReFCo
Andar/estar chispeado/ curado/ farreado/ picado/ punteado. loc. vb. Estar borracho.																																	
Sí[3]	[9]	–	–	–	–	–	–	–	–	–	+[10]	–	–	–	–	–	–	–	–	–	–	–	–	–	–	–	–
A vaquita echada. loc. adv. rur. Beber de una sola vez.[12]																																	
–	–	–	–	–	–	–	–	–	–	–	–	–	–	–	–	–	–	–	–	–	–	–	–	–	–	–	–
Domar el chivo. loc. vb. rur. Quedarse soltera la mujer.																																	
–	–	–	–	–	–	–	–	–	–	–	–	–	–	–	–	–	–	–	–	–	–	–	–	–	–	–	–
Quedarse con el cominillo /pica. loc. vb. Estar alguien con recelo o intriga																																	
–	–	–	–	–	–	–	–	–	–	–	–	–	–	–	+	–	–	–	–	–	–	–	–	+[13]	–	–	–

tabla 3

Dicc. esp. generales				Dicc. americanismos y países vecinos					Dicc. argentinismos					Dicc. regionalismos resto del país							Dicc. fraseols esp					Dic. fr. americ			Diccionarios fr. argentinos				
DRAE	EDI	DEA	DUE	DGA	DA	DECh	MPEU	DP	DHA	ID	DAAHB	DEAr	DRS	ART	DASvJ	VC	CEVS	VRFP	ReGlE	1078OR	DR	PChi	MDU	DFHA	DMLC	R	ReFCo
Ardiles[10] quiere la guerra. enunc. v. esp. Para llevar adelante una empresa, es necesario contar con capacidad o habilidad																																	
–	–	–	–	–	–	–	–	–	–	–	–	–	–	–	–	–	–	–	–	–	–	–	–	–	–	–	–
Es al ñudo tironear cuando la cobija es corta./No hay que estirarse más de lo que dan las cobijas. enunc. v. esp. Aconseja ser previsor.																																	
[14]	[15]	–	–	–	–	–	–	–	–	–	–	–	–	–	–	–	–	–	–	–	–	–	–	–	–	[17]	–
Buey solo bien se lambe. refr. Quien no tiene ayuda, se provee los medios necesarios para su subsistencia y se da maña para defenderse.																																	
[16]	–	–	–	–	–	–	–	–	–	–	–	–	–	–	–	–	–	–	–	–	–	–	–	–	–	–	–

tabla 4

	Dicc. esp. generales				Dicc. americanismos y países vecinos				Dicc. argentinismos					Dicc. regionalismos resto del país					Dicc. fraseols esp				Dic. fr. americ			Diccionarios fr. argentinos			
	DRAE	EDI	DEA	DUE	DGA	DA	DECh	MfPEU	DP	DHA	ID	DAAH	DANB	DEAr	DRS	AT	DASyJ	VC	CEVS	VRFP	ReGlE	10 7 8 R	DR	PChi	CMDU	DFHA	DMLC	R	RefCo
Dios castiga v/pero no se le ve la guasca. refr. Inexorabilidad de la justicia divina.	–	–	–	–	–	–	–	–	–	–	–	–	–	–	–	–	–	–	–	–	–	–	–	–	–	–	–
Mal de muchos, consuelo de tunturuchos. refr. Las penas compartidas son menores.	–	–	–	–	–	–	–	–	–	12	–	–	–	–	–	–	–	–	–	–	–	+11	–	–	–	–	–
Más vale cata en mano que cien volando. refr. Aconseja aferrarse a lo cierto.	–	–	–	–	–	–	–	–	–	–	13	–	14	–	–	–	–	–	–	–	–	–	–	–	–	–	–
Champade la misma vega. loc. sust. Ninguno es peor para enemigo que el que ha sido amigo, compañero o familiar.	–	–	–	–	–	–	–	–	–	–	–	–	–	–	–	–	–	–	–	–	–	–	–	–	–	–	–
No hay que contar con la chuspasin pillar el avestruz. enunc. v. esp. No disponer de antemano de las cosas que no son seguras.	–	–	–	–	–	–	–	–	–	–	–	–	–	+	–	–	–	–	–	–	–	–	–	–	–	+15	–

NON-COMPOSITIONALITY AND THE EMERGENCE OF A NEW PHRASEOLOGICAL UNIT: AN ANALYSIS OF *HAVE UNTIL* X *TO* V*

Makoto Sumiyoshi
Setsunan University, Japan

Abstract: This paper discusses the phraseological unit *have until* X *to* V, which can be exemplified by *The banks have until the end of February to make a decision*. The discussion in this paper is organized around the following three interesting points displayed by the phraseological unit. First, the unit expresses the time-limit meaning that is usually expressed by the preposition *by*, although what is denoted by *until* is the duration meaning. Second, as far as syntax is concerned, it is difficult to resort to traditional linguistic apparatuses such as intraposition to explain the emergence of the unit. It can be argued that *have until* is chosen as a unit without regard to its internal syntactic structure. Third, corpora research reveals that the preposition *till* is infrequently employed in the unit even though traditional grammar argues that *till* and *until* are exchangeable in most cases. This can be attributed to a stress clash caused by the sequence of *have till*.

Key Words: Phraseological units, non-compositionality, *have until* X *to* V, stress clash

1. Introduction

First, consider example (1), which demonstrates the problem to be discussed in this paper:
(1) Under the terms of last month's unanimous Security Council resolution, Iraq **has until Sunday to declare** all of its biological, chemical, and nuclear weapons work, as well as its long-range missiles. Iraq says the declaration could be ready as early as Wednesday. (*The Voice of America*, Dec. 3, 2002)

The underlined part of the sentence is extremely interesting. The sequence of words, in which the *until*-prepositional phrase occupies the object position of the verb *have*, is difficult to explain in the traditional lexical grammar of *have*. It has been argued that *have* is a transitive verb followed by noun phrases in whatever meanings it expresses.

The objectives of this paper are threefold. The first is to argue that the expression *have until* X *to* V as a whole functions as a phraseological unit that means a time limit is set before someone or something does something. The second objective is to show that the meaning as well as the syntactic behavior of the phraseological unit can be characterized in terms of non-compositionality, an important defining parameter of phraseologisms, as discussed by Gries' (2008) article. Third, it is argued based on corpora searches that *till* is not usually used in the unit in place of *until*, which is the result of the avoidance of a stress clash (Schlüter 2005).

2. Prerequisites

2.1 Terminology

Formulaic or multi-word expressions have been referred to with a wide variety of names (Wray 2002: 8ff.). This proliferation of terms is a reflection of the current state of phraseology, which is subsuming a plethora of linguistic phenomena under its rubric, as pointed out by Skandera (ed.) (2007), Granger and Meunier (2008), and Granger and Paquot (2008). One reason for this wider coverage of different linguistic phenomena is that two major approaches to phraseology are now recognized, and they have developed from different origins (Granger and Paquot 2008).

One approach comes from the former Soviet Union and Eastern European countries, and the other is a British corpus-based approach to "fixed" expressions. It is the latter that has found there are much more recurrent phrases in English than anticipated, thus extending the boundary of phraseology to include a wider range of lexical sequences. The territory of phraseology has expanded so vastly that it has begun to encompass multi-word combinations that occur recurrently but are discontinuous strings with one or more free slots into which some variables are inserted. Recurrent strings of words are called "phrase-frames" (e.g., *plays a * part in, a * of*, etc. (Stubbs 2007)), "PoS-grams" (e.g., *at the end of the, as a result of the, in the middle of the*, etc.), "collostructions" (e.g., [X *think nothing of* V-*ing*], [S V O *into* V-*ing*], etc. (Stefanowitsch and Gries 2003)), and "clause collocations" (e.g., *I wonder… because*, etc. (Hunston 2002: 75)).

A motley collection of multi-word units have come into the research domain of phraseology. Accordingly, the terms to refer to each type of unit have multiplied. *Have until X to* V has a characteristic meaning and it is structurally "irregular" in that the *until*-prepositional phrase stands as an object. It has two slots which are filled by an NP and a verb, both of which have a particular semantic characteristic, as will be discussed in Section 4. The recurrent string *have until* X *to* V can be regarded as one of the newly recognized phraseological units. I use the term "phraseological unit" to refer to this configuration for the very reason that the term is a neutral one that covers a wide variety of multi-word units.

2.2 Apparatuses

2.2.1 Semantic/grammatical non-compositionality

Gries (2008) enumerates six parameters that define phraseologisms, including frequencies, lexical and syntactic flexibilities, distance, semantic compositionality, and so forth. Perhaps the most important among the six parameters, as argued by Gries (2008: 6), is compositionality, that is, whether the meaning of a composite expression can be obtained by summing up the meanings of its constituents. Often-quoted examples are *kick the bucket* and *by and large*. It is impossible to obtain the meanings of "die" or "generally speaking," respectively, by combining the meanings of each of the words that constitute these phrases. Thus, these expressions are semantically non-compositional.

In terms of internal grammatical construction, the word string *kick the bucket* is not grammatically deviant. The verb *kick* takes the object noun phrase *the bucket*, and this type of syntactic structure is normal in English sentences. There is nothing unnatural about the expression in terms of its internal structure, though the meaning of the whole unit is not only the sum of the meanings of the words employed in the composite. On the other hand, the phraseological unit *by and large* is grammatically irregular in that the preposition *by* and the adjective *large* are coordinated by the conjunction *and*, which normally links constituents of the same syntactic category. Word strings of this type are grammatically non-compositional, as Moon (1998: 8) argues.

These two aspects of non-compositionality are to be taken into consideration in the analysis of the phraseological unit *have until* X *to* V.

2.2.2 The open-choice and idiom principles

Syntactically ill-formed sequences such as *by and large* are perfectly acceptable in English. This indicates that word strings of this type are not constructed one by one based on English syntax. Rather, they are prefabricated and stored as a unit.

As Sinclair (1991: 109) argues, such phrases are not created by "complex choices ... [a]t each point where a unit is completed" This means they are not produced by the open-choice principle. Instead, phraseological units are produced by the idiom principle, whereby "a language user has available to him or her a large number of semi-preconstructed phrases that constitute single choices, even though they might appear to be analyzable into segments" (p. 110).

These two principles advocated by Sinclair are indispensable in a phraseological approach to language.

3. Data

The data given in Section 4 come mainly from corpora such as the British National Corpus (BNC). The phraseological unit *have until* X *to* V, however, does not occur frequently in the BNC. Hence, especially when frequency is any indication, I rely upon two corpora freely available on the Internet.

One is the Corpus of Contemporary American English (COCA) (http://www.americancorpus.org/) and the other is the Time Magazine Corpus (http://corpus.byu.edu/time/). Space limitations prevent me from providing all the examples and numerical data in this paper. See Sumiyoshi (2012) for detailed quantitative analyses with all the examples, tables, and figures.

4. *Have until* X *to* V: A phraseological approach

In the subsections to follow, I provide a quantitative and qualitative analysis of *have until* X *to* V in terms of non-compositionality and claim that it cannot be dealt with appropriately by traditional lexical grammar of *have*.

The expression is non-compositional both syntactically and semantically, and a phraseological approach is most useful to explain its behavior.

4.1 Frequency

First, let us consider how often the phraseological unit is used in present-day English. The three corpora were searched for all the variant forms of the expression, including tensed variants and *till*-variants.

The raw figures from the COCA are given in Table 1. *Until* is exclusively employed. *Till* is unlikely to occur, the reason for which will be discussed in Section 4.4.

Table 1. The frequency of "*have until/till* X *to* V" in the Corpus of Contemporary American English

have until X *to* V	322
have till X *to* V	5

Quirk et al. (1985: 1080) argue that "[*t*]*ill* is used in the same way as *until*." However, as is clearly demonstrated in Table 1, this is not the case for *have until* X *to* V. *Until* is chosen by default. Figure 1 shows parts of the concordance lines of *have until* X *to* V from the COCA.

1 ...They **have until** June 8, I believe it is, **to** file paperwork in this case.
2 ...Parents **have until** Thursday **to** get them their shots or file waivers,
3 ...He would **have until** June 15 **to** withdraw from the draft.
4 ...public school system **have until** June 1 **to** request a transfer if they want their child
5 ...loans and investments. # Other banks **have until** March 31 **to** join the plan,

Figure 1. Concordance lines of *have until* X *to* V from the COCA.

4.2 The syntax of *have until* X *to* V

4.2.1 Grammatical non-compositionality

As instantiated by the examples given so far, the *until*-prepositional phrase occupies the syntactic position after *have* and is followed by *to*-infinitive clauses. I emphasize that a configuration of this kind is difficult to explain reasonably using a traditional lexical approach because it has been argued, regardless of their linguistic persuasion, that the object of a transitive verb is normally a noun phrase or a nominal clause (see, for example, Quirk et al. 1985: 726). However, the transitive verb *have* in the examples above takes the *until*-prepositional phrase as its object, which is, of course, neither a noun phrase nor a nominal phrase. Wray (2002: 49) argues that "it is common for formulaic sequences to contain a word behaving in an abnormal way, (...) displaying grammatical irregularity". She exemplifies this by giving the expression *come a cropper*, in which the intransitive verb *come* takes an object. *Have until* X *to* V is an opposite phenomenon, in that a transitive verb is followed by a prepositional phrase. In the traditional language approach, the only way to "save" the analysis in this case is to assume that some kind of syntactic transformation is involved in the emergence of the expression—specifically, intraposition, whereby a syntactic element is moved leftward from the end of a sentence. As a result of this syntactic operation, the word order of the sentence changes. However, it is easy to refute this line of argument.

As Quirk et al. (1985: 690f.) argue, "[*t*]*ill* and *until* can only co-occur with durative verbs," that is, verbs that denote a period of time (such as *camp* and *work*). *Arrive*, for example, cannot co-occur with the *until*-phrase because it is not a durative verb, and the action it denotes is momentary. *Work* is acceptable because it is a durative verb. (e.g., *My girlfriend worked/*arrived there till Christmas*.) On the other hand, in sentences that contain *by*, durative verbs trigger unacceptability, whereas momentary verbs are in consonant with *by*. (e.g., *She *worked/arrived by Christmas*.). Corpora searches have made clear that verbs occurring in the *to*-infinitive clauses of *have until* X *to* V are momentary verbs (e.g., *achieve*, *agree*, *become*, *decide*, *persuade*, etc.), which are not allowed to occur with *until*-phrases.

This means that it is impossible to obtain the unit *have until* X *to* V by applying intraposition to the construction *have to* V *until* X because the latter are ill-formed if momentary verbs appear in the V slot, which can be illustrated, for example, by ungrammatical constructions such as **have to make a decision until Monday*. Hence, it is impossible to move the *until*-phrase leftward to form *have until Monday to make a decision*.

4.2.2 NPs that characteristically occur in X

Until, as a preposition, occurs almost exclusively with a temporal noun phrase, a subjectless *-ing* clause (e.g., *until leaving for...*), and either a noun phrase with a deverbal noun or some other noun phrase interpreted as equivalent to a clause (e.g., *until his death*). (Quirk et al. 1985: 691) However, NPs occurring in the X slot of *have until* X *to* V are limited to time expressions such as *five o'clock*, *Monday*, or *the end of the day*. Expressions such as *leaving for...* or *his death* do not occur in the X slot. If the open-choice principle is at work here, subjectless *-ing* clauses should also occur in the X slot of the phraseological unit. However, NPs occurring in the X slot are, in almost all cases, semantically restricted to a set of time expressions.

4.3 The semantics of *have until* X *to* V

(2) Iraq **has until Friday to accept or reject** the resolution the U.N. Security Council approved unanimously last Friday. If it does not, or falters afterward in following the tough provisions of the resolution, the United States and Britain have made clear they will attack Iraq. (COCA)
(3) Because April 15 falls on Sunday this year, investors will **have until April 16 to make** I.R.A. contributions. (COCA)

Example (2) means that Friday is the time limit that was set for Iraq to either accept or reject the resolution. Iraq is obliged to make a decision by Friday. On the other hand, example (3) means that investors are allowed to make contributions by April 16 because April 15 is a Sunday. It does not mean that obligations are imposed on investors to make contributions by April 16.

Thus, *have until* X *to* V expresses two kinds of (pragmatic) meaning. One is obligation: people have to do something by the time limit indicated. The other is a kind of permission: it is acceptable for people to do something, if they want, as long as they meet the deadline. The meaning shared by the two uses is that someone or something does something by the time limit indicated. Note that the meaning is interpreted with *by* expressing a time limit (*no later than*), though *until*, which means duration, is employed.

4.4 *Have until* X *to* V and the rhythmic alternation

Schlüter (2005) discusses phonological influences on the grammar of English based on statistical data from corpora. Citing Kager's (1989) arguments that "stressed and unstressed syllables tend to alternate at rhythmically ideal disyllabic distance" (p. 2), she schematizes the contrast between stressed and unstressed syllables in the name of the Principle of Rhythmic Alternation, which states that two adjacent stress marks are regularly spaced out by one intervening mark on the next lower level.

In some cases, this rhythmic alternation deviates from the canonical pattern. One of the deviations is the stress clash, which can be defined as "a sequence of two stressed syllables which are not separated by any unstressed syllables on the next lower level" (p. 19). Schlüter argues that "stress clashes are perceived as far more objectionable (… and that) [t]he former almost categorically necessitate compensatory measures" (p. 20). She investigates how this rhythmic alternation influences the formation of English syntactic patterns and choice of lexical items (e.g., *quite a...* vs. *a quite...*).

It can be pointed out that a stress clash may be the reason that the phraseological unit under discussion has a preference for *until*. A stress is placed on the second syllable of *until*, while *till* receives a stress without any unstressed syllable as a buffer. In the latter case, there is a sequence of two stressed syllables.

(4) a.
    X   X
X X X
have un-til X *to* V

b.
X   X
X   X
have till X *to* V

Although closer scrutiny is needed, it is now hypothesized that the difference in distribution between *till* and *until* in the phraseological unit can be attributed to the strong tendency to avoid a stress clash caused by the juxtaposition of *have* and *till*.

5. Conclusion

The paper has discussed the behavior of the phraseological unit *have until* X *to* V from different points of view. It has revealed that the phraseological unit shows irregular but intriguing syntactic characteristics along with the meaning that is characteristically denoted by the whole unit. The unit is non-compositional grammatically as well as semantically. The emergence of this type of "irregular" expression cannot be accounted for by the traditional English lexical grammar of *have*. It is reasonable to assume that the sequence of *have until* is produced as a unit expressing a time limit.

*An enlarged and revised version of this paper will appear as Sumiyoshi (2012).

6.References

GRANGER, S. & MEUNIER, F. (eds.). 2008) *Phraseology: An Interdisciplinary Perspective.* Amsterdam: John Benjamins.
GRANGER, S.. & PAQUOT, M. 2008 Disentangling the phraseological web. In: Granger and Meunier (eds.): 24-49.
GRIES, S. Th. 2008 Phraseology and linguistic theory: A brief survey. In Granger and Meunier (eds.): 3-25.
HUNSTON, S. 2002 *Corpora in Applied Linguistics.* Cambridge: Cambridge Univ. Press.
MOON, R. 1998) *Fixed Expressions and Idioms in English: A Corpus-Based Approach.* Oxford: Oxford Univ. Press.
QUIRK, R, GREENBAUM, S, LEECH, G, & SVARTVIK, J. 1985 *A Comprehensive Grammar of the English Language.* London: Longman.
SCHLÜTER, J. 2005 *Rhythmic Grammar: The Influence of Rhythm on Grammatical Variation and Change in English.* Berlin: Mouton.
SINCLAIR, J. 1991 *Corpus, Concordance, Collocation.* Oxford: Oxford University Press.
SKANDERA, P. (ed.) 2007 *Phraseology and Culture in English.* Berlin/New York: Mouton.
STEFANOWITSCH, A & GRIES, S Th. 2003 Collostructions: Investigating the interaction of words and constructions. *International Journal of Corpus Linguistics* 8:2, 209-243.
STUBBS, M. 2007 On very frequent phraseology in English. In: Fracchinetti, R. (ed.). *Corpus Linguistics 25 Years on.* 89-105. Amsterdam: Rodopi
SUMIYOSHI, M. 2012 Non-compositionality, Syntactic Irregularity and Phraseology: An analysis of "*have until* X *to* V". *Intercontinental Dialogue on Phraseology,* 1. Białystok: Uniwersytet w Białymstoku: 153-175.
WRAY, A. 2002 *Formulaic language and the lexicon.* Cambridge: Cambridge Univ. Press.

ENUNCIADOS DE VALOR ESPECÍFICO EN CONTEXTOS REALES DEL ESPAÑOL

Laura Mª Aliaga Aguza
Universidad de Alicante

Abstract: The aim of this paper is to make a pragmatic approach about *specific value statements* in Spanish. For this purpose, firstly we establish boundaries with adjacent structures, as *idiomatic phrases* and *sayings*. Secondly, we will focus on the practical analysis of such structures. In this way, we will try to reach appropriate conclusions.

Key Words: Specific value statements, Spanish phraseology

Con este estudio, pretendemos trazar unas ligeras ideas sobre los *enunciados de valor específico*, tratando de obtener conclusiones sobre su uso pragmático, pero para ello primero nos centraremos en la diferenciación de estas estructuras para, posteriormente, poder llevar a cabo un estudio más concreto.

¿Qué es un *enunciado de valor específico*? En primer lugar, debemos establecer qué entendemos por *enunciado de valor específico* puesto que, por una parte, existen diversas denominaciones para este tipo de estructuras como *frase proverbial* utilizada por autores como Casares 1969, Zuluaga 1980, Sevilla Muñoz 1988, Ruiz Gurillo 1997 o *locuciones oracionales*, término acuñado por García – Page 2008; y, por otra parte, estas estructuras poseen límites difusos al encontrarse en la frontera con respecto a otras unidades como son *locuciones* y *refranes*.

En cuanto a la terminología hemos seguido la de Corpas Pastor (1996) que a su vez se inspiró en Arnaud (1991: 11, *énoncé phrastique lexicalisé à valeur spécifique*). El motivo por el cual hemos adoptado el término *enunciado de valor específico* y no otro, viene suscitado a partir de su forma, nacimiento y uso. Esto es, *enunciado* ya que poseen sentido completo y no funcionan como elementos de una oración y *valor específico*, puesto que nacieron de una situación concreta y sólo se pueden utilizar en momentos paralelos (que simulen) al acontecimiento donde se crearon.

En segundo lugar, es necesario realizar una caracterización de los rasgos distintivos de estas unidades, puesto que comparten características tanto con las *locuciones* como con los *refranes*. Para ello, hemos recopilado las ideas que han ofrecido Casares (1969), Sevilla Muñoz (1988), Corpas Pastor (1996) y García- Page (2008). De este modo, haciendo una síntesis podemos realizar una primera aproximación a lo que es un *enunciado de valor específico*. Esto es, estas estructuras se caracterizan por ser expresiones que no requieren elaboración, se originan por un acontecimiento histórico o una anécdota que se utilizará de forma autónoma y estará relacionada con el contexto puesto que evoca una situación pasada. En otras palabras, un *enunciado de valor específico* nace de forma espontánea a partir de una situación concreta y posteriormente pasará al acervo lingüístico para ser utilizada en situaciones similares a la que le dio origen. De este modo, el *enunciado* no ofrecerá un valor de verdad general, ya que su significado no aporta una enunciación cierta en cualquier situación, sino que simplemente puede considerarse como verdadero en el contexto donde se utiliza. Sin embargo, es conveniente señalar que esta definición es vaga e inconcreta, puesto que con ella podemos confundir estas unidades con otras. Por este motivo, para poder caracterizar con más precisión estas estructuras hemos establecido unas pruebas que actúan a modo de filtro siguiendo tanto a Arnaud (1991) como a Corpas (1996 y 1998) que nos permitirán discernir, principalmente, entre los *refranes* y los *enunciados*, por un lado, y las *locuciones* y los *enunciados*, por otro, además de otras estructuras colindantes del universo fraseológico español. Así, según las características que podremos asignar a cada estructura en función de estas pruebas, podremos clasificarlas en su grupo correspondiente. Se trata de nueve filtros con los que podemos ir descartando estructuras hasta obtener una clasificación. Los dos primeros, fijación e institucionalización, poseen carácter excluyente. Mientras que el resto, idiomaticidad, sustitución léxica, imposibilidad de conjugar el verbo, autonomía sintáctica, autonomía textual, valor de verdad general y anonimato, se aplicarán de forma sucesiva. De este modo, las unidades que posean fijación, institucionalización, idiomaticidad, sustitución léxica o posibilidad de conjugar el verbo y anonimato serán *locuciones*; las estructuras que se caractericen por su fijación, institucionalización, significado literal, imposibilidad de conjugar el verbo, autonomía sintáctica, autonomía textual, valor de verdad general y anonimato serán *refranes*; y, por último, dentro de los *enunciados de valor específico* encontraremos dos tipos:

1) *Enunciados de valor específico* con significado idiomático caracterizados además por poseer fijación, institucionalización, imposibilidad de conjugar el verbo, autonomía sintáctica, autonomía textual y anonimato como *Ancha es Castilla*. Este tipo de unidades se sitúa cerca de la frontera de las *locuciones*.

2) El segundo tipo de *enunciados* se caracterizaría por los mismos rasgos que el anterior con una modificación, ya que no tendría significado idiomático, sino literal. Dentro de este grupo encontraríamos, a su vez, dos tipos de significado; uno, totalmente literal como *Cualquier tiempo pasado fue mejor*, que los sitúa cerca de los *refranes;* y, otro, con significado motivado como *De tal palo, tal astilla,* es decir, estructuras que, no poseyendo totalmente significado literal, puede inferirse al relacionar su significado con su origen.

Por lo tanto, podemos afirmar que los *enunciados de valor específico* lindan en la frontera de las *locuciones* debido a su idiomaticidad y, además, se sitúan cerca de los *refranes* por su significado literal. De ahí, que estas estructuras posean rasgos coincidentes con dos unidades que no están relacionadas entre sí. En el centro encontraríamos aquellas estructuras con significado motivado

Esta delimitación que hemos realizado de los *enunciados de valor específico* nos ha servido para ver su uso pragmático. Esto es, a la hora de someter a análisis a estructuras que podrían clasificarse como *enunciados*, por un lado, hemos podido realizar una clasificación satisfactoria y, por otro, hemos estudiado su uso en un contexto real. De este modo, hemos establecido unas características pragmáticas comunes a los *enunciados de valor específico* como que pueden admitir unas modificaciones mínimas a causa de tratarse de unidades que poseen un uso concreto dentro de contextos reales, ya que simulan una situación pretérita. Por otro lado, y a causa de su forma de nacimiento, su uso más colectivo es el de afirmar algo, por lo que forman actos de habla indirectos asertivos. Además, por este mismo motivo, poseen un carácter anafórico, puesto que se utilizan como una conclusión a la afirmación anteriormente mencionada en el discurso.

A continuación vamos a centrarnos en el análisis de dos estructuras, ambas con el sustantivo pan, para comprobar cómo actúan en el discurso (los rasgos anteriormente mencionados). Por un lado, *con su pan se lo coma* con significado idiomático y, por otro, *dame pan y dime tonto* con significado literal - motivado. Para ello, partiremos del significado semántico que ofrece el diccionario y comprobaremos si este significado difiere del aportado en contextos reales extraídos del corpus CREA. La elección de este corpus estriba, por un lado, en que se trata de un corpus muy accesible; y, por otro, puesto que ofrece tanto textos escritos como orales. Posteriormente, observaremos otros usos pragmáticos como son la deixis discursiva, los actos de habla y las modificaciones que aparecen en dichos contextos.

En primer lugar nos centraremos en la estructura *con su pan se lo coma*, que como ya hemos dicho posee un carácter más idiomático. En el corpus *CREA* la hemos encontrado en tres casos, uno en prensa y dos en novelas. Por otra parte, la hemos consultado en seis diccionarios diferentes, *CVC, DFH, DR, DFEM, DFDEA* y *DRAE*. De ellos, aparece registrada en cuatro (*DFH, DFEM, DFDEA, DRAE*) como indiferencia o desinterés hacia lo que le ocurra a otra persona a causa de su conducta. El significado de esta expresión en contextos reales equivale al ofrecido por los diccionarios como podemos ver en (1)

(1) Le están robando la imagen a José María Aznar y no hay derecho. No por él, que allá con su pan se lo coma, sino porque había muchas ganas de algo más en el horizonte inmediato que la herencia felipista[1].

Como se puede apreciar el emisor le otorga a la expresión una función explicativa, ya que con ella intenta hacernos ver que, pese a estar tratando el tema, le son indiferentes las consecuencias que pueda haber para el sujeto, y que en cierto sentido, las tiene merecidas por su conducta.

En cuanto a la deixis discursiva encontramos un carácter anafórico porque primero se enuncia el hecho "le están robando la imagen" y posteriormente se refiere a ese acontecimiento mediante el *enunciado*. De este modo el emisor utiliza la estructura como conclusión, esto es, el autor del texto, pretende mostrar, con la utilización de la estructura, que el hecho en sí no le importa y pasa a centrarse en el tema del texto, que en este caso serían el resto de consecuencias ajenas al sujeto.

Por otro lado, en lo referente a los actos de habla, siguiendo la terminología de Searle (1969), se trata de un acto de habla indirecto asertivo, ya que el autor del texto utiliza la unidad fraseológica como afirmación, en este caso, de la indiferencia que siente hacia lo que le pueda ocurrir a Aznar.

Por último, nos parece conveniente señalar que en ninguno de los casos registrados aparece ninguna modificación de la expresión analizada.

Pasamos ahora a estudiar el *enunciado de valor específico* con significado literal - motivado, para lo cual hemos elegido, *dame pan y dime tonto*. En este caso, hemos encontrado dos ejemplos registrados, uno en el corpus *CREA* y otro en el *CVC*. Se trata de un caso oral y de una novela. En lo concerniente a los diccionarios esta estructura aparece en dos de ellos (*CVC* y *DR*) como expresión que critica o defiende que una persona consiga beneficios a pesar de ser maltratado por ello. El significado que podemos sacar del ejemplo

---

[1] REAL ACADEMIA ESPAÑOLA: Banco de datos (CREA) [en línea]. *Corpus de referencia del español actual*. < http://www.rae.es > [8 de abril de 2010], *El Mundo*, Consuelo Álvarez de Toledo, *Bajo la inercia,* 1996.

del *CREA* es el de justificación de la acción realizada por el emisor, anteponiendo el resultado a los medios empleados para obtenerlo, como podemos ver en (2).

(2)... y los domingos a las nueve y estábamos todo el día y nos los españoles y nos íbamos a los apartamentos de las canadienses, americanas, las francesas sobre todo, las canadienses y las americanas manejaban pelas. Y nosotros cada español mil pesetas que era para para la semana. Y la las canadienses nos daban cien dólares por pasar dos días con ellas. Estábamos hechos hasta chulos y todo. Era lo último a lo que se podía llegar, pero en fin, yo dame pan y dime tonto, ¿comprendes?[2] ...

En este caso el hablante utiliza la unidad fraseológica con función justificativa, tratando de dar una mayor importancia al beneficio que a las acciones realizadas para conseguirlo, en concreto, restándole importancia al hecho de haber llevado a cabo acciones moralmente reprobables si con ello conseguía un importante beneficio económico como compensación.

En lo referente a la deixis discursiva, posee carácter anafórico puesto que primero relata los hechos, para posteriormente terminar con la unidad fraseológica, resaltando que lo más importante era el dinero. De este modo, el emisor utiliza la expresión con un fin conclusivo, ya que, además de venir introducido por el conector discursivo *en fin,* le sirve para hacer entrever la razón por la cual el sujeto realizaba esa acción

Por lo que respecta a los actos de habla, se trata de un acto de habla indirecto asertivo, ya que el emisor lo utiliza para afirmar su indiferencia ante las acciones que tuviese que realizar mientras estas llevasen aparejado un beneficio suficiente, en este caso, mientras las extranjeras continuasen pagando.

En cuanto a las modificaciones, debemos señalar que en los ejemplos consultados no hemos encontrado ninguna modificación registrada. Pese a ello, nos gustaría comentar que existen modificaciones como *dame pan y llámame tonto* o *dame pan y llámame can.*

Como hemos visto en las dos estructuras analizadas ambas comparten las características pragmáticas enunciadas al principio, esto es, carácter anafórico, acto de habla indirecto asertivo y, en el segundo caso, posibles modificaciones. Además, ambas estructuras poseen el mismo fin concreto, es decir, en los dos casos el emisor utiliza los *enunciados de valor específico* a modo de conclusión de alguna de las ideas citadas anteriormente. Sin embargo, cada una ofrece una función distinta relacionada con su significado. En el primer caso, apreciamos una función explicativa de la indiferencia que suscitan las posibles consecuencias de un hecho para el sujeto de la estructura, mientras que en el segundo, se trata de justificar ciertos hechos que podrían no ser aceptados pero que conllevan un beneficio.

Por último, nos parece conveniente señalar, que este estudio supone un esbozo del uso pragmático de los *enunciados de valor específico,* ya que, desde nuestro punto de vista, la dificultad para delimitarlos con claridad por su parecido con otras estructuras colindantes, hacen del mundo de los *enunciados de valor específico,* un campo donde hoy en día, queda mucho por ahondar.

---

[2] REAL ACADEMIA ESPAÑOLA: Banco de datos (CREA) [en línea]. *Corpus de referencia del español* <http://www.rae.es> [8 de abril de 2010], oral, vehículo público, conversación entre pasajeros, Madrid - Barajas, 1991.

Bibliografía

ARNAUD, P. J. L. 1991 "Réflexions sur le proverbe", *Cahiers de lexicologie* 59: 5-27.
CASARES, J. 1969 *Introducción a la lexicografía moderna*, Madrid: Gredos.
CORPAS PASTOR, G. 1996 *Manual de fraseología española*, Madrid: Gredos.
CORPAS PASTOR, G. 1998 "Criterios generales de clasificación del universo fraseológico de las lenguas, con ejemplos en español y en inglés". In: Alvar Ezquerra, M. & Corpas Pastor, G. (eds.). *Diccionarios, frases, palabras*. Málaga: Universidad: 157-187.
GARCÍA-PAGE, M. 2008) *Introducción a la fraseología española. Estudio de las locuciones.* , Barcelona: Anthropos.
RUIZ GURILLO, L. 1997 *Aspectos de fraseología teórica española*. Valencia: Universidad.
SEVILLA MUÑOZ, J. 1988 *Hacia una aproximación conceptual de las paremias francesas y españolas*. Madrid: Editorial Complutense.
ZULUAGA, A. 1980 *Introducción al estudio de las expresiones fijas*, Studia Románica et Lingüística 10, Frankfurt /Bern: Peter Lang.

Diccionarios consultados

CVC. Refranero Multilingüe. http://www.cvc.cervantes.es/lengua/refranero/
DFH: Diccionario de Frases Hechas; RBA, Larousse Editorial, Barcelona, 2001.
DR: Diccionario de Refranes; RBA, Larousse Editorial, S. A., Barcelona, 2001.
DFEM: Diccionario Fraseológico del español moderno; Fernando Varela, Hugo Kubarth. Gredos. Madrid, 1994.
DFDEA: Diccionario Fraseológico documentado del español actual locuciones y modismos españoles; Manuel Seco, Olimpia Andrés, Gabino Ramos; Aguilar lexicografía, Santillana Educación, S. L., Madrid, 2004.
DRAE, 2001. (vigésima segunda edición) www.rae.es
REAL ACADEMIA ESPAÑOLA: Banco de datos (CREA) [en línea]. *Corpus de referencia del español actual.* <http: //www.rae.es> [8 de abril de 2010].

AREAS OF SIMILARITY AND DIFFERENCE IN LEGAL PHRASEOLOGY: COLLOCATIONS OF KEY TERMS IN UK AND POLISH COMPANY LAW

Łucja Biel
University of Gdansk

Abstract: The paper discusses areas of similarity and difference in the phraseology of key terms in UK and Polish company law. The analysis is based on two comparable corpora of company law legislation. Similarities are motivated by the shared COMPANY-IS-A-PERSON metaphor and related conceptual scenarios, while differences arise from their system-specific instantiations, conditions-effects scripts and linguistic restrictions.

Keywords: Phraseological equivalence, contrastive phraseology; legal terminology.

Legal language is well-known (notorious?) for its formalism, rituals, petrification, and standardisation (cf. Mattila 2006: 83). Formulaicity, which is present in legal variants of probably all languages due to the way the legal discourse works, seems to be well suited for corpus analysis, with its potential to identify recurrent patterns. Yet it is somewhat surprising that, apart from a few isolated studies, legal phraseology has not been studied systematically either by linguists or translation scholars. Most studies of legal language analyse its complex syntactic structures, modality, speech acts, genres and terms (which attract most attention in cross-linguistic research due to their incongruity between legal systems). The neglect of collocations is not restricted to legal language but extends to all types of language for specific purposes (LSP). As noted by Kjær, specialised phraseology is under-researched, being treated by phraseology studies "as a special case, as an exception from the rule, belonging, at best, to the periphery of the discipline of phraseology" (2007: 506).

1. Collocations from a cross-linguistic perspective

With the advent of corpus linguistics, research on general language collocations has been thriving and has recently shown interest in the contrastive perspective, especially due to strong interest from second language learning, bilingual lexicography, and translation studies. Translation studies have shown interest in collocations for a number of reasons. First of all, collocations have proven to be a source of difficulty in translation and a frequent error: the translator "will be 'caught' every time, not by his grammar, (...) not by his vocabulary, (...) but by his unacceptable or improbable collocations" (Newmark 1988: 180), which may happen both in translation into and out of one's mother tongue, with the risk of a collocational error being higher in specialised languages than in the general one (Bahumaid 2006: 147). The reason why collocations cause problems for translators is that their patterns differ across languages, a fact which has been long acknowledged in the literature:

> [D]ifferences in collocational patterning among languages are not just a question of using, say, a different verb with a given noun; **they can involve totally different ways of portraying an event**. Patterns of collocation reflect the preferences of specific language communities for certain modes of expression and certain linguistic configurations; they rarely reflect any inherent order in the world around us. (...)

> *This is not to say that collocations do not often reflect the cultural setting in which they are embedded. Some collocations are in fact a direct reflection of the material, social, or moral environment in which they occur.* (Baker 1992: 49, emphasis mine)

On the one hand, phraseology may be motivated by culture-specific ethnotheories and cultural scripts (Goddard 2003), while, on the other hand, it may be "related to more or less universal aspects of the human mind" and the common cultural heritage (Colson 2008: 193). As a result, collocational ranges of equivalent words, argues Larson, do not match totally but overlap to a certain degree (1984). Cross-linguistic differences also concern semantic prosody known to be language-specific to a certain degree.

The second reason for the surge of interest in collocations within translation studies concerns the hypotheses of translation universals, in particular those related to what Chesterman refers to as T-universals, i.e. the textual fit between translations and naturally occurring non-translated language (2004: 6-7), which assume that the distribution of lexical features is marked in translation. One of the hypotheses is Mauranen's untypical collocation whereby translated language is marked by collocations and colligations which are possible but rare in the target language and has few combinations which are frequent in the spontaneous target language (2006: 97). In order to verify the untypical collocation hypothesis (which has not been examined in LSP so far) and reduce source language distortions of collocations, it is necessary, as a preliminary step, to study how collocations behave in non-translated language.

2. Legal terms and phrasemes

In the traditional objectivist approach to terminology (General Theory of Terminology) terms are defined as linguistic units that refer to discrete concepts, which are its object of study. In more recent socio-cognitive and communicative approaches, terms, or rather terminological units, are only special meanings of lexical units. In her approach (Communicative Theory of Terminology) Cabré Castellví defines terminological units as multifaceted multidimensional polyhedrons which, as "units of knowledge, units of language and units of communication" (2003: 183) have three viewpoints: "the cognitive (the concept), the linguistic (the term) and the communicative (the situation)" (2003: 187). Terminological units, above all, express and synthesise specialised knowledge and fit into its organised structure (2003). Hence, legal terminological units may be seen as prompts or points of access to legal knowledge structures (Biel 2009: 177). This semasiological approach is compatible with corpus-based methodologies which study how terminological units behave in context.

Legal terms are well known to show incongruity between legal systems. There is a close relation between the language and the law; legal terminology has a system-bound nature due to the fact that legal knowledge and concepts are usually the product of a national legal system with its distinct history, patterns of reasoning and responsiveness to the needs of a particular nation (Šarčević 1997: 232); terminological units are hence embedded in cultural and cognitive models (Biel 2009: 180). Kjær argues that legal reasoning is based on the if-then mental model where a legal term connects legal conditions with effects and functions as "a reduced representation of legal rules" (2000: 146), such conditions-effects scripts being regulated by statute. For these reasons full equivalence is rare in legal translation.

The fact that terminological units are system-bound rather than language-bound may be illustrated by terminological differences between UK and US company law, both of which use the English language and belong to the common law tradition (see Table 1).

UK	US
company	corporation
company law	corporate law
general meeting	shareholders' meeting
memorandum of association	articles of incorporation
articles of association	bylaws
promoter	incorporator

Table 1. Differences between selected key terms of UK and US company law

While some terminological units are shared (e.g. *board of directors, secretary, officer, proxy voting*), others are distinct (e.g. most notably the highest-ranking key term *company* (UK) versus *corporation* (US)). The differences not only concern terms but extend to legal phrasemes, which are also system-bound. For example, equivalent terms may collocate with distinct adjectives (*extraordinary general meeting* (UK) versus *special shareholders' meeting* (US)), verbs (*to register articles of association* (UK) versus *to file articles of incorporation* (US)) or may employ their own patterns to form more specific multi-word terms (*public company limited by shares* (UK) versus *publicly-held corporation* (US)). The incongruity of terminology and phraseology will certainly be higher: 1) between distinct languages, and 2) between legal systems that belong to common law and civil law traditions, as is the case with UK and Polish company law, respectively. The latter was modelled on German company law in the early 20th century and shaped by other continental traditions in the post-Communist transformation period.

In legal language the boundary between a term and a phraseme is blurred. Many terms combine with other lexical units, either as nodes or collocates, to form more specific terminological units, called multi-word terms (e.g. director - *board of directors, directors' meeting, shadow director, managing director, directors' remuneration report*), which in turn develop their own collocations. Both the term/phraseology distinction and multi-word terms have been a problematic issue (cf. L'Homme et al. 2003: 156); as Kjær criticises, too much attention is paid to the term/phraseology distinction at the expense of "outlining overall theories of word combinations, comprising all types of 'more or less' stable word combinations" (2007: 506). It would be more appropriate to look at these categories as not discrete, with legal terms and phrasemes forming a continuum. As noted by Shelov long ago, terms display various degrees of terminologicality (qtd. in Thelen 2002:196).

Legal phrasemes have various degrees of stability due to legal constraints (cf. Kjær 2007: 509). They re-occur in national legislation, which is the central, most prototypical genre, a constitutive text type (Kjær 2000: 139). This genre determines legal practice and reproductive text types, such as contracts, judgments and other texts used in legal practice (Kjær 2000: 140). In reproductive text types prefabs made of terms and their collocations establish intertextual links to constitutive texts (legislation), where their meaning is stabilised. Take for example Polish *naruszyć warunki* (lit. to disturb conditions), which is used in the Polish Civil Code in the meaning of *to breach conditions of a contract*. This phrase has a popular colloquial variant, *złamać warunki* (lit. to break conditions), which is not used in legislation and is not capable of prompting the relevant provision of the Code and the conditions-effects script regulated therein. Intertextual links function as "implicit quotation from other text in a genre chain in the legal domain" (Kjær 2007: 512).

3. Corpus-based contrastive analysis of company law collocations

The study has been carried out with WordSmith Tools 5.0 on two comparable corpora with the fundamental legislation, i.e. constitutive text type, which regulates company law in Poland and the UK. The Polish corpus consists of *Kodeks spółek handlowych* [Code of Commercial Partnerships and Companies] (52,068 tokens; 4,263 types); while the UK corpus includes the *Companies Act 2006* and *Table A* (318,087 tokens; 3,905 types). The purpose of this study is to examine legal collocations of the highest-ranking key terms in UK and Polish company law with a view to gaining an insight into the nature of similarity and difference.

3.1 Key terms in company law

Key words are lexemes which have become cognitively salient through their repetitive, unusually frequent use. They characterise a given text in that they "are used over and over in the text and are crucial to the theme or topic under discussion. (...) Key words are most often words which represent an essential or basic concept of the text" (Larson 1984: 177). In legal texts key words are in most cases key terms (or their components). Key terms have been isolated with the Wordlist and Keyword functions against reference corpora and adjusted for case endings. The following words have the highest keyness:
- EN: 1. *company*; 2. *director*; 3. *share*; 4. *auditor*; 5. *registrar*; 6. *meeting*; 7. *accounts*; 8. *register*; 9. *resolution*; 10. *report;* 11. *member*; 12. *name*; 13. *default*; 14. *copy*; 15. *vote*.
- PL: 1. *spółka*; 2. *wspólnik*; 3. *akcja*; 4. *kapitał*; 5. *zgromadzenie*; 6. *zakładowy*; 7. *zarząd*; 8. *uchwała*; 9. *akcjonariusz*; 10. *walne*; 11. *rejestrowy*; 12. *statut*; 13. *nadzorcza*; 14. *likwidator*; 15. *udział*.

Since company law regulates companies, the highest ranking key term is, as may be expected, *company* in the UK corpus and *spółka* [partnership/company] in the Polish corpus, and their keyness factor is substantially higher than that of other key terms. The second highest key term in the English corpus is *director*, which functionally matches *zarząd* (management board) and *nadzorcza* (adjective: supervisory — a collocate of *rada* (board)). The second highest key term in the Polish corpus is not connected with the company's management but with its ownership structure — *wspólnik*, a partner or a member in private companies, who is referred to as *akcjonariusz* (rank 9) in public companies. *Wspólnik* collocates with *zgromadzenie* (rank 5, meeting) to form *zgromadzenie wspólników*, a general meeting in private companies, its parallel in public companies being *walne zgromadzenie* (the adjective *walne* has rank 10). The ownership structure seems to be less salient in the UK corpus as *member* ranks 11 and *meeting* is 6th; however, the latter refers not only to the meeting of members (*general meeting*) but also to the meeting of directors (Polish uses a distinct term in this sense — *posiedzenie*). Other shared terms include *resolution* (9) and *uchwała* (8); *registrar* (5) and *register* (8) versus the Polish adjective *rejestrowy* (12), which collocates with *sąd* (court), *sąd rejestrowy* being a functional equivalent of *registrar*; *share* (3) versus *akcja* (3, a share in a public company), *udział* (15, a share in a private company), *kapitał* (4, capital) and its collocate — the adjective *zakładowy* (6, *kapitał zakładowy*/share capital). English terms which do not have Polish equivalents of matching high keyness are: *auditor* (4), *accounts* (7), *report* (10), *name* (12), *default* (13), *copy* (14) and *vote* (15), which may suggest that English focuses more on reporting and control. As regards Polish terms, there is only *likwiaator* (14), since *statut* (12) has a partial equivalent in *articles* (19).

Another notable difference is that due to the higher lexico-grammatical flexibility of English lexemes, the English keywords are all nouns, except for *vote*, which is both a noun and a verb. In contrast to Polish, English nouns frequently premodify other nouns (heads) in complex nominal phrases, especially in specialised discourse (nominal adjectivation for conciseness, cf. Gotti 2005: 73). The Polish list includes four adjectives (*zakładowy, walne, rejestrowy, nadzorcza*), which in principle collocate only with one node each to form two-word terms: *kapitał zakładowy, walne zgromadzenie, sąd rejestrowy* and *rada nadzorcza*. As already noted, legal terms combine with other lexical units to form more specific multi-word terminological units and, as the corpus analysis shows, the key terms are especially productive in this respect, appearing in collocations either as nodes (especially head nouns in nominal phrases, e.g. *treasury shares*) or collocates (in particular modifiers of head nouns, e.g. *share capital*). These collocations may express intraterm relations, such as: type (*private company limited by shares, opting-out resolution*), member-whole (*director* v. *board of directors*), part-whole (*udział w kapitale zakładowym* v. *kapitał zakładowy*). Languages arbitrarily choose a way of expressing intraterm relations: while one language may have a multi-word term (*company name*), another language may have a single term (*firma*) without any explicit reference to the basic key term.

3.2 COMPANY-IS-A-PERSON conceptual metaphor

In contrast to general language, the central and most frequent type of legal phrasemes, as argued by Kjær, is not idioms but "semantically transparent multi-word terms and collocations with a specialized legal sense" (2007: 509). This is in particular valid for the language of the law — the data from the corpus show that it tends to avoid vivid idioms which are more frequent in legal language (i.e. metalanguage of the law), e.g. *to lift the veil*. However, this does not mean that the language of the law is non-figurative — on the contrary, it contains many abstract concepts, and in order to deal with them (by referring, quantifying, grouping, etc., cf. Lakoff and Johnson 1980: 25) ontological metaphors are needed. In the case of company law, the underlying ontological conceptual metaphor is that of the COMPANY IS A PERSON, which personifies a company. Shane, who discusses the American version of this metaphor (CORPORATION IS A PERSON), notes that "the edification of the corporation to the status of a person is one of the most enduring institutions of the law and one of the most widely accepted legal fictions" (2006: 57). It may be expected that this conceptual metaphor will be shared by most (if not all) legal systems, although it may be differently elaborated.

Thanks to this personification, companies are comprehended in terms of human experience and motivations: following its incorporation, a company becomes a separate legal entity — a legal *person*, a *body* corporate; it has governing *bodies*, a *head* office and a *head* officer. The metaphor is productive with activity verbs: a company *carries* on business, *holds* shares; *enters* into a transaction/an agreement; it may *commit* an offence, be sued or be required to *act*. Another group of productive collocates comprises those referring to the cognitive sphere — a company may *know*, have *reasonable* cause to believe, *reasonably* consider, be *willing* to provide for..., be *guilty* of an offence, have capacity/power, have an opinion (*in the opinion of the company*) or be *satisfied* that... An interesting elaboration of this metaphor is the conceptualisation of relations between companies in terms of family relations, e.g. subsidiaries have a *parent* company. This metaphor is more productive in informal legal English, where a company may have a *sister* or *daughter* company. Although a similar elaboration may be found in informal legal Polish, e.g. *spółka matka* (lit. mother company) and *spółka córka* (lit. daughter company), it does not appear in the language of the law, where *spółka matka* is referred to exclusively as *spółka dominująca* (lit. dominant company). The COMPANY IS A PERSON metaphor is, as expected, present in Polish: a company is an *osoba prawna* (lit. legal person) and has *osobowość prawna* (lit. legal personality; not found in the UK corpus). The equivalent of *body* is not explicitly found either in reference to a company or its governing bodies; the latter are referred to as *organy spółki* (lit. organs of the company), which however reflects the conceptualisation of a company as a body, with *zarząd* (management board) and *rada nadzorcza* (supervisory board) being comprehended as its internal parts. Collocates with activity verbs are well represented: a company *prowadzi działalność* (lit. carries on activity), *udziela informacji* (lit. gives information), *wzywa wspólników* (lit. calls in partners), *pozywa* and *jest pozywana* (lit. sues and is sued), *występuje z wnioskiem* (lit. steps out with a request/makes a request). Compared to English, there are relatively few collocates related to the cognitive sphere: a company *dowiaduje się o szkodzie* (lit. learns about a loss), has *tajemnice* (lit. secrets), *dobrowolnie uiszcza należności* (lit. pays its dues of its own free will). An interesting elaboration is the Polish equivalent of *bankrupt – upadły*, and its nominal form, *upadłość* – where a bankrupt company is conceptualised as a person who has fallen down; this image is absent in English. Unlike in English, Polish does not explicitly assign the concept of guilt to a company.

3.3 Cognitive scenarios as a source of similarity and difference

Company law is based on cognitive scenarios that reflect the way companies function in the modern business world. The prototypical scenario, which exists both in UK and Polish company law, is the life-of-a-company scenario, derived from the COMPANY IS A PERSON metaphor. It regulates how a company is set up, how and where it is registered, what its governing bodies are, how they are constituted and take decisions, what filing obligations a company has, how a company develops through mergers or divisions, and how it is wound up and dissolved. Given their high frequency and nominal form, the key terms are prominent participants of the scenario. They are embedded in the scenario via collocates, in particular verbal ones which allow them to enter into relations with other terms. The shared scenario seems to be a source of similarity in phraseology. It may result in full functional equivalence with similar meaning and imagery or, more frequently, with similar meaning but different imagery. The former may be illustrated by: *to call/convene a general meeting* v. *zwołać walne zgromadzenie*; *single-member company* v. *spółka jednoosobowa* (lit. one-person company). The latter includes: *to appoint/remove a director* v. *powołać/odwołać członka Zarządu* (lit. call/recall a member of the Management Board); *to form a company* v. *utworzyć/zawiązać/zawrzeć spółkę* (lit. to create/tie/conclude a company); *joint holder of the share* v. *współuprawniony z akcji* (lit. co-beneficiary from the share). Although the phrases are equivalent in meaning, they may cause difficulty in translating since source language interferences may hinder retrieval of natural collocations in the target language.

More genuine difficulty in translating appears when the difference concerns meaning rather than imagery, which is the case of partial equivalence or zero equivalence. Although the life-of-a-company scenario is present in UK and Polish company law, it is shared at a generic level and differences appear at system-specific instantiations and elaborations of the scenario. One such elaboration reflects the perception of companies in UK and Polish law. The former makes a clear-cut distinction between companies and partnerships, which are regulated by separate legal acts, while Polish has a single term *spółka* which covers all types of companies and partnerships regulated in a single act. Yet at the terminological level UK law has a single scenario for all companies, treating private and public companies as two variants of the same organisation (Mayson et al 2006: 64-65); it uses uniform terminology for both types of companies: *share, member, Memorandum & Articles of Association, General Meeting*. By contrast, Polish has six different scenarios for each type of partnership or company, described separately in the Commercial Code, and uses distinct terminology for partnerships/private companies and for public companies: *udział* v. *akcja* (share), *wspólnik* v. *akcjonariusz* (member), *umowa spółki* v. *statut spółki* (memorandum and articles), *zgromadzenie wspólników* v. *walne zgromadzenie* (general meeting), respectively. In contrast to English, Polish treats them as distinct concepts and as such they develop their own collocations, as is the case with *umowa* and *statut spółki*. *Umowa spółki* (lit. contract of the company) collocates with *zawrzeć umowę* (lit. to conclude a contract), *wypowiedzieć* ~ (lit. to terminate by notice), and *naruszyć* ~ (lit. to breach), while *statut* collocates with *sporządzić* ~ (lit. to prepare), *podpisać* ~ (lit. to sign), and *zatwierdzić* ~ (lit. to approve).

Differences also occur due to system-specific elaborations at a micro level when a shared term has diverse conditions-effects scripts or realises a unique part of the scenario which does not have a parallel in the other language and, in consequence, its collocational range differs, as in *to disqualify a director, to keep a register of directors*. Another interesting difference appears when one term corresponds to two terms in the other language, e.g. UK companies have a unitary board structure (*board of directors*) while Polish companies have a dual board structure (*zarząd* and *rada nadzorcza*). *Board of directors* collocates with *appoint* while Polish again develops distinct collocates in this meaning: *powołać Zarząd* (lit. to call a Management Board) and *ustanowić Radę Nadzorczą* (lit. to establish a Supervisory Board).

The most prominent example of zero equivalence is observed when a term exists only in one legal system and does not have a functional equivalent in the other, e.g. *secretary, company names adjudicator, shadow director, prokura*. In this case the entire part of the scenario is missing (*to appoint a secretary of the company, to hold the office of* ~; *to discharge the functions of* ~; *register of secretaries*); these are conceptual lacunas which are most challenging to translate and are usually approximated through literal equivalents, description and explicitation. These techniques may contribute to the phenomenon of untypical collocation as translators may resort to possible but rare prefabricated units.

3.4 Language-specific restrictions of patterns

The analysis shows that some differences are caused by linguistic constraints, with Polish showing more preference for analytical constructions, e.g. *wykonać prawo głosu przez pełnomocnika* (lit. exercise one's voting right through a representative) compared to the synthetic *vote by proxy*. In consequence, nominalisation (buried verbs) is frequent, especially in complex post-modification patterns as in *walne zgromadzenie w sprawie zatwierdzenia sprawozdania finansowego* (lit. annual general meeting for the purpose of approving a financial statement). Against this background, English patterns tend to be synthetic, with nominal pre-modification, e.g. *accounts meeting*, or verbal post-modification as in *application to court to cancel resolution*, whose Polish equivalent has a nominal structure: *powództwo o uchylenie uchwały* (lit. claim for revoking a resolution).

4. Conclusions

As shown above, even though Polish company law and UK company law are shaped by different legal traditions, they demonstrate some areas of similarity. First of all, they share a substantial percentage of key terms, which suggests that similar concepts are cognitively salient. Secondly, their phraseology is motivated by the COMPANY IS A PERSON conceptual metaphor and related cognitive scenarios, in particular the life-of-a-company scenario, which reflect the way in which companies operate in the modern business world. Yet full equivalence is rare and it is more likely to observe partial or zero equivalence due to system-specific instantiations and elaborations of the generic scenarios, including conceptual lacunas. Collocational patterns are also subject to language-specific restrictions. Because of the differences collocations are a source of difficulty in translation, and hence require more research and focus in legal translator training.

The study has been financed with research grant no. 2251/B/H03/2010/38 (2010-2011) from the Polish Ministry of Science and Higher Education.

5. Bibliography

BAKER, M. 1992 *In Other Words. A coursebook on translation.* London/New York: Routledge.

BAHUMAID, S. 2006 "Collocation in English-Arabic Translation". *Babel* 52(2): 133-152.

BIEL, Ł. 2009 Organization of background knowledge structures in legal language and related translation problems. *Comparative Legilinguistics. International Journal for Legal Communication* 1: 176-189.

CABRÉ CASTELLVÍ, M. T. 2003 "Theories of terminology. Their description, prescription and explanation". *Terminology* 9(2): 163-199.

CHESTERMAN, A. 2004 "Hypotheses about translation universals". In: Hansen, G., Malmkjær K. & Gile, D. (eds.) *Claims, Changes and Challenges in Translation Studies. Selected contributions from the EST Congress, Copenhagen 2001.* Amsterdam/Philadelphia: John Benjamins: 1-13.

COLSON, J. P. 2008 "Cross-linguistic phraseological studies: An overview". In: Granger, S. & Meunier, F. (eds.) *Phraseology. An Interdisciplinary Perspective.* Amsterdam/Philadelphia: John Benjamins: 191-206.

GODDARD, C. 2003 "Thinking across languages and cultures. Six dimensions of variation." *Cognitive Linguistics* 14(2/3): 109-140.

GOTTI, M. 2005 *Investigating Specialized Discourse.* Bern: Peter Lang.

KJÆR, A. L. 2000. "On the Structure of Legal Knowledge: The Importance of Knowing Legal Rules for Understanding Legal Texts". In: Lundquist, L. & Jarvella, R. J. (eds) *Language, Text, and Knowledge. Mental Models of Expert Communication.* Berlin/New York: Mouton de Gruyter: 127–161.

KJÆR, A. L. 2007 "Phrasemes in legal texts". In: Burger, H., Dobrovol'skij, D., Kühn, P. & Norrick, N. R. (eds) *Phraseologie/Phraseology: Ein internationales Hand-buch der zeitgenössischen Forschung/An International Handbook of Contemporary Research.* Vol. 1. Berlin/New York: Walter de Gruyter: 506-516.

L'HOMME, M.-C.; U. HEID & SAGER, J. C. 2003 "Terminology during the past decade (1994-2004). An Editorial Statement". *Terminology* 9(2), 151-161.

LAKOFF, G. & JOHNSON, M. 1980 *Metaphors We Live By.* Chicago: University of Chicago Press.

LARSON, M. L. 1984 *Meaning-based Translation: A Guide to Cross-Language Equivalence.* Lanham: University Press of America.

NEWMARK, P. 1981. *Approaches to Translation.* London/New York: Prentice Hall.

MATTILA, H. E. S. 2006 *Comparative Legal Linguistics.* Aldershot: Ashgate.

MAURANEN, A. 2006 "Translation universals". In: Brown, K. (ed.) *Encyclopedia of Language and Linguistics.* Vol. 13. Oxford: Elsevier: 93-100.

MAYSON, S. W., FRENCH, D. & RYAN, C 2006 *Mayson, French and Ryan on Company Law 2006-07.* 23 Ed. Oxford: OUP.

ŠARČEVIĆ, S. 1997 *New Approach to Legal Translation.* The Hague: Kluwer Law International.

TOURISME, SANTE ET BIEN-ETRE : ANALYSE EN PHRASEOLOGIE CONTRASTIVE DE QUELQUES EXPRESSIONS DU FRANÇAIS ET DE L'ITALIEN

Rosa Cetro
Università di Brescia
Université Paris Est

Abstract: In this paper, we proceed to a contrastive phraseological analysis of some compound nouns containing the French word *tourisme* or its Italian equivalent *turismo* and dealing with health and wellness. The aim of this research is to find which of these compound nouns is the most suitable to describe the tourism sector including thermalism, thalassotherapy and climatotherapy in both languages. After searching for these compound nouns in dictionaries, encyclopaedias, press and on Web pages, we have compared them syntactically and semantically to establish their degree of equivalence. This comparison done, we explain the reasons of our final choices.

Key words: Compound nouns, tourism terminology, health terminology, thermalism terminology, French phraseology, Italian phraseology

0. Introduction

Le tourisme international a récemment connu d'importants développements dans les secteurs de la santé et de la remise en forme, qui sont considérés comme de nouveaux types de tourisme. La nécessité de les nommer a produit, dans plusieurs langues, de nouveaux noms composés. A titre d'exemples, nous citons *well-being tourism* pour l'anglais, *tourisme de santé* pour le français, *turismo medical* pour l'espagnol, *turismo del benessere* pour l'italien. Dans cet article, nous focalisons notre attention sur le français et l'italien. Le sujet de notre thèse étant l'étude terminologique du domaine touristique incluant thermalisme, thalassothérapie et climatisme, nous avons mené une recherche pour trouver le nom composé qui pouvait être, d'après nous, le plus adapté à définir ce domaine dans les deux langues. Les étapes de cette recherche ont été : 1) le repérage de ces noms composés dans différents types de sources ; 2) l'analyse comparée de ces noms composés en français et en italien sur les plans syntaxique et 3) sémantique pour établir leur degré d'équivalence, en nous appuyant sur les occurrences repérées dans le corpus.

1. Présentation des sources

Les sources utilisées pour le repérage de ces noms composés constituent un ensemble assez hétérogène, qui inclut des dictionnaires, des encyclopédies, des corpus de presse en ligne et des pages Web. Pour ce qui concerne les sources lexicographiques et encyclopédiques, la recherche a été limitée à des ouvrages des vingt dernières années. Pour la langue française, nous avons choisi : le *TLFi* (*Trésor de la Langue Française informatisé* : http://atilf.atilf.fr/tlf.htm), le *Lexis* (2009), le *Grand Robert de la Langue Française* (2001), le *Nouveau Littré* (2006), le *Nouveau Petit Robert* (dans les éditions de 1995 et 2009), le *Petit Larousse Illustré* (1993), le *Grand Larousse Universel* (1993). Les sources italiennes sont : le

Vocabolario della lingua italiana Treccani (1994), *La piccola Treccani: dizionario enciclopedico* (1997), le *DISC* (*Dizionario Italiano Sabatini Coletti*) (1997), le *GRADIT : Grande Dizionario Italiano dell'uso* (1999), le *Grande dizionario della lingua italiana* (2002) de S. Battaglia, le *Vocabolario della lingua italiana* de Devoto et Oli (2004) et le Zingarelli - *Vocabolario della lingua italiana* (2006).

Pour la presse française, la recherche a été lancée dans la base de données Factiva (www.factiva.com). Factiva regroupe les archives de la plupart des magazines et quotidiens français. Pour les quotidiens italiens, la recherche a été menée directement depuis les sites de ces quotidiens : *La Repubblica, Il Giornale, La Stampa, Il Corriere della Sera, L'Unità, Il Sole 24 ore*. Depuis ces archives, il est possible d'accéder également aux archives de magazines appartenant aux mêmes groupes éditoriaux, comme par exemple : *Il Venerdì, D la Repubblica, Corriere Salute, Tutto Scienze*.

Passant aux sites et pages Web, nous avons sélectionné des sites d'organismes officiels (tels que les deux Ministères du Tourisme et les sites de régions françaises et italiennes, ou le site de l'ENIT[1]) ou de publications spécialisés dans le tourisme (comme la revue française *Espaces*[2]), outre le moteur de recherche Google.

2. Méthodes utilisées pour le repérage des noms composés

Pour repérer ces noms composés nous avons d'abord consulté les sources lexicographiques et encyclopédiques. Ensuite, nous avons lancé la recherche par expression exacte dans les archives de presse en ligne, sur les sites spécialisés dans le tourisme et sur le moteur de recherche Google[3]. De la totalité des résultats Google, nous n'en avons retenu que les plus pertinents, qui sont fournis par un calcul automatique de Google excluant les pages à contenu similaire. Nous indiquons dans le tableau ci-dessous les noms composés repérés avec le nombre de résultats pertinents de Google produits par la recherche (menée en mai 2010). Nous avons décidé de ne pas ajouter à ces chiffres les résultats des archives de presse, car certaines de ces pages apparaissent déjà dans la recherche Google. Comme la disponibilité des pages Web peut varier si l'on relance la recherche à intervalles réguliers, force est de constater que le nombre de résultats affichés pourrait changer en cas de nouvelle recherche. Il faut donc considérer les résultats suivants comme des résultats approximatifs :

Noms composés français	Noms composés italiens
Tourisme médical (625 résultats)	Turismo del benessere (702 résultats)
Tourisme de santé (566)	Turismo sanitario (604)
Tourisme thermal (542)	Turismo termale (565)
Tourisme de bien-être (243)	Turismo medico (366)
Tourisme sanitaire (196)	Turismo terapeutico (187)
Tourisme thérapeutique (118)	Turismo della salute (163)
Tourisme curatif (13)	Turismo curativo (36)

---

[1] Ente Nazionale Italiano del Turismo (l'Organisme national italien du tourisme) : www.enit.it
[2] Revue en ligne : www.revue-espaces.com.
[3] Des critères de restriction pour la langue et le pays ont été sélectionnés.

3. Le cadre théorique de référence : la notion de nom composé

Avant de passer à la comparaison syntaxique et sémantique des noms composés repérés, nous présentons le cadre théorique auquel nous faisons référence. Nous reprenons la notion de nom composé telle qu'elle a été formulée par Gaston Gross dans son volume *Les expressions figées en français* (1996)[4]. Nous en avons choisi des extraits qui nous semblent particulièrement adaptés à résumer la notion de nom composé. Tout d'abord, l'auteur nous dit que « les noms composés ont les mêmes fonctions syntaxiques que les noms simples mais, du point de vue de leur structure interne, ils présentent cette contradiction qu'ils fonctionnent comme une unité, alors qu'ils sont constitués de plusieurs éléments lexicaux, que leur sens soit transparent ou opaque » (1996 : 28). Une autre propriété fondamentale des noms composés, selon Gross, est l'absence de libre actualisation des éléments composants: « A la différence des groupes nominaux libres, dont chaque élément lexical peut recevoir une actualisation (détermination) autonome, les noms composés ont une détermination globale » (1996 : 32). Les exemples suivants pourront aider à mieux illustrer cette citation. Comparons les deux suites Nom Adjectif *tourisme développé* et *tourisme thermal*. Si la première accepte l'insertion d'un modificateur adverbial, *très* dans l'exemple a) et *de plus en plus* dans l'exemple b), entre le Nom et l'Adjectif, l'insertion de ces mêmes modificateurs n'est pas acceptable pour la séquence *tourisme thermal*, qui sera donc considérée comme un nom composé.

    a) un tourisme très développé
    * *un tourisme très thermal*
    b) un tourisme de plus en plus développé
    * *un tourisme de plus en plus thermal*

L'impossibilité de ses éléments composants à être actualisés implique qu'un nom composé est une non-prédication: « Le fait que dans le nom composé aucun élément ne puisse être actualisé montre qu'il n'est pas le siège d'une prédication » (1996 : 33). Nous montrons cette autre caractéristique des noms composés à l'aide des exemples suivants : si la phrase c) est acceptable, il n'en est pas de même pour la phrase d), où *région administrative* est un nom composé.

    c) Une région qui est boisée
    d) * *Une région qui est administrative*

G. Gross résume ainsi les caractéristiques des noms composés : « De façon […] générale, il n'y a pas de manipulations syntaxiques entre les différents éléments d'un nom composé » (1996 : 34).

4. Repérage et emploi de ces noms composés dans les sources

Aucun des noms composés listés dans le tableau au paragraphe II n'est inclus dans les dictionnaires de langue français. Seule la forme *tourisme thermal* est répertoriée dans le *Grand Larousse Universel*, dictionnaire encyclopédique. De façon générale, la définition de *tourisme* fournie par les dictionnaires de notre ensemble n'envisage pas la possibilité d'un déplacement pour des raisons de santé[5]. Contrairement aux sources françaises, parmi les

---

[4] G. Gross, *Les expressions figées en français*, Paris, Ophrys, 1996.
[5] Comme nous le fait remarquer Alberto Bramati que nous remercions, plus le nom composé
    montre une corrélation à la notion de santé (comme par exemple *tourisme médical* et

sources lexicographiques et encyclopédiques italiennes, le *Vocabolario Treccani* et le *Dizionario Enciclopedico Treccani* incluent dans la définition de *turismo* la possibilité de se déplacer dans un autre lieu pour se faire soigner. Toutefois, aucune de ces formes n'est enregistrée.

5. Analyse comparée des noms composés dans les deux langues

Sur le plan syntaxique, les formes repérées peuvent être regroupées dans deux catégories, qui sont d'ailleurs les catégories de noms composés les plus fréquentes : 1) la catégorie *N de N* (Nom de Nom), dont *tourisme de santé* constitue un exemple ; et 2) la catégorie *N Adj* (Nom Adjectif), où l'adjectif est morphologiquement relié à un nom par dérivation (*Adj-n*), comme *tourisme sanitaire*.

L'organisation syntaxique des séquences *N Adj* est identique dans les deux langues, comme le montrent, par exemple, les noms composés *tourisme thérapeutique/turismo terapeutico*.

En revanche, les suites *N de N* de l'italien se différencient par la présence d'un *Ddéf* (déterminant défini) entre la préposition *di* et le deuxième *N* : *tourisme de bien-être/turismo **del** benessere*.

La similarité de la structure syntaxique de ces noms composés dans les deux langues laisserait supposer aussi leur équivalence sur le plan sémantique, qui demande toutefois à être vérifiée. Pour ce faire, nous procéderons à l'analyse comparée de ces séquences : d'abord nous comparerons les noms composés montrant une équivalence sémantique totale, ensuite nous passerons en revue les noms composés partiellement équivalents ou non équivalents. L'équivalence sera établie à partir des exemples tirés des archives de presse ou des pages Web et listés dans des mini tableaux, les exemples français dans les cellules de gauche et les exemples italiens dans les cellules de droite. Lorsque les deux exemples se trouvent sur la même ligne, les noms composés partagent une même acception, tandis que la présence d'une cellule vide est l'indice d'une non-équivalence sémantique entre les deux langues.

Parmi les noms composés qui montrent une équivalence totale, nous avons :
1) **tourisme thermal/turismo termale** : outre la même structure syntaxique *N Adj*, ces noms composés partagent aussi la même définition, qui pourrait être la suivante : le fait de se déplacer dans une station thermale dans un but curatif.

| « Les futures infrastructures routières sont vécues comme une aubaine pour développer le **tourisme thermal** d'Eugénie-les-Bains. » (*Sud Ouest*, 8/01/2009) | « Il **turismo termale**, come fenomeno moderno, vede la nascita di importanti stazioni termali e di strutture ricettive ad alto livello. » (http://www.relax.it/turismo_termale.htm) |

tourisme sanitaire), plus on s'éloigne de la définition de *tourisme* telle qu'on la retrouve dans les dictionnaires: le fait de voyager, de parcourir par son plaisir un lieu autre que celui où l'on vit habituellement. Nous envisageons vérifier cette hypothèse ultérieurement.

2) **tourisme de bien-être/turismo del benessere** : malgré la différence dans la structure syntaxique (*N de N* contrastant avec *N de Ddéf N*), ces noms composés ont la même définition : le fait d'effectuer un séjour dans une station thermale ou un centre de thalassothérapie dans un but de détente et de remise en forme.

« Que la Tunisie soit aujourd'hui la première destination méditerranéenne d'un **tourisme de bien-être** [...] n'a donc rien de surprenant.» (*Le Figaro*, 25/10/2001)	« Accanto verrà realizzato un centro spa con acque termali sotterranee, [...] in modo che il Gottardo venga inserito nei circuiti del **turismo del benessere**. » (*Il Giornale*, 11/06/2005)

3) **tourisme de santé/turismo della salute**, qui représente un cas différent par rapport aux deux précédents, s'agissant d'un nom composé polysémique. En effet, il est utilisé pour désigner deux types de phénomènes, souvent dans une même source journalistique : d'un côté, il est synonyme de *tourisme thermal* (sens 1), de l'autre il désigne les déplacements à l'étranger pour des soins à moindre coût ou pour éviter les délais d'attente (sens 2). Malgré cette polysémie, l'équivalence est totale.

Sens 1 : « Un rapport sur "l'industrie touristique européenne", publié en mars 2004, insiste ainsi sur [...] sur le renforcement du **"tourisme de santé"** (thalassothérapie, cures thermales etc.). » (*Le Monde*, 21/08/2005).	Sens 1 : « Nelle 12 principali località termali le cure vere e proprie sono diminuite dal 10 al 45 per cento, mentre sono in aumento solo i trattamenti rivolti al benessere psico-fisico, il cosiddetto **turismo della salute**. » (*La Stampa*, 17/11/1995).
Sens 2 : « Cette opération "coup de poing" [...] n'affecte pas les autres négoces lucratifs du **"tourisme de santé"**, comme ces cliniques qui promettent de guérir le cancer. » (*Le Monde*, 3/07/2002)	Sens 2 : « Senza contare gli introiti del **turismo della salute** : un fenomeno recente, che ha visto migliaia di stranieri arrivare a Cuba, ad esempio, per interventi di chirurgia oculare. » (*Il Corriere della Sera*, 30/01/2006)

Passons en revue maintenant les noms composés qui ne sont que partiellement équivalents : ils ont tous la même structure syntaxique (*N Adj*) et sont polysémiques, à l'exception de *tourisme sanitaire* :

4) **tourisme médical/turismo medico** : ces noms composés ont deux acceptions en commun : les déplacements vers des pays moins riches pour des soins médicaux (chirurgicaux, dentaires, etc.) à moindre coût (sens 1) ; les trafics d'organes des pays pauvres vers les pays riches (sens 2). Toutefois, ***turismo medico*** peut revêtir un sens supplémentaire, et désigner les hospitalisations à l'étranger pour des pratiques interdites dans le pays d'origine, comme les transplantations à base de cellules souches embryonnaires (sens 3). L'équivalence sera donc partielle.

Sens 1 : « Le boom du **tourisme médical** a commencé en Thaïlande il y a un peu moins de dix ans. En pleine crise économique, les hôpitaux privés ont trouvé dans les patients étrangers un moyen de survivre. » (*La Croix*, 2/07/2008)	Sens 1 : « [...] Polonia e Ungheria [...] sono diventate una meta fissa del cosiddetto **turismo medico**, ossia di coloro che fanno un viaggio all' estero per sottoporsi a cure mediche di qualche genere. » (*Repubblica*, 11/01/2008)
Sens 2 : « Sans parler des organes entiers - poumon, foie, rein, cœur, pancréas... - dont la pénurie favorise le **tourisme médical** et les trafics sordides [...]. Ces produits et sous-produits s'échangent d'un bout à l'autre de la planète en colis postaux. » (*L'Express*, 11/12/2008)	Sens 2: « Quindici anni di galera per chi torna da un paese del Terzo mondo con un organo di cui non può provare la provenienza [...]. È questa la proposta-choc di I. Marino, [...] per stroncare il fenomeno del **turismo medico** illegale. » (*L'Espresso*, 30/05/2007)
	Sens 3 : « «Quel "sì" rappresentava la speranza per tante persone costrette, come mio padre, a un **turismo medico** che è abominevole. Lui si era battuto per un uso terapeutico delle cellule embrionali che da noi, forse, sarà accettato tra vent'anni» » (*Corriere della Sera*, 25/08/2005)

5) **tourisme sanitaire/turismo sanitario** : *tourisme sanitaire* est monosémique et désigne le fait de se déplacer à l'étranger pour des soins médicaux moins chers et/ou pour réduire les temps d'attente. Il peut donc être considéré comme correspondant à la deuxième définition que nous avons donnée pour *tourisme de santé*. Ce sens est revêtu aussi par *turismo sanitario* qui, en revanche, est polysémique et peut renvoyer aussi aux hospitalisations dans d'autres régions italiennes ou aux voyages à l'étranger pour la procréation assistée. Cette polysémie empêche donc une équivalence totale.

« Selon les estimations de l'association turque du **tourisme sanitaire**, sur les 20 millions d'étrangers venus visiter la Turquie l'an dernier, 200.000 auraient joint vacances et santé. [...] Le succès actuel de la Turquie concerne surtout les soins ophtalmologiques. » (*La Tribune*, 3/04/2006)	Sens 1 : « Per altro, rendendo più abbordabile il conto del dentista, il Consiglio vuole anche scoraggiare il "**turismo sanitario**" all'estero, in particolar modo in Ungheria e Polonia, dove chi tira a fatica la fine del mese va per risparmiare. » (*Il Giornale*, 7/02/2009)
	Sens 2 : « Il servizio sanitario è spesso così scadente da costituire un rischio per la vita e da incoraggiare, in chi può, un **turismo sanitario** interregionale. » (*Repubblica*, 11/08/2009)
	Sens 3 : « Non costringete le vostre elettrici a fare **turismo sanitario** per la procreazione assistita. » (*La Stampa*, 16 /05/2004)

6) **tourisme thérapeutique/turismo terapeutico** : malgré leur faible nombre d'occurrences, *tourisme thérapeutique* et *turismo terapeutico* renvoient à des pratiques disparates. La définition de *tourisme thérapeutique* dépend des sources (soit presse, soit sites et blogs). Dans la presse, il peut renvoyer : 1) aux cures psychologiques (presse, sens 1) ; 2) aux hospitalisations à l'étranger pour des raisons économiques ou de disponibilité de soins (presse, sens 2). En ce qui concerne les attestations de sites et blogs, on remarque que *tourisme thérapeutique* peut correspondre à *tourisme thermal* (sites et blogs, sens 1). Ce changement de sens selon les sources semble ne pas concerner *turismo terapeutico*, qui a deux acceptions : 1) les transplantations à base de cellules souches (presse, sens 1) ; 2) le tourisme thermal (sites et blogs, sens 2). L'équivalence des deux noms composés ne pourra être que partielle.

Presse, sens 1 : « Du coup, le commerce du **tourisme thérapeutique** est devenu prospère et varié : psychanalyse freudienne, thérapies familiales, gestalt-thérapie, programmation neuro-linguistique (PNL), au supermarché du psychisme, il n'y a que l'embarras du moi. » (*L'Express*, 20/08/2003)	
Presse, sens 2 : « Sous le terme de **tourisme thérapeutique**, les experts regroupent les personnes qui se rendent dans des pays étrangers pour bénéficier de soins ou de traitements pour des raisons économiques ou de disponibilité médicale. » (*Les Echos*, 15/12/2005).	Presse, sens 1 : « Dunque sul piano del dibattito mondiale l'opzione di utilizzare cellule staminali non dice nulla. [...] Quando le nuove ricerche daranno i primi risultati, comincerà il **turismo terapeutico**. » (*La Stampa*, 27/08/2000)
	Presse, sens 2 : « In tempi più recenti con lo sviluppo del **turismo terapeutico** e con il crescente interesse alla cultura del benessere le Terme di Acqui hanno iniziato un processo di rinnovamento in grado di rispondere alle moderne e rinnovate esigenze della clientela. » (*La Stampa*, 25/10/2009)
	Sites et blogs, sens 1 : «Alimentato da una antiscientifica campagna mediatica mondiale [...] a favore dell'impiego di staminali adulte, il "**turismo terapeutico**" per il trattamento di gravi malattie mediante il "miracoloso" trapianto di cellule è un fenomeno che non conosce confini. » (http://www.terranews.it/news/2009/12/v ere-malattie-false-guarigioni-la-truffa-delle-staminali-adulte)

Sites et blogs, sens 1 : « Le **tourisme thérapeutique**. Au XIXe siècle, prédomine un discours médical et hygiéniste qui contribue à légitimer auprès des rentiers [...] saisons d'hiver en Méditerranée, thermalisme, bains de mer. » (http://gallica.bnf.fr/dossiers/html/dossiers/VoyagesEnFrance/themes/Tourisme4.htm)	Sites et blogs, sens 2 : « Tale forma di **turismo terapeutico** si è affermato in Liguria quando ormai era stata superata la teoria medica che i bagni di mare dessero tanto più beneficio quanto più la temperatura dell'acqua fosse fredda. » (http://www.sociologia.unimib.it/v2/DATA/Insegnamenti/2_2224/materiale/riuso%20strutture%20turismo%20sociale.pdf)

Nous présentons maintenant un cas de non-équivalence sémantique :
7) **tourisme curatif/turismo curativo**. Même structure syntaxique (*N Adj*), mais définition différente: si *tourisme curatif* désigne les séjours au contact de la nature pour se soigner et/ou se ressourcer, *turismo curativo* est synonyme de *tourisme thermal*. Nous avons remarqué que dans l'espace francophone méditerranéen *tourisme curatif* renvoie au thermalisme. Les deux noms composés ne sont cependant pas équivalents.

« Dans cette optique, on voit se développer un **tourisme curatif** qui propose d'envoyer les populations touchées par ces maux se régénérer au contact des éléments naturels. » (www.cairn.info/load_pdf.php?ID_ARTICLE=SOC_077_0005)	
	« A proposito di terme : ingenti incentivi statali incoraggiano in particolare lo sviluppo del **turismo curativo**, con l'ammodernamento delle strutture termali già esistenti [...] e con la costruzione di nuove. » (http://www.lagazzettaweb.it/Pages/rub_viag/2002/turismo/r_tur_02-02.html)

Nous avons repéré assez fréquemment deux autres couples de noms composés. L'un, partiellement équivalent, a une structure syntaxique *N de N* avec une extension en *et de N* :
8) **tourisme de santé et de bien-être/turismo della salute e del benessere**. Le nom composé français est monosémique et désigne le thermalisme, la thalassothérapie et le climatisme. Le nom composé italien comporte deux acceptions, pouvant désigner, outre le *tourisme thermal*, aussi les hospitalisations à l'étranger.

Sens 1 : « **Tourisme de santé et de bien-être**. Poids du thermalisme dans l'économie touristique. » (titre d'un dossier de presse du Ministère français du Tourisme :	Sens 1: « Wellness Tourism [...] ospiterà wellness hotel, alberghi termali e destination spa, che alimentano l'offerta del **turismo della salute e del benessere** in un segmento di mercato in costante ascesa. »

http://www.tourisme.equipement.gouv.fr/fr/n avd/dossiers/taz/att00002082/tourisme_sante _bien_etre07.pdf)	(http://www.informazione.it/c/9D1FA814 -C71A-459A-AC1D- D5505EE7CDF0/Viaggio-al-centro-del- benessere-BENe-svela-tutti-i-colori-del- wellness)
	Sens 2 : « **Turismo della Salute e del Benessere** : Diamo voce ad una odontoiatria per tutti, in Italia!! Perché recarsi nei paesi extracomunitari con tutti i rischi che questo comporta? Noi ti offriamo servizi a prezzi inferiori e con la sicurezza di strutture, materiali e personale italiani. » (http://www.pansepol.it/PDF/Turismo_sal ute2008.pdf)

L'autre, totalement équivalent, a une structure *N Adj* avec une extension en *et de N* :
9) **tourisme thermal et de bien-être/turismo termale e del benessere** : les deux renvoient au thermalisme, à la thalassothérapie et au climatisme.

« Le **tourisme thermal et de bien-être** est un secteur très porteur au Portugal. » (site de la revue *Espaces* : http://www.revue- espaces.com/librairie/6962/le-tourisme- thermal-bien-etre-portugal.html)	« Le potenzialità del **turismo termale e del benessere** nelle regioni montane e la risposta strategica dell'Austria. » (http://www.trentinosalute.net/UploadD ocs/1581_006.pdf)

6. Conclusions

Après cette phase comparative, la résolution de la problématique : choisir le nom composé désignant, en français et en italien, le domaine touristique qui inclut thermalisme, thalassothérapie et climatisme. Pour ce faire, nous nous sommes appuyée sur deux critères : 1) la monosémie et 2) l'autorité des sources consultées.

Pour le français, notre choix porte sur ***tourisme de santé et de bien-être***, dont la structure syntaxique est *N de N* plus une extension en *et de N*. Ce nom composé satisfait la condition de monosémie et est attesté sur le site du Ministère français du Tourisme, ainsi que sur d'autres sites d'organismes officiels et dans la revue *Espaces*. Pour l'italien, nous retenons ***turismo termale e del benessere***, dont la structure syntaxique est *N Adj* plus une extension en *et de Ddéf N*. Monosémique, il est attesté dans la presse, sur le site de l'ENIT et sur de nombreux sites de régions italiennes ou d'organismes officiels.

Nous expliquons pourquoi nous avons exclu tous les autres noms composés. Pour la langue française, nous n'avons retenu ni *tourisme thermal* ni *tourisme de bien-être*, malgré leur monosémie : ils seraient peut-être insuffisants à la définition du domaine concerné. Ces mêmes raisons nous amènent à exclure aussi leurs équivalents italiens *turismo termale* e *turismo del benessere*. *Tourisme thermal et de bien-être*, bien que monosémique, est très rare et ne peut pas être retenu. Nous sommes obligée de rejeter *tourisme curatif*, *tourisme médical*, *tourisme sanitaire* et *tourisme thérapeutique* car leur définition ne recouvre pas notre domaine d'intérêt.

Pour la langue italienne, nous excluons pour des raisons de polysémie *turismo della salute e del benessere*, *turismo medico*, *turismo sanitario* et *turismo terapeutico*. *Turismo curativo* est rejeté pour la rareté de fréquence dont il est attesté, bien qu'il ait le thermalisme comme seul renvoi.

Pour résumer, notre domaine d'intérêt s'appellera **tourisme de santé et de bien-être** en français, mais ***turismo termale e del benessere*** en italien.

6. Bibliographie

A.A.V.V. 1993 *Grand Larousse Universel*, vol. 15, Paris: Larousse.
A.A.V.V. 2005 *La Piccola Treccani: dizionario enciclopedico*, vol. XII, Roma: Istituto della Enciclopedia Italiana fondata da Giovanni Treccani.
BATTAGLIA, S. 2002 *Grande dizionario della lingua italiana*, vol. XXI, Torino: UTET.
BLUM, C. (dir.) 2006 *Le Nouveau Littré 2006*, Paris, Garnier.
DE MAURO, T. 1999 *Grande dizionario italiano dell'uso*, vol. VI, Torino: UTET, 1999.
DEVOTO, G., OLI, G. 2004 *Dizionario della lingua italiana*, a cura di Serianni L. e Trifone M., Firenze: Le Monnier,.
DUBOIS J. (dir.) 2009 *Le Lexis : dictionnaire érudit de la langue française*, Paris, Larousse.
GROSS, G. 1996 *Les expressions figées en français*, Paris: Ophrys.
MAUBOURGET, P. (dir.) 1993 *Le Petit Larousse Illustré*, Paris: Larousse.
REY, A. (dir.) 2001 *Le Grand Robert de la Langue Française*, Paris: Le Robert.
REY, A.; & REY-DEBOVE J. (dir.) 1995 [2009] *Le Nouveau Petit Robert*, Paris: Le Robert.
SABATINI, F. & COLETTI, V. 1997 *Disc. Dizionario Italiano Sabatini Coletti*, Firenze: Giunti
ZINGARELLI, N. 2006 *Vocabolario della lingua italiana,* Bologna: Zanichelli.

BIER, SCHWEIß UND TRÄNEN - THE ACTIVATION OF ASSOCIATIVE NETWORKS BY LEXICAL SUBSTITUTIONS IN PHRASEOLOGICAL UNITS

Sylvia Jaki
University of Munich

Abstract: Newspapers and advertisements are replete with modified phraseological units. The aim of this paper is to analyse the mechanisms of one specific type of modification, lexical substitution. Using lexical substitution, writers can exploit various strategies on different meaning and form levels, in order to play with a large number of associations that are connected with both the canonical and the modified form. For the researcher, this implies looking at the formal, semantic and contextual relations between *substituens* and *substituendum*. Furthermore, exploring which relations hold between the meanings of the entire canonical and modified forms will prove to be as essential as reflecting upon the factors that influence modifiability, in particular figurativity.

Key words: Associative networks, phraseological variation, idiom modifications, antiproverbs.

0. Introduction

Modifying phraseological units (PUs) is trendy. And it is fun. While modification is of course nothing new, but has a very long tradition, I dare say that it has never been more popular than today. Every time you open a German daily newspaper, no matter whether it is a tabloid or broadsheet, you are likely to come across at least one headline containing a modified phraseological unit such as

> ***Latein ist tot – es lebe Latein*** 'Latin is dead – long live Latin' or
> [*Der König ist tot – es lebe der König* 'the King is dead – long live the King']
> ***Quatsch mit Quote*** 'nonsense with ratings'
> [*Quatsch mit Soße* 'nonsense with sauce' = 'stuff and nonsense'].

In investigating lexical substitution of this type, this paper is part of a larger project which combines more traditional analytical approaches with theories from Cognitive Linguistics. After a description of the data collected for this study (Section 1) and a survey of the relations between the substituting and substituted elements (Section 2), the focus will lie on some of the important cognitive effects resulting from the relation between the meaning of the original version and the modified version of the PU (Section 3).

1. Starting point

As copywriters and journalists display a distinct predisposition for manipulating PUs, it is not surprising that research on modification centres mainly around advertising and newspapers (Balsliemke 2001, Bass 2006, Ptashnyk 2009, Sabban 1998 etc.). Analyses emphasize both the different mechanisms of modification and their effect on the recipient. Recently, approaches to modification, just like phraseology in general, have experienced a cognitive turn (Langlotz 2006, Mena Martínez 2006, Omazić 2005). One of the major challenges has become combining the findings of Cognitive Linguistics with the more traditional analytical approaches, in order to provide a more comprehensive insight into modification theory and to investigate restrictions on modifiability which might go beyond Dobrovol'skij's claim (1997: 75) that the only precondition imposed on modification is recognizability[1].

I will focus on the principles underlying what is probably the most common and most popular type of modification, namely lexical substitution. To this end, 120 German PUs (60 figurative and 60 non-figurative) containing 173 modifications (100 found in the non-figurative and 73 in the figurative PUs) have been collected. The material is taken from German daily newspapers like *Sueddeutsche Zeitung* or *Frankfurter Allgemeine Zeitung*; but some instances are also derived from magazines like *Der Spiegel* and other sources, such as advertisements or private conversations. I will use the term phraseological unit in a wide sense, to cover proverbs, idioms, common places, routines and binominals as well as advertising slogans, film/ book/ song titles and familiar quotations.

2. Mechanisms of substitution: relations between *substituens* and *substituendum*

Before we can look at the cognitive effects of lexical substitutions it is important to set up a systematic framework describing the relations between *substituens* and *substituendum*. These can generally be of three different types: paronymic, semantic, and contextual.

Paronymy, i.e. formal similarity, occurs in a large number of instances, since using paronymy is certainly the most efficient way to allude to a PU while using a contextually more suitable word. It is a broad term ranging from homonymy and the substitution of one or more graphemes to the simple maintenance of the number of syllables (see Prędota 2002). Homonymy proper is very rare and appears in my sample only once (*Hier steh' ich nun, ich armes Tor* 'Here now I stand, me poor goal' [*Hier steht ich nun, ich armer Tor* 'Here now I stand, me poor idiot']). Mere homophony is used three times, e.g. in the following advertisement for the organic pastries of a big supermarket: *Unsere REWE Bio Backwaren geben sich die Ähre* 'Our REWE organic pastries give themselves the ear (of corn)' [*sich die Ehre geben* 'do themselves the honour of']. What is more common, is the substitution of one or two graphemes, for instance in *Spende gut, alles gut* 'all's well that donates well' [*Ende gut, alles gut* 'all's well that ends well']. Formal similarity is less obvious when only a minor part of the *substituendum* is maintained, such as the prefix *ab-* in *Abhören und Tee trinken* 'listen on and drink tea' instead of *Abwarten und Tee trinken* 'wait and drink tea' (= 'wait and see'). One form of formal similarity that is widely used is sticking to the given numbers of syllables to keep the rhythm of the canonical form, which plays an important role in the remembering of proverbs or slogans. Even though little of the morphological and graphematic substance is maintained in the following examples, we easily recognize the PU alluded to, like in *Was lange schmort schmeckt doppelt gut* 'What stews for a long time tastes twice as good' [*Was lange währt, wird endlich gut* 'What takes a long time ends well' = 'patience is rewarded']. Overall, paronymy was found in 104 modifications (out of 173).

---

[1] See the following authors for an analysis of what must be maintained to obtain recognizability: Lenz 1998: 211-123; Omazić 2004: 628.

Semantic relations, which also support readers in their endeavour to retrieve the original version, were observed in a total of 58 modifications, and are thus less pervasive than relations of formal similarity.

The semantic relations existing between the substituting and substituted elements are manifold (see figure 1). The most frequently used relation in the present data collection is antonymy, followed by cohyponymy and cases where the two elements share at least one striking semantic feature. Another semantic relation that is still relatively common is specification. Contiguity occurs as well, but less frequently. Strangely enough, synonymy – or more precisely 'real' synonymy, i.e. semantic quasi-identity which is firmly established in the lexicon rather than just created in context (see below), – does not seem to play a role: it only appears once, namely in *Schöner die Promis nie nerven* 'VIPs never annoy more pleasantly', where, apart from other substitutions, *süßer* from the canonical form *Süßer die Glocken nie klingen* 'the bells never sound more pleasant' (a Christmas carol) has been replaced by *schöner*. [2] Even though it is in contrast to Ptashnyk's (2001) (at least implicit) suggestion that synonymy is highly relevant for substitution, this finding may not be too surprising after all, given that the major function of modifications in newspaper headlines is to attract the reader's attention and therefore to be eye-catching. Since replacing an element by a synonym is possibly not the most efficient device for achieving this, it seems only logical that synonymy between *substituens* and *substituendum* is rather rare.

Relation	Canonical form	Modified form
Antonymy	**Vertrauen** ist gut, Kontrolle ist besser. 'Trust is good; checking is better.'	**Misstrauen** ist gut, Kontrolle ist besser. 'Distrust is good; checking is better.'
Cohyponymy	Auf den **Hund** gekommen 'Come to the dog'	Auf die **Kuh** gekommen 'Come to the cow'
Semantic specification	Ich bin dann mal **weg** 'Then I'm just gone'	Ich bin dann mal **offline** 'Then I'm just offline'
Contiguity	**Adel** verpflichtet 'Noblesse oblige'	**Herkunft** verpflichtet 'Ancestry obliges'
Shared features (INTENDED HARM)	Sport ist **Mord** 'Sport is murder'	Sport ist **Rufmord** 'Sport is slander'

(1) Semantic relations between *substituens* and *substituendum*

---

[2] Nevertheless, this example shows that the relationships existing between the substituting and substituted form should not be overestimated. In many modifications, various elements have been replaced – there context and rhythm play a far more relevant role. Thus, the near-synonymy of *schön* and *süß* can be considered as a mere coincidence, conditioned by contextual and rhythmical aspects.

Contextual synonymy is one of a set of **contextual relations** to be dealt with next.[3] It can be defined as a similarity between two elements which can only be observed in a specific context. Contextual synonymy, which is, at least in my view, not separated clearly enough from 'real' semantic synonymy by Ptashnyk (2001: 438-441), actually does appear in my data, and this might explain her claim.[4]

Apart from contextual synonymies like the book title *Gott ist rund* 'God is round' instead of *Der Ball ist rund* 'the ball is round' (the book deals with soccer, which people worship like a god), other contextual relationships, contextual antonymy and specification, were detected.[5] Contextual antonymy, in contrast to semantic antonymy, means that the substituted and the substituting elements are only contrasting in a given context, as in *Wer wagt, gerinnt* 'He who dares something will clot' [*Wer wagt, gewinnt* 'He who dares something will win']. *Gewinnen* 'to win' and *gerinnen* 'to clot' are only antonymous in so far as *gerinnen* is used as 'to fail' – a meaning this lexeme normally does not have. What is more widespread than the rare cases of antonymy is contextual specification. The *substituens* can either be a more specific version of the *substituendum* on the literal level – both with figurative and non-figurative units – or on the level of figurative meaning: while *Populist* refers to the accused person in the modification *Im Zweifel für den Populisten* 'giving the demagogue the benefit of the doubt' of *Im Zweifel für den Angeklagten* 'giving the defendant the benefit of the doubt', the substitution *Lieber die knackige Erbin in der Hand als die Millionärin auf dem Dach* 'better the sexy heiress in the hand than the millionairess on the roof' [*Lieber den Spatz in der Hand als die Taube auf dem Dach* 'better the sparrow in the hand than the pigeon on the roof' = 'it is better to choose the smaller benefit over the greater, but more risky one'] specifies at the figurative level. The modification indicates what the smaller benefit one can have in this context is, namely the good-looking heiress, and the greater benefit one might not be able to obtain, the millionairess.

In most cases, however, there is no such contextual semantic relationship between the *substituendum* and its more suitable counterpart. Contextualisation without an obvious connection between the concerned elements typically occurs when names are replaced, for example in *Merkel allein zu Haus* 'Merkel is at home alone' [*Kevin allein zu Haus* 'Kevin is at home alone'[6]] or *Berlin denkt, Paris lenkt* 'Berlin thinks, Paris directs' [*Der Mensch denkt, Gott lenkt* 'man thinks, God directs'], but goes far beyond this case (*Sie kamen, kämmten,*

---

[3] That contextual relations should be distinguished from semantic ones is important, particularly because they sometimes contrast in the same modification (even though this is quite rare). In *Den Vampir mit dem Werwolf austreiben* 'to cast out the vampire with the werwolf' [*den Teufel mit dem Beelzebub austreiben* 'to cast out the devil with Beelzebub' = 'to replace one evil with another'], for instance, *vampire*, *werewolf*, *devil* and *Beelzebub* are cohyponyms with the hyperonym *incarnations of the evil*. In this specific context, however, they can be considered as synonyms, since they all have they meaning 'evil'.
[4] Another explanation for this might be that she classifies cases as modifications that I would consider to be variations. With variation, however, synonymy plays a considerable role (Ptashnyk 2001; 2009).
[5] The category of contextual relations does not occur in Sabban (1998). Interestingly, she classifies what I call contextualisation under paronymy. In my view, this is rather infelicitous as there is indeed no formal similarity involved (Sabban 1998: 245-258).
[6] The original film title in English is *Home Alone*.

siegten 'they came, combed, conquered' [*Er/Ich kam, sah, siegte* 'he/ I came, saw, conquered']).

3. Mechanisms of substitution: Relations between the canonical and the modified meaning

In the previous section I have largely followed the traditional structuralist practice of focussing on possible relationships between *substituens* and *substituendum*. From a cognitive point of view, however, what may reveal more about the nature of lexical substitution and its potential for punning is an analysis of how substitutions can alter a PU's meaning in context, for it reflects how a whole network of associations is evoked by modification.

On the one hand, the meaning, in the narrow sense, of the original and the modified form can be identical, with the only difference being that the new form provides more contextual information. [7] From this perspective, modification could be considered not just as the manipulation of an existing form, but as an adaptation of a form established in the system (at the level of *langue*) to the current context (*parole*). In a sense, this can be seen as resulting in a contextual 'improvement', which seems to be a good explanation why lexical substitution is so common. To take up an example discussed before, *Den Vampir mit dem Werwolf austreiben* constitutes such a case. Compared to the canonical form *Den Teufel mit dem Beelzebub austreiben*, the meaning 'to replace one evil with another' is unaltered. As the article following this headline deals with vampire films, the modified version is much better suited to the context. The same goes for *Huhnglaublich, aber war* 'chicken+believable, but true', which is a modification of *Unglaublich, aber wahr* 'unbelievable, but true'. Both have more or less the same meaning, but while the original is contextually neutral, the modification indicates to the recipient that the following text will be about chicken.

On the other hand, modification can lead to a crucial manipulation of meaning. With figurative PUs, this means that the phraseological meaning often vanishes, and that the form is consequently to be taken literally. *Werben bis der Arzt kommt* 'advertise until the doctor comes' is a modification of *feiern bis der Arzt kommt* 'party until the doctor comes', with the latter meaning 'to party excessively'. Generally speaking, some kind of phraseological model or schema meaning 'excessively' already seems to have developed from the original PU, which can be filled with various verbs. Ironically, *werben bis der Arzt kommt* does not mean 'to advertise excessively' in the context of the present headline, but something like 'Eastern Germany has to make huge efforts to attract doctors to their depopulated areas'. This means that the contextualized modified PU only alludes to the schema or model of the figurative source PU but has to be understood non-figuratively. Although non-figurative units are less complex since they do not provide a second level of meaning (the phraseological meaning), there also seem to be considerable differences concerning the degree of meaning alteration. A crucial manipulation may be achieved when a new frame or thematic field is associated with the modification, for example in *Bier, Schweiß und Tränen* 'beer, sweat and tears' [*Blut/Angst, Schweiß und Tränen* 'blood/fear, sweat and tears'], where the frame hard work is backgrounded by and at the same time blended with (cf. Fauconnier and Turner 2002) a different frame, beer festivals. In other cases, so much of the canonical form is changed (of

---

[7] This cateogory corresponds more or less to Mena Martínez's "occasional phraseological synonymy" (Mena Martínez 2006: 132).

both figurative and non-figurative units) that there is only a loose association with the canonical form and meaning. As an illustration, let us look at *Wer später bremst, fährt länger schnell* 'He who brakes later will drive fast longer', which is a modification of the film title *Wer früher stirbt, ist länger tot* 'He who dies sooner will be dead longer'. The alteration is substantial, as most of the original version is modified. What is maintained, however, is its rhythmical model and sentence structure.

Somewhere in between these two poles, identity of meaning on the one hand, and deconstruction of meaning on the other, lie what I refer to as *minor manipulations of meaning*. With both figurative and non-figurative units, this occurs when modification does not open up a new frame or thematic field, as in *Misstrauen ist gut, Kontrolle ist besser* 'distrust is good; checking is better' [*Vertrauen ist gut, Kontrolle ist besser* 'trust is good; checking is better'] or *Der Ball ist bunt* 'the ball is multicoloured' [*Der Ball ist rund* 'the ball is round']. In other cases, alterations of meaning might be little striking because the canonical form and/or meaning still remains co-present, which applies mostly in the case of figurative units. This does not mean that modifications of this type are less subtle. *Schlau wie Bohnenstroh* 'as smart as bean straw', for instance, is meant to designate a starlet who, in order to promote her career, plays the smart businesswoman. However, as the reader will automatically activate the canonical form *dumm wie Bohnenstroh* 'as stupid as bean straw' (= 'very stupid'), they might not be able to prevent themselves from co-associating stupidity with the modification, which is, of course, exactly the journalist's intention. While co-associations can basically occur with all lexical substitutions, it depends on the context to what extent the canonical meaning is suppressed. In this example, the link to stupidity is very strong because most readers would judge this starlet to be of a rather limited intelligence, due to her manner in a casting show for models. Thus, it is a very felicitous modification, implicitly stating something that should not be said explicitly in a newspaper headline.

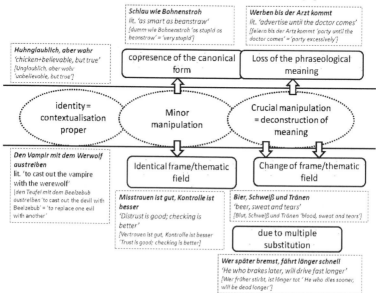

(2) Relations between the meaning of the canonical and the modified form

To sum up, there are various degrees of meaning alterations resulting from lexical substitution.[8] If it has to be admitted that the categories of the model (see figure 2) do not show clear-cut boundaries, this is only a reflection of the enormous variability of the phenomenon and the creativity of its 'users'. Consequently, at times it will not be easy to determine whether a modification still has the same meaning as the original, and people will also not always agree whether a specific modification has to be read entirely literally or if the canonical meaning is still remotely present. But this uncertainty lies in the very nature of modification: what makes it so popular is that the whole set of associations that belong to both the canonical and the modified form are not activated in exactly the same way by each recipient. The author can play with these individual activation processes, particularly with the ambiguity between literal and phraseological meanings (see Dobrovol'skij 2008: 310), which is a good way to keep one's messages more ambiguous and thus more attractive for the reader.

4. Summary and outlook

As this paper has shown, a usage-based approach is extremely helpful in giving a realistic account of what happens in lexical substitution. As there seem to be no absolute restrictions on modifiability, theoretically "anything goes". However, some types of lexical substitution will be used more frequently, and some will be perceived to be better types of modifications than others. When we look at the observed frequencies of semantic relations between substituted and substituting elements, for instance, synonymy virtually does not appear at all. I have also tried to highlight that a clear distinction of the different form and meaning levels (by distinguishing semantic and purely contextual relations as well as the different degrees of meaning alterations) has to take place in order to account for the different associations that play a role in lexical substitution. Nevertheless, these different degrees are not intended to be categories where each substitution fits in unequivocally. This is due to the fact that substitution plays with ambiguity by opening up a broad network of associations. Which associations are activated by the recipients while understanding a modification is always individual to a certain degree. What this paper has also indicated implicitly is that figurativity constitutes one major factor influencing the mechanisms of lexical substitution. As non-figurative units cannot play with the ambiguity between literal and phraseological meaning, they rely on different devices of meaning alteration. In contrast to their literal counterparts, which can only play with frozenness, lexical substitutions of figurative PUs can exploit both frozenness and figurativity. This might be the reason why this type of modified PUs shows a higher tendency towards forming phraseological schemas.

However, these findings should be considered with caution, since they are based on a fairly small data sample. The following aspects would be desirable for future research: first and foremost, the use of a much larger data base, particularly with respect to the importance of frequency ratings. Furthermore, the relevance of the dichotomy figurative – non-figurative should be analysed more comprehensively, including considerations about how specific types of motivation influence lexical substitution. While the analytical categories used in this paper

---

[8] Ptashnyk has established a similar classification for modifications in general, coming, however, to largely different results with respect to its subcategories (Ptashnyk 2009: 156f). The scope of this paper, unfortunately, does not permit a comparison.

may prove to be helpful for the description of lexical substitution, they are certainly not sufficient for giving a comprehensive account of the cognitive mechanisms that structure the production and reception of such modifications. Therefore it is indispensable to look more closely at the different types of conceptual blending[9] involved in lexical substitution; and it would make equal sense to explore experimentally how different recipients activate different associations when trying to understand the same lexical substitution.

---

[9] See Delibegović Džanić/ Berberović 2010, Langlotz 2004 and Omazić 2005 for the importance of conceptual blending in phraseology and particularly modification theory.

6. References

BALSLIEMKE, P. 2001 „*Da sieht die Welt schon anders aus.*" *Phraseologismen in der Anzeigenwerbung: Modifikation und Funktion in Text-Bild-Beziehungen*, Baltmannsweiler.

BASS, N. 2006 „*Muescht Knorr probiere, s'gaht über's Schtudiere!*" *Phraseologismen und Modifikationen in der Anzeigenwerbung 1928-1998*, Baltmannsweiler.

BURGER, H. 1991 "Phraseologie und Intertextualität", in: Ch. Palm (ed.), *Europhras 90*, Uppsala: 13-27.

DELIBEGOVIĆ, N.D. & BEBEROVIĆ, S. 2010 "Conceptual integration theory and mentonymy in idiom modifications". In: J. Korhonen;, W. Mieder; E. Piirainen & R. Piñel (eds.), *Phraseologie global – areal – regional*, Tübingen: 397-408.

DOBROVOL'SKIJ, D.O 1997 *Idiome im mentalen Lexikon: Ziele und Methoden der kognitivbasierten Phraseologieforschung*, Trier.

DOBROVOL'SKIJ, D.O. 2008 "Idiom-Modifikationen aus kognitiver Perspektive". In: Kämper, H. & Eichinger, L. M. (eds.), *Sprache – Kognition – Kultur. Sprache zwischen mentaler Struktur und kultureller Prägung*. Berlin/ New York: 302-322.

FAUCONNIER, G. & TURNER, M. 2002 *The Way we Think. Conceptual Blending and the Mind's Hidden Complexities*, New York.

LANGLOTZ, A. 2004 "Conceptual Blending as a Principle of Idiom Structure and Variation". In: Palm-Meister, Ch. (ed.), *EUROPHRAS 2000*, Tübingen: 263-272.

LANGLOTZ, A. 2006 *Idiomatic Creativity*, Amsterdam.

LENZ, B. 1998 "'Bilder, die brutzeln, brennen nicht'. Modifizierte sprachliche Formeln in Zeitungsüberschriften und die grammatischen Bedingungen ihrer Rekonstruktion". In: Hartmann, D. (ed.) *"Das geht auf keine Kuhhaut": Arbeitsfelder der Phraseologie (Akten des Westfälischen Arbeitskreises Phraseologie/ Parömiologie 1996)*, Bochum: 199-214.

MENA MARTÍNEZ, F. 2006 "Occasional Phraseological Synonymy". In: *International Journal of English Studies* 6 (1): 131-158.

OMAZIĆ, M. 2004 "Imagery in Phraseology". In: B. Lewandowska-Tomaszczyk & A. Kwiatkowska (eds.), *Imagery in Language. Festschrift in Honour of Professor Ronald W. Langacker*, Frankfurt / Berlin/ Bern: 625-633.

OMAZIĆ, M. 2005 "Cognitive linguistic theories in phraseology". *Jezikoslovlje* 6 (1-2): 37-56.

PRĘDOTA, S. 2002 "Phonische Mittel bei der Bildung von Antisprichwörtern" . In: Hartmann, D. & Wirrer, J. (eds.), *Wer A sägt, muss auch B sägen. Beiträge zur Phraseologie und Sprichwortforschung aus dem Westfälischen Arbeitskreis*, Baltmannsweiler: 341-349.

PTASHNYK, S. 2001 "Phraseologische Substitution und ihre Funktionen im Text". In: *Wirkendes Wort* 3: 435-454.

PTASHNYK, S. 2009 *Phraseologische Modifikationen und ihre Funktionen im Text. Eine Studie am Beispiel der deutschsprachigen Presse*, Baltmannsweiler.

SABBAN, A. 1998 *Okkasionelle Variation sprachlicher Schematismen: eine Analyse französischer und deutsche Presse- und Werbetexte*, Tübingen.

DIE AREALE VERBREITUNG SOG. PHRASEOLOGISCHER „HELVETISMEN"

Britta Juska-Bacher
Stefan Meier
Basel[1]

Abstract: The spatial distribution of phraseological helvetisms is not clearly defined. On the basis of empirical data gathered from about 1000 questionnaires from Switzerland, Germany and Austria we show that in lexicographical practice the term helvetism is used for different types of phrasemes: a first group which is exclusively known in (all areas of) Switzerland, a second group which is also known in Austria and/or parts of Germany, and a third group which is only known in some parts of Switzerland. We suggest that these different areal distributions should be considered by adding an element to the term helvetism, e.g. austro-helvetism, regional helvetism. For these classifications empirical data play an essential role.

Key words: Empirical data, helvetism, spatial distribution, German phraseology

1. Was ist ein „phraseologischer Helvetismus"?

Einschlägige Wörterbücher, wie diejenigen von Meyer (1989), Ammon et al. (2004) und der Dudenredaktion (2008), enthalten eine Reihe von Phrasemen, die als „Helvetismen" bezeichnet werden. Grundlage dieser Einstufung ist die areale Begrenzung der Mehrwortverbindungen auf die Deutschschweiz (z.B. Burger 1995: 13, allgemein zu lexikalischen Helvetismen siehe Haas 2000: 100). In der Forschungsliteratur wird darüber hinaus die Erfüllung weiterer Kriterien als relevant erachtet:

1. Die Zugehörigkeit der Phraseme zur Standardsprache, d.h. nicht zum Dialekt (z.B. Ammon 1995: 251–3, Burger 1995: 13),[2]
2. ihre Kodifizierung in Wörterbüchern (Ammon 1995: 251–3),[3]
3. ihre Verankerung im Sprachbewusstsein der Sprechenden (Koller 1999: 156)[4] sowie
4. ihre allgemeine Gebräuchlichkeit in der Deutschschweiz (Burger 1995: 14, Koller 1999: 156).

---

[1] Die Beiträge der Autor(inn)en: BJB: Studiendesign, Datenerhebung, Auswertung, Verfassen dieses Artikels, SM: Kartengestaltung.

[2] Burger betont verschiedentlich (1996: 464, 1998: 50, 2007: 218) die Schwierigkeiten der Zuordnung von Phraseologismen zu Standard vs. Dialekt. Die hier vorgestellte empirische Studie bestätigte dieses Problem: einige Probanden gaben dialektale Formen der Phraseme an.

[3] Hier stellt sich natürlich die Frage, wie phraseologische Helvetismen in Wörterbücher gelangen. Dabei ist von den drei Möglichkeiten: 1. die Übernahme aus anderen Wörterbüchern, 2. Expertenwissen und 3. empirische Überprüfung anhand von Korpusanalysen oder Probandenbefragungen, die letztgenannte die aufwändigste, aber zugleich die verlässlichste.

[4] Zweifel an diesem Bewusstsein äußert Burger (1998: 71–75).

In diesem Artikel beschränken wir uns auf den erstgenannten, arealen Aspekt. Es sei aber an dieser Stelle erwähnt, dass die Phraseme der hier vorgestellten empirischen Studie in Meyer (1989), Ammon et al. (2004) und/oder Dudenredaktion (2008) als phraseologische Helvetismen verzeichnet sind und damit die Kriterien der Kodifizierung in Wörterbüchern (Punkt 2) und der Zugehörigkeit zur Schweizer Standardsprache (Punkt 1) prinzipiell erfüllen. Rückfragen bei den an der Untersuchung beteiligten Studierenden (siehe Kapitel 3) und Anmerkungen von den Teilnehmenden der Befragung machten allerdings wiederholt auf Unsicherheiten bei der Zuordnung des phraseologischen Materials zur Standardsprache aufmerksam (vgl. dazu auch Fußnote 2). Die erhobenen Daten schließlich geben Hinweise auf die allgemeine Bekanntheit der abgefragten Phraseme in der Deutschschweiz (Punkt 4, siehe Kapitel 4) und auf die Verankerung dieser Einheiten im Sprachbewusstsein (Punkt 3).[5] Die Erfüllung dieser weiteren Kriterien spricht also nicht gegen eine Einstufung der betrachteten Phraseme als Helvetismen. Was bleibt, ist die Frage nach ihrer arealen Erstreckung, die wir auf den folgenden Seiten beleuchten wollen. Eine zentrale Frage in diesem Zusammenhang ist, wie ein Phrasem zu klassifizieren ist, wenn die nationale Grenze deutlich über- oder unterschritten wird. Dieses Problem spricht bereits Burger (2007: 209–210) an[6]:

> Die Begriffe „Helvetismus" und „Austriazismus" müssten bei einer genaueren Betrachtungsweise noch differenziert werden: Sowohl in Österreich wie in der Schweiz gibt es Phraseologismen, die zwar als Österreich- bzw. Schweiz-typisch gelten, die aber – vor allem aufgrund der großräumigen dialektologischen Verhältnisse im bairisch-österreichischen und im alemannischen Raum auch in den angrenzenden deutschsprachigen Gebieten verwendet werden.

2. Bekanntheitsgrade als Grundlage für die areale Erstreckung eines Helvetismus

Von vornherein von der Definition als Helvetismus ausgeschlossen werden können Phraseme, die einen relativ hohen Bekanntheitsgrad außerhalb der Schweiz haben (ab der Hälfte der Probanden bekannt). Sie werden als gemeindeutsche Phraseme bezeichnet. Unter Annahme eines Bekanntheitsgefälles bezwischen der Schweiz und Deutschland bzw. Österreich lassen sich drei Typen von Phrasemen als Helvetismen einstufen, für die im Ergebnisteil (Kapitel 4) jeweils Belege angeführt werden:
1. Phraseme, die innerhalb der Schweiz der Hälfte der Befragten oder mehr bekannt und außerhalb der Schweiz (nahezu) unbekannt sind (= eindeutige Helvetismen).
2. Phraseme, die innerhalb der Schweiz mindestens der Hälfte der Befragten und außerhalb der Schweiz einer Minderheit bekannt sind. Wenn sich diese Minderheit auf bestimmte Regionen konzentriert,[7] sollte diese Region in die Bezeichnung aufgenommen werden, z.B. Austro-Helvetismen (für in Österreich und der Schweiz bekannte Phraseme), Bavaro-Helvetismen (im bayrischen Sprachraum und in der Schweiz bekannt), Alemannismen (in

---

[5] Das Dutzend Phraseme, dessen Status als Helvetismus abgefragt wurde, wurde von 50% der Schweizer Probanden als Schweizer Eigenheit eingestuft.

[6] Entsprechend zu Austriazismen siehe Földes (1992: 11).

[7] Wenn die Phraseme hingegen im gesamten deutschsprachigen Raum einen Bekanntheitsgrad von 21–40% haben, ist ihr Status als Helvetismus zweifelhaft.

Baden-Württemberg und in der Schweiz bekannt) oder auf den süddeutschen Sprachraum beschränkte Phraseme (Baden-Württemberg, Bayern, Schweiz, Österreich.[8]
4. Phraseme, die innerhalb der Schweiz einer Minderheit bekannt oder (nahezu) unbekannt sind, wobei sich die Bekanntheit auf eine bestimmte Region konzentriert, und außerhalb der Schweiz nahezu unbekannt sind (= regionale Helvetismen).

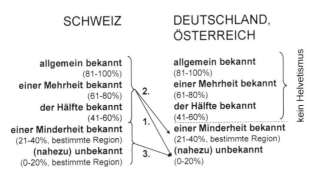

Abb. 1: Bekanntheitsgrade eines Phrasems inner- und außerhalb der Schweiz: 1. eindeutige Helvetismen, 2. z.B. Austro-Helvetismen, Bavaro-Helvetismen, Alemannismen oder auf süddeutschen Sprachraum beschränkte Phraseme, 3. regionale Helvetismen

3. Material und Methoden der empirischen Untersuchung

Die im Folgenden beschriebene Online-Befragung[9] wurde im Frühlingssemester 2009 im Rahmen eines Methodenkurses mit Germanistikstudierenden der Universität Basel durchgeführt.[10] An dieser Befragung zur Bekanntheit von phraseologischen Helvetismen haben sich rund 1000 Personen beteiligt, von denen 981 bei der Auswertung berücksichtigt werden konnten.[11] 863 von ihnen stammten aus der Schweiz (bis auf Obwalden wurden alle Deutschschweizer Kantone abgedeckt), 118 aus Deutschland, Österreich und Liechtenstein. Gefragt wurde im Multiple-choice-Verfahren nach der Form (Ergänzungstests) bzw. Bedeu-

---

[8] Weitere Kombinationen innerhalb des süddeutschen Sprachraums (Austro-Alemannismen, Bavaro-Alemannismen, Austro-Bavaro-Helvetismen sowie weitere, aller Wahrscheinlichkeit nach weniger häufige Kombinationen mit nicht direkt angrenzenden (Bundes-)Ländern, die wegen der geringen Teilnehmerzahlen in dieser Untersuchung zusammengefasst wurden (siehe Kapitel 4), sind selbstverständlich möglich, sollen hier aber unberücksichtigt bleiben.

[9] Da in dieser Studie eine möglichst genaue räumliche Zuordnung der Probanden (zu Kantonen bzw. Bundesländern) und damit ihrer Angaben vorgenommen werden sollte, wurde mit einer Informantenbefragung gearbeitet. Zur Methode der Online-Befragung sowie zu ihren Vor- und Nachteilen siehe Juska-Bacher (2010).

[10] Ihnen allen danke ich für ihr Interesse an diesem Thema und ihren Einsatz bei der Erarbeitung, Diskussion und Verbreitung des Fragebogens.

[11] Es wurden nur Daten derjenigen Probanden verwendet, für die eine eindeutige Zuordnung zu einem deutschsprachigen Land möglich war (d.h. sie mussten den größten Teil ihres Lebens im betreffenden Land verbracht haben und dort auch sozialisiert worden sein).

tung von 29 größtenteils helvetischen sowie wenigen gemeindeutschen[12] Phrasemen. Im folgenden Kapitel werden exemplarisch die Ergebnisse zur arealen Erstreckung von fünf der abgefragten phraseologischen Helvetismen vorgestellt.

4. Empirische Daten zur arealen Erstreckung von phraseologischen Helvetismen

Ein erster Blick auf die Bekanntheit der fünf exemplarischen Phraseme (siehe Abb. 2) zeigt, dass sie nach dem bisherigen lexikografischen Standard, der eine deutlich größere Bekanntheit inner- als außerhalb der Schweiz verlangt (siehe Kapitel 2), relativ klar als Helvetismen einzustufen sind. Zweifel, ob die Differenz groß genug ist, kommen evtl. beim vierten Phrasem (von unten) in Abb. 2 mit einer Bekanntheit von 99% innerhalb der Schweiz und 56% außerhalb der Schweiz auf. Die signifikant höhere Bekanntheit dieser Phraseme in der Schweiz im Vergleich zu den anderen deutschsprachigen Ländern lässt sich auch mit Hilfe eines t-Tests ($p = 0.02$) nachweisen.

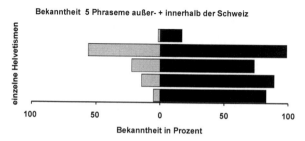

Abb. 2: Bekanntheit der fünf exemplarischen Phraseme innerhalb (schwarze Balken rechts, durchschnittlicher Bekanntheitsgrad 72%) und außerhalb der Schweiz (graue Balken links, durchschnittlicher Bekanntheitsgrad 20%)

Zu den folgenden Karten (Abb. 3–7): Die Schweizer Daten werden nach Kantonen wiedergegeben. Die bundesdeutschen Daten werden drei Regionen zugewiesen: dem an die Schweiz angrenzenden Bundesland Baden-Württemberg und dem an Österreich angrenzenden Bayern; die nördlicheren Bundesländer werden unter „Rest Deutschland" zusammengefasst. Die österreichischen (und Liechtensteiner) Daten wurden wegen der geringen Probandenzahlen jeweils zusammengefasst.[13]

---

[12] Als „gemeindeutsch" wird ein Phrasem bezeichnet, das in allen drei Vollzentren des Deutschen verbreitet ist.
[13] Österreich: 5 Probanden aus Vorarlberg, Oberösterreich, Kärnten und dem Burgenland; Liechtenstein: 7 Probanden.

Beispiel 1: *jmd. hat einen Ecken ab*[14]

Dieses Verbalphrasem mit der Bedeutung „jmd. ist nicht ganz normal", das man im übrigen deutschen Sprachraum in der Variante *jmd. hat ein Rad ab* kennt[15], wird von Ammon et al. (2004) als Helvetismus klassifiziert, in Meyer (1989) und in Dudenredaktion (2008) ist es nicht enthalten. Die Daten unserer empirischen Untersuchung zeigen in der Deutschschweiz einen hohen Bekanntheitsgrad (kartografische Darstellung siehe Abb. 3), in zwei Dritteln der Deutschschweizer Kantone ist es allgemein bekannt, im Wallis ist es nur einer Minderheit, in den übrigen Kantonen einer Mehrheit der Probanden bekannt (zu den Bekanntheitsgraden vgl. Abb. 1). Außerhalb der Schweiz ist es – abgesehen von Liechtenstein – (nahezu) unbekannt. Nach der in Kapitel 2 vorgeschlagenen Klassifizierung (Abb. 2) ist das Phrasem *jmd. hat einen Ecken ab* eindeutig als Helvetismus einzustufen.

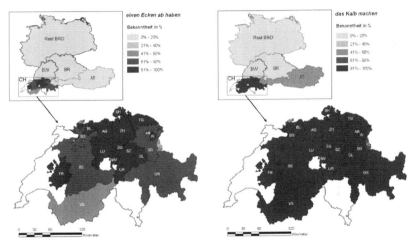

Abb. 3: Bekanntheit von *jmd. hat einen Ecken ab* inner- und außerhalb der Schweiz

Abb. 4: Bekanntheit von *das Kalb machen* inner- und außerhalb der Schweiz

Beispiel 2: *jmd. macht das Kalb*

Dieses Verbalphrasem ohne strukturell ähnliche gemeindeutsche Variante ist sowohl in Meyer (1989) als auch in Ammon et al. (2004) und der Dudenredaktion (2008) als Helvetismus aufgeführt. Die Probandenangaben belegen, dass *jmd. macht das Kalb* („ausgelassen sein, sich närrisch geben") in der Deutschschweiz in allen Kantonen allgemein

---

[14] Die Nennformschreibung folgt Korhonen (2001).
[15] Burger (1995: 17f) unterteilt drei Kategorien von Helvetismen: 1. Schweizer Phraseme, die strukturelle Varianten von binnendeutschen Phrasemen darstellen (z.B. *dastehen wie der Esel am/der Ochs vorm Berg*), 2. eigenständige Schweizer Phraseme ohne strukturell ähnliche phraseologische Äquivalente (z.B. *jmdm. nimmt es den Ärmel rein* „jmdn. packt es") und 3. falsche Freunde mit gleicher Struktur, aber unterschiedlicher Bedeutung (z.B. *jmdm. die Stange halten* „sich gegen jmdn. behaupten" vs. „jmdn. nicht im Stich lassen").

262 Britta Juska-Bacher & Stefan Meier

bekannt, in Liechtenstein einer Mehrheit (71%) und in Österreich der Hälfte (60%) bekannt ist. In Deutschland ist es mit einem Bekanntheitsgrad zwischen 2 und 14% (nahezu) unbekannt (siehe Abb. 4). Nach der in Abb. 2 angeführten Klassifizierung und in Abweichung von den Wörterbuchangaben ist *jmd. macht das Kalb* als Austro-Helvetismus einzustufen.[16]

Beispiel 3: *Jetzt jagt es den Zapfen ab.*

Dieses Phrasem (nach der Klassifizierung Burgers 2007: 39–41 eine feste Phrase), wiederum ohne gemeindeutsche Variante, wird von Ammon et al. (2004) als Helvetismus klassifiziert, in Meyer (1989) und Dudenredaktion (2008) ist es nicht verzeichnet. Die Visualisierung der Befragungsdaten in Abb. 5 zeigt ein uneinheitlicheres Bild für die Schweiz als für die vorangehenden Phraseme. In den deutschsprachigen Westschweizer Kantonen Fribourg, Bern, Solothurn und Wallis sowie in Schwyz und Appenzell Ausserrhoden (wie auch in Liechtenstein) ist es allgemein bekannt, in den Nordschweizer Kantonen (Baselland, Baselstadt, Aargau, Luzern, Schaffhausen, Zürich, Zug, Thurgau, St. Gallen) der Mehrheit der Befragten, in den übrigen Kantonen der Hälfte oder weniger bekannt. Im übrigen deutschsprachigen Raum ist *Jetzt jagt es den Zapfen ab.* in der Bedeutung „Jetzt reicht es!" (nahezu) unbekannt, nur in Bayern kennt es die Hälfte der Befragten (50%). Diesen Daten zufolge und mit Blick auf die vorgeschlagene Klassifizierung ist die Wörterbuchangabe zu korrigieren und dieses Phrasem als Bavaro-Helvetismus einzustufen.

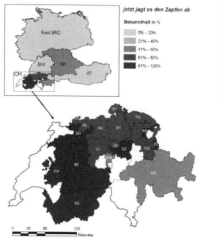 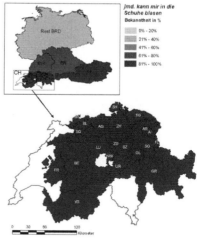

Abb. 5: Bekanntheit von *Jetzt jagt es den Zapfen ab.* inner- und außerhalb der Schweiz

Abb. 6: Bekanntheit von *jmd. kann mir in die Schuhe blasen* inner- und außerhalb der Schweiz

---

[16] Eine gewisse Vorsicht ist in dieser Untersuchung aufgrund der beschränkten Teilnehmerzahl aus Österreich geboten.

Beispiel 4: *jmd. kann mir in die Schuhe blasen*[17]

Dieses Verbalphrasem ohne strukturell ähnliche gemeindeutsche Variante (mit der gleichen Bedeutung wie *jmd. kann mir den Buckel runterrutschen*), ist in den Wörterbüchern von Meyer (1989) und Ammon et al. (2004) als Helvetismus angegeben. In Dudenredaktion (2008) wird mit der gleichen Bedeutung die Variante *er/sie [...] kann mir den Schuh/die Schuhe aufblasen* (ohne Angabe der arealen Erstreckung) genannt. Die aufgrund der relativ hohen Bekanntheitszahlen außerhalb der Schweiz (56%) zu Beginn dieses Kapitels formulierten Zweifel, dieses Phrasem als Helvetismus einzustufen, lassen sich durch einen Blick auf die räumliche Verteilung der Probanden, die diese Einheit kennen, rechtfertigen. In der Schweiz wie in Österreich (und Liechtenstein) ist *jmd. kann mir in die Schuhe blasen* mit einem Bekanntheitsgrad zwischen 97 und 100% allgemein bekannt, in Baden-Württemberg und Bayern ist es einer Mehrheit der Befragten (62% bzw. 75%) bekannt. Im übrigen deutschsprachigen Raum wurde es nur von einer Minderheit (35%) als bekannt angegeben (siehe Abb. 6). Der in Abb. 2 angeführten Klassifizierung zufolge ist die Einstufung dieses Phrasems als Helvetismus in den Wörterbüchern ungenau, es müsste vielmehr als im gesamten süddeutschen Sprachraum geläufig eingestuft werden.

Beispiel 5: *das Feuer im Elsass sehen*

Dieses Verbalphrasem ohne gemeindeutsche Variante[18] („große Schmerzen haben") ist nur bei Ammon et al. (2004) angeführt und als Helvetismus eingestuft, in den beiden anderen Wörterbüchern ist es nicht enthalten. Unseren Probandenangaben zufolge ist dieses Phrasem nur in wenigen Regionen der Schweiz bekannt, es wurde – wegen seiner räumlichen Nähe zum Elsass nicht ganz überraschend – in den nordwestlichen Kantonen Baselland und Baselstadt, Aargau und Schaffhausen sowie im Wallis von einer Minderheit (21–40%) als bekannt angeführt (siehe Abb. 7). In den übrigen Schweizer Kantonen sowie im restlichen deutschsprachigen Raum war es (nahezu) unbekannt (in der Schweiz: 0–19%, in Österreich, Deutschland und Liechtenstein: 0–4%). Gemäß der oben vorgeschlagenen Klassifizierung (Abb. 2) sollte statt wie bei Ammon et al. (2004) von einem Helvetismus eher von einem regionalen Helvetismus gesprochen werden.

---

[17] Die in Abb. 2 aufgeführte Kategorie Alemannismus kommt im Material nicht vor.
[18] In der Befragung wurden vereinzelt Formen wie *Feuer/Sterne in Holland sehen* angegeben. Ob es sich hierbei um gängige Varianten handelt, müsste gesondert untersucht werden. In den hier genannten Wörterbüchern sind diese Formen nicht aufgeführt.

264 Britta Juska-Bacher & Stefan Meier

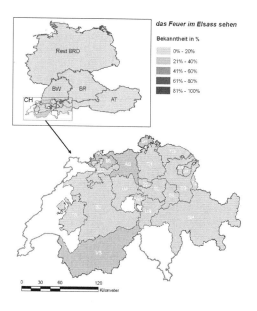

Abb. 7: Bekanntheit von *das Feuer im Elsass sehen* inner- und außerhalb der Schweiz

5. Versuch einer Ausdifferenzierung des Begriffs (phraseologischer) Helvetismus

Diese kurze Beschreibung und kartografische Darstellung empirischer Daten zur Bekanntheit phraseologischer Helvetismen diente einerseits der Prüfung der Klassifizierung als „Helvetismus" in Wörterbüchern auf der Grundlage ihrer arealen Verbreitung. Exemplarisch wurde anhand der Verbreitung von fünf Phrasemen aufgezeigt, dass die in den Wörterbüchern vorgenommenen (übrigens nicht einheitlichen) Klassifizierungen, die auf der einfachen Formel „Verbreitung in der Schweiz >> Verbreitung außerhalb der Schweiz" beruhen, der Wirklichkeit nicht immer gerecht werden. Andererseits wurde ein erster Versuch der Ausdifferenzierung des Helvetismenbegriffs vorgenommen (die nicht auf Phraseme beschränkt ist). Eine solche ist relevant, sobald die Verbreitung der sprachlichen Einheiten nicht mit den Staatsgrenzen zusammenfällt. Vorgeschlagen wurde, neben die eindeutigen Helvetismen (nur in der deutschsprachigen Schweiz bekannt) eine Gruppe von Helvetismen zu stellen, die über die Schweiz hinaus bekannt ist und diese anderen Verbreitungsräume in der Bezeichnung zu berücksichtigen, z.B. Austro-Helvetismus, Bavaro-Helvetismus etc. Für eine letzte Gruppe, die nur in bestimmten Regionen der Schweiz bekannt ist, wurde die Bezeichnung als regionale Helvetismen vorgeschlagen. Für diese Klassifizierungen sind empirische Daten, ob anhand von Korpusanalysen (zur Verwendung) oder Befragungen (zur Kenntnis oder Verwendung) unerlässlich.

Die Daten zur Bekanntheit der in dieser Studie wenigen abgefragten Phraseme zeigen eine Tendenz, dass die Dialekträume einen geringeren Einfluss als die Staatsgrenzen haben (vgl. dazu auch Polenz 1999, Hofer 2003). So ließ sich im Material kein Beispiel für ein Phrasem finden, das nur in der Schweiz (, Liechtenstein) und in Baden-Württemberg (alemannischer Raum) bekannt wäre, auch zwischen Österreich und Bayern gab es keinen auffälligen Zusammenhang. Die Bekanntheit der Phraseme in Liechtenstein war derjenigen in der Schweiz sehr ähnlich.

6. Bibliographie

AMMON, U. (1995). *Die deutsche Sprache in Deutschland, Österreich und der Schweiz. Das Problem der nationalen Varietäten.* Berlin/New York.

AMMON, U. et al. (2004). *Variantenwörterbuch des Deutschen. Die Standardsprache in Österreich, der Schweiz und Deutschland sowie in Liechtenstein, Luxemburg, Ostbelgien und Südtirol.* Berlin.

BICKEL, H. (2006). „Das Internet als linguistisches Korpus". In: *Linguistik online* 28,3. 71–83.

BURGER, H. (2007). *Phraseologie. Eine Einführung am Beispiel des Deutschen.* Berlin.

BURGER, H. (1998). „Helvetismen in der Phraseologie – Vorkommen und stilistische Funktionen". In: Dietrich Hartmann (Hrsg.). *„Das geht auf keine Kuhhaut". Arbeitsfelder der Phraseologie. Akten des Westfälischen Arbeitskreises Phraseologie/Parömiologie 1996 (Bochum).* Bochum. 49–80.

BURGER, H. (1996). „Zur Phraseologie des Schweizerdeutschen". In: Jarmo Korhonen (Hrsg.). *Studien zur Phraseologie des Deutschen und des Finnischen II.* Bochum. 461–488.

BURGER, H. (1995). „Helvetismen in der Phraseologie". In: Heinrich Löffler (Hrsg.). *Alemannische Dialektforschung: Bilanz und Perspektiven.* Tübingen, Basel. 13–25.

CLYNE, M. G. (1992). *Pluricentric languages. Differing norms in different nations.* Berlin.

Dudenredaktion (Hrsg., 2008). *Redewendungen. Wörterbuch der deutschen Idiomatik.* Mannheim/Leipzig/Wien/Zürich.

FÖLDES, C. (1992). „Zu den österreichischen Besonderheiten der deutschen Phraseologie". In: Csaba Földes (Hrsg.). *Deutsche Phraseologie in Sprachsystem und Sprachverwendung.* Wien. 9–24.

HAAS, W. (2000). „Die deutschsprachige Schweiz". In: Jachen C. Arquint et al.: *Die viersprachige Schweiz.* Zürich/Köln. 57–138.

HOFER, LORENZ (2003). „Phraseologismen im Wörterbuch der nationalen Varianten der deutschen Standardsprache". In: Harald Burger et al. (Hrsg.). *Flut von Texten – Vielfalt der Kulturen. Ascona 2001 zur Methodologie und Kulturspezifik der Phraseologie.* Baltmannsweiler. 479–490.

JUSKA-BACHER (2010). „SDS-Exploratoren und Online-Befragung – Lässt sich im Methodenmix ein Wandel in der Schweizer Dialektlandschaft nachweisen?" In: Helen Christen et al. (Hrsg.). *Dialektologie: Wege in die Zukunft.* Stuttgart: Steiner Verlag. 279–293

KOLLER, W. (1999). „Nationale Sprach(en)kultur der Schweiz und die Frage der „nationalen Varietäten des Deutschen"". In: Andreas Gardt et al. (Hrsg.). *Sprachgeschichte als Kulturgeschichte.* Berlin/New York. 133–170.

KORHONEN, J. (2001). *Alles im Griff. Homma hanskassa.* Helsinki.

MEYER, K. (1989). *Wie sagt man in der Schweiz? Wörterbuch der schweizerischen Besonderheiten.* Mannheim.

POLENZ, P. VON (1999). „Deutsch als plurinationale Sprache im postnationalistischen Zeitalter". In: Andreas Gardt et al. (Hrsg.). *Sprachgeschichte als Kulturgeschichte.* Berlin/New York. 116–132.

„DER APFEL FÄLLT NICHT *LEICHT* VOM STAMM". ASPEKTE DER SPRACHSTÖRUNGEN BEI ALTERSDEMENZ

Liliana Mitrache
Universität Uppsala

Abstract: The linguistic research on language at the old age developed in the last two decades. An interesting aspect of this research is the connection between dementia and language disturbances. Dementia is a syndrome, due to disease of the brain, usually of a chronic or progressive nature, in which there is disturbance of multiple higher cortical function including memory, thinking, orientation, comprehension, calculation, language and judgment.

A typical language disturbance of senile dementia, which belongs to the early disease stage, is „the concretism ". This term describes the inability of the patient to understand abstract expressions, the words are understood only in their literal or strict sense. In my investigation I light up this aspect of language disturbance in senile dementia. My analysis uses proverbs and idioms, which are based upon neuropsychological tests, accomplished in the medical-geriatric competence centre Felix Platter-Hospital in Basel, Switzerland.

Proverbs and idioms lose their ambiguity, are often still understood only in their literal meaning. Surprisingly the dementia patients can often completely reconstruct literally the proverbs, which they know from former time, if they read/hear the beginning of the proverb. However the patients understand the proverbs only at the concrete level, therefore also the possible deviations in the word choice. For example „The apple never falls far from the tree" (Germ.: "Der Apfel fällt nicht weit vom Stamm") loses here its metaphorical meaning and allows the surprising substitution of the adjective „far "with „easily ". It is also obvious that the patient imagines a concrete situation: "The apple never falls *easily* from the tree" (Germ.: "Der Apfel fällt nicht *leicht* vom Stamm"). The logical „explanation "of the concrete action is the picture of an apple, which falls from the tree only if it is ripe. The patient associates probably to earlier accumulated experience or knowledge. This case comes from a larger material corpus where further interesting examples of idiomatical deviation are analyzed.

Key words: Language disturbance, senile dementia, proverbs, concretism

1. Einleitende Bemerkungen. Sprache und Alter

Sprache ist ein typisch menschliches und soziales Phänomen. Sie spiegelt die Lebensäußerungen einer Gesellschaft wider und dient als Zeichensystem, um Gedanken und Gefühle auszudrücken. Sprache zählt also zu dem wichtigsten Ausdrucks- und Kommunikationsmittel des Individuums in der Gesellschaft, sie ermöglicht nicht nur Kontakte in einer Gruppe, sondern verleiht dem Sprecher eine Identität, bzw. eine Gruppenzugehörigkeit.

Das quantitative und qualitative Akkumulieren der Sprachkompetenz ist individuell und geht auch im hohen Alter weiter. Wie aber wird die Sprache, beziehungsweise die Ausdrucksfähigkeit des Individuums beeinflusst, wenn die Alterskrankheit Demenz eintritt? Demenz wird als ein Syndrom beschrieben, das aus mehreren Symptomen besteht. Demenz ist die

Folge einer fortschreitenden Krankheit des Gehirns mit Störung vieler Funktionen einschließlich Gedächtnis, Denken, Sprache, Orientierung, Auffassung, Rechnen, Lernfähigkeit und Urteilsvermögen. Die kognitiven Beeinträchtigungen werden gewöhnlich von Veränderungen der emotionalen Kontrolle, des Sozialverhaltens oder der Motivation begleitet. Das Syndrom Demenz manifestiert sich gewöhnlicherweise spät im Leben und ist oft progressiv. Die Prävalenzrate für Demenz ist z. B. mit 70 Jahren zwischen 2 bis 5%, während sie mit 90 Jahren schon bei 30% liegt. Die häufigste Demenzursache ist die Alzheimerkrankheit, bei der pathologische Eiweiße im Gehirn abgelagert und dabei die eigenen funktionstüchtigen Hirnzellen ersetzt werden. Die Alzheimerdemenz nimmt ab dem Alter von 70 Jahren an Häufigkeit stetig zu und betrifft mehr als die Hälfte aller Demenzen. Andere Formen von Demenz sind: vaskuläre Demenz, Demenz bei Parkinson-Syndrom u.a. Die Sprachstörungen gehören zu den früheren Manifestationen der Krankheit. In wie weit ein schlechteres Bildungsniveau leichtere Grade der Sprachstörungen eher manifest werden lässt, ist unklar. Die Gedächtnisstörung bei Demenzpatienten wird immer mit Störung in mindestens einem der folgenden Bereiche begleitet: Sprache (medizinisch genannt: Aphasie), Handeln (Apraxie), Erkennen (Agnosie) und exekutive Funktionen.

Die linguistische Forschung, die sich mit dem Thema Alter im Sinne von „Bejahrtheit" und Sprache beschäftigt, ist jung und hat sich erst in den letzten zwei Jahrzehnten entwickelt. Entstanden ist diese Forschung in Großbritannien, Kanada und in den Vereinigten Staaten. Der erste große Versuch sich mit dem Thema „Sprache, Kommunikation und Alter" auseinanderzusetzen, fand in Freiburg, Deutschland 1996 statt, anlässlich der Tagung der Deutschen Gesellschaft für Sprachwissenschaft. Zu weiteren wichtigen Beiträgen zu der neuen Forschung im deutschsprachigen Raum zählt auch der Sammelband „Spracherwerb und Lebensalter" von 2003, herausgegeben von Annelies Häcki Buhofer.

2. Sprichwörter und Demenz

Folgende Untersuchung wird sich mit einem interessanten Aspekt der Sprachstörungen bei Altersdemenz beschäftigen, u.zw. der Beeinträchtigung des Abstraktionsvermögens. Sprichwörter bilden, aufgrund ihrer speziellen Struktur, eine ideale Basis für die Beleuchtung dieses Phänomens/dieser Sprachauffälligkeit.

Sprichwörter werden wahrscheinlich oft schon im Kindesalter erlernt. Um die metaphorische Sprache verstehen zu können, muss sich das Kind in einer späteren Entwicklungsphase seines Erstspracherwerbs befinden.

Es wird angenommen, dass man die Umstände, unter denen ein Ausdruck in der Kindheit (oder später) erworben wird, häufig in Erinnerung behält. Auf die Frage nach der typischen Verwendungssituation des Sprichworts soll der Proband häufig an die erste Situation, in der er es gehört hat, referieren (Burger 1989:119; Ruef 1995:18).

Wie funktioniert das Erinnern der erlernten Sprichwörter und der eventuellen Assoziationen zur Zeit des Sprichworterwerbs, wenn sich die Gefragten/Probanden an dem anderen Ende ihrer evolutionären Reise befinden und an Demenz leiden?

Schon in der Anfangsphase haben die Patienten Schwierigkeiten, bei bildhaften Ausdrücken das Gemeinte aus dem Gesagten abzuleiten, wie auch Humor und Ironie zu erkennen. Grundlage für meine Analyse sind Sprichwörter und Redewendungen, die sich auf neuro-psychologische Tests stützen, durchgeführt im medizinisch-geriatrischen Kompetenzzentrum Felix Platter-Spital in Basel, Schweiz.

Sprichwörter gehören zu dem allgemeinen Kulturgut eines Volkes und werden sowohl mündlich als auch schriftlich an kommende Generationen übermittelt.

Sprichwörter werden als eine Subklasse der Phraseologismen betrachtet (Burger 1998:100). Sie bilden abgeschlossene, ganze Sätze, die als selbstständige *Mikrotexte* (Burger) oder *Mini-Texte* (Fleischer) funktionieren. Aus lexikalischer Perspektive charakterisieren sich die Phraseologismen und hier werden natürlich die Sprichwörter mitgerechnet, durch die *Festigkeit der Wortverbindung*. Das bedeutet, dass sie aus mehreren selbstständigen Lexemen bestehen, die eine neue lexematische Einheit bilden. Im Extremfall zeigt sich die Festigkeit dadurch, dass die lexikalischen Elemente in der Wortverbindung nicht ausgetauscht werden können, ohne dass sich die Bedeutung der Verbindung gänzlich ändert oder sinnlos wird. So ein Beispiel ist der Phraseologismus „Er hat nicht alle Tassen im Schrank" mit der Bedeutung, nicht bei Verstand sein'. Substituiert man dagegen das Substantiv „Tassen" mit „Kleider", einem Substantiv, das eine völlig andere Bedeutung hat und trotzdem in den oben gegebenen Kontext passt, verändert sich auch die Bedeutung des Satzes völlig. Die Komponenten des Satzes: „Er hat nicht alle Kleider im Schrank" bilden jetzt eine freie Fügung (Mitrache 1999:84).

Aus semantischer Ebene betrachtet, brauchen die Sprichwörter keine textlinguistische Anpassung an einen Kontext (Burger 1998:100). Sie werden im Volksmund als Sätze in fixierter Form überliefert, die oft eine verallgemeinerte Lebenserfahrung in bildlicher Formulierung zum Ausdruck bringen. In der Kommunikation werden sie als Texte aus dem Gedächtnis zitiert.

Aus der Perspektive der Sprachproduktion werden die Sprichwörter als relativ stabile Einheit (wie alle Phraseologismen) abgerufen, ohne dass sie eine textlinguistische Anpassung an einen Kontext benötigen. Aus der Perspektive der Rezeption heißt dies, dass sie gewöhnlicherweise kontextfrei verstanden werden (Burger 1998:100).

Sprichwörter erfüllen die Grundmerkmale des Phraseologismus, denn sie sind polylexikalisch fest und kennen unterschiedliche Grade an Idiomatizität.

Es gibt Sprichwörter mit nur einer Lesart, wie z. B.: *Geld macht nicht glücklich* oder *So ist das Leben*.

Aufschlussreich für die gegenwärtige Analyse sind die Sprichwörter, die zwei Lesarten erlauben, wie z. B.: „Der Apfel fällt nicht weit vom Stamm", oder „Lügen haben kurze Beine". Sprichwörter mit doppelter Lesart sind genau wie Phraseologismen oder Idiome, lexikalisierte Mehrworteinheiten und fungieren als fixierte Mini-Texte. Durch Demotivation wird die wörtliche Bedeutung der Konstituenten aufgehoben. Aus semantischer Perspektive gilt, dass die Gesamtbedeutung eines Sprichwortes bzw. Phraseologismus nicht der Summe der Bedeutungen der einzelnen Komponenten entspricht, sondern sie bedeutet mehr und/oder etwas anderes. Ein metaphorisches Idiom oder Sprichwort hat nur eine Bedeutung, nämlich die paraphrasierte, kennt aber zwei Lesarten, eine wörtliche und eine phraseologische. Metaphorisch heißt, dass die phraseologische bzw. sprichwörtliche Bedeutung aus der wörtlichen ableitbar ist (Mitrache 2006:29).

Eine wichtige Eigenschaft der Sprichwörter, die in den Tests mit Demenzpatienten vorkommen, ist ihre Doppeldeutigkeit, ihre Metaphorizität. Gerade diese metaphorische Bedeutung vermögen die Patienten nicht mehr zu erkennen. In der frühen Phase der Demenzkrankheit verlieren die Patienten die Fähigkeit zu abstrahieren, verstehen nicht mehr die Mehrdeutigkeit sprachlicher Äußerungen. Sie kennzeichnen sich beim Sprachverständnis durch Konkretismus, d.h. alles wird nur wörtlich verstanden. Der Begriff „Konkretismus"

stammt aus der medizinischen Sprache und bezeichnet eine typische Sprachauffälligkeit der Demenz in dem frühen Krankheitsstadium.
Die befragten Patienten sind zwischen 75 und 94 Jahre alt. Die meisten wurden mit einer leichten bis mittelschweren Alzheimerdemenz diagnostiziert. Es sind 14 Personen insgesamt, davon vier Männer und zehn Frauen. Ihre Schulausbildung variiert zwischen 7 und 12 Schuljahren. Leider kann eine umfassende Schulausbildung wenig behilflich sein, wenn die Demenz sich schon manifestiert hat. Die Erkrankten zeigen dieselbe Symptome. Es kann sein, dass die Leute, die gebildet sind, sich die Krankheit eher erklären können und früher Hilfe suchen. Sie können auch unterschiedliche Verhaltensstrategien entwickeln, die ihre Sprachschwierigkeiten maskieren. Eine Strategie wäre z. B. in einem Dialog weniger zu sprechen, oder nur dann den Satz aussprechen, wenn sie sicher sind, dass sie ihn gut beherrschen.

3. Analyse der Tests

Im frühen Krankheitsstadium erscheinen auch die Störungen zum Textverständnis.
Sprichwörter und Redewendungen verlieren ihre Doppeldeutigkeit, werden oft nur in ihrer konkreten bzw. wörtlichen Bedeutung verstanden. Erstaunlicherweise können die Demenzpatienten Sprichwörter, die sie von früher kennen, oft wörtlich völlig rekonstruieren, wenn sie beispielsweise den Anfang des Sprichwortes lesen/hören.
In dem ersten Teil des durchgeführten Tests zum Erkennen von bekannten Sprichwörtern bekommen die Patienten nur den Anfang des Sprichwortes aufgeschrieben. Erwartet wird, dass sie folgende Sprichwörter richtig vervollständigen können:
1. Wer anderen eine Grube gräbt
2. Stille Wasser
3. Der Apfel fällt
4. Man muss das Eisen schmieden

Wie schon aus dem Anfang der hier angegebenen Sprichwörter festzustellen ist, handelt es sich um solche, die einen hohen Verbreitungsgrad bzw. Bekanntheitsgrad haben. Die kulturelle Zugänglichkeit der verwendeten Sprichwörter ist natürlich eine obligatorische Voraussetzung des Tests.
Die vollständige Form der Sprichwörter, die für die Demenzpatienten als Untersuchungsgrundlage dienen, ist folgende:
1. Wer anderen eine Grube gräbt, fällt selbst hinein. Die Bedeutung des Sprichwortes ist: *wer anderen zu schaden versucht, schadet sich dadurch oft nur selbst.*
2. Der Apfel fällt nicht weit vom Stamm (ugs.; schrezh.) – mit der Bedeutung: *jmd. ist in den negativen Anlagen den Eltern sehr ähnlich.*
3. Stille Wasser gründen/sind tief – mit der Bedeutung: *äußerlich zurückhaltende, ruhige Menschen haben oft überraschende [Charakter]Eigenschaften.*
4. Man muss das Eisen schmieden so lange es heiß ist – mit der Bedeutung: *man darf unter günstigen Umständen nicht versäumen, seine Chance konsequent zu nutzen.*
(Duden Bd.11, Redewendungen und sprichwörtliche Redensarten)
Unterschiedliche empirische Studien, die die Mündlichkeit von Sprichwörtern in deutscher Hochsprache untersucht haben (Baur/Chlosta 1996:22, Mieder 1992:16) kommen zum größeren Teil zu den gleichen Sprichwörtern, die sich durch eine hohe Frequenz des Bekanntheitsgrades kennzeichnen. Nicht unerwartet ist, dass auf der Liste von ungefähr 50

Sprichwörtern, die allgemein bekannt sind, auch zwei von den Sprichwörtern der gegenwärtigen Analyse aufgezählt sind: „Der Apfel fällt nicht weit vom Stamm" und „Wer anderen eine Grube gräbt, fällt selbst hinein".

Die Antworten sind je nach Schweregrad der Demenz unterschiedlich. In einem frühen Krankheitsstadium sind die Patienten noch imstande sowohl diese Sprichwörter richtig zu rekonstruieren als auch ihre Bedeutung zu erkennen. Das Sprachverständnis wird sehr früh beeinträchtigt und bleibt im weiteren Verlauf nur noch auf der konkreten Ebene. Wenn das demenzielle Syndrom einen mittleren Krankheitsstadium erreicht hat, erkennt der Patient auch das Sprichwort nicht mehr.

Interessant sind die Erklärungen, die die Patienten bei der Produktion eines solchen Sprichwortes geben:
1. Das Sprichwort „Wer anderen eine Grube gräbt, fällt selbst hinein" wird auf das konkrete Bild einer Grube reduziert. In der Erklärung des Patienten wird sogar die Gefahr ausgedrückt: *„Wenn man jemandem weh tut, kann dieser direkt reinfallen...ein Übel bekommen"* (Frau, 82 Jahre, 12 Jahre Ausbildung). Erstaunlicherweise ist sogar ein Teil der übertragenen Bedeutung in der Erklärung zu erkennen, u. zw. die Intention jemandem zu schaden. Die Tatsache, dass diese negative Intention sich dann auf sich selbst zurückkehrt, ist aber in dieser Erklärung nicht mehr vorhanden.

Im folgenden Fall gilt die Ergänzung des Patienten zum Sprichwort auch als Erklärung der Bedeutung: *Wer anderen eine Grube gräbt: gräbt sich selber* (Frau, 81 Jahre, 12 Jahre Ausbildung). Auch wenn die ursprüngliche Form nicht mehr korrekt wiedergegeben wurde, enthält die Erklärung zum Sprichwort eine Art konzentrierte und direkte Beschreibung der eigentlichen Weisheit, die das Sprichwort vermittelt. Die Idee des „sich selbst Schaden zufügen" ist hier vorhanden, dennoch ist es schwer nachzuweisen, ob der Patient jetzt die konkrete oder die übertragende Bedeutung meinte.

Ein weiteres Beispiel zum wortwörtlichen Verstehen des Sprichwortes ist der Kommentar zu „Wer anderen eine Grube gräbt – *wird zu müde*" (Frau, 85J., 10J. Ausb.). In diesem Beispiel kann die Patientin das Sprichwort wörtlich wiedergeben, kennt aber nicht mehr seine Bedeutung. Interessant ist, dass sie trotzdem versucht, dem Sprichwort eine logische Erklärung auf der konkreten Ebene zu geben. Die Müdigkeit erscheint hier als die logische Folge einer physischen Anstrengung.

2. Im folgenden Beispiel erkennt der Patient die metaphorische Bedeutung des Sprichwortes „Der Apfel fällt nicht weit vom Stamm" nicht mehr. Es gelingt ihm aber das Sprichwort mit einer Abweichung wörtlich zu rekonstruieren: „Der Apfel fällt nicht *leicht* vom Stamm" (Frau, 86 J., 12J. Ausb.). Das Adjektiv „weit" aus dem Sprichwort wird mit dem Adjektiv „leicht" substituiert. Die Vorstellung von der Bedeutung liegt bei dem Patienten nur auf der konkreten Ebene und wird auf das Bild des Apfels reduziert, der nicht zu weit weg vom Stamm fallen kann. Wieder ein Versuch einer logischen Erklärung zum Bild.

Folgender Patient ergänzt richtig das Sprichwort „Der Apfel fällt nicht weit vom Stamm", erkennt aber seine übertragene Bedeutung nicht. Er versteht es als konkretes Bild und hat dafür eine logische Begründung: *„weil der Apfel reif ist"* (Frau, 79J., 9J. Ausb.).

Die Erklärungen zu dem richtig erkannten Sprichwort können unterschiedlich sein. Sie gehen alle von dem konkret ausgedrückten Bild aus und enthalten eine Art von logischer Begründung, die individuell ist.

Weitere Beispiele: „Der Apfel fällt nicht weit vom Stamm, *denn er kann nicht 15 Meter vom Stamm weg fallen. 15 Meter vom Stamm weg nach Äpfeln suchen bringt nichts.*"

(Mann, 82J., 12J. Ausb.). Die genaue Antwort hier – „15 Meter" - stützt sich anscheinend auf eigene Lebenserfahrung bzw. eigene Lebenskenntnisse und enthält dadurch aus der Perspektive des Patienten eine logische Begründung.

Eine andere Erklärung zu dem Sprichwort ist: *„Wenn der Apfel nicht weit vom Baum fliegt.... man kann ihn wiederfinden, er ist nicht weit weg."* Die Begründung hier bleibt logisch, obwohl sich auch eine gewisse Verwirrung in der Antwort versteckt.

Weniger logisch sind aber folgende zwei Beschreibungen, die sich auf die konkrete Bedeutung des Sprichwortes beziehen: 1. *„Wenn der Apfel da steht und der Apfel herunter fällt"* (Frau, 85J, 9 J.Ausb.) und 2. *Der Apfel hat Kontakt mit dem Stamm* (Frau, 81J., 12J. Ausb.).

3. Das nächste Sprichwort „Stille Wasser gründen tief" wird vom Patienten richtig vervollständigt. Die Erklärung zu der Bedeutung des Sprichwortes bleibt wieder nur auf der konkreten Ebene: *„Nicht jedes Seelein, das aussieht wie ein Seelein ist auch eines...es könnte auch eine tiefe Pfütze sein, die einen herunterreist"*. (Frau, 85J, 12J. Ausb.) Der Überraschungsmoment aus der übertragenen Bedeutung, nämlich die unerwarteten menschlichen Charaktereigenschaften, ist hier in dem konkreten Bild wiederzuerkennen. Hinter der stillen Oberfläche der Menschen, die sich nicht offen äußern, verbirgt sich mehr als man denkt. In der konkreten Erklärung des Patienten verändert sich ein Seelein in eine tiefe Pfütze, die plötzlich gefährlich wird und einen herunterreist. Das Sprichwort erweckt negative Gefühle beim Patienten und die übertragene Bedeutung scheint hier noch latent vorhanden zu sein, auch eine gewisse Logik in der Erklärung.

Völlig auf der konkreten Ebene ist die Erklärung *„Wenn Wasser ruhig ist, und es tief ist."* (Frau, 85J., 12J. Ausb). Sie erscheint als eine logische Folge zu der Aussage „Stille Wasser gründen tief."

4. Keine Ausnahme ist die Erklärung des Sprichworts: „Man muss das Eisen schmieden, solange es heiß ist" (Mann, 87J., 10J. Ausb.). Der Patient setzt auf der konkreten Ebene die Idee fort und schlussfolgert logisch: *Kaltes Eisen lässt sich nicht schmieden...* Frühere Erfahrungen bzw. Kenntnisse scheinen hier noch aktiv zu funktionieren.

Eine idiomatische Abweichung findet im nächsten Beispiel bei dem Vervollständigen des Sprichwortes: „Man muss das Eisen schmieden solange es *weich* ist." (Mann, 89J., 10J. Ausb.). Überraschenderweise erkennt der Patient noch richtig die übertragene Bedeutung des Sprichwortes.

4. Schlussbemerkungen

Die Beispiele stammen aus einem größeren Materialkorpus, in dem sich viele weitere interessante Fälle der idiomatischen Abweichung nachweisen lassen. Die Fragen zu dem Erkennen und Erklären von bekannten Sprichwörtern sind Teil einer umfassenden Untersuchung mit Tests u.a. zu der phonematischen und verbalen Flüssigkeit, die die Sprachstörungen bei Demenzpatienten erläutern.

Die Beeinträchtigung der Fähigkeit abstrakt zu denken, findet schon am Anfang der Krankheit statt. Diese Feststellung gewinnt an Bedeutung, wenn man die Untersuchungen zum dem Erstspracherwerb in Betracht zieht. Das Vermögen zu abstrahieren entwickelt sich in einer späteren Entwicklungsphase bei den Kindern. Mit ungefähr 6 Jahren fangen sie an die Mehrdeutigkeit sprachlicher Äußerungen zu verstehen, verwenden bewusst Witze, Sprachspiele und Metaphern. Zu dieser Zeit wird auch der Sinn für Ironie und Humor entwickelt. Es heißt, dass sie erst jetzt auch Sprichwörter, Redewendungen und die metaphorische Sprache verstehen. Das Vermögen zu abstrahieren ist also eine relativ spät erworbene Sprachfähigkeit im Kinderalter und gerade diese Fähigkeit gehört zu den ersten Sprachverlusten bei Demenzkrankheit.

Wie aus den hier angegebenen Beispielen hervorgeht, gelingt es den Patienten die Sprichwörter wortwörtlich zu rekonstruieren. Das in einer früheren Lebensphase auswendig Gelernte, vielleicht in der Kindheit oder Jugend bleibt noch aktuell am Anfang der Demenzkrankheit. Der metaphorische Inhalt der Sprichwörter dagegen wird konkret verstanden, wobei das Interessante ist, dass die konkreten Erklärungen zu den rekonstruierten Sätzen meistens noch auf einer logischen Ebene liegen.

Außer der Beeinträchtigung der Fähigkeit zu abstrahieren, haben die Patienten Schwierigkeiten Witze und Ironie zu verstehen. Das Problemfeld wird ausführlich in einer weiteren Untersuchung behandelt.

5. Literatur

BAUR, R.S. & CHLOSTA, C. 1996 „Welche Übung macht den Meister? Von der Sprichwortforschung zur Sprichwortdidaktik". *Fremdsprache Deutsch Heft* 15: 17-24.

BROWN, J- & HILLAM, J. 2004 *Dementia. Your Questions Answered*. Edinburgh, London, New York, Oxford, Philadelphia, St. Louis, Sydney, Toronto.

BURGER, H. 1998 *Phraseologie. Eine Einführung am Beispiel des Deutschen*. Berlin.

HÄCKI BUHOFER, A. (Hrsg.) 2003 *Spracherwerb und Lebensalter*. Tübingen und Basel.

FLEISCHER, W. 1997 *Phraseologie der deutschen Gegenwartssprache*. 2. durchges. und erg. Auflage. Tübingen.

MIEDER, W. 1992 Sprichwort – *Wahrwort!? Studien zur Geschichte, Bedeutung und Funktion deutscher Sprichwörter*. Frankfurt am Main.

MITRACHE, L. 1999 *Intertextualität und Phraseologie in den drei Versionen der Panne von Friedrich Dürrenmatt. Aspekte von Groteske und Ironie*. Uppsala.

MITRACHE, L. 2006 *Metaphern in literarischen Übersetzungen. Eine vergleichende Analyse der sechs Übersetzungen von Strindbergs Roman Hemsöborna*. Uppsala.

MITRACHE, L. 2010 „Spracherwerb und Sprachverlust. Phänomene von Sprachstörungen im hohen Alter". *Studia Neophilologica* 82/1: 91 – 99. Uppsala.

RUEF, H. 1995 *Sprichwort und Sprache: am Beispiel des Sprichworts im Schweizerdeutschen*. Berlin.

LAS UNIDADES FRASEOLÓGICAS IRÓNICAS: UN ESQUEMA FRASEOLÓGICO EN ESPAÑOL

G. Angela Mura
Universidad Complutense de Madrid

Abstract: In this paper we aim to demonstrate the different discursive functions carried out by the Spanish phraseological scheme *¿será por + X?*. Drawing on theories developed by GRIALE (Grupo de Investigación para la Pragmática y la Ironía del Español) - a research group focused on pragmatics and the use of irony in Spanish - based at the University of Alicante, we can observe the different uses of this phraseological scheme, which includes future values, negative values and references to probability.

Key words: Phraseological scheme, irony, pragmatics, negation, Spanish phraseology

1. INTRODUCCIÓN

Este trabajo se propone analizar los valores discursivos que adquiere una unidad fraseológica (UF) concreta en español, *¿será por + X?*, que pertenece a una categoría específica de UFs situada en la periferia de la fraseología, la de los esquemas fraseológicos. Al tratarse de una parcela de la fraseología en la cual aún reina cierta imprecisión, previamente es necesario reflexionar acerca de esta clase heterogénea de unidades y precisar, aunque de forma sucinta, qué se entiende por esquema fraseológico y perfilar sus rasgos tanto formales como funcionales. Para ello nos servimos de una definición de *esquema fraseológico* que elaboramos en un trabajo anterior:

«Formalmente, los esquemas fraseológicos se componen de un módulo sintáctico fijado en el que se insertan uno o más constituyentes libres cuyo paradigma antes de integrarse en el discurso no es cerrado ni inventariable. A nivel funcional representan actos lingüísticos cuyo significado sólo se activa en el ámbito de la interacción comunicativa en la que aparecen o, lo que es lo mismo, significan sólo en el momento de su empleo» (Mura, 2008).

A continuación observamos cómo se manifiesta la ironía en este tipo de UFs y lo hacemos mediante una reflexión acerca de la relación que se instaura entre estas peculiares estructuras y el concepto pragmático de ironía. Si aplicamos, pues, la propuesta de Timofeeva (2009) sobre la clasificación de los diversos tipos de usos de las UFs con valor irónico a la categoría de los esquemas fraseológicos, la propia naturaleza de estas estructuras hace presuponer que se podrían reunir bajo la etiqueta de *fraseología contextualmente irónica*. En otros términos, la ironía fraseológica no forma parte de la constitución interna convencional de la UF, sino que se origina gracias a determinadas condiciones contextuales que permiten la lectura irónica de la estructura en cuestión.

Tomando en consideración tales hechos, nos detenemos en el estudio del comportamiento pragmático del esquema fraseológico español *¿será por + X?* y corroboramos el análisis apoyándonos en distintos corpus de referencia: el *Corpus oral de la variedad juvenil universitaria del español hablado en Alicante* de Dolores Azorín Fernández y Juan Luis Jiménez Ruiz, el *Corpus de conversaciones coloquiales* de Antonio Briz y el Grupo Val.Es.Co., el corpus COLA (*Corpus Oral de Lenguaje Adolescente*) de la Universidad de Bergen, el corpus C-ORAl-Rom (*Integrated reference corpora for spoken* *romance languages*) y el *Corpus de Referencia del Español Actual* (CREA) de la Real Academia Española. En los casos en que los corpus de referencia no proporcionen datos exhaustivos, utilizamos como fuente el buscador Google, seleccionando las fuentes encontradas de acuerdo con los criterios preestablecidos.

2. ASPECTOS FORMALES: LA SEMI-FIJACIÓN DEL ESQUEMA FRASEOLÓGICO

Formalmente, el esquema fraseológico español *¿será por + X?* se presenta como una construcción compuesta por dos partes netamente separadas: la primera parte, encabezada por el verbo *ser* en futuro de indicativo en 3ª persona singular seguido por la preposición causativa *por*, es totalmente fija; la segunda parte, constituida por un sustantivo, que puede ser tanto común como propio y aparece generalmente en plural (a menos que se trate de un sustantivo incontable), es libre y varía según el contexto discursivo en el que se emplea.

Así pues, esta estructura está compuesta por un fragmento fijo que introduce la unidad fraseológica y un elemento perteneciente a la técnica libre, que se presentan necesariamente en este orden:

Parte fija → *será* = verbo *ser* en futuro de indicativo, 3ª persona singular
+ *por* = preposición
Parte libre → *X* = sustantivo (plural o no contable)

Normalmente, el esquema fraseológico analizado constituye una intervención aislada que aparece precedida y seguida por una pausa. Se pronuncia con entonación interrogativa y, en ocasiones, exclamativa, y suele constituir una secuencia de inserción que se inserta en una secuencia argumentativa.

La observación de un ejemplo extraído del corpus de referencia -un artículo periodístico sobre el funeral de la princesa Diana de Gales- nos ayudará a ilustrar las características formales descritas.

(1) «"Goodbye, England's Rose, que siempre florezcas en nuestros corazones. Eras la gracia que aparecía donde vidas habían sido rasgadas. Eras la voz de nuestro país y arrullabas a los que sufren... Ahora estás en el cielo y las estrellas cantan tu nombre." El primer pop que ha sonado en la milenaria abadía de Westminster. Humedeció los ojos. Ni la competencia de pamelones -desbancaban a los ennegrecidos casquetes- pudo disimularlo. Se enrojeció la fácilmente emotiva Bernardette Chirac, la única con traje cruzado ante la abundancia de trajecitos de chaqueta con una sola fila de botones como el lucido por Hillary Clinton bajo un <u>sombrerito</u> algo echado para atrás, en fieltro, similar a los llevados con mayor costumbre - **¡será por sombreros o bolsos!**- por la Reina Isabel y su hermana Margarita, con un lazo trasero en raso animando el tocado».

[CREA. Época, 15/09/1997: *La princesa del pueblo entierra a la princesa de Gales*]

Como vemos, la construcción fraseológica *¡será por sombreros o bolsos!* refleja los rasgos anunciados anteriormente, a saber:

• Se compone de una parte fija (*será por*) seguida por una parte libre (*sombreros o bolsos*). Si nos fijamos en la segunda parte del esquema, notamos que la libertad combinatoria depende totalmente del contexto comunicativo específico, pues en este caso el hablante

retoma la palabra *sombrero* pronunciada en la intervención precedente y añade otro término, *bolsos*, que acentúa la fuerza de sus palabras.
- En este fragmento el aislamiento de la intervención está marcado por los signos de exclamación, que indican también la entonación de la expresión, y por dos guiones que encierran el esquema, que indican el carácter independiente propio de esta estructura.
- Constituye una secuencia de inserción incrustada en una secuencia argumentativa, pues es como si el hablante, durante su disquisición sobre un evento celebrado en la abadía de Westminster, abriese un paréntesis para hacer un comentario personal y lo cerrase inmediatamente después siguiendo con su descripción del evento.

3. ASPECTOS FUNCIONALES: LOS VALORES DISCURSIVOS DEL ESQUEMA FRASEOLÓGICO

Una primera aproximación al esquema fraseológico *¿será por + X?* nos permite observar que estamos ante una construcción interrogativa que se usa para negar y cuyas inferencias negativas funcionan como indicador de un sentido irónico. Asimismo, observando el verbo que sustenta la expresión, podemos intuir que se trata de una construcción que presenta una lectura modal. Para demostrar estas intuiciones y describir los valores pragmático-discursivos del esquema, nos apoyamos en los estudios sobre la interrogación retórica, la negación, la ironía y la modalidad, aspectos que, como veremos, están estrictamente relacionados entre ellos.

¿Será por + X? es una interrogación y, en concreto, una interrogación retórica, pues se manifiesta como una expresión interrogativa que carece de la expectativa de una respuesta (Dumitrescu, 1994). Como sugiere Sánchez López (1999: 2605), la interrogación retórica funciona como un *inductor negativo*, es decir, como aquellos «elementos que comparten la propiedad de crear entornos sintácticos en los que pueden aparecer términos de polaridad negativa». De acuerdo con el título de este trabajo, centramos nuestra atención sobre el valor irónico del esquema fraseológico objeto de estudio.

3.1. La fraseología al servicio de la ironía
El concepto de negación implícita, el valor de negación y las inferencias negativas que se desprenden atendiendo a una lectura idiomática del esquema fraseológico analizado, funcionan en el discurso como un indicador de ironía, es decir, permiten interpretar el sentido irónico del esquema a partir de la inversión del significado de los términos que lo componen, ya que se infiere justo lo contrario de lo que dicen las palabras[1].

¿Será por + X? → No es por + X

Si se da a entender lo contrario de lo que se dice, inevitablemente se viola el requisito previo de sinceridad entre el hablante y el oyente del que habla Grice, pues se produce una violación de la máxima conversacional de cualidad con la que se afirma que la contribución del hablante a la conversación ha de ser verdadera, y, de manera más específica, no hay que proporcionar información falsa. Como hemos observado anteriormente, adoptando la propuesta de Timofeeva (2008: 213) sobre los diversos tipos de uso de unidades fraseológicas para conseguir ironía, incluimos el esquema *¿será por + X?* en la categoría de las *unidades fraseológicas contextualmente irónicas*, aquellas que adquieren la implicatura irónica

---

[1] Adoptamos la concepción de ironía propuesta por el Grupo GRIALE (www.griale.es).

únicamente en determinadas condiciones contextuales. En estas expresiones, observa Timofeeva (2008: 214), «su significado convencionalizado no recoge inferencias irónicas y, por tanto, no origina el entorno irónico», pues «la ironía se origina como una implicatura conversacional particularizada».

Como veremos, los ejemplos recogidos en el corpus parecen demostrar que en este caso la ironía se ha convencionalizado y ha pasado a formar parte del significado codificado de la expresión. Seguiría, de este modo, el proceso que Escandell (2007: 127) denomina *convencionalización de contenidos implícitos*, pues algunas expresiones, entre las que incluimos el esquema fraseológico analizado, al emplearse en contexto adquieren valores añadidos que proceden de la interacción entre el contenido estrictamente lingüístico y la información extralingüística. En ocasiones tales valores secundarios contextuales pueden llegar a consolidarse y estabilizarse, convirtiéndose de este modo en parte integrante del significado intrínseco de la unidad. En este caso concreto, se ha producido una codificación del significado irónico de la unidad fraseológica, que se ha desarrollado paralelamente al proceso de *fraseologización*, término acuñado por Ruiz Gurillo (1997: 104) para designar «el proceso por medio del cual, gracias a la fijación en algún grado y en ocasiones a la idiomaticidad, parcial o total, se constituye una unidad fraseológica».

La observación de las distintas fases por las que pasa el enunciado *¿será por + X?* antes de codificar su significado irónico, nos permite explicar la evolución del significado propio de algunas unidades fraseológicas irónicas. Como veremos, por lo general, cuando la combinación es libre y, en consecuencia, no representa una unidad fraseológica, posee un significado literal y no es irónica; cuando la combinación es fija, es decir, es una unidad fraseológica, tiene un significado idiomático y es irónica:

a. Sintagma libre → no UF → significado literal → no irónico
b. Sintagma fijo → UF → significado idiomático → irónico

3.2. Los tres usos del esquema fraseológico

Aplicamos este razonamiento a la construcción *¿será por + X?*. El corpus testimonia tres usos diferentes del esquema que conviven simultáneamente. Podemos considerar la coaparición de los tres significados como un síntoma de que la construcción está evolucionando en este momento. Para explicar este fenómeno sincrónicamente, atendemos a las propiedades descritas por Hopper (1991), que propone cinco principios de gramaticalización -estratificación, divergencia, especialización, persistencia y descategorización- para explicar la convivencia de los diversos usos de una estructura. En este caso concreto, es posible aplicar el principio de estratificación:

«Within a broad functional domain, new layers are continually emerging. As this happens, the older layers are not necessarily discarded, buy may remain to coexist with and interact with the newer layers» Hopper (1991: 22).

Según este principio, la coexistencia de dos o más formas (o significados) en el mismo periodo histórico representa una etapa indispensable y necesaria en los procesos de gramaticalización. Pues, la continua aparición de estratos nuevos -entendidos como usos distintos de una misma estructura- conlleva una situación de coexistencia e interacción entre los estratos más antiguos y los estratos que van apareciendo. Es lo que ocurre con la estructura *¿será por + X?*, que, actualmente, presenta tres acepciones distintas simultáneas, lo que nos hace suponer que la estructura se encuentra en una fase de evolución.

Atendiendo a los diversos usos que manifiesta dicha expresión, proponemos una distinción entre tres funciones diferentes que, adoptando la terminología empleada por Ruiz Gurillo (2009: 376) en un contexto de tipo diacrónico, van desde un significado léxico, concreto y objetivo hasta un significado pragmático, abstracto, basado en el emisor, pasando por valores hipotéticos, de probabilidad, que han facilitado los usos irónicos y negativos. Presentamos a continuación las tres funciones diferentes del esquema que nos ocupa, partiendo del uso menos frecuente para llegar al uso más corriente.

3.2.1. Función como elemento temporal

¿Será por + X? puede presentar un significado concreto que tiene un claro valor temporal de futuro: el verbo *será* indica la certeza de algo que ocurrirá en un tiempo futuro y la preposición *por* denota un valor causal. El significado objetivo que se desprende del conjunto de los elementos que componen la expresión es el de posterioridad, pues es una predicción de hechos futuros: *pasará X a causa de X*. Se trata de un significado léxico literal que no posee ninguna connotación pragmática, como muestra el ejemplo (2):

(2) Banco Mundial advierte sobre alzas en alimentos y energía. El Apocalipsis **será por hambre**. Robert Zoellick en su último discurso previene sobre disturbios sociales graves en 33 países del orbe. Nicaragua en la mira y la consigna es: ¡Que los precios bajen ya!
[http://www.elnuevodiario.com.ni/nacionales/12553]

Como vemos, estamos ante una previsión de un evento (*el Apocalipsis*) que ocurrirá en algunos países a causa del hambre, si no se procederá a bajar los precios de los alimentos y de la energía.

3.2.2. Función como elemento hipotético

Frecuentemente, este valor de certeza, de predicción segura y evidente, evoluciona hacia un valor de probabilidad. Con el verbo *será* el hablante ya no hace una previsión cierta de algo que ocurrirá en el futuro, sino que usa este tiempo verbal para distanciarse de lo que dice; hace una suposición sobre el presente, no afirma con certeza y seguridad. *¿Será por + X?*, en este caso, no marca distancia temporal sino distancia epistémica, como vemos en (3), una conversación entre amigos que discuten acerca del comportamiento de los gatos cuando están en celo:

(3) MALCC2J03: 1[tronco sabéis que ya a la gata de <navn>Pati</navn> tronco es como una puta en <navn>Galapagar</navn> tronco]
MALLC2J02: 1[ponerla un pañal]
MALCC2J03: ya a ningún gato quiere subir a la terraza a a follar con ella tronco
MALCC2J03: antes subían mazo... y hasta que ha {tenío|tenido} este celo que nunca les dejaba dormir a nadie por la noche pero es que no subía ningún gato
MALCC2J03: <navn>Pati</navn> estaba desesperada que quería subir a un gato de la calle para que para que la dejase embarazada sabes/
MALCC2J03: que no o es rarísimo pero no iba ningún gato
MACCL2JO1: sabes por qué/

MACCL2JO1: que la lleven al veterinario los ga hay algunos animales que cuando el el o sea cuando el otro sexo los otros su ligue vamos
MACCL2JO1: tiene alguna enfermedad o alguna cosa lo rechazan
NOSPEAKER: <música/>
MACCL2JO1: 2[si saben que está enfermo o cualquier cosa por instinto si ellos lo detectan por el olor porque la ven algo o por cualquier cosa]
MALCC2J03: 2[jo pues será eso...ah] [...]
MACCL2JO1: que la lleve al veterinario por si está mala por si tiene algo
MALCC2J03: 2[no lo sé, me lo contó hace ya mazo]
MACCL2JO1: 2[si los gatos no suben es muy raro porque los gatos no tienen la conciencia de e esta ha {follao|follado} con muchos sabes/]
MALCC2J03: 1[ya pero la terraza de <navn>Pati</navn> se suben todos sabes está a una altura tal y ven a una gata en celo y vamos]
MACCL2JO1: 1[pero les da lo mismo...claro y si no han venido está vez]
MACCL2JO1: y si no han venido esta vez **será por algo** tronca que la lleve e y ya está
[COLA.M. malcc2-11.htm 15-Mar-2007 16:05 523K]

Al utilizar la expresión *será por algo*, MACCL2JO1 no hace referencia a un hecho futuro, sino que hace una suposición sobre el presente, pues desconoce la causa por la cual los gatos no han subido a la terraza de su amiga Pati donde había una gata en celo, pero afirma que tiene que haber una motivación precisa. Como vemos, cambia la perspectiva: se pasa de valores temporales (futuro) a valores modales (probabilidad), pero seguimos en un nivel donde el significado es literal, no idiomático: *puede que la causa sea X*.

3.2.3. Función como elemento negativo

En este tercer apartado analizamos los casos en que *¿será por + X?* presenta un significado pragmático, abstracto y basado en el emisor. La mayoría de los ejemplos registrados por el corpus de referencia muestran esta acepción del esquema, que, como vimos anteriormente, niega la proposición que parece afirmar -*no es por + X*-, comportándose como un término de polaridad negativa.

El ejemplo que presentamos a continuación es una buena muestra de la codificación de las inferencias negativas que conllevan la lectura irónica del esquema fraseológico. En el artículo de (4), el periodista denuncia los abusos de poder y la corrupción de algunos políticos e ironiza acerca de la ley del silencio de la prensa, pues los medios actúan más de armas de distracción masiva que de denuncia y movilización.

(4) ... los plátanos de Canarias, dos chalés en lugar de uno. Dos chalés que son recuelos de otros chalés. A Luis Roldán, el ex director general de la Guardia Civil, recordarán que le dieron órdenes de que sacara papeles sobre sus prósperas propiedades inmobiliarias, que el tío tiene que ser un mago, si yo fuera las Koplowitz, me lo llevaba de director general para seguir pegando pelotazos en esta España de los barquinazos y los banestazos. Genio de los negocios, virtuoso del honesto y corto sueldo, con esa vista especulativa que Dios le dio, se ha levantado Roldán un capital a brazo, como hacían el chocolate los benedictinos, pero tiene tantos chalés que se le olvidan, los va arrojando como el sabio de las yerbas del poema.
Ahora le sacan dos chalés más, en Rota, que edificaron precisamente unos constructores que hicieron varios cuarteles para la Benemérita, pero mire usted qué casualidad, el mundo efectivamente es un pañuelo. Como siempre ocurre, **¿será por chalés?** Un chalé en Navarra,

otro en Aravaca, parcelas por allí, pisos de lujo por acá, terrenos, dúpleses, plazas de garaje... De 1,6 millones escriturados en propiedades inmobiliarias, suelo que se pisa, cuando era concejal socialista en Zaragoza, a una pelota de 184 millones cuando ha salido de la Dirección General de la Guardia Civil. Oímos hablar de los chalés como el que oye llover, nos llega a parecer lo más normal del mundo. No se explica lo inexplicable, estamos completamente insensibilizados ante la ética y estética del chalé. Don Luis Roldán sigue gozando de excelente salud civil, pero ahora quieren matar al reportero mensajero, Luis Cervero-Jesús Mendoza, ante los tribunales. El fin siempre es callar a los medios... José Luis Gutiérrez, enhorabuena por lo tuyo.

[CREA. El Mundo, 30/01/1994: ANTONIO BURGOS: El Fin y los Medios]

En este fragmento, *¿será por chalés?* representa una unidad fraseológica que ha fijado su forma y su significado irónico y, por consecuencia, funciona como un indicador de que el contexto en el que se inserta puede ser irónico. En el texto de (4) encontramos también otros elementos que ayudan a captar que se trata de un discurso irónico: obsérvese, por ejemplo, la gran cantidad de unidades fraseológicas empleadas (*levantarse un capital a brazos, el mundo es un pañuelo, como el que oye llover*, entre otras) y el uso de sufijos aumentativo (*pelotazos, barquinazos, banestazos*)[2].

4. CONSIDERACIONES FINALES

Recapitulando estas ideas, hemos observado que el esquema fraseológico *¿será por + X?* puede adquirir valores diferentes y muestra usos distintos que van desde valores temporales -como vimos en § 3.2.1- a valores modales -como muestran los ejemplos incluidos en § 3.2.2. y § 3.2.3.- o, adoptando los términos de Rojo y Veiga (1991: 2894), de valores rectos a valores dislocados (o desplazados). Más concretamente, el grupo descrito en § 3.2.1 engloba aquellos usos donde la construcción posee un valor temporal central de futuro, en § 3.2.2. hemos insertado los esquemas que presentan un valor adicional de probabilidad y en § 3.2.3. pasamos a un valor estrictamente modal de negación irónica.

Lejos de la pretensión de llevar a cabo un análisis de tipo cuantitativo, el corpus nos permite afirmar que la cantidad de esquemas que pertenecería al primer grupo de nuestra clasificación es realmente exigua, pues no fue tarea fácil encontrar contextos de uso donde la construcción *¿será por + X?* presentara un valor recto de futuro que denota certeza epistemológica y viene a indicar la predicción de la causa de un evento futuro. Son más numerosas las ocurrencias que pertenecen al segundo grupo, es decir, los esquemas usados para expresar un valor hipotético de probabilidad. Pero la gran mayoría de los ejemplos registrados en el corpus se adscribe al tercer grupo, donde la unidad fraseológica adquiere su significado pragmático de negación y actúa como indicador de ironía.

---

[2] Hemos subrayado en el texto los elementos que funcionan como indicadores de ironía.

5. BIBLIOGRAFÍA

AZORÍN FERNÁNDEZ, D. & JIMÉNEZ RUIZ, J. L. (1997): *Corpus oral de la variedad juvenil universitaria del español hablado en Alicante*. Alicante: Instituto de Cultura Juan Gil-Albert.
BRIZ, A. & Grupo Val.Es.Co. (2002): *Corpus de conversaciones coloquiales*. Madrid: Arco Libros.
BUSTOS, E. (1986): *Pragmática del español: negación, cuantificación y modo*. Madrid: UNED.
CALSAMIGLIA BLANCAFORT, H. & TUSÓN VALLS, A. (1999): *Las cosas del decir. Manual de análisis del discurso*. Barcelona: Ariel.
COLA. *Corpus Oral de Lenguaje Adolescente*. Universidad de Bergen. En línea: http://www.colam.org
CONTRERAS, H. (1999): "Relaciones entre las construcciones interrogativas, exclamativas y relativas". In: Bosque, I. & Demonte V. (eds.), *Gramática descriptiva de la lengua española*, Madrid: Espasa: vol 2: 3253-3322.
C-ORAL-ROM. *Integrated reference corpora for spoken romance languages*. En línea: http://lablita.dit.unifi.it/coralrom/intro.html
CREA. *Corpus de Referencia del Español Actual*. En línea: http://corpus.rae.es/creanet.html
DUMITRESCU, D. (1994): «Estructura y función de las preguntas retóricas repetitivas en español». In: Villegas, J. (ed.), *De historia, lingüísticas, retóricas y poéticas. Actas Irvine-92, Asociación Internacional de Hispanistas*, Vol. I: 139-147.
ESCANDELL VIDAL, M. V. (1999): "Los enunciados interrogativos. Aspectos semánticos y pragmáticos". In: Bosque, I. & Demonte, V. (eds.) *Gramática descriptiva de la lengua española*, Madrid: Espasa: vol. 3: 3929-3992.
ESCANDELL VIDAL, M. V. (2004): *Fundamentos de semántica composicional*. Barcelona: Ariel.
ESCANDELL VIDAL, M. V. (2007): *Apuntes de semántica léxica*. Madrid: UNED.
GARCÍA-MEDALL, J. (2006) (ed.): *Fraseología e ironía. Descripción y contraste*. Lugo: Axac.
HOPPER, P. J. (1991): "On some principles of grammaticization". In: Traugott, E. C. & Heine B. (eds.) (1991): *Approaches to grammaticalization*. Amsterdam/Philadelphia: John Benjamins: vol I: 17-35.
LÓPEZ GARCÍA, Á. (1991): *La negación y los verbos modales*. Logroño: Consejería de Educación, Cultura y Deportes.
MARTINELL, E. (1992): «Preguntas que no preguntan». *Estudios de lingüística*, 8: 25-33.
MARTÍNEZ VÁZQUEZ, M. (ed.) (2003): *Gramática de construcciones. Contrastes entre el inglés y el español*. Huelva: Grupo de Investigación Gramática Contrastiva.
MICHAELIS, L. A. (2004): «Type shifting in construction grammar: an integrated approach to aspectual coercion», *Cognitive Linguistics*, 15/1: 1-67.
MOESCHLER, J. (1993): «Négation: presupposition, implicature et inference invitée». In: *Colloque La négation*, Paris: Université de Paris-10.
MOESCHLER, J. & REBOUL, Anne (1994): *Diccionario enciclopédico de pragmática*. Madrid: Arrecife.

MURA, G. A. (2008): *Forma y función de los esquemas sintácticos fraseológicos pragmáticos. Estudio contrastivo español-italiano.* Trabajo de Investigación. Universidad Complutense de Madrid.

MURA, G. A. & RUIZ GURILLO, L. (2010): «De la construcción a la fórmula: estudio contrastivo español-italiano de un esquema fraseológico», *Cuadernos de Filología Italiana*, vol. 17, pp. 45-64.

OTAOLA OLANO, C. (1988): «La modalidad (con especial referencia a la lengua española)», *Revista de Filología Española*, LXVIII : 1/2, pp. 97-117.

PRADO IBÁN, Mª E. (1999): "Interpretación discursiva y explicaturas". In: Fernández González, J., Fernández Juncal, C., Marcos Sánchez, M., Prieto de los Mozos, E. & Santos Río, L. (eds.): *Lingüística para el siglo XXI*, vol. II, Salamanca: Universidad.

QUIROGA MUNGUÍA, P. (2006): "*¿Me estás diciendo que no?* Fraseología contrastiva de la negación en español e italiano". In: García-Medall, J. (ed.), *Fraseología e ironía*, Lugo: Axac.

RIDRUEJO, E. (1991): "Modo y modalidad. El modo en las subordinadas sustantivas". In: Bosque, I. y V. Demonte (dirs.), *Gramática descriptiva de la lengua española*, Madrid, Espasa, vol 2, pp. 3209-3252.

RODRÍGUEZ ROSIQUE, S. (2008): "Una propuesta neogriceana". In: Ruiz Gurillo, L. & Padilla García, X. A. (eds.), *Dime cómo ironizas y te diré quién eres*, Frankfurt: Peter Lang: 109-132.

ROJO, G. & VEIGA, A. (1991): "El tiempo verbal. Los tiempos simples", en Bosque, I. & Demonte V. (eds.): *Gramática descriptiva de la lengua española*. Madrid: Espasa, vol. 2: 2867-2934.

RUIZ GURILLO, Leonor (1997): *Aspectos de fraseología teórica española*. Valencia: Universitat.

RUIZ GURILLO, L., MARIMÓN, C., PADILLA, X. A. & TIMOFEEVA, L. (2004): «El proyecto *Griale* para la ironía en español: conceptos previos», *ELUA*, 18: 231-242.

RUIZ GURILLO, L. (2006): *Hechos pragmáticos del español*. Alicante: Universidad.

RUIZ GURILLO, L. (2006): "Fraseología para la ironía en español". In: De Miguel, E., Palacios, A. & Serradilla, A. (eds.): *Estructuras léxicas y estructuras del léxico*. Frankfurt, Peter Lang: 129-148.

RUIZ GURILLO, L. & PADILLA GARCÍA, X. A. (2009): *Dime cómo ironizas y te diré quién eres*. Frankfurt: Peter Lang.

RUIZ GURILLO, L. (2009): "La gramaticalización de unidades fraseológicas irónicas". In: Ruiz Gurillo, L. & Padilla García, X. A. (eds.), *Dime cómo ironizas y te diré quién eres*, Frankfurt: Peter Lang: 371-390.

RUIZ GURILLO, L. (2009): «¿Cómo se gestiona la ironía en la conversación?». *RILCE*, 23/2: 363-377.

RUIZ GURILLO, L. (2010): «Interrelaciones entre gramaticalización y fraseología en español». *Revista de Filología Española*, XL/1: 173-194.

SÁNCHEZ LÓPEZ, C. (1999): "La negación". En Bosque, I. & Demonte V. (eds.), *Gramática descriptiva de la lengua española*, Madrid: Espasa, vol 2: 2561-2634.

SANCHO CREMADES, P. (1999): "Análisis contrastivo de la fraseología: la expresión del rechazo del discurso previo en catalán y español". In: Fernández González, J.; Fernández Juncal, C.; Marcos Sánchez, M.; Prieto de los Mozos, E. & Santos Río, L. (eds.): *Lingüística para el siglo XXI*, vol. II, Salamanca: Universidad.

SANZ ALONSO, B. (1996): *La negación en español*. Salamanca: Ediciones Colegio de España.

TIMOFEEVA, L. (2008): "Las unidades fraseológicas". In: Ruiz Gurillo, L. & Padilla García X. A. (eds.), *Dime cómo ironizas y te diré quién eres*, Frankfurt: Peter Lang: 193-217.

TRAUGOTT, E.C. & HEINE, B. (eds.) (1991): *Approaches to grammaticalization*. Vol I & II. Amsterdam/Philadelphia: John Benjamins.

STILISTISCHER FEHLGRIFF ODER FUNKTIONALE MODIFIKATION? DER PHRASEOLOGISMENGEBRAUCH IN SARAH KUTTNERS *MÄNGELEXEMPLAR* (2009)

Ulrike Preußer
Bielefeld

Abstract: Literary texts continually represent revealing corpora for investigating the functions of idioms - so far the focus was mostly on texts in which the use of idioms, particularly the use of modifications, happens in an allocable reflected and pointed way in this area. In some literary texts such a use is, however, quite doubtable. Therefore, the article on hand tries to attempt to reveal the implemented modifications of Sarah Kuttner's *Mängelexemplar* in such a way as to differentiate if these can be classified either functional or unmotivated.

Key words: Phrases in literature, modifications, pragmalinguistics, literary criticism.

1. Ein stilistischer Erklärungsversuch

Bei der Frage nach der Qualität eines literarischen Werks – also der Frage: ist das wirklich gut? – handelt es sich einerseits um eine viel gestellte, andererseits um eine vor allem struktural absolut verpönte und zu guter Letzt um eine eigentlich nicht zu beantwortende. Um sich auch nur einem Teilbereich von so etwas wie 'Qualität' anzunähern, muss man normativ werden, also festsetzen, was gemacht werden darf und was nicht, damit ein Qualitätsmerkmal erfüllt ist, und das ist eigentlich schon von Anfang an eine Absage an jede Form von Avantgarde im Speziellen, an literarische Entwicklungsprozesse im Allgemeinen und letztlich an Kunst an sich. Um also nicht der Kunst ein ungewolltes Bein zu stellen und um nicht in die Normativitätsfalle zu tappen, ist es zunächst vonnöten, vorsichtig zu formulieren: Es geht im Folgenden um keinen Absolutheitsanspruch, auch wenn eine Voraussetzung formuliert wird, die in gewisser Weise ein Gütekriterium darstellt. Doch geschieht dies dieser kleinen Vorrede eingedenk so wenig festschreibend wie möglich und so sehr an Funktionalität orientiert wie notwendig. Es soll also im Folgenden darum gehen, inwiefern man feststellen kann, ob ein kleiner sprachlicher Ausschnitt (die Phraseologie im engeren Sinne) eines literarischen Textes als funktional oder als unmotiviert bezeichnet werden kann und damit letztlich als qualitativ besser oder schlechter.

2. Sarah Kuttners *Mängelexemplar* (2009): Der Roman und eine kurze Skizzierung seiner sprachlichen Gestaltung

Untersuchungsgegenstand der folgenden Überlegungen soll der 2009 erschienene erste Roman *Mängelexemplar* der als Viva-Moderatorin bekannt gewordenen Sarah Kuttner sein. Doch warum ist ausgerechnet dieser ein gutes Beispiel für die Frage nach der Qualität der sprachlichen Gestaltung eines literarischen Textes? Bezeichnender Weise wurde er von der Presse äußerst gespalten aufgenommen. Einerseits handele es sich um ein Buch, das sich auf „sensible Weise mit dem Tabuthema 'Depression'" beschäftige, andererseits konstatiert z.B. Sonja Pohlmann in Orientierung an im Text eingearbeiteten Phraseologismen am 29.03.2009 im Tagesspiegel: „Trotzdem kommt darin leider allzu oft die Moderatorin durch, die lieber einen schlechten Witz als gar keinen macht. In »Mängelexemplar« bedeutet das: Lieber einen schlechten Satz als gar keinen. »Es ist zum Mäuse-Melken mit Philipp«, heißt es an einer Stelle. »You can get it if you really want it [sic]. Ich wante vermutlich nicht really genug«, an einer anderen." Offensichtlich stört die Kritikerin insbesondere der Umgang mit Phraseologismen und ihren Modifikationen, auch wenn sie es nicht genauer umschreibt oder benennt – ein Ansatzpunkt, den es sich durchaus lohnt weiterzuverfolgen. Doch zuvor soll eine kurze Skizzierung der narrativen und sprachlich-stilistischen Gestaltung des Textes erfolgen, um die Bemerkung Sonja Pohlmanns etwas ausbauen zu können.

Zunächst präsentiert der Roman den Krankheitsverlaufs einer Depression, indem intern fokalisierend der Blickwinkel der 26-jährigen Karo wiedergegeben wird, die auch als autodiegetische Erzählerin fungiert. Der gesamte Text ist im Präsens verfasst, was die Unmittelbarkeit des Erzählten bewirkt. Der Roman beginnt mit einem bis S. 10 reichenden Abschnitt, der chronologisch betrachtet die Gegenwart des Erzählenes markiert – Karo schildert hier ihren offensichtlich nicht ersten Besuch bei einem Psychotherapeuten, der ihr aus ihren aktuellen Gefühlen der Verzweiflung heraushelfen soll. Die folgenden Kapitel bis S. 250 stellen eine Analepse in das vergangene Jahr dar, aus der ersichtlich wird, wie Karo vor dem Offenbarwerden ihrer Depression gelebt hat (in einer nicht funktionierenden Beziehung), wie sich die Entdeckung ihres psychischen Problems schließlich äußert (Abbruch der nicht funktionierenden Beziehung) und welche therapeutischen Schritte sie im Anschluss in die Wege leitet (Beginn einer Psychotherapie). Ab S. 250 liegt eine Wiederaufnahme der Gegenwart vor, die eine Lösung Karos psychischer Probleme nahelegt, indem sie sich auf ihren mittlerweile neuen Partner im Rahmen einer festen Paarbindung vertrauensvoll einlässt. Am Ende des Romans ließe sich konstatieren: Geändert hat sich nichts, obwohl die erfolgreiche Partnersuche dies suggerieren möchte – weder an Karos Einstellung, noch an ihrer Lebensführung, die nach wie vor allein auf eine möglichst dauerhafte Paarbindung fixiert ist. Dabei reflektiert Karo ihr Verhalten und ihre Empfindungen ständig und beschreibt sie bildreich – was durch die Einbindung zahlreicher Phraseologismen, Metaphern, Allegorien und Vergleiche erreicht wird – und selbstironisch, indem Übertreibungen und bildhafte Vergleiche zur Deskription eines verzerrten Selbstbilds verwendet werden. Karo meint, zwischen der Binäropposition von Krankheit und Gesundheit und damit zwischen den Polen Normalität und Anormalität zu oszillieren. Sie möchte sich immer wieder im Bereich des 'Normalen' verorten, indem sie sprachlich Normalitätsdiskurse aufgreift (sprachlich Vorgeformtes bzw. Phraseologismen), die sie schließlich aber doch nur erneut an ihrer seelischen, psychischen Normalität (d.h. Gesundheit) zweifeln lassen, was überwiegend an der Modifikation des Vorgeformten deutlich wird. Karo changiert so zwischen Elementar- und Spezialdiskursen, indem Phraseologismen im engeren Sinne und (innovative) Metaphern als Ausgangspunkte und Gestaltungsmittel für längere Allegorien genutzt werden und einen Dialog mit der Normalität erzeugen. Karos Leben ist auf den Kopf gestellt – um das kenntlich zu machen, bedient sie sich ausufernder, aber traditioneller oder gesellschaftlich anerkannter sprachlicher Bilder, die in Form von Metaphern ihre Lebenszusammenhänge in 'normale' Bahnen lenken (sollen). Die Logik der Technik und auch die von Körperfunktionen wie auch die sie stets umgebende Mediensprache, dienen dabei häufig als sprachliche Vorlagen bzw. Bild- und Formulierungsspendebereiche. Sie stellen Eckpfeiler eines als normal empfundenen Lebens dar, denn wie auch ihre Psychiaterin Frau Dr. Kleve erklärt, steht „ein ausgeglichenes [und damit ist an dieser Stelle ein 'normales' Leben gemeint, U.P.] auf fünf Säulen [...]: Familie, Liebe, Wohnung, Beruf und Freunde stützen es." (Kuttner 2009: 94). Von diesen fünf Säulen hat Karo in kurzer Zeit mindestens drei verloren: Liebe und Beruf, einige Freunde und über einen längeren Zeitraum auch die Familie. Insofern erscheinen die in den Text eingearbeiteten Phraseologismen und ihre Modifikationen durchaus als motiviert – im Einzelfall zeigt sich aber, dass der Produktionsaufwand vieler dieser Sprachspiele sehr hoch ist, während ihre semantische Funktionalität sehr gering bleibt und häufig nicht über den produzierten Satz hinaus reicht. Insofern könnte man sogar behaupten, dass die modifizierten Phraseologismen die Kohärenz des Textes eher unterbrechen als weiterführen. Es ließe sich nun vermuten, dass sich die oben beschriebene Unsicherheit und Ungewissheit der Protagonistin auch in ihrer – höchst privaten, da intern fokalisierten Erzählweise widerspiegelt. Genau das erfolgt aber nicht – keine unzuverlässige Erzählerin tritt uns in dem Roman entgegen. Mittels einer solchen wäre es möglich gewesen, die witzige und sprachlich opulente Darstellungsweise zu durchbrechen, indem sie irgendwann als Selbstlüge kenntlich gemacht wird, sodass eine tatsächliche Änderung der Einstellung erfolgen könnte, die ein Entkommen aus der als repressiv empfundenen Gefühlswelt ermöglichen würde. Die Erzählerin in *Mängelexemplar* ist jedoch eine ihrer selbst in hohem Maße gewisse, die trotz der Unmittelbarkeit der gewählten Erzählweise stets genau über sich Bescheid zu wissen scheint. Selbst auf Gedankengänge, die ihr ihre Psychotherapeutin nahelegt, reagiert sie ziemlich selbstbewusst:

> Anette meint, dass ich mich zu sehr von Liebe abhängig mache, dass mir auch Freunde und Familie das Gefühl geben können, dass eine Beziehung nur die Olive im Martini ist, aber mal ehrlich: Martini ohne Olive ist scheiße. Und Philipp ist zwar definitiv keine Olive, aber zum jetzigen Zeitpunkt würde ich auch die Sardelle, die Philipp ist, in meinen Martini hängen (Kuttner 2009: 114).

Karo ist sich erstaunlich genau darüber im Klaren, wie sie ist und was sie nach welchen Maßstäben bewertet – und daran zweifelt sie zu keinem Zeitpunkt – im Gegenteil: Ihre Perspektive auf die Welt, ihre stete Suche danach, in Beziehung stehen zu können ist ein unhintergehbares Kontinuum, das niemals hinterfragt wird. Karos Weltgefüge gerät also streng genommen vielleicht ins Wanken, es bricht jedoch nicht wirklich zusammen, was eine tatsächliche Neuorientierung möglich gemacht hätte. Insofern kokettiert Karo auch nur mit dem vermeintlichen Normalitätsverlust, statt dass ein solcher tatsächlich manifest werden würde.

Die gewählte Erzählinstanz vermittelt zum einen Unmittelbarkeit (kurze Zeitspanne, über die sich die erzählte Zeit erstreckt, Präsens), zum anderen wird jedoch durch das offensichtliche Selbstbewusstsein der Protagonistin außerdem der Eindruck erweckt, dass die Geschichte aus viel größerer zeitlicher Distanz erzählt wird, als das tatsächlich der Fall ist. Einzig eine größere zeitliche Distanz zu dem emotional einschneidenden Erlebnis könnte jedoch eine selbstbewusste Perspektive hinlänglich plausibilisieren. Diese Unausgewogenheit könnte als Begründungsansatz für die negative Kritik an dem Roman herangezogen werden. Sie schlägt sich auch – wie bereits kurz erwähnt wurde – in der Sprachverwendung nieder, die an steter Pointenproduktion orientiert zu sein scheint; ein Vorgehen, das wiederum auf den ersten Blick dem Charakter der stets witzelnden Karo, die es nicht schafft, sich ihren Problemen und Ängsten zu stellen, zu entsprechen scheint, auf den zweiten jedoch deutlich macht, dass zur Konstruktion eines solchen Charakters außerdem noch gehören würde, dass diese offensichtliche Fassade als eine solche – zumindest implizit – kenntlich gemacht und nicht durch eine selbstgewisse Erzählposition unterlaufen wird.

Im Folgenden soll unter Berücksichtigung des eine mögliche Negativkritik plausibilisierenden Befunds der partiellen erzählerischen Unstimmigkeit bzw. Unglaubwürdigkeit, die durch eine andauernde 'Pointenproduktion' im Sinne von selbstzweckhaften Sprachspielen untermauert wird, der Frage nachgegangen werden, inwiefern modifizierte Phraseologismen als funktionale Veränderungen oder stilistische Fehlgriffe klassifiziert werden können.

3. Stilistischer Fehlgriff und funktionale Modifikation – Definitionen

Wenn im Titel des Beitrags die Frage aufgeworfen wird, ob der Phraseologismengebrauch in Sarah Kuttners Roman als 'funktional modifizierend' zu beschreiben sein könnte oder eher als 'stilistischer Fehlgriff', dann muss zunächst geklärt werden, was mit diesen beiden Begriffen gemeint sein soll.

Emmy Kerkhoff versteht unter Stil Folgendes: „Wir sehen Stil als das in den Einzelheiten eines Werkes Übereinstimmende, die Einheit in der Vielheit, welche sich bei aller Variation im Einzelnen gleichbleibt. Er ist ein durch verschiedene Werkschichten hindurchgehendes Kontinuum" (Kerkhoff 1962: 15). Dieser Stilbegriff trifft im Wesentlichen das, was hier als Minimum in Bezug auf den Phraseologismengebrauch angenommen werden soll: Eine strukturell eindeutige Verwendung von Modifikationen insofern, als dass bei allen Abweichungen im Einzelfall doch ein übergeordnetes Prinzip sichtbar wird, das anhand dieser Form der Sprachverwendung eine eigene Semantisierung deutlich werden lässt. Bei Arno Schmidt, Elfriede Jelinek, Günter Grass und Ernst Jandl lassen sich solche funktionalen Modifikationsstrategien durchaus nachweisen.

Unter einer 'funktionalen Modifikation' wird im Folgenden eine semantische und/oder formale Modifikation verstanden, die motiviert in dem Sinne ist, dass sie einem speziellen (semantischen und/oder formalen) Zweck dient, der wenigstens über den Satz hinausgeht, wenn möglich jedoch die Meso- oder Makrobene des Textes umfasst.

Als 'stilistischer Fehlgriff' wird im Folgenden eine Modifikation bezeichnet, die nicht im o.g. Sinne motiviert ist.

4. Beispiele für stilistische Fehlgriffe und funktionale Modifikationen

Zunächst sollen einige Beispiele für funktionale Modifikationen angeführt und analysiert werden. Anhand dieser lässt sich erörtern, welche konkreteren Eigenschaften diese aufweisen, damit sie als solche bezeichnet werden können.

4.1 Funktionale Modifikationen

Nach dem ersten Besuch bei einer Psychotherapeutin ist Karo geradezu euphorisch und schildert ihren ersten Eindruck wie folgt:

> Vielleicht bin ich nur *wie ein oller Weisheitszahn*. Ich habe die ganze Zeit *leise unter einer Schicht Haut vor mich hin geeitert*, und jetzt hat jemand *die Wunde aufgeschnitten*. Das *schmerzt und eitert und stinkt* erst mal vorübergehend noch stärker, aber nun befasst sich jemand mit dem Problem. *Man wird die Wunde säubern und dann langsam ausheilen lassen*. Es geht los! Der erste Schritt zur Besserung! *The first cut is the deepest*. Andererseits, was weiß Cat Stevens schon von so was (Kuttner 2009: 29).

Hier findet die semantische Modifikation des englischsprachigen Sprichworts (das hier als Geflügeltes Wort eingesetzt wird) *The first cut ist he deepest* statt. Karo verwendet es nicht den habitualisierten Sprichwortsituationen gemäß, um einem aktuellen Liebeskummer Ausdruck zu verleihen (da sie sich ja auch noch nicht von ihrem Freund Philipp getrennt hat), sondern, um die Metapher der Wunde (oder vielleicht sogar das implizierte Sprichwort *Die Zeit heilt alle Wunden*) auf der denotativen Ebene weiterzuführen. Damit ist das Sprichwort in seiner wörtlichen Bedeutung aktualisiert verwendet worden. Diese Modifikation wäre also insofern nicht als unmotiviert zu bezeichnen, als dass sie die fortgeführte Metapher (Allegorie) der Wunde mit einem Sprichwort regressiv transgeneralisierend abschließt – allerdings nur, um diese Funktionen mit dem nachgestellten Satz wieder in Frage zu stellen (= semantische Modifikation, die eine Allegorie beendet und sinnstiftend überhöht).

Auch an folgendem Textbeispiel, in welchem Karo ihre hoch emotional Wesensart beschreibt, lässt sich deutlich machen, dass die formale und semantische Modifikation durchaus motiviert erfolgt: „*Kleinigkeiten machen mich irre, wegen einer Mücke werde ich zum Elefanten. Und nicht zu einem dieser Pixar-Elefanten, sondern zu einen von jenen, die aus Rache töten*" (Kuttner 2009: 14). Interessant an der Verwendung ist hier das Zusammenspiel von Modifikation und ursprünglichem verbalen Phraseologismus: Es werden die beiden Lexeme „Mücke" und „Elefant" aus ihrem ursprünglichen Relationsverhältnis (*aus einer Mücke einen Elefanten machen*) herausgelöst und in ein neues gestellt, das auf der denotativen Ebene eine Kausalbeziehung wiedergibt. Die neue phraseologische Bedeutung ('aus nichtigem Anlass ausflippen') hat durchaus noch einen Bezug zum Ausgangsphraseologismus, da die phraseologische Bedeutung „aus etwas Kleinem etwas Großes machen" auch in der Modifikation noch präsent ist, ja, in gewisser Weise ihre Aktualisierung das Verständnis der semantischen Modifikation wesentlich mitbestimmt. Karos Verhalten lässt sich damit beschreiben, dass sie 'aus einer Mücke einen Elefanten macht', wenn sie 'wegen einer Mücke zum Elefanten wird'. Durch diese Dialogizität, die zwischen Ausgangsphraseologismus und Modifikation besteht (die Modifikation wäre damit die Stimme der Selbsterkenntnis, der Ausgangsphraseologismus die Stimme der von außen erfolgenden Gesellschaftskritik), entsteht die enge Verzahnung zwischen beiden, die eine starke Motiviertheit dieser kontextspezifischen Veränderung und ihrer Vorlage deutlich macht (= Dialogizität zwischen Ausgangsphraseologismus und Modifikation). In Bezug auf die Kontexteinbettung lässt sich feststellen, dass die Modifikation progressiv transgeneralisierend eingesetzt ist, da im Anschluss die Schilderung einer Situation erfolgt, in der die Protagonistin 'aus nichtigem Anlass ausflippt' (=formal-semantische Modifikation, die sinnstiftend überhöhend wirkt).

Im folgenden Beispiel, das das Wiedersehen von Karo und Philipp auf dem Bahnhof beschreibt, nachdem er einige Tage in seinem Heimatort verbracht hat, liegt eine Kontamination aus der Modifikation *schlechte Miene zum guten Spiel machen* (*gute Miene zum bösen Spiel machen*) und dem verbalen Phraseologismus *keine Miene verziehen* vor: „*Philipp verzieht die schlechte Miene zum guten Spiel nicht und haucht einen flüchtigen Kuss in die Nähe meines Mundes*" (Kuttner 2009: 46). Der Ausgangsphraseologismus bedeutet 'etwas notgedrungen hinnehmen, sich den Ärger nicht ansehen lassen'. Die Modifikation in *schlechte Miene zum guten Spiel machen* erfolgt 1. durch eine Vertauschung der positiv bzw. negativ konnotierten, binäroppositionellen Adjektive und 2. durch die Substitution des Adjektivs 'böse' durch das Adjektiv 'schlecht', das zwar semähnlich, aber weit entfernt von semgleich ist ('schlecht' wird verwendet in Bezug auf die Laune, die hier im Hintergrund mit assoziiert wird). Die Kontamination mit *keine Miene verziehen* erzeugt eine situationsspezifisch treffende Beschreibung auf der wörtlichen wie auch der phraseologischen Bedeutungsebene: Philipp macht das Gegenteil von *guter Miene zum bösen Spiel*, denn die Voraussetzungen dafür sind gänzlich verkehrte. Er lässt sich seinen Ärger ansehen, obwohl das Theaterspiel, das er und Karo ihre Beziehung nennen, tatsächlich gut ist – immerhin kann sich Karo tatsächlich in Wiedersehensfreude hineinsteigern, wenn es unmittelbar zuvor heißt: *„[...] und pünktlich mit Philipps Zug fahren auch wieder liebevolle Gefühle in den Bahnhof meines Herzens ein"* (Kuttner 2009: 45). Philipp hat also schlechte Laune, die in der schlechten Miene ihren wortwörtlichen Niederschlag findet, aber auch in der konnotierenden Lesart von 'Miene' als 'Haltung' präsent wird. *Keine Miene verziehen* vermittelt vor allem die Stetigkeit, mit der die schlechte Laune zur Schau gestellt wird und dient insofern der Verstärkung (= formal-semantische Modifikation, die durch Kontamination und Umkehrung die konkrete Situation modellierend beschreibt und bewertet).

Die exemplarisch herausgegriffenen Beispiele geben einen kleinen Einblick in die Vielseitigkeit der nachvollziehbar funktionsorientierten Einbettung von modifizierten Phraseologismen, deren Eigenschaften sich wie oben gezeigt umschreibend erfassen lassen. Die im folgenden Abschnitt aufgeführten Beispiele besitzen diese Eigenschaften offensichtlich nicht.

4.2 Stilistische Fehlgriffe / Unmotivierte Modifikationen

Im folgenden Textausschnitt wird Karos Reaktion auf die erste Diagnose ihrer Psychotherapeutin beschrieben:

Ich habe gerade noch genug Zeit, ein wenig enttäuscht zu sein über die Kürze dieser Diagnose, und dann fange ich an zu <u>weinen</u>. Als ob in meinem Inneren irgendetwas <u>aufgedreht</u> wird, <u>fließt es überraschend aus mir heraus</u>. Ich <u>schluchze los wie ein Kind</u>. Alles in mir ist plötzlich klein und traurig. Eine nahezu beschämend <u>große Woge von Weltschmerz</u> rüttelt mich durch. Ich <u>fühle mich wie ein Surfer, der unter einer Welle</u> verbummelt geht. <u>Überall Wasser, überall viel</u>. Und weil ich keine Zeit verlieren möchte, denke ich schon während der <u>Überschwemmung</u> hektisch darüber nach, wie ich <u>so unter Wasser geraten</u> konnte. Und verblüffender Weise habe ich keinerlei Ahnung. Ich gehe im Geiste alle akuten Probleme durch, um zu sehen, <u>auf welchen Topf der nasse Deckel gehört</u>. Aber keiner scheint zu passen (Kuttner 2009: 23-24).

An diesem Beispiel sieht man gleich Mehreres – die Verwendung von Metaphern, Vergleichen und Phraseologismen und die einigende Zusammenführung in einem gemeinsamen Bildspendebereich bzw. über Monosemierung: Zum einen wird das Denotat 'sich in starker körperlicher Reaktion zeigende Traurigkeit', das mit den Signifikanten „weinen" und „schluchzen" und „traurig" und „Weltschmerz" auch tatsächlich benannt wird, aktiviert. Im Rahmen der Tätigkeit des Weinens findet im folgenden Text eine Monosemierung auf das Sem [flüssig] bzw. [Wasser] statt, die durch mehrere Vergleiche und Metaphern erzeugt wird, die zu Beginn mit dem Bild der sich öffnenden Schleusen arbeiten, dann mit einer Analogie zum Meer und schließlich zum Ertrinken. Dabei wird nicht nur Bezug genommen auf die Tränenflüssigkeit an sich, sondern auch noch eine konnotative Lesart aktiviert, wie an *unter Wasser geraten* deutlich wird. Diese Wortverbindung bezeichnet zum einen das 'Unterwassergeraten' der Augen und zum anderen im übertragenen

Sinne den Kontrollverlust, der mit der über dem Kopf zusammenschlagenden Woge in Verbindung steht. Insofern könnte man hier durchaus von einer Motivierung sprechen. Am Ende des Abschnitts findet sich dann jedoch noch ein Phraseologismus, genau genommen ein formal und semantisch modifiziertes Sprichwort: *Auf jeden Topf passt ein Deckel*. Im Textauszug wird dieses Sprichwort gleichsam als bekannt vorausgesetzt – es wird nur über die beiden Lexeme „Topf" und „Deckel" aktualisiert (und über einen Verwendungszusammenhang, in dem die Zusammengehörigkeit beider Küchenutensilien eine tragende Rolle spielt). Die Modifikation ist tiefgreifend: Sie besteht formal in der Herauslösung der beiden Lexeme „Topf" und „Deckel" und der Verbindung mit einem semähnlichen Verb (statt „passen" „gehören"). Die Satzwertigkeit des Sprichworts ist durch den Gebrauch aufgehoben, da er in eine Nebensatzkonstruktion eingebaut wird. Zudem findet neben Tilgung und Substitution auch noch eine Erweiterung statt, indem das Lexem „Deckel" um das Adjektiv 'nass' ergänzt wird. Das Adjektiv schafft hier die Anschlussmöglichkeit an den zuvor eröffneten Bildspendebereich „Wasser" und motiviert in Bezug auf den Kontext auch die semantische Modifikation. Während das Ausgangssprichwort im Zusammenhang mit einer bis dato erfolglos verlaufenen Partnersuche Anwendung findet ('Jeder findet einen zu ihm passenden Partner'), wird es im aktuellen Textzusammenhang unmittelbar auf einen anderen Kontext übertragen; es bleibt dadurch eigentlich nur das Ursprungsbild des Zueinanderpassens erhalten, denn Karo überlegt, wie sie ihre Tränenzufuhr einordnen und dadurch stoppen kann. Damit fungiert als 'Topf' das Ursprungsproblem, das Karo nicht finden kann, und als 'nasser Deckel' Karos Tränen, denen eine Ursache zugeordnet werden muss. Auch wenn Karo im Verlauf der Erzählung durchaus deutlich macht, dass sie nicht allein sein kann, dass sie auf Partnersuche ist und diese nicht immer erfolgreich verläuft, ist im zitierten Textausschnitt keine Verbindung zur phraseologischen Bedeutung des Sprichworts herstellbar, was den Rekurs darauf unmotiviert erscheinen lässt. Der fehlende semantische Anschluss zeigt sich zunächst in der nicht erfolgenden Aufnahme weder des dem Sprichwort zugrunde liegenden Relationsverhältnisses (im Sinne der Sprichwortidee) noch der sprichwortimmanenten Gebrauchsrestriktionen. Sie zeigt sich noch deutlicher in dem nur wenige Semähnlichkeiten aufweisenden, diffusen tertium comparationis, das herangezogen werden muss, um den zu stoppenden Tränenfluss mit 'Topf' und 'Deckel' in Verbindung bringen zu können (= formal-semantische Modifikation ohne semantischen Zugewinn, unpassende Gebrauchssituation, keine Berücksichtigung des Relationsverhältnisses im Sinne der Sprichwortidee).

Das nächste Textbeispiel zeigt eine formale Modifikation ohne semantische Modifikation. Der sprachliche Produktionsaufwand steht in keinem Verhältnis zu einer sachlichen oder sprachlichen Pointe; es wird auch nicht die Anschlussfähigkeit an den Kontext erhöht. Vielmehr wird eine Anschlussfähigkeit erzwungen, indem der umgangssprachliche phraseologische Vergleich *passen wie Arsch auf Eimer* auf das Anbahnen einer Beziehung angewendet wird: *„Es ist nicht so, dass ich aktiv auf der Suche war, aber in Beziehungen zu sein, fand ich schon immer toller, als es nicht zu sein, und ich war es gerade nicht, <u>also passte da wohl der Arsch der Gelegenheit auf meinen Eimer</u>"* (Kuttner 2009: 39) Warum wird an dieser Stelle ein Phraseologismus verwendet? Warum wird dieser auch noch modifiziert, indem er (doppelt) expandiert wird? Der vulgärsprachliche phraseologische Vergleich hätte seine Funktion auch in der Ursprungsform vollständig erfüllt; es entsteht keine Ambiguität und die Referenzen laufen ins Leere: Was bedeutet „passte […]

auf meinen Eimer"? „Auf meinen Eimer" der Situation? (= formale Modifikation ohne erkennbare Verbesserung der Anschlussfähigkeit, unpassende Gebrauchssituation).

Im letzten zu betrachtenden Beispiel beschreibt Karo erneut ihren psychisch-emotionalen Zustand: „*Die ganzen Gefühle, mit denen ich plötzlich meinen Körper teilen muss, nerven wie Drahtseile. Sie kommen sich ständig in die Quere*" (Kuttner 2009: 113). Hier wird ein verbaler Phraseologismus bzw. ein phraseologischer Vergleich, der ein Substantiv präzisiert (*Nerven wie Drahtseile [haben]*), allein durch Satzstellung und eine Abweichung der Groß- und Kleinschreibung („nerven wie Drahtseile") zu einem phraseologischen Vergleich, der ein Verb näher umschreibt, umfunktioniert. Die Bedeutung dieses formalen Wortspiels scheint zunächst sekundär zu sein, muss doch die Bedeutung über einen Nachsatz („Sie kommen sich ständig in die Quere") erst hergestellt werden. Selbst mit dieser Erklärung bleibt der semantische Gehalt sehr gering, der erzeugte Vergleich aufgrund des weit entfernten tertium comparationis wirkt daher unnötig. Das kann daran liegen, dass keine Verbindung mit dem Ausgangsphraseologismus nahegelegt wird: Während die ohnehin bereits metaphorischen 'Nerven' mit den Semen [stark], [besonders dick], [haltbar] u. ä. in Verbindung gebracht werden und sich hier gleich über mehrere Seme eine Verbindung zu großer Geduld herstellen lässt, ist die Gleichsetzung des Verbs' nerven' (also sich von etwas gestört fühlen) mit 'Drahtseilen' nur sehr mühsam herzustellen. Inwiefern könnte man sich von Drahtseilen genervt fühlen? Das verbindende Sem liegt so weit entfernt, dass der Zusammenhang mit dem bereits zitierten Nachsatz „Sie kommen sich ständig in die Quere" erklärt werden muss. Und selbst diese Erklärung erschließt sich in ihrer Bildhaftigkeit nicht vollends: Inwiefern können Drahtseile (die gemäß ihrer Prägung im etablierten phraseologischen Vergleich die Seme [stark], [dick], [fest] u. ä. führen) sich in die Quere kommen? – Der stilistische Fehlgriff läge damit im kaum wahrnehmbaren und daher erläuterungsbedürftigen tertium (= formal-semantische Modifikation ohne semantischen Zugewinn).

Die oben präsentierten Beispiele zeigen einen deutlich wenig bzw. nicht motivierten Gebrauch von Modifikationen. Die solcherart modifizierten Phraseologismen scheinen daher überwiegend der eingangs so genannten 'Pointenproduktion' zu dienen: Sie stellen die Aufmerksamkeit des Lesers auf sich ziehende Sprachspiele dar, die keinen darüber hinaus gehenden semantischen Mehrwert produzieren und keine Reichweite, die über den jeweiligen Satz hinaus geht, besitzen.

5. Fazit

Wertungsfragen sind ein heikles Thema, dem man sich stets vorsichtig und mit dem Bemühen um größtmögliche Transparenz hinsichtlich der zugrunde gelegten Kriterien nähern sollte. Im vorliegenden Beitrag wurde dieser Überlegung durch Konzentration auf einen kleinen sprachlichen Ausschnitt (Modifikationen), einer möglichst genauen Definition der zugrunde gelegten Begriffe (stilistischer Fehlgriff und funktionale Modifikation) und einer kontrastiven Analyse ausgewählter Textbeispiele, die als funktional bzw. als unmotiviert klassifiziert werden können, begegnet.

6. Literaturverzeichnis

BERNSTEIN, N. 2010 „Phraseologismen bei Nicanor Parra und Ernst Jandl". In: Korhonen, Jarmo et al. (Hrsg.). *EUROPHRAS 2008. Beiträge zur internationalen Phraseologiekonferenz vom 13.-16.08.2008 in Helsinki.* Helsinki: Universität Helsinki, 198-206.

BURGER, H. 2007 *Phraseologie. Eine Einführung am Beispiel des Deutschen.* 3. Neu bearbeitete Auflage. Berlin: Erich Schmidt Verlag.

KERKHOFF, E. L. 1962 *Kleine deutsche Stilistik.* Bern/München: Francke.

KUTTNER, S. 2009 *Mängelexemplar.* Frankfurt/Main: S. Fischer Verlag.

LINK, J. 2009 *Versuch über den Normalismus. Wie Normalität produziert wird.* 4. Auflage. Göttingen: Vandenhoeck & Ruprecht.

MARTINEZ, M. /SCHEFFEL, M. 2007 *Einführung in die Erzähltheorie.* 7. Auflage. München: Verlag C.H. Beck.

NÜNNING, A. (Hrsg.) 1998 *Unreliable Narration: Studien zur Theorie und Praxis unglaubwürdigen Erzählens in der englischsprachigen Erzählliteratur.* Trier: WVT.

PREUSSER, U. 2004 „Phraseologismen in literarischen Texten – Zwischen Linguistik und Literaturwissenschaft". In: Földes, C./Wirrer, J. (Hg.) (2004). *Phraseologismen als Gegenstand sprach- und kulturwissenschaftlicher Forschung.* Baltmannsweiler: Schneider Verlag Hohengehren (= Phraseologie & Parömiologie 15), 267-284.

PREUSSER, U. 2005 „Das ist ein weites Feld ... – Phraseologismen in der Literatur des Deutschunterrichts". In: *Der Deutschunterricht* 5/2005; 62-71.

PREUSSER, U. 2007 *Aufbruch aus dem beschädigten Leben. Die Verwendung von Phraseologismen im literarischen Text am Beispiel von Arno Schmidts »Nobodaddy's Kinder«.* Bielefeld: Aisthesis Verlag (= Phrasemata III).

POHLMANN, S. 2009 „Mängelexemplar". In: *Der Tagesspiegel* vom 29.03.2009: http://www. tagesspiegel.de/kultur/literatur/maengelexemplar/1484994.html (zuletzt besucht am 20. 08.2010).

MOTIVACIÓN FÓNICA EN LOS FRASEOLOGISMOS ITALIANOS

Justyna Pietrzak
Universidad Complutense de Madrid

Abstract: In this paper, the main phonic/rhythmic devices, like pace, heap, alliteration, paranomasia and apophony, are analyzed in the phraseological units. A classification of the phraseological units is proposed according to the phonic motivations, and, finally we study some phraseological units whose only motivation is phonic.

Key words: Phraseology, Italian phraseology, phonic motivation, phono-symbolism.

1. Introducción

En los estudios fraseológicos no se suele conceder la suficiente atención a la faceta fónica de los fraseologismos. De hecho, los principales manuales de fraseología, dedican a este argumento muy pocas o incluso ninguna página[1] lo que es debido ante todo al hecho de que, al abordar el estudio de las unidades fraseológicas, se atiende en primer lugar a sus aspectos semánticos, sintácticos o culturales y por otro lado, porque quizás esté aún vigente la creencia que relaciona la artificiosidad formal sólo con el universo paremiológico. Sin embargo, el papel que el aspecto fónico desempeña en la creación y fijación de las unidades fraseológicas es innegable, por lo cual el propósito de esta presentación es dar a conocer en primer lugar en qué manera el ingrediente fónico se manifiesta en los fraseologismos y ofrecer en segundo momento una reflexión sobre su influencia en la formación y fijación de los mismos. En el presente estudio centramos la atención en las unidades fraseológicas de la lengua italiana. El corpus de datos que hemos manejado está compuesto por un conjunto representativo de unidades fraseológicas extraídas de las siguientes obras: las recopilaciones fraseológicas *Frase fatta capo ha* de G. Pittàno, *Dizionario dei modi di dire della lingua italiana* de B. M. Quartu (2000), *Capire l'antifona* de Turrini, y de los diccionarios generales *Dizionario della lingua italiana* (DISC) de F. Sabatini y V. Coletti (2006) y *Vocabolario della lingua italiana* (lo ZINGARELLI) de M. Dogliotti y L. Rosiello (1997).

2. Procedimientos fónico-rítmicos en las locuciones

En primer lugar nos interesa identificar los principales procedimientos fónico–rítmicos que configuran los modismos y locuciones italianos. Entre ellos destacan ritmo, rima, aliteración, *derivatio* e iteración, paronomasia y apofonía.

---

[1] A. Zuluaga dedica un breve capítulo a este fenómeno (1980: 115-120), mientras que Corpas hace unas pocas observaciones sobre dicho argumento (1996:111-116) y Dietz (*Rhetorik in der Phraseologie*) le dedica tres subcapítulos (1999:352-363).

2.1. Ritmo

A pesar de lo que se suele creer, en el universo de la fraseología la presencia del ritmo acentual no está restringida sólo y exclusivamente a los refranes (García- Page Sánchez, 2008: 331), aunque sí es verdad, que dicho fenómeno se aprecia especialmente en ellos.

El carácter versificado es el rasgo fundamental del refrán y cabe recordar que la abrumadora mayoría de este tipo de paremias está configurada por algún esquema rítmico. En cambio, en el caudal de las locuciones, la disposición rítmica se observa sólo en algunos casos, ante todo en los binomios, es decir unidades compuestas por dos lexemas unidos a través de conjunciones coordinadas o encorsetados en un esquema preposicional[2]. Si este tipo de locuciones posee propiedades rítmicas, esto se debe principalmente a la simetría que presenta su estructura.

A continuación ofrecemos un breve repertorio de los esquemas rítmicos fundamentales que presentan las unidades fraseológicas del corpus considerado.

Los ritmos trocaicos, la alternancia binaria de una tónica y una átona (Di Pietro, 2000: 13) se dan en las unidades como: *calma e gesso*; *essere come cane e gatto*; *chiaro e tondo*; *fare conto tondo, a corpo morto*; *a mano a mano*; *di padre in figlio*; *a scappa e fuggi*.

El ritmo anfibráquico, la secuencia de tres sílabas, de las cuales la tónica es la penúltima (Di Pietro, 2000: 13), puede ser ejemplificada por las siguientes unidades: *d'amore e d'accordo*; *essere un asino calzato e vestito*.

El ritmo dactílico, la secuencia de tres sílabas, de las cuales la tónica es la primera (Di Pietro, 2000: 13) se aprecia en: *Apriti Sesamo!*

La disposición rítmica es perceptible también en: *Qui lo dico e qui lo nego!* ; *non fare né caldo né freddo*; *non avere né capo né coda*; *non avere né casa né tetto*; *non essere né carne né pesce*; *non stare né in cielo né in terra*; *essere più di là che di qua*; *non farsi né in là né in qua*.

El ritmo, la secuencia regulada de sílabas tónicas y átonas contribuye al establecimiento de vínculos de cohesión y a la formación de una unidad compacta y cerrada facilitando su fijación (Zuluaga, 1980: 118). Además, el ritmo, en muchos casos que hemos expuesto arriba, está reforzado por paralelismos formales o repetición de miembros comunes, como la conjunción *né*, las preposiciones *in*, *di*, etc.

2.2. Asonancia, consonancia y rima

Los elementos que indudablemente refuerzan el ritmo son la rima, la consonancia y la asonancia. También la rima es un elemento adscrito tradicionalmente al dominio del refrán. Existe, sin embargo, un número cuantitativamente significativo de fraseologismos que también utilizan la rima, la consonancia o asonancia, en su configuración.

Por asonancia entendemos identidad de los sonidos vocálicos en la terminación de dos palabras llanas, a partir de su última vocal acentuada. Cabe distinguir entre dos tipos de asonancia: perfecta, la cual cumple a rajatabla dicha definición, y asonancia imperfecta, en el caso de la cual la identidad de los sonidos vocálicos concierne tan sólo a las vocales tónicas, mientras las átonas son diferentes. Existe también un tercer tipo de asonancia que se da entre

---

[2] Para más detalles hacer acerca del fenómeno del binomio consúltese García-Page Sánchez, 2008, 329-334 y F. Čermák (2010).

las vocales tónicas e átonas de una palabra llana y otra esdrújula. En la palabra esdrújula la sílaba intermedia resulta casi imperceptible para el oído y por consiguiente "vocalmente" no influyente (Di Pietro, 2000: 61-63).

Los ejemplos de la asonancia perfecta son: *basta e avanza*; *difendere a spada tratta* (a-a) ; *far carte false, a gambe levate* (a-e) ; *alti e bassi*; *armi e bagagli* (a-i); *Aspetta e spera!* (e-a); *a denti stretti* (e-i); *a prima vista* (i-a); *fare a bocca e borsa* (o-a); *essere il padrone del vapore* (o-e); *da pochi soldi, fare gli occhi dolci* (o-i); *vedersi a colpo d'occhio*; *fare conto tondo*; *a corpo morto, rimetterci l'osso del collo* (o-o); *nudo e bruco* (u-o).

La asonancia entre una palabra esdrújula y una llana puede ser ejemplificada en: *soffrire come un'a(ni)ma dannata* (a-a); *essere suo(ce)ra e nuora* (o-a).

La asonancia imperfecta está reflejada en: *fare a palle e santi* (a-e, a-i); *a rotta di collo* (o-a, o-o); *andare d'amore e d'accordo* (o-e, o-o); *per amore o per forza* (o-e, o-a).

En el caso de la consonancia se trata de la identidad de las consonantes a partir de la vocal tónica de dos palabras, independientemente de la diversidad de sonidos vocálicos (Di Pietro, 2000: 63-64). A modo de ejemplo nos pueden servir los siguientes fraseologismos: *giocare a carte scoperte*; *essere casa e chiesa*; *a destra e a sinistra*; *fare il finto tonto*.

Por rima entendemos la identidad de todos los sonidos a partir de la vocal acentuada (Di Pietro, 2000: 60): *essere più la spesa che l'impresa*; *non avere né amore né sapore*; *annessi e connessi*; *tra il lusco e il brusco*;*nato e sputato*; *fare nomi e cognomi*; *nudo e crudo*.

Al igual que el ritmo, también la asonancia, consonancia y rima son unos elementos de suma importancia al fijar un enunciado. Como dice Zuluaga, la rima "remite a algo ya percibido" (1980: 117), la rima presente en el segundo componente remite a la del primero, creando un vínculo de cohesión entre los miembros implicados y desempeña al mismo tiempo un papel importante desde el punto de vista mnemotécnico contribuyendo a la fijación del texto. También el juego de asonancias y consonancias tiene la misma función de crear correspondencias fónicas entre los elementos de una secuencia, aunque su fuerza es menor en comparación con la rima.

2.3. Aliteración

Un artificio fónico que las unidades fraseológicas esgrimen con frecuencia es la aliteración. Es decir, la repetición de la misma consonante o vocal o a veces sílaba al principio o en el interior de varias palabras (Spang, 1984: 154); si la iteración del mismo fonema se da en posición inicial de palabra se habla de *homeopróforon* o *parhómeon* (Mayoral, 1994: 61-62); la repetición de la misma sílaba en el comienzo se denomina *dysprophoron* (Garavelli, 1988: 315).

Los ejemplos de homeopróforon son: *fortunato come un cane in chiesa*; *stare come il cane alla catena*; *capitare tra capo e collo*; *essere tutto casa e chiesa*; *non avere né capo né coda*; *essere fuori fase*; *far finta*; *far fuori*; *far furore*; *in fretta e furia*; *mettere a ferro e fuoco*; *fare fuoco e fiamme*; *grande e grosso*; *cercare in lungo e in largo*; *promettere mari e monti*; *non avere né occhi né orecchie*; *né punto né poco*; *essere una palla al piede*; *suonare sempre la stessa solfa*; *vivo e vegeto*; *fare sera e sabato*; *scritto sulla sabbia*; *scaldare una serpe in seno*; *a viva voce*.

A modo de muestra de dispróforon citamos: *fare a bocca e borsa*; *salvare capra e cavoli*; *mettere la corda al collo*; *a questi lumi di luna*; *fare da Marta e da Maddalena*; *fare pari e patta*; *alzare le vele al vento*.

Sonidos repetidos en diferentes posiciones se aprecian en: *star seduto su due sedie* (d, e, s, u); *cadere dalla padella nella brace* (a, ,d, e, l); *mettere il coltello alla gola* (a, l, o, t); *contro corrente* (c, e, n, o, r, t); *con la coda dell'occhio* (c, o); *essere più tondo dell'o di Giotto* (o); *spremere come un limone* (m); *Alla larga* (a, l); *mettere alle strette* (e, t); *essere la Verità rivelata* (ve, ri, ta, la)[3]; *ormai la frittata è fatta* (a, f, t).

Cabe señalar que la mayoría de los fraseologismos en los que se aprecia la figura retórica de la aliteración son también ya mencionados binomios. También la aliteración, como cualquier figura de repetición, es un importante factor adicional de cohesión y compactación entre dos términos en contacto.

2.4. *Derivatio*, iteración

Entre los fraseologismos es posible encontrar aquellos cuya estructura está caracterizada por la repetición de dos lexemas, de los cuales uno contiene morfemas derivativos (Mayoral, 1994: 106-107; Spang, 1984, 158-159) o por la iteración de la misma palabra (Mayoral, 1994: 109-110). Al primer grupo pertenecen unidades cuyos componentes comparten una base léxica común con la sufijación o prefijación de uno de los elementos, como se puede apreciar en las unidades recaudadas: *batti e ribatti*; *fare il pelo e il contropelo*; *lasciare il certo per l'incerto*; *dai e ridai*; *fare e disfare*; *flussi e riflussi*; *fritto e rifritto*; *essere più realista del re*; *lacci e lacciuoli*; *andare dal letto al lettuccio*; *fare figli e figliastri*.

La iteración de la misma palabra se da en: *a mano a mano*; *da uomo a uomo*; *colpo su colpo*; *a goccia a goccia*; *pian piano*; *man mano*; *il fior fiore*; *lì per lì*; *dai e dai*; *far a giova giova*; *dire pane al pane e vino al vino*.

Cabe mencionar que la mayoría de los fraseologismos aquí mencionados pertenece también al grupo de los binomios.

2.5. Paronomasia

En la base de algunas locuciones están los juegos paronomásticos. Paronomasia es la vecindad de palabras fónicamente parecidas, independientemente del parentesco etimológico, pero diferentes en cuanto a significado (Spang, 1984: 156-157): *spendere e spandere*; *volere o volare*; *onori e oneri*; *capire fischi per fiaschi*; *non avere né arte né parte*; *dalle stalle alle stelle*; *prendere Roma per Toma*; *volente nolente*

2.6. Apofonía

De forma más bien esporádica en la configuración de los fraseologismos interviene la apofonía consistente en alternar vocales de una misma secuencia: *di riffa o di raffa*; *fare a ruffa raffa*; fare *berlicchi e berlocche*; *così o cosà*; *a ghirigoro*.

2.7. Mezcla de figuras

Muy frecuentemente en una sola unidad fraseológica se concentra el juego de diferentes recursos fónicos de los que hemos hablado antes: *fare a bocca e borsa* – aparte de la

---

[3] En este caso se trata de un anagrama (véase Mayoral, 1994:74).

aliteración la locución presenta la misma disposición rítmica y asonancia perfecta (o, a); *non stare né in cielo né in terra* – la disposición rítmica está reforzada por la repetición de los elementos *né, in* y la asonancia imperfecta.

Los procedimientos de configuración material de la expresión que acabamos de mencionar suelen pasar desapercibidos en el acto comunicativo, ya que en la codificación y la decodificación de un mensaje lingüístico se suele fijar la atención en primer lugar en el contenido y la gramaticalidad (Zuluaga, 1980: 115). Sin embargo, la función que por su carácter iterativo desempeñan el ritmo, la rima, la aliteración, paronomasia, la simetría, etc. resulta primordial en la creación de vínculos de cohesión entre los miembros de la expresión. Por otro lado, la estructura artificiosa que es la repetición, en sus diferentes formas, constituye un recurso mnemotécnico nada despreciable para fijar y codificar la unidad fraseológica.

3. Tipos de relaciones entre los aspectos fónico y semántico de los fraseologismos

Ahora bien, es verdad que gran parte de las unidades fraseológicas no presenta ningún tipo de artilugios retórico-fónicos y la base de su motivación es puramente semántica. Sin embargo, existe un grupo de locuciones en las cuales entre el aspecto fónico y semántico de sus componentes se establece una especie de relación. Entre ellos destaca el grupo de los binomios, cuya estructura, como ya hemos visto, es muy propicia a acoger diferentes tipos de artificios sonoros.

En fraseologismos como *prendere lucciole per lanterne*; *sano e salvo*; *non avere né arte né parte*, se puede apreciar un juego equilibrado de los dos aspectos. Entre los lexemas se instaura una relación semántica lógica y transparente, que al mismo tiempo se ve reforzada por las figuras fónicas. Otros ejemplos de este tipo serían *dalle stelle alle stalle*; *fare il finto tonto*; *in lungo e in largo*; *prendere fischi per fiaschi*; *onori e oneri*, etc.

En el segundo grupo el acoplamiento de dos o más términos viene dictado meramente por los rasgos fónicos que prsentan. Su motivación semántica se ve relegada a un segundo plano, si no es que quede quebrantada por completo a nivel sistémico. La creación y cohesión de la unidad *volere o volare* se sustenta en primer lugar en la aliteración y consonancia. Sólo tras la fijación de la formación se produce, como consecuencia de ella, una especialización semántica de sus componentes. Comprárense también *o mangi la minestra o salti la finestra*; *tra il lusco e il brusco*; etc.

Por último, señalaremos la existencia del grupo de fraseologismos donde la búsqueda de efectos fónicos se convierte en su única razón de ser, un verdadero juego, que lleva a la formación de creaciones léxicas caprichosas - muchas veces debidas a la desfiguración de palabras existentes - que fuera de la determinada locución no funcionan de manera autónoma en el sistema, como es el caso de *Toma* en *promettere Roma e Toma*. Aquí el factor semántico está en un primer momento excluido por completo de este juego y sólo después, en apoyo a las figuras de antonimia o sinonimia las "neoformaciones", palabras idiomáticas o diacríticas, adquieren valores semánticos (*così o cosà*; *far berlicche o berlocche*; *parlare in quinci e squinci*)[4].

---

[4] Véase para este fenómeno en español, García-Page (2008:360-361).

4. Desfiguración fónica de grupos léxicos latinos

Las palabras idiomáticas motivadas fónicamente no sólo son el fruto de transformaciones caprichosas forjadas sobre la base del primer elemento dentro de la pareja binómica. Un cierto número de unidades fraseológicas ha surgido como resultado de la desfiguración fónica de grupos léxicos latinos. Este hecho se explica porque el latín ha sido la lengua oficial utilizada en la liturgia de la Iglesia Católica durante varios siglos hasta que, bien entrado el siglo XX, el Concilio Ecuménico Vaticano II (que se celebró entre los años 1962-65), sustituyó al latín por las lenguas vernáculas. El pueblo fiel, ignorante del latín, pero expuesto a oír ciertas fórmulas repetidas veces durante la celebración de los oficios, al no ser capaz de segmentar ese *continuum fónico* en formas léxicas, lo interpreta de manera libre y disparatada dando pie a nuevas creaciones. Estas adaptaciones populares de una palabra o un grupo de palabras latinas se pueden documentar también en otros idiomas europeos, por ejemplo en español, en la expresión: *de bóbilis bóbilis* (*de vobis, vobis*, fórmula que utilizaban los mendigos para pedir limosna) (Buitrago, 2007: 179). [5]El resultado de deformaciones de este tipo en italiano son los siguientes fraseologismos: *andare in visibilio* o *mandare in visibilio* – entusiasmarse o entusiasmar a alguien, embelesarse o embelesar. El origen de la expresión *in visibilio* se halla en el comienzo del Credo cristiano: *Credo in unum Deum, patrem omnipotentem, factorem caeli et terrae, visibilium omnium et invisibilium*, donde el término *invisibilium*, la forma del genitivo plural de *invisibilis*, ha sido separado en dos elementos *in visibilio*, adquiriendo el valor semántico equivalente a gran número de cosas, cosas maravillosas, increíbles, emocionantes (Pittàno, 1992: 29; Sabatini, Coletti, 2006: 2984; Dogliotti, Rosiello, 1997: 1995).

El fraseologismo *andare a maravalle / maravalde*, hoy en desuso, equivalente a morirse, es la adaptación vulgar de un pasaje del canto *Libera me, Domine*, en la liturgia de difuntos: *Dies illa, dies irae, calamitatis et miseriae, dies magna et amara valde [Día aquel, día de ira, de calamidad y miseria, día grande y muy amargo]* donde la parte final *amara valde*, ha sido fundida en *maravalle* con el aféresis de la vocal *a* y la asimilación progresiva del grupo consonántico *ld*, aunque existe también la variante, *maravalde*, en la cual no se produjo la asimilación (Dogliotti, Rosiello, 1997: 1030; Pittàno, 1992; 26; Quartu, 2000: 288). Con *maravalle* o *maravalde* se indicaría entonces el lugar donde va aquel que muere, siguiendo el esquema de otros fraseologismos que significan fallecer y que están compuestos por el verbo *andare* y el complemento circunstancial de lugar: *andare all'altro mondo*; *andare al mondo di là*; *andare al mondo dei più*; *andare all'aldilà*; *andare alle ballodole*; *andare al macello*; *andare a porta inferi*; etc. No está excluido que en la creación de la variante asimilada *maravalle* haya también influido el componente semántico del lexema *valle*, existente en el sistema.

El mismo significado tiene la unidad fraseológica *andare a patrasso*, donde el término *patrasso* es el resultado de la derivación fónica del acusativo plural *patres* presente en la fórmula latina procedente de la Biblia: *ire ad patres* – ir a los antepasados, morir. La derivación consiste en la adición de la sílaba epitética *so* con la geminación del sonido *s* y en la sustitución de la vocal *e* por *a*, con lo que se produce la repetición de la misma vocal de la primera sílaba (Dogliotti, Rosiello, 1997: 1260; Pittáno, 1992: 27; Quartu, 2000: 380; Sabatini; Coletti, 2006: 1861).

---

[5] Para más ejemplos en español véase García-Page (2008:360).

También en la expresión *Qui sta / Ora viene il busilli(s)* – Aquí está la dificultad – el término *busilli(s)* es la corrupción de un grupo léxico latino *in diebus illis* - en aquellos días - con el cual comienzan muchos episodios del Evangelio (Buitrago, 2007: 270; Dogliotti, Rosiello, 1997: 263; Pittàno, 1992: 242; Sabatini, Coletti, 2006: 356).

Existen por fin fraseologismos en cuyo origen están las expresiones del latín no necesariamente eclesiástico, como *promettere Roma e Toma*; *prendere Roma per Toma*; *fare il nesci*; *valere un ette*, etc. En *promettere Roma e Toma* - "prometer el oro y el moro", el segundo término del binomio *Toma* podría haber surgido como fusión de la conjunción *et* y el pronombre *omnia* de la unidad latina *promittere Romam et omnia* (*prometer Roma y todo*) con la intermediación de un proceso de asimilación asonántica con el primer componente del binomio *Roma* que provoca la caída del grupo silábico *ni*. Lo mismo se refiere a la unidad *prendere Roma per Toma* - tergiversar, tomar el rábano por las hojas (Pittàno, 1992: 239; Quartu, 2000: 453). En *fare lo nesci*, *nesci* viene de la segunda persona singular del indicativo *nescis* del verbo *nescire* – no saber (Dogliotti, Rosiello, 1997: 1146; Pittàno, 1992: 50; Quartu, 2000: 322; Sabatini, Coletti, 2006: 1674). *Valere un ette* – donde *ette* viene de la conjunción latina *et* con la sílaba epitética *te* y la expresión indica valer poca cosa (Dogliotti, Rosiello, 1997: 645; Pittàno, 1992: 203; Sabatini, Coletti, 2006: 922).

5. Conclusiones

A modo de conclusión recordemos que en las locuciones, al igual que en los refranes, aunque en menor medida, están presentes diferentes artilugios fónicos, entre ellos el ritmo, la rima, asonancia, consonancia, aliteración, iteración, apofonía, etc. Las figuras mencionadas están basadas en la repetición de algún elemento: un sonido, un lexema, una palabra, la disposición acentual, etc., repetición que es una de las fórmulas pragmáticas más eficaces en el proceso de la fijación y conservación de la unidad en la memoria colectiva.

Por otro lado, hemos podido observar que la motivación fónica, que en la mayoría de los casos actúa junto al aspecto semántico reforzando a este último, desempeña pues un papel secundario respecto a la faceta semántica (*andare d'amore e d'accordo*). Sin embargo, entre el caudal locucional italiano se hallan también casos donde el alineamiento de ciertos términos se puede explicar sólo por cuestiones fónicas, rima (*tra il lusco e il brusco*), paronomasia (*volere o volare*), etc. Otro tipo de motivación fónica es dado por algunas palabras diacríticas o idiomáticas. Las palabras diacríticas son unidades que no existen en el sistema de manera autónoma, sino que están encorsetados en unas estructuras determinadas: locuciones, refranes, etc. Aquí se encuentran por un lado, neoformaciones apofónicas (*così o cosà, non dire né a né ba,*) y por otro creaciones que son el resultado de la deformación de procedencia latina.

Cabe señalar por último, que el tipo de unidades fraseológicas que representa más artilugios fónicos, como hemos podido constatar a lo largo de la investigación, son los llamados binomios. Lo que no debe extrañar dada su específica estructura simétrica.

6. Bibliografía

BUITRAGO, A. 2007 *Diccionario de dichos y frases hechas*. Madrid: Espasa Calpe.
ČERMÁK, F. 2010 "Binomials: Their Nature in Czech and in General". In: J. Korhonen et al. (eds.), *Phraseologie global - areal - regional*. Tübingen: G.Narr Verlag: 309-315.
CORPAS PASTOR, G. 1996 *Manual de fraseología española*. Madrid: Gredos.
DI PIETRO, R. 2000 *Fonosimbolismo e vocalità poetica*. Arezzo: Helicon.
DIETZ, H.U. 1999 *Rhetorik in der Phraseologie*. Tübingen: Niemeyer.
DOGLIOTTI, M. & ROSIELLO, L. 1997 *Vocabolario della lingua italiana* (lo ZINGARELLI). Bologna: Zanichelli.
GARAVELLI, B. M: 1988 *Manual de retórica*. Madrid: Cátedra.
GARCÍA-PAGE SÁNCHEZ, M. 2008 *Introducción a la fraseología española. Estudio de las locuciones*. Barcelona: Anthropos.
MAYORAL, J. A. 1994 *Figuras retóricas*. Madrid: Síntesis, D.L.
PITTANO, G. 1992 *Frase fatta capo ha. Dizionario dei modi di dire, proverbi e locuzioni di italiano*. Bologna: Zanichelli.
QUARTU, B. M. 2000 *Dizionario dei modi di dire della lingua italiana*. Milano: Rizzoli
SPANG, K. 1984 *Fundamentos de retórica*. Pamplona: EUNSA.
SABATINI, F. & COLETTI, V. 2006 *Dizionario della lingua italiana* (DISC). Milano: Rizzoli. Larousse.
TURRINI, G. *et al.* (eds.) 1995 *Capire l'antifona. Dizionario dei modi did dire con esempi d'autore*. Bologna: Zanichelli.
ZULUAGA OSPINA, A. 1980 *Introducción al estudio de las expresiones fijas*. Frankfurt: Peter Lang.

EL NOMBRE PROPIO PROVERBIAL EN LA COMPARACIÓN ESTEREOTIPADA

Mario García-Page
UNED, Madrid

Abstract: The main aim of this paper is to study some stereotyped comparatives containing a proverbial proper name that points out their typically Spanish origin. These expressions are *más feo que Picio, más listo que Cardona, más tonto que Abundio, escribir más que el Tostado, tener más cuento que Calleja,* and *saber más que Lepe.*

Key words: similes, stereotyped comparisons, Spanish phraseology, proper names, onomastic idioms

1. Introducción

Las unidades fraseológicas no son sólo productos lingüísticos, sino que son también productos culturales. Son hechos culturales porque, directa o indirectamente, expresan la cultura de un pueblo o de una nación, manifiestan sus propiedades idiosincrásicas: su historia, sus habitantes, sus usos y costumbres, su religión, sus tradiciones, su folclore, sus ciudades o municipios y su arquitectura y paisaje, el idioma incluso...

Considerando que es fundamentalmente el léxico el componente lingüístico que puede describir mejor la cultura del pueblo, vamos a fijar nuestra atención en una de las estructuras léxicas posiblemente más llamativas o peculiares por la impronta / huella de fórmula proverbial que imprime / deja y el rango de prototipo asociado a la cultura de un pueblo que puede llegar a adquirir: el nombre propio de persona o antropónimo proverbial; más concretamente, el nombre propio que aparece en las comparativas estereotipadas. No cabe duda de que las expresiones que contienen un nombre propio proverbial, sea de persona, de lugar, de institución, etc., sea éste real o ficticio, están entre las más representativas y apropiadas para transmitir los valores culturales y pintar la sociedad de un periodo histórico. Locuciones y comparaciones fraseológicas como *hablar como Castelar, más bajito que el Fari de rodillas, viajar más que el baúl de la Piquer, más feo que el sargento de Utrera, tener más orgullo que don Rodrigo en la horca, como el alma de Garibay, más tonto que Perico el de los palotes, como Pedro por su casa, armarse la Marimorena, ver menos que Pepe Leches, más tonto que Pichote, tener más moral que el Alcoyano, irse por los cerros de Úbeda, estar entre Pinto y Valdemoro, estar en Babia, ser Jauja,* etc., amén de centenares de refranes que podrían citarse –en especial, los llamados refranes geográficos (*Quien fue a Sevilla, perdió su silla; En Miravete, mira y vete,* etc.)–, son nítidas manifestaciones lingüísticas de la cultura española, instrumentos de información cultural, indicadores intraculturales.

Hay, claro está, expresiones que contienen nombres proverbiales que informan de hechos interculturales o transculturales, que traspasan la frontera de un único pueblo o nación, como *más ladrón que Caco, más rico que Creso, más viejo que Matusalén, saber más que Calepino, ser más listo que Merlín, ser un Adonis, más feo que Esopo, tener más paciencia que el santo Job, más listo que Papús, armarse un Tiberio, el paso del Rubicón, pasar por las horcas caudinas, todos los caminos llevan a Roma...* Pese a carecer de señas de identidad específicas del pueblo español, estas expresiones podrían considerarse también indicadores intraculturales en la medida en que forman parte del acervo colectivo y son unidades de la gramática o la fraseología de la lengua española.

Junto con las expresiones idiomáticas con nombres propios proverbiales, existe un conjunto de frases que vierten información cultural a través esencialmente de sus constituyentes léxicos. Estos constituyentes léxicos pueden agruparse en campos léxicos, y corresponden a diferentes esferas o ámbitos de la realidad: el sistema monetario, la religión, las tradiciones, el folclore, los objetos de la vida cotidiana, el vestuario, los aperos de labranza, las profesiones, los juegos, etc. Dichos elementos permiten en algunos casos fijar la cronología, la clase de sociedad del momento, etc. Es el caso de locuciones como *estar sin blanca, pagar a toca teja, hacer la peseta, más largo que una peseta de hilo, ser más delgado que el canto de un duro, mirar la pela, valer cuatro perras (gordas), andar de zocos en colodros, irse de picos pardos, ponerse el mundo por montera, saltarse a la torera, a ojo de buen cubero, pintar menos que peón de caminero, tomar a alguien por el pito del sereno, haber moros en la costa, confundir las churras con las merinas, más contento que unas castañuelas, cantar las cuarenta, no dar pie con bola, más largo que un mayo, más chulo que un ocho, durar menos que un pirulí en la puerta de la iglesia, tener más granos que una paella, colgar el sambenito, más visto que el TBO, más aburrido que el NODO, dar más vueltas que la bola del telediario*, etc.

Entre los constituyentes léxicos que connotan la "nacionalidad" hispánica de la locución están las palabras idiomáticas o diacríticas. Son palabras genuinas o endémicas de la fraseología española, formas idiosincrásicas de lo español, como muestran las locuciones *en un santiamén, en un periquete, a traque barraque, ni oxte ni moxte, sin ton ni son, al tuntún, al alimón, a espetaperro, que si patatín que si patatán, en vilo…*

2. Comparativas estereotipadas con nombre propio de persona

Para la ocasión, hemos seleccionado las siguientes construcciones comparativas que contienen un nombre propio proverbial de carácter intracultural restringido a lo español, es decir, que designa un personaje de la cultura española: *más feo que Picio, más listo que Cardona, más tonto que Abundio, escribir más que el Tostado, tener más cuento que Calleja y saber más que Lepe*. Para el relato biográfico de estos personajes nos hemos servido de las principales obras de folcloristas y recopiladores de estas fórmulas proverbiales, que, a su vez, se han basado en otros autores u obras (José María Sbarbi, Vicente Vega, etc.), como, por ejemplo, José María Iribarren en *El porqué de los dichos*, M. Barrios en *Repertorio de modismos andaluces*, Doval en *Del hecho al dicho* y Luis Junceda en *Del dicho al hecho*, M. Candón y F. Bonet en *A buen entendedor*, Buitrago en *Diccionario de dichos y frases hechas* o Rafael Escamilla en *Origen y significado de las más usuales frases hechas de la lengua castellana*. De hecho, algunos de estos estudios no son nada originales, pues copian literalmente lo que otros antes han dicho.

2.1. Más feo que Picio

Todos los estudiosos coinciden en señalar que Picio es un personaje real de principios del siglo XX, un zapatero granadino, natural del pueblo de Alhendín, que, al volverse extremadamente feo (calvo, con picaduras y pústulas en la cara, etc.), se retiró a Lanjarón donde, para que no lo reconocieran, se tapaba la cara con un pañuelo; desacreditado en esta población, regresó a Granada, donde murió. En lo que no hay coincidencia es si la fealdad tiene su origen en los sufrimientos padecidos durante su encarcelamiento (Buitrago) o en la impresión o sorpresa que le causó el indulto en el último momento de la condena a muerte (Iribarren, Barrios, Doval, Candón y Bonet). Tampoco hay precisión a la hora de señalar si es un crimen o no la causa de la condena ni si es el autor real o sólo supuesto del crimen: "condenado a muerte por un crimen" (Doval), "condenado a muerte, según parece injustamente" (Buitrago), "el cual, por un delito que no precisan los informes, había sido sentenciado a la última pena" (Barrios), "fue condenado a la última pena" (Iribarren).

2.2. Más listo que Cardona

No todos los libros antes citados recogen esta expresión. El significado de la palabra *listo* es, al parecer, determinante para asociar la expresión con un personaje y acontecimiento o con otro. Para Iribarren, que critica la interpretación del diccionario académico, según la cual la voz *listo* es asimilada a la listeza o sabiduría, y para Doval, el significado de *listo* es el de «raudo», que entronca con la forma presta de huir de Castellón y refugiarse en la ciudad de Cardona (Barcelona) el vizconde de Cardona, amigo del infante don Fernando, al enterarse de que éste fue ordenado matar por su hermano, el rey Pedro IV de Aragón (1363). Esta versión es la única que ofrece también Buitrago. Sin embargo, los otros dos autores señalan, además, otro personaje histórico que permitiría vincular la palabra *listo* a la sabiduría; se trata del fraile Antonio de Fortch de Cardona, que, según Iribarren, en opinión de Grimaldi, era hijo del almirante marqués de Guadalete (valido de la reina Ana, madre del futuro rey Carlos II el Hechizado) y una mujer valenciana, y fue famoso por su belleza, ingenio, vasta cultura y tacto en los negocios.

2.3. Más tonto que Abundio

Siendo una de las comparaciones más comunes en la lengua española coloquial, no aparece recogida en la mayoría de los diccionarios o compilaciones de dichos y frases hechas (por ejemplo, no aparece en Iribarren, Barrios, Junceda, Escamilla, Candón y Bonet...). No hay certeza sobre la existencia real de este personaje proverbial. Buitrago sólo proporciona la información confusa e imprecisa de que "algunos afirman que el famoso Abundio vivió en Córdoba a principios del siglo XVIII y que su bien ganada fama se debe a que pretendía regar todo un cortijo 'con el solo chorrillo de la verga'".

2.4. Escribir más que el Tostado

La comparación hace referencia, según Iribarren, a Alonso Tostado, llamado Alonso de Madrigal, por haber nacido en Madrigal de las Altas Torres (Ávila), y *el abulense*, por haber sido obispo de Ávila. Vivió siendo rey Juan II de Castilla. Fue catedrático en la Universidad de Salamanca y asistió al Concilio de Basilea (1431). Murió en 1454 (aunque, según Doval, fue en 1453). En la descripción coinciden los demás autores. Buitrago añade que fue consejero del rey Juan II. El dicho alude realmente a la cantidad de libros que escribió ("sus obras publicadas en latín constan de veinticuatro tomos en folio, habiendo dejado otras muchas en castellano", Iribarren; Doval añade: "y otras tantas inéditas en ambos idiomas") y a su memoria prodigiosa ("era capaz de recitar sin equivocarse pasajes bíblicos extensísimos y toda la *Summa theologica*, de santo Tomás de Aquino", Buitrago).

Resulta curioso que, haciendo cálculos de las páginas que podría haber escrito de ser cierto lo que dice el epitafio en verso sobre su tumba, los autores no se pongan de acuerdo en la cifra exacta de pliegos escritos: 53880 (Iribarren, siguiendo a Rodríguez Marín); 55845 (Buitrago); 70225 (Cejador).

2.5. Tener más cuento que Calleja

Calleja es, como casi todos los indicados hasta ahora, un personaje histórico real, de carne y hueso, y no producto de la ficción. Todos los autores coinciden en señalar que este individuo se llamaba Saturnino Calleja Fernández (1855-1915) y fue autor de numerosos libros y, sobre todo, editor.

Calleja fundó la Asociación de Librería de España, y, luego, su propia editorial, en 1875. La mayoría de los libros editados era de orientación pedagógica o bien cuentos infantiles. Según Candón y Bonet, entre sus cuentos más conocidos están *Testigos con alas*, *El anillo de Giges*, *Las tres preguntas*, *El tesoro del Rey de Egipto*, *El traje de moda* y *Chin-Pirri-Pi-Chin*.

2.6. Saber más que Lepe

El sustantivo *Lepe* puede no designar el pueblo onubense, lugar paradigmático en la fraseología y folclore de la lengua española. Hay dos posibles teorías al respecto de esta expresión, aunque la mayoría de los autores apuesta por esta primera que ahora se relata.

Lepe es el primer apellido de Pedro de Lepe y Dorantes (Dirantes o Durantes, para otros autores), escritor y prelado nacido en Sanlúcar de Barrameda en 1641 y muerto en Arnedillo en 1700, obispo primero de Calahorra y luego de La Calzada a principios de 1687. Es autor de libros como las *Cartas Pastorales*, recopiladas y publicadas por Herrera y Graguera en 1720, y del *Catecismo católico*, que se hizo casi tan famoso en su época como el del padre Astete (1608).

Por su gran sabiduría y notoriedad, fue incluido en el *Catálogo de Autoridades de la Lengua*, de la RAE.

La incertidumbre sobre la autoría verdadera que da sustento a este dicho se cierne ante la opinión de otros estudiosos, como el historiador Pedro Voltes (en su obra *El reverso de la Historia*, 1993), quien sugiere que el nombre *Lepe* de la comparación hace alusión a Juan de Lepe, un famoso aventurero natural del pueblo de Lepe, nacido en el seno de una familia humilde, de quien se cuenta que, una vez establecido en la corte inglesa tras diversos viajes en ultramar y haberse granjeado la amistad del rey Enrique VII, fue capaz de ganar, gracias a su astucia e ingenio, la corona de Inglaterra en una apuesta de cartas. También se dice que sus restos reposan en el convento franciscano de Nuestra Señora la Bella.

3. Bibliografía

ARORA, S. I. 1977 *Proverbial comparison and related expression in Spanish*. Berkeley: University of California Press.
BARRIOS, M. 1991 *Repertorio de modismos andaluces*. Cádiz: Universidad.
BUITRAGO JIMÉNEZ, A. 1995 *Diccionario de dichos y frases hechas*. Madrid: Espasa Calpe.
CABALLERO y RUBIO, R. 1942 *Diccionario de modismos (frases y metáforas)*. Buenos Aires: Librería El Ateneo.
CANDÓN, M. y F. BONET 1993 *A buen entendedor. Diccionario de frases hechas de la lengua castellana*. Madrid: Anaya/Mario Muchnik.
DOVAL, G. 1995 *Del hecho al dicho*. Madrid: Ediciones del Prado.
ESCAMILLA, R. 1996 *Origen y significado de las más usuales frases hechas de la lengua castellana*. Madrid: Grupo Libro.
GARCÍA-PAGE, M. 1996 "Más sobre la comparativa fraseológica en español". *LEA* 18/1: 49-77.
GARCÍA-PAGE, M. 2008 "La comparativa de intensidad: la función del estereotipo". *Verba*, 35: 143-178.
GARCÍA-PAGE, M. 2008 "Propiedades sintácticas de la comparativa estereotipada en español". *Romanistische Jahrbuch* 59: 339-360-
GARCÍA-PAGE, M. 2008 *Introducción a la fraseología española. Estudio de las locuciones*. Barcelona: Anthropos.
GARCÍA-PAGE, M. 2010 "Aspects sémantiques de la comparative proverbiale espagnole du type *fuerte como un toro*" (en prensa).
IGLESIAS OVEJERO, Á. 1986 "El estatuto del nombre proverbial en el refranero". *RFR*, 4: 11-50.
IRIBARREN, J. M. 1995 [1955] *El porqué de los dichos. Sentido, origen y anécdota de los dichos, modismos y frases proverbiales de España con otras muchas curiosidades*. Pamplona: Gobierno de Navarra.
JUNCEDA, L. 1991 *Del dicho al hecho*. Barcelona: Obelisco.
RODRÍGUEZ MARÍN, F. 1899 *Mil trescientas comparaciones populares andaluzas*. Sevilla.

PONIENDO EN EVIDENCIA: AN ANALYSIS OF IDIOMATICITY IN LIGHT VERB CONSTRUCTIONS IN LATIN AMERICAN SPANISH

Louisa Buckingham
University of Nizwa, Oman

Abstract: This study of Spanish light verb constructions (LVCs), or *construcciones con verbo soporte*, examines the relative idiomaticity of the noun component of LVCs and discusses the relationship between idiomaticity and the degree of morphosyntactic fixedness of the construction. The examples analysed were extracted from a seven-million-word corpus of contemporary newspaper texts from seven Latin American countries, and were limited to constructions with light verbs dar, poner, tener and tomar. Results demonstrate that idiomaticity is not always a prerequisite for morphosyntactic fixedness and that even fully idiomatic LVCs may display degrees of structural variation.

Key words: Light verb constructions; newspaper language; formulaic language, idiomaticity

1. Introduction

This study examines the relationship between idiomaticity and morphosyntactic fixedness in selected light verb constructions (LVCs). The analysis is based on data extracted from a corpus of newspaper texts in Latin American Spanish comprising seven million words. In most language-specific studies of LVCs, introspective approaches have predominated to date, and previous research on Spanish LVCs[1] has not been an exception to this (Alonso Ramos, 2004; Blanco Escoda, 2000; Bosque, 2001; De Miguel, 2008); data-driven studies employing a contemporary corpus, such as Bustos Plaza (2005) and Buckingham (2009), are still a rarity.[2] Corpus-based descriptions of language have an advantage over intuition-based descriptions in that they are able to provide evidence of (*inter alia*) the relative frequency of particular formal features, dialectal differences, and creative uses of language. On occasion, corpus examples of language may run counter to intuition-based assertions regarding a structure's formal characteristics.

Following Pamies Bertrán's (2007) classification of fixed multi-lexical units, I consider LVCs to be a type of verb-noun collocation which contains a collocate (the light verb) with an idiomatic meaning. This idiomatic element distinguishes them from verb-noun collocations in which both components are semantically transparent (e.g. *pedir disculpas*). Within the

---

[1] LVCs are usually known in Spanish as *construcciones con verbo soporte* (Blanco Escoda, 2000; Romero Ganuza, 2007), *construcciones con verbo de apoyo* (Alonso Ramos, 2004; De Miguel, 2008), or *construcciones verbonominales* (Bustos Plaza, 2005); other denominations may also be found.

[2] The earliest corpus studies of light verb constructions I have identified are Dubský (1965), in which formal features of, what the author calls, *sintagmas verbo-nominales* are discussed using data from literary corpus (word-count not given), and Panzer (1968), who studied the equivalent structures in German (*Funktionsverbgefüge*) in a modest corpus of newspaper texts of just over 30,000 words.

category of idiomatic verb-noun collocations a further distinction can be made between verbs which are 'semantically tailored' (c.f. Allerton, 2001) and those which are desemanticised. In the former case, the collocate expresses a particular 'tailored' meaning in combination with a limited number of nouns (e.g. *levantar + embargo, entredicho* etc.). With respect to LVCs, however, the collocate is desemanticised[3]; its primary function is to enable the meaning of the noun to be expressed as an event or action, and it usually combines with a large number of nouns, often quite arbitrarily. Verb-noun combinations involving a light verb and an eventive noun are, thus, always partially idiomatic in that the verb expresses a figurative meaning. They may, however, also be fully idiomatic; that is, both components may be used idiomatically (e.g. *tomar tierra*)[4]. Some studies have treated these combinations as LVCs (e.g. in Alonso Ramos, 2004; Buckingham, 2009, among others), but the distinction between partially idiomatic and fully idiomatic LVCs has not been explored in the literature.

Pamies Bertrán (2007) discusses the co-occurrence of idiomaticity and morphosyntactic fixedness with regard to multi-lexical units. He demonstrates that fixedness does not necessarily imply idiomaticity, while conversely, all idiomatic multi-lexical units exhibit degrees of morphosyntactic fixedness. Whilst his analysis does not specifically address LVCs, it does focus on phrases and compound lexemes which function as a single lexeme, and collocations. While partially idiomatic LVCs (i.e. where the light verb is the only idiomatic component) correspond to idiomatic verb-noun collocations, as previously discussed, it is not clear how fully idiomatic LVCs (i.e. in which both the noun and verb are idiomatic) may be categorised. Given that these constitute a single morphosyntactic unit with a figurative meaning, it would seem that they more closely resemble idiomatic verb phrases, according to the classification proposed by Pamies Bertrán (2007), than idiomatic verb-noun collocations.

This study explores the relationship between morphosyntactic fixedness and idiomaticity; it uses corpus data to investigate the varying degrees of fixedness that accompany partially and fully idiomatic LVCs. To this end, an examination is undertaken of formal characteristics of frequently occurring LVCs which contain the light verbs *dar, poner, tener, tomar*. The results enable the identification of the relative frequency of occurrence of particular morphosyntactic features and provide an overview of the degree of formal variation possible with each example. The morphosyntactic features selected for analysis include verb form, distance between components, adjectival and relative clause modification, and determiner use, although other aspects (such as the nominalisation of LVCs) are discussed where relevant. This description of formal characteristics is followed by a brief discussion of the degree of idiomaticity expressed by the noun, as exhibited in corpus examples. Although brief mention is made of dialectal differences (the corpus comprises data from seven Latin American dialects), the relatively modest size of this corpus precludes an analysis of diatopic variation. The corpus does enable, however, an indication of the relative degree of frequency of LVCs in newspaper texts as a discourse genre.

The paper is structured as follows. In the following sub-section I provide a definition of LVCs which is used to identify corpus examples. Definitions of LVCs rarely coincide in the literature, and I concede *a priori* that the approach used here will inevitably differ in some

---

[3] On this point I differ from Allerton (2001), who considers the light verb (or thin verb as he terms it) "to be semantically tailored to fit the meaning of the base" (p.222).

[4] These examples are classified by Bustos Plaza (2005) as compound lexical units on account of their advanced stage of lexicalisation.

respects from that of other studies. This is followed by a brief description of the corpus and the methodology used to identify and extract LVCs. In section 3, selected morphosyntactic features and the idiomaticity of common LVC types is discussed. Section 3 ends with a general discussion, which is followed by the conclusion in section 4.

1.1 Definition of LVCs

Definitions of LVCs found in the literature vary but they are not usually language specific. This section draws on definitions for LVCs as formulated in studies in Spanish, Portuguese, Italian, German and English. Narrower definitions may differentiate LVCs from support verb constructions (e.g. Butt, 2003), or may restrict LVCs to constructions consisting of a light verb and noun complement, excluding constructions with a prepositional object such as *poner de manifiesto* (e.g. Bustos Plaza, [2005, 2006] calls these constructions *combinaciones atributivas*). Broader approaches may admit constructions with a copular verb (Allerton, 2001; Athayde, 2003; Blanco Escoda, 2000; Cattell, 1983; Pfleiderer et al., 2000), or nouns which are not eventive that would be treated here as verb-noun collocations (e.g. *poner la lavadora* in Martín del Burgo, 1998:183). Some scholars (e.g. Blanco Escoda, 2000:5) also include verb-noun collocations such as *practicar un deporte, soplar el viento*. The verbs contained in such combinations do not conform to the definition of a light verb used in this study. The approach taken in this study is as follows.

The central group of LVCs comprises constructions consisting of a light verb (also known as a support, function, desemanticised or delexicalised verb[5]) and a deverbal (or, more rarely, deadjectival, e.g. *tener la oportunidad*) noun. A clear semantic differentiation can be made between the verb when used as a full verb and a light verb. In contrast to its meaning when used as a full verb, the desemanticised nature of the light verb means that that noun is the central carrier of meaning within the construction. A light verb undergoes selectional restrictions and cannot usually be substituted for a synonym in the manner that a full verb may. For instance, *dar* as a full verb may be considered synonymous with *entregar* and an antonym of *tomar*. These semantic relations are not retained by *dar* as a light verb (e.g. *dar un beso, *entregar un beso, *tomar un beso*).

The noun is the principal carrier of meaning in the construction. In prototypical examples of LVCs, the noun is semantically transparent and is used with the same meaning in the LVC and in free combinations (e.g. *tomar control*). In most cases the noun arbitrarily selects its light verb collocate[6]. This gives rise to a potential lack of interlinguistic correspondence (e.g. *poner una queja; make a complaint*) and even the lack of an intralinguistic consistency. The light verb in *poner una queja*, for instance, is not predictable; other nouns semantically related to *queja* do not take this light verb (e.g. *hacer un reproche)*. Even nouns which share the same root may not always take the same light verb (e.g. *hacer una petición; interponer un pedimento*).

---

[5] See Hanks et al. (2006) for a discussion on terms used to refer to light verbs.
[6] Nevertheless, light verbs may combine with nouns from specific semantic sets (e.g. *dar + golpe, manotazo, cachete, bofetada*).

LVCs are a syntactic and semantic unit and can usually be replaced by a single verb. The relationship between the LVC and the corresponding verb may be one of four types[7]: there may be morphological and semantic correspondence (*poner una queja, quejarse*); the correspondence may be semantic but not morphological (*dar una clase, enseñar*); morphological but not semantic (*tomar medidas, medir*); or finally, the LVC may have no simple verb correspondence (*hacer una huelga*). With respect to the first type of correspondence, due to the polysemy of the simple verb, the LVC will usually correspond to only one of its meanings (Allerton, 2001:225; Alonso Ramos, 2004:131). For instance, *hacer una precisión* corresponds to *precisar* in the sense of "*fijar o determiner de modo preciso*" but not in the sense of "*ser necesario o imprescindible*"[8].

The conceptualisation of LVCs followed in this study includes constructions in which the noun is embedded in a prepositional phrase (e.g. *tomar en consideración*). In these examples, the preposition is also desemanticised, losing its original spatial reference (Allerton [2001] uses the term "thin" prepositions). In the following examples, the (a) desemanticised nature of the preposition '*en*' is contrasted with (b) its full meaning: (a) *el proyecto fue puesto en marcha;* (b) *puso el billete en su cartera.*

Considerable differences exist in the degree of morphosyntactic variation possible with individual LVCs. There may be restrictions on article use, limitations on modifiability by adjectives, a prepositional phrase or a relative clause. Word order may be invariable; and restrictions may exist on the noun functioning as the surface subject of a passive construction, or on the replacement of the noun by an interrogative pronoun. Conversely, some LVCs may admit these variations in structure.

2. Methodology

A large number of LVCs exist in both Spanish and English, but they do not necessarily occur frequently in corpora (c.f. Allerton [2001:30] and Stevenson et al. [2004:4]). An examination of the morphosyntactic or textual features of LVCs usually requires very large corpora, particularly if data on less frequent examples are sought.[9] As the focus of this study is limited to a selection of frequently occurring LVCs, a relatively modest corpus suffices. A seven-million-word corpus was compiled for this purpose from newspaper texts from seven Latin American countries: Argentina (AR), Chile (CL), Colombia (CO), Costa Rica (CR), Mexico (MX), Peru (PE) and Venezuela (VE). (The two-letter country abbreviation is used after all examples cited from our corpus to indicate origin.) Each country-specific sub-corpus totals just over one million words. The newspaper texts, comprising a broad array of registers (from sport through to the economy), were selected from the electronic version of newspapers published on-line between June 2007 and August 2009. In Buckingham (2011) a more detailed description of the corpus compilation procedure is provided.

---

[7] For a fuller discussion of this point, see Bustos Plaza (2005), Martín Mingorance (1998) or Pirea & Varela (1999).

[8] Meanings are taken from the online dictionary of the Real Academia Española (www.rae.es).

[9] Stevenson et al. (2004), for example, use Google as a data base rather than the British National Corpus (100 million words) in order to compile a sufficient number of types for particular LVC tokens.

Two verbs known be very frequent in LVCs (*dar, tener*) and two known to be less frequent (*poner, tomar*) were selected for this study. This variation in frequency was established in an initial study using a smaller corpus (1.4 million words) of written scholarly texts (Buckingham, 2008). The electronic corpus software WordSmith Tools 4.0 (Scott, 2004) was used to identify all LVCs with a common light verb. To this end, a file was loaded containing all grammatical forms of each light verb. The results were sifted through manually to separate LVC tokens from instances of idioms and other verb-noun combinations. Each LVC was tagged with an abbreviation representing the noun (as the main carrier of meaning), which subsequently facilitated the creation of frequency lists.

The selection of the most common LVC types for further analysis was guided by two criteria. Although frequency of occurrence was an important consideration, some of the most frequent types did not display sufficient morphosyntactic variation to warrant further analysis. For instance, *darse cuenta, tener en cuenta* and *tomar en cuenta* were largely invariable with regard to word order, distance between components, adjectival modification, determiner use, adjectival modification and number. In the case of *darse cuenta*, fixedness was also accompanied by idiomaticity (i.e. both verb and noun components were used figuratively; the meaning *percatarse* is not present in either the noun *cuenta* or the homologous verb *contar*). In the latter examples, the noun *cuenta* corresponds to one of the meanings of the homologous verb *contar* (e.g. "*Y cuente usted que saldremos a la calle...*") and can only be considered partially idiomatic. The types selected for further analysis were frequent and they displayed a degree of variation in form. These were the following: *dar cuenta, dar un paso, dar una repuesta, poner un ejemplo, poner énfasis, tener la oportunidad, tener una relación, tomar una decisión, tomar una medida, tomar posesión*. Four additional LVCs related (at least in form) to examples listed here are also briefly discussed: *dar paso, dar respuesta, tener oportunidad, tener relación*.

3. Results

The corpus contained 20,893 LVC tokens. Tokens with the light verb *tener* were most frequent (11,498), followed by *dar* (4809), *tomar* (2656) and *poner* (1930).[10] The most frequent types for each light verb in each sub-corpus are displayed in the Appendix. Due to space limitations, the results are limited to the first five positions of highest frequency. As can be deduced from these data sets, certain LVC types appear with high frequency across all sub-corpora. Interestingly, this is more likely to be the true of LVCs with *tomar* and *poner*, light verbs with a lower number of tokens, than with *tener* and *dar*, light verbs with a higher number of tokens. *Tomar una medida, tomar una decisión, tomar en cuenta, poner fin* and *dar cuenta* rank highly in all seven sub-corpora, while *poner en marcha, poner en riesgo* and *dar un paso* rank highly in all but one.

The results from this study permit a comparison of frequency of LVCs across different genres. This newspaper corpus contains almost twice as many tokens as a similarly-sized corpus of written scholarly texts compiled for a previous study (Buckingham, 2009). The corpus of written scholarly texts (comprising texts from both Peninsular and Latin American Spanish dialects) contained a total of 11,362 tokens, distributed as follows: *dar* (1663); *poner*

---

[10] Numbers in round brackets are used throughout this paper to refer to the number of occurrences of a particular LVC or light verb in the corpus.

(1625); *tener* (6899); *tomar* (1175). Interestingly, in contrast to the other three light verbs, the number of tokens for *poner* remained relatively stable in both corpora.

3.1 Analysis of selected morphosyntactic features
3.1.1 LVCs with light verb *dar*
3.1.1.1 Dar cuenta

Dar cuenta appears a total of 154 times in the corpus, occurring most frequently in Dar/AR (32) and Dar/MX (31), and least often in Dar/CR (11). The light verb appears with overwhelming frequency in the third person singular present (85) and past (26) tenses. The first person appears only twice (in plural: *dimos*). Little variation is found in the noun phrase. Adjectival modification appears only twice [1], [2][11]. Though extremely infrequent, *dar cuenta* may appear with a determiner (2) [2], [3] or in plural (2) [4], [5].

[1] Pero solo excepcionalmente los medios **dan cuenta** detallada de las votaciones. (Dar/PE)
[2] "Todos son dignos", lanza antes de partir a **dar su cuenta** municipal. (Dar/CL)
[3] Zaldívar, inicia la ceremonia pidiendo permiso a la sala para que la Presidente **dé su cuenta** del presente año y ofrece la palabra a la Mandataria. (Dar/CL)
[4] "Estoy disponible a **dar cuentas** aquí y dónde tenga que **darlas**", manifestó. (Dar/CL)
[5] "Carlos Salinas es del PRI... por ello creo que es ese partido el que debe ser sometido a juicio y **dar cuentas** de sus gobiernos", señaló Martínez. (Dar/MX)

3.1.1.2 Dar el/un paso

Dar el/un paso appears a total of 179 times in the corpus, occurring most frequently in Dar/CL (38) and Dar/CR (33), and least often in Dar/VE (13). The light verb appears in a great variety of forms, with the most frequent being the infinitive (33), and the third person in present (13) and past (25) tenses. The present continuous (*está dando pasos*) is surprisingly frequent (16), and the past participle form, as seen in [6], is not uncommon (6).

[6] Gracias **al paso dado** ayer, los ticos se meten por quinta vez en unas semifinales de la Copa. (Dar/CR)

The noun appears in both singular and plural forms, although the singular is more frequent. Whereas a determiner is optional with a plural noun, the singular noun requires a determiner. (*Dar paso* with no determiner is a different LVC; see the discussion below.) The single occurrence of *dar el paso* with no determiner [7] appears within the title of a newspaper article, and the determiner has been omitted from *paso* and other nouns in the sentence (*congreso, ingreso*) for the sake of economy of style. This reinforces the importance of examining context when using corpus examples to generate descriptions of use.

---

[11] Numbers in square brackets refer to examples provided in this paper of the concordance line containing the LVC under discussion.

[7] Congreso **da** primer **paso** para aprobar ingreso de Venezuela a Mercosur. (Dar/AR)
The order of the light verb and noun is flexible, as examples [8]-[10] illustrate, and no distinct preference for order is discernable in this corpus. This flexibility facilitates the formation of passive [8] and relative clause [9] structures. The light verb and noun components may appear at some distance from each other, although only four examples occur in the corpus where five words or more separate the two components [8]-[10]. (Sinclar [1991] considers a distance of up to four words between collocational components to be usual.)

[8] **Los** primeros **pasos** "preventivos" para atajar "las vulnerabilidades" del régimen ya **fueron dados** a través de las inhabilitaciones de los opositores que puntean en las encuestas, como Leopoldo López y Enrique Mendoza. (Dar/VE)
[9] Tras firmar el convenio de constitución de Petroandina, Chávez recalcó que es solo "**el** primer **paso** de los mil" que su país y Bolivia deben **dar** juntos. (Dar/MX)
[10] **El** primer **paso** en la búsqueda de recuperar la soberanía tributaria, en Colombia, **lo dio** el alcalde de Barranquilla. (Dar/CO)

A further factor evidencing the combination's high degree of compositionality is the frequent occurrence of adjectival modification of the noun. Almost half of all examples carry an adjective (93 in total appear), and in some cases the noun is modified twice [11], [12]. The adjective may in turn be modified by an adverb [13].

[11] Aseguró que su gobierno sigue "**dando pasos** firmes y decididos en el combate a la criminalidad y a la delincuencia en el país. (Dar/MX)
[12] Sebastián Piñera **dio un paso** necesario y fundamental, al empezar a separar formalmente sus intereses económicos y políticos. (Dar/CL)
[13] Algunos sostienen que Fernández podría **dar el paso** políticamente arriesgado de acordar con los tenedores de bonos que no entraron en la reestructuración de la deuda soberana para reducir los costos financieros del país. (Dar/CL)

Dar un paso displays considerable morphosyntactic variation. In all examples in this corpus, however, the action expressed by the noun, *"movimiento al andar"*, is purely metaphoric as no actual physical movement is involved; as a constituent of an LVC, *paso* expresses the meaning *"adelantamiento que se hace en cualquier situación"*[12].

Related in form to *dar un paso*, *dar paso* appears 59 times in the corpus. It displays a high degree of morphosyntactic invariability: the order of components is fixed, the article is absent and no modification of the noun occurs. In the majority of cases, the noun is used metaphorically and expresses the meaning of *"permitir el paso o el acceso"*[13] in an abstract rather than literal sense (as seen in [14]).

[14] La Conferencia Mundial contra el racismo celebrada en Durban, Sudáfrica en 2001 **dio paso** al reconocimiento formal de los afrodescendientes en la región. (Dar/MX)

---

[12] Real Academia Española (www.rae.es).
[13] Real Academia Española (www.rae.es).

3.1.1.3 Dar la/una respuesta

Dar la/una repuesta appears a total of 56 times in the corpus, most frequently in Dar/VE (22) and least often in Dar/AR (3). The light verb occurs most frequently in the infinitive (20) and the third person in present (7) and past (16) tenses. Other forms also occur, albeit in reduced numbers: the first person plural in present (1), past (2) and future (1) tenses, and first person singular in past tense (1). The noun *respuesta* appears with equal frequency with the definite and indefinite article and may appear without a determiner when the noun is in plural [15].

[15] Indignado por las medidas tomadas por el gobierno, comenzó a **dar respuestas** a las decenas de llamadas de los turistas argentinos. (Dar/AR)

The usual order of components (V+N) may be reversed, giving greater prominence to the noun [16]. This operation may lead a greater distance between components than five words [17].

[16] Uno se pregunta si CNN se presta a esos juegos mágicos pero **la respuesta la dio** el mismo Chávez al denostar todo el tiempo a la CNN. (Dar/CR)
[17] **La respuesta** que mi admirado amigo Gaetano Pandolfo **ha dado** a las observaciones que hice sobre un artículo suyo, es una especie de invitación a que discutamos la persona de don Oscar Arias. (Dar/CR)

Adjectival modification of the noun is relatively frequent. Of the 25 adjectives appearing with this LVC, some are cases of multiple modification; [18] is an unusually complex example. While the adjective usually follows the noun, it may also precede it [19]. Finally, the noun may appear as a complement of a quantifying noun phrase [20].

[18] El comisario general Trosel señaló: "**dimos una respuesta** rápida, oportuna, efectiva y eficiente en un hecho en el cual cuatro jóvenes venezolanos perdieron la vida". (Dar/VE)
[19] Medité por unos segundos, antes de **dar una** apresurada **respuesta** y le dije: 'Todavía no'. (Dar/CO)
[20] Dijo que su propuesta puede **dar parte de** la respuesta al tema de las asimetrías tan marcadas que existen en la región. (Dar/MX)

Dar la/una respuesta contrasts syntactically and, to some extent, semantically with *dar respuesta*. This LVC does not admit a determiner and the noun is always in singular; adjectival modification, while not frequent, is possible, however. Semantically, the difference is not always clear cut, however. Various examples of *dar respuesta* with adjectival modification occur in the corpus which, semantically, closely approximate *dar la/una respuesta* [21] - [23].

[21] Consideró "insuficientes" las explicaciones de ambos ministros al considerar que no **dieron "respuesta** satisfactoria" a las preguntas formuladas por el Partido. (Dar/PE)
[22] Ahora, esa emisora quedará fuera del aire porque no se le **dio respuesta** oficial a su trámite. (Dar/VE)

[23] El senado **dará respuesta** pronta a los interrogantes de la representante. (Dar/CO)

3.1.2 LVCs with light verb *poner*

3.1.2.1 Poner énfasis

The LVC *poner énfasis* appears 53 times in the corpus, occurring most frequently in Pon/CL (15) and least frequently in Pon/CR (1). The light verb occurs with almost equal frequency in present (18) and past (19) tenses, with the infinitive form also well represented (8). A limited number (15) and variety of adjectives modify the noun: *mayor, especial, igual, inmediato, creciente*. The adjective may appear in the pre- or post-modifying position [24], [25].

[24] Para ello, se **pondrá** especial **énfasis** en el reforzamiento de las estructuras sociales básicas. (Pon/MX)

[25] Recuperar el control pleno en territorios endémicamente afectados por las actividades delictivas, **poniendo énfasis** especial" en el reforzamiento de las estructuras sociales básicas. (Pon/MX)

The corpus contains twelve tokens of this LVC with a singular noun (no instances of plural occur) with an article (only one of which is the indefinite article). In most cases involving the definite article, the noun precedes the verb [26]. Other forms of determiner are used such as *tanto, mucho* and *demasiado* [27]. The corpus contains only one token in which the noun without a determiner precedes the verb [28]; rather, the adjective *igual* is used, which (unlike *mismo*), obviates the need for a determiner. Of the eleven cases in which the noun precedes the verb, five are cases of constructions with *estar*, as seen in [26].

[26] **El énfasis estaría puesto** en la celebración de la literatura y no en el legítimo incentivo de las transacciones comerciales. (Pon/CL)

[27] Y también incomprensible que el Gobierno, que tanto **énfasis pone** en la seguridad, ignore esa iniciativa ciudadana. (Pon/CO)

[28] Igual **énfasis puso** al recordarnos que "los derechos humanos surgen de nuestra razón de ser peruanos" (Pon/PE)

Poner énfasis admits considerable morphosyntactic variation. The noun is semantically transparent and its meaning corresponds to that of the related verb *enfatizar*. The light verb is the only idiomatic constituent of this LVC.

3.1.2.2 Poner el/un ejemplo; poner como ejemplo; poner de ejemplo

Viewed as a group, these constructions appear 47 times in the corpus: *poner el/un ejemplo* (14); *poner como ejemplo* (30); *poner de ejemplo* (3). Variation in tense and person is equally represented: the third person singular in present (13) and past (18) tenses is still the most common verb form, together with the infinitive (7), but the first person singular (4) and third person plural (1) also appear. In the case of *poner el/un ejemplo*, both definite (6) and indefinite (8) articles occur. A plural noun appears only occasionally in the cases of *poner como ejemplo* (2) and *poner el/un ejemplo* (2), and only two cases of adjectival modification (*buen* and *verdadero*) occur across all forms [29]. *Poner el/un ejemplo* is also the only variant which admits modification by a relative clause, as illustrated in example [30].

[29] El gobierno de México **ha puesto como** <u>buen</u> **ejemplo** la cooperación con Petrobras en materia energética. (Pon/MX)

[30] Es fácil comprender que todos **los ejemplos** que **pongamos** nos demuestran una y otra vez la raíz emocional de las discusiones. (Pon/PE)

Poner un ejemplo and its variants admit varying degrees of morphosyntactic variation. The noun is semantically transparent and its meaning is closely related to the verb *ejemplificar*. The light verb is the only idiomatic constituent of this LVC.

3.1.2.3 Other LVCs with *poner*

Other frequent LVCs with *poner* (*poner fin, poner en marcha, poner a disposición, poner en riesgo*), exhibit little morphosyntactic variation across all sub-corpora. *Poner fin* (137) displays almost complete invariability: the order of components is fixed and a determiner or adjectival modification are absent. LVCs with a prepositional complement are very common with *poner*; this structure displays a high level of fixedness and adjectival modification is rare. Of the 67 examples of *poner a disposición* only one case of adjectival modification occurs (*entera*); none occurs with *poner en marcha* (279). This LVC, however, occurs relatively frequently in the nominalised form *puesta en marcha* (94). Although not present in this corpus, nominalised forms are possible with other examples of *poner* + prepositional complement, such as *la puesta en peligro, la puesta en riesgo, la puesta a disposición*. Some LVCs with a prepositional complement exhibit greater formal flexibility; for example, in the case of *poner en riesgo* and *poner en peligro* the noun may precede the verb, although such examples are infrequent (e.g. *procederán contra la empresa por* <u>*el peligro en que puso*</u> *a los vecinos*). This is not possible with *poner a disposicion* or *poner en marcha* (e.g. **la marcha en que fue puesta el proyecto*).

With respect to the relative degree of idiomaticity of the LVCs cited here, the noun component expresses a closely related meaning in other contexts without the light verb (e.g. *evaluaron la marcha del proyecto*). In such cases, the light verb is the only component displaying idiomaticity.

3.1.3 LVCs with light verb *tener*

3.1.3.1 Tener la/una oportunidad

Tener la/una oportunidad appears 230 times in the corpus, most frequently in Ten/CO (50) and least frequently in Ten/AR (18) and Ten/CL (18). The light verb appears most frequently in the present third person plural form (31), but other tenses are well represented. It appears with similar frequency in the first person singular (4 present; 10 past) and plural (10 present; 3 past), although examples in third person are more numerous (22 present; 25 past). It admits a variety of determiners, the most frequent being the definite article. All sub-corpora contain a modest number of tokens in which the noun appears in singular without a determiner [31],

[32]. Little or no semantic difference is discernable between these examples of *tener oportunidad* and *tener la oportunidad* in [33].

[31] Aunque no preparé a Dayana Mendoza, **tuve oportunidad** de darle unos consejos. (Ten/VE)
[32] Los empresarios chilenos **tendrán oportunidad** de participar en mesas redondas sectoriales con sus pares. (Ten/CR).
[33] Ruiz **tendrá la oportunidad** de disputar la fase previa de la Champions. (Ten/CR)

The noun may appear in plural (40) and one occasion of relative clause occurs [34]. Adjectival modification of the noun is not uncommon (37), and most usually appears as a premodifier [35]. (Only five cases of the adjective in postmodifier position occur [43].) The indefinite article only occurs together with adjectival modification in this corpus [35], [36].

[34] No entienden la necesidad de millones de argentinos que no **tuvieron la oportunidad** que sí **tuvieron** otros de nacer en grandes centros urbanos. (Ten/AR)
[35] El gobierno **tiene** ahora **una** magnífica **oportunidad** para llamar a un diálogo abierto y constructivo. (Ten/MX)
[36] Los líderes del G8 **tuvieron una oportunidad** única que podría no volverse a presentar. (Ten/CO)

Based on the examples in this corpus, *tener oportunidad* appears to be a variant of *tener la oportunidad* which exhibits a greater degree of morphosyntactic fixedness. This is not accompanied by an increase of idiomaticity of the noun, however. In the case of both examples, the light verb is the only idiomatic component.

3.1.3.2 Tener la/una relación

Tener la/una relación appears 185 times in the corpus. It is equally well represented in all sub-corpora, occurring most frequently in Ten/CL (37) and least frequently in Ten/CR (20). The light verb occurs in a wide variety of forms, most frequently in the infinitive (49) and the third person singular present tense (48). The first person plural present tense is also relatively common (33). With regard to the noun phrase, both definite and indefinite articles occur, although the noun is frequently used in plural without a determiner (94). The noun may also appear as a complement within a modifying noun phrase [37]. Adjectival modification of the noun is frequent (138) and always occurs in this corpus when an indefinite article is used. Multiple modification of the noun is not uncommon [38]-[40]. Adjectives appear in both pre- and post-modifying positions and may in turn be modified by an adverb [40].

[37] Moyano negó que **tuviera** algún tipo de **relación** con los cambios de funcionarios y ministros del gobierno. (Ten/AR)
[38] **Tiene una** estrecha y permanente **relación** con el primer plantel. (Ten/CO)
[39] **Tenemos una relación** comercial bastante ínfima con Chile. (Ten/CL)
[40] Chile y Bolivia **tienen una** históricamente complicada **relación** bilateral. (Ten/CL)

Closely related in form to *tener una relación*, *tener relación* appears 46 times, most commonly in Ten/CO (10) and Ten/CR (10) and least frequently in Ten/MX (2). The light verb appears most frequently in the third person singular (24) and plural (14) present tense, followed by the infinitive (13). This token possesses a high degree of fixedness: the noun does not occur in plural, does not admit a determiner, and the order of components is usually fixed; [41] is the single exception to this in our corpus. Adjectival modification is possible, and the majority of the 19 occurrences are of *buena* (10) and *directa* (6). When carrying an adjectival modifier, semantically, this LVC appears to be interchangeable with *tener una/la relación* [42], [43].

[41] Deben hablarles también de sus compañeros de trabajo y qué **relación tiene** con ellos. (Ten/PE)

[42] Precisamente, el actor **tiene** muy buena **relación** con el director de la cinta. (Ten/CR)

[43] Este fenómeno en Venezuela se podría decir que **tiene relación** directa con la corrupción de los gobiernos de turnos. (Ten/CO)

In the case of both *tener una relación* and *tener relación*, the light verb is the only idiomatic element. The greater degree of fixedness of the latter type is not accompanied by increased idiomaticity of the noun.

3.1.4 LVCs with light verb *tomar*

3.1.4.1 Tomar la/una decisión

Tomar la/una decisión appears a total of 744 times, occurring most frequently in Dar/CL (146) and Dar/AR (131), and least often in Dar/PE (81). The light verb appears overwhelming in the infinitive (223), while the third person singular present (48) and past (101) tenses are also common. Overall, a wide variety of verb forms are found, with future tenses and subjunctive forms represented, although they are not necessarily numerous. Of interest is the frequency of the nominalised light verb (120), most usually in singular, as seen in [44]. This LVC displays considerable morphosyntactic variation: variation in determiner, number and in the order of components [45]-[47], pronominalisation of the noun [47] and modification by relative clause [46]. Adjectival modification occurs (57), although not with the frequency of other LVCs with a similar degree of compositionality. Only three cases occur in which the adjective precedes the noun [48]. The nominalisation of the light verb enables this also to receive adjectival modification [44], although this occurs only once. The light verb and noun almost always appear contiguously or within a distance of four words (see Sinclair, 1991); examples such as [45] where the distance is greater are rare in this corpus.

[44] En simultáneo con su esposa, Kirchner interviene cada vez más en **la toma de decisiones** diaria. (Tom/AR)

[45] **Las decisiones** sobre la incorporación a la Organización **son tomadas** en base a consensos. (Tom/AR)

[46] Chávez pudo distanciarse de **decisiones** delicadas que se **tomaron** en el país. (Tom/VE)

[47] **La decisión** fue autónoma, **la tomé** yo. (Tom/AR)
[48] Todos los gobiernos tienen problemas, cometen errores, **toman** <u>buenas y malas</u> **decisiones**. (Tom/CL)

Four examples occur where the noun appears within a quantifying noun phrase such as *una serie de* [49], [50].

[49] El actual fiscal Iguarán **tomó** <u>una serie de</u> **decisiones** que afectaron a muchos funcionarios del Gobierno. (Tom/CO)

[50] Sin duda, el eje de la definición interna del partido del sol azteca fue <u>el conjunto</u> de **decisiones que se tomaron** a partir del conflicto electoral del 2006. (Tom/MX)

This idiomaticity present in this LVC is limited to the light verb. The noun exhibits a close semantic correspondence to the homologous verb.

3.1.4.2 Tomar la/una medida

Tomar la/una medida appears 486 occasions fairly evenly across all sub-corpora. It occurs most frequently in Tom/AR (107) and Tom/MX (85), and least frequently in Tom/CR (35). The light verb appears overwhelmingly in the infinitive (157), while forms in third person singular and plural, in past and present tenses appear between 20 and 30 times. The noun appears frequently in plural without a determiner, but the definite article is common when the noun precedes the verb [51]. The indefinite article in singular (2) and plural (3) form is uncommon [52], [53]. The corpus contains five occurrences of the noun within a quantifying noun phrase [54].

[51] **Las medidas** anunciadas como parte del Plan Anticrisis profundizan el proceso recesivo y van en dirección contraria a <u>las</u> que **están tomando** otros países. (Tom/VE)

[52] Al no haberlo, venimos pidiéndole al Alcalde que **tome** <u>unas</u> **medidas** urgentes para blindar la contratación del metro de Bogotá. (Tom/CO)

[53] Pero ya en la segunda inspección pudo ver cómo la empresa había **tomado** <u>una</u> drástica **medida** para aminorar los efectos de la crisis. (Tom/CL)

[54] La Argentina **ha tomado** <u>una serie de</u> **medidas** de prevención y organización del sistema sanitario para el caso de ingreso del virus al país. (Tom/AR)

Adjectival modification of the noun is relatively frequent, with 150 occurrences within the corpus. The vast majority of examples are of post-modification, but pre-modification of the noun occurs on eight occasions [55]. Occasionally, the noun may be modified by two adjectives [56]. The most common adjectives are the following: *necesaria* (22), *preventiva* (12), *importante* (8). Other adjectives such as *adicional*, *drástica*, *pertinente*, *urgente*, *unilateral* appeared on fewer than five occasions.

[55] Añadió que "hay que **tomar** <u>nuevas</u> **medidas** para proteger aún más nuestro sector externo." (Tom/PE)

[56] Se deben **tomar medidas** <u>inmediatas y contundentes</u> para restablecer a Zelaya en el poder. (Tom/AR)

The meaning of *medida* does not correspond to the homologous verb *medir*, but may be equated with *disposición*. Unlike *dar cuenta* and *dar paso*, however, the noun *medida* retains this meaning also in other contexts (e.g. *las medidas de contención del gasto no fueron muy eficaces*). The light verb is the only idiomatic component of this LVC.

3.1.4.3 Tomar posesión

Tomar posesión appears 55 times in the corpus, most frequently in Tom/MX (21) and least frequently in Tom/CR (1). The light verb appears most commonly in the nominalised form as part of a compound noun phrase (22), as can be seen in [57]-[59]. The corpus contains one example of the nominalised light verb in plural [58]. Otherwise, the light verb appears most frequently in infinitive (14), and simple past third person singular (6).

[57] Casualmente ocurrió justo un día antes de **la toma de posesión** de Felipe Calderón. (Tom/MX)
[58] Espero que cerremos noviembre con **tomas de posesión** en todas las gobernaciones. (Tom/VE)
[59] Me uní a otros líderes de todo el mundo para celebrar la histórica **toma de posesión** del Presidente electo Funes. (Tom/VE)

This LVC evidences a high degree of morphosyntactic fixedness. The order of components is invariable, and the noun does not admit a determiner, variation in number, pronominalisation or adjectival modification. The corpus contains only one example of adjectival modification of the nominalised light verb [59]. Both constituents of this LVC are used idiomatically. The meaning of '*ocupar un cargo*' is not conserved by the noun in other contexts (e.g. **la posesión de Felipe Calderón fue el gran acontecimiento del año*).

3.2 Discussion

This analysis of morphosyntactic features of the more common examples of LVCs in our corpus has revealed a number of interesting aspects. Of the more syntactically flexible examples, such as *dar la/una respuesta, tener la/una relación, tomar la/una decisión*, the verb and noun components usually appear within a short distance of each other, if not contiguously; examples in which the intervening space is superior to four words are an exception. Thus, their potential to admit intervening elements is seldom realised, or only in a limited fashion. With the exception of *dar el paso* and *tomar una decisión*, these LVCs tend to appear in the unmarked word order of V+N. Further, despite admitting adjectival modification, this is not necessarily common (e.g. *tomar una decisión*). In the case of *tener relación* and *dar respuesta*, adjectival modification can have the effect in narrowing the semantic gap between these LVCs and their counterparts with a determiner (*tener una relación, dar una respuesta*). Some LVCs, particularly those with light verb *tomar* and *poner*,[14] appear regularly in nominalised form, particularly *tomar posesión* (22 of 55 occurrences), and *tomar una decisión* (120 of 744 occurrences) and *poner en marcha* (94 out

---

[14] The corpus contains 155 instances of nominalised LVCs with the light verb *tomar*, and 116 with light verb *poner*.

of 279 occurrences). Other LVCs which occur relatively frequently in the nominalised form but which have not been discussed here are *poner en funcionamiento* (15 of 38 occurrences), and *poner en libertad* (7 of 24 occurrences).

A high degree of morphosyntactic fixedness is often present where the LVC is fully idiomatic. This was seen in the case of *tomar posesión, dar cuenta* and *dar paso*. In these cases, the meaning of the homologous verb (*poseer, contar, pasar*) is different from the meaning expressed by the LVC, and the noun (*posesión, cuenta, paso*) is not used with the same meaning in other contexts. At the most, the noun could be said to express the action designated by the verb in a metaphorical sense. Both components of these LVCs can be considered to be idiomatic. Fixedness is not always accompanied by idiomaticity, however; in the case of *tener relación* the noun is closely related semantically to *relacionarse* and it occurs in other contexts with the same meaning. In some instances, a semantically related verb may not exist. The meaning of the noun in *tomar una medida* cannot be equated with that of the verb *medir*. The noun is used frequently in other contexts with the same meaning and is not idiomatic.

4. Conclusion

This study of LVCs in a seven-million-word corpus of newspaper texts examined the occurrence of both frequent and unusual examples with a view to providing a broad-ranging discussion on the morphosyntactic features of LVCs in Latin American Spanish. Almost 21,000 tokens were identified in our corpus; the most productive light verb proved to be *tener* and least productive *tomar*. A comparison of corpus results from this study and those from a previous study using a written scholarly corpus of the same dimension reveals that LVCs are considerably more common in newspaper texts than in scholarly writing. No difference was found in the order of frequency of the light verbs in the two studies, however.

The analysis undertaken of formal and semantic aspects LVCs began with an initial distinction between partially and fully idiomatic examples. While all LVCs are partially idiomatic on account of the desemanticised nature of the LVC, in some instances the noun, too, is used figuratively. The analysis undertaken in this study demonstrated that LVCs exhibiting greater morphosyntactic fixedness are not necessarily fully idiomatic. For example, despite the relatively high degree of morphosyntactic fixedness exhibited by *dar respuesta* and *tener oportunidad*, the nouns in these examples were not used figuratively. Corpus examples indicated that, in certain contexts, these LVCs can be used interchangeably with their respective homologous variant with a determiner. Conversely, in some fully idiomatic examples, such as *dar cuenta, tomar posesión*, idiomaticity does not imply complete morphosyntactic fixedness; even in these cases, degrees of structural variation are still possible, at least in the context of the genre used here, newspaper texts.

Appendix: List of most frequent LVCs for each light verb[15]

Dar
AR: dar cuenta 32; dar un discurso 12; dar una explicación 18; dar un paso 16; dar marcha atrás 16; dar muestras 11
CL: dar un paso 38; dar una señal 24; dar cuenta 16; dar un ejemplo 14; dar una respuesta 10
CO: dar un paso 28; dar cuenta 19; dar una orden 19; dar una respuesta 12; dar inicio 11; dar un resultado 10
CR: dar un paso 33; dar un resultado 25; dar una oportunidad 22; dar una razón 21; dar declaraciones 19
MX: dar cuenta 31; dar un paso 21; dar un resultado 21; dar detalle 16; dar un golpe 13; dar una oportunidad 13; dar origen 12; dar un impulso 12; dar una muestra 12
PE: dar un paso 30; dar cuenta 26; dar un resultado 21; dar una oportunidad 16; dar una explicación 16; dar un despliegue 13; dar un apoyo 11; dar una razón 11
VE: dar respuesta 22; dar cuenta 19; dar un golpe 18; dar un resultado 17; dar detalles 16; dar muestras 16; dar una respuesta 16

Poner
AR: poner en marcha 44; poner fin 35; poner en juego 23; poner en duda 20; poner en riesgo 20; poner énfasis 13
CL: poner en marcha 21; poner el énfasis 15; poner a disposición 15; poner de acuerdo 14 ; Poner en riesgo 14; poner fin 11; poner en duda 11; poner en peligro 7
CO: poner en marcha 35; poner fin 21; poner en riesgo 14; poner a disposición 11; poner en práctica 11; poner de manifiesto 9
CR: poner en práctica 21; poner en peligro 15; poner fin 13; poner en duda 11; poner en riesgo 11; poner a prueba 10
MX: poner en marcha 55; poner en riesgo 33; poner fin 31; poner a disposición 14; poner un ejemplo 14
PE: poner en marcha 22; poner a disposición 13; poner de acuerdo 11; poner fin 11; poner en riesgo 10; poner el énfasis 10; poner en peligro 8
VE: poner a la orden 16; poner fin 15; poner en peligro 12; poner en marcha 11; poner de manifiesto 10

Tener
AR: tener en cuenta 76; tener un problema 54; tener una relación 40; tener un impacto 30, tener un objetivo 25
CL: tener un problema 55; tener una relación 37; tener una capacidad 33; tener una posibilidad 25; tener acceso 24
CO: tener en cuenta 100; tener una oportunidad 50; tener una razón 38; tener acceso 34; tener una relación 31
CR: tener una capacidad 66; tener un problema 49; tener una oportunidad 40; tener una razón 29; tener una posibilidad 27

---

[15] The number following each LVC refers to the frequency of the LVC in the respective country-specific sub-corpus. Only the five highest ranking types are listed.

MX: tener un problema 55; tener acceso 52; tener una capacidad 44; tener una oportunidad 47; tener un impacto 34
PE: tener en cuenta 56; tener un problema 44; tener una relación 43; tener acceso 28; tener una capacidad 28; tener un efecto 20
VE: tener un efecto 45, tener una oportunidad 43; tener una capacidad 37; tener un problema 36; tener una relación 35

Tomar
AR: tomar una medida 107; tomar una decisión 131; tomar en cuenta 18; tomar nota 9; tomar conciencia 8
CL: tomar una decisión 146; tomar una medida 68; tomar en cuenta 31; tomar contacto 7; tomar la iniciativa 6
CO: tomar una decisión 95; tomar una medida 39; tomar conciencia 9; tomar en cuenta 8; tomar posesión 7
CR: tomar una decisión 96; tomar en cuenta 81; tomar una medida 35; tomar una acción 13; tomar una fotografía 11; tomar posesión 11
MX: tomar una decisión 110; tomar una medida 85; tomar en cuenta 49; tomar posesión 21; tomar una acción 19
PE: tomar una decisión 81; tomar una medida 71; tomar en cuenta 52; tomar el control 13; tomar una acción 11
VE: tomar una decisión 85; tomar una medida 81; tomar en cuenta 77; tomar una acción 20; tomar conciencia 9; tomar posesión 9

References

ALLERTON, D.J. 2001 *Stretched verb constructions in English*. Florence: Routledge.
ALONSO RAMOS, M. 2004 *Las construcciones con verbo de apoyo*. Madrid: Visor Libros.
ATHAYDE, Mª. F. 2003 *A estrutura semântica das construções com verbo-suporte preposicionadas do português e do alemão*. Unpublished doctoral thesis, Coimbra: Universidade de Coimbra.
BLANCO ESCODA, X. 2000 Verbos soporte y clases de predicados en español., *Lingüística Española de Actualidad*, 22(1), 99-117.
BUCKINGHAM, L. 2008 Spanish support verb constructions from a learner perspective. *Estudios de lingüística inglesa aplicada*. Universidad de Sevilla, 8: 151-179.
BUCKINGHAM, L. 2009 *Construcciones con verbo soporte en un corpus especializado*. Studien zur romanischen Sprachwissenschaft und interkulturellen Kommunikation, Vol. 60. Frankfurt am Main: Peter Lang.
BUCKINGHAM, L. 2011 *Poniendo de manifiesto:* Spanish light verb constructions in Latin American newspapers. *Corpora*, 6(2): 201-226.
BOSQUE, I. 2001 Sobre el concepto de 'colocación' y sus límites. *Lingüística Española de Actualidad*, 23(1): 9-39.
BUSTOS PLAZA, A. 2005 *Combinaciones verbonominales y lexicalización*. Frankfurt am Main: Peter Lang.
BUSTOS PLAZA, A. 2006 Combinaciones atributivas del tipo "poner en movimiento" y diccionario. In: M. Alonso Ramos (ed.), *Diccionarios y fraseología*, 89-100. Anexos de revista de lexicografía. A Coruña: Universidad de La Coruña.
BUTT, M. 2003 The light verb jungle. http://www.ai.mit.edu/people/jimmylin/papers/Butt03.pdf.
CASTILLO CARBALLO, Mª A. 2001 Colocaciones léxicas y variación lingüística: implicaciones didácticas. *Lingüística Española de Actualidad*, 23(1): 133-143.
CATTELL, R. 1983 *Composite predicates in English*. Sydney: Academic Press.
DANLOS, L. 1992 Support verb constructions: Linguistic properties, representation, translation. *Journal of French Language Studies*, 2: 1-31.
DE MIGUEL, E. 2008 Construcciones con verbos de apoyo en español. De cómo entran los nombres en la órbita de los verbos. *Actas del XXXVII Simposio Internacional de la Sociedad Española de Lingüística*, Pamplona: Servicio de Publicaciones de la Universidad de Navarra.
DUBSKÝ, J.F. 1965 Intercambio de componentes en las formas descompuestas españolas. *Bulletin Hispanique*, 67(7-4): 343-352.
HANKS, P, URBSCHAT, A. & GEHWEILER, E. (2006). German light verb constructions in corpora and dictionaries. *International Journal of Lexicography*, 19(4): 439-457.
ÍRSULA PEÑA, J. 1994 *Substantiv-Verb Kollokationen: Kontrastive Untersuchungen Deutsch-Spanisch*. Frankfurt am Main: Peter Lang.
LANGER, S. 2009 *Funktionsverbgefüge und automatische Sprachverarbeitung*. Munich: Lincom Europa.
LAPORTE, E., RANCHOD, E. M. & YANNACOPOULOU, A. 2008 Syntactic variation of support verb constructions. *Lingvisticae Investigationes*, 31(2): 173-185.
MARTÍN DEL BURGO, M. C. (1998). Tener, coger, poner y dar como verbos de soporte. *Interlingüística*, 9, 179-184.

MARTÍN MINGORANCE, L. (1998). Las unidades singtagmáticas verbales en inglés y en español. Metodología de análisis. In: A. Marín Rubiales (ed.), *El modelo lexemático-funcional. El legado lingüístico de Leocadio Martín Mingorance*, 19-31. Granada: Universidad de Granada.

MELERO, M., & GRACIA, O. (1990). Construcciones de verbo soporte. In: Álvarez Martínez (ed.), *Actas del Congreso de la Sociedad Española de Lingüística, XX aniversario*, vol. 2, (pp. 653-667), Madrid: Gredos.

PAMIES BERTRÁN, A. (2007). De la idiomaticidad y sus paradojas. In: Germán Conde (ed.), *Nouveaux apports à l'étude des expressions figées*, 173-204, Cortil-Wodon, Belgique: InterCommunications & E.M.E. (Collection *Proximités – Didactique*).

PANZER, U. (1968). Kompositionsbildung und Streckverben in der politischen Berichterstattung der Presse. *Muttersprache*, 97-122.

PIERA, C. & VARELA, S. (1999). Relaciones entre morfología y sintaxis. In: I. Bosque, V. Demonte, (eds.) *Gramática descriptiva de la lengua española*. Vol. 3, 4367-4422. Madrid: Espasa.

PFLEIDERER, B., RAFFA, M. & STROMBOLI, C. (2000). Funktionsverbgefüge im Italienischen. *PhiN* 13, 73-106.

ROMERO GANUZA, P. (2007). La delimitación de las unidades fraseológicas en la investigación alemana y española. *Interlingüística*, 17, 905-915.

SINCLAIR, J. (1991). *Corpus, concordance, collocation*. Oxford: Oxford University Press.

SCOTT, M. (2004). Wordsmith Tools 4.0. Oxford: Oxford University Press. Available online: http://www.lexically.net/wordsmith.

STEVENSON, S., FAZLY, A. & NORTH, R. (2004). Statistical measures of the semi-productivity of light verb constructions. In: *Proceedings of ACL-04 workshop on Multiword Expressions: Integrating Processing*, 1–8.

LÉXICO Y FRASEMAS FIGURADOS DEL ACEITE Y LA ACEITUNA EN ÁRABE MODERNO

Yara El Ghalayini
Mahdi Fendri
Universidad de Granada

Abstract: This paper aims at studying the notional domain of olive tree in the Arabic language (Tunisian dialect). The cultural impact of this tree is of high importance for research in semantics and figurative phraseology. We analyze here the figurative names of 21 Tunisian varieties of this plant.

Key words: Olive tree, agriculture, terminology, figurative language, metaphor, metonymy.

1. Introducción:

El cultivo del olivo es una de las actividades más antiguas que ha realizado el hombre a través de su historia. Esta planta se cultivaba hace ya 5000 años en la zona de Persia antigua y Mesopotamia (Loukas & Krimbas 1983). De allí se extendió por toda la cuenca mediterránea que hoy en día se considera como el ámbito principal de este cultivo (Rallo, 2005). El olivo contribuyó ampliamente al desarrollo de la civilización en esta región del mundo ya que ocupaba un lugar privilegiado, no sólo a nivel económico sino también a nivel cultural y espiritual.

El impacto cultural de este árbol se considera como un campo interesante para la investigación en lingüística y especialmente en fraseología, para lenguas como el español (Jurado, 2004; Pamies & Tutáeva 2010). Estas circunstancias animan a realizar trabajos lingüísticos y fraseológicos relacionados al ámbito oleícola en otras lenguas y culturas de la región mediterránea. En este contexto, el presente trabajo dedica su atención al campo nocional del olivo/aceite en la lengua árabe, más concretamente en un dialecto magrebí. Se ha estudiado el caso de Túnez ya que este país se considera como un país oleícola tradicional y es el segundo productor mundial de aceite de oliva fuera de la Unión Europea (Consejo Oleícola Internacional 2010). Allí el olivo ocupa la mayor parte de las tierras cultivadas y por lo tanto tiene un impacto socio-económico y cultural considerable (Jardak 2006).

En el presente trabajo se ha estudiado el simbolismo cultural subyacente de los nombres de las variedades de olivo utilizados por los agricultores en las distintas regiones de Túnez. Las variedades estudiadas pertenecen a una colección nacional que ha sido establecida tras un programa de prospección realizado en diversas regiones de Túnez (Trigui et al. 2006). Dicha colección ha servido de base para la publicación de un primer catalogo de variedades autóctonas de Túnez donde se especifican los caracteres agronómicos y morfológicos de cada una de ellas (Trigui et al. 2002). En este estudio, se propone analizar el sentido figurado de 21 nombres de variedades de olivo cultivadas en Túnez.

¿Que significa el término *variedad*? Dentro de la misma especie del olivo, cuyo nombre científico es *Olea europaea L.*, existe una multitud de variedades, llamadas también cultivares, que son unos tipos de olivos distintos que difieren genéticamente unos de otros. En el olivo, las diferencias entre variedades se manifiestan especialmente a nivel de los frutos (aceitunas), en términos de tamaño, forma, color, sabor etc.. o también se manifiestan en los árboles mismos, atendiendo a diferencias en la dimensión del árbol, su aspecto, su producción, su adaptación al frío o a la sequía etc. (Barranco et *al.* 2004). En base a esto los agricultores han ido seleccionando desde ya hace mucho tiempo los árboles más sobresalientes. Y entonces reproducían árboles idénticos que luego se van a llamar variedades (*Ibid.*). Más adelante, a cada variedad se ha atribuido un nombre según los rasgos que resultaban más llamativos para los agricultores. Estos nombres también se utilizan por los científicos a la hora de llevar a cabo sus trabajos de identificación, catalogación y conservación de las variedades, hoy en día existen en el mundo más de 2000 variedad de olivo (Rallo 2005).

2. El fruto

2.1. Metáforas (intra)vegetales

Existen varios grupos metafóricos en los nombres de las variedades dependiendo del contenido figurado presente en cada uno de dichos nombres. En primer lugar, se destacan los nombres que se basan en el fruto y precisamente en su forma, con la curiosa peculiaridad de que el nombre de un vegetal a menudo procede del de otro vegetal, de modo que el "dominio fuente" no es distinto del "dominio meta" en estas proyecciones.

El nombre تفاحي **toffahi** que significa en árabe "manzana" incluye una figuración que viene del hecho de que la forma del fruto de esta variedad recuerda la forma de un fruto de una otra especie del entorno que es la manzana. Entonces, los agricultores llaman a esta variedad **toffahi** porque, según ellos, la forma del fruto de este árbol se parece mucho a la manzana. El mismo tipo de figuración se destaca con el nombre de una otra variedad: انجاصي حشيشينة **injassi hchichina**, donde *hchichina* es el nombre de la zona, y *Injassi* significa en árabe "fruto con forma de pera". Existe también una variedad de una otra zona distinta situada en el sur de Túnez (La zona de Gafsa) que lleva exactamente la misma figuración: انجاصي قفصة **injassi gafsa**., también alusiva a la forma de pera. La misma metáfora ha sido utilizada independientemente en dos zonas completamente distintas.

Destaca otra variedad cuyo nombre incluye la imagen de otro vegetal basada en la forma del fruto, en este caso, el dátil. La variedad se llama شملالي بلحي **Chemlali balhi**, donde *balhi* significa "fruto con la forma de un dátil". Igual que en el caso destacado anteriormente, la misma figuración es utilizada por otros agricultores de una zona distinta del país. Efectivamente, existe una variedad en la zona de Sfax que se llama بلحي سيق **balhi Sig**, donde *balhi* hace referencia a la forma del dátil. El nombre figurado *injassi* se utiliza al mismo tiempo en las zonas de Sfax y Gafsa mientras que *balhi* se utiliza en las zonas de Sfax y Mednine.

2.2. Metáforas animales

Otro grupo de imágenes alude a ciertos animales presentes en el entorno del agricultor. En la zona de Kasserine, existe una variedad con el nombre منقار الرقمة **mingar el ragma** donde *mingar* significa "**pico**" y *ragma* designa a un buitre endémico de la región. La forma de este fruto evocaría el pico de este buitre autóctono de la región de Kasserine. También existe en la misma región una variedad llamada بيض حمام **bith hmem**, cuyo nombre significa "huevos de paloma", por su forma. En ambos casos, los nombres figurados populares se basan en rasgos relacionados con pájaros del entorno. En la región del Norte de Túnez, y precisamente cerca de la capital, se utiliza otro zoomorfismo para llamar a una variedad de aceituna. El nombre ناب جمل **nab jmal** significa "dientes de camello"..

2.3. Otras imágenes del fruto

Otros rasgos inspirados del entorno aparecen en estos nombres figurados. La variedad صوابع علجية **souabaa Algia** cuyo nombre significa en árabe "dedos de Algia" se cultiva en la zona de Kasserine. Algia es un nombre característico de la mujer campesina en Túnez. Entonces, para los agricultores de la región, los frutos de esta variedad recuerdan la forma de los dedos de una mujer (metáfora, anatómica antropomórfica). La variedad جمري بوشوكة **jemri bouchouka** cuyo nombre incluye dos figuraciones a la vez se cultiva en la región de Mednine; *jemri* significa "color del carbón encendido" y *bouchouka* significa "fruto con espina". Efectivamente, el fruto de esta variedad tiene como un pezón de color rojizo. En la zona de Sfax, existe una variedad llamada زربوط الوزير **zarbout Louzir**, donde *Louzir* es el nombre de la finca y *zarbout* significa "trompo".

2.4. Metonimias y antonomasias

Otro grupo de figuraciones, basadas en el aspecto del fruto, aluden a categorías mayores. Por ejemplo, la variedad الشهلة **ech-chahla** de la zona de Sfax, cuyo nombre significa "fruto bonito" (tiene un llamativo degradadado cromático y unos puntos, que parecen ornamentales, en su superficie). También ocurre en el nombre de la variedad كبيرة اللوزير **kbiret Louzir** originaria de la región de Sfax, *Louzir* es el nombre de la finca y *kbiret* significa "fruto grande" (por sus llamativas dimensiones). Lo mismo ocurre con otra variedad de la región de Sfax, cuyo nombre es خشينة سيق **khchinet Sig** (Sig es el nombre de la finca). Los agricultores utilizan palabra *kechinet* que significa "fruto gordo" para distinguir esta variedad. Igualmente, el nombre de la variedad سمني جبنيانة **semni Jbeniana** originaria de la misma región de Sfax (*Jbeniana* es el nombre de la zona) hace referencia al tamaño del fruto, *semni* también significa "fruto gordo" (las palabras سمين y خشين **smin** y **kechin** son sinónimas en el dialecto tunecino). Otras figuraciones relacionadas con el fruto no se basan ni en la forma, ni el aspecto del fruto, sino sobre su olor o su sabor. El nombre de la variedad مسكي **meski**, originaria de una zona situada cerca de la capital, significa "fruto perfumado". Efectivamente este tipo de aceituna se caracteriza por su olor agradable y se usa exclusivamente para aceituna de mesa y no para aceite. Un caso parecido es el de la variedad بسباسي **besbessi**, de la misma zona, y cuyo nombre significa "fruto con sabor de Hinojo", otra planta muy típica de esta región.

3. El árbol

Existe otro tipo de figuraciones que no se basa sobre el carácter del fruto sino sobre caracteres del árbol mismo. En el nombre de la variedad ذكار نفطي **dokhar Nafti** de la región de Mednin, *dokhar* significa "**árbol macho**" mientras que la palabra *Nafti* hace referencia a la zona. Se llamó así porque la propiedad que caracteriza esta variedad es su abundante producción de polen. Esta misma propiedad se ha usado también por otros agricultores para atribuir un nombre a una variedad distinta llamándola ذكار بن فردأن **dokhar Ben Guerdène** donde *dokhar* es "árbol macho" y *Benguerdène* hace referencia a la zona. Del mismo modo que se ha comentado anteriormente, existe una repetición de la misma imagen en la fitonimia popular de los agricultores de distintas zonas.

Por último, destaca otro caso de figuración donde el carácter del árbol que ha llamado la atención del agricultor no era su producción de polen sino su alta producción de aceitunas y por lo tanto le han dado el nombre de **ontha,** es decir, "árbol hembra (fértil)". La misma imagen se observa en otra zona muy alejada con la variedad *chaibi ontha* basada en el mismo rasgo.

4. Conclusiones

Como conclusión de este trabajo se puede decir que el estudio del campo nocional del olivo/aceite es particularmente interesante porque por una parte, ese cultivo es milenario y fuertemente anclado en la cultura de toda la región mediterránea. También, como el cultivo del olivo sigue siendo relativamente tradicional en Túnez, la mayoría de las variedades están difundida sólo en torno al área donde aparecieron por la primera vez. Por ello, los nombres utilizados están estrechamente relacionados con el ámbito cultural local. Por otra parte, existe una gran diversidad en cuanto a los nombres de variedades ya que existen en el mundo más de 2000 variedades con más de 3000 denominaciones distintas, sin contar las que todavía no se han descrito ni clasificado.

En este estudio llevado a cabo sobre 21 nombres de variedades de olivo de Túnez se ha destacado:

1- La presencia de una diversidad considerable en cuanto al contenido figurado de los nombres de las variedades.
2- Las figuraciones detectadas están estrechamente relacionadas con el entorno rural que rodea el agricultor.
3- Los agricultores utilizan los rasgos que les parecen más llamativos para atribuir los nombres a las variedades.

Por otra parte, la utilización de los nombres científicos para llamar a las variedades de olivo genera hoy en día muchos casos de confusión característicos de los olivares de los países oleícolas tradicionales. Los científicos también intentan adaptar el sistema tradicional de denominación, hay variedades distintas que llevan el mismo nombre (homonimias). Los investigadores que están llevando a cabo trabajos de catalogación de los recursos genéticos se ven obligados a tomar decisiones para adoptar un nombre de una variedad u otro. Esto puede abrir una vía de colaboración interesante entre la biología, la agronomía y la lingüística, para un mejor conocimiento de este patrimonio todavía poco estudiado.

5. Bibliografía

BARRANCO, D.; FERNANDEZ-ESCOBAR, R. & RALLO, L.: 2004 *El cultivo del olivo*. 5ª ed. Madrid: Mundi-Prensa.

BARRANCO, D.; TRUJILLO, I. & RALLO, L.: 2005 "Elaiografía Hispánica". En: Rallo L. et al. (eds). *Variedades de olivo en España*. Madrid: Mundi-Prensa.

C.O.I: 2007 Consejo Oleícola Internacional: http://www.internationaloliveoil.org/

F.A.O: 2006 Food and Agriculture Organization: http://apps3.fao.org/wiews/olive/oliv/

I.N.S: 2007 Institut National de la Statistique (Tunisie).

JARDAK, T.: 2006 "The olive industry in Tunisia". *Special seminar: the olive industry in the Mediterranean countries*. 35-46.

JURADO, A.: 2004 *Las voces y refranes del olivo y del aceite*. Madrid: C & G.

LOUKAS, M. & KRIMBAS, C.B.: 1983 "History of Olive cultivars based on their genetic distances". *Journal of Horticultural Science*, 58: 121–127.

PAMIES, A.: 2008 "Productividad fraseológica y competencia metafórica (inter)cultural". *Paremia*, 17, pp. 41-58.

PAMIES, A.: 2010 "Paremias del olivo y cultura mediterránea", *I Giornata Siciliiana di Studi Ispanici del Mediterraneo*. Università di Catania. 6 de mayo de 2010 [en prensa].

PAMIES, A. & TUTÁEVA, K. 2010 "El árbol como referente linguo-cultural". In: Mellado, C. et al. (eds.) *La fraseografía del S. XXI*. Berlin: Frank & Timme: 169-190

RALLO L.; BARRANCO D.; CABALLERO JM.; DEL RIO C.; MARTIN A.; TOUS J & TRUJILLO, I. (eds.): 2005 *Variedades de olivo en España*. Madrid: Mundi-Prensa.

TRIGUI, A.; MSALLEM, M.; YENGUI, A.; BELGUITH, H.; KHECHEREM, J.; MELIÈNE, A.; MALEK, S.; BOUSSELMI, A, SAMET, A. & TRABELSI, E.: 2002 *Oliviers de Tunisie*, vol. 1. Tunis: Ministère de l'Agriculture, République Tunisienne; IRESA, Institut de l'Olivier.

TRIGUI, A.; YENGUI, A. & BELGUITH, H.: 2006 "Olive germplasm in Tunisia". *Olea*, 25. 19-23.

6. Anexo

جمري بوشوكة
Jemri Bouchouka – Jemri: Fruto con color de carbón encendido / Bouchouka: fruto que presenta una Espina

زربوط لوزير
Zarbout Louzir - Trompo de la zona del Louzir

Léxico y frasemas figurados del aceite y la aceituna en árabe moderno   335

منقار الرقْمة
Mengar Erragma – Pico de Buitre

الشهلة
Ech-chahla – La guapa

LA FRASEOLOGÍA ESPECIALIZADA DEL ÁREA CIENTÍFICA Y SOCIOECONÓMICA DEL OLIVAR Y EL ACEITE DE OLIVA: ENTRE LA TRADICIÓN Y LA MODERNIDAD

Esteban Tomás Montoro del Arco
Universidad de Granada

Abstract: The existing language of oliviculture and elaiotechnics makes evident the significant development of this specialised field over the past decades. The progressive industrialisation and professionalization of this sector has progressively given rise to a new terminology that is updating the old jargon and is undergoing important normalisation processes. The present work focuses on the concept of 'olive oil' and the variety of terms with which it has been designated across the history up to the present times.

Key words: Terminology; agriculture; olive tree; specialized phraseology

0. Introducción

El predominio de Andalucía (y de Jaén en particular) en la producción mundial de aceite de oliva data de la época de los establecimientos del Imperio romano en Hispania. Fue en el valle del Guadalquivir donde se concentró la mayor producción de aceite de oliva, lo que contribuyó a que la Bética se convirtiera en una de las provincias más ricas y fecundas de Roma. Desde entonces hasta ahora, las alabanzas del aceite han sido constantes y han ido aumentando conforme se han ido constatando sus beneficios. Desde muy antiguo se ha empleado el aceite como medicina y en la actualidad se dedica también parte de la producción a la elaboración de jabones de alta calidad. Pero quizá sus usos alimentarios sean los más conocidos, ya que constituye uno de los productos gastronómicos más importantes de la tan celebrada "dieta mediterránea".

El desarrollo secular de todo tipo de actividades en torno al olivo conlleva un rico y extenso léxico que estuvo a punto de desaparecer junto con los hablantes más ancianos: afortunadamente, los investigadores de la Universidad de Granada Juan Martínez Marín y Juan Antonio Moya Corral —alentados por Gregorio Salvador— se preocuparon por recogerlo a finales de los 70 antes de su previsible pérdida y realizaron encuestas en veinticuatro localidades de la provincia de Jaén en busca del léxico (y ocasionalmente la fraseología) relacionado con el olivar y la almazara. Fruto de ello fue un libro que ha de guardarse como un tesoro: *El léxico del olivo y la almazara en la provincia de Jaén* (1982). Moya Corral explica, más de veinticinco años después, la oportunidad de dicho trabajo:

> *La fortuna no es de quien la busca, es un regalo que los dioses dejan en el camino de los viajeros, es un bien inesperado que no suele percibirse sino algún tiempo después de disfrutarlo. Esto fue, probablemente, lo que nos ocurrió a nosotros. No estaba en nuestros cálculos que, pocos años después, gran parte de la cultura tradicional del olivo y, prácticamente, toda la relacionada con la producción de aceite iba a desaparecer. Durante el período de recogida de datos existía en la provincia de Jaén solo una almazara –o, al menos, nosotros tuvimos noticias de la existencia de solo una– que había modernizado el sistema de fabricación. La verdad es que el cambio*

que se iba a operar en el espacio cultural al que me refiero se inició inmediatamente y fue relativamente breve. La década de los 80 supuso una fuerte conmoción para los olivareros, los aceituneros y, sobre todo, para los trabajadores de las almazaras y las orujeras. El proceso de mecanización se inició y también se finalizó en la década de los 80. En esos diez años dejaron de usarse los molinos de piedras y todas las otras máquinas vinculadas con el viejo modo de extracción de aceite. En su lugar se fueron instalando unos ingenios controlados electrónicamente que, si bien modificaban en profundidad el método de extracción de aceite, respetaban, en gran medida, las fases de producción. El proceso pudo ser, incluso, más rápido, pero se ralentizó al objeto de que los trabajadores que requerían las viejas almazaras fueran acomodándose en las nuevas fábricas de aceite o en otros ámbitos de trabajo. Hubo convulsión, qué duda cabe, pero el cambio terminó por instalarse. (Moya Corral 2006: 259)

En efecto, la industrialización ha supuesto el abandono de determinadas prácticas, pero también ha llevado aparejada una incipiente expansión del mercado del aceite; y, como toda actividad, una terminología propia. Esta no está en peligro de extinción pero sí entraña un cierto peligro: el de la creación neológica desordenada que dificulte la comunicación entre expertos. Como antaño, este hecho tampoco ha pasado desapercibido para los lingüistas, que se han percatado a tiempo de la necesidad de sistematizar y regular los términos que acompañan al aceite en su periplo por los mercados internacionales y por distintos ámbitos profesionales.

El proyecto de investigación OlivaTerm (Roldán Vendrell 2010) reúne actualmente a un equipo multidisciplinar formado por trece investigadores de las universidades de Jaén y de Granada, especializados en lingüística, terminología, traducción, lengua española, lengua inglesa, lengua china, comercio, agricultura e informática. Nuestro objetivo general es recopilar, sistematizar y presentar la terminología del ámbito del olivar y el aceite de oliva para facilitar la comunicación entre especialistas, mediadores lingüísticos (redactores, traductores e intérpretes) y empresarios del sector, y ayudar a paliar los problemas de comunicación que entrañan las transacciones comerciales internacionales. La selección de lenguas para este proyecto (español/inglés/chino) responde al perfil de los destinatarios del vocabulario y a las funciones que éste ha de cumplir[1].

El resultado esperado del proyecto será un vocabulario trilingüe, en formato electrónico, que garantice el acceso rápido a la información y que permita la gestión de un gran número de términos en las tres lenguas seleccionadas. Cada *ficha terminográfica* o entrada del diccionario ofrecerá, entre otras informaciones, el término en español, la información

---

[1] El trabajo pretende, en primer lugar, servir a la comunidad científica y empresarial española, proporcionándole la terminología adecuada para llevar a cabo la comunicación especializada en lengua española; en segundo lugar, va dirigido a la comunidad internacional y por ello tiene en cuenta la lengua inglesa, dada la importancia que tiene como lengua de especialidad y factor de comunicación mundial; por último, este proyecto se propone, de manera muy especial, ayudar a resolver los problemas de comunicación con el mercado chino, por las extraordinarias perspectivas de expansión que este mercado representa para el sector oleícola en la actualidad.

gramatical correspondiente, su equivalencia en inglés, su equivalencia en chino[2], la definición del término, un contexto de uso real, las referencias de la definición y del contexto y su abreviatura y sinónimos cuando corresponda.

1. La fraseología especializada

La lematización y definición de los términos constituye uno de los aspectos que merece mayor reflexión, especialmente cuando se trata de términos pluriverbales, pues en ello se da una serie de dificultades que deriva en gran parte de su especial morfología. Su detección automática aún plantea muchas dificultades y no existe consenso ni en cuanto a sus características definitorias ni en cuanto a su denominación.

Es necesario, para empezar, distinguir entre fraseología especializada y fraseología común o general. El hecho de utilizar el mismo término para referirse a ambas constituye ya un obstáculo innecesario y, por ello, se utilizan términos que marcan la diferencia: así se explican opciones como *fraseología especializada, terminología fraseológica o fraseoterminología*, por citar solo algunas. Los estudiosos de la fraseología de la lengua general no coinciden ni en cuanto a la delimitación de las unidades que deben considerarse fraseológicas ni en cuanto a las cualidades, necesarias y suficientes, que éstas deben presentar para ser consideradas como tales. De igual modo, en el ámbito de la terminología, existen múltiples trabajos teóricos y metodológicos en los que tampoco se observa acuerdo[3].

Concretamente en el modelo teórico de la Teoría Comunicativa de la Terminología (TCT) (Cabré 1999) la fraseología especializada se integra como una más de las posibilidades formales de las *unidades de conocimiento especializado* (UCE), las cuales pueden ser vehiculadas mediante "unidades de significación especializada que se corresponden con unidades discursivas (textos), con unidades morfológicas (morfemas), con unidades léxicas (términos y otras unidades léxicas de contenido especializado) o bien con unidades fraseológicas (combinación de unidades léxicas)" (Lorente 2002). Por añadidura, desde la TCT se considera, acertadamente, que las unidades especializadas no pertenecen a un ámbito de especialidad en exclusiva, sino que su carácter especializado deriva de su uso en textos de especialidad.

Tomando estos postulados como referencia, en el proyecto OlivaTerm partimos de un corpus textual representativo cuya sección en español consta de 571 textos especializados. El concepto de 'aceite de oliva', en torno al que se estructura todo nuestro trabajo, constituye ya de por sí un gran reto lexicográfico. Como es habitual en los lenguajes de especialidad, la terminología del aceite de oliva proviene de un medio laboral tradicional que contrasta con la progresiva industrialización y profesionalización del sector. Esto obliga a establecer un diálogo con el pasado para determinar qué términos y/o conceptos tradicionales han permanecido vigentes y forman parte del caudal terminológico habitual manejado por los expertos y qué otros han dejado de utilizarse o han perdido su carácter técnico. En lo que sigue presentaremos una muestra de la fraseoterminología tradicional relacionada particu-

---

[2] Tanto en caracteres chinos como en *hanyu pinyin*, es decir, utilizando el sistema de transcripción fonética más habitual de la lengua china, basado en una representación en alfabeto latino de los sonidos del mandarín estándar moderno.

[3] No es objeto de este estudio adentrarnos en dicha discusión epistemológica. Remitimos para ello a la bibliografía existente al respecto: *vid.* Gläser (1994-5), Lorente, Bevilacqua, Estopà (1998) o Pavel (1993).

2. Aceite, aceites y aceites de oliva

2.1. En español tenemos dos raíces relativas al fruto líquido de la oliva: una voz culta, procedente del latín, *óleo* (OLĔUM 'jugo del fruto de la oliva'), que está presente en términos derivados como *oleícola, oleico, oleaginoso,* etc.; y una palabra de origen árabe, *aceite,* que procede del ár. hisp. *azzáyt* (este del ár. clás. *azzayt,* y éste, a su vez, del arameo *zaytā,* vid. DRAE 2001), y que significa también, por sí mismo, 'jugo de la aceituna'. El actual fraseotérmino *aceite de oliva* supone, pues, una redundancia desde un punto de vista etimológico, si bien imperceptible ya para el usuario medio[4]. Es, además, el de más temprana datación en el DH (1960) y presenta variantes o usos vacilantes relativos al número y género gramatical del árbol (oliva/olivas/olivo)[5] del que procede el fruto:
(1)   *Aceite de oliva, olivas* u *olivo* (1280): 'el que se obtiene del fruto del olivo'[6].
El carácter hiperonímico de la palabra *aceite* —esto es, su mayor *extensión*—, se refleja en uno de los tempranos fraseotérminos recogidos por el DH en la parte sintagmática de la entrada *aceite*:
(2)   *Aceite común* (1498): 'generalmente el de oliva. En algún caso el de linaza'.
El *aceite* es concretamente un tipo de *grasa vegetal* extraído del fruto del olivo, pero en español se extendió como representante de la grasa que se extrae de otras semillas, en función de los beneficios que se han asociado siempre con el fruto de la aceituna[7]. Como consecuencia, encontramos un patrón de formación de nuevos términos por el procedimiento

---

[4] Como es sabido, este tipo de redundancias no es extraña y se debe al debilitamiento o pérdida de significado que sufren algunas palabras a lo largo de su evolución: lo encontramos en el propio término *agricultura,* donde el componente añadido *agro* 'campo' está ya presente en el concepto inicial de *cultura*. Hablar de *aceite de girasol* es, *sensu stricto,* incongruente, pues equivaldría a *'jugo de aceituna de girasol'.

[5] Como es sabido, el fruto del *olivo* (árbol) se conoce como *aceituna*. No obstante, en Jaén se utiliza preferentemente *oliva* para referirse al árbol: "la designación jiennense por antonomasia es *oliva,* la cual ocupa prácticamente toda la provincia, salvo la zona suroccidental [...] en donde se emplea *olivo*. [...] En castellano se emplearon ambas formas hasta el Siglo de Oro, momento en que se generalizó la forma *olivo;* ello determinó que la otra denominación, *oliva,* quedase relegada a zonas dialectales" (Martínez Marín y Moya Corral 1982: 166). Como es sabido, en algunas zonas dialectales también se conoce como *oliva* a la aceituna.

[6] En cada referencia al DH, acompañaremos el fraseotérmino de la primera datación y el significado que señala el diccionario.

[7] Esta preponderancia ha sido constante desde el mundo grecolatino, como señalan Mataix y Barbancho (2007: 728): "La importancia en el mundo grecorromano del aceite de oliva supuso la relegación de las demás grasas. Otros aceites vegetales utilizados fueron los de almendra, nuez, ricino, sésamo, cártamo, rábano y *Ben*. Ocasionalmente se usaban en la alimentación pero sobre todo en la perfumería y medicina. [...] Los grecorromanos usaron pocas grasas animales en la alimentación. Las de pato, gallina, oca, cabra, oveja y vaca se empleaban para la medicina y la industria".

de *sintagmación*, cuyo resultado, frente a los de la fraseología general (tendente a la opacidad y la escasa productividad), resulta transparente y productivo (Montoro del Arco 2008): la base *aceite* recibe una especificación de la planta de la que procede —directa o indirectamente— a través del esquema sintáctico [*aceite* + *de* + sustantivo], y nombra así todo tipo de grasas vegetales. En el DH encontramos los siguientes fraseotérminos de este tipo:

(3) *Aceite de abeto/beto* (1521): 'abetinote, resina que se extrae del abeto'.
(4) *Aceite de almendras* (1495): 'El que se obtiene de este fruto'.
(5) *Aceite de anís* (del Pimpinela Anis) (1782): 'aguardiente anisado y con gran cantidad de azúcar, lo que le hace muy espeso'.
(6) *Aceite de cada* o *cade* (1853): 'miera, producto que se obtiene del enebro'.
(7) *Aceite de canime, canimé* (canine, cabina), *cabime, camíbar* (1607): 'nombre de cierto producto medicinal, generalmente identificado con el *bálsamo de copaiba*, que se extrae de diversas plantas del género Copaifera'. También *aceite de palo* (1764).
(8) *Aceite de lentisco* (1515): 'especie de almáciga que se obtiene de la planta de este nombre'. También *aceite de mata* (1495).
(9) *Aceite de linaza, de lino* o *de linoso* (1593): 'el que se extrae de las semillas del lino y se emplea como laxante, en pintura y con otros fines'.
(10) *Aceite de María* (1563): 'bálsamo de María, resina de calaba o calambuco'.
(11) *Aceite de nabo* (1882): 'el que se extrae de la semilla del chicalote'.
(12) *Aceite de palma* (1851): 'el que se extrae del fruto de cierta palmera, conocida por el nombre de *corojo de Guinea*, y que se emplea en medicina como emoliente y para hacer jabón'.
(13) *Aceite de ricino* (1851): 'el que se obtiene de las semillas de la planta de este nombre'. También *aceite de castor* (1802) y *aceite de palma Cristi/Christi* (1826).

Hoy día se prefiere denominar *aceites* a las grasas líquidas en general, sea cual sea su naturaleza (aunque fundamentalmente es vegetal), y se reserva el término *grasas* a las de consistencia sólida (animal y otras)[8]: gracias a la asociación con el aceite de oliva, los consumidores suelen relacionar las primeras con propiedades saludables de diversa índole, mientras que las segundas suelen provocar rechazo (sea este justificado o no) (Carpio Dueñas 2009). Asimismo, dentro de los *aceites* vegetales, los *aceites de oliva* se oponen a los llamados *aceites de semillas* (*aceite de girasol, aceite de colza, aceite de cacahuete, aceite de corozo*, etc.).

Al margen de estas denominaciones, algunos aceites vegetales se fueron especializando en una función concreta, lo que generó nuevos términos para referirse a ellos. El aceite de oliva (ejemplo 1), nuevamente, se erigió como prototipo para los usos alimentarios. Así lo reflejan denominaciones como las siguientes:

(14) *Aceite de comer* (1782): 'el que se emplea en la alimentación; generalmente el de oliva'[9].
(15) *Aceite dulce* (1853): 'Aceite de olivas'.

---

[8] La consistencia líquida del aceite de oliva ya hizo que se asociara el término aceite con cualquier producto líquido y graso, como ocurre con el *aceite de azufre* ('antigua denominación del ácido sulfúrico', 1680).

[9] Aunque curiosamente, según señala el DH, en América Central, Colombia y Puerto Rico el aceite de comer es 'el que, generalmente con alcanfor, se emplea en fricciones; nunca se come'.

Por el contrario, el de linaza, de peor calidad que el de oliva (aunque también identificado ocasionalmente como *aceite común*, *vid.* ejemplo 2), se utilizaba en el alumbrado y por ello se denomina —por analogía con *aceite de comer*— *aceite de arder*:
(16)   *Aceite de arder* (1817): 'El que se destina al alumbrado, generalmente el de linaza'.
No deja de sorprender, por ello, que uno de los términos especializados hoy día para las denominaciones oficiales del aceite de oliva, organizadas según los parámetros de calidad de organismos oficiales como el Comité Oleícola Internacional o la Unión Europea, sea *aceite de oliva virgen lampante*, fraseotérmino cuyo último formante (*lampante*) procede precisamente del uso de un aceite de oliva de peor calidad (*vid.* ejemplo 25) para el alumbrado mediante lámparas (Montoro del Arco y Roldán Vendrell e. p.).

En realidad, la versatilidad del aceite de oliva hizo que desde un principio se destinara a múltiples usos, distintos de los alimentarios. Por ejemplo, entra en la composición de cosméticos o en la elaboración de productos farmacéuticos, como reflejan los siguientes fraseotérminos documentados:
(17)   *Aceite de Aparicio* (1547) 'Preparación medicinal vulneraria inventada en el siglo XVI por Aparicio de Zubia y cuyos ingredientes son: aceite de oliva, trementina de abeto, vino blanco, trigo, hipérico, valeriana y cardo bendito'.
(18)   *Aceite de ladrillo* o *ladrillos* (1516): 'líquido empireumático resultante de la destilación del aceite de oliva mezclado con polvo de ladrillo'.
(19)   *Aceite de manzanilla* (1438): 'el que se obtiene por infusión de las flores secas de esta planta en aceite de oliva'.
(20)   *Aceite de raposa, raposo, vulpino, zorro* o *çorro* (1581-1606): 'preparado al que se atribuían propiedades medicinales y que se obtenía cociendo un zorro en aceite de olivas'.
(21)   *Aceite alcanforado* (1851): 'solución de alcanfor en aceite de olivas'.
(22)   *Aceite cocido* (1817): 'se aplica a diversos aceites que se obtienen haciendo cocer materias de distinta procedencia, como aceitunas, nueces, linaza, etc.'
(23)   *Aceite rosado* (1330?): 'preparación medicinal que se obtenía por infusión de rosas en aceite de olivas'.
(24)   *Aceite violado* (1498): 'preparación medicinal hecha a base de aceite y probablemente de violetas'.

2.2. En efecto, no todos los aceites obtenidos de la aceituna eran iguales y siempre existieron diferencias según su calidad. Los boticarios, en particular, usaban un tipo de aceite cuya escasa calidad provenía de la falta de maduración de las aceitunas, conocido como
(25)   *Aceite de agraz* (1495) / *aceite onfacino, onfancino, omphacino, omphancino, vnfancina* (del ár. *unfaq*) (1498): 'el que se obtiene de las aceitunas sin madurar, aceite onfacino'.
Debido también a las condiciones poco favorables de extracción (contacto con el aire, temperaturas altas, etc.), este aceite tenía una acidez muy alta y más que para la alimentación se empleaba como combustible o como cosmético (*vid.* ejemplos 19, 23 y 24).

La calidad del aceite fue mejorando conforme se incorporaron los avances tecnológicos a su proceso de extracción. En un principio, el principal modo de obtención del aceite libre de la pulpa de la aceituna fue la *presión*. Al comienzo se emplearon los pies y las manos y este aceite se conoció como
(26)   *Aceite de talega* (1513): 'el que se saca con solo pisar las aceitunas metidas dentro de una talega'. También denominado, significativamente, *aceite de pie* (1803).

Los métodos de presión fueron evolucionando y permitieron hacer un aceite cada vez mejor. Así, se logró un incremento en la presión a través de la *molturación*, que permitía romper el hueso y mejorar la separación del aceite. Más adelante se observó que si se añadía agua caliente a la masa resultante y se la sometía nuevamente a presión se obtenía una mezcla de agua y aceite que era fácilmente separable por decantación. Sin embargo, añadir agua caliente suponía obtener un líquido de peor calidad, de modo que comienzan a diferenciarse dos tipos de aceite: uno de mejor calidad, obtenido por una primera presión y sin ayuda de agua caliente, que se denominó *aceite virgen*, denominación que ha llegado hasta nuestros días e incluso actúa como hiperónimo de un conjunto específico de aceites de oliva (*aceite de oliva virgen extra, aceite de oliva virgen, aceite de oliva virgen lampante*, vid. Montoro del Arco y Roldán Vendrell e. p.):

(27)   *Aceite virgen* (1817): 'el que sale de la aceituna al exprimirla por primera vez en el molino, y sin repasos en prensa con agua caliente'.

Y otro, de peor calidad, obtenido a partir de la acción del agua caliente y la decantación, que se conoció de muy diversas formas, con más intensidad a finales del siglo XIX:

(28)   *Aceite de hojuela* (1770): 'el que se saca de las balsas donde se recoge el alpechín de la aceituna'.

(29)   *Aceite de heces* (1865): 'es el aceite de olivas que se obtiene del bagazo o residuo de prensar la aceituna'.

(30)   *Aceite de infierno* (1884): 'el que se recoge en el pilón llamado infierno y que es de inferior calidad'.

Es en el primer tercio del siglo XX, conocido como la "edad de oro del olivar español" (Zambrana 1987: 69), cuando se regula oficialmente la producción y comercialización. Nace una fuerte competencia entre las empresas oleícolas y las instituciones españolas limitan la entrada de grasas vegetales distintas a la del aceite de oliva, al tiempo que hacen los primeros esfuerzos normativos orientados a preservar la autenticidad de uno de los productos nacionales más importantes para el país.

Uno de los primeros textos en los que se acomete esta tarea es el *Real Decreto-ley de 8 de junio de 1926* relativo a "El régimen de los aceites de oliva o comestibles", en el que se establecen oficialmente no solo criterios de calidad (como el que distingue un tipo de aceites de oliva de menos de 5 grados de acidez frente a los de más de 5 grados) sino también términos como *aceites de orujo* y *aceites de oliva mezclados*. Tras la Primera Guerra Mundial, se consolidó la industria refinadora, de forma que el *refino* hizo aptos para el consumo los aceites defectuosos y facilitó el uso industrial de otros aceites. Y, como siempre, implicó nuevas denominaciones y categorías que atendieran a los distintos *aceites de oliva refinados*. Este proceso no ha sido del todo satisfactorio, en tanto que, por ejemplo, se ha llegado a un sistema en el que *aceite de oliva* es un hiperónimo que subsume un hipónimo homónimo (*vid.* más detalles en Montoro del Arco y Roldán Vendrell e. p.).

Ya en el siglo XX se introdujo un procedimiento de obtención del aceite de oliva más novedoso, el de la *centrifugación*, que ha cambiado totalmente las denominaciones. La centrifugación es una operación basada en la utilización de una maquinaria específica (el *decánter*) que, por efecto de la fuerza centrífuga, permite la *separación de fases* en virtud de la diferente densidad de las mismas. Estas *fases* son el resultado de la acción del decánter que, en el sistema de centrifugación *de tres fases*, tiene tres salidas por las que salen separadamente el orujo (*fase sólida*), el alpechín (*fase acuosa*) y el aceite con algo de humedad (*fase oleosa*). Este sistema, no obstante, ha sido modernizado y en la actualidad la mayoría de las almazaras utiliza un sistema de dos fases, en el que el decánter tiene solo dos salidas por las que salen respectivamente el aceite con algo de humedad (*fase líquida*) y el orujo mezclado con agua (*fase sólida* o *alperujo*). El término *fase* es utilizado por los expertos para designar realmente al aceite de oliva en alguno de los momentos del proceso de centrifugación, por lo que *fase oleosa, fase líquida* y *fase sólida* constituyen también términos especializados para designar al fruto de la aceituna en otra de sus dimensiones.

3. Conclusión

En este trabajo hemos querido mostrar un ejemplo de los problemas a los que intentamos dar respuesta en el proyecto OlivaTerm, valiéndonos de la compleja y abigarrada red de relaciones que implica un fraseotérmino tan básico para nuestro proyecto como es el de *aceite de oliva*. En él convergen, por ejemplo, los significados parciales de sus elementos componentes, pues tanto *aceite* como *oliva* son polisémicos y han ido modificando su significado a través de la historia. La pérdida del valor etimológico de *aceite*, en particular, posibilitó que entrara en la composición de términos pluriverbales para designar líquidos grasos de diversa índole. Aparte, los términos pluriverbales para designar al 'aceite de oliva' son muy diversos (*aceite de oliva, aceite de olivas, aceite de olivo, aceite de comer, aceite dulce, aceite de agraz, aceite virgen, aceite onfacino, aceite de heces, aceite de hojuela, aceite de infierno, aceite de oliva virgen, aceite de oliva virgen lampante, fase líquida*, etc.). Aunque pueden coincidir en la sincronía actual, pertenecen a épocas diversas y se integran en sistemas conceptuales distintos, pues no tienen los mismos referentes: estos han ido cambiando con el incremento progresivo de la tipología de aceites de oliva merced a los avances tecnológicos del sector oleícola.

4. Bibliografía

CABRÉ, Mª T. 1999 *La terminología: representación y comunicación*. Barcelona: Institut Universitari de Lingüística Aplicada, Universitat Pompeu i Fabra.

CARPIO DUEÑAS, A. 2009 "El aceite de oliva y oliva virgen. Componentes saludables". Consejo Económico y Social de la Provincia de Jaén y Universidad de Jaén, *El Aceite de Oliva Virgen, alimento saludable*. Jaén: Diputación Provincial:17-34.

[DH] = Real Academia Española 1960 *Diccionario histórico de la lengua española / proyectado y dirigido inicialmente por Julio Casares*, vol. 1 (A-Alá), Madrid: Real Academia Española.

[DRAE] = Real Academia Española 2001 *Diccionario de la lengua española*. Madrid: Espasa Calpe.

GLÄSER, R. 1994/95 "Relations between Phraseology and Terminology with Special Reference to English". *ALFA* 7/8: 41-60.

LORENTE, M. 2002 "Terminología y fraseología especializada: del léxico a la sintaxis". In: Guerrero, G. & Pérez Lagos, L. (eds.), *Panorama actual de la terminología*, Granada: Comares: 159-180.

LORENTE, M., BEVILACQUA, C. & ESTOPÀ, R. 1998 "El análisis de la fraseología especializada mediante elementos de lingüística actual". In: *Actas del VI Simposio Iberoamericano de Terminología: Terminología, Desarrollo e Identidad nacional*, La Habana [Disponible en <http://www.riterm.net/actes/6simposio/lorente.htm>, consulta: 20/03/ 2010].

MARTÍNEZ MARÍN, J. & MOYA CORRAL, J.A. 1982 *El léxico del olivo y la almazara en la provincia de Jaén*. Granada: Universidad.

MATAIX VERDÚ, J. & BARBANCHO CISNEROS, F.J. 2007 "El aceite de oliva en la alimentación mediterránea". In: *I Congreso de la Cultura del Olivo*. Jaén: Instituto de Estudios Giennenses: 707-764.

MONTORO DEL ARCO, E.T. 2008 "Relaciones entre Fraseología y Morfología: las formaciones nominales pluriverbales". In: Almela Pérez, R. & Montoro del Arco, E. T. (eds.), *Neologismo y morfología*, Murcia: Universidad: 65-90.

MONTORO DEL ARCO, E.T. & ROLDÁN VENDRELL. M. [en prensa] "Las denominaciones del aceite de oliva en los reglamentos oficiales: evolución, normalización y problemas terminológicos". In: Sinner, C. (ed.), *Comunicación y transmisión del saber entre lenguas y culturas*.

MOYA CORRAL, J.A. 2006 "Sobre el léxico del olivo y la almazara". In: Moya Corral, J. A. & Sosinski, M. (eds.), *Lexicografía y enseñanza de la lengua española. Actas de las XI Jornadas sobre la enseñanza de la lengua española*, Granada: Universidad: 259-272.

PAVEL, S. 1993 "La phraséologie en langue de spécialité. Méthodologie de consignation dans les vocabulaires terminologiques", *Terminologies Nouvelles* 10: 67-82.

ROLDÁN VENDRELL. M. 2010 "Lingüística y terminología multilingüe: OlivaTerm". In: Roldán Vendrell, M. (ed.), *Bases para la terminología multilingüe del aceite de oliva*. Granada: Comares: 1-15.

ZAMBRANA PINEDA, J. F. 1987 *Crisis y modernización del olivar español. 1870-1930*. Madrid: Ministerio de Agricultura, Pesca y Alimentación/Secretaría General Técnica.

LA PHRASÉOLOGIE DU POSITIONNEMENT DANS LES ÉCRITS SCIENTIFIQUES

Mariam Mroue
Université Stendhal-Grenoble-3

Abstract: The transdisciplinary scientific lexicon is a common lexicon for the entire scientific community, and it is related specifically to the writing and communication of scientific knowledge. This study examines the transdisciplinary collocations expressing the position of the author in his writing through a corpus of about two million words made up of scientific articles and thesis of three scientific fields: linguistics, economics and medicine. The objective of this study is to help foreign students who are proceeding their studies in the french universities to write their researches.

Key words: Phraseology, collocations, terminology.

0. Introduction

Les écrits scientifiques et universitaires font l'objet de deux projets de recherche, Scientext[1] et FULS[2] au LIDILEM[3]. Notre étude en fait partie et s'intéresse au lexique scientifique transdisciplinaire dans une perspective didactique pour l'aide à la rédaction des écrits de recherche auprès des étudiants étrangers venus étudier dans les universités françaises.

L'origine de notre travail repose sur le constat des difficultés linguistiques que rencontrent les étudiants étrangers poursuivant leurs études en France et amenés à pratiquer un nouveau genre d'écrits - l'écrit de recherche universitaire - qui conduit à des besoins linguistiques spécifiques. Nous savons qu'en matière de français de spécialité, la principale difficulté des locuteurs non natifs réside moins dans la terminologie disciplinaire que dans les habitus communicatifs et pragmatiques des discours professionnel ou scientifique. C'est pourquoi nous nous intéressons au lexique non terminologique mais spécifique à la rédaction et à la communication du savoir scientifique. Plus particulièrement, nous nous consacrons à l'étude des unités phraséologiques que sont les collocations; celles exprimant le positionnement de l'auteur/scripteur dans son écrit de recherche sont l'objet de ce travail.

Suite à une première partie introductive consacrée au lexique phraséologique transdisciplinaire et à une deuxième partie portant sur le positionnement, nous présentons certains de nos résultats obtenus à partir d'une analyse d'un corpus de deux millions de mots environ, et constitué notamment d'articles scientifiques et de thèses de trois domaines scientifiques : la linguistique, l'économie et la médecine.

---

[1] Scientext : un corpus et des outils pour étudier le positionnement et le raisonnement de l'auteur dans les écrits scientifiques, ANR piloté par le Lidilem, http://scientext.msh-alpes.fr/scientext-site/spip.php?article1

[2] FULS : Formes et Usages des Lexiques Spécialisés en vue d'exploitations didactiques en FLE et FLM, financé par le ministère de la recherche et piloté par le Lidilem, http://webtek-66.iut2.upmf-grenoble.fr/

[3] Laboratoire de Linguistique et didactique des langues étrangères et maternelles, Université Grenoble3, http://w3.u-grenoble3.fr/lidilem/labo/

1. Le lexique phraséologique transdisciplinaire

a) Définition

Le lexique transdisciplinaire est une pratique langagière propre à une communauté de discours, en l'occurrence la communauté scientifique. Il s'agit d'un lexique commun à toutes les disciplines scientifiques et se distingue par là du lexique terminologique.

Notre étude se situe dans la lignée des travaux élaborées par une équipe du CREDIF dirigée par Phal autour du « Vocabulaire Général d'Orientation Scientifique » (VGOS). Phal (1971 : 9) définit le VGOS comme suit:

> *le vocabulaire scientifique général est [...] commun à toutes les spécialités. Il sert à exprimer des notions élémentaires dont elles ont toutes également besoin (mesure, poids, rapport, vitesse, etc...) et les opérations intellectuelles que suppose toute démarche méthodique de la pensée (hypothèse, mise en relation, déduction et induction, etc.).*

L'existence d'une langue commune aux scientifiques, appelée Langue Scientifique Générale (LSG), est récemment au centre des intérêts des phraséologues. Pecman (2005 : 112) la définit ainsi :

> *la LSG est une pratique langagière spécifique à une communauté de discours composée de chercheurs en sciences exactes dont les objectifs communicatifs poursuivis émanent des préoccupations partagées par des scientifiques à travers le monde et indépendamment de leurs spécificités disciplinaires.*

Les corpus de Phal et Pecman sont limités aux disciplines des sciences exactes. Par conséquent, notre conception du lexique transdisciplinaire se démarque de celle qu'ils proposent et rejoint plutôt celle de Drouin et Tutin (Drouin, 2007, Tutin, 2007) qui décrivent « le Lexique Scientifique Transdisciplinaire » issu d'un corpus d'écrits scientifiques de trois domaines (médecine, économie, linguistique) représentant ainsi les trois sciences, expérimentale, sociale et humaine.

> *Nous définirons le lexique transdisciplinaire des écrits scientifiques comme le lexique partagé par la communauté scientifique mis en œuvre dans la description et la présentation de l'activité scientifique. Ce lexique peut être considéré comme un lexique de genre, n'intégrant pas la terminologie du domaine, mais renvoyant aux concepts mis en œuvre dans l'activité scientifique. Il transcende donc les domaines à l'intérieur d'une même famille de pratiques scientifiques [...] et présente un noyau commun significatif entre disciplines.* (Tutin, 2007)

Nous partons donc dans notre étude de l'idée de l'existence d'un lexique vecteur des connaissances et des savoirs scientifiques que tous les chercheurs indépendamment de leur domaine de spécialité partagent.

b) Collocations transdisciplinaires

Nous portons un intérêt particulier aux collocations transdisciplinaires (*faire une hypothèse, mettre en évidence, résoudre un problème, jouer un rôle, formuler une hypothèse*) pour maintes raisons tant linguistiques que didactiques :

La phraséologie joue un rôle crucial dans la construction du savoir scientifique (Gledhill, 1997). Plus généralement, sa maîtrise constitue « la clef de voûte » de l'enseignement et de l'apprentissage d'une langue étrangère (Binon & Verlinde, 2003) et son assimilation conditionne la fluidité de l'expression orale et écrite (Lewis, 2000).

Bien qu'elles soient des connaissances indispensables, les unités phraséologiques dans les écrits scientifiques n'ont pas été suffisamment étudiées et ce contrairement aux unités phraséologiques dans la langue générale. Les listes de mots simples du VGOS, présentent des limites qui peuvent être liées à la polysémie des lexèmes (Tutin, 2007), et à un manque d'approche sémantique.

Les unités phraséologiques sont peu étudiées et par conséquent peu enseignées. Or les observations des écrits d'étudiants montrent bien qu'il y a soit un sous-emploi de ces unités, soit une connaissance partielle et approximative empêchant un réemploi correct.

Les dictionnaires phraséologiques n'existent que pour la langue générale et bien qu'ils soient des outils précieux, ils ne constituent pas une aide efficace pour la rédaction scientifique.

Tous ces constats nous ont par conséquent amené à nous concentrer uniquement sur l'étude des collocations transdisciplinaires et pour ce faire nous avons opté pour une description sémantique en la matière. Dans un premier temps, notre choix s'est porté sur le positionnement.

2. Le positionnement

Pour justifier notre intérêt pour le positionnement, il convient de nous pencher sur les exigences de l'écrit universitaire. L'une d'entre elles consiste, pour l'étudiant, à se forger une opinion personnelle sur la base de ses lectures, en faisant montre d'esprit critique aussi bien vis-à-vis des travaux d'autrui que vis-à-vis de ses propres travaux a priori ; autrement dit, les discours d'autrui ne doivent pas être montrés « tels une collection de pièces dans une vitrine attestant un travail accompli » (Reuter, 2001) mais doivent participer à la construction d'un savoir nouveau. L'acculturation au discours universitaire devrait amener l'étudiant, après une première phase qui consiste à s'approprier des savoirs, à adopter une posture réflexive vis-à-vis des autres travaux de recherche afin de se construire un savoir personnel prouvant que s'est opérée « *une rencontre, via l'activité langagière, entre le questionnement de départ de l'étudiant et les discours déjà-là* » (Rinck, 2004). L'acculturation suppose donc, entre autres, la maitrise du positionnement qui participe considérablement au développement d'une identité "énonciative" et "rédactionnelle".

Par ailleurs, il s'agit d'un processus assez complexe, régi par des tensions d'ordre linguistique, socioculturelle, psycholinguistique, et d'autres non traitées ici. Le sentiment de sécurité/insécurité, dominance/soumission, vis-à-vis des prédécesseurs y influe largement ainsi que l'idée traditionnelle autour de l'objectivité d'un discours scientifique et l'amalgame qui se fait avec la neutralité. Nombreux étudiants ne connaissent pas la distinction entre un énoncé objectif qui exprime un point de vue assumé par le scripteur et un énoncé neutre qui n'exprime aucune prise de position face au discours d'autrui. Par conséquent, dans un souci d'objectivité, les étudiants citent dans leurs écrits les discours de leurs prédécesseurs sans les commenter.

Notre recherche se concentre uniquement sur la dimension linguistique de ce processus. Notre hypothèse de travail est qu'en montrant aux étudiants les différents moyens linguistiques et formes de positionnement nous pourrons les aider à maitriser -linguistiquement- ce phénomène, et par conséquent à préparer leur affiliation à la communauté des chercheurs dans le cadre de leurs écrits de recherche.

3. Les collocations exprimant le positionnement: analyse de corpus

Deux dimensions sont à prendre en considération dans un travail de recherche : l' « own work » et le « other work » (Teufel & Moens, 2000). Le chercheur novice devrait apprendre à se positionner face au savoir construit avant d'écrire et donc d'expliciter ses idées et ses apports novateurs. Dans le schéma suivant inspiré d'une étude effectuée par Teufel et Moens (2000), nous illustrons les formes par lesquelles se traduirait une prise de position.

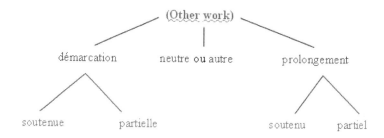

Schéma 1 : le positionnement

Le positionnement peut donc consister soit en un prolongement des travaux antérieurs, soit en une démarcation. L'objectif de notre travail est de présenter aux étudiants novices des moyens linguistiques leur permettant de répondre à cette exigence de l'écrit scientifique. Afin de vérifier comment les locuteurs natifs se positionnent, nous nous sommes basés sur un corpus d'écrits scientifiques de chercheurs confirmés. Notre base de données est constituée des corpus KIAP-LIDILEM[4], de 2 millions de mots environ, regroupant trois disciplines scientifiques: la linguistique, l'économie, la médecine. Il est constitué d'articles de revues spécialisées, de thèses et rapports de recherche.

Nous avons pu établir des listes de collocations verbales exprimant les deux faces du positionnement :
- le "prolongement"*(ex: retenir l'idée de, affirmer avec quelqu'un, saluer une démarche, etc...)*
- la "démarcation"*(rejeter l'hypothèse de, émettre une réserve, présenter une limite, etc..)*

Par conséquent nous pouvons affirmer que le positionnement n'est pas uniquement synonyme de "rejet". En plus, il existe une variété de formules et tournures linguistiques permettant aux

---

[4] Le corpus est formé d'une partie du corpus KIAP (Projet mené à l'université de Bergen de janvier 2002 à juin 2006) enrichie par d'autres écrits au Lidilem.

étudiants de prendre davantage position sans devoir forcément évoquer une polémique ou se sentir en insécurité vis à vis des chercheurs confirmés.

a) Lexique transdisciplinaire exprimant la démarcation : quelques résultats

Grâce à l'utilisation conjointe des logiciels Antconc, Nooj et des concordanciers et dictionnaires, nous[5] avons pu établir une liste de 42 collocations de démarcation, ou plutôt réseaux de collocation de démarcation.

Ces deux exemples montrent bien que la démarcation est moins une affaire de collocations qu'une affaire de réseaux collocationnels : en effet, il est rare de voir un verbe systématiquement associé à un nom spécifique et un seul. Nous avons repéré des « verbes de démarcation » s'associant de manière quasi-indifférente à un champ ou réseau sémantique spécifique (idée, théorie, thèse, argument, approche…). En d'autres termes, la démarcation sera le plus souvent exprimée à l'aide d'un verbe démarcateur suivi d'une lexie appartenant à une classe sémantique spécifique dont les éléments fonctionnent essentiellement par synonymie (théorie – thèse), voire hyperonymie ou hyponymie (théorie – argument) (approche/modèle – notion). Les lexies de cette classe sémantique pourraient être regroupées sous la dénomination adoptée par Tutin (2005) : « objets construits par l'activité scientifique ».

Certaines collocations ont un sens plus prégnant que d'autres. Certains expriment la volonté de se démarquer totalement (rejeter une théorie, abandonner l'hypothèse), d'autres impliquent une démarcation partielle (nuancer une idée), d'autres enfin signifient moins une remise en cause qu'une « mise en discussion » qui finalement pourrait aboutir soit à un prolongement soit à une démarcation (mettre en doute).

Nous constatons aussi que les collocations de démarcation se trouvent pour l'essentiel dans les corpus d'économie et de linguistique. Nous pouvons donc émettre l'hypothèse qu'en économie, la démarcation, ou tout du moins le débat d'idée, font partie intégrante des usages de la discipline. En linguistique également, mais de manière moins marquée. En revanche, la médecine n'emploie que rarement ce lexique démarcatif, ce qui signifie peut-être qu'il s'agit d'un domaine plus consensuel, moins empreint d'une logique de démarcation.

Un autre constat parait pertinent, celui qui touche à la présence de collocations de démarcation précédées de syntagmes verbaux introductifs. *Exemples :*
Ceci nous incite à…
- contester cette hypothèse
- nuancer ce résultat
Ceci nous conduit à …
- rejeter l'hypothèse
- remettre en question l'évaluation
- nuancer quelque peu ce diagnostic

Les structures repérées ci-dessus permettent certainement à l'écrivant de donner à son refus, du moins à sa démarcation, un caractère scientifique puisque objectif et non personnel. Ainsi, un énoncé de type : *« ceci nous incite à contester l'hypothèse de X »* signifie que ce n'est pas le scripteur qui choisit de contester X - le « je » est absent du propos - mais que c'est la nature objective des faits scientifiques qui l'*amène* et l'*oblige* – malgré lui, pourrait-on dire,

---

[5] L'étude sur la démarcation est réalisée en collaboration avec Ingreed Chavez en 2008.

ou du moins, indépendamment de lui – à contester X. Ces structures donnent donc la possibilité d'installer une distance entre le chercheur et ses propos, de « dépersonnaliser » son avis divergent et de situer sa démarcation dans le champ de la science et non pas celui de la polémique.

b) Lexique transdisciplinaire exprimant le prolongement, quelques exemples :

Concernant le prolongement, nous nous contentons dans cet article de vous présenter quelques exemples que nous jugeons intéressants au plan didactique.

« *Retenir +....* »
- une démarche: « nous retenons la démarche pragmatique proposée par Fleurbaey et Michel »
- une idée: « on retient ici l'idée que la construction du sens ne se résume pas à un choix dans une liste d' items lexicaux ».
- une approche: « l'approche déterministe a été retenue pour cette étude ».
- une solution: « la solution de Milner est cependant à retenir ».

Ces différents exemples permettront aux étudiants de prendre conscience des variations que peuvent prendre les collocations.

« *Reprendre +...* »
- une démonstration: « cet annexe reprend une démonstration de Karlin et Carr [1962] en ajoutant à leur modèle le choix du facteur travail en tant que facteur de production ».

Dans cet exemple, nous repérons un prolongement auquel s'ajoute une proposition d'une nouveauté.

- une idée: « il semble donc pertinent de reprendre l'idée de Fericelli et Khan selon laquelle la théorie du salaire d'efficience peut bénéficier de le notion de rémunération de efficience, grâce à l'ensemble des composants de le rémunération global (Fericelli et Khan , 2000) ».

Il est à noter dans cet exemple la forme impersonnelle qui nous rappelle les structures repérées ci-dessus dans l'étude consacrée à la démarcation. Avec cette forme, le scripteur se décharge presque de toute responsabilité impliquée par son positionnement.

Ces exemples montrent les variations syntaxiques que peut subir une collocation de type V-N : en plus de la construction directe, nous avons recensé des constructions à la forme passive et d'autres à la forme pronominale. Ils illustrent aussi les différentes formes du prolongement (prolongement partiel ou total).

Ces exemples ainsi que les différents constats établis lors de notre analyse de corpus (*par ex : le repérage des structures de type syntagmes verbaux introductifs + collocations de démarcation*), nous ont conduits à insister sur la nécessité d'envisager l'enseignement de ces unités phraséologiques en contexte.

Il n'est évidemment pas question de les enseigner sous forme de liste. Les listes que nous élaborons serviront à fournir des éléments pour établir par la suite une didactique de la phraséologie transdisciplinaire. C'est en effet au contact de différents textes scientifiques – présentant les collocations dans des contextes variés mais significatifs – qu'un ancrage cognitif sera rendu possible (Binon & Verlinde, 2004).

Notre étude est une première approche du lexique phraséologique exprimant le positionnement. Nous sommes conscients que l'enseignement de ce lexique n'aboutirait pas automatiquement à la maîtrise de ce processus et que d'autres facteurs (socioculturels et psycholinguistiques) y interviennent. Cependant nous sommes convaincus qu'une sensibilisation des étudiants à cette problématique et à ce lexique et une explication des différentes formes et stratégies du positionnement ne peuvent être que productives pour les aider dans leurs écrits universitaires.

4. Bibliographie

BINON J. & VERLINDE, S. 2003 « Les collocations : clef de voûte de l'enseignement et de l'apprentissage du vocabulaire d'une langue étrangère ou seconde ». *La lettre de l'AIRDF* n°33: 31-36.

BINON, J. & VERLINDE, S. 2004 « L'enseignement/apprentissage du vocabulaire et la lexicographie pédagogique du français sur objectifs spécifiques (FOS) : le domaine du français des affaires ». *ELA,* n° 135: 271-283.

CAVALLA, C 2010 « Les écrits universitaires des étudiants étrangers : quelles normes présenter? ». In: Bertrand O. &Schaffner I. (eds), *Quel français enseigner ? La question de la norme dans l'apprentissage / enseignement*. Paris: Editions Ecole Polytechnique: 153-161.

DROUIN, P. 2007 « Identification automatique du lexique scientifique transdisciplinaire ». *Revue française de linguistique appliquée*, n° XII-2: 45-64.

GLEDHILL, C. 1997 « Les collocations et la construction du savoir scientifique ». *ASP,* 15/18: 85-104.

PECMAN, M. 2005 « Les apports possibles de la phraséologie à la didactique des langues étrangères ». *ALSIC* n°8: 109-122.

PHAL, A. 1971 *Vocabulaire général d'orientation scientifique (V.G.O.S.) - Part du lexique commun dans l'expression scientifique*. Paris: Didier/ Crédif.

REUTER, Y. 2001 « Je suis comme un autrui qui doute. Le discours des autres dans l'écrit de recherche en formation ». *Lidil*, n° 24: 13-27.

RINCK, F. 2004 « Construire la problématique d'un rapport de stage : les difficultés d'étudiants du second cycle. *Pratiques: théorie, pratique, pédagogie*, 121/122: 93-110.

TEUFEL, S. & MOENS, M 2000 « What's yours and what's mine: Determining Intellectual Attribution in Scientific Text ». In: *Proceedings of the 2000 Joint SIGDAT Conference on Empirical Methods in Natural Language Processing and Very Large Corpora*. Hong Kong.

TUTIN, A. 2005 « Collocations du lexique transdisciplinaire des écrits scientifiques: annotation et extraction des propriétés syntaxiques ». In: *Phraseologie 2005, La phraséologie dans tous ses états. Colloque interdisciplinaire: 13-15 octobre 2005*. Louvain-la-Neuve: Université Catholique.

TUTIN, A. 2007 « Présentation du numéro *Autour du lexique et de la phraséologie des écrits scientifiques* ». *Revue française de linguistique appliquée*, n° XII-2: 5-14.

TUTIN, A. 2007 « Modélisation linguistique et annotation des collocations : une application au lexique transdiciplinaire des écrits scientifiques ». In: Koeva, S.; Maurel D. & Silberztein, M. (eds), *Formaliser les langues avec l'ordinateur : de Intex à NooJ*, Besançon: Presses Universitaires de Franche Comté: 189-215.

LEWIS M. 2000 *Teaching Collocations, Further Developments in the Lexical Approach*. London: Language Teaching Publications.

ESTUDIO DE LA VARIACIÓN TOPOLECTAL DE LAS UFE EN EL ÁMBITO DEL DERECHO PENAL ESPAÑOL E HISPANOAMERICANO

Alejandro Pastor Lara
Universität München
Encarnación Tabares Plasencia
Universität Leipzig

Abstract: In this paper we would like to present a systematic analysis of the main differences in the lexical selection of Spanish legal collocations in relation to their counterparts in the different legal systems of the rest of the spanish-speaking countries. Therefore we have built up a corpus of specialized texts consisting of the criminal codes of all Spanish-speaking countries from Latin America and Spain. For the practice of translation topolectal variations in the field of specialized collocations are very important because usually the terms do not always select the same basis in the different legal systems that share Spanish as official language or the same collocation is not always used in the same communicative situations and with the same meaning. Finally to illustrate these aspects of topolectal variation, in the last part of our paper we present the differences in the collocational patterns of the term 'pena' (sentence) throughout the different legal systems.

Key words: specialized phraseological units, phraseological variation, topolectal variation, Criminal Law

1. Introducción

El objetivo de nuestro trabajo es, mediante la exploración de corpus de textos especializados compuesto por los códigos penales de todos los países de habla española de América Latina y de España[1], analizar cuáles son las principales diferencias en la selección léxica que las colocaciones jurídicas españolas presentan en relación con sus homónimas en los distintos sistemas jurídicos hispanoamericanos.

    A un traductor que no dispone de la competencia terminológica adecuada para enfrentarse a textos especializados jurídicos no siempre le resulta fácil encontrar en las aplicaciones terminográficas al uso el equivalente más adecuado para el término que ha de traducir. La información gramatical y, sobre todo, combinatoria que ofrecen los diccionarios, muy a menudo, insuficiente, asistemática y poco rigurosa, dificulta al traductor la tarea de resolver cómo utilizar una determinada unidad terminológica dentro de un contexto de uso concreto. Estas complicaciones que encuentra el traductor se agravan aún más cuando el

---

[1] Hemos de aclarar que hemos utilizado un corpus tan vasto porque nuestra intención es realizar un trabajo más amplio a medio plazo que refleje la variación fraseológica intralingüística relevante para el traductor que tenga que habérselas con textos jurídico-penales. Aquí solo pretendemos ofrecer una muestra de los cambios fraseológicos motivados por factores geográficos. Por ello, solo vamos a hablar básicamente de un tipo de UFE, al que luego aludiremos y únicamente pondremos algunos ejemplos de sus realizaciones en los textos jurídicos mencionados. Tampoco vamos a aludir en esta ocasión a cuestiones de frecuencia de uso.

objetivo no es traducir un término, ya sea este monoléxico o poliléxico, sino una unidad fraseológica, ya que, debido a las interrelaciones semánticas que se establecen entre sus diferentes constituyentes en una lengua, se hace muy difícil saber cuál puede ser la unidad fraseológica equivalente en la lengua de llegada, si es que realmente se trata de un fraseologismo.

Aunque en el "lenguaje" jurídico, como lenguaje de especialidad, no es pacífico hablar de "idiomaticidad" en el sentido en que se utiliza para las unidades fraseológicas de la lengua general, sí es importante destacar el hecho de que en las colocaciones especializadas jurídicas, la relación que se establece entre la base y el colocado es puramente arbitraria y fijada en el sistema de la lengua a través del uso que de ellas hacen los especialistas, lo que hace que para una misma base la elección de los colocados que funcionan con ella difiera notablemente en una y otra lengua. Estas diferencias en la selección del colocado por parte de la base no sólo se hacen patentes desde una perspectiva interlingüística sino que también desde la perspectiva intralingüística, y muy especialmente en el caso del español, lengua común de los diferentes sistemas jurídicos de los países donde es lengua oficial, el traductor se encuentra con la dificultad añadida que suponen para el desarrollo de su labor las diferentes variaciones topolectales que una misma unidad fraseológica puede presentar en cada uno de los diferentes sistemas jurídicos.

Coincidimos con Caro Cedillo (2004: 41) al considerar que, aunque las unidades fraseológicas especializadas (en adelante UFE) son unidades fijadas en la norma en el sentido coseriano del término, en el nivel de sistema, al igual que el resto de unidades monolexemáticas de la lengua, presentan variaciones diasistemáticas que un traductor debe conocer para el ejercicio de su actividad.

El terreno de las variaciones diatópicas que presentan las diferentes unidades fraseológicas es un terreno poco explorado, ya que tradicionalmente la dialectología ha centrado sus investigaciones en intentar establecer fronteras geográficas para las áreas dialectales que presenta una misma lengua. Para el establecimiento de estas fronteras o isoglosas la dialectología tradicional se ha basado en criterios de tipo fonético o fonológico, criterios morfológicos e incluso criterios léxicos, dejando siempre a un lado las propiedades semánticas a la hora de establecer variedades de una misma lengua. Esto explica que exista un enorme déficit en investigación sobre las variaciones dialectales que presentan las unidades fraseológicas ya sean estas propias de la lengua general o de la lengua especializada (Piirainen 2007). Al mismo tiempo, los estudios de fraseología contrastiva no suelen tratar con el fenómeno de la limitación geográfica de las diferentes unidades fraseológicas individuales que estudian, sino todo lo contrario. Desde la perspectiva de la investigación fraseológica tradicional se suele partir de la idea de un grupo homogéneo de unidades, que son comunes a la lengua como conjunto, independientemente de las diferentes variedades regionales (Piirainen 2007). Esta concepción de la fraseología es inaplicable a una lengua como el español, que está conformada históricamente por un número considerable de dialectos.

En este último caso, los estudios se han ido ampliando gracias al interés creciente por la fraseología, que originó, sobre todo a partir de los años 80 del siglo XX, entre otros factores, una ampliación del concepto de Terminología (Desmet 1994), siendo que hoy es un ámbito de análisis más en la investigación terminológica[2].

2. Nuestro concepto de UFE

Existen distintas consideraciones de UFE, como ocurre también con el fenómeno en la lengua general. En primer iugar, se puede constatar punto de vista que parte de los planteamientos de la Lexicología y de la Lexicografía para reconocer automáticamente las UFE y poder así representarlas en productos terminográficos mono, bi o multilingües (Hausmann 1990; Benson; Benson & Ilson 1996; Heid 1992, entre otros; L´Homme 1995); en segundo lugar, existe una perspectiva terminológica, que surge, en parte, de los modernos enfoques dentro de la Terminología (Socioterminología, Teoría Comunicativa de la Terminología, entre otros), siendo que esta aproximación al fenómeno considera que las UFE están formadas por el término y sus coocurrentes, por lo que el término es siempre el núcleo de la unidad (Picht, 1990a y b; Bevilacqua 1996; Lorente; Bevilacqua & Estopà 2002; Pavel 1993; Blais 1993). Una tercera tendencia, cuyos representantes más conspicuos son Roberts (1994/1995) y Gouadec (1994), reputa UFE no solo sintagmas, sino también, y principalmente, aquellas expresiones formularias u oraciones o fragmentos propios de un dominio especializado. Son unidades que pueden llegar a ser una o varias frases completas en las que hay elementos invariables y variables.

Nuestra opinión es que las tres tendencias son aprovechables, puesto que, si atendemos a las dos primeras, aunque sigan caminos distintos, llegan a una misma tipología morfosintáctica para las UFE, considerándolas básicamente como sintagmas nominales, verbales, preposicionales y adjetivales. Y teniendo en cuenta la tercera podremos ampliar el campo de acción de la fraseología especializada con un provecho enorme para la traducción, puesto que se identificarían y analizarían unidades prototípicas (expresiones-marco Gülich & Krafft 1998) de un género textual concreto que facilitaría mucho la producción de textos en la lengua extranjera. Es decir, desde una perspectiva práctica y aplicada entendemos que deberían tenerse en cuenta el mayor número de unidades que presenten prototipicidad y especificidad, aparte de cierta fijación y grado de frecuencia dentro de los distintos tipos de discursos especializados, siendo, por lo demás, que, si siguiéramos el famoso criterio del centro y la periferia, propio de la fraseología de la lengua general, diríamos que las combinaciones, fundamentalmente verbonominales, cuyo núcleo es una UT constituirían el centro dentro de la fraseología especializada y estas unidades mayores que pueden estar constituidas por un término o no estarían más cerca de la periferia.

3. Variación fraseológica y traducción jurídica

Según Kjaer (2007), muchos fraseólogos se han mostrado hasta ahora reticentes a estudiar en detalle las combinaciones de palabras propias de los textos especializados, porque la comprensión en detalle de su significado y funcionamiento dentro del discurso es inseparable de un conocimiento profundo de la ciencia o profesión concreta que se pretende estudiar. En

---

[2] Véanse a este respecto Cabré & Estopá & Lorente (1996), Bevilacqua & Lorente & Estopá (1998), Cabré (2005), Tabares Plasencia & Pérez Vigaray (2007) y Tabares Plasencia & Ivanova (2010).

este sentido, Greciano (1995) argumenta que tanto el tema como la lengua configuran el texto especializado. Esto implica que no se pueda analizar la lengua de un texto especializado sin tener en cuenta la interdependencia que se establece entre la fraseología y el contexto social y profesional en el que se usa. Por tanto, como propone Sandrini (1996), para analizar una unidad cualquiera, ya sea esta fraseológica o terminológica, de un ámbito concreto del saber humano, primero hay que estudiar qué función representa la unidad que nos proponemos estudiar dentro del ámbito específico del que es propia.

En este mismo sentido, tenemos que asumir que el Derecho es un sistema nocional vinculado a un discurso y este a una sociedad concreta, con una historia determinada. Ello implica normalmente su "carácter monocultural" (Thiry 2005:1), esto es, el hecho de que no suela ir más allá de las fronteras nacionales (Gémar 2002:166). Esta premisa es especialmente importante por lo que respecta a la Traducción jurídica puesto que a través de la lengua española se vehiculan veinte ordenamientos jurídicos diferentes (Tabares& Ivanova 2010). Por tal circunstancia, para el traductor jurídico es muy importante encuadrar las unidades fraseológicas del texto que tiene que traducir en el marco del sistema jurídico-cultural de partida e intentar adecuarlo al marco del de llegada. No queremos sino recordar aquí que cuando se traduce un texto jurídico también se debe realizar una tarea de terminología y fraseología comparadas (Thoiron et al. 1996:512-513), que debería orientarse a satisfacer las expectativas terminológicas y fraseológicas de los receptores del texto (Tabares Plasencia& Ivanova 2010).

4. Variación fraseológica en torno al término "pena"

En la última parte de nuestra exposición, a partir de los sentidos 'castigar a alguien& ser castigado alguien' hemos querido investigar, en los distintos códigos penales objeto de análisis, cuáles eran las combinaciones más frecuentes (utilizadas con el mismo sentido y en el mismo contexto) y, en caso de ofrecer variación, si esta variación era relevante para un traductor y qué otros cambios de orden paradigmático o sintagmático, también de relevancia, para el traductor se producen.

Resulta interesante cómo en todos los códigos se recoge la unidad *imponer (una/la) pena* a alguien con el sentido de 'castigar', salvo en Cuba donde se utiliza el sinónimo de pena *sanción penal*. Naturalmente, por cuestiones de espacio solo vamos a reproducir algunas muestras textuales de algunos de los códigos:

(1) **CP-ES**[3]
Artículo 144
El que produzca el aborto de una mujer, sin su consentimiento, será castigado con la pena de prisión de cuatro a ocho años e inhabilitación especial para ejercer cualquier profesión sanitaria, o para prestar servicios de toda índole en clínicas, establecimientos o consultorios ginecológicos, públicos o privados, por tiempo de tres a 10 años.
Las mismas penas se impondrán[4] al que practique el aborto habiendo obtenido la anuencia de la mujer mediante violencia, amenaza o engaño.

---

[3] Hemos optado por colocar tras esta abreviatura, más o menos generalizada para Código Penal en el mundo hispánico, el código del país según la norma ISO 3166-1, para distinguir cada una de las unidades de nuestro corpus.

(2) **CP-PE**
Artículo V.- Garantía Jurisdiccional
Sólo el Juez competente puede **imponer penas** o medidas de seguridad; y no puede hacerlo sino en la forma establecida en la ley.

(3) **CP-AR**
Art. 151.- **Se impondrá la misma pena** e inhabilitación especial de seis meses a dos años, al funcionario público o agente de la autoridad que allanare un domicilio sin las formalidades prescriptas por la ley o fuera de los casos que ella determina.

(4) **CP-CU**
ARTÍCULO 2.1. Sólo pueden sancionarse los actos expresamente previstos como delitos en la ley, con anterioridad a su comisión.
2. A nadie puede **imponerse una sanción penal** que no se encuentre establecida en la ley anterior al acto punible.

A pesar de que esta UFE es bastante constante en el corpus que nos ocupa, lo cierto es que hay algunos detalles de su empleo que creemos destacables. Normalmente, el hecho de que el término *pena* como núcleo de la unidad pueda combinarse con *imponer* suele implicar que los elementos que forman parte de su misma clase semántica (p.e. hipónimos del tipo: *prisión, inhabilitación, privación del derecho X*, etc.) puedan coocurrir también con él. Sin embargo, aunque esto es así en algunos de los textos legales estudiados, en otros, la combinación *imponer* directamente con el hipónimo no se da nunca como es el caso del CP de España, Costa Rica, Nicaragua y El Salvador:

(5) **CP-ES**
Artículo 142
(...)
2. Cuando el homicidio imprudente sea cometido utilizando un vehículo a motor, un ciclomotor o un arma de fuego, **se impondrá** asimismo, y respectivamente, **la pena de privación del derecho a conducir vehículos a motor y ciclomotores o la privación del derecho a la tenencia y porte de armas**, de uno a seis años.

(6) **CP-NI**
Art. 153 **Lesiones gravísimas** Quien causare a otro, por cualquier medio o procedimiento la pérdida o inutilidad de un órgano o miembro principal o de un sentido, la impotencia, la esterilidad, una grave deformidad o una grave enfermedad somática o psíquica, **se impondrá pena de prisión** de tres a diez años.

(7) **CP-SV**
Art. 132.- El homicidio culposo será sancionado con prisión de dos a cuatro años.

---

[4] La negrita es nuestra en todos los ejemplos.

Cuando el homicidio culposo se cometiere mediante la conducción de un vehículo, **se impondrá así mismo la pena de privación del derecho a conducir o a obtener la licencia respectiva** por un término de dos a cuatro años cuando ello sea requerido.

Frente a, por ejemplo:

(8) **CP-CO**
Artículo 109. *Homicidio culposo*. (...) Cuando la conducta culposa sea cometida utilizando medios motorizados o arma de fuego, **se impondrá igualmente la privación del derecho a conducir vehículos automotores y motocicletas y la de privación del derecho a la tenencia y porte de arma**, respectivamente, de tres (3) a cinco (5) años.

(9) **CP-MX**
ARTÍCULO 142. Al que ayude a otro para que se prive de la vida, **se le impondrá prisión** de uno a cinco años, si el suicidio se consuma. Si el agente prestare el auxilio hasta el punto de ejecutar él mismo la muerte, la pena aplicable será de cuatro a diez años de prisión.

Asimismo, consideramos también de interés que, aparte de la UFE arriba mencionada, se utilicen en algunos de los textos legales de nuestro corpus otras con el sentido de 'recibir un castigo' como *sufrir pena* (o sus hipónimos) que son completamente desconocidas en los otros, como en CP de España. Así:

(10) **CP-EC**
Art. 2.- Nadie puede ser reprimido por un acto que no se halle expresamente declarado infracción por la Ley penal, ni **sufrir una pena** que no esté en ella establecida.

(11) **CP- PY**
Artículo 69.- Cómputo de privación de libertad anterior
1° Cuando el condenado **haya sufrido prisión preventiva** u otra privación de libertad, éstas se computarán a la pena privativa de libertad o de multa.

(12) **CP-VE**
ARTICULO 118. Es reo de parricidio, quien diere muerte a alguno de sus ascendientes o descendientes, a su cónyuge o a la persona con quien hace vida marital, y **sufrirá la pena de treinta (30) a cuarenta (40) años de reclusión**.

En otros casos, se prefiere *incurrir en pena* (o sus hipónimos) como variante de la unidad anterior (en los casos en los que se utiliza en el mismo texto) o de variación cuando se utiliza como forma sinonímica de la anterior en otro de los textos:

(13) **CP-CO**
Artículo 27. *Tentativa*. El que iniciare la ejecución de una conducta punible mediante actos idóneos e inequívocamente dirigidos a su consumación, y ésta no se produjere por circunstancias ajenas a su voluntad, **incurrirá en pena** no menor de la mitad del mínimo ni mayor de las tres cuartas partes del máximo de la señalada para la conducta punible consumada.

(14) **CP-EC**
Art. 13.- El que ejecuta voluntariamente un acto punible será responsable de él, e **incurrirá en la pena** señalada para la infracción resultante, aunque varíe el mal que el delincuente quiso causar, o recaiga en distinta persona de aquella a quien se propuso ofender.

(15) **CP-CR**
Artículo 246 bis.- Incurrirá en las penas previstas en el artículo 246 quien cree un peligro común para las personas o los bienes, mediante la emisión, propagación o el impacto de sustancias o productos químicos tóxicos o peligrosos, agentes o toxinas de carácter biológico o sustancias similares o radiaciones de material radiactivo.

Otro ejemplo interesante lo tenemos para expresar el contenido 'establecer un castigo concreto y determinado dentro del marco penal correspondiente'. En la mayoría de los textos analizados nos encontramos con las unidades *fijar* y *determinar la pena*:

(16) **CP-PY**
(...)
2° **Al determinar la pena**, el tribunal sopesará todas las circunstancias generales en favor y en contra del autor y particularmente: los móviles y los fines del autor; la actitud frente al derecho; la intensidad de la energía criminal utilizada en la realización del hecho;

(17) **CP-NI**
Cuando en aplicación del acuerdo condicionado el imputado o acusado colabore eficazmente con la administración de justicia, el Juez **fijará la pena acordada**, que en ningún caso podrá ser menor a la mitad del límite mínimo del delito o delitos de que se trate.

En algún supuesto también recogimos, no obstante, la unidad *individualizar la pena*:

(18) **CP-MX**
ARTÍCULO 71
(...)
En estos casos, el juzgador **individualizará la pena** tomando como base el nuevo marco de referencia que resulte del aumento o disminución.

(19) **CP-ES**
Artículo 66
(...) 1ª. Cuando no concurrieren circunstancias atenuantes ni agravantes o cuando concurran unas y otras, los jueces o tribunales **individualizarán la pena** imponiendo la señalada por la ley en la extensión adecuada a las circunstancias personales del delincuente y a la mayor o menor gravedad del hecho, razonándolo en la sentencia.

Lo que resulta también curioso en este caso es que, en muchos de los textos podemos encontrar la nominalización de la UFE *individualizar la pena*, *individualización de la pena*, aunque no la unidad verbonominal misma, lo cual puede implicar un la terminologización de la dicha nominalización. Véanse los siguientes ejemplos:

(20) **CP- CO** Artículo 59. *Motivación del proceso de **individualización de la pena***. Toda sentencia deberá contener una fundamentación explícita sobre los motivos de la determinación cualitativa y cuantitativa de la pena.

(21) **CP-PA**
Capítulo V
Aplicación e **Individualización** de las Penas
Para terminar, nos referiremos al proceso relativo al 'cambio de un castigo o sanción por otros, normalmente menos graves' que prevén casi todas las legislaciones modernas en determinados casos. Para la expresión de tal contenido hemos constatado la presencia de las siguientes UFE en los textos estudiados:
Convertir la/una pena (o sus hipónimos)

(22) **CP-PE**
Artículo 52.- Conversión de la pena privativa de libertad
En los casos que no fuera procedente la condena condicional o la reserva del fallo condenatorio, **el Juez podrá convertir la pena privativa de libertad** no mayor de dos años en otra de multa, o la pena privativa de libertad no mayor de cuatro años en otra de prestación de servicios a la comunidad o limitación de días libres, a razón de un día de privación de libertad por un día de multa, siete días de privación de libertad por una jornada de prestación de servicios a la comunidad o por una jornada de limitación de días libres.

Conmutar la/una pena (o sus hipónimos)
(23) **CP-CR**
ARTÍCULO 69.-
Cuando a un delincuente primario se le imponga pena de prisión que no exceda de un año, el Juez **podrá conmutarla por días multa,** cuyo monto fijará atendiendo a las condiciones económicas del condenado.

Sustituir la/una pena (o sus hipónimos)
(24) **CP- ES**
Artículo 88
1. **Los jueces o tribunales podrán sustituir,** previa audiencia de las partes, en la misma sentencia, o posteriormente en auto motivado, antes de dar inicio a su ejecución, las penas de prisión que no excedan de un año por multa o por trabajos en beneficio de la comunidad (...).

5. Conclusión

Nos hubiera gustado poder ofrecer más ejemplos, no solamente variación de unas determinadas unidades sino también del comportamiento de las mismas en los textos trabajados, pero, desgraciadamente, no disponemos de más espacio para ello. Desde un punto de vista traductológico es interesante tener en cuenta todas las transformaciones posibles y constatables en los textos de una UFE y comprobar si también es posible verificar variaciones motivadas por factores dialectales en estas transformaciones, pues realmente son las restricciones de transformación las que más problemas crean a los que aprenden una lengua de especialidad o a los que deben traducir textos especializados. Por lo demás, nuestra intención ha sido mostrar cómo la conciencia de variación topolectal en el ámbito de la traducción jurídica y por lo que se refiere a la fraseología es fundamental para mejorar su calidad, en general. Esperemos que ello sea posible en el futuro.

6. Bibliografía

BENSON, M.; BENSON, E. & ILSON, R. 1996 *The BBI combinatory dictionary of English*. Amsterdam: John Benjamins.

BEVILACQUA, C. 1996 "Do domínio jurídico-ambiental: proposta de critérios para seleção e tratamento de unidades fraseológicas". In: *Actas del V Simposio Iberoamericano de Terminología: Terminología, Ciencia y Tecnología*, México (1996). http://www.riterm.net/actes/5simposio/cleci.htm (consulta: 15.02.2010).

BLAIS, E. 1993 "Le phraséologisme. Une hypothèse de travail". *Terminologies Nouvelles* 10: 50-56.

CABRÉ, M. T. 2005 "Recursos lingüísticos en la enseñanza de lenguas de especialidad". In: Gómez de Enterría, J. (coord.): *V Jornada- Coloquio de la Asociación Española de Terminología AETER*, Universidad de Alcalá de Henares (2004). http://cvc.cervantes.es/obref/aeter/conferencias/cabre.htm (consulta: 18-01-2010).

CABRÉ, M. T.; ESTOPÁ, R.; LORENTE, M. 1996 "Terminología y fraseología". In: *Actas del V Simposio Iberoamericano de Terminología: Terminología, Ciencia y Tecnología*, México (1996). http://www.riterm.net/actes/5simposio/cabre5.htm (consulta: 18-01-2010).

CARO CEDILLO, A. 200*Fachsprachliche Kollokationen. Ein übersetzungsorientiertes Datenbankmodell Deutsch-Spanisch*. Tübingen: Narr.

DESMET, I. 1994 "Terminologia, desenvolvimento e ensino/aprendizagem das LSP. O valor heurístico do plano textual na investigação. In: *Actas del IV Simposio Iberoamericano de Terminología: Terminología y Desarrollo*, Buenos Aires (1994). http://www.riterm.net/actes/4simposio/desmet.htm (consulta: 13.02.2010).

GÉMAR 2002 "Le plus et le moins-disant culturel du texte juridique. Langue, culture et équivalence". *Meta* XLVII (2) : 163-176.

GOUADEC, D. 1994 "Nature et traitement des entités phraséologiques. Terminologie et phraséologie. Acteurs et aménageurs". In: Gouadec, Daniel (ed.): *Actes du deuxième Université d'Automne en Terminologie*. Paris: La Maison du Dictionnaire: 164-193.

GRÉCIANO, G. 1995 "Fachfraseologie". In: Metriech, H. et al.: *Rand und Band. Abgrenzung undVerknüpfung als Grundtendenzen des Deutschen*. Tübingen: G. Narr: 183-195.

GÜLICH, E.; KRAFFT, U. 1998 "Zur Rolle des Vorgeformten in Textproduktionsprozessen". In: Wirrer, Jan (ed.): *Phraseologismen. Text und Kontext*. Bielefeld: Aisthesis: 11-32.

HAUSMANN, F.J. 1990 "Le dictionnaire de collocations". In: Hausmann, Franz Josef et al. (eds.): *An International encyclopedia of lexicography*. Berlin & New York: de Gruyter: 1010-1019 (vol. 1).

HEID, U. 1992 "Décrire las collocations: deux approches lexicographiques et leur application dans un outil informatisé". *Terminologie et traduction* 2/3. Bruxelles: Commission des Communautés Européennes, Service de Traduction: 523-548.

KJAER, A.L. 2007 "Phrasemes in legal texts". In: Burger, Harald (ed.): *Phraseologie: ein internationales Handbuch zeitgenössischer Forschung*. Berlin& New York: de Gruyter: 506-516.

L'HOMME, M.C. 1995 "Processing word combination in existing term banks". *Terminology: International Journal of theoretical and applied issues in specialized communication* 2 (1). Amsterdam: John Benjamins: 141-162.

LORENTE, M.; BEVILACQUA, C. & ESTOPÀ, R. 2002 "El análisis de la fraseología especializada mediante elementos de la lingüística actual". In: *Terminologia, desenvolvimento e identidade nacional. VI Simposio Iberoamericano de Terminología* (La Habana, novembro de 1998). Lisboa: ILTEC-Ediçoes Colibri: 647-666.

PAVEL, S. 1993 "La phraséologie en langue de spécialité. Méthodologie de consignation dans les vocabulaires terminologiques". *Terminologies Nouvelles* 10: 67-82.

PICHT, H. 1990a "LSP phraseology from the terminological point of view". *Terminology science & research: Journal of International Institute for Terminology Research* 1 (1-2). Viena: International Network for Terminology: 33-48.

PICHT, H. 1990b "A Study of LSP phraseological elements in spanish technical texts". *Terminology science & research: Journal of International Institute for Terminology Research* 1 (1-2). Viena: International Network for Terminology: 49-58.

PIIRAINEN, E. 2007 "Dialectal phraseology: Linguistic aspects." In: H. Burger, D. Dobrovolskij, P. Kuehn, and N. Norrick (eds.): *Phraseology. An International Handbook of Contemporary Research*. Berlin, New York: De Gruyter, Vol. 1: 530-540.

ROBERTS, R. 1994/1995 "Identifying the Phraseology of LSPs". *ALFA* 7/8: 61-73.

TABARES PLASENCIA, E.& PÉREZ VIGARAY, J.M. 2007 "Fraseología terminológica: Estado de la cuestión y ejemplo de análisis contrastivo". *RFULL* 25: 567-578.

TABARES PLASENCIA, E.& IVANOVA, V. 2010 "La variación topolectal en Terminología. Implicaciones para la traducción jurídica español↔alemán". In: Varela Salinas, María José (ed.): *Panorama actual del estudio y la enseñanza de discursos especializados*. Bern: Peter Lang: 67-93.

THIRY, B. 2005 "La Terminología a la luz de una investigación en Derecho". *Cahiers de Recherche de l'École de Gestion de l'Université de Liège* 2005/10/03 (consulta: 10/02/2010) URL: http://www.hec.ulg.ac.be/FR/recherche/activites/working-papers.php

THOIRON, Ph. et al. 1996 "Notion d''archiconcept' et dénomination". *Meta* XLI (4): 512-524.

Corpus (Códigos Penales)

CP-AR: (Argentina) http://www.jusneuquen.gov.ar/share/legislacion/leyes/codigos_nacionales/CP_aindice.htm
CP-BO: (Bolivia) http://www.oas.org/juridico/spanish/gapeca_sp_docs_bol1.pdf
CP-CL: (Chile) http://www.pericia.cl/Leyes/codigo_penal.pdf
CP-CO: http://www.oas.org/Juridico/MLA/sp/col/sp_col-int-text-cp.pdf (Colombia)
CP-CR: (Costa Rica) http://www.upoli.edu.ni/icep/legis-mesoamerica/C%f3digo%20Penal%20Costa%20Rica.pdf
CP-CU: (Cuba) http://www.cubapolidata.com/gpc/gpc_codigo_penal_de_cuba.html
CP-DO: (República Dominicana) http://www.suprema.gov.do/codigos/Codigo_Penal.pdf
CP-EC: (Ecuador) http://www.oas.org/juridico/MLA/sp/ecu/sp_ecu-int-text-cp.pdf
CP-ES: (España) http://noticias.juridicas.com/base_datos/Penal/lo10-1995.html
CP-GT: (Guatemala) http://www.lexadin.nl/wlg/legis/nofr/oeur/arch/gua/CodigoPenal.pdf
CP-HN: (Honduras)
　　http://www.sic.gob.hn/transparencia/documentos/Leyes/Codigo_Penal.pdf
CP-MX: (México) http://www.unifr.ch/ddp1/derechopenal/legislacion/l_20080616_63.pdf

CP-NI: (Nicaragua)
http://legislacion.asamblea.gob.ni/Normaweb.nsf/%28$All%29/1F5B59264A8F00F9062 57540005EF77E?OpenDocument
CP-PA: (Panamá) http://www.unifr.ch/ddp1/derechopenal/legislacion/l_20080630_02.pdf
CP-PE: (Perú) http://www.lexadin.nl/wlg/legis/nofr/oeur/lxweper.htm
CP-PR: (Puerto Rico) http://www.ramajudicial.pr/leyes/codigopenal.htm
CP-PY: (Paraguay) http://www.unifr.ch/ddp1/derechopenal/legislacion/l_20080616_71.pdf
CP-SV: (El Salvador)
://www.csj.gob.sv/leyes.nsf/c8884f2b1645f48b86256d48007011d2/29961fcd868286340 6256d02005a3cd4?OpenDocument
CP-UY: (Uruguay) http://www.parlamento.gub.uy/Codigos/CodigoPenal/Cod_Pen.htm
CP-VE: (Venezuela)
http://www.cianz.org.ve/archivos/LeyesyReglamentos/LEYESPENALES/CODIG%20O PENAL.pdf

DIE PAAR KRÖTEN, DAS SIND DOCH ALLES NUR PEANUTS!
EINE ANALYSE ZUR INTRA- UND INTERLINGUALEN ÄQUIVALENZ PHRASEOLOGISCHER EINHEITEN IN PRESSETEXTEN

Christine Schowalter
Landau

Abstract: This paper is dedicated to the *toad* (ger. *Kröte*). In the German language a very small amount of money can be metaphorical designed as *Kröten* but nowadays as *Peanuts* as well. A first analysis concentrates therefore on the question if the two metaphors are similar and in which manner they could whether or not be replaced by each other. A second enquiry focuses then on the idiom *to swallow a toad* (ger. *eine Kröte schlucken*) and its cross-linguistic equivalence between several languages as English, German, French, Italian, Spanish and Portuguese. This part is thus based on articles from newspapers published in various countries in 2009.

Key words: Intralinguale Äquivalenz von Kröten und peanuts; interlinguale; Äquivalenz von eine Kröte schlucken, avaler un crapaud, ingoiare un rospo, engolir um sapo, tragarse el sapo; international Pressesprache, politische Berichterstattung

1. Sind *Kröten* wirklich *Peanuts*? Die Frage nach der intralingualen Äquivalenz

Seit das englische Fremdwort *Peanuts* zum Unwort des Jahres 1994[1] gekürt wurde, zählt es auch im Deutschen zum allgemein bekannten Sprachgebrauch. Dies lässt sich nicht nur mittels mehrerer Nachweise in der Wochenzeitung DIE ZEIT verifizieren, sondern auch anhand des Eintrags als eigenständiges Lemma im Duden (^{21}1996: 556) überprüfen. Dort sind *Peanuts* mit der Bedeutung: *„ugs. für* Kleinigkeiten; unbedeutende Geldsumme" aufgeführt[2]. Dagegen kann die Bezeichnung *Kröten* im Deutschen auf eine sehr viel längere Tradition zurückblicken, denn bereits im Mittelniederdeutschen lässt sich diese Relation belegen (vgl. DWB 1873: 2419). Die Klangähnlichkeit zwischen mhd. *krot(e)* und ndd. *Groten* 'Groschen' kann hier als recht naheliegender Beweggrund für diesen Zusammenhang angenommen werden (vgl. Kluge ^{23}1999: 489).

Im 19. Jahrhundert erfolgt im Englischen die metaphorische Übertragung von *peanut* zunächst auf „persons or things regarded as mean, paltry, insignificant, or contemptible" (DAE 1960: 1703). Die Konversion vom Nomen zum transitiven Verb *to peanut* als *„to make small or insignificant"* ist seit 1884 belegt. In der festen Wortverbindung *Peanut politics* ist die Bedeutung „political action inspired by mean or narrow motives" ab 1887 lexikalisiert. Im Jahre 1897 lässt sich über die Mehrworteinheit „peanut gallery" ('billige Plätze') wiederum eine erstmalige Bedeutungsspezifizierung hin zu Geld feststellen. Die Pluralform des Nomens spielt in der übertragenen Wortbedeutung bis dahin aber ganz offensichtlich keine Rolle, denn

---

[1] Vgl. die Auflistung der Gesellschaft für deutsche Sprache: www.gfds.de/aktionen/wort-des-jahres/unwoerter-des-jahres/
[2] In der 5. Auflage von 1990 des Dudens, Bd. 5 (Das Fremdwörterbuch) fehlt der Eintrag noch, ab der 6. Auflage, die 1997 veröffentlicht wurde, ist er verzeichnet.

alle Lemmata sind noch im Singular angegeben (vgl. DAE 1960: 1704)[3]. Heute nun werden *Peanuts* sowohl in der Bedeutung „a: something small, inconsequential, or of little value" als auch im Sinne von „b: a very petty sum of money usu. in comparison to the total amount involved" (WID 1993/1961: 1661) verwendet.

Gemeinsam ist den beiden Metaphern demnach, dass sie im informellen Sprachgebrauch als Bezeichnung für wenig Geld eingesetzt werden und dann stets im Plural stehen. Beide haben zudem noch als Herkunftsbereich die Natur vorzuweisen, so dass einer wechselseitigen Austauschbarkeit eigentlich nichts im Wege stehen sollte. Mittels einer Pressetextanalyse, die anhand von Artikeln aus der deutschen Wochenzeitung DIE ZEIT angefertigt wurde und einen Zeitraum von 1977 bis 2010 umfasst, soll dieser Frage nun einmal etwas genauer nachgegangen werden.

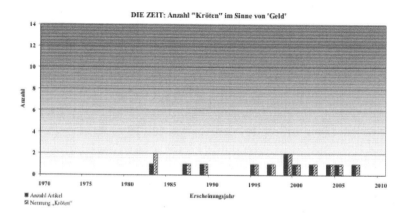

Beide Ausdrücke lassen sich in der Presseberichterstattung herausfiltern, allerdings kommen sie in ganz unterschiedlicher Häufigkeit vor.

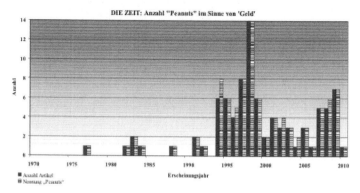

[3] Die New York Times berichtet allerdings vom legendären Aufstieg eines Harry M. Stevens (1856-1934), der mittels kluger Geschäftsideen „a bag of peanuts into a million dollars" verwandelt haben soll (28.09.1955: 43), so dass sich die unmittelbare Bedeutungsbeziehung zwischen Geld und *Peanuts* schon früher zeigen lässt.

„Kröten" als Bezeichnung für kleinere Geldbeträge erzielte während des Untersuchungszeitraums von immerhin 40 Jahren lediglich 13 Nennungen, "Peanuts" erhielt in derselben Bedeutungsvariante dagegen 94 Treffer. Zeigen lässt sich in dieser Darstellung vor allen Dingen, dass ein singuläres Ereignis wie das berühmt gewordene Zitat des Vorstandssprechers der Deutschen Bank[4], der im Jahr 1994 eine hohe Geldsumme geringschätzig als „Peanuts" bezeichnet hatte, geradezu eine Modewelle auslöste und sich die Metapher seitdem einer großen Beliebtheit erfreut.

In welchen Kontexten sind die beiden Metaphern nun aber am ehesten anzutreffen und lassen sich dabei vielleicht auch typische Umgebungen herausfiltern? Laut dem LDR werden die *Kröten* vor allem mit dem Indefinitpronomen *paar* kombiniert und sind als Mehrworteinheit in dieser Verknüpfung auch lexikographisch erfasst (vgl. LDR 1994: 346). Die Überprüfung der Einheit im Projekt Wortschatz der Uni Leipzig[5] ergibt in der Konsequenz eine hohe Trefferquote (142). In den untersuchten Artikeln von DIE ZEIT entsprechen nun rund 60% diesem Muster: „mit den paar *Kröten* nicht auskommen" (vgl. 15.05.1987).

Ganz anders liegt der Fall bei *Peanuts*, denn in dessen indirekter oder direkter Nachbarschaft findet sich das Adverb nur (17%), so bspw., wenn es im Korpus heißt „alles nur *Peanuts*" (01.07.1988) oder auch „kriegen nur *Peanuts*" (22.08.1997). Etwa gleich oft werden geringe Werte zu hohen Geldsummen in Beziehung gesetzt:

(1) „Das sind doch *Peanuts* [...]. Wohl wahr. Im Vergleich zu den täglichen Milliardenumsätzen ist das ein läppischer Betrag" (20.10.1995) oder

(2) „Denn das Extrageld [...] kostet vergleichsweise wenig. Letztlich sind das *Peanuts*." (23.12.2008).

Allerdings finden sich die entsprechenden Wortformen („im Vergleich zu"; „vergleichsweise") im Unterschied zu den Ergebnissen des Leipziger Projekts Wortschatz in den analysierten Texten sowohl in linker als auch in rechter Nachbarschaft zur gesuchten Metapher:

(3) „alles nur *Peanuts* im Vergleich zu dem" (01.07.1988) bzw.

(4) „Doch im Vergleich zum Reingewinn [...] sind diese Kosten wahrlich *Peanuts*" (13.09.1996).

Deutlich wird hier aber vor allem, dass die Definition des Dudens als „Kleinigkeit; bes. als unbedeutend erachtete Geldsumme" (vgl.[7] 2001: 742) zu kurz greift, denn ganz offensichtlich wird auch im Deutschen häufig auf die ursprüngliche Konstellation zurückgegriffen. Der Substitutionstest zeigt schließlich, dass trotzdem die Grammatikalität der Sätze erhalten bleibt, die Metaphorizität der Worteinheiten sich im Kontext des jeweils anderen Kandidaten verändern kann:

(5) „Das Geld war von den Rentenanstalten bereitgestellt, die Schecks an Rentner, die im Ausland leben, abgeschickt worden. Dann kümmerte sich niemand mehr drum. Das ist nun wirklich kein Wunder, wissen wir doch längst: Das sind alles „*Peanuts*". [Substitution: Das sind alles „*Kröten*".] Wer mag Banken verübeln, daß sie ein paar Millionen versehentlich behalten, die die Empfänger nicht abholen" (13.05.1994).

---

[4] Vgl. DIE ZEIT v. 05.08.1994: „Vorstandssprecher Hilmar Kopper, der wegen seiner unbedachten Bemerkung von den peanuts aus dem Pleitefall Schneider zu Recht viel Prügel einstecken mußte.

[5] *Projekt Deutscher Wortschatz,* online zu finden unter: http://wortschatz.uni-leipzig.de/

Nachdem die Anführungszeichen in diesem Beispiel (5) auf eine übertragene Bedeutung verweisen, die Kombination mit „alles" aber ungewöhnlich ist, kann die Verwendung von „Kröten" hier auf zwei Varianten referieren: 1. 'geringer Geldbetrag'; 2. 'etwas Unangenehmes akzeptieren müssen'. Bedeutung 1 erweist sich als widersprüchlich zu dem nachfolgenden „Millionen", so dass die Bedeutung 2 in den Vordergrund rückt und damit die Mehrworteinheit „Kröten schlucken" aufscheint, die nun aber auch nicht so recht zum referierten Sachverhalt passen will.

(6) „Wir, die wir unsere paar *Kröten* [Substitution: Wir, die wir unsere paar *Peanuts*] mühsam verdienen und für unsere Angehörigen sorgen müssen. Wir wollen uns unser Geld nicht für windige Geschäfte und nochmals wertlosen Plunder aus der Tasche jagen lassen" (11.01.2007).

Im Beispiel (6) nun, zeigt sich die potentielle Substituierbarkeit von *Kröten* durch *Peanuts* und löst damit die festgefügte Relation zwischen den einzelnen Komponenten der Redewendung „ein paar Kröten" auf, ohne dass sich die lexikalisierte Bedeutung wesentlich verändert. Der Ausdruck „ein paar Peanuts" kann hier also durchaus als äquivalent zu „ein paar Kröten" angesehen werden: Festzuhalten bleibt demnach, dass die Metapher *Peanuts* als äquivalent zu *Kröten* gelten kann, dies aber nicht für den umgekehrten Fall zutrifft. Folglich handelt es sich hier auch um keine reziproke Substituierbarkeit. Aufgrund der zunehmenden Präsenz von *Peanuts* könnte die Metapher *Kröten* in der Bedeutung 'geringer Geldbetrag' in Zukunft zudem völlig verschwinden, da die Einführung von Euro und Cent im Jahr 2002 die Bezeichnung *Groschen* bereits weit aus dem Sprachbewusstsein verdrängt hat und so die Grundlage für die Korrelation zu *Kröten* verloren geht. Wenngleich ihre metaphorische Bedeutung innerhalb dieser Konstellation auch schwindet, gewinnt sie mittels der Redewendung *Kröten schlucken* dafür immer mehr an Relevanz.

Abb. 1: Gemeinsame und unterscheidende Bedeutungskomponenten bei *Kröten* und *Peanuts*.

2. Wo schluckt man denn heute noch Kröten? Die Frage nach der interlingualen Äquivalenz

Gerade in Deutschland wird die Redewendung *Kröten schlucken* oft und gerne von Politikern verwendet und erscheint dementsprechend häufig in der Presseberichterstattung. Die Artikel in der Wochenzeitung DIE ZEIT bilden dabei keine Ausnahme. Im Untersuchungszeitraum von 1970 bis Mitte 2010 konnte *eine Kröte schlucken* bzw. *Kröten schlucken* immerhin 139mal nachgewiesen werden. Die Bedeutung der Redewendung ist bei Röhrich als 'Unangenehmes hinnehmen müssen' lexikographisch erfasst (1992: 894), der Duden fügt darüber hinaus noch die Komponente 'sich mit einer lästigen Sache abfinden' hinzu (³2008: 453). Die Belege, die innerhalb eines Zeitraumes von fast 40 Jahren publiziert wurden, folgen

dieser Bedeutungszuweisung problemlos, allenfalls ließe sich hier noch der Aspekt der 'Kompromissbereitschaft' ergänzen:
(7) Gemessen an den Ausgangspositionen der beiden Seiten ist der Vertrag ein fairer Kompromiß. „Man *muß ja immer eine Kröte mitschlucken*, wenn der andere eine schluckt." (14.08.1970)
In keinem der Nachweise konnte die Facette 'Demütigungen, Beleidigungen, Kränkungen einstecken müssen' auch nur ansatzweise herausgefiltert werden, so dass eine Bedeutungsrelation zwischen frz. *avaler des couleuvres* und dt. *Kröten schlucken* – wie es Bárdosi/Ettinger/Stölting in ihrem Wörterbuch vorschlagen (vgl. ³2003: 53) – nicht verifiziert werden kann.

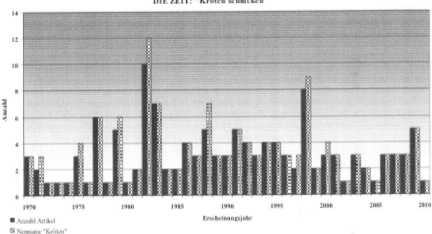

Allerdings scheint gerade bei dieser Redewendung einiges in Verwirrung geraten zu sein, denn selbst im *Trésor de la Langue Française informatisé*[6] finden sich unter den Lemmata *crapaud* und *couleuvre* folgende Erläuterungen:

Avaler un crapaud. 'Faire contre son gré une chose, un acte désagréable, pénible.'
Syn. *avaler un/des couleuvre(s).*
Avaler des couleuvres. 'Subir des affronts ou éprouver des difficultés sans se plaindre.'

In der direkten Gegenüberstellung der beiden Bedeutungen wird offensichtlich, dass die beiden Phraseologismen kaum synonym sein können. Zwar sind frz. *affronts* bzw. dt. *Kränkungen* in der Tat schwierig zu akzeptieren, aber nicht jede unangenehme Entscheidung, die getroffen werden muss, impliziert zwangsläufig eine Beleidigung oder gar Demütigung. Im Gegenteil, das o.a. Beispiel (7) verdeutlicht ja gerade mittels des erzielten Kompromisses den gegenseitigen Respekt der Beteiligten. Wenngleich nun keine Äquivalenz zwischen den beiden Mehrworteinheiten festzustellen ist, so könnte man das *Natternschlucken* (frz. *avaler des couleuvres*) freilich als eine Intensivierung des *Krötenschluckens* (frz. *avaler des crapauds*) auffassen.

---

[6] Vgl. auch die entsprechenden Lemmata im GRLF sowie im DFL.

Die Übersetzung einer solchen Mehrworteinheit erweist sich dann als einfach, so Albrecht, wenn „eine in einer Sprache entstandene Wendung in andere Sprachen übernommen wurde: *eine Kröte schlucken, avaler un crapaud, ingoiare un rospo*", hätten daher „mehr oder weniger die gleiche Bedeutung" (2005: 119).

In Anlehnung an die Analysekriterien, die Dobrovol'skij/Piirainen für den Vergleich von Phraseologismen vorschlagen (vgl. 2005: 67ff), soll hier daher eingehender überprüft werden, inwieweit sich die Redewendung *eine Kröte schlucken* in anderen Sprachen als äquivalent erweist. Als Grundlage der Untersuchung dienen Pressetexte aus international renommierten Tageszeitungen, die im Jahre 2009 online publiziert wurden. Erstaunlicherweise konnten für das Englische oder Französische weder in *The New York Times* noch in *Le Figaro* entsprechende Belege für *to swallow a toad* respektive *avaler un crapaud* gefunden werden. Eine Verifizierung in den einschlägigen Wörterbüchern blieb für das Englische[7], aber auch für das Spanische[8] erfolglos, für das Französische konnten entsprechende Belege immerhin in den großen Lexika nachgewiesen werden[9]. Widersprüche ergeben sich hieraus zu den analysierten Pressetexten, denn die Redewendung sp. *tragarse el sapo* lässt sich für das Jahr 2009 in 23 Artikeln von *El País* herausfiltern und erreicht damit im Vergleich zu den anderen Zeitungen den höchsten Wert. In Anbetracht eines solchen Resultats, liegt die Vermutung nahe, dass im Spanischen für Redewendungen andere Quellen zu konsultieren sind. Tatsächlich ergibt aber erst die Recherche im *Diccionario del Español actual* einen lexikografischen Nachweis, nämlich: *tragar(se) un sapo: 'aguantar una contrariedad sin exteriorizarlo'* (1999: 4037).

Zeitung[10]	Land	Redewendung	Artikelanzahl 2009	Sprache	Lexikografischer Nachweis
FR	D	eine Kröte schlucken	9	D	√
NYT	USA	to swallow a toad	---	E	---
LF	F	avaler un crapaud	---	F	√
EP	ES	tragarse el sapo	23	SP	√
LR	I	ingoiare un rospo	8	I	√
DDN	PT	engolir um sapo	13	PT	√
			insg. **53**		

Tab. 1: Anzahl der Artikel, die die Redewendung *Kröte schlucken* im Jahre 2009 enthalten

In den französischen Lexika ist die Mehrworteinheit wiederum erfasst, in den Artikeln von *Le Monde* des Jahres 2009 aber nicht zu ermitteln. Und schließlich konnte für das Englische kein Hinweis auf eine figurative Bedeutung ausgemacht werden: Weder ließ sich ein entsprechender Beleg in den Artikeln von *The New York Times* finden noch in den Lexika.

---

[7] Webster's kennt zwar den wörtlich gemeinten *toadeater*, aber keine figurative Bedeutung, *to swallow a toad* findet dort jedenfalls keine Erwähnung (vgl. WID 1961/1993: 2402).
[8] Im *Diccionario de la lengua española* der *Real Academia Española* fehlt das Lemma.
[9] Resultat der Recherche im TLF, GRLF und im DFL.
[10] FR: Frankfurter Rundschau; NYT: The New York Times; LF: Le Figaro; EP: El País; LR: La Repubblica; DDN: Diário de Notícias.

Für das Deutsche, Italienische und Portugiesische ließ sich die Redewendung dagegen problemlos in Artikeln und Wörterbüchern nachweisen.

In welchen konkreten Erscheinungsformen zeigt sich die Redewendung nun aber in der Presseberichterstattung? Auch dies ist für die jeweiligen Sprachen verschieden, denn während die italienischen Beispiele die geringste Varianz aufweisen und bei 9 Belegen nur zwei unterschiedliche Ausformungen erkennen lassen, erhöht sich deren Anzahl bei den portugiesischen *Diário de Notícias* auf 7 Varianten, in der *Frankfurter Rundschau* auf 8 in *El País* sogar auf 17 verschiedene Versionen. Die Unterschiede sind dabei oft nur minimal, wie bspw. ein Wechsel vom bestimmten zum unbestimmten Artikel oder auch von der Singular- zur Pluralform. Größere Aussagekraft haben diese Ergebnisse freilich, wenn man sie noch ins Verhältnis zur Anzahl der Belege setzt: Die größte Stabilität ist dann bei den italienischen Nachweisen, die höchste Variabilität gleichermaßen bei den spanischen und deutschen Mehrworteinheiten festzustellen.

Anhand einer thematischen Analyse lassen sich hier nun noch weitere Besonderheiten herausarbeiten. So erzielt die Redewendung in der politischen Berichterstattung in den untersuchten Artikeln bei allen Sprachen hohe bzw. höchste Werte. In der portugiesischen und deutschen Presse erscheint sie zudem häufiger in der Rubrik Sport, in der italienischen ebenso in der Wirtschaftsberichterstattung. Insgesamt wird die Mehrworteinheit vor allem in der informierenden, nur selten in der meinungsbetonten Presse verwendet. Alles in allem kann also die Feststellung von Röhrich, dass die Redewendung „Kröten schlucken" „ungemein häufig in der politischen Sprache" vorkommt, nun auch auf andere Sprachen ausgeweitet werden (1992: 894):

Sprachen	**D**	**I**	**SP**	**PT**	**Gesamt**
Zeitung	Frankf. R.	La Repubbl.	El País	Diário d. N.	
Artikelanzahl	9	8	23	13	53
Nachweise	11	9	24	13	**57**
Rubriken:					
Politik	6	3	18	7	**34**
Wirtschaft	---	3	2	---	5
Bildung	---	---	2	---	2
Sport	3	2	1	5	**11**
Meinung	2	1	1	1	5

Tab. 2: Thematische Analyse zur Redewendung *Kröte schlucken* in verschiedenen Sprachen.

Inwieweit lassen sich nun die Phraseologismen bei all den herausgearbeiteten Differenzen und Gemeinsamkeiten sprachenübergreifend aber als tatsächlich äquivalent ansehen? Legt man die hier anvisierten Kriterien zu Grunde und fordert sowohl den lexikografischen Nachweis als auch Belege des allgemeinen Sprachgebrauchs, so kann folgende Bilanz gezogen werden.

Dt. *eine Kröte schlucken*, it. *ingoiare un rospo*, pt. *engolir um sapo* und selbst sp. *tragarse el sapo* erfüllen die Anforderungen voll und ganz, denn die jeweiligen Mehrworteinheiten lassen sich sowohl in Wörterbüchern als auch mehrfach in Pressetexten finden. Demnach kann hier tatsächlich Äquivalenz konstatiert werden, die dann natürlich auch die Übersetzung vereinfacht. Im Unterschied zur Feststellung von Albrecht (2005: 119), lässt sich die französische Redewendung *avaler un crapaud* jedoch keineswegs als übersetzungsäquivalent zu *eine Kröte schlucken* akzeptieren, denn wenngleich beide auch lexikografisch erfasst sind, so ist die französische Mehrworteinheit im allgemeinen Sprachgebrauch doch nicht präsent. Nicht *avaler un crapaud* sondern *avaler la pilule* ist hier die äquivalente Redewendung, die nun wiederum im Deutschen und im Englischen eine direkte Entsprechung haben, nämlich: *eine bittere Pille schlucken* respektive *to swallow a bitter pill*:

(8) „The Senate Republican leader, Mitch McConnell of Kentucky, said Mr. Obama needed support from every Democrat because the bill had 'virtually no appeal to any Republican senator.' - 'Here we are a few weeks before Christmas, with Democrats trying to squeeze every single one of their members *to swallow a pretty bitter pill* for the American people,' Mr. McConnell said" (The New York Times, 07.12.2009)

3. Zusammenfassung

Im Deutschen lässt sich eine kleine unwichtige Geldsumme mit der Metapher *Kröten* bezeichnen, im Englischen sind dies wiederum nichts als *peanuts*. Seit dieser Ausdruck nun einen Skandal auslöste und daher von der Gesellschaft für deutsche Sprache zum Unwort des Jahres 1994 gewählt wurde, erfreut er sich im Deutschen großer Beliebtheit. Die Analyse hat nun aber gezeigt, dass beide nicht einfach gegenseitig ausgetauscht werden können. Während *peanuts* von den Sprachnutzern mit steigender Tendenz verwendet wird, erscheint *Kröten* eher selten in der Presseberichterstattung. Diese stehen aber wiederum als Teil der Redewendung *Kröten schlucken* im Mittelpunkt der politischen Berichterstattung. Übersetzungsäquivalenz konnte hier für einige der untersuchten Sprachen, jedoch nicht für alle, festgestellt werden. Andere Redewendungen füllen in einem solchen Fall dann die bestehende Leerstelle im jeweiligen Sprachsystem aus.

6. Bibliographie

A Dictionary of American English 1960 London. (DAE)
ALBRECHT, J. (2005). *Übersetzung und Linguistik*. Tübingen.
AYTO, J. ³2010 *Oxford Dictionary of English Idioms*. Oxford.
BÁRDOSI, V./ ETTINGER, S./ STÖLTING, C. ³2003 *Redewendungen Französisch / Deutsch. Thematisches Wörter- und Übungsbuch*. Tübingen/Basel.
Chambers Dictionary of Etymology (2003/1988). New York. (DET)
Diccionario de la lengua española ²²2001 online unter: http://buscon.rae.es/draeI/ (DLESP)
Dictionnaire de français „Littré": http://littre.reverso.net/dictionnaire-francais (DFL)
DOBROVOL'SKIJ, D./PIIRAINEN, E. 2005 *Figurative Language: Cross-cultural and Cross-linguistic Perspectives*. Amsterdam/Boston.
Der Duden, Bd. 1 ²¹1996. *Rechtschreibung der deutschen Sprache*. Mannheim/Leipzig.
Der Duden, Bd. 5 ⁵1990; ⁶1997, ⁷2001). *Das Fremdwörterbuch*. Mannheim/Leipzig.
Der Duden, Bd. 11 ³2008. *Redewendungen*. Mannheim/Leipzig.
Grand Robert de la langue Française électronique online unter: http://lerobert.demarque.com/fr/fr/dictionnaire-en-ligne/ (GRLF)
GRIMM, J. / GRIMM, W. 1873 *Deutsches Wörterbuch* Bd. 5. Leipzig. (DWB)
KLUGE, F. (²³1999). *Etymologisches Wörterbuch der deutschen Sprache*. Berlin.
MARTINS BARATA, A. 1989 *Dicionário Prático de locuções e expressões peculiares da língua portuguesa*. Braga.
MÜLLER, K. (Hrsg.) 1994 *Lexikon der Redensarten*. München. (LDR)
RADICCHI, S. ³1985 *In Italia. Modi di dire ed espressioni idiomatiche*. Roma.
RÖHRICH, L. 1992 *Das große Lexikon der sprichwörtlichen Redensarten* Bd. 2. Freiburg.
SECO, M./ ANDRÉS, O. / RAMOS, G. 1999 *Diccionario del español actual* Bd 2. Madrid.
The Oxford English Dictionary 1970/1933 Oxford.
Trésor de la Langue Française informatisé: online unter: http://atilf.atilf.fr/tlf.htm (TLF)
Webster's Third New International Dictionary (1993/1961). Cologne. (WID)

A NEW STATISTICAL CLASSIFICATION OF SET PHRASES

Jean-Pierre Colson
Institut libre Marie Haps (Brussels) /
Université catholique de Louvain (Louvain-la-Neuve)

Abstract: Traditional classifications of set phrases based on semantic criteria are confronted with the problem of borderline cases and cannot be easily verified on large corpora nor used for automatic extraction. In this paper, a purely statistical classification is proposed, based on the association between the element parts of n-grams and on the frequency of the combination.

Key words: collocations, phrasemes, automatic extraction, corpus-based phraseology

1. Introduction

Phraseology has largely contributed to making set phrases a central issue in linguistic theory and practice. It should be recalled, however, that the scope of phraseology is not restricted to pure idioms or phrasemes, but also includes formulaic language, routine formulae, clichés, collocations and all sorts of weakly idiomatic phrases, that are considered by Burger (1998) as *phraseology in the broad sense*. As far as frequency is concerned, it has been shown that the great bulk of set phrases in most texts precisely belongs to this weaker part of phraseology, while fully idiomatic phrases (*phrasemes*) are rather rare in corpora (Moon,1998; Colson, 2007). It comes therefore as no surprise that corpus and computational linguistics, in which statistics play a crucial part, have devoted more attention to frequent combinations. Most recent works start from a very broad notion of set phrases, for which the generic term is often *collocation*[1]. Contrary to the semantic approach followed by many researchers in phraseology, most corpus and computational linguists now use a purely statistical definition of collocations (taken as set phrases in the broadest sense), and they mainly refer to Hoey (1991), who was inspired by Sinclair (1991) when he wrote that collocations are defined as *"the relationship of a lexical item with items that appear with greater than random probability in its (textual) context"*. The advantage of this formulation is that it focuses on an objective, reproducible criterion (statistical probability) for defining set phrases in the broad sense. If we apply it to a linguistic corpus, we find many different constructions corresponding to this definition: proper nouns (*Mount Rushmore*), compound nouns (*city breaks*), idioms or phrasemes (*spill the beans*), routine formulae (*long time no see*), proverbs, sayings, clichés (*it takes two to tango*), quotations (*mock the time with fairest show*), song or films titles (*Gone with the wind*)... While statistics yield a very broad palette of apparently unrelated constructions, it should be stressed that there is a crucial common ground between

---

[1] In Burger (1998), collocations are just one category of set phrases, defined as weakly or partly idiomatic constructions. In corpus and especially computational linguistics, 'collocation' is mainly used as the generic term for all set phrases, corresponding to German 'Phraseologismus'.

them: they are *recognised by native speakers as belonging together*. The advantage of statistics is only to make the identification of set phrases more objective, and to open the way for an automatic extraction of all set phrases.

2. New perspectives for the automatic extraction of set phrases

Since the publication of Church and Hanks (1990), there have been numerous attempts at extracting *collocations* in the broad sense (set phrases). Almost all those studies, however, are limited to binary combinations (bigrams) and all the possible statistical scores (for an overview, see Evert, 2004) have shown their limitations: the performance of the scores is generally low (Deane, 2005) and it is only better if additional grammatical criteria are added (Pazos Bretaña & Pamies Bertrán, 2008). There are very diverse results when different scores are used and an extension to trigrams or higher grams is not easy (Heid, 2007).

In Colson (2010a; 2010b), two different exploratory methods are proposed for the automatic extraction of trigrams or higher grams from large corpora. Both methods rely on the use of a web search engine. The second method is based upon the average proximity between the grams as a measure of association, and the easiest way of applying it is the analysis of web search results (for a full report, see Colson, 2010b). Equation (1) below summarises the way the score is computed:

(1)
$$WPRn(Sx) = \frac{Fe(GR2, GR3 \ldots GRn)}{x}$$

The principle is fairly simple: users can verify the collocational (fixed) character of a combination by typing them WITHOUT quotation marks on a web search engine (in this experiment, www.yahoo.com). A program then checks the proportion of EXACT matches in the first results sent back by the search engine (in this case 100); the score is divided by x (x being the number of results yielded). Thus, as expressed by equation (1), the Web proximity score (*WPR*) at gram level *n* for a given sample of size x is the division of the exact frequency for those grams (*Fe*) by x. In other words, the score will be close to 0 if a given n-gram is not fixed, and it will be closer to 1 if a combination is fixed. The threshold level has been experimentally set at 0.15 for considering a combination as (at least partly) fixed. The originality of this approach is that it starts from the real proximity of grams in huge corpora, and not from statistical contingency tables; it can besides be used for grams of size 2 to 10 (or even higher). The method was tested (Colson 2010b) on a list of 4,000 collocations mentioned by dictionaries, and on a set of 340,000 fivegrams extracted from the Web1T, a huge English corpus of 1 trillion words (10,000 times the British National Corpus) made available by Google.[2]

---

[2] The Web1T is distributed by the Linguistic Data Consortium, http:www.ldc.upenn.edu/. It consists of 6 DVDs. The n-grams were generated from about 1 trillion word tokens from the Web and the corpus is therefore called the Web1T. The Web1T can be easily manipulated by several free programs, such as SSGNC (http:code.google.com/p/ssgnc/wiki/Introduction). The Computation Linguistics group of the University of

The efficiency of automatic extraction algorithms is traditionally measured by precision and recall. The precision score measures whether all n-grams that were identified as set phrases are indeed set phrases, whereas recall will check if all set phrases have been extracted by the algorithm.[3] Both the precision and the recall score obtained in Colson (2010b) are above the average: 0.965 for precision and 0.915 for recall.

The *Web Proximity score (WPR)* presented in equation (1) above looks simple, but it actually triggers the complex algorithms developed by web search engines. This offers the advantages of speed and huge corpus size.

Table 1 below presents the results obtained with both scores for a number of trigram combinations starting with *face the*[4]. The frequency of those trigrams on the Yahoo! search engine is also mentioned.

Trigrams	WPR-score	Yahoo! Frequency
Face the music	0.77	3,690,043
Face the truth	0.61	1,910,039
Face the facts	0.47	2,250,017
Face the challenge	0.45	2,400,017
Face the vicissitudes	0.44	1,011
Face the indignity	0.39	2,110
Face the ravages	0.33	2,700
Face the unthinkable	0.17	25,700
Face the storm	0.16	53,300
Face the consequences	0.14	2,090,273
Face the crowd	0.06	108,002
Face the window	0	37,900

Table 1. Proximity scores and frequency for trigrams with 'face the'

Osnabrück (http:www.cogsci.uni-osnabrueck.de/~korpora/ws/cgi-bin/Web1T5/Web1T5_freq.perl) offers a very useful tool on its Web site.

[3] Precision and recall rely on the relationship between the elements that should have been detected and were indeed found, called the true positives (tp), the elements that were detected but wrongly, the false positives (fp); and the elements that were not detected and should have been, the false negatives (fn). This yields the following formulas:

$$\text{Precision} = \frac{tp}{tp + fp} \text{ and Recall} = \frac{tp}{tp + fn}$$

[4] The search is here limited to this exact form (in the infinitive), with no words between the grams.

The figures in table 1 show that the last two trigrams (*face the crowd, face the window*) receive a much lower *WPR*. They are clearly less fixed from a semantic point of view as well. If we set the threshold level for the score at 0.15, we can see that all fixed trigrams from the table are recognised as such. Table 1 also suggests that frequency is not a good criterion for extracting (and defining) set phrases. *Face the music* indeed receives both the highest *WPR*-score and the highest frequency, but *face the vicissitudes, face the indignity, face the ravages*, for instance display a much lower frequency than *face the consequences*, and correspond however to a higher *WPR*-score.

The Web1T offers additional evidence that raw frequency on large corpora is not a valid criterion for extracting set phrases. Table 2 presents the most frequent fivegrams from the Web1T ending with the noun *argument*. Obviously, most of them are not set phrases in any sense.

14898331	PUN PUN PUN supplied argument
889940	NUM warning PUN supplied argument
127110	NUM warning PUN invalid argument
98867	pointer targets in passing argument
94064	for the sake of argument
66454	<S> warning PUN invalid argument
54076	wrong datatype for second argument
32681	builtin and then its argument
30981	PUN PUN PUN the argument
27022	PUN PUN PUN first argument
25963	both sides of the argument
25231	warning - UNK param argument
18018	PUN PUN the first argument
16455	politics PUN essays PUN argument
14866	ordered submitted without oral argument
14239	<S> warning PUN missing argument
14223	PUN PUN warning PUN argument
13110	has been deprecated - argument
13009	PUN warning PUN passing argument
11657	<S> it is the argument
11543	<S> there is an argument
11487	this is not an argument
10926	determined unanimously that oral argument
10895	the i - th argument
10871	- merge UNK PUN argument

Table 2. Most frequent fivegrams from the Web1T ending with 'argument'

3. Toward a statistical classification of set phrases

Although the Web Proximity score presented in the preceding section should still be confirmed by further evidence, it may be interesting to take a look at the classification of set phrases that derives from it. If we start from a semantic classification of set phrases (Burger, 1998), it is obvious that the most fixed, idiomatic, opaque or figurative constructions such as *spill the beans* will be considered as the clearest cases of phraseology. At the other end of the spectrum, we will find partly idiomatic combinations (weak collocations, grammatical patterns and communicative formulas).

The first results obtained with the *WPR*-score partly confirm this distinction. Indeed, strongly fixed phrases (usually called *phrasemes* or *idioms*) receive a very high score, no matter what their frequency is. Table 3 below displays the *WPR* and the frequency (on Yahoo!) of 12 common English phrasemes[5].

Phrasemes	*WPR-score*	*Yahoo! Frequency*
A taste of his own medicine	0.57	266,003
Butterflies in my stomach	0.66	377,008
Cat got your tongue?	0.63	320,005
Down for the count	0.51	1,760,013
Draw the line	0.50	9,670,146
Easier said than done	0.97	6,510,107
Every cloud has a silver lining	0.66	541,008
Fish out of water	0.78	4,210,028
Get it off your chest	0.80	2,890,203
Give it a whirl	0.69	2,130,022
Life in the fast lane	0.75	2,630,031
Needle in a haystack	0.80	422,015
Spill the beans	0.61	2,910,029

Table 3. WPR-score and Web frequency for common English phrasemes

It is again quite clear from table 3 that frequency and *WPR*-score are two different things: the highest *WPR*-scores (*Easier said than done, Get it off your chest, Needle in a haystack, Fish out of water, Life in the fast lane*) are not the most frequent phrasemes; besides, *Needle in a haystack* is 22 times less frequent than *Draw the line*, but its *WPR*-score is much higher.

Table 4 presents the results for a number of constructions that belong semantically to the category of *collocations* (as defined by Burger, 1998), i.e. partly idiomatic phrases.

---

[5] In this list, the phrasemes have been reduced to the stable part, for instance *Needle in a haystack* and not *Finding a needle in a haystack*, because several variants are possible (e.g. *Looking for a needle in a haystack*).

Collocations	WPR-score	Yahoo! Frequency
A business deal	0.27	1,070,034
Carry out a plan	0.31	94,402
Changed his mind	0.51	6,850,107
Come to an agreement	0.60	4,420,082
Earn a living	0.63	7,740,116
Make a comparison	0.38	1,470,017
Meet the requirements	0.15	17,600,207
Take advantage of	0.73	287,003,946
Turn a deaf ear to	0.32	330,005

Table 4. WPR-score and Web frequency for common English collocations

To complete the picture, another test was carried out about the adjective collocations in combination with the noun *criticism*. In order to make a valid comparison possible with the traditional statistical scores, part of the WaCky English corpus[6] (a portion of 10 million words) was parsed and indexed by the program Xaira tools (developed by Oxford University[7]) and the Z-score was computed for all adjectives preceding the noun. Table 5 displays, for the top of the list, the Z-score, the frequency on the WaCky English corpus, the *WPR*-score computed on the Web, and the Yahoo! frequency.

Collocations (+ criticism)	Z-score	WaCky Frequency	WPR-score	Yahoo! Frequency
Textual	219.3	11	0.97	1,640,001
Literary	164.7	19	0.91	17,000,107
Withering	130.0	1	0.83	215,016
Constructive	123.8	7	0.85	13,600,405
Subverting	82.2	1	0.02	5
Incessant	61.3	1	0.91	13,001
Harshest	55.4	1	0.90	159,016
Stinging	49.1	1	0.73	329,004
Fruitless	47.4	1	0.09	94
Scathing	47.4	1	0.80	1,150,015
Malicious	41.3	2	0.55	8,561

[6] The WaCky project (Baroni et al., 2009) is a huge corpus of 2 billion words assembled from the Web (http:wacky.sslmit.unibo.it/doku.php?do=show&id=start); it is available for English, Italian, German and French.
[7] For the documentation, see: http:www.oucs.ox.ac.uk/rts/xaira/

Outspoken	36.0	1	0.71	139,009
Severe	26.5	3	0.85	942,012
Practical	26.1	5	0.70	85,301
Strongest	22.1	1	0.88	101,001
Valid	19.7	2	0.54	503,017
Implicit	19.1	1	0.80	86,601
Bitter	16.4	1	0.45	82,400
Excessive	16.4	1	0.50	38,200
Unfair	16.1	1	0.59	561,004
Damaging	15.9	1	0.27	15,400
Heavy	15.2	2	0.85	1,280,064
Substantial	14.7	2	0.77	62,800
Subtle	13.6	1	0.65	25,501
Silent	13.0	1	0.09	1,420
Slight	12.3	1	0.84	84,204

Table 5. Z-score, WPR-score and Frequency for adjective collocations with 'criticism'

Table 4 and 5 confirm that frequency alone is not a good criterion for the degree of association. Table 5 also shows that the corpus of 10 million words was not sufficient for extracting many examples of adjective collocations with *criticism*, and that the Z-score is less efficient than the *WPR-score*.

If we use the *WPR*-score as a statistical criterion for the classification of set phrases, we then come to the conclusion that this does not totally corroborate the semantic classification: combinations that are strongly fixed, idiomatic, non-compositional or opaque such as those in table 3 display *WPR*-scores that are often higher than those of less idiomatic phrases (table 4), but binary collocations, on the other hand (table 5), show very high scores as well. As to frequency, it depends a lot on each combination, and no frequency threshold can therefore be established for the classification of set phrases. It is true that many collocations reach frequency figures above those of phrasemes, but *spill the beans*, for instance, is three times more frequent than a common collocation such as *severe criticism*.

Obviously, the fact that the statistical classification does not really confirm the semantic one, does not mean that the latter is not valid. It is just an indication that the semantic criteria cannot be used as a basis for a statistical classification, nor for the automatic extraction of set phrases. Investigating the theoretical implications of this point would carry us too far, but the matter is certainly related to the complex interplay of meaning, structure and frequency in language.

From a practical point of view, the algorithm used in this paper establishes a statistical classification of set phrases that reflects their degree of association. Frequency is an important additional criterion for checking if the combination is common or not. The statistical classification may then look as in table 6 below[8]; the only relevant distinctions within set phrases are: degree of association (no association, low, medium or high association) and frequency (low, medium or high). If there is no association (*WPR*-score lower than 0.15), the combination does not qualify as a set phrase; a low association (*WPR*-score between 0.15 and 0.34) but a medium or high frequency may be sufficient to have borderline cases (indicated as '+/-' in table 6), while a medium or high association (*WPR*-score equal to or higher than 0.35) always results in a set phrase. In that case, frequency is an additional indication of how common the set phrase is. A very high association score combined with a high frequency is indicated as '++' in the table.

COMBINATIONS	ASSOCIATION				FREQUENCY			SET PHRASE
	NO	Low	Mediu	Hig	Low	Medium	High	
Constructive				+		+		++
Down for the count				+	+			+
Face the consequences		+				+		+/-
Face the crowd	+					+		-
Face the facts			+			+		+
Face the music				+		+		++
Face the ravages		+			+			-
Face the unthinkable		+			+			-
Face the window	+				+			-
Fruitless criticism	+				+			-
Give it a whirl				+		+		++
Make a comparison			+			+		+
Meet the requirements		+				+		+/-
Severe criticism			+		+			+
Silent criticism	+				+			-
Spill the beans			+			+		++
Turn a deaf ear to		+				+		+/-
Withering criticism			+		+			+

Table 6. A statistical classification of a few word combinations

[8] In this table, the threshold for low association has been set at a minimal *WPR*-score of 0.15, for medium at 0.35 and for high at 0.60. As for frequency, the figures in this paper were computed from the web, so we set the thresholds rather high: from 100,000 occurrences for medium frequency and from 1,000,000 occurrences for high frequency.

4. References

BARONI, M., BERNARDINI, S., FERRARESI, A. & ZANCHETTA, E. 2009 The WaCky Wide Web: A collection of very large linguistically processed Web-crawled corpora. In: *Journal of Language Resources and Evaluation,* 43 (3): 209-226.

BURGER, H. 1998 *Phraseologie. Eine Einführung am Beispiel des Deutschen.* Berlin: Erich Schmidt Verlag.

CHURCH, K. W. & HANKS, P. 1990 Word association norms, mutual information and lexicography. In: *Computational Linguistics* 16: 22–29.

COLSON, J.-P. 2007 The World Wide Web as a corpus for set phrases. In: Burger, H.; Dobrovol'skij, D.; Kühn, P. & Norrick, N. R. (eds.), *Phraseologie / Phraseology. Ein internationales Handbuch der zeitgenössischen Forschung / An International Handbook of Contemporary Research.* Berlin / New York: Walter de Gruyter: Vol. 2: 1071-1077.

COLSON, J.-P. 2008 Cross-linguistic phraseological studies: An overview. In: Granger, S. & Meunier, F. (eds.), *Phraseology. An interdisciplinary perspective.* Amsterdam / Philadelphia: John Benjamins, 191-206.

COLSON, J.-P. 2010a The Contribution of Web-based Corpus Linguistics to a Global Theory of Phraseology. In: Ptashnyk, S., Hallsteindóttir, E. & Bubenhofer, N. (eds.), *Corpora, Web and Databases. Computer-Based Methods in Modern Phraselogy and Lexicography.* Hohengehren, Schneider Verlag: 23-35.

COLSON, J.-P. 2010b Automatic extraction of collocations: a new Web-based method. In: S. Bolasco, S., Chiari, I. & Giuliano, L., *Proceedings of JADT 2010,Statistical Analysis of Textual Data, Sapienza University , Rome, 9-11 June 2010.* Milan: LED Edizioni: 397-408.

DEANE, P. 2005 A nonparametric method for extraction of candidate phrasal terms. In: *43d Annual Meeting of the Association for Computational Linguistics.* University of Michigan.

HEID, U. 2007 Computational linguistic aspects of phraseology. In: Burger, H.; Dobrovol'skij, D.; Kühn, P. & Norrick, N. R. (eds.), *Phraseologie / Phraseology. Ein internationales Handbuch der zeitgenössischen Forschung / An International Handbook of Contemporary Research.* Berlin / New York: Walter de Gruyter: Vol. 2: 1036-1044.

HOEY, M. 1991 *Patterns of Lexis in Text.* Oxford University Press.

MOON, R. 1998 *Fixed Expressions and Idioms in English.* Oxford: Clarendon Press.

PAZOS BRETAÑA, J.-M. & PAMIES BERTRÁN, A. 2008 Combined statistical and grammatical criteria for the retrieval of phraseological units in an electronic corpus. In: Granger, S. & Meunier, F. (eds.), *Phraseology. An interdisciplinary perspective.* Amsterdam / Philadelphia: John Benjamins: 391–406.

SINCLAIR, J. 1991 *Corpus, Concordance, Collocation.* Oxford: Oxford University Press.

LA JERGA DE LOS ESTUDIANTES BRASILEÑOS UNIVERSITARIOS: LA TRIBU Y LA ALDEA

Ortiz Álvarez, M.L.
Ribeiro Câmara A. P.
Universidade de Brasília

A vida não me chegava pelos jornais nem pelos livros
Vinha da boca do povo na língua errada do povo
Língua certa do povo
Porque ele é que fala gostoso o português do Brasil
Manuel Bandeira

Abstract: Our study aims at examining slang as a group's linguistic resource, more specifically, youth slang in a university context, its dynamism and its immense potential for reflecting socio-cultural practices and values. Therefore, the slang we intended to investigate is the one that the "tribe" of university students, created by them in order to relate to their peers inside their restricted environment. In order to reach our goals, we collected slang expressions from genuine *Orkut* web material and from recorded interviews with university students. We analyzed those expressions in relation to their origin and meaning, as well as to their role in this emerging specific context.

Key words: Brazilian slang, university slang, *Orkut*.

1. Introducción

Toda lengua es esencialmente dinámica, es decir, no constituye un sistema cristalizado y definitivo, por el contrario, está siempre modificándose, viviendo un proceso continuo de combinación, composición y perfeccionamiento. El lenguaje constituye una entidad viva en constante mudanza, siendo sus usuarios los que determinan esas transformaciones lingüísticas, condicionadas por diversos factores: regionales, sociales, intelectuales etc. Uno de los registros lingüísticos del léxico es la jerga común, objeto de análisis de este estudio. Tal jerga caracteriza un determinado grupo social, predominantemente en su modalidad oral y registro informal. En este sentido, Oliveira (2001 : 109) afirma que "*de un modo general, podemos considerar como princípio el hecho de que un vocablo es aceptado como elemento de la lengua, a partir del momento en que pasa a expresar los valores de un determinado grupo social y, sobre todo, satisfacer sus necesidades de comunicación*"(traducción nuestra). Así, la actuación social de los hablantes favorece la ampliación léxica por medio de vocablos y expresiones algunas utilizadas de forma restricta por determinados grupos sociales.

2. La jerga

El diccionario Michaellis (1998: 1034) trata la *gíria* (jerga) como lenguaje especial de un grupo perteneciente a una clase o a una profesión, o como el lenguaje de grupos marginalizados. Ya el diccionario Aurélio (1999: 989) complementa la definición antes apuntada con la expresión "lenguaje de malhechores, etc.", usada para no ser entendidos por otras personas. Para Cardona (1991: 159), [la jerga es una] *variedad lingüística compartida por un grupo restringido (por edad o por ocupación) y hablada para excluir de la comunicación personas extrañas y para reforzar el sentimiento de identidad de los que pertenecen al grupo.*

De acuerdo con Ortiz (2007), la jerga se refiere a un conjunto de vocablos y expresiones, características de ciertos grupos socio-profesionales y clases sociales, a la que se recurre cuando el lenguaje corriente no consigue dar respuesta a ciertas necesidades de comunicación, o cuando se desea mantener alguna cosa en secreto dentro de un grupo restringido de personas. En general la jerga se utiliza para lograr la comunicación entre indivíduos que realizan actividades en común, con el objetivo de evitar que el mensaje pueda ser captado por otras personas ajenas al grupo. Es un tipo de lenguaje gremial o de convivencia. Así, en los grupos que lo pratican, desempeña una función especial: es un seña identitaria gremial, sirve como marca de ese grupo. Por tanto, existen tantas jergas cuantos grupos las utilicen: jóvenes, medicos, policias, roqueeros, marginales, etc. Esa jerga es utilizada en muchas ocasiones como forma de defensa del grupo frente a otros grupos, mayores o menores, y para mantener su identidad como grupo así como la de sus respectivos miembros.

Dauzart (1946) afirmaba que el proceso de formación de la jerga es un hecho absolutamente normal de la propia evolución de las lenguas y está ligado a un fenómeno social concreto, ésta se enriquece o empobrece, en casos extremos aparece o se extingue, dependiendo del auge o disminución de los aspectos sociales relacionados. Generalmente la jerga tiene su origen asociado a los grupos marginalizados y su finalidad era establecer un tipo de comunicación que sólo podria ser entendida por quien dominase tal código, quedando, así, fuera de la norma social. Por tener estrecha vinculación con la lengua oral y con la norma coloquial de la lengua, ser utilizada en actividades cotidianas, y no encuadrarse en la norma culta, su uso, esencialmente en la lengua escrita, es censurado por muchos gramáticos. Pero aparece en la lengua escrita, en los textos literarios, en la caracterización de determinados personajes o en textos publicados en revistas y periódicos, con la intención de interactuar con un determinado grupo social. No obstante, la creación y duración de la jerga depende de su aceptación y empleo por parte de los usuarios durante sus interacciones diarias. En ese caso se dice que la jerga "cuajó" (*pegou*) y a partir de entonces, su permanencia en la vida cotidiana de un grupo es imprevisible.

De este modo, la jerga es un instrumento de comunicación caracterizado por su riqueza, espontaneidad y fuerza de expresión, atestiguando las frecuentes mudanzas sociales, las conquistas tecnológicas y la modificación de los modos de vivir de una determinada comunidad. Por esa razón, la jerga requiere una renovación constante, porque muchas veces el uso excesivo desgasta sus palabras, que pasan rápidamente al dominio público, incorporadas a la lengua coloquial, pasando a formar parte de la vida cotidiana. Tienen como característica encubrir, enmascarar, ser conocidas por pocos, por tanto todo eso exige, en consecuencia, continuas modificaciones. Esa fluidez hace que algunas caigan en desuso o se vuelvan *anticuadas*, o *superadas* en poco tiempo, aunque eso no elimina el resurgimiento de muchas de ellas. Por ejemplo, la palabra *bacana* en portugués que parece aún estar *en la onda*, dependiendo del contexto en que es utilizada. A veces nos acostumbramos a "medir" las diferentes generaciones por el tipo de jerga que usan, pues los jóvenes son más permeables a las constantes innovaciones.

3. La jerga juvenil

En muchas ocasiones la jerga se identifica por el comportamiento de los grupos más agresivos, por ejemplo, los jóvenes, marcados por la insatisfacción, la rebeldía y el espíritu de irreverencia con el objetivo de marcar su oposición y hostilidad con relación a comportamientos estereotipados. Así, en toda parte, la juventud construye formas propias de existencia, de comunicarse entre si y con los otros, de forma más dinámica y explosiva. La proliferación de esos estilos muestra que los jóvenes forman un segmento dentro de la sociedad y luchan por buscar su auto-afirmación. Por tanto, la jerga puede funcionar como mecanismo de catarsis social, una manera para que los individuos liberen sus frustraciones y su rechazo de las injusticias, por medio de ironía, humor, agresividad, y la oposición a todo lo que remite a los valores establecidos por la sociedad y a los tabúes morales cristalizados por la tradición (Preti 2000).

En el caso de los jóvenes, refiriéndose a la situación específica del lenguaje de los estudiantes, Mônica Rector (1975: 101) resalta: *la jerga de los estudiantes es un lenguaje especial, propio de un grupo social y generacional. Se trata de términos y expresiones que se refieren a una determinada actividad. En el caso de los estudiantes, el lenguaje empleado tiene la intención de no ser comprendidos, principalmente por sus profesores, y para ser identificados como alumnos.* Se asemeja a lo que I. Iordan (p. 632-34) llama "argot": a) pertenece a una categoría social determinada, a un grupo de individuos que, junto con la jerga, usan la lengua común, y b) puede ser utilizada con la finalidad de no ser comprendida por aquellas personas que no pertenecen al respectivo grupo. Tiene la intención de "impresionar" y "llamar la atención" de los no iniciados, sobre todo de los universitarios.

Los adolescentes priorizan el uso de la jerga para integrarse en grupos formados por jóvenes, como afirma Calvet (2002: 114,) al decir que "*la jerga de los adolescentes responde parcialmente a un deseo de convivencia en el seno de un grupo de la misma edad*". Esa interacción, además del modo de hablar, se caracteriza también por la manera de vestirse, por las músicas y por los símbolos registrados en los *graffiti*.

Si comparásemos la juventud actual con la de los años 70, notaríamos una diferencia significativa entre la jerga que la caracteriza pues reflejan la ideología y comportamiento de las respectivas generaciones, con sus ideales, juicios y prejuicios. Marcos Bango (2006) en un artículo publicado en la revista *Presença Pedagógica*, discute dos tipos de discurso que se contraponen; el discurso científico y el discurso de sentido común. El primero remite a teorías de la lingüística moderna y considera las variaciones lingüísticas como un proceso, y el segundo, está cargado de prejuicios sociales y opera con la noción de error (juicios de valor). Así, es evidente que el sentido común predomina con relación a las practicas lingüísticas, una vez que el hablante puede inconscientemente indicar su origen, así como el grupo social al cual pertenece o en el cual participa (Calvet, 2002), lo que de cierta forma contribuye para reforzar la actitud de (pre)juicio del hablante.

Conocemos el proceso de tribalización que ocurre en nuestra sociedad y que creó un terreno abonado para el crecimiento y expansión de la jerga. Según Rector (1994), la indiferencia social conlleva a la formación de grupos, o bandas, pues es a través de esos grupos como se gana identidad cultural. Considerando ese proceso de tribalización que está íntimamente asociado a la jerga, decidimos añadir al título de nuestro trabajo las palabras "tribu y aldea". La tribu se refiere a los universitarios, el grupo que contemplaremos en nuestro estudio, y la aldea, al lugar en que ellos se encuentran y donde conviven, la universidad. En este trabajo procuramos desvincular la jerga del concepto de vocabulario de pícaros o malhechores, la tratamos sin el prejuicio que siempre le fue atribuido, pues ella es un recurso lingüístico, y es también usada por otros grupos, como por ejemplo, médicos y otros especialistas, y no sólo por marginales. En nuestra opinión, la jerga nunca será sinónimo de empobrecimiento del idioma, sino de riqueza semántica y léxica, por su expresividad, creatividad, su carácter humorístico, y se puede reconocer cómo a través de ella podemos entender las vivencias, inquietudes y concepciones de los grupos que coexisten en nuestra sociedad.

Las dos preguntas que orientaron nuestro estudio y análisis fueron: ¿Cuál es el papel y función de la jerga juvenil dentro del contexto universitario? ¿Qué significados metafóricos están detrás de las preguntas que fueron elaboradas para alcanzar nuestro objetivo principal de examinar la jerga como recurso lingüístico de un grupo, más específicamente la jerga dentro del ambiente universitario brasileño? Para analizar la jerga usada en la universidad, su comportamiento y sus funciones, contamos con el auxilio de un cuestionario y entrevistas realizadas con alumnos de una universidad pública del Distrito Federal, así como con textos producidos por universitarios en el *sitio de relacionamiento Orkut*.

4. La investigación

Definir lo que es jerga es hasta hoy una tarea ardua. Podemos observar que muchos confunden los términos *jerga* y *argot* aunque poco a poco estos estén siendo definidos ampliamente y de forma más clara. De acuerdo con Mônica Rector (1975) algunos autores como Lázaro Carreter y Amadeu Amaral colocan como equivalentes las palabras *jerga* y *argot*. Sin embargo, otros como Dino Preti y la propia Mônica Rector consideran que esos dos términos no son equivalentes. Otros autores como Mattoso Câmara (1956) considera el argot un aspecto de la jerga *lato sensu* en su modalidad más vulgar. Con relación a la confusión entre los términos jerga y argot ocurre probablemente por causa del término francés *argot* que, en algunos momentos es traducido como jerga, en otros como argot. Entendemos la jerga como el vocabulario restringido y específico de un determinado grupo social que posee, a veces inconscientemente, un carácter críptico. La principal función de la jerga es la comunicación, paralelamente a la de preservación de identidad y de defensa de un grupo. Entre las características de la jerga tenemos: 1) Su breve pervivencia; 2) la expresividad; 3) la metaforicidad, a través de la relación de semejanza entre el sentido propio y el figurado; 4) la idea de síntesis presente en cada vocablo. Según un material publicado en la revista "*Super Interessante*" en marzo de 1996, intitulada *Essa gíria é da hora!*, la jerga es definida como "aquel vocabulario que lo dice todo sin gastar mucha saliva"; 5) la codificación, o sea, el carácter críptico; 6) sirve como mecanismo de defensa de un determinado grupo social;7) es mantenedora de identidad social de un grupo.

De acuerdo con Celso Cunha (2004) también pueden ser características de la jerga la premeditación, la intencionalidad, la interdicción léxica y la consciencia del lenguaje. Basándonos en estudios de Dino Preti (1983) dividiremos la jerga en dos grandes grupos. La *jerga de grupo* y la *jerga común*. La de grupo es aquella que carga consigo la característica de *signo de grupo*, es elemento de auto-afirmación, de identificación, de defensa y preservación de clase. Ya la jerga común es aquella que no está más ligada al hecho de pertenecer a un grupo social, pues cuando la jerga de grupo pierde su carácter de *signo de grupo* y pasa a ser usada y entendida en el lenguaje popular se transforma en jerga común y deja de ser jerga de grupo. En ese trabajo dimos especial atención a la jerga de grupo.

Siendo la jerga universitaria el tema central de análisis de nuestro estudio, en ese tópico trataremos de entender las relaciones existentes entre la tribu (la juventud), la aldea (la universidad) y la jerga. Primero, necesitamos conocer y comprender el mundo de los jóvenes, quienes son. El concepto de juventud está ligado a la noción de edad y de generación. Según Foracchi (1972) la existencia humana, en sus diferentes etapas, está marcada por su ritmo biológico (edad y envejecimiento), y para cada una de esas etapas tenemos un comportamiento peculiar que las caracteriza. La juventud constituye, por tanto, una etapa de la vida humana, tanto por su ritmo biológico, como por la peculiaridad de sus acciones y actitudes. Esto quiere decir que *juventud* corresponde una generación dentro de nuestra sociedad, formada por individuos de edades afines, que poseen un estilo específico de comportamiento y que "comparten un acervo común de experiencias, situaciones de vida y oportunidades de trabajo" (op. cit.: 20-21).De acuerdo con Foracchi (1972), la juventud refleja las crisis del propio sistema, y en el comportamiento de esos jóvenes se observan omisiones, contradicciones y beneficios de nuestra configuración social. Y es de esa crisis de donde nacen las manifestaciones y respuestas de los jóvenes, entre las cuales podemos citar varios ejemplos: el tipo de vestimenta, el peinado, las maneras de relacionarse y, sobre todo, la forma de expresarse. De acuerdo con Mônica Rector (1994), una de las consecuencias o causas de ese conflicto de generaciones es la diversificación del lenguaje; los jóvenes usan la 'norma joven' para que los padres y otras personas no los entiendan, y así crean una actitud lingüística de oposición y de consciente agresión a la lengua estándar. Lo que es necesario entender es que los jóvenes, viviendo con la crisis que sobre ellos recae, generan comportamientos presentes desde la adolescencia y que se extienden a la vida universitaria llegando muchas veces hasta la fase adulta. De esas manifestaciones surgen las actitudes de ruptura de lo convencional, entre las cuales incluimos la jerga.

4.1 Metodología

La metodología empleada para realizar nuestra investigación es la cualitativo-interpretativa que busca describir los fenómenos de forma cualitativa, mostrando sus características específicas de acuerdo con el contexto donde se detecta el fenómeno estudiado, así como de sus participantes. En algunos momentos utilizamos también datos cuantitativos. Durante la lectura y análisis de los diccionarios decidimos observar como los universitarios entendían la jerga. Para tal elaboramos un cuestionario con cuatro preguntas dirigidas a investigar la definición y carácter de la jerga de acuerdo con la opinión de los jóvenes.

Usamos diccionarios de lengua general, fácilmente encontrables en bibliotecas públicas y particulares y mini-diccionarios que estudiantes de todos los niveles acostumbran a usar. Después de la lectura y selección de diccionarios procuramos también seleccionar textos producidos por universitarios. Nuestro primer objetivo era trabajar con textos de periódicos y de revistas escritos por alumnos de la universidad, ya que existe un periódico interno publicado por la Facultad de Comunicación y elaborado por estudiantes. Posteriormente, percibimos que no alcanzaríamos nuestro objetivo, ya que el lenguaje utilizado en esos textos era formal. Por esa razón, decidimos trabajar con textos de *orkut*. La universidad pública donde fue realizado este estudio posee una *comunidad de relacionamiento* en la web de *Orkut* con 28.300 miembros (hasta julio de 2009). Seleccionamos para lectura y análisis los temas producidos entre julio de 2008 y julio de 2009, relacionados a asuntos de la vida universitaria, y que tuviesen entre 10 e 150 *posts*.

*Orku*t es una comunidad virtual afiliada al Google, creada el 22 de enero de 2004 con el objetivo de ayudar a sus miembros a crear nuevas amistades, a relacionarse con amigos (no necesariamente en el sentido literal de la palabra, sino desde el punto de vista de las afinidades compartidas, y a participar en otras comunidades sobre los más diversos asuntos. El nombre *Orkut* tiene su origen en el proyectista jefe, Orkut Büyükkokten, ingeniero del Google. Tales sistemas, como éste adoptado por su proyectista, también son llamados *redes sociales*. El *Orkut* se compone de tres partes principales: *perfil, mis amigos* y *mis comunidades*. Es junto al *perfil* donde se localizan los mensajes propios y declaraciones de sus participantes, habiendo un *link* para los mensajes.

4.2. Los cuestionarios y la entrevista

Al analizar los cuestionarios nos impresionaron algunas de las respuestas y decidimos entonces trabajar los datos de manera cualitativo-cuantitativa. Los cuestionarios fueron sometidos a 128 alumnos de diferentes cursos y turnos, de los cuales 127 respondieron, sólo 1 cuestionario fue entregado en blanco. De esos 127 alumnos que respondieron, solamente 4 fueron escogidos para la entrevista que duraba entre 15 y 20 minutos, la disponibilidad de tiempo por parte de los entrevistados era pues necesaria, de manera que decidimos trabajar con un número reducido de personas. Esos alumnos tenían entre 20 y 30 años, tres de ellos son del Curso de Letras y uno es del Área de Ciencias Exactas. El objetivo de la entrevista era recolectar eventuales jergalismos utilizados durante la entrevista para su posterior análisis. Fueron realizadas aproximadamente 27 preguntas, relacionadas con la vida universitaria en general. Para la entrevista nos basamos en el cuestionario elaborado por Mônica Rector en su libro "*A linguagem da juventude: uma pesquisa geo-sociolingüística*" (1975) que está relacionado con la comprensión general del vocabulario usado por jóvenes en diferentes situaciones, no sólo dentro del contexto universitario. Como nuestro objetivo era específicamente la jerga en la universidad, muchas preguntas fueron descartadas.

4.3. Analizando los datos

Durante el análisis de las definiciones de *jerga* en los diccionarios, observamos una gran cantidad de definiciones erróneas y algunas, en nuestra opinión, tendenciosas o con prejuicios. Por esa razón, nuestra primera pregunta del cuestionario fue "Nos gustaría saber como definiría la palabra jerga. ¿Qué significa la jerga para usted?" Como se trata de una pregunta subjetiva, las estadísticas son aproximadas. De los 127 alumnos que respondieron el cuestionario, 47, 65% definieron jerga como *vocabulario específico de un grupo*; 17,18% la asociaron al lenguaje informal, lo que no deja de ser verdad, aunque resulte incompleto; 7,81% la definieron como *vocabulario específico de jóvenes;* 17,18% colocaron definiciones variadas, entre ellas podemos observar: confusiones entre jerga y regionalismo, entre jerga y neologismo, entre jerga y expresión idiomática, entre otros. Esos resultados muestran que las definiciones erróneas o cargadas de prejuicios no se limitan a los diccionarios. No obstante, la mayoría definió la jerga como vocabulario de un determinado grupo social. Fue mencionado anteriormente que la jerga, en una definición bastante básica, sería el vocabulario restringido a un determinado grupo social. De esta forma los universitarios constituyen un grupo social, por tanto una jerga universitaria. Basándonos en ese hecho, elaboramos la segunda pregunta "Usted, como universitario, ¿considera que existe una jerga universitaria exclusiva, usada solamente por jóvenes universitarios y diferente de aquella usada por otros jóvenes que no son universitarios? ¿Por qué?" El 43,31% respondió que no. 53,9% que sí y 0,78% que no sabían. La gran mayoría que marcó *sí* justificó su respuesta afirmando que por causa de situaciones específicas por las cuales pasa un determinado grupo surge una jerga específica que otras personas no pueden entender. Los que respondieron *no* eran alumnos que en la primera pregunta no asociaron la jerga al vocabulario exclusivo de un determinado grupo social.

También queríamos evaluar el nivel de entendimiento de los universitarios sobre algunas características de la jerga. La tercera pregunta es sobre el carácter críptico de la jerga ¿"Usted considera críptica la jerga universitaria (usada por usted y sus amigos)? O sea, ¿es usada para esconder algún significado y para que otras personas no entiendan? ¿Por qué? ¿Para qué?" Ningún alumno marcó la alternativa *siempre,* 58,59% marcaron a *veces,* 38,28% marcaron *nunca* y 3,12% respondieron *no lo sé*. Los que marcaron *a veces* lo justificaron afirmando que en algunas situaciones es necesario el uso de un vocabulario críptico para que otras personas no nos entiendan, confirmando así el papel defensivo de la jerga. Aquellos que marcaron la opción *nunca,* en su gran mayoría, no justificaron su opción, pero los que lo hicieron afirmaron que no hay necesidad de jerga críptica en el contexto universitario. Es importante resaltar que el carácter críptico es una característica inmutable de la jerga de grupo. El relativismo que existe con relación a este aspecto es que la jerga de un grupo puede ser considerada más o menos críptica cuando es comparada con la de otro grupo. Así, afirmamos que la jerga universitaria es críptica, no tanto como la de un grupo de presidiarios, por ejemplo, mas nunca podremos negar que es críptica. Pero ¿todas las palabras del vocabulario usado por un determinado grupo son crípticas? Sí, en determinado momento: cuando ésta nace. Aún cuando intencionalmente los miembros del grupo no quieran esconder nada, otras personas que no pertenecen a ese grupo desconocerán su significado, simplemente porque no estaban en el contexto en que fue creada. Sabemos que la jerga de grupo se puede tornar una jerga común, pero no podemos olvidar que toda jerga común fue primeramente jerga de grupo y críptica.

La cuarta y última pregunta, también a respecto a las características de la jerga fue sobre la intencionalidad de la misma. "¿Considera Vd. que la jerga universitaria (usada por usted y sus amigos) es premeditada, o sea, creada intencionalmente para que sólo ustedes entiendan? ¿Por qué?" El 2,3 % marcaron *siempre;* 37,5% marcaron *a veces*; 57,03% marcaron *nunca;* 3,1% respondieron *no sé*. Los alumnos que marcaron *siempre* y *a veces* justificaron su respuesta afirmando que la jerga sería premeditada cuando ellos quisieran mantener el significado de la palabra exclusivamente entre los miembros del grupo o cuando quisieran hacer, a propósito, un chiste con un colega o profesor, colocar un apodo, por ejemplo. Los alumnos que marcaron *nunca* afirmaron que no creían en la premeditación ni en la creación intencionada, porque la jerga es espontánea, y nace de la creatividad de sus usuarios, de manera natural. Esa pregunta fue motivada primeramente por una duda nuestra, pues la expresividad es una característica de la jerga y de los fraseologismos, constantemente asociada al humor, inclusive al humor negro. A partir de ahí, nos planteamos si esas características (expresividad, espontaneidad, creatividad, humor) podrían ser combinadas con premeditación, de manera que decidimos colocar esa pregunta en el cuestionario. A través del análisis de las respuestas de los alumnos, parece que la premeditación no concuerda con las demás características citadas anteriormente, no obstante una palabra puede ser premeditada y creativa o premeditada y tener sentido de humor, ironía, etc. Pero la premeditación, a diferencia del carácter críptico, no es una característica inmutable de la jerga de grupo. En este sentido la respuesta "correcta" para la premeditación habría sido, en nuestra opinión, *a veces* puesto que algunos jergalismos pueden ser premeditados, p.ej., un apodo para un colega, para poder referirse a él sin que otras personas se den cuenta.

4.4. Los temas del *orkut* y las entrevistas

Además de los cuestionarios y entrevistas decidimos colectar las jergas universitarias, y para eso usamos "tópicos" del *orkut*. Descubrimos que una gran cantidad de jergalismos usados por los universitarios forman parte de la jerga común. Queremos destacar que no podríamos separar la jerga usada por los universitarios de la estudiantil en general. La jerga universitaria seria una especie de "matiz" de la jerga estudiantil, puede haber elementos que las diferencien, pero hay muchos otros que son comunes. La siguiente figura ilustra la situación de la jerga dentro del contexto universitario:

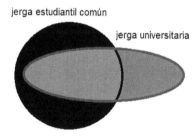

La esfera achatada representa la jerga universitaria y engloba parcialmente la que representa la jerga estudiantil general, pues los universitarios, obviamente, ya fueron alumnos de enseñanza media y primaria, por ello tienen un buen conocimiento de la jerga estudiantil general. Pero lo efímero de la jerga hace que los universitarios, en el transcurso del tiempo, no entiendan algunas usadas por alumnos que no son universitarios. La parte azul representa la jerga de grupo, la jerga universitaria exclusiva, a la que los alumnos o jóvenes no universitarios, normalmente, no tienen acceso y no consiguen comprender. Ya la parte de la esfera roja que está dentro de la esfera negra representa la jerga que es común a los dos grupos. No nos parece sensato afirmar (incluso porque no investigamos profundamente ese respecto) que la jerga juvenil y la estudiantil son equivalentes, pero concordamos en que las dos están bastante próximas. Mostramos aquí un pequeño corpus de vocablos pertenecientes a la jerga universitaria recogidos en las entrevistas y de los temas del *orkut*. Mostramos los vocablos y las debidas explicaciones para cada una de ellos (en portugués):

5. Corpus

Açougueiro: aluno do curso de medicina.
Adistração: trocadilho com administração. Referência, segundo eles, ao pouco estudo dos alunos da administração.
Aiqueternura: trocadilho com arquitetura. Segundo os alunos, o trocadilho foi criado para fazer referência à delicadeza dos alunos de arquitetura.

Batateiro: *aluno do curso de agronomia.*
Biolorgia: *trocadilho com biologia. De acordo com os alunos, esse trocadilho surgiu por causa das festas realizadas pelos alunos que cursam biologia.*
Bixo: *aluno novato no meio universitário.*
Boiologia: *trocadilho com biologia.*
Capa-gato: *aluno do curso de veterinária.*
Calourada: *festa ou recepção dada aos alunos novos.*
Calourice: *atitude de aluno novato.*
Calouro: *aluno novato no meio universitário*
Carniceiro: *aluno do curso de medicina.*
CO – centro de orientações: *trocadilho com centro olímpico. Esse trocadilho é usado para enganar os alunos novatos que pedem informações. O centro olímpico da universidade onde fizemos a pesquisa fica distante do local onde as aulas da maioria dos cursos são ministradas. Assim, os alunos novos se perdem ou caminham muito até descobrirem que foram enganados.*
Cozinheiro: *aluno do curso de química.*
Deuses do Olímpio: *alunos que estudam no monte Olímpio (ver: monte Olímpio).*
Frutinha: *aluno do curso de nutrição.*
Monte Olímpio: *maneira de referir-se à faculdade de ciências sociais aplicadas que geograficamente está localizada em lugar mais elevado.*
Ordenhaboi: *aluno do curso de veterinária.*
Peão: *aluno do curso de agronomia.*
Pedagorda: *trocadilho com pedagoga. Termo usado para referir-se às alunas do curso de pedagogia.*
Pedreiro: *aluno do curso de geologia.*
PH: *trocadilho com ph (potencial hidrogeniônico, grandeza que indica a acidez, neutralidade ou alcalinidade de uma solução líquida) para referir-se ao pessoal das humanas.*
Pica-pau: *aluno do curso de engenharia florestal.*
Reles mortais: *alunos que não fazem parte do monte Olímpio, ou seja, que não estudam na faculdade de ciências sociais aplicadas.*

Además de esos jergalismos, en nuestras entrevistas identificamos un código usado por los alumnos para expresar las veces que repitieron una determinada disciplina. La primera forma es el uso de los términos *mestre, doutor* y *Ph.D*. *Mestre* se utiliza para la primera vez que se repite una disciplina, *doutor* para la segunda y *Ph.D.* para la tercera. Otra forma de informar cuántas veces el alumno repitió es usando un sistema numérico. Si la materia no posee secuencia, el alumno colocará el número de veces que la está repitiendo. Si la materia posee secuencia, como *Cálculo 3* o *Grego 2*, el alumno va a colocar un numero más, *Cálculo 3.1* o *3.2*. Después de realizar el análisis concluimos que la metáfora desempeña un papel de destaque en la formación de la jerga universitaria. Para Rector (1994) la metáfora consiste en la transferencia de una palabra hacia un campo semántico al que no pertenece, pero en la que hay una relación de semejanza con el objeto designado, entre el sentido propio y el figurado. Muchas veces esa relación de semejanza es usada con frutas, verduras o animales, como en el caso del alumno de ingeniería forestal chamado de *pica-pau* (pájaro loco). Observamos que en otras ocasiones, crean palabras nuevas a través de semejanza fonética con la palabra original, por ejemplo: *aiqueternura* para arquitectura, *biolorgia* para biología, *pedagorda* para pedagoga. En algunos momentos son usados los jergalismos con sentido irónico o peyorativo, pues hay una actitud agresiva con relación a los colegas de otros cursos o a los colegas recién ingresados. Pero también hay una actitud humorística que puede ser observada, principalmente en el código usado para indicar la cantidad de veces que el alumno repitió una disciplina.

6. Consideraciones finales

El análisis reveló que la función de la jerga dentro del contexto universitario es mantener y resguardar la identidad de los alumnos de cada curso. Vimos también que esa jerga refleja la gran rivalidad que existe entre ellos. Hay rivalidad entre los alumnos novatos y los que ya están graduándose, entre los de ciencias humanas y ciencias exactas, así como entre los de cada curso. Cuando iniciamos la investigación pensábamos que las "hostilidades" estarían dirigidas hacia los profesores, sin embargo al concluir el estudio descubrimos que las mayores rivalidades son entre los propios alumnos. La jerga está presente para mantener la identidad y como mecanismo de defensa de la tribu y de cada grupo que se forma en ella. Concluimos también que en la *aldea* (universidad) hay una gran *tribu* (los universitarios) formada por familias (cada grupo que surge: alumnos de química, novatos, etc.), y que cada familia se resguarda en su *oca*[1]. Mas a pesar de esas divisiones, ellos no dejan de constituir una tribu, cada uno en su *oca*, mas sabe que pertenece a la tribu y la conoce, se identifica como miembro de ella. Constatamos también que el uso de la jerga les da a sus usuarios un sentimiento de superioridad, sirve como signo de grupo, contribuyendo así para la auto-afirmación. Cuando el significado de esa jerga sale del ámbito del grupo, nuevos términos son creados para que se mantenga su carácter criptográfico. De esa forma, el estudio sobre la dinámica de renovación léxica es relevante, pues a través de ella observamos más claramente las transformaciones que ocurren dentro del sistema de valores grupalmente compartidos y vinculados a las necesidades sociales de grupo.

---

[1] Nombre de las grandes chozas colectivas indígenas en Brasil.

7. Referencias Bibliográficas

BAGNO, M. 2006 "Nada na língua é por acaso: ciência e senso comum na educação em língua materna". *Presença Pedagógica*, setembro. [Acesso em 02 de julho de 2009] em <http://www.marcosbagno.com.br/conteudo/textos.htm/>.

CALVET, L. J. 2002 Variações diastráticas, diatópicas e diacrônicas: o exemplo da gíria. *Sociolingüística: uma introdução crítica*. São Paulo: Parábola, 4ª ed.

CÂMARA JR, J. M. 1956 *Dicionário de fatos gramaticais*. Rio de Janeiro: Ministério da Educação e Cultura, Casa de Rui Barbosa.

CARDONA, G. R. 1991 *Diccionario de lingüística*. Barcelona: Ariel.

CUNHA, C. F. da. 2004 "Em torno dos conceitos de gíria e calão". In: Pereira, Cilene da Cunha. *Sob a Pele das Palavras*. Rio de Janeiro: Nova Fronteira /Academia Brasileira de Letras.

DAUZART, A. 1946 *La vida del lenguaje*. El ateneo.

FORACCHI, M. M. 1972 *A juventude na sociedade moderna*. São Paulo: Pioneira.

MICHAEILIS. 1998 *Moderno dicionário da língua portuguesa*. Rio de Janeiro: Reader's Digest & São Paulo: Melhoramentos.

OLIVEIRA, A M. P. P. de. 2001 "Regionalismos brasileiros: a questão da distribuição geográfica". In: Oliveira, A. M. P. P. de & Isquerdo, A. N. (orgs.) *As ciências do léxico: lexicologia, lexicografia, terminologia*. Campo Grande, MS: Ed. UFMS: 109-115.

ORTIZ ALVAREZ, M. L. 2007"A gíria juvenil em três contextos latino-americanos: Cuba, Brasil e Chile". *Revista Contextos. Estudios de Humanidades y Ciencias Sociales*. Año IX, n. 18, nov. (UMCE, Santiago de Chile): 21-38.

PRETI, D. 1984 *A gíria e outros temas*. São Paulo: T. A. Queiroz.

PRETI, D. 1983 *A linguagem proibida: um estudo sobre a linguagem erótica*. São Paulo: USP.

PRETI, D. 2005 "Dino Preti: um pesquisador pioneiro, premiado e... coisa inédita nos meios acadêmicos... muito humilde". *Letra Magna. Revista eletrônica de divulgação científica em língua portuguesa, linguística e literatura*. São Paulo, 15 de março de 2005. Entrevista com Ranira Cirelli Appa. <http://www.letramagna.com/dinoentre .htm> [Acesso em: 26 jan. 2009].

RECTOR, M. 1975 *A linguagem da juventude: uma pesquisa geo-sociolingüística*. Petrópolis: Vozes.

RECTOR, M. 1994 *A fala dos jovens*. Petrópolis: Vozes.

QUOTATIONS OR ANONYMOUS PHRASEMES –
THAT IS THE QUESTION!

Sixta Quassdorf
University of Basel

Abstract: The article addresses the question of the relationship between quotations and phrasemes. Simple answers cannot be given, as quotations are a pragmatic rather than an structural phenomenon, i.e. their "existence" is context-sensitive. However, diachronic studies of usage reveal how word strings that are marked as quotations (or strongly resemble word strings in a literary work) are used outside their original context; they show if and how these word strings change over time and what these changes tell us about their phraseological status. A sample study of the line "I must be cruel, only to be kind" from Shakespeare's *Hamlet* demonstrates that besides the emergence of deviating, but recurrent formal and semantic properties, increased usage in new discourse contexts is especially indicative of a this development from a poet's word to a phraseological unit.

Key words: quotations, formulae, winged words, propositional collocations.

1. Quotations, phrasemes and the question

Definitions of quotations commonly rely on a non-linguistic criterion: the known origin. The *Oxford English Dictionary* (OED) defines quotations as "[a] passage quoted from a book, speech, or other source; (in modern use *esp.*) a frequently quoted passage of this nature" (sense 5.a). The logical tradition in philosophy puts it differently: quotations *mention* something,[1] i.e. they draw the addressee's attention to something "other than its extension" (Saka 1998:126). This *something* is prototypically the known source including its associated connotations.

Phrasemes are defined by linguistic criteria, most commonly by the structuralist view that a phraseme is a polylexical semantic unit, whose components are habitually combined (cf. Burger 2003: 14). Frequency of occurrence (usage-based theories), mental storage and retrieval as a whole (psycholinguistic/cognitive approaches) or co-occurrence above probability (corpus-linguistics) are further criteria which are differently highlighted depending on the theoretical approach to language. Phrasemes and quotations overlap according to the structuralist approach as they generally consist of more than one word.

However, the OED provides a further aspect to quotations, i.e. reproduction and repetition. Apart from the passage above "a frequently quoted passage", the verb 'to quote' is defined by: "[t]o reproduce or repeat a passage from (a book, author, etc.); to repeat a statement by (a person); to give (a specified person, body, etc.) as the source of a statement" (2. a). In other words, a link to the usage-based approach is established as repetition entails frequency.

Some quotations are very often reproduced and have become so popular that the phraseological criteria of frequency and co-occurrence above probability pertain without a

---

[1] The use-mention distinction was introduced by Willard Van Orman Quine in Mathematical Logic (1940).

doubt. A case in point is the hackneyed "to be or not to be" from *Hamlet's* great soliloquy (act 3, scene 1).[2] Its structure *to X or not to X* has become a productive construction in apparently almost all languages of the world (cf. Hohl/Langlotz 2009).[3] The construction has preserved its *mentioning* property, even though the individual language user might not know that the phrase actually derives from *Hamlet*: if some serious origin was not assumed and the clash with the often trivial application was not felt, the humorous effect could not be achieved that often accompanies its reproduction. We may possibly speak of a conventionalised quotation here.

However, conventionalised quotations are rare. Other frequent quotations have only partly maintained the link to their origin or lost it altogether. They therefore appear today more commonplace or anonymous, such as "mind's eye" (act 1, scenes 1 and 2) and "sea of troubles" (act 3, scene 1). Accordingly, these expressions are no longer felt to meet the criterion of the known origin; they are simply *used*, as the philosophical term describes it: the meaning of the words is all that needs to be understood, their extension is sufficient, no second layer, no *mention*, is implied or presupposed. Meyer calls these expressions *borrowings* to distinguish them from quotations proper (cf. Meyer 1961: 13f.).

Unfortunately, the *use/mention* or *quotations/borrowings* distinction is in practice not stable and fixed, but dynamic. The same expression may be quoted or borrowed or just casually be identical depending on the circumstances. It is not a property of a phrase but a pragmatic usage phenomenon. Moreover, there are today habitual linguistic units which are similar to the wording in a literary artefact and we may wonder about their relationship. The question that arises then is how we can determine the phraseological status of a quotation.

2. Criteria of analysis

Frequency will provide information on usage despite specific differences in actual performance. What is more, frequency entails that a quotation is better accessible. According to the definition, the **context** of access to quotations is specific: a quotation is usually learned or created by contact with cultural artefacts, be it directly or indirectly via schooling or quotation anthologies. However, the more a string of words (taken from a context worth *mentioning*) is *used* rather than *mentioned*, the more its connection to the specific context of the cultural artefact may be lost. The more the quotation is encountered in different contexts, the more it will be felt to be a 'normal' and 'anonymous' linguistic item of the *langue*. This process is, however, a historical development. Therefore, the analysis needs to be based on **diachronic** data.

Moreover, we have to consider that **linguistic properties** of the original phrase may have induced people to use the phrase as a frequent quotation in the first place: its rhetorical make-up may enhance memorability; salience of keywords or constructions may have attracted the addressee's attention; the ratio between lexical and grammatical words may influence the ease or difficulty to embed it into new contexts. These linguistic properties may also influence **formal stability and variability**. One must not believe that quotations in common language are rendered verbatim (cf. also Clark/Gerrig 1990). However, if quotations become phraseologized,

---

[2] All examples in this article refer to Shakespeare's Hamlet, which has been chosen as the prototypical literary artefact.
[3] Construction in the sense of Construction Grammar, cf. Croft 2002.

a certain degree of recurrent variants will develop to suit the cognitive advantage of using phrasemes (cf. Wray 2008). On the other hand, certain stable formal features serve as self-reflective recognition point or implicit signals, such as bits of archaic language or salient constructions like *to X or not to X* (cf. Hohl/Langlotz 2009). In conjunction with the historical approach, lineages of these 'recognition points' become traceable.

Explicit **quotative signals** by metalinguistic or typographical means, such as 'to quote Shakespeare,' 'to use the poet's words' or quotation marks are neither a necessary nor a sufficient condition for quotations. The presence or absence of signals partly depends on the genre and the period. In fictional genres, explicit marking is the exception rather than the rule; recognising covert references is part of the pleasure of reading. In Elizabethan and Jacobean times, one recycled good ideas and expressions of one's fellow writers as a matter of course without bothering about source attribution or copyright (cf. Bruster 2000: 15-27 and Footnote 7 p. 214).[4] However, analysing signals within one genre and period sheds light on the treatment of certain phrasemes: e.g. if in early British newspapers "there is the rub" (act 3, scene 1) is marked as a quotation already in 1722, but other occurrences of *Hamlet*-like verbal combinations are not, we may be justified in concluding that the latter were neither felt nor meant as a quotation, i.e. they were created independently from *Hamlet*. Furthermore, persistently lacking signals after a period of more or less explicit marking can be interpreted in two ways: a) the quotation is so well known that no marking is necessary ("to be or not to be"); b) the quotation is more *used* than *mentioned* and has more or less lost the link to its original source, i.e. it is turning from a quotation into a fully-fledged phraseme (see section 3.2.).

The **semantics** of the phrase also helps to distinguish quoted variants from other similar expressions, e.g. the distinction between the noun *kind* and the adjective *kind*: the co-occurrence of *cruel* and *kind* in *a cruel kind of* is different from the contrast expressed by the adjectives *cruel* and *kind*, which is again different - as I will show below - from the oxymoron implied in "I must be cruel, only to be kind" (act 3, scene 4). Secondly, **semantics** may also be indicative of the phraseological status of a quotation. For instance the Hamletian phrase "it is a custom more honour'd in the breach than the observance" (act 1, scene 4) has broadened its meaning over time: whereas originally "the custom" is negatively connoted and as such the phrase expresses the opinion that it is good to breach bad rules, the negative connotation of the subject noun erodes over time so that today the phrase frequently describes the simple observation that certain rules are not observed (cf. Quassdorf 2009:6). These so-called misquotations, if they occur repeatedly, demonstrate that the direct link to the play has been severed and that it is frequently *used* as an 'anonymous' phraseological unit.

3. Exemplary analysis

For the sample study, I selected a line from *Hamlet,* act 3, scene 4:

(1) I must be cruel, only to be kind.

---

[4] A look at the data in the HyperHamlet database of quotations from and allusion to Shakespeare's Hamlet seems to confirm this assumption: only 8 out of 314 references from the 17th century are explicitly marked as quotations or allusions to Hamlet. On the other hand, those eight clearly attributed quotations strongly mark Shakespeare's Hamlet as an extraordinary work of fiction which was considered worth to be overtly referred to.

The line is characterised firstly by a bipolar structure, which makes it formally complex. Secondly, the line is also conceptually complex: it expresses an oxymoron - two contrastive notions are blended into one. Thirdly, the line contains only two lexical words, which are therefore easily discernible as keywords. Forthly, the keywords alliterate and thus enhance the rhetoric form. Consequently, we do not only have an oxymoron, but the rhetoric figure of paronomasia. Thanks to its rhetoric sophistication, the precondition for easy memorizing is given. Memorability is further enhanced by the fact that the oxymoronic concept is not an entirely new idea, but it had been common currency for centuries, cf:

(2) For whom the Lorde loueth, him he chasteneth (The Bible, proverbs 3,12).

However, in contrast to the wording in the Bible, Shakespeare found a more concise way of denoting this paradox-like conduct: two relatively common adjectives are linked by auxiliaries and a few common grammatical words. As such it has the potential of being integrated into "normal" language without marking a breach in style.

3.1 Authorship and semantics

The first question to tackle is to what degree Shakespeare coined the line. Was the mere combination of the keywords Shakespeare's invention, or did they already appear in earlier texts? Therefore, older Bible translations were searched for *cruel**[5] and checked for co-occurring lemmas. 52 tokens were found in the Bishop's Bible from 1568, 69 in the Geneva Bible from 1587. In both cases, *cruel* or *cruelty* is never combined with *kind* and *kindness*, but if a contrast is expressed it is expressed by *good*, *mercy(ful)* and *compassion*. A proximity search was not possible; the search *kind** was not carried out because of the polysemic nature of *kind*. Furthermore, *Literature Online* (LION), which also contains antedating texts, was searched with the proximity search *cruel NEAR.5 kind* (i.e. wordspan = 5, including spelling variants, authors living between 500 and 1550). The search yields 27 tokens, 21 of which are a combination of nominal *kind* with *cruel* (*a cruel kind of*). However, if we extend the search to authors born by 1600, i.e. contemporaneous writers or slightly younger authors than Shakespeare, we find already more than 50% adjectival combinations, i.e. 48 out of 90 tokens use the adjectives *kind* and *cruel* to denote a contrast as in example (3):

(3) And not be cruell where he may be kinde (Nicholas Breton, 1545?-1626?).

According to these data, the combination of the adjectives *cruel/kind* seems to have gained in currency around the turn of the 17th century. It is therefore possible that *Hamlet* (first performance presumably in 1601) gave that alliterating choice of words a boost, but it is just as possible that it developed independently.

However, if we add the semantic criterion 'oxymoron' as a filter to gain more clarity, we find one clearly antedating example:

---

[5] The asterisk is a so-called wildcard and stands for any number of additional letters to capture derivative word forms or spelling variants such as cruelty, cruell, cruelle etc.

(4) Or be more cruel, love, and so be kind (Queen Elizabeth I, 1568-1570).

The combination of the adjectives for expressing oxymoronic meaning was obviously not Shakespeare's invention. Still, Queen Elizabeth's oxymoron may not necessarily have become widely known: her poems were not published at the time. The possibility remains that the oxymoron was made popular for repetition by the success of *Hamlet,* even though it was not a Shakespearean coinage.[6] Antecedent texts yield an ambiguous result as to the actual coinage of the keyword combination for contrastive use. However, the antecedent data draw attention to the fact, that there is more to be taken into account than the mere formal combination of the keywords: there is obviously a distinction in usage between contrastive and oxymoronic meaning.

3.2 Signals

Adding the criterion of signalling in postdating texts, we find that ten out of 14 oxymora in the *17th and 18th c. Burney Collection of Newspapers* (BBCN) are explicitly marked for quotation, whereas the simple contrastive combinations of the keywords are not. There are three early unmarked oxymora, which, however, occur in poems (i.e. we have to take into account the genre-related reluctance towards overt references in poetic language). However, from 1770 onwards ten out of the 11 oxymora in the BBCN, which occur all in non-fictional contexts, are explicitly signalled to be quotations. We may therefore be justified to assume that the oxymoronic phrasing, in contrast to the mere contrastive combination, was felt to be linked to Shakespeare's line "I must be cruel, only to be kind:"

(5) I finish the present letter with an assurance that
"I am only cruel to be kind;"
(*General Evening Post*, London, Thursday, September 13, 1770).

(6) I reply, that a Whole is greater than a Part, and plead with Hamlet, that
"I must be cruel only to be kind."
(*Public Advertiser*, London, Wednesday, February 12, 1772).

(7) The Duke of Richmond […] wished not to employ Savages, who wantonly tortured our fellow-subjects […] and were then to be defended on the ground of having been "cruel only to be kind,"
(*Morning Chronicle* and *London Advertiser*, London, Monday, December 8, 1777).

The results in the *Times Digital Archive 1785-1985* (TDA) provide converging evidence: the early *cruel/kind* oxymora of the 81 valid hits (i.e. adjectival co-occurrence) are all explicitly signalled to be quotations. However, formal deviance and abbreviations from clause to verb phrase are soon observable:

---

[6] This phenomenon of "mediated" quotations can repeatedly be observed; cf. "to the manor born" which most British people will link to a popular BBC TV series of the 1970s, although the expression itself is already recorded in the early 19th century (cf. HyperHamlet); it is a pun based on the line "Although I'm native here and to the manner born" from Hamlet, act 1, scene 4.

(8) they would have done wisely to have been "cruel only to be kind," (*The Times*, October 11, 1791).

It is only in 1879, i.e. more than 100 years after its first appearance in the newspaper collection that the oxymoronic line appears without any marking:

(9) at times we must even be cruel in order to be kind. (*The Times*, May 14, 1879).

In other words, it took at least a century that the phrase gained either independence from its Shakespearean source, or such familiarity that explicit marking became superfluous. The fact, however, that the *Cambridge Dictionary of Idioms* and other similar reference works list 'cruel to be kind' as an idiom without mentioning the Shakespearean origin, may support the first interpretation.

3.3 Formal patterns

Possibly because of the slow progress from loosing its *mentioning* quality, the formal development of variants is prototypical: at a first stage the oxymoron is almost always marked and rendered near-verbatim. This stage lasted some 100 years in British newspaper English as exemplified by *The Times*. Then quotative signals are gradually reduced, while patterned variants arise. The following three constructions are repeatedly found in TDA:

(10) cruel only to be kind (27 out of 81 hits, first time 1770)
(11) cruel in order to be kind (9 out of 81 hits, first time 1879)
(12) cruel to be kind (42 out of 81 hits, first time 1860 in a title, unmarked; first time in the body of text 1901, after 1924 always unmarked).

The three patterns can be equalled to a gradual weakening of emphasis: the original *only* puts a strong and exclusive emphasis on the positive purpose of the cruel behaviour, which is still felt, though less strongly, in the substitutive variant *in order to*, but given up altogether by the omission of the adverb.[7] The criteria of marking, semantics, formal stability and frequency across time draw a rather clear picture about which *cruel/kind* combinations can be unambiguously linked to Shakespeare's *Hamlet*, i.e. the constructions (10), (11) and (12). If we compare this with contemporary data, the interpretation seems conclusive: The proximity search of the keywords in the *Corpus of Contemporary American English* (COCA) draws a similar picture: from the 25 adjectival combinations, expressed contrasts often appear freely combined, cf. ex. (13) (this intuition is backed by the low MI-value of -1.61). We feel only

---

[7] There is a forth structure though, which might be connected: cruel kindness. This expression uses the same keywords and condenses the oxymoron to its extreme. Cruel kindness first appears in LION in the 1620s, i.e. after Hamlet's first performance, in TDA in 1819, i.e. almost 50 years later than the verbal phrase variant. 78 out of 81 tokens of cruel kindness in TDA occur within the following 100 years. It was apparently a catchword especially in political discourse and parliamentary debates in the second half of the 19th century. However, it is never marked for quotation; therefore the link to Shakespeare remains contestable.

confident about the oxymoronic structures including the copular construction 'to be kind,' cf. ex. (14), (15) and (16), as being related to the Shakespearean line:

(13) You're cruel, and she is kind!
(14) Sometimes one has to be cruel to be kind.
(15) Being Cruel to Be Kind: Don't Indulge Your Partner's Woes
(16) Cruel to be kind, it's a very good sign. Cruel to be kind means that I love you.

Even though intuition is obviously not necessarily wrong and sometimes the only means to establish certain connections (cf. Talmy 2007, Wray 2008), the look at historical data has been able to provide clarifying facts.

The historical link is mainly traceable through explicit source indication, as the keywords are little conspicuous. It is noteworthy that the oxymoronic meaning is rather stable and serves as a recognition point: we also find very different structures expressing the oxymoron, which are marked for quotation. Structural independence, however, can as yet not be verified: searches for a (partial) open slot structure such as *(must) be adjective only to be adjective* were not successful in contemporary databases (COCA, BNC). As such the three variants (10)(11) and (12) have to be interpreted as form-meaning pairs, i.e. they are constructions.

This is not to say that individual cases of word play might not considerably deviate from these three patterns and also weaken the meaning to a simple opposition. As mentioned in the first section, what is actually retrieved from which base form is an individual psycholinguistic and pragmatic process, which is open to any form of creativity, even to the extreme of using just one single salient feature. However, the question at hand is concerned with the relationship between quotations and phrasemes: as such the historically established patterns of variation show firstly, that the quotation has obviously been modified according to contextual needs and hence *used*, and secondly, that a process of formal fixation must have taken place independently from the source text.

3.4 Contexts

Although the chosen corpora imply a bias towards journalistic language, we may nevertheless be justified in assuming that the many topics reported and commented on in the media reach a large part of a language community. Secondly, the many readers of newspapers or magazines are concerned with these subjects and familiar with the discourse, and thirdly, they understand (and possibly feel a certain appeal towards) newspaper language. In other words, although journalistic language has its specific traits, it is strongly audience-directed and, moreover, a wide-spread and far-reaching register of a language.

Newspapers offer different discursive contexts as they cover a wide range of subjects. Therefore they are generally subdivided into thematic sections. The Times is divided into the sections news, politics&parliament, business&finance, law, sport, featured articles, editorials, letters to the editor, reviews, art & entertainment and a few more. News and editorial are thematically a 'mixed bag;' it may therefore not come as a surprise that we find about 60 % of the chosen Shakespearean line in these two segments. Reviews come next with 17%. This finding may not be a surprise either, as the genre is closely linked to cultural issues and a more elaborated language may be expected. However, one may not have anticipated that cruel/kind appeared in that segment only in 1903; it was preceded by news and editorials, sports and advertisements (cf. figure 2). In other words, one has to be careful with "natural" assumptions about genres being prone to use certain quotations as a matter of course; discourse characteristics may simply depend on temporary fashions. The occurrences in the letters to the editor (cruel/kind 4%, first occurrence in 1859) imply that the expression belongs to the active phrase stock of a part of the readers. Figure 2 shows that the line spreads into more and more newspaper subjects over time, i.e. the broadening of contexts during the phraseologization process is clearly traceable.

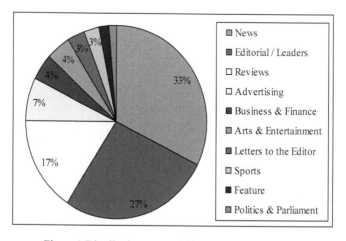

Figure 1 Distribution across different thematic contexts

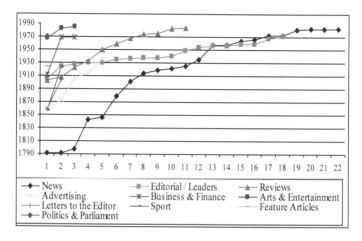

Figure 2 Thematic distributions over time

4. Conclusions

At the beginning of this article we asked whether we can determine the phraseological status of a quotation and how we go about to determine that a certain polylexical unit derives from a quotation, especially if the constituents of the phraseme/quotation are rather inconspicuous.

The answer is partly obvious and trivial: the historical approach allows us to trace lineages and verify connections among expressions. As such the study has shown that the co-occurrence of the keywords 'cruel' and 'kind' is not sufficient, but that further criteria need to be added.[8] Overt marking for quotation has proved to be the most informative criterion. The evolution from quotation to phrasal unit seems to start, indeed as expected, from marked, near-verbatim renditions, which over time gradually lose their quoting signals, while in the same time variants develop. The historical approach provides, moreover, some evidence for our hypothesis that spread into more varied discourses and phraseologicalization are related: the expression has increasingly been *used* in more and more discourses over time, i.e. it can be learned without ever reading Shakespeare. Recurrent changes in meaning, form and usage imply an independent development.

However, a caveat is appropriate here: this process might be genre-related. Obviously, the rules of quoting in literature are very different from the ones in newspapers. A more fine-grained genre analysis is necessary in a future study. Nevertheless, within the genre of British newspaper language the development seems prototypical and confirms general historical observations in the phraseology of a language and follows cognitive considerations of ease of effort. Moreover, thanks to the fact that in quotation studies the base form is known, quotation studies feed into general phraseological research and are able to confirm hypotheses made in that domain, such as formal reduction and weakening of meaning (cf. Burger/Linke 1998: 746-748; 750-752). On the other hand, as long as *Hamlet* is read, the base form will be found side by side with derived forms and conventionalization of variant forms will take longer; discussions in the internet about misquotations exemplify a conservative attitude and are worth another follow-up study.

---

[8] In other cases, if the keyword combination is more salient such as in "Though this be madness, yet there is method in't" (act 2, scene 2), the mere co-occurrence suffices as recognition point (according to an unpublished study of this line).

5. References

5.1 Primary references

BRETON, N. 1545?-1626? "Another". *The Works in Verse and Prose of Nicholas Breton: For the First Time Collected and Edited: With Memorial-Introduction, Notes and Illustrations, Glossarial Index, Facsimilies, &c. By the Rev. Alexander B. Grosart.* Blackburn: Printed for Private Circulation by T. and A. Constable. 1879. Literature Online. Basel: Universitätsbibliothek.

QUEEN ELIZABETH I. "On Monsieur's Departure". *The poems of Queen Elizabeth I.* Ed. Leicester Bradner. Providence, Rhode Island: Brown University Press, [1964]. Literature Online. Basel: Universitätsbibliothek.

5.2 Secondary references

BRUSTER, D. 2000 *Quoting Shakespeare: Form and culture in early modern drama.* Lincoln (Neb.): University of Nebraska Press,.

BURGER, H. 2003 *Phraseologie: Eine Einführung am Beispiel des Deutschen.* 2., überarb. Aufl. Berlin: E. Schmidt.

BURGER, H & LINKE, A. 1998 "40 Historische Phraseologie". In: W. Besch, A. Betten, O. Reichmann & S, Sonderegger (eds.): *Sprachgeschichte. Ein Handbuch zur Geschichte der deutschen Sprache und ihrer Erforschung.* 2., vollständige neu bearbeitete und erweiterte Auflage. 1. Teilband. Berlin/New York: Walter de Gruyter: 743-755.

CLARK, H. H., & GEERIG, R. J. 1990 "Quotations as Demonstrations". *Language* Vol. 66. No. 4: 764–805.

CROFT, W. 2002 *Radical construction grammar: Syntactic theory in typological perspective.* Oxford: Oxford University Press.

HOHL, T. R. & LANGLOTZ, A. 2009 "The Grammar of 'To Be or Not to Be'". In: Cs. Földes (ed.), *Phraseologie disziplinär und interdisziplinär.* Tübingen: Günter Narr: 155-166.

MEYER, H. 1961 *Das Zitat in der Erzählkunst: Zur Geschichte und Poetik des europäischen Romans.* Stuttgart: Metzler.

QUASSDORF, S. 2009 " 'On quoting ...' - a corpus-based study on the phraseology of well-known quotations". In: M. Mahlberg, V. González-Díaz & C. Smith (eds.), *Proceedings of the Corpus Linguistics Conference CL2009, University of Liverpool, UK, 20-23 July 2009* [http://ucrel.lancs.ac.uk/publications/cl2009/]. Last access 24 August 2010.

SAKA, P. "Quotation and the use-mention distinction", *Mind* 107.425 (1998): 113-35. [http://mind.oxfordjournals.org/cgi/reprint/107/425/113]. Last access: 24 August 2010.

TALMY, L. 2007 "Foreword [comparing introspection with other methodologies]". In: M. Gonzalez-Marquez; I. Mittelberg; S. Coulson & M. Spivey (eds.). *Methods in Cognitive Linguistics: Ithaca.* Amsterdam: John Benjamins.

WRAY, A. 2008 *Formulaic Language: Pushing the Boundaries.* Oxford: Oxford University Press.

5.3 Databases and dictionaries

BBCN -17th/18th Century Burney Collection Newspapers. British Library and Gale Cengage Learning.[http://find.galegroup.com.proxy.nationallizenzen.de/bncn/start.do?prodId=BBCN&userGroupName=1gbv] Last access 24 August 2010

BNC -*The British National Corpus*, version 3 (BNC XML Edition). 2007. Oxford University Computing Services. [http://www.natcorp.ox.ac.uk/] Last access 24 August 2010.

COCA -Davies, Mark. *The Corpus of Contemporary American English*: 410+ million words, 1990-present [http://www.americancorpus.org]. Last access 24 August 2010.

HYPERHAMLET. Corpus of references to and quotations from Shakespeare's Hamlet. [www.hyperhamlet.unibas.ch] Last access 24 August 2010.

LION - *Literature Online*. [http://lion.chadwyck.co.uk]. Last access 24 August 2010.

MCCARTHY, M. et al. *Cambridge International Dictionary of Idioms*. Cambridge: Cambridge University Press, 1998.

OED - *The Oxford English Dictionary*. Online Edition. [http://dictionary.oed.com]. 24 August 2010.

TDA -*The Times Digital Archive 1785 - 1900*. The Times and Gale Cengage Learning. [http://infotrac.galegroup.com.proxy.nationallizenzen.de/itw/infomark/0/1/1/purl=rc6_TTDA?sw_aep=1gbv]. Last access 22 August 2010.

THE BIBLE. [http://www.studylight.org]. Last access 22 August 2010.

WO FLINTEN IM KORN UND HUNDE BEGRABEN LIEGEN. ZUR EPOCHENSPEZIFISCHEN VERWENDUNG VON PHRASEOLOGISMEN IN MODERNER LYRIK

Nils Bernstein
Universität Wuppertal

Abstract: In the recent research of phraseology there has been a lot of disagreement with Lutz Röhrich's hypothesis of proverbs as the "rhetoric of the simple man" (*Rhetorik des einfachen Mannes*, Röhrich 1991:48). However, the use of many phraseological units, especially of conversational routines, is not adequate in the rather elaborated language of poetry. The counting of phraseological units in an anthology of ten volumes of German Poetry (ed. by Walther Killy et.al.) documents that they are very frequent in Modern Poetry of the 20th century. The increased frequency of occurrence can be used as a criterion for discriminating the language of poetry from everyday speech. Furthermore it proves the tendency of using colloquial language in Postmodern Poetry in terms of a deviation of concepts of conventional poetics. The article finally shows that phraseological units can be found in certain epochs of literary history.

Key words: Phraseology in poetry, stylistics of phraseological units, categories of poetry.

0. Einleitung

Lutz Röhrichs Gleichsetzung sprichwörtlicher Redensarten mit einer „Rhetorik des einfachen Mannes" (Röhrich 1991, S. 48) ist in der aktuellen Phraseologie-Forschung vielfach widersprochen worden. Dennoch eignen sich viele Phraseologismen, insbesondere Routineformeln, nicht für den Gebrauch in – tendenziell elaborierterer – Gedichtsprache, sondern eher für den Gebrauch in Alltagssprache. Durch eine Frequenzanalyse einer zehnbändigen Lyrik-Anthologie (hg. von Walther Killy u.a.) lässt sich belegen, dass Phraseologismen gehäuft in Moderner Lyrik des 20. Jahrhunderts auftreten. Diese Vorkommenshäufigkeit bietet sich als Beschreibungskriterium für Gedichtsprache an und gilt als Beleg einer zunehmenden Kolloquialisierung der Lyrik der Zweiten Moderne. Im Verständnis einer Deviationsästhetik lässt sich der Phraseologismengebrauch als Abweichung von konventionellen Poetologie-Konzepten mit der damit einhergehenden Innovationskraft beschreiben. Darüber hinaus dienen Phraseologismen als epochenspezifisches Charakterisierungsmerkmal.

1. Textkorpus und Hypothesen bei der Sichtung

In seinem Buch zu einer Philosophie von Kunst namens *The transfiguration of the commonplace* zitiert Arthur C. Danto ein Beispiel, um das intuitive Kunstverständnis zu erläutern: Wenn man einen kunsttheoretisch ungeschulten Mann in ein Warenhaus schicken würde und ihm den Auftrag erteilte, all jene Waren, die Kunst darstellen, herauszuholen, so würde er damit aller Wahrscheinlichkeit nach erfolgreich sein und das heraussuchen, was auch ein Kunsttheoretiker herausgesucht hätte (vgl. Danto 1984, S. 100).[1] Überträgt man dieses Beispiel auf die Lyriktheorie so würde dies bedeuten, dass ein Laie, der mit dem Auftrag versehen wird, aus einer Buchhandlung all jene Werke herauszusuchen, die seinem Verständnis von Lyrik entsprechen, ebenso treffsicher auswählen wird, wie dies eine Literaturwissenschaftlerin oder ein Literaturwissenschaftler tun würde. Das Alltagsverständnis von dem, was ein Gedicht ist, weicht, wenn überhaupt, nur geringfügig von dem ab, was philologisch als Gedicht definiert wird.

Provokant formuliert heißt das, eine Diskussion darüber, was ein Gedicht ist, könnte in einer Kneipe genau so produktiv sein, wie in einem germanistischen Oberseminar. Das hieße dann aber auch, dass in der Literaturwissenschaft keine gültigen Definitionsvorschläge gemacht worden sind. Die gelegentliche Verwirrung bestätigt dies zunächst. „What one person calls poetry another may call noise", erklärt Brett Bourbon in seiner tastenden Beantwortung der Frage „What Is a Poem?" (Bourbon 2007, 142). Und laut Jan Mukařovský „ist zu schließen, daß überhaupt keine Eigenschaft die Dichtersprache ständig und allgemein charakterisiert." (Mukařovský 1974, 144). Diesem Fatalismus stehen eindeutige Definitionsvorschläge gegenüber.

Das lyrische Gedicht sei „Einzelrede in Versen" (Lamping 1989, 63), stellt Lamping in einer Verquickung aus Form- und Sprachtheorie fest und schließt damit Kompositionen der Konkreten Poesie oder Peter Handkes viel diskutiertes Beispiel *Die Aufstellung des 1. FC Nürnberg vom 27.1.1968* eindeutig aus. Hans-Georg Kemper erklärt dagegen: *„Lyrik ist formdominant 'verdichtete' (Vers-)Rede."* (Kemper 2009, S. 40, Hervorhebung im Original). Ein Gedichtbeispiel, in dem pragmatisch-kommunikative Phraseologismen zentral sind, soll die unterschiedlichen Standpunkte illustrieren. Die eröffnenden und abschließenden Verse von Enzensbergers Gedicht *Einführung in die Handelskorrespondenz* (1983) lauten:

> *„Mit freundlichen Grüßen*
> *Mit grämlichem Hüsteln*
> *Mit christlichem Frösteln*
> *Mit fiesen Grimassen*
> *Mit geilen Finessen [...]*
> *Mit fröhlichem Knirschen*
> *Mit kreischenden Flüchen*
> *Mit freundlichen Grüßen"*
> (Enzensberger nach Thalmayr 2005, S. 50f).

Es ist deutlich erkennbar, dass hier schlicht die alltagssprachliche Routineformel *Mit freundlichen Grüßen*, die original im ersten und letzten Vers angeführt ist, anspielungsreich modifiziert wird, wobei die morpho-syntaktische Struktur gleich bleibt und die anfängliche Assonanz zunehmend verfremdet wird. Nach Lampings Definition lässt sich der vorliegende Text von lyrischen Gedichten ausschließen, da Einzelrede „eine einzelne, in sich geschlossene Äußerung" (Lamping 1989, 64) darstelle, was hier nicht der Fall ist. Kemper zufolge hingegen lässt sich die Einführung in die Handelskorrespondenz noch der Gattung Lyrik

---

[1] Das Zitat stammt aus William Kennicks Aufsatz *Does traditional Aesthetics rest on a Mistake?* (1958).

zuschlagen, da „auch das Sprach- und Lautmaterial in einem Bild- oder Lautgedicht" (Kemper 2009, 40) bei ihm Berücksichtigung findet.

Im Folgenden soll die Problematik der Beschreibbarkeit von Gedichtsprache mithilfe einer quantifizierenden Auswertung von Phraseologismen betrachtet werden. Zu diesem Zweck wurde die von Walter Killy u.a. herausgegebene Anthologie *Deutsche Lyrik von den Anfängen bis zur Gegenwart in zehn Bänden* gesichtet und dabei gezählt, in wie vielen Gedichten ein oder mehrere Phraseologismen vorkommen. Dabei wurde ein erweiterter Begriff von Phraseologismen zu Grunde gelegt, sodass auch Routineformeln, Sprichwörter, Geflügelte Worte und Zwillingsformeln gezählt wurden. Kollokationen hingegen wurden nicht berücksichtigt. Besonderes Augenmerk fand die Zeit vom Barock bis zum Jahre 2000. Der Vorteil der annalistisch sortierten Killy-Anthologie ist ihr verhältnismäßig großer Umfang, denn in den letzten sieben Bänden, vom Barock bis zur Gegenwart also, sind dort genau 2421 Gedichte verzeichnet. Der so genannte *Große Conrady* hingegen enthält unter Berücksichtigung des gesamten Zeitraums der Lyrikgeschichte etwa 2200 Gedichte, der von Ludwig Reiners herausgegebene *Ewige Brunnen* gar „nur" 1660 Gedichte. Ein weiterer Vorteil ist, dass die Auswahl der Anthologie nicht etwa ausschließlich kanonisierte Lyrik enthält, sondern versucht wird, einen historisch-exemplarischen Eindruck der Lyrikgeschichte zu vermitteln. Nicht das, was wir heute noch lesen, sondern das, was damals tatsächlich gedruckt und rezipiert wurde, möchten die Herausgeber über die historische Distanz hinweg der heutigen Leserschaft vermitteln. Wie Jürgen Stenzel, der Herausgeber des fünften Bandes, also der Lyrik von 1700 bis 1770, im Vorwort anmerkt, handelt es sich nicht um eine „Blumenlese" sondern um eine Zusammenstellung, die „neben dem künstlerisch Gelungenen und dem von der Geschichte Kanonisierten auch mittelmäßige Gebrauchslyrik, Mißlungenes und Kurioses" (Stenzel 2001, S. 5) enthalte.

Aus diesem Grund lassen sich aus den vorliegenden Gedichten Rückschlüsse auf die damalige Gedichtsprache ziehen. Ferner wurde auch die kleinere, von Hay und Steinsdorff herausgegebene Anthologie *Deutsche Lyrik vom Barock bis zur Gegenwart* gesichtet, die etwas mehr als 300 Gedichte enthält und eine Auswahl der Gedichte der Killy-Anthologie darstellt. Und für eine Überprüfung der zeitgenössischen Lyrik wurde das von Ron Winkler herausgegebene *Neubuch. Neue junge Lyrik* ausgewertet, in dem 25 nach 1972 geborene Autorinnen und Autoren mit vier bis sieben Gedichten vertreten sind.

Bei der Frequenzanalyse der in den Gedichten vorkommenden Phraseologismen wurden zwei Hypothesen aufgestellt:
(1) Phraseologismen sind tendenziell Eigenschaft lyrikuntypischer Sprachverwendung, da sie dem konventionellen Ansatz sprachlicher Originalität widersprechen.
(2) Bestimmte Epochen, bestimmte Strophenformen, bestimmte Metren und bestimmte Autoren lassen Phraseologismenabstinenz erwarten, wohingegen Lyrik nach 1945 u.a. aufgrund erhöhter metasprachlicher Reflexion zu einer höheren Vorkommenshäufigkeit von Phraseologismen tendiert.

Die im Titel angeführten Phraseologismen hat Morgenstern in zwei berühmten Gedichten remotiviert. Um diese beiden Phraseologismen zu bemühen, geht es mir um die Überlegung, ob bei der Verwendung von Phraseologismen in Lyrik eine weitere Eigenschaft zur Beschreibung von Lyriksprache verborgen ist, also um die Frage, ob hier ein weiterer Hund der Lyriktheorie begraben ist, der uns davon abhält bei der Definition des Gedichtes gleich die Flinte ins Korn zu werfen.

2. Daten zu Phraseologismenfrequenz und Phraseologismendichte

In den meisten definitorischen Ansätzen zu einer Lyriktheorie werden die Eigenschaften „Liedhaftigkeit, Kürze, Abweichung von der Alltagssprache und Versform" (Burdorf 1997, 6) genannt. Zweifellos lassen sich bei Phraseologismen ebenso wie bei freien Lexemen die verschiedensten Stilebenen feststellen (vgl. Mohr-Elfadl 2006, 297-313, v.a. 298-300). Doch gerade die „Dominanz der Mündlichkeit in der Phraseologie" (Stein 2007, 221) steht im Widerspruch zur Abweichungsästhetik und spricht gegen den Gebrauch von Phraseologismen in Lyrik, was in Sonderheit für die Routineformeln geltend zu machen ist. Weder Routine noch Formelhaftigkeit lassen eine Abweichung von Alltagssprache erwarten. „Wer Routineformeln gebraucht, hält sich an das Erprobte, Bewährte, an das Gewohnte." (Donalies 2009, S. 99). Tatsächlich findet man bei den im sechsten Band der Killy-Anthologie (*Gedichte 1770-1800*) aufgenommenen Oden nur bei einer einen Phraseologismus. In dem Band sind 30 Oden verzeichnet, deren Paradigma des weihevollen, lyrisch-erhabenen Duktus mit anspruchsvoller Stilhöhe im Widerspruch zu einer Verwendung sprachlich wenig originärer fest geprägter Mehrwortverbindung zu stehen scheint. Im Falle der Verse, die im elegischen Distichon verfasst sind, verhält es sich im genannten Band ähnlich. In keinem einzigen der neun im elegischen Distichon stehenden Gedichte kommt ein Phraseologismus vor. Die Lyrik Hölderins und Klopstocks hat nachhaltig die Odenform des 18. und 19. Jahrhunderts sowie schließlich die bei uns heute vorherrschenden Vorstellungen exemplarischer Oden beeinflusst. Bei 24 Klopstock-Gedichten und 33 Hölderlin-Gedichten findet man lediglich zwei Gedichte Klopstocks, die nicht-idiomatische Phraseologismen enthalten und eines von Hölderlin, das eine Phraseoschablone aufweist. Die beiden Dichter neigen zumindest zufolge den in der Anthologie vertretenen Gedichten zu Phraseologismenabstinenz.

Eine Auswertung der Phraseologismenfrequenz zunächst nach Jahrzehnten und schließlich nach Literaturepochen erlaubt weitere Aussagen. Erstere Angabe ist in den folgenden vier Diagrammen illustriert[2]:

---

[2] Etwas verwirrend ist, dass das so genannte Zaunpfahlproblem von den Herausgebern der Anthologie nicht konsequent berücksichtigt wurde. So beginnt etwa der vierte Band der Anthologie richtigerweise mit dem Jahr 1601, wenngleich der Titel *Gedichte 1600-1700* lautet. Der Band schließt mit einem Gedicht von 1700 und der Folgeband setzt wiederum mit vier Gedichten aus dem Jahr 1700 ein. Diese Ungenauigkeit zieht sich durch die gesamte Anthologie. In den hier angeführten vier Diagrammen zum 17., 18., 19. und 20. Jahrhundert beginnt beispielsweise das 17. Jahrhundert mit dem Jahr 1601 und endet mit dem Jahr 1700.

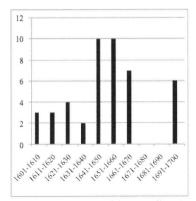
Phraseologismendichte 17. Jahrhundert (Killy u.a.)

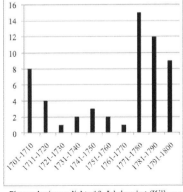
Phraseologismendichte 18. Jahrhundert (Killy u.a.)

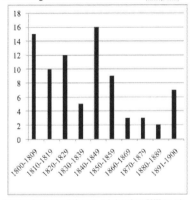
Phraseologismendichte 19. Jahrhundert (Killy u.a.)

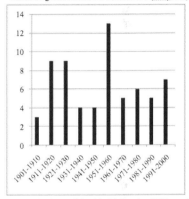
Phraseologismendichte 20. Jahrhundert (Killy u.a.)

Unter literaturgeschichtlichem Gesichtspunkt hingegen ist eine quantifizierende Annäherung an die Phraseologismenfrequenz bzw. -dichte vor allem dann interessant, wenn man sie nach Literaturepochen aufgliedert. Im vorliegenden Fall wird auf eine – in einem anderen Zusammenhang durchaus gerechtfertigte – Diskussion strittiger Epochenbegriffe verzichtet und die Einteilung nach Gero von Wilperts einschlägigem *Sachbuch der Literatur* zu Grunde gelegt. Abgesehen von Klassik und Romantik wurden im Folgenden jene Epochen berücksichtigt, die keine Datierungsüberschneidung mit anderen Epochen aufweisen. Wilpert datiert dabei folgendermaßen: Barock (1600-1720), Aufklärung (1720-1785), Klassik (1786-1805), Romantik (1798-1830), Realismus (1850-1890), Expressionismus (1910-1925). Als Vergleichszahl wurde der relationale Phraseologismendichte nach Killy u.a. die absolute Frequenz nach der Anthologie von Hay/ Steinsdorff gegenübergestellt. Die Dichte berechnet sich aus der Anzahl der Gedichte mit einem oder mehreren Phraseologismen geteilt durch die Anzahl der im jeweiligen Zeitraum aufgenommenen Gedichte. Um die Datierungsüberschneidung der Romantik auszugleichen, wurden bei der Auswertung lediglich jene Gedichte berücksichtigt, die eindeutig exemplarischen Vertretern dieser Epoche zuzuschlagen sind. Bei der (Weimarer) Klassik wurden jene Gedichte des Zeitraums gezählt, die von den beiden Hauptvertretern Goethe und Schiller stammen. Für die epochenspezifische und relationale Phraseologismendichte nach Killy u.a. und die epochenspezifische und absolute Phraseologismenfrequenz nach Hay/ Steinsdorff ergibt sich folgende Verteilung:

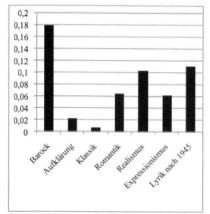
Phraseologismendichte (Killy u.a.)

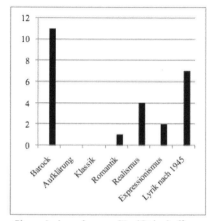
Phraseologismenfrequenz (Hay/ Steinsdorff)

Insbesondere die hohe Frequenz im Barock und in der Lyrik nach 1945 ist auffällig. Die hohe Vorkommenshäufigkeit von Phraseologismen im Barock ist nicht allein dem Umstand geschuldet, dass diese 120 Jahre der Lyrikgeschichte andauernde Epoche natürlich einen entsprechenden Umfang in der Anthologie einnimmt. In dieser Zeit stand der Gebrauch bestimmter fester Wendungen und vor allem bestimmter Parömien noch für die Belesenheit und die hohe Bildung des Autors. Phraseologismen wurden nicht hinterfragt oder reflektiert, sondern galten als „akzeptierte Weisheiten und Prinzipien" (Eismann 2007, 321). In den 45 Gedichten mit Phraseologismen, die sich im vierten Band der Killy-Anthologie finden (*Gedichte 1600-1700*), sind allerdings nur acht Phraseologismen enthalten, die Idiomatizität aufweisen. Ferner finden sich darunter 29 Zwillingsformeln (etwa „Tag vnd Nacht", „gantz vnnd gar" oder „hin und her"), die interpretatorisch nicht in relevanter Weise zu analysieren sind. Interessant ist dagegen, dass in der Lyrik des 19. Jahrhunderts Zwillingsformeln zu finden sind, die zur Beibehaltung des Versmaßes und/ oder des Reimschemas modifiziert werden. Dies ist etwa in dem Gedicht *In der Frühe* (1828) der Fall, in dem Eduard Mörike die Komponenten einer Zwillingsformel vertauscht, um den Reim zu erhalten: „Es wühlet mein verstörter Sinn/ Noch zwischen Zweifeln her und hin" (Killy u.a. 2001, Bd. 7, S. 330). Eine dreifache Modifikation der Zwillingsformel *Tag und Nacht* (Plural, Vertauschung der Komponenten, Elision des den Plural markierenden 'e') nimmt Christian Friedrich Scherenberg in seinem Gedicht *Galeerenpoesie* (1856) vor, um sowohl Reimschema als auch Versmaß zu erhalten: „Sie singen eintönig ab eine Geschicht',/ Zum Lied geworden wie verlor'ne Klage:/ Frei wurde mal Einer – Sie glauben's nicht,/ Doch singen sie es *alle Nächt' und Tage.*" (Killy u.a. 2001, Bd. 8, S. 225, Hervorhebung im Original).

Im zehnten Band der Killy-Anthologie (*Gedichte von 1961-2000*) finden sich unter den 23 Phraseologismen hingegen mit immerhin 12 idiomatischen Phraseologismen weit mehr übertragen zu verstehender Mehrwortverbindungen, als im Barock. Eine Auswertung der von Ron Winkler herausgegebenen Zusammenstellung *Neubuch. Neue junge Lyrik* bestätigt die erhöhte Tendenz zur Verwendung von Phraseologismen auch für die zeitgenössische Lyrik junger Dichterinnen und Dichter. Bei den 139 Gedichten sind 15 Gedichte mit einem oder mehreren Phraseologismen zu zählen, was eine Dichte von 0,108 ergibt. Eine Dichte von mehr als 0,1 – jedes zehnte Gedicht enthält also einen oder mehrere Phraseologismen – ist als verhältnismäßig hoch einzustufen. Diese Schwelle wird in der Lyrik der Romantik und des Expressionismus unterschritten. Auffällig ist, dass in der Lyrik nach 1945 phraseologisches Sprachmaterial themenentfaltend verwendet wird, Phraseologismen damit also oftmals die Grundlage einer Strophe oder gar eines kompletten Gedichtes bilden. Sie werden oftmals durch *verba dicendi* eingebettet und ihr literaler Wortsinn wird häufig kritisch reflektiert. Insgesamt korreliert die Reflektion von Phraseologismen mit der Zunahme an metasprachlicher Thematisierung in der Lyrik nach 1945. Das abschließend angeführte Gedicht *Amtliche Mitteilung* (1962) von Volker von Törne (Killy u.a. 2001, Bd. 10, S. 20) dient als Beispiel für eine thementfaltende Verwendung von Phraseologismen bei gleichzeitigem kritischen Hinterfragen ihres Inhaltes.

Die Suppe ist eingebrockt:
wir werden nicht hungern.
Wasser steht uns am Hals:
wir werden nicht dürsten.
Sie spielen mit dem Feuer:
wir werden nicht frieren.
Für uns ist gesorgt.

In dem Gedicht dienen die Phraseologismen als kritische Stellungnahme. Törne remotiviert in diesem Paradebeispiel eines Gedichtes der engagierten Lyrik drei verbale, idiomatische Phraseologismen durch den Zusatz im jeweils zweiten Vers der Strophen: Die eingebrockte Suppe verhindert den Hunger, das bis zum Hals stehende Wasser den Durst und das Spiel mit dem Feuer das Frieren. Allerdings werden alle drei Phraseologismen nur auf wenig wünschenswerte und zu vermeidende Situationen angewandt, wohingegen das Abwenden von Hunger, Durst und Kälte durchaus positiv ist. Das ebenso fest geprägte und damit zum Bestand der Phraseologie zählende Fazit im abschließenden Vers *für jmdn. ist gesorgt* ist eine ironische Stellungnahme zu den gegebenen gesellschaftlichen oder gesellschaftspolitischen Verhältnissen, die derart beklagenswert sind, dass eben nicht die (wirtschaftliche) Zufriedenheit eine totale Passivität nach sich ziehen soll. Im Gegenteil enthält das korrekte Verständnis des idiomatischen Inhaltes der angeführten Phraseologismen in dieser dadurch ganz und gar nicht *amtlichen* Mitteilung zwischen den Zeilen einen Appell zum politischen Handeln gerade trotz der Saturiertheit zu Zeiten des wirtschaftlichen Aufschwungs im Wirtschaftswunderdeutschland.

3. Zusammenfassung

Die Auswertung der Phraseologismenfrequenz und -dichte in einer umfangreichen Gedichtanthologie nebst Überprüfung der gewonnenen Werte anhand von zwei weiteren Gedichtbänden erbringt einen zweifachen Erkenntnisgewinn. Zum Einen erfolgt damit eine epochenübergreifende Annäherung an die Gattung der Lyrik, die in der Phraseologieforschung bislang – im Gegensatz zu erzählender Literatur – „eher stiefmütterlich behandelt worden" (Eismann 2007, S. 324) ist. Zum Anderen dient diese Auswertung einer erneuten

Differenzierung von Gedichtsprache und Alltagssprache. Die Aporie besteht dabei mitunter darin, dass Sprache kein allein der Kunst vorenthaltenes Medium ist. Die Sprache, die im Alltag verwendet wird, dient auch der Produktion literarischer und lyrischer Texte. Dadurch unterscheiden sich Schriftsteller von Künstlern anderer Betätigungsfelder, etwa von Malern oder Musikern. Denn Töne und Farben werden in alltäglicher Kommunikation nicht als Medium benutzt, Sprache dagegen schon. Die Sprache der Literatur bildet dadurch eben kein „sekundäres modellierendes System" (Lotman 1993, S. 39), wie Jurij Lotman es in seiner einflussreichen Studie *Die Struktur literarischer Texte* behauptet hat.

Die Gedichtsprache enthält sich nicht von vornherein des Gebrauchs von Phraseologismen. Die Phraseologie gehört zu jenem Sprachsystem, dessen sich auch eine jede Autorin und ein jeder Autor beim Verfassen von Gedichten bedient. Jedoch konnte gezeigt werden, dass ein epochal bedingter Unterschied zwischen den Auffassungen von Gedichtsprache und der damit zusammenhängenden Phraseologismentendenz besteht. Bestimmte Bereiche der Literatur- und Lyrikgeschichte neigen zu Phraseologismenabstinenz, etwa Epochen wie die Klassik, bestimmte Autoren wie der klassische Goethe und der klassische Schiller, Klopstock oder Hölderlin, bestimmte Strophenformen wie die Ode oder bestimmte Metren wie das elegische Distichon. In der Lyrik ab 1900 und insbesondere in der Lyrik ab 1945 ist ein gehäufter Phraseologismengebrauch zu verzeichnen, der im Einklang mit einer Zuwendung zu metasprachlicher Reflexion und zunehmender poetologischer Reflexivität überhaupt in der jüngeren Lyrikgeschichte steht (vgl. Hildebrand 2003, S. 5). Die erhöhte Vorkommenshäufigkeit von Phraseologismen unterstreicht eine Annäherung an Alltagssprache, eine Tendenz der allgemeinen Kolloquialisierung und einen Bruch mit dem lyrisch-weihevollen Ton eines heutigentags überkommenen *poeta-vates*-Konzepts.

4. Literatur

BOURBON, B. 2007 „What Is a Poem?". *Modern Philology* 105 Heft-Nr. 1: 27-43.
BURDORF, D. 1997 *Einführung in die Gedichtanalyse*. 2. Aufl. Stuttgart/ Weimar.
DANTO, A. C. 1984 *Die Verklärung des Gewöhnlichen. Eine Philosophie der Kunst*. Übers. von Max Loser. Frankfurt/ M.
DONALIES, E. 2009 *Basiswissen Deutsche Phraseologie*. Tübingen/ Basel 2009.
EISMANN, W. 2007 „Phraseme in literarischen Texten und Autorenphraseologie". In: Burger, H. u.a. (Hgg.): *Phraseologie. Ein internationales Handbuch der zeitgenössischen Forschung. Handbücher zur Sprach- und Kommunikationswissenschaft* Bd. 28.2. Berlin/ New York: 316-329.
HAY, G. und VON STEINSDORFF, S. (Hgg.) 2007 *Deutsche Lyrik vom Barock bis zur Gegenwart*. München.
HILDEBRAND, O. 2003 „Einleitung". In: Ders. (Hg.): *Poetologische Lyrik von Klopstock bis Grünbein. Gedichte und Interpretationen*. Köln u.a.
KEMPER, H. G. 2009). *Komische Lyrik – lyrische Komik. Über Verformungen einer formstrengen Gattung*. Tübingen.
KILLY, W. u.a. (Hgg.) 2001 *Deutsche Lyrik von den Anfängen bis zur Gegenwart in zehn Bänden*. München.
LAMPING, D. 1989). *Das lyrische Gedicht. Definitionen zu Theorie und Geschichte der Gattung*. Göttingen.
LOTMAN, J. M. 1993 *Die Struktur literarischer Texte*. 4. unverändert. Aufl. München.
MOHR-ELFADL, S. 2006 „Zur phraseologischen Stilanalyse literarischer Texte". In: Burger, H. u.a. (Hgg.): *Phraseology in Motion I. Akten der Internationalen Tagung zur Phraseologie* (Basel, 2004). Baltmannsweiler: 297-313.
MUKAŘOVSKÝ, J. 1974, [1948] „Über Dichtersprache". Übers. von Herbert Grönebaum. In: *Ders.: Studien zur strukturalistischen Ästhetik und Poetik*. München: 142-199.
RÖHRICH, L. 1991). *Lexikon der sprichwörtlichen Redensarten*. Freiburg u.a.
STEIN, S. 2007 „Mündlichkeit und Schriftlichkeit aus phraseologischer Perspektive". In: Burger, H. u.a. (Hgg.): *Phraseologie. Ein internationales Handbuch der zeitgenössischen Forschung. Handbücher zur Sprach- und Kommunikationswissenschaft Bd. 28.2* Berlin/ New York, S. 220-236.
STENZEL, J. 2001, [1969] „Einleitung". In: Killy, W. u.a. (Hgg.): *Deutsche Lyrik von den Anfängen bis zur Gegenwart in zehn Bänden. Bd. 5: Deutsche Lyrik 1700-1770*. München: 5-12.
THALMAYR, A. 2005*eraus mit der Sprache. Ein bisschen Deutsch für Deutsche, Österreicher, Schweizer und andere Aus- und Inländer*. München/ Wien.
WILPERT, G. VON 2001 *Sachwörterbuch der Literatur*. 8., verb. und erw. Aufl. Stuttgart.
WINKLER, R. (Hg.) 2008 *Neubuch. Neue junge Lyrik*. München.

NUR ÜBER MEINE LEICHE! - ¡POR ENCIMA DE MI CADÁVER! ENUNCIADOS FRASEOLÓGICOS ALEMANES Y ESPAÑOLES QUE EXPRESAN RECUSACIÓN

Mª Luisa Schilling
Universidad Complutense de Madrid

Abstract: The article offers a contrasted analysis of the German and Spanish psycho-social recusation routine formulas used to verbalize the linguistic expressions of denying and refusing. Furthermore it analyses the linguistic structure of these routine formulae, both in German and Spanish, as well as it's ilocutive value. Finally it includes a contrasted analysis of the final results and offers a wide range of total and partial equivalences between both languages.

Key words: routine formulae, formulaic language, refusal forms, Spanish phraseology, German phraseology

Hace ya varios meses, la Dra. Consuelo Moreno y yo comenzamos a preparar el presente trabajo, pero desgraciadamente a ella se la llevó en octubre del año pasado una enfermedad y no le dio tiempo nada más que a recopilar el material correspondiente a toda la parte española del corpus. El estudio que les presento aquí pretende ser un homenaje y un recuerdo muy especial a mi compañera de tantos años.

El trabajo se enmarca dentro de un estudio más amplio llevado a cabo por diferentes miembros del equipo de investigación fraseológica de la UCM, IDIOMAT, estudio que abarca tanto el plano teórico como el práctico de nuestro objeto de investigación. Algunos de los resultados ya fueron dados a conocer por las doctoras Balzer y Piñel, autoras de la parte teórica del análisis, en el congreso de Europhras 2008 de Helsinki y en la "VI. Internationale Arbeitstagung, Romanisch-deutscher und Innerromanischer Sprachvergleich" celebrado en Innsbruck en septiembre del mismo año.

Siguiendo con la clasificación de las fórmulas rutinarias que proponen Balzer y Piñel hemos llevado a cabo un análisis contrastivo de las fórmulas rutinarias psico-sociales de *recusación* alemanas y españolas que sirven para verbalizar el acto de habla de *negar* o *rechazar*.

El material que conforma el corpus procede de diccionarios fraseológicos tanto alemanes como españoles, de obras monográficas o de consulta y de testimonios directos de hablantes nativos.

Dada la limitación de tiempo propia de una comunicación, nos centraremos en presentar y comentar los aspectos relacionados con la forma lingüística de los enunciados de las fórmulas rutinarias mencionadas y su valor ilocutivo. Paralelamente comentaremos algunos aspectos relacionados con el análisis contrastivo de los resultados obtenidos, que ha permitido proponer posibles equivalencias totales o parciales entre ambas lenguas.

En la mayoría de los casos en este estudio se parte de las fórmulas de recusación en alemán y, por ello, prácticamente todas las frases contextualizadas están en esta lengua. Aunque, de nuevo para no exceder los límites de esta comunicación, no incluimos ejemplos de uso de todas las fórmulas rutinarias, sino sólo de aquellas que son más representativas. Estas oraciones contextualizadas proceden en su mayoría del Duden 11, *Redewendungen.*

Wörterbuch der deutschen Idiomatik y del *Lexikon der Redesarten* de Klaus Müller. En cada caso proponemos además una posible equivalencia de la fórmula rutinaria en español, si bien, como es de suponer, ambas lenguas no coinciden siempre en la forma ni en la imagen que evocan. En un menor número de casos se parte de la fórmula de recusación española y no traducimos los ejemplos de uso porque ya proponemos una equivalencia en la otra lengua.

Fórmulas rutinarias psico-sociales

Nuestro día a día está lleno de hábitos y rutinas, ya que repetimos con frecuencia, y casi siempre de forma inconsciente, aquello que hacemos o decimos en determinados contextos, lo que se refleja en el frecuente uso de fórmulas rutinarias. Como mencionamos más arriba, el presente estudio se centra aquí en las fórmulas psico-sociales que son aquellas que desempeñan funciones que facilitan el desarrollo normal de la interacción social, o bien funciones de expresión del estado mental y de los sentimientos del emisor. (Corpas 1997)

De acuerdo con las definiciones de Corpas, Burger, Coulmas, Balzer y Piñel y Valero, las fórmulas rutinarias presentan las siguientes características:

- Son unidades fraseológicas estereotipadas del discurso que forman una sucesión de palabras estable, que se repiten en la comunicación diaria, que aparecen en situaciones comunicativas claramente delimitadas, que tienen una estrecha relación con el contexto pragmático en el que aparecen y que se utilizan de acuerdo con unos comportamientos sociales compartidos por toda la comunidad de un mismo ámbito lingüístico y cultural.

- Las fórmulas de recusación expresan, en general, desacuerdo con lo dicho por el interlocutor, aunque con diversos matices, como por ejemplo el de negar, de rechazar, de rehusar por inadmisible o no creíble una proposición o de expresar disconformidad irónicamente. (Corpas 1997).

1. Valor locutivo

Las fórmulas de recusación alemanas y españolas analizadas en el corpus presentan muy diferentes estructuras formales pues, al tratarse habitualmente de una reacción frente a una observación de un interlocutor en una situación comunicativa concreta, pueden aparecer como oraciones independientes, como oraciones compuestas, como expresiones elípticas o como informaciones añadidas a lo que ya ha dicho el interlocutor. Así desde el punto de vista formal para el alemán en este corpus hay que diferenciar:

1.1 Exclamaciones:
sonst noch was! - ¡lo que faltaba!
Meine Eltern könnten doch jetzt zu uns ziehen, oder? – *Sonst noch was!* Dann ziehe ich aber aus! (Du)
Ach was! - ¡Qué va!
Du hast wohl schlechte Laune heute? – *Ach was*! Ich bin bloß hundemüde. (Du)
Para estos dos ejemplos proponemos una equivalencia con verbo en español. Además, como vemos en el último caso, en el contexto de las fórmulas de recusación ambas lenguas cuentan también con interjecciones impropias o palabras pertenecientes a otras categorías gramaticales que han sido lexicalizadas como interjecciones. Con frecuencia nos encontramos expresiones

con elementos interrogativos, aquí *was* o *qué*, ambos con valor de interjección y combinados con otro elemento. O como los siguientes ejemplos:
    nichts da! - ¡de eso nada [monada]! / Nanay del paraguay
    Was heißt hier Kaffeetrinken? *Nichts da*! Jetzt wird erst das Geschirr gespült! (Du)
    I wo! -¡Nada de eso!
Sintagmas nominales exclamativos:
    Irrtum vom Amt! -¡Craso error!
    Ich soll das gesagt haben? *Irrtum von Amt*, mein Lieber! (Du)
En éste y en los siguientes ejemplos coincide parcialmente las dos lenguas.
    Quatsch mit Soße!- ¡Tonterías! ¡Pamplinas! ¡Chorradas!
    nicht um alles in der Welt – por nada del mundo, ni por todo el oro del mundo
    Nicht um alles in der Welt wollte sie ihm an diesem Ort begegnen (Du)
Exclamaciones en forma de sintagma verbal, aquí en participio:
    nicht geschenkt! – ¡ni regalado!
    Windows Vista? *Nicht geschenkt*!

1.2. Oraciones

1.2.1 Fórmulas de recusación en oraciones enunciativas completas en alemán, y a menudo con construcciones de infinitivo en español:
    Davon kann gar keine Rede sein! - ¡de eso ni hablar!
    Ich soll dir Geld leihen? *Davon kann gar keine Rede sein*! Zahl erstmal deine alten Schulden zurück! (Mü)
    Ich denke gar nicht daran, (das zu tun) – ¡ni pensarlo!
    Ich denke gar nicht daran, hinter dir herzuräumen. Bring dein Zimmer gefälligst selbst in Ordnung! (Mü)
    Da lachen ja die Hühner! – ¡no me hagas reír!
    Für dieses Auto wollen Sie noch 10.000 Mark? *Da lachen ja die Hühner*! Schauen Sie sich die Rostkiste doch einmal genau an! (Mü)
En los tres ejemplos anteriores coinciden en las dos lenguas las imágenes a las que aluden los verbos: hablar, pensar y reír.
    Er kann mir mal im Mond begegnen! – ¡Anda y que le den dos duros!
    Der Egon, dieser blöde Kerl, *der kann mir mal im Mond begegnen*! Mit dem hat man doch nichts als Ärger! (Mü)
También en este caso se trata de una interjección impropia en español en esa forma verbal combinada con las conjunciones "anda y que".

1.2.2. Fórmulas de recusación expresadas por medio de oraciones en imperativo:
    Rutsch mir den Buckel runter! - ¡Vete a freír espárragos / a hacer puñetas / a tomar viento!
    Deine ewigen Vorwürfe reichen mir jetzt. *Du kannst mir mal den Buckel runterrutschen*! (Mü)
    Geh mir weg mit…! - ¡Quita p'allá con …! / ¡déjame de…! / ¡vete al cuerno!
    Geh mir weg mit Kinderkriegen! Es gibt schon genug Kinder auf der Welt! (Mü)
    Mach keine [faulen] Witze! - ¡no me cuentes chistes / historias!

Deine Mutter will zu uns ziehen! *Mach keine faulen Witze*! Wo soll sie denn in unserer Zweizimmerwohnung hausen? (Mü)
En todos estos ejemplos coinciden las oraciones de imperativo en ambas lenguas, si bien las imágenes a las que aluden algunos de ellos son totalmente diferentes en alemán y en español. En términos generales hemos recogido más ejemplos de expresiones de recusación en imperativo en español que en alemán, muchas de cuales al aparecer en una construcción negativa se expresan en español con el correspondiente verbo en subjuntivo como requiere la negación del imperativo en esta lengua. Incluso se ha documentado alguna expresión indirecta del imperativo con "sollen" en alemán y la conjunción "que" en español:

Soll er doch sehen, wo er bleibt! - ¡que se busque la vida!
en las que se expresa la insolidaridad y el rechazo.

Dicha construcción iniciada con una conjunción y equivalente a un imperativo también se documenta en alemán:

Dass ich nicht lache! – ¡No me hagas reír!
Ich soll deine Schuhe putzen? *Dass ich nicht lache*! (Du)

1.2.3. También hemos documentado fórmulas de recusación alemanas en contextos interrogativos. Las equivalencias propuestas a veces coinciden formalmente en las dos lenguas y otras no:

wie komme (käme) ich dazu (das zu tun)? - ¡a mí no me pidas eso!
Wie kommst du mir [eigentlich] vor? - ¿de qué vas?
Ich soll für dich im Betrieb anrufen und behaupten, dass du krank bist? *Wie kommst du mir eigentlich vor*! (Du)

expresiones que se utilizan para expresar protesta y rechazo ante lo que se acaba de oír por considerarlo insolente y descarado.

Wo haben wir denn zusammen Schweine gehütet? - ¿cuándo hemos comido juntos?
Esta unidad fraseológica rutinaria se dice para atajar y rechazar a alguien que empieza a tratarle a uno con excesiva confianza. La imagen es totalmente distinta en ambas lenguas pero tiene un significado idéntico y coincide también la forma interrogativa de ambas oraciones.

1.2.4. Las siguientes fórmulas de recusación son básicamente reacciones ante aquello que acaba de decir el interlocutor y, por ello, es frecuente que la respuesta se exprese con una oración elíptica, aquí como una sucesión de palabras estable y estereotipada, en la que se han elidido uno o varios de sus miembros:

Ach woher denn! / ach wo / i wo! / wo werd' ich denn! - ¡qué va! / ¿qué dices? / Ni hablar / De ninguna forma
que se utilizan para negar rotundamente lo que acaba de mencionar el interlocutor.

Du willst dich doch nicht nach sechs Kognaks noch ans Steuer setzen? - *Wo werd' ich denn*! Ich lass mir ein Taxi kommen.(Du)

O el siguiente ejemplo:

Du kannst mich [mal] kreuzweise - ¡que te den!
con el que se expresa desprecio y rechazo. En la forma alemana está elidido tanto el infinitivo que acompaña al adverbio modal como un local y en la española se prescinde del local, resultando dos fórmulas que aunque no son idénticas en ambas lenguas, coinciden totalmente en el significado y en el nivel de lengua grosero.

1.3. Negación:

1.3.1. Expresión explícita de la negación:
Aunque estamos analizando fórmulas que se utilizan en actos de habla que expresan negar y rechazar, no siempre nos encontramos con la expresión explícita de la negación. Sin embargo, en el siguiente ejemplo no cabe ninguna duda de lo que se quiere transmitir:
 Nein! Siebenmal nein! - ¡no y no!

1.3.2. Por el contrario encontramos en ambas lenguas múltiples expresiones sin negación explícita, por ejemplo:
 Das kannst du deiner Großmutter erzählen! - ¡cuéntaselo a tu abuela!
que muestra un paralelismo en ambas lenguas y sirve para expresar incredulidad ante algo dicho por otro. Tanto en alemán como en español hay muchas variaciones de esta fórmula rutinaria.
 das könnte dir so passen! - ¡qué más quisieras! / ¡que te crees tú eso!
 Das könnte dir so passen, mich mit den Kindern allein lassen und in die Kneipe gehen! (Du)
Ambas fórmulas se usan para rechazar algo como pretensión imposible del interlocutor, con el mismo matiz burlón, de ironía.
 El caso totalmente opuesto es la expresión española
 ¡Sí, hombre! ¡Sí, pero menos!
en la que la negación y la rebaja de las pretensiones del otro se expresan por medio de una afirmación explícita que transmite un alto grado de ironía. Aquí conviene comentar que entre las interjecciones impropias, en español se utiliza con frecuencia el sustantivo "¡Hombre!" o "¡Mujer!", como acabamos de ver en el ejemplo anterior.

1.3.3. Esta expresión de la ironía se repite en muchas de estas fórmulas rutinarias, en las que aunque explícitamente se dice justo lo contrario, por el contexto queda claro que con ellas se quiere negar o rechazar lo propuesto.
 So siehst du aus! - ¡qué más quisieras!
 Während du dich amüsierst, soll ich zu Hause bleiben und auf die Kinder aufpassen? *So siehst du aus*! (Du)
 Das wäre ja noch schöner! - ¡lo que faltaba!
 Ob ich dir mein Auto leihe? *Das wäre ja noch schöner*! Wo du mir doch erst neulich eine Beule reingefahren hast! (Mü)
 Du bist gut! - ¡estás tú fresco! /¡estás tú bueno! /¡vas listo!
 Ich soll dir das Geld leihen? *Du bist gut*! Wann hast du mir denn mal geholfen? (Du)

1.4. Las fórmulas rutinarias de recusación pueden aparecer en diferentes lugares del discurso: generalmente se encuentran abriendo o cerrando una oración, pero también encontramos algunas dentro de la misma, en particular cuando se trata de refuerzos de la negación. Así, por ejemplo:

 Mit mir war *nicht die Bohne* los. Ich war bloß irgend so ein Idiot. (Du)
que equivaldría en español a "nada en absoluto".

2. Función ilocutiva

En este análisis nos hemos centrado en las fórmulas rutinarias de recusación que se utilizan en actos de habla de negar y de rechazar y hemos ampliado dicha fuerza ilocutiva a los matices que conllevan 'estar en desacuerdo', 'negar el conocimiento', es decir, 'ignorar', 'expresar la disconformidad', 'rectificar el error del otro', 'invitar a la desaparición' que entendemos como un rechazo, y algunos juicios y críticas. Aplicando la clasificación que proponen Balzer y Piñel, la fuerza ilocucionaria de los ejemplos de recusación de este corpus se estructura de la siguiente manera:

2.1. Entre las fórmulas expresivas, aquellas que utiliza el emisor para expresar su actitud y sus sentimientos, distinguimos:

2.1.1. las fórmulas expresivas que cumplen la función de desaprobar y, por tanto, de negar, como por ejemplo
Das kommt nicht in die Tüte! / Das kommt nicht in Frage! / Nichts da! / Ach was! / I wo!
y sus posibles equivalencias en español
Ni hablar del peluquín / Nanay del Paraguay / Nasti de plasta / Naranjas de la China / ¡de eso nada! / De ninguna manera / De ningún modo / ¡Tararí que te vi! / ¡no hay tu tía! / ¡Qué va!
Ich soll deine Mutter am Bahnhof abholen? *Das kommt gar nicht in die Tüte*! Du weißt doch, dass wir ständig Streit miteinander haben! (Mü)

2.1.2. Aquellas fórmulas expresivas que tienen la función de replicar y de comunicar la ignorancia y el desconocimiento del emisor. Son las fórmulas expresivas de respuesta a una observación del interlocutor. En los ejemplos del corpus se utilizan para transmitir ignorancia:
Was weiß ich! -¡yo qué sé! / ¡qué se yo!
Wo ist bloß mein gelber Pullover? – *Was weiß ich*, pass doch besser auf deine Sachen auf! (Du)
Gott weiß - ¡Dios sabe! / ¡Sabe Dios!
Gott weiß, wie lange das dauern kann! (Du)
Este último con invocación a la deidad, como en las fórmulas emocionales que veremos más adelante.
Da bin ich überfragt! – ¡Ahí me has pillado! / ¡Ni idea!
Wieso hat die Firmenleitung das erfahren? will Janda wissen. - *Da bin ich überfragt*, sagt Leo. (Du)

2.1.3. Las fórmulas expresivas que se usan para transmitir disconformidad y crítica al interlocutor, a una tercera persona no presente o a alguna situación. Entre éstas incluimos también expresiones irónicas con las que se comenta o critica algo que acaba de decir el interlocutor y que se considera intolerable o falto de razón.
Das fängt ja heiter an! - ¡pues sí que empezamos bien! / ¡Pues sí que estamos buenos!
Das fängt ja heiter an! Das Benzin ist gleich alle und weit und breit keine Tankstelle in Sicht! (Mü)
Das hab ich gerne! - ¡en eso estaba yo pensando!
Das hab ich gerne, mit meiner Nagelschere Packpapier schneiden! (Du)

En el siguiente ejemplo tenemos una expresión de reproche contra alguien que critica a otro por un defecto que él mismo tiene.
    Du hast es gerade nötig (etw. Bestimmtes zu tun / zu sagen) - ¡mira quién fue a hablar!
    Du hast es gerade nötig, mich aufzufordern, langsam zu fahren! Dabei rast du selber immer wie ein Irrer, sobald man dich ans Steuer lässt! (Mü)
    Incluimos aquí también las expresiones de insolidaridad y desinterés
    das ist nicht mein Bier! - Eso no es asunto mío
    Ich soll hier den Dreck wegmachen? *Das ist nicht mein Bier*! (Mü)

2.2. Las fórmulas directivas tienen como fin mover al receptor a actuar.

2.2.1. Fórmulas de requerimiento para acabar con algo, finalizar un acto.
    Jetzt ist aber Feierabend! -¡Se acabó lo que se daba!
    Jede Nacht erst nach zwei nach Hause kommen und meistens stockbetrunken – *damit ist jetzt Feierabend*, mein Lieber! (Du)

2.2.2. Fórmulas para invitar a la desaparición que son las fórmulas directivas que tienen como fin mover al receptor a marcharse.
    Geh'/ scher' dich zum Kuckuck / zum Henker! - ¡Ahueca el ala! / ¡Que te des el piro! ¡Déjame en paz!
    Geh zum Kuckuck mit deiner ständigen Nörgelei! (Du)

2.3. Fórmulas asertivas o representativas son aquellas con las que el hablante transmite información que él considera cierta y que emplea para reforzar la sinceridad de sus afirmaciones.
    Nur über meine Leiche!- Por encima de mi cadáver…
    Du willst also Kunstmaler werden! Da kann ich nur sagen: *Nur über meine Leiche*! Zuerst must du einmal einen Beruf erlernen, der dich ernähren kann. (Mü)
    Keine zehn Pferde bringen mich dazu - Ni atado…
    Keine zehn Pferde bringen mich dazu, mich bei ihm zu entschuldigen. Schließlich hat er mit dem Streit angefangen! (Mü)
Estas unidades fraseológicas rutinarias asertivas manifiestan en ambas lenguas la decisión irrevocable del emisor de oponer resistencia a algo por estar seguro de encontrarse en lo cierto.

2.3.1. Algunas fórmulas asertivas se emplean para negar y rechazar de manera más fuerte que la mera desaprobación que hemos mencionado entre las fórmulas expresivas. Entre otras se incluye aquí la expresión de incredulidad, "no me creo lo que dices, no exageres". Algunas de estas construcciones tienen un equivalente total en las dos lenguas.
    Das kannst du deiner Großmutter erzählen! – ¡[Eso] se lo cuentas/ cuéntaselo a tu abuela!
    Du willst plötzlich in Latein eine sehr gute Note erhalten haben? *Das kannst du deiner Großmutter erzählen*! (Mü)
    Mach keine (faulen) Witze!- ¡No me cuentes historias / chistes! / ¡A otro burro con esa albarda!
    Nun mach mal halblang -¡Menos lobos! /¡no te pases!/¡Para el carro!
    Nun mach mal halblang, zwanzig Euro für einen Stehplatz ist ein bisschen zu viel! (Du)

2.3.2 Si con las fórmulas asertivas el emisor transmite información que él considera cierta, también las empleará para rectificar el error de su interlocutor y decirle que se equivoca:
Irrtum vom Amt! / Weit gefehlt! / - ¡Craso error!
Ich soll das gesagt haben? *Irrtum vom Amt*, mein Lieber! (Du)

2.4. Fórmulas emocionales a través de las cuales los hablantes hacen partícipes de sus sentimientos a sus interlocutores y expresan un estado de ánimo; dentro de este grupo se incluyen las invocaciones a la deidad:
Gott bewahre/behüte! – ¡Dios me libre!
que significa la negación absoluta.
Ich und heiraten, *Gott bewahre*! (Du)

2.5. Fórmulas de veredicto con las que el hablante emite un juicio acerca de su interlocutor y que también emplea para reprochar, rechazar y protestar.
Das ist doch keine Art! – ¡No son formas!
Plötzlich in mein Schlafzimmer zu stürzen und die Vorhänge aufzureißen, das *ist doch keine Art*! (Du)

3. Conclusión

Podemos resumir que el valor locutivo de las formulas rutinarias psico-sociales de recusación presenta en las dos lenguas estructuras formales muy diferentes pues, al tratarse habitualmente de una reacción frente a una observación de un interlocutor en una situación comunicativa concreta, aparecen como oraciones independientes, como oraciones compuestas, como expresiones elípticas o informaciones añadidas a lo que ya ha dicho el interlocutor. El análisis formal ha hecho patente que la recusación se expresa con exclamaciones (ya sean interjecciones o sintagmas más o menos amplios), oraciones imperativas, oraciones interrogativas y oraciones enunciativas. Es frecuente el uso de la ironía para expresar la recusación y, por tanto, se han documentado tanto expresiones negativas, como explícitamente afirmativas. La correspondencia entre el alemán y el español depende del contexto comunicativo, pero hay algunas fórmulas rutinarias de recusación con un equivalente total o parcial en ambas lenguas.

El valor ilocutivo de las expresiones recogidas en el presente corpus se ajusta prácticamente a la clasificación propuesta por las doctoras Balzer y Piñel. Hemos incluido los matices que conllevan 'estar en desacuerdo', 'negar el conocimiento', es decir, 'ignorar', 'expresar la disconformidad', 'rectificar el error del otro', 'invitar a la desaparición' que entendemos como un rechazo, y algunos juicios negativos y críticas. También hemos asignado algunas fórmulas de rechazo y negación a apartados que inicialmente no se relacionan con la recusación, como por ejemplo el apartado de fórmulas emotivas y de invocación a la deidad. Los ejemplos documentados demuestran que esta función está presente en este apartado en las dos lenguas analizadas. Para posteriores ocasiones queda abierto el análisis de este corpus teniendo en cuenta otros valores de la comunicación interactiva, como son el contexto sociocultural, la relación social entre el emisor y el destinatario, la dimensión temporal y el portador de la responsabilidad.

4. Bibliografía

AUSTIN, J. L. 1962 *How to Do Things With Words*. Cambridge, Mass.
BURGER, H. 1998 *Phraseologie. Eine Einfürung am Beispiel des Deutschen*. Berlín.
BALZER, B. & R. PIÑEL 2009 "Vorschlag eines klassifikatorischen Modells für Routineformeln psycho-sozialer Art". In: Korhonen, J., Mieder, W., Piirainen, E., & Piñel, R. (eds.): *Phraseologie global – areal – regional. Akten der Konferenz EUROPHRAS 2008 vom 13.–16.8.2008 in Helsinki*. Tübingen: 269-275
CORPAS PASTOR, G. 1997 *Manual de fraseología española*. Madrid.
COULMAS, F. 1979 "On the Sociolinguistics Relevance of Routine Formulae". *Journal of Pragmatics* 3: 239-266.
DUDEN 11 1992 *Redewendungen und sprichwörtliche Redensarten. Wörterbuch der deutschen Idiomatik*. Mannheim.
DUDEN 11 2002 *Redewendungen. Wörterbuch der deutschen Idiomatik*. Mannheim.
SECO, M.; O. ANDRÉS & G. RAMOS (2004): *Diccionario fraseológico documentado del español actual*. Madrid.
MÜLLER, K. 2001 *Lexikon der Redesarten*. Niedernhausen.
SOSA MAYOR, I. 2006 *Routineformeln im Spanischen und im Deutschen. Eine pragmalinguistische kontrastive Analyse*. Wien.
VALERO GARCÉS, C. 2001 "Las fórmulas rutinarias en la comunicación intercultural: la expresión de emociones en inglés y en español y su traducción". In: Cruz, I.de la; Santamaría, C.; Tejada, C. & Valero,C. (eds.), *La lingüística aplicada a finales del s. XX*. Alcalá de Henares.

PINTADAS Y FRASEOLOGÍA

María del Carmen Ugarte García
Universidad Complutense de Madrid

Abstract: Graffiti as long with other manifestations of the new culture are being observed by paremiologists, mainly in USA as a vehicle for the dissemination of new and old proverbs. In Spain, and in Spanish, the study of the graffiti has been an exception, although some researches have seen the need to pay some attention to them. In this communication external and internal form of graffiti are reviewed. The external form uses similar mnemonic mechanisms that proverbs to attract the attention. Relating themes, we have extracted some examples about women and liberty.

Key Words: Spanish phraseology, graffiti, proverbs, anti-proverbs

1. Introducción

En el 2007, habiendo solicitado la colaboración del Departamento de Lengua del I. E. S. Juan Martín el Empecinado (Aranda de Duero, Burgos, [España]) para que los alumnos aportaran refranes conocidos en sus pueblos e intentar profundizar así en el conocimiento de la lengua y cultura locales, uno de los alumnos, Ismael González, Martínez (1.º E. S. O), del pueblo de Arandilla, hizo una curiosa aportación bajo la rúbrica «Refranes del vino y las viñas»:

Prende la vid, no los arroyos (frase hecha, no me la ha dicho nadie, lo pone en el frontón).

Efectivamente, un año después, allí, en el frontón de Arandilla, aunque con el texto un poco cambiado, pero sin duda identificable, pude fotografiar la pintada (imagen) que había llamado la atención del joven alumno de E. S. O. hasta el punto de haberla incluido en el trabajo escolar junto a otras paremias más tradicionales facilitadas por sus familiares.

Frontón de Arandilla (Burgos)

Los paremiólogos estadounidenses vienen prestando atención desde hace algunos años a este tipo de manifestaciones: «Proverbs and *their structures* are used in graffiti, on bumper stickers, and of course also on that ubiquitous T-shirt with its proverbial slogans» (Mieder, 2004: 251), [subrayado nuestro], por lo que creímos que un intento de aplicar criterios de análisis paremiológico a las pintadas de este lado del charco, principalmente aquellas escritas en español, podría resultar interesante y seguir avanzando así en los estudios paremiológicos.

En nuestro país, los profesores Vigara Tauste y Reyes Sánchez (1996) ya habían prestado atención al lenguaje de las pintadas, mayormente en sus aspectos sociolingüísticos y de comunicación, aunque apuntaban en su trabajo algunos rasgos (resaltados en la cita), que podrían ponernos asimismo en la pista del análisis paremiológico:

A primera vista, graffiti y pintadas se limitan a ser mensajes visuales anónimos y de escaso contenido informativo, *cuyos motivos,* plasmados casi siempre en paredes «ajenas» y espacios urbanos, *se repiten, aparentemente, hasta la saciedad.* Pero ésta es sólo una primera impresión superficial.

Diez años más tarde, un trabajo publicado por la Universidad de Alcalá (Angulo Manso, 2006) pone de relieve a la vez el olvido y la importancia que el estudio de las pintadas tienen dentro de las culturas populares, inventariando en un espacio geográfico reducido, 92 de estos textos y apuntando ya la originalidad de algunos de ellos, aunque la novedad, precisamente, consiste más en los continentes que en los contenidos:

El objetivo de este trabajo es el de recoger un material literario escasamente prestigioso, muy desatendido, que suele ser obviado en los estudios de lengua y literatura. Estamos acostumbrados a pensar que literatura es aquello que se encuentra escrito, editado, publicado, que ha superado los filtros del canon establecido por editores, críticos, lectores. Pero ¿qué sucede con esas otras manifestaciones de la lengua que no tienen formato de libro? Mi intención aquí es dejar constancia de una literatura efímera, cuyo destino es el olvido si no hay quien la recoja y la reivindique. Se trata de textos que no están impresos en hojas de papel ni en páginas web, sino que se encuentran en *lugares muy poco convencionales.* Nos estamos refiriendo, claro está, a los *graffiti* o pintadas que encontramos en muros, postes, puertas, columpios, y en un sinfín de lugares más. Sobre todo, en las puertas de los servicios de edificios públicos y de negocios.

Si bien podemos decir que las pintadas estaban ya presentes en la Antigüedad revelando en algunos casos datos importantes para el conocimiento de esas épocas, es en la segunda mitad del siglo XX, y ligados a distintos movimientos juveniles, cuando las pintadas y *graffitis* parecen haber tomado la calle e irrumpido plenamente en la cultura, aunque siempre, preciso es resaltarlo, al margen de la llamada cultura oficial, manteniendo su punto de marginalidad. Sin embargo, no cabe duda de que están ahí, y de que forman parte tanto de la cultura como de la lengua viva.

Las pintadas se vindican a sí mismas como la voz del pueblo, como un espacio de libertad en el que la gente libre puede decir lo que piensa, sin censuras de ningún tipo. Es el propio pueblo el que se anima:

- a expresarse, a no callarse: *Barrio no te calles*;
- a hacerlo sin el corsé económico de imprentas y detentores oficiales de medios de comunicación: *Las paredes son la imprenta del pueblo;*
- a vindicar la expresión artística en sí misma: *Nunca podréis callar el spray* y *El spray es un arte.*

Pasamos a continuación a analizar algunas de las características del lenguaje de las pintadas, el ver cómo lo hacen, qué temas son los preferidos y qué medios utilizan.

2.Características lingüísticas

2.1.Temporalidad

Quizá detrás de la lengua hablada, los textos de las pintadas sean los que en términos generales menos permanencia presenten. Podemos decir que, salvo excepciones, son textos efímeros y que permanecerán lo que permitan los agentes atmosféricos y las políticas de limpieza municipales y privadas, aunque afortunadamente podremos salvar algunos de ellos gracias a la cámaras fotográficas o a las labores de inventario como el realizado por la profesora Angulo Manso (2006). Esa temporalidad no parece detener a los *escritores*, que estarán dispuestos a dejar su testimonio, aunque solo sea por unos segundos o minutos.

En en una de las nevadas ocurridas en el invierno madrileño del 2010, pudimos constatar cómo los escritores habían aprovechado el material maleable de la nieve para dejar constancia de sus firmas (VICTOR), sus declaraciones de amor (I LOVE YOU) o incluso de su amor maternal (MAMA TE QUIERO), como podemos ver en la foto que Xosé Castro compartió con sus amigos de Facebook (imagen). Tampoco nos son desconocidas las palabras escritas en la arena de la playa a la espera de que las olas se las lleven en poco segundos.

Por nimias o carentes de valor paremiológico que puedan presentar estos textos sencillos, veremos más adelante que pueden ser la base para fórmulas más complejas.

3.Estructura externa

Empecemos por la forma externa, lo que nuestro ojo o el objetivo de la cámara captan:

Viejos lemas, lo nuevo y lo viejo

En numerosas ocasiones lo más fácil es trasladar a este «nuevo» soporte los viejos lemas, el objetivo inmediato es la publicidad, las paredes como periódico del pueblo, no solo para escribir en él sino también para leer.

Obrero muerto, patrón colgao [+ dibujo de una horca], viejo lema anarquista del que podemos encontrar distintas muestras en documentos de los años ochenta, que se siguen hasta la actualidad: «Hasta aquí hemos llegado / ¡A obrero despedido, / Patrón colgado!», así termina el poema titulado *Reflexiones de un parado* que circula por foros de Internet comprometidos con la causa obrera.

No hay camino para la libertad, la libertad es el camino [+ A anarquista + ~~comunidad libertaria~~ (tachado)]. A propósito de este lema, diremos que aparece incluido en el refranero de María Gil, de 86 años, que lleva recogidos por mera afición más de 9.000 refranes. En concreto la frase que nos ocupa hace el número 2.863. Al comentarle que esta frase aparece en una pared en su mismo pueblo, y que estrictamente hablando no es un refrán, ello negó rotundamente que la hubiera sacado de ninguna pared, sino mas bien que la había leído en algún libro o haberla oído, como la mayoría de sus refranes, y que en cuanto a si no era un refrán, que «sin duda encerraba mucho de sabiduría».

En ocasiones para producir el efecto de atraer al paseante, las unidades frásicas tradicionales se desautomatizan para producir esa llamada de atención. Es el caso de un buzón de correos en Madrid (imagen) en el que encontramos pintado: *Tengo sed y tengo hambre*, cuando la colocación a la que estamos acostumbrados, por influencia bíblica es, *tengo hambre y sed*. La inversión de elementos y el nuevo medio consiguen el objetivo.

Chamberí (Madrid)

La rima

Sin duda, al igual que ocurre en las paremias populares y en muchos de los eslóganes, la rima es uno de los recursos más empleados en las pintadas para captar la atención, y a la vez retenerlas en la memoria. Las pintadas largas suelen disponerse en dos o más líneas:
    Tu ke te quejas de burgueses y de nuevos rikos deja de konsumir las drogas ke les llenan los bolsillos
y no es raro que introduzcan símbolos matemáticos en su composición:
    alcaldillos + especuladores= parques de ocio "Urbanizaciones"

Paralelismos y anáforas

Un buen ejemplo de estos mecanismos lo encontramos en esta pintada hallada en las paredes de la facultad de Filología de la UCM coetánea de las protestas del plan Bolonia:
    Si no tú ¿Quién? Si no ahora ¿Cuándo? Si no aquí ¿Dónde?

Otros recursos

Retruécano: El ya mencionado *No hay camino para la libertad, la libertad es el camino* y *O estado rouba, / rouba o Estado*. Antítesis: Encontramos este otro ejemplo también en la lengua portuguesa, tan próxima al español en cuestiones paremiológicas: *A liberdade vive cuando o estado morre*. Aliteración: *Mujer ni sumisa ni devota Te quiero libre, linda y loca* y *Solo solos somos libres*.

Dialogismos y wellerismos

La profesora Angulo Manso (2006: 2-3) observa acertadamente la existencia de cadenas de mensajes que demuestran la existencia de una comunicación (diálogo) alternativa en las pintadas. En nuestro caso, la contestación, un añadido en realidad, puede convertir el mensaje original, con frecuencia totalmente neutro o incluso anodino, en un mensaje completamente diferente. Veamos un par de ejemplos:
    Una declaración de amor convencional: *Te kiero Tamara,* se convierte en toda una reivindicación al constatar la respuesta de la supuesta amada: *Pero Kiereme bien!* [+ símbolo feminista].
    Dos únicas palabras componen un sencillo lema político: *Andalucía libre*. Ahora bien, si una segunda mano, como nos prueba la diferente caligrafía, añade otras dos: *de precariedad*, el mensaje es totalmente diferente: *Andalucía libre de precariedad*.

Estructura profunda

Tras esta aproximación a las pintadas en su estructura externa, pasamos ahora, aunque sea brevemente, a ocuparnos de su estructura profunda, de qué temas nos hablan las pintadas.

Contexto

Como en todo texto, el contexto en el que está hecha la pintada es fundamental para su correcta interpretación, para que el mensaje pueda captarse. En este caso hablaremos de un contexto espacial —el lugar u objeto sobre el que se ha pintado— y el contexto temporal. Sin lugar a dudas, el primero será determinante y formará en muchos casos parte del mensaje. En cuanto al segundo, ya hemos visto que las pintadas suelen ser efímeras, pero cuando superan permanecen en el tiempo, su significado real se diluye (veremos un caso claro más adelante).

Las paredes están llenas de reivindicaciones sociales, pero el derecho a la educación parece cobrar más fuerza si se estampa, precisamente, en las paredes de la facultad de Ciencias de la Educación: *Los/as obreros/as también keremos estudiar. No LOU. Defiende tus derechos.*

El mobiliario urbano se presta bastante a ser el soporte de este tipo de mensajes. La leyenda *Vota aquí* resultaría completamente neutra si no se hubiera escrito sobre un *cubo de basura* o en el *borde del registro de una alcantarilla*.

Igualmente, un anuncio en una céntrica avenida de Buenos Aires llamaba la atención del viandante utilizando la atractiva figura de un joven y un exultante corazón (love) *I love New Year* (imagen); una vez más, el rotulador popular cruzó el corazón para poner las cosas en su sitio: *Sí, Porque / tienes platita para gastar putito / pero la gente / se caga de hambre*.

Anuncio en Buenos Aires

La leyenda *Viva la vejez, salud y alegría* nos pasaría totalmente desapercibida de no haber sido pintada en la pared de un popular centro de la tercera edad, justo al lado de un banco donde los viejos suelen salir a solazarse. Nótese que estamos acostumbrados a utilizar en este caso el eufemismo *¡Viva la juventud!* para animar a las personas mayores con buena forma física y mejor ánimo. En este caso, la mano anónima ¿juvenil? ha piropeado sin ningún tipo de rodeo a los usuarios del centro.

Más allá va sin duda la mano que en la pared trasera de la catedral de Granada ha escrito: *Monumento a la decadencia del espíritu.*

La profesora Angulo Manso (2004: 3) advierte antes de iniciar su inventario de pintadas acerca de la ideología que se manifiesta en muchas de ellas:

Una advertencia final pero muy importante: la ideología que reflejan estas inscripciones anónimas es, demasiadas veces, agresiva, violenta, brutal. Abundan las imprecaciones y los insultos contra las mujeres, contra los hombres, contras las personas homosexuales, contra los extranjeros, contra quienes tienen determinada opción política. Pese a ello, y aunque, naturalmente, no nos identificamos con los contenidos de tales mensajes, creemos que su registro y transcripción son pertinentes desde el punto de vista histórico, sociológico, etnográfico. Reflejan modos de pensar, de sentir, que no por reprobables merecen ser obviados o silenciados en el ámbito de las ciencias sociales. Al contrario, igual que sucede con las enfermedades del cuerpo, cuanto más conocidas sean estas enfermedades del alma, tanto más eficaces podrán ser las respuestas y los remedios que en el ámbito educativo y social se les puedan dar.

Sobre el lenguaje agresivo y violento, ya apuntado arriba, volveremos a incidir, pero en cuanto a los temas en sí, creemos que presentan algunos matices nuevos que difícilmente se presentaban en otras formas de expresión, constituyendo en esto las pintadas una auténtica novedad y un campo sociolingüístico de investigación todavía virgen.

Temas

Es por ello que nos hemos preguntado si hay unos temas más proclives que otros a ser tratados en las pintadas. Sin duda, son los temas políticos y sociales, seguidos de las declaraciones de amor, los que ocupan buena parte de ellas, pero su ámbito es mucho más amplio y en todo caso presentan temas de preocupación muy actuales.

En cualquier caso, los viejos temas, también presentes, adoptan y saben adaptarse a las nuevas formas de expresión. Pongamos como ejemplo *Temo el silencio de los buenos*. No sabía lo que me había llamado la atención de esta frase, pero al llegar a casa, mi madre (83 años) corroboró lo que me rondaba por la cabeza: *Del agua mansa, líbreme Dios, que de la brava ya me libro yo*. El viejo refrán había dado paso a un verso libre más acorde con el siglo XXI, pero el espíritu, el mensaje, la advertencia, seguía siendo el mismo.

La libertad

Viendo la cantidad de pintadas que reivindican la libertad individual o colectiva podría pensarse que vivimos rodeados de cadenas y mordazas, que las pintadas no han sido recogidas en países democráticos, sino en otros en los que los derechos fundamentales se restringen. Sin duda, la libertad es un valor en alza. Muchas de estas pintadas van acompañadas de la firma anarquista, se reivindica la libertad a la vez que se ataca al Estado.

Si la tradición se preocupaba sobre todo de la libertad personal, el libre albedrío, *el buey suelto bien se lame*, desde las paredes se reclama la libertad, física en este caso, de alguien que ha sido encarcelado, *Libertad para fulano*, pero sobre todo se reclama la libertad como valor universal y absoluto: *La libertad es ser libre desde nosotros mismos*. Ya hemos visto otros ejemplos más arriba y veremos todavía algún otro.

La mujer toma la palabra

Es difícil saber quién ha sido el autor material de una pintada, pero no nos cabe duda de que el espíritu, las reivindicaciones y las propias palabras que muestran muchas de las pintadas, a veces en series dentro de un espacio urbano delimitado, nos lleva a constatar la creciente presencia de la mujer en el mundo de las reivindicaciones callejeras: La estampación *Mujeres, las calles son nuestras* (Gaelx: 2319078082) aparece en varias fotos del álbum *Lucha feminista* de (Gaelx: 2006-2010). En el álbum de esta autora pueden verse distintas, a menudo también reivindicando esa libertad de la que hemos hablado, ahora como grupo: *Nos queremos libres* (Gaelx, 4607733748), o parafraseando los anuncios de la higiene femenina, doble tinta, doble grafía (Gaelx, 4379474106):

Ni somos finas, ni estamos seguras... [en tinta roja] chavala, espavila [sic], el cerebro no se depila.

Personalmente, y en el barrio de Estrecho de Madrid pude fotografiar una serie de pintadas feministas reivindicativas algunas con textos bastante violentos y agresivos contra el «patriarcado agresor»: *Tijeras xa todas*, y a modo de firma unas tijeras; y si es preciso se acude a la rima para fijar el mensaje: *Si es aburrido, mata a tu marido*. Sin duda la violencia contra la mujer que se hallaba en muchos refranes clásicos se ve igualada y hasta superada por estas nuevas voces populares y anónimas.

Un ejemplo más de las reivindicaciones femeninas unidas a las imágenes violentas, para dar más énfasis al mensaje, sin faltar la rima: *La diferencia / que puede haber / entre un parto / y otro, es la misma que / hay entre una violación / desgarradora y un buen polvo*. Para entender esta pintada tenemos que encuadrarla en el tiempo; aunque la foto fue tomada con posterioridad, y todavía puede leerse, fue realizada para reivindicar la anestesia epidural en los partos en un tiempo en que las autoridades sanitarias regionales eran remisas a facilitarla de forma gratuita.

Conclusiones

Ciertamente no podemos decir que cualquier pintada, pueda ser analizada aplicando criterios fraseológicos; tampoco presentan todas ellas unas características textuales que las permitan encuadrar en una clase determinada de textos, pero en un número de ellas hallamos una cierta proximidad a las paremias, y en su caso a una utilización voluntaria de unidades frásicas de uso generalizado.

Al igual que las paremias populares, podemos decir que muchas de las pintadas, portadores de una cierta sabiduría o consejo, nacen con vocación de ser recordadas y repetidas, sirviéndose para ello tanto de la rima como de otros recursos estilísticos tales como paralelismos, retruécanos, antítesis...

En algunos casos el viejo y clásico consejo ha sido redactado y actualizado con un lenguaje más del siglo XX y XXI; en otros se han tratado de buscar nuevos temas separándose completamente de la tradición.

Pese a lo que algunos autores manifiestan acerca de la repetición de estos mensajes, lo cierto es que salvo en el caso de las realizadas con molde, las personales presentan nula o mínima repetición. Parece importar más que muchos ojos las lean que que muchos labios las repitan, y ello a pesar de los mecanismos aludidos. No obstante, vemos que algunas de ellas, aunque sea tímidamente, están empezando a pasar a otros ámbitos del lenguaje, por lo que sin duda habrá que tenerlas en cuenta en los estudios futuros sobre fraseología.

Bibliografía

ANGULO MANSO, M. 2006 "Inscripciones, pintadas y graffitis en calles y servicios: literatura efímera, ideología del pueblo". *Culturas Populares. Revista Electrónica 2* (mayo-agosto 2006), <http://www.culturaspopulares.org/textos2/articulos/manso.htm>, [consulta: 07/08/2010].
GAELX 2006-2010 *Galería de Gaelx* en Flickr, <http://www.flickr.com/photos/gaelx/>, [consulta: 07/08/2010].
MIEDER, W. 2004 *Proverbs: a handbook*. Westport (Conn.): Greenwood Press.
VIGARA TAUSTE, A. M. & REYES SÁNCHEZ, F. 1996 "*Graffiti* y pintadas en Madrid. Arte lenguaje y comunicación". *Espéculo*, 4, [consulta: 07/08/2010]: <http://www.ucm.es/info/especulo/numero4/graffiti.htm>.

LES ADJECTIVAUX ACTUALISATEURS : ÉTUDE CONTRASTIVE FRANÇAIS/ ARABE

Monia Bouali
Université de Kairouan

Abstract: The "adjectivals" are multi-word collocations or idioms performing the same function than adjectives (G. Gross: 1991). According to their use, they can be predicative (*être en colère* :*to be in anger: "to be angry") or non-predicative (*de fer*: *of iron: "iron"). Previous linguistic studies generally focus on the first category. In this work, we are specifically interested into adjectival collocations that realize the actualization of predicates, or arguments, in the elementary sentence. Whatever they be predicative or argumental, the *adjectivals* assume identification criteria specific to each use. We intend to describe the functioning of these items from a contrastive French / Arabic point of view

Key words: Adjectival idioms, adjetival collocations, actualization, fixedness, Arabic phraseology.

0. Introduction

Bien qu'elles soient deux langues typologiquement éloignées, le français et l'arabe présentent beaucoup de points de convergence. L'étude des adjectivaux actualisateurs est une occasion pour mettre en relief certaines de ces interférences. La catégorisation même de ces items comme des locutions adjectivales qui ont les mêmes critères d'identification de l'adjectif simple ou de la صفة [sifɛ] en arabe, est un fait de langue qui rend compte de l'un de ces points communs. Il faut préciser que nous faisons cette étude dans le cadre de la théorie des classes d'objets adoptée au laboratoire de linguistique LDI (Lexiques, Dictionnaires, Informatique) en vue du traitement automatique des langues et de l'étude de corpus parallèles. Il sera tout d'abord question d'établir les critères d'identification des adjectivaux en tant que séquences figées qui peuvent être prédicatives ou non prédicatives; ensuite, nous nous pencherons sur un type particulier d'adjectivaux qui est identifié *à priori* comme des adjectivaux non prédicatifs actualisateurs. Il s'agit de mettre en évidence leur statut en français et en arabe en établissant une grille de propriétés qui leur sont propres. Après et à partir d'un jeu sur un corpus parallèle français/ arabe, nous comptons proposer une taxinomie de ces adjectifs composés actualisateurs qui varient entre classifieurs et intensifieurs.

1. Les adjectivaux

Les adjectivaux s'identifient comme des séquences figées qui ont le même fonctionnement qu'un adjectif. Il s'agit de locutions adjectivales telles qu'*à la mode*. Par ailleurs, tout comme l'adjectif ou la صفة [sifɛ] en arabe, l'adjectival ou le صفاتي [sifɛti:] peut occuper les positions attribut, apposition ou épithète. Par exemple l'unité polylexicale *à la mode* fonctionne comme un tout qui a les mêmes propriétés que l'unité unilexicale *élégante* :

Léa est (élégante, à la mode)
Léa, (élégante, à la mode), a séduit tout le monde
Léa est une fille (élégante, à la mode)
Elle peut aussi recevoir les marques de l'intensité :
Léa est très (élégante, à la mode)
Ainsi qu'elle peut être pronominalisée en *le*, pronom invariable :
*Léa est à la mode et elle **le** restera toujours*
Mais, il faut préciser que parmi ces critères certains identifient l'adjectif ou l'adjectival comme prédicatif, d'autres le classent en tant que non prédicatif. C'est pourquoi, une première typologie de ces locutions s'impose : les prédicatifs et les non prédicatifs.

1.1 Les adjectivaux prédicatifs

Tout comme pour les adjectifs simples, les adjectivaux peuvent être prédicatifs ou non prédicatifs selon qu'ils répondent aux critères de prédicativité ou non. Les critères de prédicativité sont l'actualisation en *être* et la pronominalisation en *le*. Soient les adjectivaux *en colère, en acier, de fer, de bonne humeur*. Seuls *en colère* et *de bonne humeur* sont identifiés comme des adjectivaux prédicatifs :
   en colère /N0:<hum>
      Luc est en colère, Léa l'est aussi.
   de fer/ <santé>
      Luc a une santé de fer.
      *sa santé est de fer.
      *sa santé est de fer, sa volonté l'est aussi.
L'étude[1] de ces adjectivaux prédicatifs a montré qu'ils sont susceptibles d'être événementiels ou non événementiels dans la mesure où les premiers acceptent seulement l'actualisation en *être* et qu'ils sont réfractaires aux marqueurs aspectuels de changement d'état comme *devenir, tomber*, etc. Les unités *de bas étage* et *dans les bras de Morphée* sont toutes les deux prédicatives, mais la première n'accepte en aucun cas une actualisation autre qu'en *être*, marqueur d'état, alors que la seconde peut être actualisée par *être, tomber*, etc.
   de bas étage /N0 :<hum>
      Luc est de bas étage.
      *Luc est devenu de bas étage.
   dans les bras de Morphée/ N0 :<hum>
      Il est dans les bras de Morphée.
      Il est tombé dans les bras de Morphée.

1.2 Les adjectivaux non prédicatifs

Dans le cadre de notre étude, les adjectivaux non prédicatifs se définissent comme les locutions adjectivales qui :
   - ne répondent pas aux critères de prédicativité mentionnés ci-dessus;

---

[1] Cette étude a été menée dans le cadre de notre thèse qui a porté sur l'actualisation aspectuelle des adjectivaux prédicatifs. Ce travail s'intitule L'actualisation aspectuelle des adjectivaux prédicatifs : le cas du changement d'état. Décembre 2007. LDI, Paris13.

- n'ont pas la capacité de sélectionner des arguments;
- ne sont pas en mesure de rentrer dans les structures en *être*.
en acier/<objets>
    Un plateau en acier
    *ce plateau est en acier
    *ce plateau est en acier, cette table l'est aussi.

Mais, ce statut d'adjectival non prédicatif demeure équivoque malgré ces critères d'identification par opposition à ceux d'adjectival prédicatif. En effet, une unité appartenant à une phrase élémentaire doit nécessairement avoir l'une des trois fonctions suivantes prédicat, argument ou actualisateur. Par ailleurs qualifier une unité de non prédicative pourrait relever de deux statuts ou bien de celui d'argument ou de celui d'actualisateur. Certains adjectivaux non prédicatifs sont des «actualisateurs». Soient *de fer, de béton, à air, à essence,* etc.

2. Les adjectivaux actualisateurs

à vapeur, à son zénith, à son apogée, à domicile,, à jet continu, à armature métallique, à la carte, à la pelle, à cent balles, au beau fixe, en accordéon, en vrille, de choc, de moineau, de première urgence, de haut vol, de peu, en grand tralala,, de longue date, de cet acabit, de singe, sans mélange, sur l'oreiller, etc.

Les adjectivaux actualisateurs sont des unités polylexicales qui prennent la charge d'actualisation des prédicats ou des arguments dans une phrase élémentaire. Ce qui fait qu'ils peuvent être actualisateurs de prédicats ou actualisateurs d'arguments. Selon qu'ils fassent partie des uns ou des autres, ces unités s'attribuent deux fonctions : ils sont soit des «intensifieurs» de classes sémantiques de prédicats soit des classes d'objets d'arguments ou des «classifieurs» de classes d'objets d'arguments.

2.1 Adjectivaux actualisateurs de prédicats

    Luc a une santé de béton.
    La joie de Luc est à son comble.

De béton, à son comble actualisent respectivement <santé> et <joie>. Ces phrases sont paraphrasables par :
    Luc a une très bonne santé
    La joie de Luc est très grande

Tout comme les groupes ADV+ ADJ *très grande* et *très bonne*, les adjectivaux *de béton, à son comble* actualisent les prédicats cités ci-dessus.

2.2 Adjectivaux actualisateurs d'arguments

    Luc est un patron de choc.
    Léa est une femme de cœur.
    Luc propose du pain à gogo.

A priori et selon le corpus d'unités polylexicales adjectivales non prédicatives, que nous avons recueilli dans *Frantext* et *Le Monde*, les adjectivaux actualisateurs d'arguments sont beaucoup plus nombreux que ceux actualisateurs de prédicats. Ils sont généralement sélectionnés par des classes d'objets d'arguments. Certains rentrent dans un paradigme pour indiquer une classe ou une sous-classe de la classe d'objets en question, d'autres relèvent du domaine de la quantification.

3. Vers une typologie des adjectivaux actualisateurs

Outre la subdivision des adjectivaux actualisateurs en actualisateurs de prédicats et actualisateurs d'arguments, une autre taxinomie s'impose comme transversale opérant sur tous les adjectivaux actualisateurs. Il s'agit de l'opposition adjectivaux intensifieurs/ adjectivaux classifieurs.

3.1 Adjectivaux intensifieurs

Les adjectivaux actualisateurs à valeur intensive marquent un degré élevé de la propriété exprimée par le nom auquel ils se rapportent. Il s'agit d' «un cas particulier de quantification». Les locutions *de fer, à son comble* dans les exemples qui suivent marquent un haut degré. Il s'agit tout d'abord d'un type particulier de quantification. La paraphrase effectuée précédemment dans le cadre de phrases élémentaires a montré qu'il s'agit d'une intensification

Luc a une santé de fer.
La joie de Luc est à son comble.

Dans ce cas, nous parlons d'«une quantification intensive» et par la suite d'adjectivaux intensifieurs. Soit le schéma de phrase suivant:

<classes sémantiques de prédicats> + adjectival intensifieur
<santé> + *de fer/ de béton.*

3.2 Adjectivaux classifieurs

Ces adjectivaux n'indiquent pas vraiment des propriétés des entités désignées par le nom, mais entrent dans un paradigme et permettent ainsi d'indiquer un sous-ensemble dans un ensemble.

à air
 (chambre, manchon, perforatrices, carabines, filtre, pistolet, moteur, sifflet, pompe, tramways, bateau)
à vapeur
 (voiture, cuisson, tramways, machine, locomotive)
à essence
 (voiture, pompe, briquet, machine, tramways)

Les adjectivaux *à air, à essence, à vapeur* actualisent différentes classes d'arguments. Mais ils sont parfois sélectionnés par les mêmes arguments comme l'exemple de <tramways> qui peut être actualisé par *à air, à vapeur ou à essence*. Ces actualisateurs d'arguments permettent de lister des types de *tramways (tramways à air, tramways à vapeur, tramways à essence)*, c'est-à-dire des sous-classes de tramways dans la classe même de <tramways>. Il s'agit de classifier les entités qui sélectionnent ces unités polylexicales. Soit le schéma suivant :

<classes d'objets d'arguments> + adjectival classifieur
<*machines*>   *à air, à vapeur, à essence*

4. Les adjectivaux actualisateurs en arabe

L'un des enjeux du traitement automatique des langues naturelles est la traduction automatique. Une étude contrastive permet de cerner les similitudes et les différences de fonctionnement d'un même fait de langue dans deux langues éloignées. Ainsi entre français et arabe[2] se définissent les adjectivaux actualisateurs ou les صفاتيّات محيّنة [sifɛ:tijɛ:t muhɛjjina] comme un point de convergence.

L'adjectif se définit en arabe comme une entité simple qui porte sur le nom. Dans l'exemple suivant, جميل [ʒami:l] est un adjectif qualificatif :

سامي جميل
[sami: ʒami:l]
sami-beau
sami est beau

Il s'agit d'une phrase nominale selon l'analyse grammaticale traditionnelle où le خبر [xabar], équivalent de prédicat en français, est un adjectif صفة [sifɛ]. Le صفاتي [sifɛ:ti] est une unité polylexicale qui a le même fonctionnement qu'une صفة [sifɛ].

Une صفة [sifɛ] peut être prédicative ou non prédicative. Le صفاتي [sifɛti] aussi. Il est prédicatif, lorsqu' :
- il est susceptible d'occuper la position [xabar];
- il est pronominalisable par des éléments invariables comme هكذا [hɛ:keðɛ] كذلك [keðɛ:likɛ].

Il est non prédicatif lorsqu'il est réfractaire à ces deux critères. Soient les deux adjectivaux من حديد et على أتم الاستعداد :

* سامي على أتم الاستعداد وسيبقى عليه
*[sami: ʕɛlɛ ʔɛtɛm lʔistiʕdɛ:d wa sɛjabqa ʕɛlɛjhi]
*sami-sur-toute-préparation-et-rester-futur-sur-elle]
*Sami est tout prêt et il y restera.

سامي على أتم الاستعداد وسيبقى كذلك دائما
[sami: ʕɛlɛ ʔɛtɛm listiʕdɛ:d wa sɛjabqa hɛ:keðɛ: dɛ:ʔimɛn]
sami-sur-toute-préparation-et-rester-futur-comme ça-toujours
Sami est tout prêt et il le restera toujours.

صحّته من حديد
[sihhatuhu min hɛdi:din]
Santé-sa-de-fer
Il a une santé de fer.

من حديد et على أتم الاستعداد sont deux unités polylexicales qui ont le même fonctionnement qu'une صفة [sifɛ] en arabe. Le premier est un adjectival prédicatif, le deuxième est non prédicatif. Ce dernier relève des adjectivaux actualisateurs qui sont classés à leur tour en actualisateurs intensifieurs et actualisateurs classifieurs. Soit l'échantillon de corpus suivant :

---

[2] Nous précisons que nous appliquons ici la règle des quatre lignes et que nous présentons à chaque fois l'exemple, sa transcription phonétique, sa traduction littérale et sa traduction en français.

من حديد/ [min ħedi:d]/ de-fer/ de fer
من ذهب/ [min ðɛhɛb]/ de-or/ d'or/ en or
من نار/ [min na:r]/ de-feu/ de feu
من طين/ [min ti:n]/ de-argile/ en argile
بالفواكه الجافة/ [bilfɛwɛkih lʒɛffɛ]/ aux-fruits-secs/ aux fruits secs

4.1 Les actualisateurs d'arguments

Tout comme pour le français, les adjectivaux actualisateurs d'arguments en arabe sont généralement sélectionnés par des classes d'objets d'arguments. Par exemple la classe des <مرطبات> / <patisseries> sélectionnent les deux unitésبالشكلاطة/ au chocolat etبالفواكه الجافة/ aux fruits secs :

مرطبات بالشكلاطة
[muratabɛt biʃʃocla:ta]
Pâtisserie-au-chocolat
Pâtisserie au chocolat

مرطبات بالفواكه الجافة
[muratabɛt bilfɛwɛkih elʒɛffɛ]
Pâtisserie aux-fruits-secs
Pâtisserie aux fruits secs

Les adjectivaux classifieurs mettent en évidence des types de l'entité en question. Il s'agit de deux classes de <pâtisseries> dans ce cas.

4.2 Les actualisateurs intensifieurs

L'expression de l'intensité en arabe peut être traduite par les adjectivaux intensifieurs. En effet, le même exemple du français *Il a une santé de fer* existe en arabe et c'est l'exemple type d'un adjectival actualisateur intensifieur :

صحّته من حديد
[sihhatuhu min ħedi:d]
Santé-sa-de-fer
Il a une santé de fer

5. Conclusion

Pour conclure, nous présentons l'exemple d'un proverbe tunisien qui comporte une actualisation particulière faite grâce à des adjectivaux actualisateurs métaphoriques qui restent à étudier dans le cadre de l'actualisation prédicative;

كان الكلام من فضة، السكات من ذهب
[kɛn ilklɛm min fiḍḍa, eskɛt min ð hɛb]
Si-la parole-être- d'-argent-le silence-être-présent-d'or
Le silence est d'or.

Par ailleurs, la théorie des classes d'objets permet de réviser certaines notions et parfois de recatégoriser les unités lexicales selon des paramètres nouveaux comme l'exemple de ces unités polylexicales qui étaient longtemps considérées comme des groupes prépositionnels.

Les adjectivaux existent en langue arabe que ce soit en dialectal tunisien ou en arabe littéral. Ils ont la syntaxe des adjectifs simples et leur fonctionnement répond aux critères définitoires de ces derniers. Cependant, la liste de ces unités lexicales reste à déterminer et à étudier d'une manière systématique et exhaustive.

6. Bibliographie

BOUALI, M. 2007 *L'actualisation aspectuelle des adjectivaux prédicatifs : le cas du changement d'état*, Thèse de doctorat en Sciences du Langage de l'Université Paris-13, Laboratoire LDI (Lexiques, Dictionnaires, Informatique).

GROSS, G, 1991 «Typologie des adjectivaux». In: Harro Stammerjohann (éd.) *Analyse et synthèse dans les langues romanes et slaves*, Tübingen: Gunter Narr.

MEJRI, S. 1997 *Le figement lexical. Descriptions linguistiques et structuration sémantique*, Tunis: Publications de la Faculté des lettres de la Manouba.

MEJRI, S. 2004 «Les séquences figées adjectivales». In Jacques Francois (éd.) *L'adjectif en français et à travers les langues*. Caen: Presses Universitaires: 403-412.

MEJRI, S. 1998 «Structuration sémantique et variations des séquences figées». In: Actes du colloque *Le figement lexical*. Tunis: 103-112,

OUERHANI, B. (2004). *Les verbes supports en arabe moderne*, Thèse de Doctorat, Tunis: Université de La Manouba.

OUERHANI, B. [à paraître] «L'actualisation comme outil de classement sémantique des prédicats nominaux en arabe», *Le traitement du lexique. Catégorisation et actualisation*, p. 154-167, Sousse: Faculté des lettres et sciences humaines.

OUERHANI B. 2005 La phrase nominale arabe : analyse traditionnelle et structuration prédicative. In: *La terminologie: entre traduction et bilinguisme, journée scientifique de formation et d'animation régionale. Hamamet,Tunisie 2004.*

RIEGEL, M. (1985). *L'adjectif attribut*, Paris: P.U.F.